PRAISE FOR *GATES*

"Bill Gates has become a symbol of many things, from good old American inventiveness to weird, secretive power-wielding. Stephen Manes and Paul Andrews have put the complicated pieces together in a revealing and nicely droll way. Anyone interested in how computers have remade the world, anyone curious about how Bill Gates has made his fortune, anyone who loves—or hates—Microsoft's Windows will enjoy this impressive book."

—James Fallows, *The Atlantic*, author of *More Like Us*

"A real knockout! *Gates* is so clear and exciting that anyone can enjoy it, yet so crammed with detail that computer fanatics will have their eyes opened about how their business—and Bill Gates—*really* work. Manes and Andrews know their stuff: They've laid the myths to rest, they've provided amazing new revelations, and they've written the first serious book about the computer industry that you simply can't put down."

—Paul Somerson, *PC/Computing*, formerly of *MacUser*, author of *PC Magazine's DOS Power Tools*

"Part history, part biography, part computing, *Gates* tells how a man turned a byte into a dollar, a language into an obsession, and a program into a bestseller. Here's the complete story of the man who built a universe from his keyboard and an empire from his software."

—Clifford Stoll, author of *The Cuckoo's Egg*

"Scrupulously researched, overflowing with detail, and just plain fun, *Gates* is must reading for anyone interested in an accurate history of Microsoft, and learning what's gone right—and what's gone wrong—in the personal computer industry."

—Charles Petzold, *PC Magazine*, author of *Programming Windows*

"Finally, the real book on Microsoft's Gates! . . . The real Book of Bill has arrived . . . a potent biography . . . a compelling story."

—*Newsweek*

"A hot read . . . The best account yet of the 37-year-old software titan who has become America's richest man . . . The good stuff starts on page one. . . . Manes and Andrews deserve credit for trying to show Gates's complexity rather than blithely simplifying him, as most previous profiles have done."

—*Fortune*

"The definitive work . . . Gets beyond the cliché of Gates the billionaire nerd . . . *Gates* is particularly good at providing insights into what sets Mr. Gates apart."

—*The New York Times*

"Fast-paced, informative . . . riveting . . . Pioneering on the high-tech frontier, Mr. Gates embodies the stirring American symbol of a self-made man calling his own shots. At the same time, his success is so fantastic that it inspires envy, suspicion, and awe in both friend and foe."

—*The Wall Street Journal*

"An impressive account of the life of the Microsoft chairman . . . as interesting and important as [Microsoft's] story is, this massive biography is perhaps more interesting for its portrait of Gates as a complex character . . . meticulously researched . . . Well-written, with much of the drama and suspense of a novel. . . ."

—*The Washington Post*

"The most complete and most colorful account yet of the meteoric rise of the nation's No. 1 software company . . . embellishes events with provocative detail and puts them in context."

—*Business Week*

"The definitive book on the USA's oddest, richest person . . . Read *Gates* for a sophisticated look at the software industry's dominant figure."

—*USA Today*

"A real gem . . . The book takes us behind the scenes as Gates uses the power of deftly worded contracts to quickly squeeze out rivals and even finagle his partner. . . . Manes and Andrews provide insights."

—*San Francisco Chronicle*

"We should thank our lucky stars for authors Stephen Manes and Paul Andrews. These journalists and personal computer experts have given us a rare and exacting look at America's richest man—who just happens to head the world's largest software company."

—*Rocky Mountain News*

"Rich with anecdotes and details that are so painstakingly documented it's hard to imagine a more thorough job . . . Should be required reading for any new hire in the personal computer industry, especially those who want to understand what has made Microsoft the dominant power it is. Ultimately, *Gates* is a thorough history of a business that has changed the way we work and play."

—*Seattle Times*

"A remarkable story of a complex and highly talented individual made all the more interesting because of the close links between Gates's career and the evolution of the computer."

"Manes and Andrews have produced a valuable primer on the computer industry, its cast of strange characters and its even stranger array of corporate cultures. . . ."

"While this isn't the first book written about Gates, it's by far the best—complete, balanced, insightful, and well-documented."

"From now on, this estimable effort will be mandatory reading for whoever writes about Gates. . . . In documenting the rise of Gates, Manes and Andrews provide a valuable history of the computer and software industries that grew up with him."

"The book methodically separates the real from the apocryphal. Future writers will thank Manes and Andrews for their reporting . . . the bio of record."

"The book not only is the story of a man of vision, but it also is about the explosive growth of a new industry—software—in which he was something of a pioneer. And it paints the most complete picture yet of Gates, who has remained something of an enigmatic figure despite spending a lot of his time in the public eye."

"Gates succeeds . . . Its authors' admirable depth of knowledge and their anecdotes are ultimately more revealing of both the industry and the man . . . Gates lets the reader determine whether the man is in fact an obnoxious bully, or simply smart and successful."

"Gates is a comprehensive account of the early years of personal computing, a crazy time . . . a high-tech story told in the language of the streets . . . an informative look at a generalissimo of the information revolution."

". . . the definitive picture of 'the real Bill Gates.' "

"Scrupulous, balanced, and thoroughly engaging . . . a tour-guided voyage through historic events behind the transformation of an information industry and age."

—*Toronto Star*

"Fascinating inside look at what made a billionaire out of Gates while still, incredibly, in his 30s."

—*Copley News Service*

"Manes and Andrews combine authoritative discussions of technology with a clear and entertaining prose style. . . . Most interesting is the glimpse of the turbulent 20-year history of the computer industry."

—*Publishers Weekly*

"An illuminating, unsentimental biography . . . a like-it-is portrait of an archetypal nerd who built a world-class business empire . . . An exhaustive report on an aging whiz-kid whose consequential life story is far from over."

—*Kirkus Reviews*

"Refreshing . . . Rich with detail, this book is thorough and not always laudatory of Gates."

—*Library Journal*

"Two veteran reporters take off the rose-colored glasses to show the young tycoon at his best . . . and worst. . . . This warts-and-all portrait of a businessman as a celebrity reveals Gates' temper, childishness, and disregard for employees, as well as his brilliance and work acumen."

—*Booklist*

"An impressively detailed chronicle of the man and his company . . . Independent and scrupulously documented . . . the authors do an outstanding job."

—*PC Magazine*

"Solid information . . . An engrossing narrative."

—*Byte*

"The Bill Gates story is inextricably linked with the history of the PC industry. And that's where the book shines. . . . The most satisfying explanation we're likely to get for quite a while as to why—and how—lightning from the PC revolution struck Bill Gates."

—*Information Week*

"Definitive . . . The intertwined history of the man and the industry is fascinating . . . engrossing . . . What a story!"

"The best biography of Bill Gates . . . the definitive work to date, both well-written and accurate . . . A fascinating, detailed, warts-and-all account of the accumulation of America's largest private fortune by, arguably, the single most important person in computer history."

"The hot book of the new year for anyone who follows the computer industry."

"A rich and wonderfully captivating account of the birth of an industry that changed the world . . . Manes and Andrews successfully weave together what are now two interrelated tales: the development of both Bill Gates and the microcomputer industry. . . . The book captures those early years of computing so well that you can almost feel the excitement and power. . . . Manes and Andrews should also be applauded for presenting technical information about the emerging technologies of the time that should neither intimidate nor insult the reader."

"The ultimate Bill Gates book . . . dismisses old myths and adds new seasoning to the Gates legend, as fact is separated from fiction with extraordinary detail. This history book tells a story that is as fascinating as the American dream."

"Manes and Andrews have written not just a biography, but a history of the microcomputer industry . . . that is at once entertaining and informative. Whether you work with business or computers, or are simply curious for details on how the wealthiest man in America made it to the top, *Gates* should be at the top of your reading list."

". . . the best-researched and most-detailed history of desktop computing ever written. It's ostensibly about Billion-Dollar Bill, but Microsoft's history starts with the Altair in 1975 and touches literally every aspect of desktop computing to happen since then.

"And Gates is an interesting guy, one you have to admire without necessarily wanting to play bridge with him. . . . He is quintessentially American, and I doubt a better portrait of him will be painted than this one. . . ."

GATES

HOW MICROSOFT'S MOGUL

▼

REINVENTED AN INDUSTRY—

▼

AND MADE HIMSELF

▼

THE RICHEST MAN IN AMERICA

STEPHEN MANES
AND
PAUL ANDREWS

A TOUCHSTONE BOOK
PUBLISHED BY SIMON & SCHUSTER INC.
NEW YORK   LONDON   TORONTO   SYDNEY   TOKYO   SINGAPORE

TOUCHSTONE
Rockefeller Center
1230 Avenue of the Americas
New York, New York 10020

Designed by Claire Naylon Vaccaro
Manufactured in the United States of America

10 9 8 7 6 5 4 3 2 1

Library of Congress Cataloging-in-Publication Data is available.

ISBN 0-671-88074-8

Illustration credits: 1: Jim Ball; 2, 3: © *Seattle Times;* 4, 5, 6, 10, 11: Courtesy of Mary and Bill Gates; 7:
Wallace Ackerman Studio; 8, 9: Lakeside School; 13: Photo by Jungle Jim Productions, courtesy of Paul
Gilbert; 15: Photo by Tim Rogers, © 1992 Stephen Manes and Paul Andrews; 16: Reprinted from
POPULAR ELECTRONICS, January 1975, copyright © 1975, Ziff-Davis Publishing Company; 19: The
Computer Museum, Boston; 20: Courtesy of Monte Davidoff; 22, 23, 28, 29, 30, 31, 32, 34, 35: Courtesy
of Bob Wallace; 24: Courtesy of Ric Weiland; 25, 26, 33: Courtesy of Microsoft; 27: Courtesy of Miriam
Lubow; 36: Courtesy of Jack Sams; 38: Photo by Dale Blindheim, © 1992 Stephen Manes and Paul
Andrews; 39: Photo by Barry Wong, © *Seattle Times;* 40, 54: Courtesy of Charles Simonyi; 41: Courtesy of
Jill Bennett; 42, 46, 48: © 1984 Ann E. Yow; 43: © 1986 Ann E. Yow; 44: © 1990 Ann E. Yow; 45, 47:
© 1988 Ann E. Yow; 49, 50: © 1987 Ann E. Yow; 51: © 1992 Ann E. Yow; 52: Mike Siegel/SYGMA; 53:
Photo by Mark Harrison, © *Seattle Times;* 55: Doug Wilson; 56: Copyright © Aerolist Photographers Inc.,
1-800-852-3686.

Excerpts from Joseph Weizenbaum, *Computer Power and Human Reason,* copyright © 1976, reprinted by
permission of W. H. Freeman and Company.

for Susan
——S.M.

for Cecile
——P.A.

CONTENTS

The computer programmer . . . is a creator of universes for which he alone is the lawgiver. . . . No playwright, no stage director, no emperor, however powerful, has ever exercised such absolute authority to arrange a stage or a field of battle and to command such unswervingly dutiful actors or troops.

—JOSEPH WEIZENBAUM,
Computer Power and Human Reason

PROLOGUE

WITNESS THE
TRANSFORMATION!

On the otherwise unremarkable day of May 22, 1990, William Henry Gates—often called III, in actuality IV, and legally just William Henry—was about to transform the computer industry one more time. As he rocked back and forth in the wings of Manhattan's City Center Theater, the hyperkinetic, tousle-haired thirty-four-year-old computer programmer, tycoon, Harvard dropout, and multibillionaire was about to deliver the most important presentation of his presentation-filled career. Bill Gates, co-founder, chairman, and chief executive officer of Microsoft, number-one personal computer software company in the known galaxy, was about to announce the latest incarnation of Microsoft Windows. It was a product that had been released four or five times before to less than stunning success. But now . . .

Witness the transformation!

It was the theme of the day, the slogan for the biggest, splashiest software rollout yet concocted. It was emblazoned on posters, flyers, buttons. It sounded like the mantra of some bizarre religious cult—which in some ways it was. When you got right down to it, this whole Windows thing had been basically an act of faith, Bill Gates's faith in his vision of the future of computers —a faith that had taken him to the very top of the industry and transformed him into a national figure in the class of such inventor-promoter plutocrats as Thomas Edison, Henry Ford, and Howard Hughes.

As the throng of press, industry-watchers, analysts, and customers filed into the auditorium, the giant screen above the stage displayed only the classic `C:\>` prompt that signified dull old MS-DOS. That essential "operating system" software served as a sort of butler for other programs, controlled virtually every IBM PC and compatible ever made, and had long been the underpinning of the Microsoft fortune. Now Windows was designed to wipe that prompt off the screen and take DOS into the future.

With Japanese long-term tenacity, Bill Gates had steered this pet project through half a dozen incarnations over seven itchy years to response that had been anything but deafening. It wasn't easy to get people excited about a program designed, like DOS, mainly to run other programs, and that was pretty much what Windows was. Yet as he waited near a loudspeaker pumping out the mindlessly hard-driving music common to porn films and business "events," the high-stakes poker player in Gates knew he was about to turn up an ace.

Witness the transformation!

Transformation? Gates had seen his share of it, had created his share. On the day he was born in 1955, fewer than 500 electronic computers had existed in the entire world, their total retail value amounted to less than $200 million, and the term "software" had not yet been coined. Over the years since his junior high school days in 1968, when he first laid hands on a computer terminal, Bill Gates had transformed himself and his company again and again, bending over backward and sometimes forward to create the business, get the business, keep the business. Now Gates was personally worth more than $2 billion, his company was valued at more than $7 billion, and he owed it all to an electronic revolution he had helped create.

In the world of 1990, computers were virtually everywhere you might look —and many places you couldn't. Gates and his company had little influence on the refrigerator-size modules that symbolized Big Computing's past and still hulked in air-conditioned chambers crunching data for banks and underwriters and universities and government agencies. Microsoft and its CEO had virtually nothing to do with the millions upon millions of tiny single-chip computers— microprocessors—hidden in the guts of cars, TV sets, VCRs, radios, fax machines, copiers, telephones, popcorn poppers.

But the man and the company had made an unmistakable mark on the millions and millions of microprocessors inside the machines that had come to epitomize the word "computer" in the 1980s. To most people, "computer" now meant "personal computer," a machine that fit on desk or lap—a screen, a keyboard, a disk drive or three, perhaps a mouse, all hooked up to anything from a scanner that could decipher printed words, to a printer that could produce typographically elegant pages, to a plotter that could render architectural drawings, to a modem that could send documents across the world in a flash. And some nine out of ten of those computers—it was probably closer to ten out of ten—ran software from Bill Gates's Microsoft.

Witness the transformation!

Forget chips and circuit boards and capacitors and controllers: What transformed all that mere hardware into a device that could actually do something useful was an intangible set of commands, an intellectual product that determined whether a given machine would manipulate words, calculate sums, animate pictures, do all three at once, or do something else entirely. That behind-the-scenes puppeteer, that intellectual product, that command set, was software.

Computer software had been around since World War II, though the term was largely unknown as late as 1960. But back in 1975, Gates and his partner Paul Allen had been the very first to commercialize software for the just-born personal computer. And commercialize was the word: Whereas much early software had been developed for the sheer challenge and shared like some favorite toy, the Gates/Allen edition of BASIC—the first personal computer language—was from the outset a business proposition, something people were supposed to pay for. That idea did not sit well with the pioneer hobbyists whose lame little machines needed BASIC to become something more than high-tech doorstops.

It had been Bill Gates himself who first challenged the freebie software ethic, in a truculently capitalistic letter bemoaning that his BASIC had been ripped off, unconscionably copied, and then blithely distributed among computer hobbyists without so much as a thank-you to its authors. Never mind that young Bill had a less-than-spotless past when it came to computer freebieism, had been chastised for manipulating accounts on a time-sharing system as an eighth grader and investigated by Harvard University for running up hour upon hour of academic computer time while developing that very same for-profit BASIC. Those had been mere errors of youth. Software was business.

And what a business! From Bill's initial BASIC, the microcomputer software industry had grown to become one hell of a business, an $8 billion business heading into the stratosphere, a business with profit margins undreamed of in the world of hardware, a business that at Microsoft alone had turned hundreds of programming weenies into millionaires.

And billionaires. As the house lights dimmed in the City Center, the sometimes-boyish man waiting offstage was without doubt the wealthiest, most influential computer mogul of them all. Bill Gates owned 36 percent of the company he had co-founded, an international enterprise with a wildly diversified product line that was grossing over a billion dollars a year with no debt at all and a war chest of nearly half a billion dollars in cash. He was planning a state-of-the-art electronic whizbang of a house whose site alone cost $5 million and whose construction might take a couple of dozen million more. He was scouting investments in electronic art displays and artificial intelligence and biotechnology and who knew what else. And, most amazingly of all, in a decade of mere money-movers like Ivan Boesky and Michael Milken, Gates had earned his fortune from a company that actually made things.

Gates's reign over the kingdom of the soft extended far across the border of the hard. His decisions on which machines to back and which to ignore helped make companies and break them. Heads of firms that created computers and microprocessors—hardware—regularly made pilgrimages to Microsoft's wooded headquarters in Redmond, Washington, to sit at the feet of the master. Indeed, the company had even set an industry standard with its Microsoft Mouse—hardware.

Lavish product-rollout extravaganzas like this one had once been the almost exclusive domain of hardware companies, the IBMs and Compaqs and Apples of the industry that pushed hefty boxes of metal and plastic and silicon at thousands of bucks a pop. Today, for the first time ever, a mere hundred-dollar software program ($150 list, but only fools would pay that) was being launched with the hoopla and backing—a cool $2 million—formerly reserved for hardware costing multiple kilobucks.

Some of that $2 million had financed the satellite links that were now beaming the City Center event to Boston and Chicago and Dallas and San Francisco and Los Angeles and Toronto and Washington, D.C. Some of it had financed what the audience was watching now: Microsoft's filmic short course in computer history. The on-screen parade through the past included mostly hardware—no sense hyping the competition—yet the passing glimpses of Richard Nixon, Michael Jackson, and E.T. subtly emphasized the essential point: At bottom, software was no longer merely the offstage puppeteer that manipulated hardware. Software had become the star.

Just as the music (software) on a compact disc was the important thing and the player a mere device to extract it, just as the movie (software) on a videotape was the important thing and the player a mere device to deliver the sound and picture, computer software had become the important thing, nothing less than what you played on hardware. There was word processing software to make you a better writer, spreadsheet software to give those bottom lines panache, database software to endow you with the digital intelligence of the CIA. Desktop publishing software promised to turn you into a Gutenberg, multimedia software sounded neat even if nobody could say exactly why, business presentation software could transmogrify you into—well, a Bill Gates. Software determined what hardware was worth. Software defined hardware. Software *made* hardware.

Gates had been instrumental in making this software revolution happen. In the fifteen years since he had welcomed the dawn of personal computing, software had gone from drab functional tools custom-written for big companies to eye-popping, shrink-wrapped, hype-slathered, mass-market manna generating profit margins that bordered on the outrageous. Hardware? With few exceptions, hardware was just plain boring, a mere commodity, a fungible item of no more interest than a VCR or TV set and sold at margins almost as slim.

And if you didn't want to take Microsoft's word for it, you could believe the popular press, which had picked up on the idea that the computer industry had become the New Hollywood, complete with enormous paydays, gossip columns, stars. Among those stars, the press's designated Personal Computer Visionary had until recently been Steve Jobs, the co-founder of Apple Computer and most recently of NeXT Inc.—a hardware guy! For years the headlines had read Steve Jobs Says This, and Steve Jobs Says That, and Steve Jobs Says the Other Thing, and every once in a while Bill Gates Says Something Else Entirely. But now Steve Jobs, whose fortune was counted in mere millions with an *m*, was out in Silicon Valley hustling his latest change-the-world machine, trying to relive the dream maybe once too often, and the press's attention had passed to Bill Gates—a software guy, *the* software guy.

Now the Windows rollout would cement Bill's position as the media's designated superstar. Before the media frenzy was over, dozens of national magazines would feature him and/or Windows on their covers. "Good Morning America," "Today," *Time, Newsweek, Fortune, People, USA Today,* and nearly every computer rag on the planet would be touting Bill Gates and his wonder product.

Under the able guidance of his public relations counselors, Gates was being propelled into a curious kind of nerdy celebrityhood riddled with contradictory stories about wild womanizing on the one hand and an inability to get a date on the other, about fast cars and speeding tickets mixed with monkish workaholism, about a thirst for Dom Perignon in private but hamburgers and french fries in public. Reportedly a voracious reader, he insisted his favorite books were two novels, *The Catcher in the Rye* and *A Separate Peace,* popular largely with pimply adolescents. Described as oblivious to wealth, he was quoted boasting "I have an infinite amount of money." Although he clearly enjoyed his fame and notoriety—at his thirtieth birthday celebration he came dressed as Jay Gatsby—he was nonetheless fiercely private, choosing to dole out to the press a collection of random fabrications, exaggerations, and facts that left Gates-watchers with the same question that appeared with a photo of him in his high school yearbook: "Who is this man?"

His multiple contradictions remained unexplored. Gates, the roving bachelor, remained so close to his parents and sisters that he built a secluded vacation compound for them yet designed it to double as a site for corporate retreats. Gates, the corporate bigwig, would discuss Microsoft business over dinner with employees and then blithely split the check with them. Gates, the terrible-tongued pragmatist, remained fiercely loyal to his oldest friends, maintaining jobs for them, standing by them even through conviction and imprisonment. Bill Gates's story was never rags to riches, a Harvard friend once remarked, but riches to riches—though the initial affluence, embellished to include such fictions as a million-dollar trust fund, was now utterly insignificant.

A "high-bandwidth" intellect capable of discussing gene splicing with high-powered biotech scientists, a business wizard who at the age of twenty-three could rebuff a buyout offer from Ross Perot, Gates could just as easily lock his keys in the trunk of his rental car, lose his credit cards, and burn out car engines by ignoring the "low oil" light. Gates owned a limited-edition Porsche 959 he'd bought for $380,000 and whose value had more than doubled even though the U.S. Government deemed it unroadworthy, yet he flew coach whenever possible. Charming one minute, rude the next, Gates was hard to sum up in a sound bite, a Binary Bill of polar contradictions beginning with public shyness and private aggressiveness—some said ruthlessness—that even longtime associates found difficult to reconcile.

Witness the transformation!

On the City Center screen, a splashy MTV-style extended commercial featured a trip into a Windowsland where computing would be transformed into child's play. Microsoft called Windows an "operating environment," meaning it was designed mainly to run other programs—programs that could take advantage of its graphical user interface—"GUI," as it was known in the industry, "gooey," as it was pronounced.

A GUI gave you a symbolic representation of your desktop right up there on your computer screen, complete with little pictures called "icons"—a sheet of paper to signify a data file, a fanciful trademark to represent a program. When you worked with a document on your screen, it would look pretty much like what would emerge from your printer. You'd manipulate it all with a pointing device called a mouse. And if you were so inclined, you could divide your screen into areas called—yes!—"windows."

The GUI concept was invented neither by Bill Gates nor by Microsoft. Windows was a descendant—some would say "ripoff"—of earlier graphical user interfaces, most notably the experimental versions from Xerox's Palo Alto Research Center, better known as PARC, and the best-known and best-loved GUI of them all, the commercial version from Apple Computer's Macintosh. Compared to these rather elegant renderings of the concept, the first versions of Windows had been gauche, ugly poor relations. But now, as the mantra pointed out, Windows had undergone major cosmetic and internal surgery and emerged looking fit, trim, glamorous. Under the guidance of Windows, stodgy IBM PCs and clones would be magically transformed into lovable Macalikes.

And why not? After all, Bill Gates had been in on both the IBM PC and the Macintosh from their very inception. He was among the few people in the world who had played with both machines when they were mere prototypes, little more than circuit boards with wires sticking out all over them. So who better to perform this transformation than . . .

. . . "Ladies and Gentlemen: Bill Gates!" Despite his ill-fitting pinstripe suit and bunched-up red tie, the Boy Genius looked more like a classic businessman than ever and less like a boy. As he strode to the stage and pushed his glasses back on his nose in a characteristic gesture, he actually looked his age. On the giant screen above his head, his visage gazed out over the silent auditorium.

Gates grinned awkwardly. "Well, I'm glad to hear it's ready. This would have been a very extravagant way to announce a delay in our schedule." Even in a room ready for an icebreaker, the joke fell flat. Windows 3.0 had not been officially announced until now, but it had been delayed so often that it had become the worst-kept secret in the computer industry. The first Windows announcement, back in the PC cobwebs of 1983, had taken place a few blocks away, at the Plaza Hotel, more than two full years before the product was actually delivered. The original Windows release was so late that it was responsible for the popularization of the term "vaporware"—software that exists primarily in the minds of its developers.

But seven years in the computer business was such ancient history that few in the audience even remembered the initial delays. Over those seven years, the Windows story had been one of tepid reviews, backhanded compliments, empty hype, sluggish sales. After half a dozen incarnations, Windows was supposed to be in its grave.

Lawyers might have sounded the death knell. The very Macintoshness of Windows was the subject of a celebrated and protracted Apple lawsuit against Microsoft.

IBM might have dealt the death blow. Big Blue had refused to go along with Windows no matter how hard Bill pitched it. Instead a succession of blue suits insisted on defenestrating Windows in the process of creating the jointly developed OS/2, a bigger, stronger, more powerful system intended to do all the things Windows and MS-DOS did and many more besides.

Still, IBM was a big, loyal customer, and Bill and his old Harvard buddy, best friend, and prime lieutenant Steve Ballmer agreed they wanted its business. So Microsoft said yes, customer, you are right, we'll do it your way. In the inmost circles of Microsoft, doing things The IBM Way for OS/2 came to be known by the acronym BOGU—Bend Over and Grease Up—and was symbolized by the jar of Vaseline a group of programmers gave Ballmer for one less than happy birthday.

Now, after all these years, Windows was more alive than ever. If anybody in American business could afford the luxury of a Japanese-style long view, it was Billion-Dollar Bill. Of all the young microcomputer pioneers, he was virtually the only one left in control of his original company. Alone in the spotlight, with his face filling the screen overhead, the owlish Young Achiever with a developing middle-age wattle executed his performance stiffly, awkwardly, talking about how complicated and boring the PC had become and how the graphical Windows interface was going to transform the desktop computer into something cool, great, neat, super. Right, wags muttered: a lot like what the Macintosh had been for years now.

Theatrical smoke and flashing lights heralded a demonstration. Look, Bill said in his deadpan way. You could switch between programs without having to exit and reload. You could cut numbers from one program and paste them into another one. You could "hot-link" two programs together so that changing a number in a spreadsheet would change a total in a form letter. You could, of course, have done all those things with earlier versions of Windows, but never mind. Now there were more colors! Fancier icons! Cleaner borders! Snazzier fonts! Sexy 3-D buttons! And now you could write and run really *big* programs.

Gates even called his old buddy and colleague, the bearded, heavyset Paul Allen, to the stage for a sentimental but overscripted public reunion. After a bout with Hodgkin's disease in 1982, Allen had gone off to form Asymetrix, a new software company, and his lack of interest in publicity had made him something of a forgotten man, even though he owned a street-illegal Porsche just like Bill's, even though he was building a house as grand as Bill's, even though he owned vast property tracts in Hawaii and the Portland Trail Blazers basketball team—forgotten, perhaps, because his net worth was only half of Bill's, a paltry billion. Now, after a welcome return to Microsoft's board of directors, he was bantering awkwardly with his old friend in a rare public appearance as he demonstrated ToolBook, his software intended to make programming and animation easier. "We've come a long way in fifteen years!" Bill read from the teleprompter.

Next came the grand finale: a videotaped parade of computer-industry heavyweights, fellow hardware and software giants, even members of the computer press, praising the new Windows in unstinting gush. Even Borland's Philippe Kahn, a longtime Microsoft archenemy, joined the fun, announcing: "Windows is an important platform for the future. I never thought I would say that with a straight face!" The final shot caught Bill Gates in shirtsleeves staring at the camera, pushing his glasses back on his nose yet again, and uttering a single word: "Cool!"

The taped Gates dissolved into the real Gates, who called out the entire Windows development team, a motley crew united by their official Windows polo shirts—scraggly-haired, blue-jeaned young Smart Guys (and a couple of Gals) wandering through the aisles brandishing copies of Windows 3.0. In the days that followed, Egghead Discount Software stores would find lines of eager customers waiting outside their front doors to buy the new Windows.

Windows or OS/2? Let the market decide! It wouldn't be long before Boom-Boom Ballmer, Gates's prime lieutenant, would be pounding his fist on the tables of America's corporate boardrooms, leading not the tired old cheer

—OS/2! OS/2! OS/2!—but the stirring new one: Windows! Windows! Windows! By the end of its first year on the market, Windows 3.0 would sell more than 4 million units—more than all the Apple Macintosh computers sold since the machine was introduced in a similar hellzapoppin' rollout with a dramatic Super Bowl third-quarter TV ad in January 1984. Windows, however, would do it without TV; Bill Gates had so little interest in broadcast television that his home set and VCR did not include tuners.

Microsoft's success was so immediate and dramatic that Apple found itself beleaguered by cheap PCs running Windows and scrambled to contrive a new line of low-cost Macintoshes. Independent software developers began deserting OS/2 in droves to write Windows applications. And then came the backlash. Windows wasn't as easy to use as the initial claims led some to believe. Windows was slow. Windows didn't always work quite right. And Microsoft's emphasis on Windows made IBM feel queasy about OS/2 and the future of its relationship with Bill Gates. Windows was a home run, but a home run of a special kind—the kind that broke the neighbor's windows.

Within months the most popular industry sport would become Bill-bashing, grumbling and mumbling about unfair business practices at Microsoft— welshed deals, misinformation, disinformation. On the cover of *Business Month,* Gates's head would be satirically airbrushed onto a weight lifter's torso above the legend "The Silicon Bully: How Long Can Bill Gates Kick Sand in the Face of the Computer Industry?" Inside, competitors would compare him to GM's discredited Roger Smith, and Lotus 1-2-3 creator Mitch Kapor would call Microsoft products "unimaginative, tone-deaf, and slow."

With that issue, *Business Month* expired, but that didn't stop the talk. Competitors would bitch about how Microsoft sent teams of developers to software companies to steal corporate secrets, about how the company would get others to divulge their product plans and then go off to develop competitive products of its own. A small mouse maker would sue, howling antitrust. The Federal Trade Commission would launch an antitrust investigation, with the implied threat of breaking up Gates's carefully constructed empire. IBM and Microsoft, their relationship already on the rocks, would file formal separation papers. It would get so bad that industry luminaries would refer to Bill Gates as the Prince of Darkness, his employees as Hitler Youth.

And then it would get better. By early 1992 the stock market would value Microsoft at more than $22 billion, making Bill Gates, at more than $7 billion, the richest person in America. A single golden share of Microsoft's first private stock issue worth roughly $1 in 1981 would be worth more than $1,500; a $25 share from the 1986 initial public offering would be worth more than $750.

But all that was for later. On the day of the Windows rollout, Bill Gates and Microsoft were on top of the computer world. You could calculate your corporate budget with a Microsoft spreadsheet, display it as a slide with

Microsoft presentation software, turn it into a report with Microsoft word processing software. And if software weren't enough, you could buy Microsoft Press books, read a Microsoft magazine, wear Microsoft T-shirts, even—was it the snide joke of the Harvard dropout?—attend Microsoft University. Insiders who knew Bill's ability, his luck, his hubris, his shrewdness, his chutzpah, his downright fearlessness were certain that no matter what happened, Billion-Dollar Bill would find a way to slap a Microsoft label on it and make a buck off it.

In the audience at City Center, his mother was beaming. This transcontinental, international presentation was a significant improvement over one she remembered from fifteen years ago. At that demonstration, in the family living room, everything had gone awry, and her son had invoked her assistance in front of the baffled customer: "Tell him, Mom! Tell him it worked last night!"

No, this time everything had worked just fine. At a celebration that evening, Mary Gates told a reporter "This is the happiest day of Bill's life."

1

"THINK SMART!"

William Henry Gates was born October 28, 1955, in Seattle's Swedish Hospital. A cheerful infant, dubbed "Happy Boy" by the neighbors, he was the only son, and the second of three children, of William Henry Jr. and Mary Gates. The Northwest lineage of both parents traced back to the late 1800s, when the pioneering instinct sent opportunists and fortune hunters to the promise-filled West Coast.

Bill's great-grandfather, Pennsylvania native William Henry Gates Sr., arrived in the Seattle area in the 1880s, when the young port city was booming with expansionist fervor. In his early years, this Bill Gates reportedly ran a delivery wagon, which he used to ferry distraught victims to safety in the Great Seattle Fire of 1889, the Northwest's version of the Chicago conflagration. When gold was discovered in Alaska nine years later, Gates moved his wife and three children—two girls and Microsoft Bill's grandfather William Henry Jr. —to Nome.

The Gates clan spent more than a decade in the Last Frontier, where Bill Sr. established a furniture business and built a grubstake by mining prospectors' pockets. At the age of eight his enterprising son, known as Will, made a name for himself selling newspapers to transplanted Lower Forty-Eighters starved for the latest word from back home.

By the beginning of the Great War, the Gateses had moved back to Puget Sound, to the burgeoning navy shipyard town of Bremerton. Gates purchased a building he named the Gates Hotel and with a partner began a secondhand furniture business, the U.S. Furniture Company. Eventually selling new merchandise, the store became a fixture in downtown Bremerton.

As the business grew, young Will Gates was named manager. Tall, congenial, and popular, he joined virtually every civic organization and social club in the area. When his son, William Henry Gates III, was born in 1925, proud poppa Will walked up and down Bremerton's streets announcing the event to well-wishers.

Nicknamed "Billy," Microsoft Bill's father evinced the Gates flair for entrepreneurship at an early age. He and a neighbor kid combined to put out a newspaper, *The Weekly Receiver,* complete with classified advertisements and a sports section so respected for its accuracy it won the two thirteen-year-olds choice seats in the press box at local games. The duo sold shares to family and friends at a dime apiece; when the paper eventually folded, they repaid stockholders at the munificent rate of fifteen cents a share.

Billy Gates dropped the diminutive—and the III—from his name before he entered the army to serve in World War II. He even made it official: "On my birth certificate it said William Henry Gates III. And as I was getting ready to go into the service, I was apprehensive about that, because I had to send in a copy of my birth certificate, and I could see on all these rosters around the service in the army: 'William H. Gates III.' And I wasn't particularly crazy to give some top sergeant that line . . . So I got my name officially changed to William H. Gates Jr."

Shorn of his numerical suffix, Gates attained the rank of second lieutenant. After the war he attended the University of Washington as an undergraduate, went on to study law there, and became assistant city attorney for his native Bremerton. He also married a young schoolteacher he'd met at the UW, where the two wound up sharing fiscal duties as members of the student body Budget and Finance Committee.

Mary Maxwell, nicknamed "Giggles," was a vivacious social dynamo who had been elected secretary of the Associated Students of UW and president of the Kappa Kappa Gamma sorority, participated in the women's honorary societies Mortar Board and Totem Club, and posted the best time in the women's 1950 intramural ski meet. Energy ran in her family. While the Gates patriarch was putting together his grubstake in Alaska, Mary's grandfather was forging his financial career in southwest Washington.

James Willard Maxwell had ventured west from Lincoln, Nebraska, with more than a decade of banking already under his belt. The son of a physician who had helped lay out the town of Lincoln, Maxwell had been born in 1864 in Iowa. "The Indians really were wild," he would relate in his eighties. "At every Indian scare, my family kept moving eastward from Lincoln, Nebraska, until the family was in Iowa. Then I was born, and we went back."

Nicknamed "Willie" and "Will," both of which he detested, Maxwell spent his boyhood in Lincoln and left high school at the end of his freshman year. Later he relished telling how at age fifteen he began his banking career literally at the bottom—digging a cellar for a Lincoln bank president. Offered a salary of $16 a month, he vowed to complete the cellar in two months but wound up taking three—the sort of promise-to-delivery ratio that would later become commonplace in his great-grandson's software ventures.

In Maxwell's telling, the banker was nonetheless impressed enough to offer him the lowly position of errand boy, and he quickly worked his way up through the ranks to the position of assistant cashier. He also became friends with prominent Lincoln citizens, including the renowned orator and politician William Jennings Bryan and the future World War I General John J. Pershing, at the time an instructor at the University of Nebraska.

Although climbing Lincoln's social ladder, Maxwell felt he could shake his vexing nicknames and make a bigger mark in the uncharted but fertile commercial wilds of the Pacific Northwest. In 1892 he and his wife settled in the bustling Washington port of South Bend. At the time the town considered itself a cinch to be the terminus of the Northern Pacific Railroad and thus the Northwest's gateway to Alaska, West Coast, and Orient trade, and Maxwell knew someone had to keep track of the cash flow. He founded the American Exchange Bank, then acquired a partner and turned it into a private bank called Maxwell, Smith & Company. Before the century turned, Maxwell had served two terms as mayor of South Bend, a stint on the school board, and one term in the state legislature and had started businesses in barrel bolts and oysters.

In 1901, through the influence of a boyhood friend, Charles G. Dawes, then serving as comptroller of the currency in a career that would lead to the vice-presidency of the United States, Maxwell was made national bank examiner for a five-state district stretching from Washington to Wyoming. For six years he roamed the region, a traveling physician for the fiscally unfit. In 1906, however, it was Seattle for keeps. Maxwell served nineteen months as cashier of the National Bank of Commerce, then moved to Seattle National Bank, where he became an officer, director, and major shareholder. In 1911 he organized the National City Bank of Seattle. His career came full circle eighteen years later, when that bank merged with the National Bank of Commerce and he was named chairman of the new institution's executive committee.

Wide-mouthed, thick-lipped, bespectacled, and talkative, Maxwell distinguished himself as a public citizen in his middle and later years, serving on a variety of boards, including the Seattle Chamber of Commerce, the Federal Home Loan Bank Board, and the national board of the American Automobile Association. Every Thanksgiving he supplied a local charity with enough turkeys to feed 1,000 people. But he seemed to be proudest of his longevity as president of the Automobile Club of Washington, a position he held for twenty-five years. Although Maxwell was involved in a widely reported 1929 two-car collision in which he suffered a slight brain concussion, his car was reportedly being driven by a friend at the time. Maxwell's passion for motoring would reappear in later generations, particularly in Bill Gates's legendary adventures beyond the speed limit.

Perhaps J. W.'s greatest bequest was a Spartan work ethic and competitive spirit. Headlined "Bankers' Hours! They Mean Little to Maxwell," a 1929 *Seattle Star* story told how J. W. arrived at his office an hour earlier than the rest of the work force, despite an oppressive forty-five-minute commute by public bus from his summer home. Fifty-five years later night owl Bill Gates would lose at least one girlfriend by insisting on a "seven-hour turnaround" between leaving work in the evening and arriving back the next morning.

An avid tennis player into his seventies, J. W. organized a bank-industry tournament "and offered the loving-cup prize. Then I played for the title myself. I took a beating over that. 'You give the cup and then try to win it yourself—fine thing,' people scoffed. I'd have given anything to win, but I never did." Anything to win? That attitude would again and again be ascribed to J. W.'s great-grandson.

Maxwell kept working through his eighty-fifth birthday, telling associates he was too busy to think of retirement. A year later he was reportedly accumulating magazine covers of pretty girls to paper his garage. When he died in 1951, he had amassed a fortune appraised at $265,000 in a widely diversified portfolio of stocks, bonds, and real estate. Five years before, his late wife, Belle Oakley Maxwell, had left an estate valued at roughly $450,000.

J. W.'s sons, Oakley and James Willard Jr., followed in their father's footsteps wearing smaller shoes. Willard, vice president of Pacific National Bank, was an early proponent of Far East trade, visiting Tokyo, Hong Kong, Saigon, and other Asian cities in a 1957 expedition that presaged his grandson's future business ties with the Orient. Oakley served as vice president of his father's National Bank of Commerce; his wife Alice achieved moderate fame as a short story writer for national magazines. Both brothers were active in United Good Neighbors, a tradition continued by Willard's daughter Mary after the organization was renamed United Way. Willard died in 1960 at the relatively young age of fifty-nine—the same age at which Oakley had passed away—leaving his wife Adelle and their daughter Mary.

Mary Maxwell and Bill Gates were married in 1951. After teaching junior high school in Bremerton for a year, Mary switched to a classroom in north Seattle when her husband joined the Seattle law firm of Skeel, McKelvy, Henke, Evenson & Uhlmann. Tall, distinguished, warm, and gracious in a manner more evocative of Southern gentility than the chilly politeness of the Pacific Northwest, Mary and Bill cut impressive figures at social and political gatherings and began to make their mark on Seattle's civic landscape. With the lack of ostentation typical of upper-crust Seattle, they lived comfortably but modestly. After a brief stay in the firmly middle-class Wedgwood neighborhood, they moved to a small, simple postwar single-story house in Seattle's pleasant but hardly exclusive View Ridge.

In 1953 Bill and Mary Gates started their family with the birth of a daughter, Kristianne, named—but not spelled—after Kristiane Rasmussen, a Norwegian immigrant whose devoted service as J. W. Maxwell's housekeeper led him to remember her in his will with $5,000 cash and $150 a month for two years.

When their second child arrived on a Friday just before Halloween, there was no question what he would be named. On Bill's birth certificate, he bears the same name as his father, no numerical designation specified. Although actually the fourth, the William Henry Gates who rose to software stardom has never referred to himself that way, nor has anyone else in the family. Three became the preferred number, especially when Grandma Adelle instantly dubbed him "Trey," the cardplayer's term for a three. But Gates also was known as "Little Bill" when he was growing up. He signed a high school yearbook "William H. Gates Jr." Eventually he would go mostly by plain "Bill Gates," using "William Gates Jr." to avoid local confusion, and reserving "William Gates III" primarily for formal business occasions.

From the start the newest Bill was a high-energy kid. Whenever his mother visited his cradle, a family heirloom on rockers, the baby would be swaying to and fro. In his early years he would spend hours riding a coil-springed hobby-horse. "I think that got to be a very comforting, comfortable kind of motion for him," his mother recalled. No doubt: He carried his rocking habit into adulthood and Microsoft, where it would become his most widely imitated personal trademark.

The Seattle of Bill's childhood was a regional hub with a lively port, a flourishing aerospace industry, and a strong sense of community. Seattle's Boeing was jetmaker to the world, but what first revealed the hardworking, unpretentious city's hidden ambitions was the 1962 World's Fair. Its theme was "Century 21." Its symbol was the soaring free-form Space Needle with its patented revolving restaurant. Its focus was technology for the twenty-first century. To young Bill Gates, it was "a huge event, a neat deal. We went to every pavilion."

The vision of the future was strikingly like the one an adult Bill Gates would see and sell twenty and thirty years later. Spurred by the Kennedy-era push for scientific achievement, the U.S. Science Exhibit had as an official goal "to stimulate youths' interest in science," and hammered it home with films and exhibits on everything from genetics to space travel. The NASA exhibit included the *Freedom* 7 capsule in which Alan Shepard had made the first manned American space flight just one year before.

Among the computer exhibits were giant IBM machines set up to translate words spoken into a microphone or calculate space satellite trajectories, and the American Library Association's Univac that stored "quotations from great books, gazetteer information, and bibliographical material." The World of Tomorrow included the office of the future, "a complete communications center with devices that project micro-mail, automatic transmission machines for correspondence and machines that communicate with one another to exchange information, freeing man for more creative pursuits." And the General Electric Pavilion presented "General Electric Living," featuring "colored television projected on large wall surfaces, the electronic home library, movies that can be shown immediately after they are taken . . . and the home computer for record-keeping, shopping and check writing." Although the adult Bill Gates would eventually work on projects that mirrored every one of these uses and would even team up briefly with General Electric on a computer project called "Homer," what impressed the six-year-old Bill Gates were things that went fast: the mile-long monorail and the Wild Mouse ride.

"He was a nerd before the term was even invented," said one former teacher. With a disregard for fashion that he would never totally abandon, the school-age Bill buttoned his shirt to the top and hiked his pants well above his waist. Gates had a high-pitched, nasal, almost squeaky voice that carried into adulthood. Small for his age, skinny, and left-handed, with big feet on an otherwise slight frame, he cut a gawky, lively figure.

Bill was usually also the youngest in his class; his October 28 birthday meant he squeaked in under the Seattle schools' November 1 enrollment cutoff. By third or fourth grade, the discrepancy with his classmates was obvious enough that his parents considered holding Trey back a year. School authorities convinced them that however slight Bill's physique or immature his personality, his mind was more than capable. By the age of nine he had read the *World Book* encyclopedia from A to Z and, his mother recalled, would chide her for insufficient intellection: "He'd never ever be ready when we were going someplace, and we'd call out to him, 'What are you doing?' "

Bill's response: "I'm thinking. I'm thinking."

"It was worse than that," according to his father. "He'd chastise us: 'Don't *you* ever think?' We didn't have a good answer to that: We weren't sure we ever did."

When it came to math drill recordings asking " 'seven plus nineteen' or 'thirteen times five,' all the other kids are going aaarrrggghhh, I can't do this, stop the record!" Gates recalled. He quickly realized he was better at figures than most of his View Ridge Elementary contemporaries. But Bill had a hard time finding challenges in school, and instead got into a variety of scrapes with teachers and administrators. Luckily his quirkiness managed to attract the attention of teachers who would overlook his erratic study habits in favor of his flashes of insight, talent, and competitiveness.

Hazel Carlson, his fourth-grade teacher at View Ridge, was known as a stern disciplinarian adept at handling very bright boys with less-than-perfect behavior records. When she had the class do outlining, Bill's initially neat sinistral hand would quickly disintegrate into a scrawl as he tried to "get as many things down on paper as he could produce in his mind." But when it came to a geography test that utterly baffled other bright kids, Bill passed with only one wrong answer. "He knew a lot about a lot of things," Carlson remembered. His IQ, which she estimated in the 160s or 170s, "was among the higher ones I've ever had."

"He loved to organize things," Carlson recalled, a preoccupation that led him to the school library, where Trey became a tracer of lost books. On the scent of a misplaced title, Bill would work doggedly through recess, to the point where his teachers would have to drag him outdoors for fresh air and exercise. His proudest moment was when he turned up with a volume deemed irretrievably lost but discovered by his sister at a slumber party. Unbeknownst to Bill, the title in question had been passed around as a "spicy" item because of a passage about one character's developing breasts.

In an essay on the theme of "How I Liked Fourth Grade," young Bill singled out as his sport of choice the game "soak 'em," a strange ritual of personal aggressiveness in which the players without the ball try to catch it and the player with the ball tries to hit the others with it. The View Ridge boys played this game hard and rough; Carlson changed the rules to equalize the competition for girls.

But Bill knew he was best at other things. "I want to get back to division because last year I was the best and I liked it very much," Bill wrote in the same essay. "I like everything but arithmatic [sic] book studing [sic] but best of all arithmatic [sic] records." In both fourth and fifth grades, Gates checked the word "scientist" when asked about future occupations.

In a one-hour class, he scrawled a fourteen-page report on the human body when, as Carlson recalled, "Most of the kids did just a page or two." Carlson saved the paper, in which Gates listed dozens of characteristics of major organs in meticulous detail: The heart, he wrote, was "shaped like a valentine," the lungs "shaped like bloon [sic]." Most important, the brain was "unreplacble" [sic]—but if he had to try, Bill wrote, "I'd ask for one that came from a smart dog."

Bill's grandmother Adelle Maxwell, known as "Gam," was there to greet him and his sister when they came home and their mother was out volunteering. That was often: Beginning early in the morning, driving out of the neighborhood at a clip worthy of her grandfather or, eventually, her son, Mary Gates was building a long record of community service. By 1966 she had become president of the Junior League and was working her way up through the ranks of the local United Way. In the 1970s she would serve on a variety of corporate and public boards, including Children's Orthopedic Hospital, Unigard Security Insurance, Pacific Northwest Bell, broadcaster KIRO, and her father's Pacific National Bank, giving her a behind-the-scenes power base equivalent to elective office or business executiveship. In 1975 she would become local chair of the

United Way and a member of the University of Washington Board of Regents, which she would later serve as president.

So Gam assumed the after-school duties, making sure to disappear just before Bill Jr. came home so that she wouldn't be seen as an intrusive mother-in-law. Neighborhood children thought of Gam as a surrogate mom, always ready with cookies and conversation when their mothers needed time off to shop or run errands.

There was a reason Adelle Maxwell dubbed her grandson "Trey": She loved games, particularly cards, and taught young Bill double solitaire, fish, gin, bridge, and a variety of other favorites. For Gam, who had been a star forward on the women's basketball team at Enumclaw High School as well as class valedictorian, games were not frivolous diversions but tests of skill and intelligence. "Very early on we played bridge," Mary Gates remembered, "and she was always saying to him, 'Think smart, think smart!' "

Games of all sorts were a constant in the competitive Gates household—everything from board games to jigsaw puzzle competitions. After dinner, the family would often play cards to see who would do the dishes. Perhaps the ultimate moment in Gatesian gaming legend came when Mary and Bill Jr. learned of her unexpected pregnancy. The parents broke the news to Trey and Kristi in Gam's living room via the medium of Hangman. Before the noose won out, the kids guessed the message: "A little visitor is coming soon." Bill's sister Libby was born in June 1964.

Adelle's intellectual quickness was a major influence on Trey. Gam often read books to the kids, and Bill became an avid reader with broad interests: Math and science books vied for his attention with such classic juvenile fiction as *Charlotte's Web, Dr. Doolittle,* and the Freddie the Pig, Tom Swift, and Tarzan series. A public library near his home had summer reading contests; as Gates recalled it, he was always first among the boys, and occasionally even first overall. But Bill felt he had to temper his competitiveness in order to be accepted:

> I remember girls always got so much better grades than boys, so it was wimpy to get good grades. So I only got good grades in reading and math. And they always had these things where they'd grade you on your ability and effort, so the goal was always to get an A3, which was the best grade with the worst effort. They'd give me like an A1, and I'd say "Come on, I didn't try at all. This is bullshit, it's an A3, and I had a messy desk and everything!"

When he did get threes in effort, his parents did not appreciate them: "You were supposed to get good grades . . . They always thought I was smart and should be doing super well." Mom and Dad rewarded A's with quarters and straight A's—his older sister Kristi always got them—with otherwise forbidden fruit: weeknight television. But bored with school, Gates balanced his good grades in math and reading with C's and D's in the lesser challenges of penmanship, citizenship, and other subjects he considered trivial. It wasn't until his college days that Gates discovered the word "precocious" could have a positive meaning; the only time the term had come up before was in phrases such as "precocious brat" or "precocious troublemaker."

In the middle of Trey's fourth-grade year, the Gateses built a spacious modern house overlooking Lake Washington three miles to the south in Laurelhurst, an understated but highly upscale community that became one of Seattle's most prominent. Both Bill and his sister Libby live in the neighborhood today; his parents are still in the same house, with a clear view of their son's grand new homesite two miles across the water.

The Gateses attended University Congregational Church, where Bible lessons did little to abate Bill's reputation as a smart but erratic cutup. But at age eleven, lured by the promise of dinner atop the Space Needle, young Bill flawlessly delivered the Sermon on the Mount to the church's pastor, the Reverend Dale Turner, after memorizing it on a two-and-a-half hour family drive to the Washington coast. Relatively few of Turner's students attempted the twenty-five-minute recitation, though Kristi Gates had mastered it two years before. Trey's mother had advised the minister that the boy had a "vise-like mind," but Turner was nonetheless impressed with Bill's understanding. "He not only repeated the passage, he showed a grasp of its message well beyond his years."

Sixth grade was a watershed for Trey as his parents and teachers struggled to find a focus for his intellect. One venture was the Contemporary Club, a group of Laurelhurst Elementary schoolchildren who got together for discussions on current events, books, and other topics in a pint-size collegiate atmosphere lacking only sherry and overstuffed sofas. The Contemporaries considered themselves "supermature sixth graders certainly at high school level in our minds," as member Stanley "Boomer" Youngs recalled it. They organized field trips to such intellectually stimulating venues as the Battelle Institute think tank at the edge of the neighborhood. And, inevitably, they competed at games. According to Youngs, "My most vivid memory is of Bill playing Risk," the board game of global domination. "You try to take over the world." It was useful preparation for the future.

So was a special sixth-grade economics class taught by Laurelhurst's principal, George Ryals, for which Bill prepared a report entitled "Invest with Gatesway Incorporated." The report was a family affair: Gam helped put together the cover, and Bill's father, who did legal work for Physio-Control, the Seattle firm that marketed the first portable defibrillator for the revival of heart attack victims, got Trey an interview with one of the company's principals.

In this portrait of the capitalist as a young man, Bill imagined himself a "young inventor" out to market a coronary care system to hospitals. "To avoid personal liabilities, I am going to incorporate," Bill wrote, though during the initial six years of Microsoft's existence as a partnership he would ignore what he had learned in grade school. Raising sufficient capital would be one problem, the young entrepreneur decided; hiring management, a sales force, and skilled workers would be another. "If my idea is good and I am able to hire good people and raise enough money," he concluded, "I should be successful." Gates was successful enough to get a dreaded A1 on the report.

"He was a goofy kid, kind of funny," recalled Bill's sixth-grade pal Lollie Groth. Assigned to recite Longfellow's "The Arrow and the Song," Bill could not get past the line "I shot an arrow in the air" without cracking up; the teacher had him sit down before the class disintegrated in giggles. At least one parent-teacher conference was called when young Trey roped other classmates into collaborating on class disturbances, and Ryals held several meetings with Bill's parents "trying to make some plans for this kid." Even putting him up front didn't get Bill's attention, said teacher Lucy Cady: "He was just bored in school. I was upset because I knew he could do better."

Summers were centered around swimming, diving, and, later, sailing, at the Laurelhurst Beach Club, a hub of neighborhood summertime activity for Seattle's upper crust. For years, there was always an idyll on the Hood Canal, a bucolic inlet south and west of Bill's father's native Bremerton. "Cheerio," a motley collection of rustic cabins near the water, became the site of an annual two-week sojourn for the Gateses and their family friends, including prominent politicians and local business and civic leaders. The compound teemed with kids, so Trey and his cronies created the Cheerio Club, roaming the woods and waters with personal flags and member numbers and special events. Each night everyone would gather around a campfire before the children marched off to bed in a parade that, each kid hoped, would wind up at his or her cabin last.

From that group evolved the annual Cheerio Olympics, an assortment of games and challenges that kept children and adults alike occupied with exchange dinners, egg tosses, three-legged races, and other wholesome fun. Enormous attention was paid to detail, from opening ceremonies with the oldest kid bedecked in a mantle of leaves and bearing a torch, down to postevent medals presented to the winners on a little metal stand.

By the time the Cheerio gang eventually broke up, Hood Canal summers remained a family tradition, since Trey's grandmother had acquired a summer home nearby. In the late 1980s Bill would develop "Gateaway," a residential complex for the whole family not far from the Cheerio site; the Cheerio Olympics would eventually serve as a model for the annual summer Microgames hosted by the Gates clan.

Throughout his grade-school years, Bill's parents tried to funnel their son's energy into organized activities. But as an all-American boy, Bill Gates was a fizzle. The character-building newspaper route for a thrice-weekly neighborhood paper did not particularly grab him. Payment was in the form of collecting a "contribution"—usually a buck or two—from customers who didn't particularly want the "dogmeat" journal anyway.

According to Gates, he devised a scam to boost his take. As a promotional gambit, a local drug-and-discount store's advertisements would include crude keys, a few of which would open a prize box at the establishment. Bill compared the keys he was supposed to deliver, determined which ones might be unique and therefore valuable, and trooped off to the store to collect his booty. In later years, Gates (perhaps in one of his tale-spinning moods) would vow that the scheme made him the proud owner of such wonderful commodities as a hula hoop, a large garbage can, and a lawnmower.

The garbage can, or one like it, would eventually become a prop for one of Bill's singular athletic talents: leaping out of a trash receptacle at one go. There were always "things like that that he would work on," his sister Kristi recalled. "He was always upset about his little toe curling in, so he'd work on it. He'd spend time holding it out so he'd have a straight toe." It was the kind of obsessive focus that even as an adult would keep his attention riveted on specific goals long after others had given them up.

Gates was a good rollerskater, a decent tennis player, a straight, fast, formless, reckless snow skier, and, especially at Cheerio, a passionate, stylish waterskier. But despite his parents' encouragement, team sports were not his calling. Gates recalled one stint as a center linebacker in an admittedly low-ranked peewee football league. In Little League baseball, his mind would wander in the lulls between pitches.

Still, in May 1966 he enjoyed the game enough to negotiate what may have been his first formal contract, giving him the right to use his sister's baseball glove on an unlimited but nonexclusive basis: "When Trey wants the mitt, he gets it." Bill paid the grand total of $5 "on acceptance of terms," signing in imitation of his father's signature with yet another variant of his name: "William H. Gates Jr. Jr." Apparently Bill was already showing interest in legal formalities: At the bottom of the page was a blank line with the legend "Witness sign here."

Scouting turned out to be the ideal outlet for his boundless energy. His father had been an Eagle Scout whose scoutmaster, Dorm Braman, later became mayor of Seattle. Bill joined Cub Scout Pack 144 and moved up to Boy Scout Troop 186. On hikes he was almost always at the head of the pack, and he held an unofficial record for "Dirty Boy" awards given to the scout whose clothes were the filthiest at the expedition's end. Bill's practice of wearing white shirts and shorts on outings apparently assisted his cause.

And the loopy, no-uniforms, laid-back style of Troop 186 may have been one of the things that attracted Bill most. Whereas other troops conducted group hikes in full regalia and devoutly arranged their tents in formal circles, Troop 186 would hike along in jeans and T-shirts and pitch camp in whatever way seemed easiest. On one memorable campout, a sudden thunderstorm flooded most of the troop's tents; while most of the wet and weary scouts huddled together for warmth under one plastic tarp, Gates and a compatriot stuck it out in their collapsed tent, giggling uproariously at their soggy plight.

The monthly Troop 186 outings, usually to the Cascade or Olympic Mountain ranges sandwiching Puget Sound, were a quixotic blend of Robinson Crusoe and Gilligan's Island. Bus rides to distant points featured floating card games wherein scoutmasters would fleece their charges out of whatever spending money Mom and Dad might have provided. A troop newsletter recounts an August 1970 Vancouver Island coastal hike where Gates injected a little of his not-universally-appreciated brand of levity:

> This return was "livened" when Bill Gates decided to jump up and down on the suspension bridge, creating the enormous mirth which you can imagine among the others on the bridge. That afternoon the scouts ventured out again into the sea, where Bill (always at the forefront) was swept into the waves and others floundered in the raging surf. All declared they had fun as they drizzled back into camp.

For all his dedication to scouting, Gates fell two or three merit badges short of making Eagle. He did achieve Life ranking, and may have earned more badges than it takes to qualify—but not the right ones. Years later, one of Bill Gates's closest female friends would characterize him in terms of scouting:

> He loved being a Boy Scout. And he goes back to these Boy Scout stories over and over and over. . . . If I have to make an image of him, it's a 12-year-old Boy Scout, and I think of those Boy Scout stories in my mind: "Where's the adventure? Where are we hiking to? Where are we marching to? What happens next?"

What happened next for Bill Gates was the adventure that turned him away from scouting, the adventure that kept him from worrying about becoming an Eagle Scout. Computers marched into his life. An obsession was born.

2

LOGGING IN

Assigned seating at lunch! Grace before the meal! Button-down seventh graders who carried little briefcases, observed a stringent dress code of jacket and tie, and called their teachers "masters"! Taking in the scene at Seattle's exclusive Lakeside School, Bill Gates thought "Holy smokes, what is this?" Bad enough that his parents were planning to send him to private school "to straighten me out," but a school with intimidating rules—well, as he told his mom and dad, "Hey, I can fail the entrance exam if I want to!"

But he didn't. "It's not the kind of thing I would do." As things turned out, that was a wise decision: Lakeside School, an all-male institution that included grades seven through twelve and catered largely to the sons of Seattle's wealthy and influential, was about to change his life in ways virtually no public school would have been able to.

Founded in 1919 as an independent elementary boarding and day school, Lakeside was no longer anywhere near a lake: In 1930 it had moved from a Lake Washington setting to its landlocked faux–New England north Seattle campus and become a middle and high school. But it did not relinquish its boarding department until 1963, and when Bill Gates arrived in 1967 it still held to many time-honored traditions and strictures—including the discipline his parents hoped for. Lakeside's talented faculty was used to challenging smart but undirected boys.

Sending Bill to Lakeside was nonetheless a difficult decision for his parents. His older sister Kristi, a straight-A student, had spent all but one year of her educational career in the public school system. Both Papa Gates and his wife were products of public education from childhood through college and beyond. Mary had been a public school teacher herself, and Bill *père* would later serve as chairman of the Seattle school levy campaign.

Still, as his mother recalled, Trey "was a person who was independent from about the time he was seven or eight years old. We were not controlling his life in any way. We were just kind of trying to hold things together and have as much influence as possible. But he was in control.''

"He didn't have any appearance of early maturity or any other particular sign. It wasn't as if he was some kind of obvious super-bright kid,'' his father remembered. "I think we recognize it better looking back than we did at the time. At the time we just thought he was trouble.''

Trey was getting into more worrisome behavioral problems at school and seemed to have little respect for the educational process. "My desk was always messy, and I didn't seem to be paying attention. I was always out there on the playground trying to form some sort of group of guys, or sort of laughing about something when you weren't supposed to be laughing.'' His mother was "anxious that he learn good study habits, get some discipline in his life, not sit around thinking all the time, but that he prepare himself to develop some kind of a good school record so that he could go to any college that he wanted to attend.'' His father "thought he was a little immature and that a little bit smaller class setting would be more supportive.'' They finally decided to place Bill at Lakeside for seventh and eighth grades, intending to have him follow the footsteps of his mother and sister at Roosevelt High, one of Seattle's top public secondary schools.

Seventh grade, beginning in 1967, was largely a year of adjustment, a matter of getting used to Lakeside's ways and a new circle of associates. Gates was a B student. His only higher grade was an A-minus in an algebra honors class where he enjoyed explaining things at the blackboard, rocking back and forth furiously as he filled the slate with his left-handed scrawl. Among the seventh- and eighth-grade Lower School students, Gates was known as a serious and sallow but talkative and sarcastic math-science guy who could get pushy and obnoxious if crossed. "There were a few sort of prototypes of nerds, and Gates was one of them,'' a classmate recalled.

For this group, "hip'' was where belt holsters held the slide rules that pricey portable calculators would soon make passé. The math-science clique was considered hopelessly square. Neither artistic nor athletic, its members were on the periphery of campus life, their particular talents considered irrelevant in a dawning age of social upheaval. Sit-ins, teach-ins, antiwar demonstrations, draft-card burnings, and protest marches were the order of the day. Math and science were for bean counters, corporate sellouts, bomb builders, napalm makers, defense contractors, emotionless rationalists, social lepers.

Yet the math-science crowd at Lakeside was about to take the first steps of the thousand-mile journey of a revolution that initially had little to do with sex, drugs, and rock 'n' roll, with breaking down the system, overthrowing the power structure, exploring the inner psyche. The linear, syllogistic nature of *this* revolution seemed the antithesis of every crazed, out-of-control, up-the-establishment hallmark of the '60s generation except one: individual empowerment.

When Bill Gates entered eighth grade in 1968, he and the other math-science whizzes were about to catch the front curl of a new wave of personal liberation through the sheer exercise of intellect. He and his companions returned to school that fall to find a clunky machine sporting a keyboard and a giant roll of yellow paper ensconced in a tiny office near the front door of McAlister Hall, the steepled brick-and-clapboard math and science building. None of the kids knew how to operate the machine or even much about what it was. But true to the ethic of their generation, they set about learning and ultimately mastering what that machine could do far better than any of the teachers or other adults associated with it.

The machine in question was an ASR-33 Teletype, the same kind of unit responsible for the characteristic clackety-clack once heard in newsrooms throughout the world and eventually relegated to the fake background clatter of news radio. The Teletype was a shotgun wedding between the waning machine era and the burgeoning age of information, a noisy, ungainly electromechanical contraption combining a keyboard, a printer, a paper tape punch and reader, and a modem that could connect the unit via telephone to the outside world.

If you pressed its plungerlike keys, the Teletype would print upper-case characters on huge rolls of $8\frac{1}{2}$-inch-wide paper. If you knew what you were doing, you could have the punch record your typing in a skinny roll of paper tape and later play it back like a player piano. But the important thing was the modem—two "mouse ear" cups that clutched a telephone handset and let you transfer messages to and from anyone with a similar machine or—and this was the important part—a time-sharing computer.

A computer! Hardly anyone understood computers back then. They were mysterious, they were impenetrable, they were just plain weird. And until the 1960s, they were almost totally unapproachable. Before then, a computer was typically a multimillion-dollar machine comprised of refrigerator-size units linked together by special cables underneath a raised floor in an air-conditioned room accessible only to initiates.

The traditional way a mere mortal interacted with a computer was to type up a program on a deck of 80-column punch cards, hand them through a little window to an operator, and come back later—days later, if you were low on the priority list—for a sheaf of fan-fold computer paper with the results. At least the hope was that it would be a sheaf. More likely it would be a single page with a doleful ERROR message announcing a mistake in programming logic or, more likely, a typographical blunder. Either way, the cycle from punch card to machine to printout would begin all over again. Debugging even a simple program, getting it to run properly, could take weeks or months.

Time-sharing changed all that. It was the first true revolution in the way people used computers. Developed in the late 1950s and early '60s, time-sharing was the clever conceit that a single computer could be used to run multiple programs at the same time. Actually, at any given instant, the computer was never running more than one program; instead it performed a clever juggling illusion, switching among the multitude faster than the eye could follow.

This was not just a revolution. It was a revelation. Forget the operator, the card decks, the wait: With time-sharing, you could sit at your teletype, bang in a couple of commands, and get an answer then and there. Time-sharing was interactive: A program could ask for a response, wait for you to type it in, act on it while you waited, and show you the result, all in "real time." There was no longer any need to show up in person at a computer site; with the help of a Teletype you could access the machine from almost anywhere. Time-sharing first took off in university settings, then blossomed so quickly that by the late 1960s, a variety of public services offered computer time to anyone with a Teletype, a phone line, and sufficient credit to open an account.

To get anything done, you also needed to understand a computer language. Designed to teach programming fundamentals and to take advantage of the interactive nature of time-sharing machines, BASIC—Beginner's All-Purpose Symbolic Instruction Code—had been developed under a National Science Foundation grant by John Kemeny and Thomas Kurtz at Dartmouth College. It first ran on May 1, 1964, at an hour typical of programming milestones—4:00 A.M.

The great thing about BASIC was simplicity. You could easily write a little program like

```
10 PRINT 2 + 2
20 END
```

Then if you typed **RUN** and pressed the return key, the Teletype would clackety-clack into action. At a blistering 110 baud, 10 characters per second —about the speed of a very fast human typist—it would print out

```
4
TIME: 0 SECS
```

To the math-science types at Lakeside, the computer was the best new toy since the slide rule. No: It was way better than that. Programming was exciting; it was smart; it was addictive. But as that **TIME** line hinted, there was one little wrinkle: It was expensive. Equipment, computer time, and file storage all cost money. The Teletype rented for $89 a month. Then came $8 an hour for on-line fees, about eight cents a second for computer processing time, and sixty cents a block for program storage. In an era when a new car could be had for less than $2,000, that was expensive even for well-off kids.

Money had been a sticking point since the very beginning of Lakeside's involvement with computers. In the fall of 1967, Edgar Horwood, director of the Urban Data Center at the University of Washington, had written to Lakeside suggesting that it look into an arrangement with General Electric's time-sharing service: "Conceivably a computer group could be started with at least some of the parents contributing for time used by their sons." Lakeside's young math and science teachers, most of whom had taken summer computer courses, took up the cause and joined with headmaster Dexter Strong to lobby actively for computer access. By the end of the school year, limited funding was agreed to, but the idea of having parents pay for computer time seemed somewhat unmanageable. So where might additional financing come from?

The answer was a group as untechnical as any: the Lakeside Mothers Club, which held an annual rummage sale that solicited directly from the affluent Lakeside parents. With merchandise several cuts above the usual flotsam, the sale raised thousands of dollars each year, leaving the Mothers Club officers with the task of divvying up the booty among worthy school causes. For 1968, one of those causes was computer access for Lakeside School.

At first the Teletype used a local access line to dial into a General Electric Mark II time-sharing system that offered only the BASIC language. Still, that was enough to get the kids started. Math teacher Paul Stocklin recalled trooping the sixteen students in his honors class into the tiny room in McAlister Hall "and explaining to them on the order of ten to fifteen minutes everything I knew about it, which was pretty doggone limited. And I remember that was the last time I knew more than those guys." Word of the setup quickly spread among the math-science elite on campus, and what became known as the "computer room" in McAlister Hall turned feverish with electronic rambunctiousness.

A runty freckle-faced eighth grader named Bill Gates quickly elbowed his way in among the upperclassmen. "I go around saying I taught him all he knows," recalled Bill Dougall, one of the teachers instrumental in bringing computer access to Lakeside. "It took him a week to pass me." At Lakeside there was no formal course in computing; a small set of people just glommed onto it, plowing their way through the rudimentary forty-two-page BASIC manual GE had provided. The GE BASIC, based on the original Dartmouth version, was pretty rudimentary itself; it lacked all but the simplest mathematical functions, it was hopeless when it came to manipulating "strings" of characters, and it had a limitation on program length. According to the GE manual, "two feet of teletypewriter paper filled with BASIC statements is about it."

Those shortcomings hardly mattered to novices still feeling their way around. Bill Gates's first program let you enter a number in any arithmetic base and convert it to a number in any other. A practical senior named Harvey Motulsky put together a program to compute grade point averages from letter grades. A chunky tenth-grade electronics expert named Paul Allen had worked on spark-shooting Van de Graaff generators, robots with ultrasonic eyes, and an "electronic amoeba" that would turn toward light, and already knew a little about computers—single "flip-flop" devices that could add one and one and get two. Allen's tall, skinny, gawky classmate Ric Weiland knew even more: He had already built a mechanical Tic-Tac-Toe computer out of surplus electrical parts. But now you could do that in software: Tic-Tac-Toe was Bill Gates's second BASIC program, using tabs, slashes, X's, and O's to simulate the game grid.

When senior class president Matt Griffin had trouble getting a 25-line BASIC program to run, teacher Fred Wright steered him to the computer room. "It was just all getting started then," Griffin later recalled. "There's this little blond kid sitting over in a chair. . . . His feet are swinging and they aren't touching the floor." Wright posed the problem. Bill Gates unhesitatingly rattled off the answer.

Though they weren't yet spending their own money, the budding programmers became wise in the ways of keeping costs down. The most important, especially as programs got longer, was the use of punched paper tape. If you logged on to the GE computer and then typed in your program, you'd be charged for every precious second. The solution was to stay off-line and type in your program with the Teletype's tape punch on, thereby putting meaningful holes in a slim yellow ribbon of paper. When the program was ready, you'd log on to the computer, feed in the tape with your program, and switch to the keyboard to interact with it. Rolls of the yellow tapes, the floppy disks of their era, quickly replaced slide rules as badges of nerdy honor at Lakeside—the bigger the better.

Still, computing was anything but free. Given the sluggishness of the computers of the day, you could mistakenly assume a program was chugging along toward an answer when in actuality it was stuck in an infinite do-nothing loop. If it took you just a minute to realize what was going on, you had blown five bucks. With processor time going for $4.80 a minute, not to mention the other charges on top of that, it wasn't impossible to run up a bill of $50 at one sitting. The school's computer budget quickly began to run dry.

Within weeks a miraculous boon suddenly appeared. A group of computer folk from the University of Washington Computer Center had banded together to found a private outfit they christened the Computer Center Corporation and quickly began referring to as Triple-C or C-Cubed. In a move that spoke megabytes about America's changing technology, they had gutted a former automobile showroom in Seattle's University District and installed the city's first state-of-the-art Digital Equipment Corporation PDP-10 time-sharing computer, one of the first commercial public-access PDP-10 systems anywhere. Now they were in the process of selling time on it to all comers, intending to cash in on such clients as the Boeing Company, which during the passenger-airline boom of the 1960s had garnered a slew of multimillion-dollar jet contracts and hastily expanded its work force to more than 100,000. And there were all sorts of other Seattle businesses—engineering firms, accountants, boatbuilders, the sky was the limit—that would need computer power too; steeped in academic computing, C-Cubed's principals had no doubts about it.

Monique Rona, a C-Cubed founder and corporate secretary whose son Tom was a year ahead of Bill at Lakeside, made the connection with the school. The C-Cubed computer was undergoing what was known as an "acceptance test," a free shakedown cruise during which the company could make certain the brand-new DEC hardware and software performed according to specifications—something it was not even close to doing upon delivery. Her idea was to bring kids in and use them to help put the system software through its paces and ferret out troublesome "bugs." She wrote the school suggesting that the Lakeside boys help test the C-Cubed computer in exchange for free time on it.

Free time? To Bill Gates, "It was manna from heaven." Free time was the computerist's holy grail. C-Cubed had no trouble luring the kids into the office on Saturday mornings, when the computer was closed to public access. They sat in a little classroom with eight teletype units—no need to worry, as at Lakeside, about impatient peers looking over your shoulder, offering useless advice, trying to get their turn at the machine. There was no need to worry about paper tape either; the whole idea was to put as heavy a load on the PDP-10 as possible, to simulate what would happen once C-Cubed had a full complement of customers and they all beat on the machine at the same time.

Rule Number One at C-Cubed was "Anything goes." The kids were encouraged to try to crash the system; that's what they were there for. As one C-Cubed veteran recalled, Bill Gates was an instant master at it:

> We'd just brought up the first release of BASIC on the PDP-10. . . . All of a sudden the system crashed.
>
> We brought the system back up. It crashed again. The system programmer was going nuts while this was going on. He finally tracked down what was happening. Gates would log on. He'd call up BASIC. BASIC would ask **NEW OR OLD**—Gates would type **OLD**. BASIC would ask **OLD PROGRAM NAME**—. And then he would type **OLD PROGRAM NAME BILL**. He should've just typed **BILL**.

The overlong answer—almost certainly deliberate, since Gates was already familiar with the **OLD PROGRAM NAME** prompt from the GE system—had overflowed a data buffer and knocked the system down. Thus Bill learned Rule Number Two: "Once you find a way to make it crash, you've got to tell us, and you can't use it again until we tell you to." And crash it did. In the early going, with a heavy user load, the system was unlikely to keep running for more than half an hour at a time. Even after software improvements, a day without at least one crash was a rarity; a trouble-free week was unheard of.

But crashes just came with the territory. Within a few weeks the kids were coming up with their own programming projects. A senior math whiz named Bob McCaw developed a casino program featuring simulated versions of black-jack and roulette. Senior Harvey Motulsky wrote a renowned Monopoly program. The software randomly rolled the "virtual" dice; Motulsky even programmed "Chance" and "Community Chest" cards. Other Lakesiders contributed their own wrinkles; even Bill Gates added a few fillips. "I just kept writing it," Motulsky would say years later, "finding bugs and fixing it. I don't remember actually playing it."

That was the sign of a born programmer: It wasn't the destination that counted, it was the trip. Thirteen-year-old Bill Gates knew the feeling exactly. Fresh from an obsession with Napoleon, who as a youth had displayed a remarkably similar personality and flair for math, Bill devised an elaborate war game that for a time occupied his every spare moment. As Paul Allen remembered it, "You'd have these armies and you'd fight battles. . . . He had these great interesting ideas, and the program kept getting bigger and bigger, and finally when you stretched it all out, it was like fifty feet of Teletype paper long. I'm not sure if it was ever finished"—it wasn't—"or what it did, but he invested a lot of time trying to figure out how it worked."

While Gates was mastering BASIC, Allen, the electronics nut two years older than Bill, became fascinated with the innards of the machine. When he told one of the programmers he wanted to learn how the computer really worked, Allen was handed a manual listing the computer's instruction set—its elemental building-block commands. After mastering that manual, Allen returned to inquire humbly how he might actually do something with the instruction set. This time the programmer gave him a manual for the macro assembler, a program that converts assembly language—mnemonic instruction codes such as **ADD A** or **MOVE I**—into the ones and zeroes of the machine language that the computer understands. But when Allen tried writing programs using the assembler, he discovered it didn't offer any way to print characters to the terminal or save them to a disk. Allen's Zen master then handed him a copy of the manual for the Monitor, the operating system program that controlled the hardware and executed input and output requests. "It was kind of a gradual process of learning."

The kids became multilingual. They learned FORTRAN, the original "high-level" English-like computer language. They fiddled with AID, a simple math-oriented language descended from a historical relic known as JOSS. They learned assembly-language programming with the MACRO-10 assembler and DDT-10, the "Dynamic Debugging Technique." They made the acquaintance of PIP, the "Peripheral Interface Program" that did such chores as copying files to their personal DECtapes, hockey-puck-size reels of magnetic tape that they carried around with their programs and data. And they discovered most of it by poring over the bone-dry loose-leaf documentation, whose rare attempts at wit were typified by a footnote in the debugger's manual: "Confusion between DDT-10 and another well-known pesticide, dichloro-diphenyl-trichloroethane ($C_{14}H_9Cl_5$) should be minimal since each attacks a different, and apparently mutually exclusive, class of bugs."

Eventually the kids' Saturday hours expanded to after-school sessions lasting until late in the evenings. Wearing their coats and ties, carrying their briefcases, they would ride the bus half an hour south from Lakeside to C-Cubed, program until they were too tired to program anymore, and grab a bus for home. For Coke and snacks they'd head next door to the mom-and-pop grocery. Across the street was Morningtown, a laid-back joint dispensing hippie wisdom along with the programmer's soul food—pizza.

Of all the kids who hung out at C-Cubed, Bill Gates was the most tenacious. At home he would literally beat his head against the wall when he was frustrated with a problem. His room was a sea of Teletype and computer paper —rolls of it, stacks of it, mixed with dirty laundry. It got to the point where the family regarded his room as an "absolute disaster." Various incentives were tried, to no avail. Eventually Mary simply removed clothing from the floor, and Trey was supposed to pay a quarter to get each item back. But as his sister Libby recalled it, "He never paid to get his clothes back. He didn't care what he wore." The ultimate solution: Bill would keep his door shut.

That didn't work for long, but for a time it turned out to be useful. After dinner, unbeknownst to his parents, Bill would sometimes pretend to go to bed, then sneak out of the house and take a ten-minute bus ride back to C-Cubed for more programming. Occasionally the buses had stopped running by the time he got out, and he'd walk the two or three miles home. "We always wondered why it was so hard for him getting up in the morning," his mother recalled. In a sibling pact, sister Kristi knew but kept mum about her brother's nocturnal whereabouts.

C-Cubed represented a haven of liberation every bit as fascinating as coffeehouses for the hip and locker rooms for the athletic. The hardware in the computer room included a huge Bryant disk drive whose horizontal spindle held two vertical disks totaling a whopping 8 megabytes of storage space within its own air-conditioned box—and crashed anytime anyone ventured within three feet of it. There were drives for the standard 9-track magnetic tapes and for the beloved DECtapes. There were a card punch, a card reader, a line printer, and even an ASR-35 Teletype, a "high-speed" model that could print an astonishing 15 characters a second.

And then there was the computer itself, a refrigerator-size central processor and rack upon rack of core memory—spiderwebs of wire and tiny ceramic rings that added up to the equivalent of roughly 128 kilobytes, about 128,000 characters, fifty times less than what today fits in a typical laptop computer. There was even another computer, a boxy PDP-8 the size of a small file cabinet, that handled communications with the outside world. By today's standards, everything was comically bulky, overengineered, underperforming; by the standards of the time, it was leading-edge technology.

"We enjoyed having those kids around," remembered Carl Young, C-Cubed's president. "They were fearless. They would attempt all kinds of things. They picked it up far faster than the ordinary working engineer would. They would say, 'What if? What if?' " The kids enjoyed hanging around the programmers, because the guys who could put the incredible machines through their paces were smart, savvy, and, well . . . cool.

Programmers were Smart Guys (and a Gal or two), perfect adolescent role models—quirky, eccentric, snide. Though they worked hard, they dressed down, stripping off their sport coats and ties when business customers weren't around and wearing T-shirts and sandals on weekends. Programmer Steve Russell, who had trained in the rarefied atmosphere of the Stanford Artificial Intelligence Labs, seemed to know all there was to know about hardware. He did. Some years before, at MIT, he had invented Spacewar, the first video game ever. Rotund mad scientist Dick Gruen, formerly DEC's Stanford systems support expert, encouraged vigilant bug reports, cultivated a snotty attitude toward software that didn't do what it was supposed to, and generally promoted fearlessness. Russell and Gruen remembered well their own high school days, when they had attended a National Science Foundation summer program that included access to a computer. At C-Cubed, Gruen recalled, "The novel thing was that we were treating high school students like real people."

Not quite. Real people had to pay for computer time. Although the crashes kept the acceptance test period dragging on and on, at some point DEC insisted that the meter start running. Years later Gates would relate the sad event: "I remember explicitly the day they ended software acceptance. They basically said, 'Okay, monkeys, go home.' " On occasion, when C-Cubed had some new program or bug fix or hardware to test—the addition of a second PDP-10 in spring 1969 caused a passel of troubles—someone would call up the school and say time was free for the evening. But otherwise Lakeside became one of C-Cubed's rare paying customers, with each student having his own password and his own account for computer time at a 20 percent educational discount. The kids paid their individual bills via an in-house checking-account system already in place at the school. Even though a monthly bill would rarely amount to more than $10, the day when math teacher Fred Wright posted the bills became a dreaded occasion. The Lakesiders had become addicted to programming, and the fixes were just too costly.

But hey, software could do anything! A real programmer couldn't be stopped merely because of a minor matter like money. By this time Gates and Allen knew the intricacies of the C-Cubed system as well as they knew their own neighborhoods. They had discovered Richard Greenblatt's classic chess game, a computer-intensive program that pushed the DEC system to its limits, and they had burned up thousands of dollars of computer time playing it and learning how you could "cheat" it. Accessing the accounting files, where the passwords were stored, seemed like just another challenge.

Exactly who accomplished the feat, exactly what they did, and exactly how they did it is shrouded in mystery. But Bill Gates and his friend Paul Allen were clearly the ringleaders. Security was minimal. If you sent the key combination Control-D—the D was for "die"—to the computer's operator, you could log off the system and log back on as the operator, giving you free run of the machine. Today such "hacking" or "cracking" is subject to stiff penalties. Back then it was often considered mischief, experimentation. The kids were testing the system, just doing a little digital shoplifting. What harm was there in appropriating unused computer time protected with only the flimsiest of barriers? To Paul Allen, "It was just like part of it was roped off, and what was in there, we really wanted to know."

Had they left it just at snooping, he and Gates might never have been discovered. But one day Fred Wright, the Lakeside math teacher most directly responsible for the computer connection, phoned Don Herrick, the C-Cubed salesman responsible for the Lakeside account, with the message that "The kids have gotten into something they shouldn't have." Wright eventually produced a roll of yellow Teletype paper with the whole computer accounting package on it, complete with account numbers, billings, passwords. Potentially the kids had total control of the system—for free.

Herrick hurried back to C-Cubed and reported the incident. Initially he was met with skepticism—after all, these were just kids playing around. But when Herrick handed the evidence to Gruen and others, they passed the word along to the Massachusetts headquarters of Digital Equipment Corporation.

Digital responded with a new version of the Monitor software. Asked to try to crack this one, the kids did it from Lakeside in about an hour and a half. After school they visited C-Cubed to show how they had managed it.

When the upper echelon at C-Cubed learned that the ring led by Gates and

Allen had manipulated the accounting files for their own benefit, they were sorely irritated—and not just at the kids. "The school was much more upset about it than we were," Herrick remembered. "Our official position was one of concern, but in the back room, it was 'Holy mackerel, if kids can do this, imagine what somebody who knew something could do.' "

Still, C-Cubed officials felt some sort of disciplinary action was necessary. Dick Wilkinson, the tall sales chief, who walked around in suits, a brush cut, and a neatly trimmed Vandyke, visited the school with another member of the C-Cubed staff in a tough-guy act that left a sober impression on at least one of the Lakeside hackers. To this day Gates remembers a "guy from the FBI" meeting with Wright and the computer trespassers. More likely the G-man was Wilkinson, who recalled, "They were changing their bills. They were giving themselves free time. We caught them redhanded. Gruen and I went out there and read 'em the riot act and banned 'em from the system. They sat there with their heads hung down."

The kids involved, including Bill and Paul, wound up being excluded from the system for the summer—a ban so significant in the mind of Bill Gates that he would later recall it to be a whole year long. But not even the ban would stop Paul Allen, whose father was associate director of the University of Washington Library. After finding a professor with a free account at C-Cubed, Allen spent part of his summer vacation programming on a terminal in the university's electrical engineering department. "When I saw Bill at the beginning of the next year, he said, 'Well, Paul, did you do any programming this summer?' I said, 'As a matter of fact, I did,' and he said, 'You didn't tell me! You had a free number and you were programming all summer?' . . . He was pretty upset."

In the fall, as Bill entered his freshman year at Lakeside—there was no longer any thought of his returning to public school—he had become a fixture in the computer room at McAlister Hall. Not everybody was impressed. Despite his own infatuation with games, Gates could "get all indignant" with some of his fellow computerphiles "that we were frivolously wasting our precious computer time" on a Star Trek game, one upperclassman recalled. "He hogged the damn thing."

Gates did not suffer fools gladly. The phrase "That's the stupidest thing I've ever heard of!" became a Gates catchphrase, recalled teacher Bill Dougall. "Bill, don't say that," Dougall would tell him, "but as it turns out, he's almost always right. When you say something stupid, he's willing to say it's stupid."

To those who didn't mesh with the scrawny, arrogant kid, he could be, one Lakesider remembered, "an extremely annoying person. He was very easy to sort of dislike. And I think that probably me and a lot of people took a little extra pleasure in sort of bumping him while passing him in the hall and basically giving him a little bit of a hard time. . . . In public school, the guy would've been killed.'' Fortunately, Lakeside was full of smart guys with weird personalities, and tolerance rather than retribution was the order of the day.

At C-Cubed Gates and Allen took a new route toward free computer time. Their strategy was to convince the programmers that they could be useful around the place. Paul was assigned to help modify the BASIC compiler, the program that took the code people wrote and converted it into the machine language the hardware understood. Bill tinkered with SYSTAT, a utility program that kept track of what was happening on the system. Ric Weiland went them one better and actually got a paying job doing programming for a suburban outfit called Logic Simulation, one of C-Cubed's few regular customers; Weiland became the envy of the group when the company loaned him a ''portable'' Teletype—the thing weighed some fifty pounds—to take home.

By this time, Bill had struck up a close friendship with a classmate named Kent Evans, the aggressively entrepreneurial son of a Unitarian minister. Whereas the other computerists tended to read such techie journals as *Popular Electronics* or *Electronics News,* Evans would carry copies of *Fortune* or *Business Week* or the *Wall Street Journal.* Eventually he and Bill Gates cadged free weekend-only accounts on which they gleefully ran up multithousand-dollar monthly tabs. Though they still had to pay for their time when logging on during school hours, the kids' computer fix was assured.

For a time, anyway. Even after Lakeside began paying, gloomy omens began appearing in C-Cubed circles. Undercapitalized from the outset, run by bright people with far more experience in academe than in business, C-Cubed was on its uppers. Lakeside was told to pay its December bills directly to a factoring firm that had bought receivables at a discount when C-Cubed needed quick cash. The C-Cubed officials began to realize that their initial expectation of selling vast quantities of computer time was simply not going to happen. Seattle entered the throes of a near depression when airlines began canceling contracts and Boeing laid off thousands of workers. Gruen bailed out of C-Cubed in January 1970. As he left the economically stricken city he saw the now-legendary billboard: ''Will the last person leaving Seattle turn out the lights?''

With few customers and mounting debts, C-Cubed was forced to find ways to skirt payment on the machines, pouncing on mistakes in invoices, bugs in the software, anything to defer its lease payments, to buy time. In February, when it defaulted on notes of over $60,000, C-Cubed had its assets and receivables assigned to ACQ Computer Corporation of Chicago. By March C-Cubed had sent Lakeside its final billing. The account of Bill Gates, number 366,2633, owed $2.03.

The new management kept the computers running twenty-four hours a day, but the inevitable shutdown was finally signaled by a repossession mixing poignance and hilarity. Gates recalled:

We're sitting there typing at the Teletypes and these guys are coming in taking the furniture and they say to stand up. We're still typing, and the guys are not gonna bring the chairs back, and all the programmers are saying "Don't worry about it, we're gonna form a new company, we're gonna get a little more money, we'll be back in business."

Outside, an office chair comically rolled down the street as if making a mad dash to escape the moving van. Left to type away on their knees, Gates and Allen downloaded all their program files from the system onto magnetic tapes. Then it was good-bye. C-Cubed had given Bill and Paul all it could: not only an apprenticeship in how to use computers, but also an object lesson in how not to run a company.

3

OPEN FOR BUSINESS

The demise of C-Cubed was like a death in the family. It left a huge gap in the lives of the hardcore Lakeside programmers. The other available time-sharing services were all based in distant cities. None offered anything like the C-Cubed package: your own terminal a short bus ride from school, the camaraderie and wisdom of experienced programmers, and, of course, free computer time.

Lakeside returned to its original provider, the General Electric Time-Sharing Service. But GE still had little more to offer than its wimpy BASIC, and by now Bill and his gang had nothing but "disdain for the guys who still were just typing in" lame BASIC programs. Besides, GE was expensive. Somewhere, somehow, the Lakesiders had to find someplace where time wasn't money.

The first candidate was the University of Washington, where the graduate center was clearly the place to be. It had leading-edge equipment—amazing stuff such as terminals that required no paper, but instead displayed characters and even crude graphics on TV-like screens. It was on these units that Bill and Paul first saw a version of Russell's Spacewar game as well as a primitive edition of a computer mouse. Cool!

But the Xerox Data Systems (XDS) Sigma V time-sharing machine was the real attraction. It was a direct competitor of the PDP-10, and Paul Allen was the first to learn how to use it:

> I just walked in there and started acting like I knew what I was doing and started using the computer, and after a while I was helping graduate students. I was like seventeen years old, and one day a professor came up to me and said, "I don't think you're in any of my classes."
> I said, "Nope."

> He said, *"Are you a graduate student?"*
>
> *I said, "No."*
>
> *And he said, "Well, you seem to be helping people here a lot, so as long as you don't cause any problems . . . fine, just keep doing whatever you're doing."*
>
> *So that was cool, except pretty soon I brought Bill there, and Bill brought Kent, and Ric came and all of us were typing . . .*

A less tolerant professor figured out what was going on, and "after that we were *persona non grata.*"

Allen's philosophy was simple: "I want to look at every computer I can, understand the software, the neat things this computer can do other computers can't." Bill Gates felt more or less the same way.

Fortunately the university's Control Data Corporation (CDC) Cyber 6400 was housed in another part of the building. Based on a design by hot-rod-computer pioneer Seymour Cray, it was a superfast machine for its day. It didn't offer time-sharing, accepting only punched-card decks, but that was better than nothing. Gates learned "You could go in there for free and just type up cards and they weren't gonna charge you and you could even run them through the printing thing and the little collator thing." And if you cultivated the student computer operators, as Bill and Paul did, you might just be able to convince them to run your programs.

At some point Lakeside itself received two computers on loan for about three months each. First came a DEC PDP-8L, a small model descended from the original PDP-8 released in 1965 and generally regarded as the first true minicomputer. It was limited in capacity and hard to program, and it lacked any way of storing information short of the Teletype's paper tape, but these cheap minis—you could get a bare-bones model for less than $10,000—were spreading the computer gospel, bringing the joys and pains of computing into more places than ever before, particularly in academic, scientific, and other research circles.

In the DEC world, software was largely free. The best source was DECUS, the DEC Users Society. It was from DECUS that Bill Gates got hold of paper tapes containing the source code to a version of BASIC and an assembler for the PDP-8. He used them to begin work on a project he considered fun: his very own edition of a BASIC interpreter.

Programs written in computer languages begin with *source code*—instructions that generally resemble English:

```
10 FOR I = 1 TO 100
20 LET Z = Z + 1
```

```
30 PRINT Z
40 NEXT I
```

Somehow those instructions must be converted to a form that makes sense to the computer. There are two basic kinds of software that can do the job: compilers and interpreters.

Both compilers and interpreters are essentially translators. A compiler, like the translator of a written speech, does the job all at once after seeing the work whole; an interpreter, like a simultaneous translator at the United Nations, works on the fly without the opportunity of knowing "what comes next."

A compiler takes source code and translates it, in one or more steps, into *object code*—a set of ones and zeroes that the computer can understand and that can run all by itself. An interpreter takes source code (or a modified version of it) and translates it one command at a time. With an interpreter, no object code is ever produced, so both the source code and the interpreter must be available in order to run the program.

Compiled programs almost always run faster than interpreted ones. But interpreted languages generally require less memory. Although the initial Dartmouth BASIC, running on relatively big GE machines, used a compiler model, memory limitations led many subsequent versions of BASIC, particularly ones written for small machines, to be interpreted. The lessons Bill Gates was learning about cramming interpreted languages into tiny spaces would pay big dividends in the years to come.

Alas, the PDP-8 had to be returned before he made much headway on his version of an interpreter for BASIC programs. Gates tried to rewrite it for a Data General Nova, a newer machine of greater capabilities but different internal architecture that arrived at Lakeside shortly thereafter. It, too, disappeared before he could get very far.

But Bill and his cohorts came to understand these small machines inside out. What they understood most intensely was how woefully underpowered the little computers were compared to the big machines they had become accustomed to. They dearly longed to get back to their cherished PDP-10s.

And in the fall of 1970, Bill's sophomore year, Lakeside got wind of a public PDP-10 in the great Northwest at a time-sharing company called Information Sciences, Inc. (ISI) 170 miles to the south in Portland, Oregon. The bearer of the news was ISI's Seattle contact, Frank Peep, who had been Lakeside's sales rep from C-Cubed when it went belly up. In lieu of his final paycheck, he had hung on to a "portable" ASR-33 Teletype, which he later sold to one William Henry Gates.

Peep signed Lakeside up with ISI for computer time on the PDP-10—computer time that went for $15 an hour, roughly double the rates C-Cubed had been charging. For Lakeside's PDP-10 experts, a return to skullduggery seemed the order of the day. Presto! The ISI system was every bit as easy to crack as C-Cubed's had been. Free computer time was a reality again.

Until the kids got caught. This time there was no "FBI man"—just Frank Peep, explaining that ISI wouldn't tolerate such shenanigans. But Peep had been a Bill Gates fan from the beginning. To him, "It was obvious from the start that he was their guiding light; it was patently obvious." Next thing they knew, ISI executives were receiving letters from an organization called the Lakeside Programmers Group.

LPG had originally been nothing more than a name, a corporate-sounding moniker that would give Kent Evans a better chance of receiving free information when he sent in the "bingo cards" that appeared in computer and electronics magazines. Paul had employed a similar ruse: He called himself Allen Systems.

Evans was Bill's closest friend. "From the beginning of the eighth grade to the end of the eleventh grade they were absolutely inseparable," recalled Kent's father, Marvin Evans. "I can remember hauling them all over town so they could bootleg computer time." Forever coming up with some grandiose new scheme for big money or instant fame, Kent was the great early influence on Bill Gates's business savvy. Evans "acted like a forty-year-old business-man," according to math teacher Wright. "He was to a great extent responsible for the whole business orientation of things."

Evans made a strong impression on Bill's father:

> Most kids grow up mostly being told about all the things that you're too young to do: "You can't do that, you couldn't possibly do that." Somehow that never was ever any influence in Kent's life, because he didn't see any limits. . . . He was fearless. . . . He'd do anything. He'd just pick up the phone and call people. He just didn't have any sense of inhibition or limit about what he could do because he was a fifteen-year-old or whatever he was at the time.

Fearlessness, the inability to see limits: Again and again people would later ascribe those qualities to Bill Gates. "I don't know how much of that is natural to him and how much he got from the influence of Kent," Bill's father would say. "They were together a lot."

Banding with Weiland and Allen under the Lakeside Programmers Group rubric, Gates and Evans wrote ISI to offer programming services in exchange for free computer time. When ISI remained unconvinced, they loaded themselves down with printouts and hopped the train to Portland to prove how good they were.

Within weeks they had hustled ISI into coming up with a project for them: a do-it-all payroll program that would entice new customers for its system. By

November 18, 1970, they had an agreement to do the payroll program in exchange for "the experience to be gained thereby." For kids desperate for free computer time, it was déjà-Cubed all over again.

ISI demanded that all the programming be done in COBOL—COmmon Business-Oriented Language, the business standard. Only Weiland knew the language; the others cracked the books and sat in on a few COBOL courses at UW. But Gates soon realized the project was far more complex than anything they'd ever tackled. "You have these labor distribution reports, and these quarterly tax reports, and health deduction reports, and if you file one thing with the government but then you change your mind or decide it was in error, the kind of mag tape you have to file is very complicated."

"It was a bitch of a program," Paul Allen recalled. And things were rocky from the outset, as teenage interpersonal dynamics got in the way of rational project management. Discovering that EDIT-10, everyone's favorite program editor, was unavailable on the ISI system, Weiland wrote a new and improved version. Named EDITX in Roman-numeral homage to the original, the editor was a programming challenge far more fascinating than the mundane payroll project, and Weiland kept "adding bells and whistles to it when Bill thought maybe I should have been doing more on the payroll program." Eventually Weiland would cut a deal with ISI to pay him royalties whenever anyone used EDITX, which pissed Bill off even more. And Allen admitted that Bill and Kent "were much more hardcore. They worked really hard on that thing."

Even the specter of C-Cubed came to haunt the enterprise. Padlocked doors and runaway chairs signaled the end to most people, but not to Bill and Kent. Watching out for the bankruptcy sale, the pair focused on the DECtapes that remained. Some of the tapes were blanks; others contained programs C-Cubed customers had worked on. Bill and Kent bought the lot for a couple of hundred bucks, a fraction of their retail value. They didn't bother mentioning the purchase to colleagues Weiland and Allen; in fact, Kent hid the tapes in the base of the Teletype at Lakeside.

Word filtered back to Weiland, who reported it to Allen, who was "really upset about this, because I thought we had been doing all this stuff as a communal project and nobody had tried to take stuff off the side or make money on the side. It was an all-for-one, one-for-all kind of thing." Allen decided to teach the whippersnappers a lesson. Without telling Bill or Kent, he took the tapes home.

The next day in the Lakeside computer room, Bill and Kent teased Paul, telling him they had something he wished he could have. Allen played dumb, hovering around the Teletype, pretending to wonder just what the tenth graders could possibly be talking about. After discovering the tapes were missing, Bill and Kent quickly deduced the culprit. The litigious Evans howled that Allen had stolen the tapes, that this was a case of theft, that he'd call the police.

"What tapes are you talking about?" Allen retorted coyly. "You mean there are some tapes you have you didn't tell me or Ric about? How'd you get those?"

A furious confrontation raged, but eventually the foursome came to terms on who would get to keep which tapes. Bill and Kent hung on to some of theirs, but rustled up a buyer for the rest—a software affiliate of the Oregon Museum of Science and Industry in Portland—and, according to Gates, "made a very good markup."

Meanwhile, the quartet was beginning to understand the true magnitude of the payroll project, particularly the documentation job, for which Kent had taken responsibility. LPG pushed to renegotiate its deal. Now the boys were to get $5 worth of computer time for every man-hour they worked.

At some point, according to Gates, the group informally agreed to a division of the spoils: Bill and Kent took four-elevenths each, Weiland two-elevenths, and Paul one-eleventh—a reflection of dissension over who was really contributing to the joint effort. From January through July of 1971, the group ran up the equivalent of more than $25,000 in billings, about 1,575 hours of computer time—an average of eight hours a day, seven days a week, or two hours a day per programmer.

Despite—or perhaps because of—the rigors of his programming exploits, Bill had begun to blossom academically; his sophomore year marked the first time he ever managed to get straight A's. Still a voracious reader, he had fallen in undying love with J. D. Salinger's *The Catcher in the Rye*. Following in his sister Kristi's footsteps, he had spent three weeks of the spring in Olympia, Washington, as a legislative page. Political and personal clout helped make it possible: Governor Daniel Evans had been a longtime family friend of the Gateses, and Bill roomed in the governor's mansion during his sojourn in the state capital.

Next Bill Gates began a cottage industry of his own. Ric Weiland's part-time employer, Logic Simulation, was contracting its services to a traffic-consulting firm. Among Weiland's programming projects was a program to create an inventory of all the street signs in Kent, Washington. With Weiland on his way to college, Gates managed to promote himself a job processing data that came from paper tapes generated by the familiar car-counting boxes attached to hoses laid across roadways.

First he agreed to take over the analysis program, producing neat reports on each day's traffic past the box, both as numbers and as a bar graph comprised of asterisks—among the earliest of Bill's personal forays into the graphical display of data. But Bill agreed to do even more: On a contract basis, he would also take responsibility for getting the data into the computer. At a piecework rate of 25 cents per tape day, he hired Lakeside kids—a seventh grader named Chris Larson would be one of the first—to count the holes in the tapes and write down the totals; some of the kids even got their mothers to help out. Bill personally keypunched the results and fed them into the program on the CDC machine at the University of Washington. Since Gates was being paid about $2 a tape day, his profit margin was handsome even if there was a lot of scutwork to do. If only it could be automated, Bill thought. . . .

But there were more important things to worry about. In August 1971, claiming dissatisfaction with the state of the payroll program and the quality of the documentation, ISI refused to give the kids the computer time it had promised. With his friend Bill in tow, an indignant Kent Evans marched down to the law offices of the senior Bill Gates, apoplectic with rage. The Lakeside Programmers Group had been taken advantage of, Evans insisted; he demanded their rightful recompense. Kent "kept wanting me to say things, as some aggressive clients will—to kind of give it to 'em because they were being treated wrong," Bill's father recalled. "He was acting kind of difficult."

In the end, Gates senior did write a lawyer's letter to ISI. Discussions among Bill, Kent, and two ISI principals led to a new written agreement between ISI and the Gates/Evans team that spelled everything out to the letter. By this time, Allen and Weiland, on their way to college, were effectively out of the picture; exactly what happened to their share of the ISI programming time remains unclear.

Apparently the kids had been doing some cracking again. One thing the agreement spelled out was what would happen if the transgressions were repeated: "In the event that we observe unauthorized access to disk areas not assigned to LPG, this agreement will be terminated *immediately*."

The reduced-force Lakeside Programmers Group was to complete the payroll program and improve its documentation so that ISI's staff could teach people how to use it. In exchange, the initial draft proposed, LPG would get $5,000 of free time (an amount that in later retellings Bill would kite to $10,000), provided it was used before the end of 1971. Gates and Evans, however, crossed out the December date and wrote in "June 30, 1972." And although originally only Bill and Kent were to be permitted to use the free time, the boys crossed out "two" and inserted "four" where the number of programmers was mentioned.

These changes, initialed by Gates, Evans, and ISI's president, provided young Bill Gates his earliest lesson in how the world could turn on a minor contractual phrase. As it turned out, LPG would make good use of virtually every last minute of computer time, practically until the stroke of midnight June 30. And by the time that amended deadline rolled around, Kent Evans would be dead.

Junior year at Lakeside brought two new interests into Bill Gates's life: cars —real ones, not the virtual vehicles on the traffic tapes—and girls. Could skirts and hot wheels compete with lines of code?

Barely. Bill began driving his parents' Mustang, a red/orange convertible that is parked in his driveway today. What he really wanted was his own car, preferably a Porsche, the vehicle of choice among Lakeside hotshots. Even an ancient, decrepit Dodge Dart would do in a pinch; that, after all, was the famous vehicle of "one of the coolest guys who ever lived," Sang Ho Lee, an exuberant exchange student from a well-to-do family in Korea who influenced Bill's attitude toward four-wheeled vehicles. Gates and Sang Ho were known for wild joy rides in the Dart, which expired after a legendary brake failure at the top of a steep viaduct near Seattle's University District. Sideswiping a guard rail to slow the car's momentum, Sang Ho survived; the car did not. His carpooling buddies, including Bill Gates, suffered the consequences when Sang Ho showed up in a tiny red Mazda with an incredibly uncomfortable backseat. Eventually Sang Ho got the Bill Gates dream machine: a Porsche 911.

The advent of girls at Lakeside—actually the merger of Lakeside with a girls' school, St. Nicholas, founded in 1910—created a whole new "operating environment" and an uneasy transition at the former bastion of masculinity, where controversy remained fierce over whether women should have been allowed. A marker commemorating the end of Lakeside's exclusive maleness was placed prominently on campus. Resembling a tombstone, it offered the female pioneers a chilly welcome.

The merger with St. Nick's created more than just emotional uncertainty for Lakeside. It also produced a class-scheduling nightmare, complicated immensely by the fact that most girls were splitting time between the Lakeside campus and the St. Nick's facility nearly ten miles away.

Until the previous year, scheduling had been done by hand: Students would arrive in the fall to find a wall full of index cards listing their assignments. To the administration, the process seemed like just the sort of linear thing a computer could handle. Simply enter names and class lists, sort by requested assignments, adjust by class size and section, and presto! Neat little printouts of each and every schedule.

Bill Gates knew better. Tapped as the logical choice to develop such a program, he chose to stay on the sidelines. This wasn't a simple problem by any means. Class sizes had to be balanced, double-period labs had to be sandwiched in with teachers' schedules—the variables, Gates realized, were endless:

I want black lit. I want dance. I want bio lab. I don't want three courses in a row. Or I want three courses in a row. Everybody has these crazy ideas about what they want, and it turns out you can't have drums upstairs and choir downstairs at the same time . . . this thing is far more complicated than you think.

When teacher Bob Haig, a former Boeing engineer, first tried to put the schedule together in the middle of the 1970–71 school year, sophomores Gates and Evans and seniors Weiland and Allen had pitched in to help teach his Lower School computer course. Haig managed to hack out a schedule for the third trimester.

But if scheduling had been a purgatory before, the merger with St. Nick's turned it into a living hell. Haig promised he would get the postmerger schedule done over the summer in time for fall trimester. But the program, developed on the University of Washington's CDC machine, turned out to be far more difficult than he anticipated. The fall schedule was a mess.

Haig plodded on. On January 30, 1972, he and another teacher went flying together north of Seattle, heading toward the Lakeside campus to take aerial photos of it. The trip ended in tragedy when their single-engine Cessna 150 crashed and burst into flames. Both men were killed.

With Haig's death the school turned again to Gates and Evans. Working with Latin teacher Kenneth Van Dyke, they managed to shoehorn the third-trimester schedule into some kind of order on the CDC machine. Then Bill and Kent cut a deal with the school. Lakeside would pay them to do the scheduling, and the boys would use their free ISI time to do it.

The program, written from scratch in FORTRAN, didn't come together any easier for them than Haig's had for him. Gates and Evans spent hour after hour in the computer room, often sleeping overnight in a classroom, out on the grass, or in the teachers' lounge. Even for kids endowed with youthful exuberance and energy, the scheduling program was a grind.

Too much of a grind, perhaps. On May 28, 1972, Kent Evans went hiking with a University of Washington basic mountaineering class on Mount Shuksan near Bellingham. The group was crossing a gently sloped snowfield when Evans tripped and fell, tried to get back up, and then tumbled over and over, six to eight hundred feet across the snow and down the Curtis Glacier. Despite shouts from other hikers, Evans inexplicably assumed the "tucked," rather than the flattened-out "arrest," position, accelerating his plummet down the slope. He hit several large rocks, apparently suffered head injuries, and died aboard a rescue helicopter.

The death of Kent Evans was a sobering blow to the school, its students, and Bill Gates. Over the previous year, Gates and Evans had become closer than ever, spending hours on the phone discussing Kent's new enthusiasms— one week the foreign service, the next week the FBI, the next week the military. Bill received the news of Kent's death in a shattering phone call from Dan Ayrault, Lakeside's headmaster. Lakeside art teacher (and future best-selling author) Robert Fulghum, like Kent's father a Unitarian minister, conducted the emotional funeral service at Lakeside's chapel, after which Bill broke down in tears.

John Knowles's *A Separate Peace,* featuring a close prep school friendship ended by accidental death, soon became the second favorite novel in the Gates library. Fifteen years later he and Allen would donate a new math-science building to Lakeside and dedicate it to the memory of their "classmate, friend, and fellow-explorer, Kent Hood Evans," whose name would grace the auditorium.

Overweight and not inclined to sports, Evans had taken the climbing class partly because "he was trying to become an athletic guy," Gates recalled. "He didn't strike me as somebody who had any business up on the slopes," another contemporary remembered. To this day, Lakesiders speculate that the untimely deaths of Haig and Evans—both apparently precipitated by fatigue—may well have been related to the inhuman demands of the scheduling program. "I will be convinced to my dying day," said Evans's father, "that it was Kent's sort of semiexhausted physical state that led to his unfortunate accident. The last conversation I had with him was trying to convince him not to go, but he had a commitment to finishing things."

So did Bill Gates. With Evans gone and the June 30 ISI time-sharing cutoff looming, he turned to his friend Paul Allen, back from his freshman year at Washington State University. The duo worked feverishly to wrap up the scheduling program, and Gates even hired a couple of classmates, Doug Gordon and Melanie Graves, paying them a couple of hundred dollars each for assistance. "I remember staying up longer than I've ever stayed up, something like forty-eight hours straight, trying to get all this stuff done," Gordon recalled. The one fringe benefit was a master key to the school that Gates copied and distributed to his workers. Gordon used it for after-hours basketball in the gym until the night watchman figured out what was going on. As for Graves, she recalled a pizza break where Bill told her, "I'm going to make a million dollars by the time I'm twenty."

The line was more than just a come-on. It was something Gates had told others, including Anne Stephens, the English teacher and drama coach who had become an ad hoc counselor to many of the students. The model? Quite possibly the film he had seen the year before on a family trip to Europe, one that would remain a favorite well into his adult years: *The Thomas Crown Affair,* a 1968 caper starring Steve McQueen as a bored, supercool multimillionaire who masterminds a $2.5 million bank robbery. In a modest leap of imagination, the broad-lipped, big-nosed Gates could see himself as a McQueen surrogate—driving a Rolls, a dune buggy, and a hard business deal. He could fantasize about seducing Faye Dunaway, a beautiful insurance investigator smart enough to beat him at chess—but not smart enough to keep him from getting away with a second heist. Best of all, Gates saw, McQueen was beating "the System," even while he worried with exquisite adolescent angst about "who I want to be tomorrow."

But the future millionaire had shorter-term goals to worry about. Despite such setbacks as being locked outside the school in a sudden Northwest downpour, Gates managed to bring the project in on deadline. By the end of June, there was still $1,000 worth of time left in the ISI kitty; just for spite, Gates and Allen ate up as much of it as they could with a meaningless program that executed a do-nothing endless loop, then shut it down as July came into view.

Over the years the scheduling program, for which he was paid $4,200, made Gates a legend at Lakeside. To avoid official censure, Gates and Allen saw to it that the headmaster's daughter Lisa always got the precise schedule she requested. For a senior English course, Bill put all the smartest kids in one session—the one he was in—and the rest elsewhere. And despite the statistical challenges of a three-to-one boy-girl ratio, he insisted that he managed to arrange his senior history class with only one other boy—"a real wimp"—and "all the good girls in the school."

Gates shepherded the scheduling program for two more years, even after he had left Lakeside, and finally turned it over to underclassman and traffic-tape helper Chris Larson. After Larson graduated in 1977—a year in which, at Bill's suggestion, he scheduled himself some otherwise all-girl classes, prompting Bill to joke that he had "first call on every sin"—the program would be taken over by teachers, including an adult Tom Rona, and radically recast for a succession of improved computers; its descendant remains in use today.

In April 1972 Brock Adams, a longtime family friend who was serving his fourth term in the U.S. House of Representatives, had advised in a letter addressed to "Trey"—whom Adams had known as a hyperkinetic sprite since the Cheerio Club days—that he had been chosen as a summer congressional page. For bright guys—at the time, no females were involved—being a page was considered a useful first step in a career path to law school, legal practice, and political office. Adams, who had served in University of Washington student politics with Bill's parents, pulled strings to make the appointment happen.

No sooner was the scheduling program finished than Gates made preparations to leave for Washington, D.C., and his first unsupervised stay away from home. Gates served as a page from July 17 to August 18, pulling down $634.58 of the taxpayers' dollars. He lived with other pages at an establishment known as Mrs. Smith's Boarding House after the proprietor, a stern grandmotherly type all too wise to her charges' ways. Bill recalled her telling his group that they were "the most unruly bunch that had ever been there," but that may have been a line she worked on every year's crop.

Summer pages were at the bottom of the heap, looked down upon by the "real" year-round pages, but Gates apparently learned most of the classic page scams, such as pouring soup down the four-story mail slots in the House and Senate Office Buildings and sending people on bogus errands to the numbered restrooms there. The greatest scam of all, in Bill's opinion, was the officially sanctioned scam of the flag page, who spent entire days raising and lowering the Stars and Stripes at the Capitol building so that the fabric could then be sent to constituents with a letter stating that the enclosed flag had flown over the United States Capitol, conveniently omitting that it had been for a couple of seconds along with scads of others.

Then came the great McGovern-Eagleton button coup, one of the many Bill Gates stories that would grow in legend over the years. As Gates told the tale to friends and reporters, he attended McGovern's first press conference after the revelation that the vice-presidential candidate had previously received electroshock treatment for depression. Although McGovern made a initial pledge of "1000 percent support" for his running mate, Gates asked some of the Democratic congressmen whether that claim was really believable. Not a chance, he was told; McGovern was just biding time to come up with a replacement.

According to Gates, "that's when it dawned on me that we could go buy those buttons and make some money." The business opportunity was simple: Buy up all the campaign buttons you could find, then resell them later when Eagleton would be dropped from the ticket. Gates recalled purchasing thousands of buttons with another page for a nickel apiece and selling them for $10 to $25 each after Eagleton withdrew on August 1.

Gates claimed his edge was a superior distribution system: Pages would wear the buttons and, when people inquired about them, offer them for sale. When a dispute arose over the strongly forbidden practice of wearing political buttons in Congress, Bill and his pals argued that collectors' items of historical value didn't count. Supposedly Fishbait Miller, the colorful doorkeeper of the House, was willing to overlook the transgression for a fistful of buttons. Gates even claimed to have given buttons to Senator Eagleton, who somehow didn't have any.

The story does not compute. Pages on the scene at the time remember no one violating the strong prohibition against wearing political buttons on the floor. If Gates sold just 2,000 buttons, that would put the gross at a minimum of $20,000—a net of perhaps ten grand, assuming fees to the page distribution system. Yet Gates remembered taking home only a couple of thousand dollars at the end of the summer.

Besides, buttons were not exactly scarce commodities. A Ferndale, New York, campaign-paraphernalia manufacturer was printing up an extra 100,000 to accommodate demand. A Liberty, New York, grocer reportedly purchased 99,000 buttons, selling batches to the Smithsonian Institution and Eagleton himself. In later years Bill's fellow pages would dimly recall buying and selling buttons, but none remembered a price of anything like $10. Advertisements from commercial vendors offered pins at about $1 each. And although Gates claimed to have attended the press conference in Washington, McGovern's "1000 percent support" announcement in fact took place halfway across the country in South Dakota.

Gaining media momentum over the years, Bill's McGovern-button "coup" seems about as likely as the "billions" of computer-simulated Monopoly games he reportedly ran in his early Lakeside days. Even his sister Kristi believed the story had been "inflated." No matter how successful or wealthy he would become, the storytelling and self-inflation would remain a part of his vaguely insecure personality, as if his actual achievements were somehow not significant enough.

In the couple of weeks remaining before his senior year at Lakeside, Gates embarked on a whirlwind tour of his eastern-seaboard college choices: Princeton, Yale, Harvard, and MIT. But he decided that MIT was "just going to be a bunch of engineering guys," so he skipped the interview and played pinball instead. He could always sit in on classes there anyway if, as he expected, he made it into Harvard.

4

PROGRAMMING UNLIMITED

By the fall of 1972, it was time to build a computer, and Paul Allen had an idea how to do it. He and Bill had already been kicking the idea around, to the point where they had engaged in discussions with a hardware guy named Paul Gilbert. Gilbert, a quiet, lanky engineering type four years older than Bill, had attended Shoreline, a public high school not far from Lakeside. Back in the C-Cubed days, he had occasionally exchanged electronic messages with Gates and other Lakesiders. Gilbert was now an electrical engineering student at the University of Washington, where he also worked in the physics lab and had access to a wide variety of electronic test equipment.

The electronics magazines Paul Allen read were suddenly full of news and hype about an amazing new product from chipmaker Intel—the 8008 chip, successor to the original but underpowered 4004. The 4004, originally designed in 1969 for an electronic calculator, had been the first programmable microprocessor chip ever produced. Its breakthrough was summed up in that single key word: *programmable*. Programmable meant that unlike every chip that came before it, the 4004 could do one task one instant and a wildly different task the next. The instrument of that transformation? Software.

The 4004 could handle only four binary digits—bits representing ones or zeroes—of information at a time, and a four-bit system wasn't even enough to handle all the characters in the alphabet. But the new 8008 handled data eight bits—one byte or character—at a time, which was more than enough. Initially it had been intended as the brains of a computer terminal, but development delays lost Intel that deal. Now the 8008 was all dressed up with no place to go, and the ads touted it as "Intel's second computer on a chip! This one's a data expert."

Intel's hype was half accurate, half exaggeration. As its ad admitted, the little sliver of silicon and wire needed at least twenty-one more chips to become a full-fledged computer. But in theory it could become the brains of one. Paul Allen got hold of the specification sheet and tried to convince Bill to write a version of BASIC for it. But Gates was skeptical: Though far outstripping the lowly 4004, the 8008 was still severely limited in its capabilities. All in all, Gates thought it would be too limited and slow to support a decent BASIC.

So instead Allen sold Gates on the idea of an 8008-based special-purpose computer that could be programmed in assembly language, hooked up to a tape reader, and used to analyze Bill's traffic tapes. Now, here was something useful, something possible, something lucrative, something that appealed to Bill Gates. He and Allen materialized at the UW physics lab and asked Gilbert if he could put such a machine together. The money prospects were uncertain; pay was not discussed. They were making Gilbert an offer he could refuse. But he didn't.

Gates and Allen went down to an electronics supply shop and ponied up $360, mostly Bill's, for a single 8008 chip. Inside the little paper box, stuck into a piece of black foam plastic, wrapped in aluminum foil, was a piece of silicon that could, with luck, drive the logic of a real computer. Gates, typically, was impressed not only with the microprocessor, but also with its cost: "Three hundred and sixty bucks for this little chip!" And he was supposed to be impressed: In keeping with the computer-on-a-chip theme, Intel had set the price to plant a subliminal reminder of IBM's popular System 360 mainframes.

Thus was born the company that Bill Gates would christen Traf-O-Data. For nearly a decade, Traf-O-Data would continue in its quest to build the dream car-counting machine, making roughly enough money—nowhere near as much as Bill would later claim—to keep the company in equipment and stationery, a letterhead featuring a whimsical logo by Paul Gilbert's brother Miles.

The logo may have been Traf-O-Data's most impressive asset. Everything seemed to work against the enterprise. No one had done the slightest bit of research to see how many customers, if any, might actually want a traffic-counting computer. No one had wondered how to go about marketing such a product. And no one had realized how long it would take for the system to begin to come together. But when it did, the frustrating Traf-O-Data experience would set the stage for Bill Gates and Paul Allen to catch the next wave of computing.

Toward the end of the year, Lakeside School senior classman Bill Gates took on a different marketing project: the selling of William Henry Gates. Potential customers? College admissions officers. Bill had scored 800 on his math SAT and five achievement tests (though only in the low 700s on the verbal SAT), and as he put it, "I wanted to know which personality of mine would appeal to the world at large."

Witness the transformation! To Harvard, he was Bill Gates, son of a prominent lawyer, someone with connections, "the guy who was into politics . . . so my whole page experience was the central part of that application." For Princeton, "I positioned myself as a computer nerd," the programming magician who could hypnotize a minicomputer or mainframe into doing anything he commanded. For Yale, he was a consummate do-gooder and sensitive artist with thespian aspirations, "the guy who did drama, the guy who was Boy Scout." It was one of the earliest displays of his chameleonlike, Thomas Crown–like ability to change his skin, to transform his persona—and, eventually, his company's—in order to "do business."

Once the applications were in the mail, Gates the nerd got a major boost. Aerospace gurus from TRW's grandly named One Space Park in Redondo Beach had won the bid on a project that had nothing whatever to do with aerospace: a massive undertaking for the Bonneville Power Administration in Vancouver, Washington, across the Columbia River from Portland, Oregon. The BPA, for whom one-time employee Woody Guthrie had years before written "Roll On, Columbia," was now entering the computer age, and RODS—Real-Time Operating and Dispatch System—was to be the nerve center of the power grid that distributed cheap, seemingly limitless electricity from the skein of hydroelectric plants that had harnessed the river's might.

A companion system would gather data from the far-flung network that began with dams and turbines and generators, ran through power lines and transformers and substations, and ended in sawmills and aluminum smelters and toasters throughout the Great Northwest. The goal was to assemble and display the data in real time—right now, give or take a couple of seconds—so that the experts running the power grid could monitor how best to keep the juice flowing without unseemly interruption.

The aerospace wizards from One Space Park had woefully underestimated the complexity of this earthbound challenge. It would take maybe six programmers a couple of years, they had originally guessed, but now the hardware was all in place and the software was—well, nobody really knew where the software was, except many bugs short and many, many days late. Since the whole thing ran on DEC PDP-10s and PDP-11s, and huge performance penalties were looming, TRW was scouring the country for crack DEC programmers, flying them in from the company's own facilities halfway across the country, hiring them away from outfits like Hughes Aerospace, contracting them as temporary help from Control Data, even borrowing them from DEC itself.

Already aboard was Bud Pembroke, the former technical chief of Portland's ISI, where he happened to have availed himself of the services of a few young DEC mavens from Seattle. Over Christmas vacation, he phoned Ric Weiland, Bill Gates, and Paul Allen with an amazing offer: How would they like to come down to Vancouver to work on the biggest DEC installation they had ever seen?

Weiland declined, but Gates and Allen had just returned home exhausted from a bitter week at Washington State University in Pullman. They had been trying to keep warm in Paul's semiheated dorm room and jump-start their get-rich-quick Traf-O-Data business. They had succeeded at neither.

At least the Traf-O-Data hardware, built by their friend Paul Gilbert, was beginning to look real. With its Plexiglas front sprinkled with switches and blinking red LEDs, the rack-size unit strongly resembled a DEC computer—the popular PDP-11 that Gilbert had taken as a physical model. Its innards were far less elegant, a hand-soldered, wire-wrapped marvel of Rube Goldberg engineering.

Gates and Allen had spurred Gilbert to get the job done. To Gilbert, Bill "had a real way of bringing you in on something and getting you totally involved in it. He kind of got me motivated, made me more motivated about that project than anything I was working on in classes. I let them really go, because it really meant a lot. Here I wasn't working for him, I wasn't his boss, I was a partner, but he had that charisma." The usually laid-back Paul Allen played the unaccustomed role of bad cop: "He would really light into me for being a little bit slow on things."

Now Allen was being slow. What he had been trying to accomplish on the Washington State University IBM System 360 was an almost alchemical feat: turning hardware into software. The goal: a program called a simulator that would cleverly mimic every last quirk of the tiny 8008 chip inside the Traf-O-Data box. In effect, the simulator would turn a big computer into a little one, and then Bill Gates could use big-computer resources to write software for the Traf-O-Data machine. But Paul Allen had not yet managed the alchemy that might turn Traf-O-Data into gold.

So when TRW made its offer, Gates and Allen jumped at it. A paid job with unlimited access to their cherished PDP-10 machines? After years of scrounging cheap or free time from whatever source they could finagle? It sounded like programming nirvana. Sure, they were supposed to be students, but finding an officially sanctioned reason for cutting classes had never been a problem before. The two friends tossed some gear into Allen's car, drove the 160 miles from Seattle south to the "other" Vancouver, and rolled up to the RODS control center.

Located just below a huge Bonneville Power substation atop a hill at the edge of a wooded glade, the concrete-and-glass building was not particularly impressive from the outside, in part because much of it was underground. But the interior! "This is the coolest facility. . . . They have this massive control room, which looks better than any TV show I've ever seen, even like 'Time Tunnel,'" Gates remembered. "They have this map on the wall that Siemens did which has little lights behind every line and every gridpoint, and they have the first color CRT [cathode ray tube] command consoles where you have all these lines. . . . You have this kind of gun-trigger cursor-control thing, and you have these little chart recorders. They have like forty of these command stations down in this place, then behind that is the big computer room where they have all these PDP-11s" for data acquisition, "and then those things would feed to the two PDP-10s, and then there's this control panel inside there which is just for the computers to say what's live and what's not."

"It's mind-blowing!" Gates recalled. "It was like a dream come true!" And if their supervisors thought, "Whoa, these are kids!"—well, these kids came with Bud Pembroke's blessing, and though some members of the team were seasoned veterans who had worked on such things as the Anti-Ballistic Missile project, there were plenty who were still only a couple of years past voting age. Besides, kids worked cheap. Gates and Allen started out at about $4 an hour—ridiculously low for programmers whose professionalism was unquestioned. But to a high school student working on a "senior project"—as Gates presented it to Lakeside in order to maintain his class standing—$4 an hour didn't seem utterly exploitive.

Besides, how many high school seniors got to work on real-world computer problems that were state of the art? No—"way beyond the state of the art," as Gates put it, "because we were trying to do this fault-tolerant PDP-10 system, where if any piece of hardware would fail we'd switch over to the backup system." How many college-bound seniors got to work with brilliant analysts like John Norton, flown in from One Space Park to audit the project, interview the suspects, review everybody's code, straighten out the screwups? To Gates, "He was a god! He would take a piece of source code home, come back and just totally analyze the thing. Just a high-IQ act."

When Bill phoned his parents to learn whether they'd received word about his Harvard application, Allen, a sophomore experienced in academic circles, gave him some portentous but unappreciated advice: "I remember telling Bill 'There are going to be some guys at Harvard who are smarter than you.' And he said, 'No way! No way!' "

But Bill's cockiness got something of a comeuppance at the RODS facility. "At first I got crappy stuff assigned to me," Gates recalled—stuff like documenting "every error message the PDP-10 could ever emit. . . . Of course, DEC had never done that, so there were three people who'd just sit there at their desk all day long just looking through these manuals trying to create these alphabetized infinite error messages." What was even more galling to Gates was that Allen was working on cool stuff, neat stuff, like the recovery module that would instantly switch the whole system over from a dying PDP-10 to a live one. Still, where else could a high school kid work and play on great computers day and night, with an endless amount of that most precious of resources, free computer time, in the bargain?

Certainly not in high school, but Gates made the best of it. When he returned to Lakeside in early spring 1973, he strutted into math class as well prepared and cocky as if he'd never left. Gates was popular with teachers, but written work was his major failing. "He hated to write the lab reports," recalled chemistry teacher Daniel Luzon Morris. "I tried to get him to get things organized. . . . He could do the work fine, he hated the writing up of it."

But he didn't mind the limelight. Under the direction of Anne Stephens, his closest friend and confidante among the Lakeside teachers, he starred in Peter Shaffer's *Black Comedy* as Brinsley, the hapless young sculptor trying in the midst of an electrical blackout—precisely what Bill in real life had been helping to prevent—to juggle his fiancée, his lover, and a potential deal with—prophetically—the richest man in the world. In *The Thurber Carnival,* he did a star turn in the monologue "The Night the Bed Fell." He got an A-minus in Love —"Love in the Western World," Stephens's literature class that included such torrid items as the adulterous passion of Tristram and Iseult. He won a National Merit Scholarship, got into all three schools of his choice with special accolades, and sent his regrets to Princeton and Yale. He accompanied his stockholder mom to IBM's annual meeting, held that year in Seattle. And, when the very idea of the senior prom led to much debate about such a traditional institution being too, uh . . . *square* for the youth of laid-back 1973 and the ultimate decision was to hold the prom but attend in offbeat attire, Bill Gates escorted the highly regarded junior Melissa Kristoferson—his *Black Comedy* costar Vicki Weeks had turned him down—and cut a dapper figure with his white frock coat, pink ruffled shirt, top hat, and cane.

After graduation, Gates tooled back to Vancouver, where he, Allen, and Weiland roomed together near the RODS facility. At the Brandywine Apartments, the less-argumentative Weiland drew the living-room couch in a furnished two-bedroom unit whose dominant feature was green shag carpet. For the summer, Gates got a raise—a big one, if you looked at it on a percentage basis, not much if you looked at it more objectively, though in later years it would inflate, with Bill as the apparent source, to "something like $30,000 a year." He also began to get better assignments, such as revising the system's backup program and bug-swatting its FORTRAN compiler. Eventually he "got involved in what was called System Integration."

The goal for the acceptance of RODS was the successful completion of a 400-hour test, during which the system could be down for roughly two minutes. So far, that goal seemed a long way off. Gates was one of the programmers who tested the system with special sets of data designed to simulate the information that would come in from here, there, and everywhere when and if the facility ever got up and running.

All-night programming became the norm, and marathon sessions were not uncommon. In the service of great program code, personal hygiene would be tossed to the winds—not that it had ever been a major concern. "We had contests," Gates recalled, "to see who could stay in the building like three days straight, four days straight. Some of the more prudish people would say 'Go home and take a bath.' We were just hardcore, writing code."

The official pick-me-up was Instant Tang. Gates and company would scoop it out of the jar and eat it raw, giving their fingertips a perpetual orangish glow. When the confines of the RODS facility became too oppressive, the programmers would clamber up the microwave tower or roam through the battery room in the basement, vehemently arguing about code, music, life. But the late-night and sometimes round-the-clock work sessions weren't entirely for the greater glory of the Bonneville Power Administration. In a fit of whimsy, Allen developed a program that turned the command-and-control terminals into giant color monitors, and Bill modified some system software to display dull program code in dazzling hues.

And the PDP-10s came in handy for business purposes other than TRW's. The most important was Allen's 8008 simulator for Traf-O-Data. He had come up with the right design now—an adaptation of the existing PDP-10 Macro Assembler and DDT debugger that would let Gates write, test, and produce 8008 code for the Traf-O-Data box using all the tools of the big DEC machine. By the end of summer the 8008 simulator was ready to roll. Traf-O-Data might just make it yet.

For the ever-competitive Gates, play was every bit as intense as work. The Japanese game of Go was a favorite pastime, and in the informal tournaments, Bill won more often than not. Chess was another matter. Paul Allen understood how to counter the aggressive Gates attack, attack, attack. And Gates hated to lose: When Allen won, Bill would angrily upset the chessboard and mutter "Just kidding."

At group outings to the local racetrack, Gates indulged his penchant for gambling. A retired jockey who lived in a colleague's building was always ready to supply horse tips that never seemed to pan out. The dog races were "totally random"; eventually Gates came up with a betting scheme based on license plates he'd seen in the parking lot.

A young Californian named Bob Barnett was one of Bill's superiors. On sunny workdays, Gates would bop into the RODS facility around noon, saunter up to Barnett's desk, and say, "Let's go waterskiing." By one or two in the afternoon, Barnett's sleek ski boat would be skimming along Vancouver's Lacamas Lake with Bill at the end of the towrope, taking off from the dock and executing turns and jumps gracefully, fearlessly, on a single ski. The afternoon would finish with a meal, and a long night of programming would commence.

"Gates was definitely the best waterskiier," Barnett recalled. But before one of his single-ski dock starts, Bill forgot to readjust the ski's footbed. Moments later he jumped the towboat's wake as he had hundreds of times before—but went sprawling into the water. When his friends hauled him into the boat, there was no doubt about it: Bill's leg was broken. The doctor who set the cast told him to come back and have it taken off in six weeks. Bill went home to Seattle to recuperate.

Three weeks later Barnett looked up from his desk and saw Bill Gates. "Where's your cast?" he asked.

Gates muttered that he'd had a Seattle doctor take it off. "Let's go skiing!"

"Show me your leg," Barnett said.

Gates did. It looked horrible, a pastiche of ugly hues. "No way," Barnett told him.

"I want to go waterskiing," Bill said firmly. "I can do it."

Barnett just shook his head.

But when it came to convincing people, Bill Gates had a whole repertoire of tricks at his disposal, everything from aggression to charm, whatever worked. By the end of the afternoon, without knowing exactly how it had happened, Barnett found himself at the helm of his boat, with Bill Gates at the end of the towrope, executing daredevil leaps, oblivious to any problems with his injured limb. It was the same fearlessness—some called it recklessness— that would later entice the waterski-crazy Gates, at a dude ranch in Montana, to attempt a dock start from a diving platform ten feet above Flathead Lake. A family photo of the event shows clearly that he didn't make it.

In their spare time at RODS, Bill and Paul reworked the Lakeside scheduling program for the coming year. Late at night when testing something on the system and encountering terrible response time, Barnett quickly learned to suspect the handiwork of Gates and Allen, who'd be running multiple iterations of the scheduler all over the system, on every spare terminal they could get their hands on. In an attempt to slow them down, Barnett would give them new assignments, but that didn't keep Bill busy for long. According to Barnett, "It took him one day to do what I considered forty hours' work."

In the fall of 1973 Paul Allen went back to Washington State. Ric Weiland returned to Stanford. And, not long before his eighteenth birthday, Bill Gates arrived at Harvard with all the clarity and vision of a typical wet-eared freshman. Although he had enough advanced placement credits to earn sophomore standing, his parents pointed out that he was young for his class and encouraged him to enter as a freshman—a decision they were later to rue.

Named a National Scholar by Harvard—he'd been offered similar honors at Yale and Princeton—Gates was invited to state his preference among roommates. When Bill requested a foreign student and a minority student, he was assigned to Harvard Yard's Wigglesworth Hall, Building A, room 11, along with Sam Znaimer, an aspiring scientist from Montreal's Jewish St.-Urbain Street neighborhood, and Jim Jenkins, a black student from Chattanooga, Tennessee.

Officially Gates intended to major in applied math. He and his Lakeside buddy Doug Gordon, a chemistry major, enrolled in Math 55 along with two math whizzes from upstairs in "Wig A"—Andy Braiterman from Baltimore and Jim Sethna from Indianapolis. Math 55 was the course for people with 800 math boards, for people who had "never met anyone else who's better . . . in mathematics, ever." The nasty problems posed by the Math 55 instructor led to weekly all-night pizza-and-problem sessions in the Sethna-Braiterman digs. It was there that Gates ruefully realized Allen was right: There were people at Harvard who were smarter—at least when it came to math.

Gates also enrolled in classes in Greek literature, social science, English history, and organic chemistry—where he earned his single worst grade at Harvard. "We were both really shocked," recalled Doug Gordon, who later became a chemist. "We were getting like D's on these exams, and that really blew us away, because we had both been pretty much straight-A students at Lakeside."

But the self-propelled Gates was also majoring in such classical studies as Pong, the simple ping-pong video game that had become a runaway hit, defined a genre, and for many people offered their first experience in interactive computing. There were also pinball games at Harvard Square's 24-Hour Rest, movies at the local revival houses, and duplicate bridge, chess, and hanging out till all hours in the morning arguing in the dorms. "Gates was a good arguer," Braiterman remembered. "He would argue about everything." One of the things he argued most emphatically about was the idea that people would have computers in their homes. Nobody would need books; you could call up what you wanted on your computer. When friends objected to the privacy implications—big brother finding out what you read, accessing your financial records, your life history—Gates pooh-poohed them and simply argued harder.

And Gates did not hesitate to become involved in academic games. Working the angles to get access to the computers he felt his experience merited, Gates cajoled, whined, and argued the keepers of the educational flame into letting him skip most of the prerequisite computer science courses. He also managed to leapfrog the machines reserved for mere undergraduates and worm his way onto the ones normally reserved for graduate students. These were situated at Harvard's Aiken Computation Laboratory under the direction of Professor Thomas Cheatham, who later described Gates succinctly: "He was a hell of a good programmer." But Cheatham found Bill's personality left much to be desired. "In terms of being a pain in the ass, he was second in my whole career here. He's an obnoxious human being. . . . He'd put people down when it was not necessary, and just generally not be a pleasant fellow to have around the place."

The lab was steeped in computer history. It was named for Howard H. Aiken, inventor of the first automatic general-purpose digital calculator, the

"Automatic Sequence Controlled Calculator" completed in 1944 and known at Harvard as the Mark-1. The lab's ancient DEC PDP-10 had supposedly spent most of the Vietnam War sitting in an army truck. When the Defense Department's Advanced Research Projects Agency (ARPA) offered it to Harvard at the height of the late 1960s' antiwar fervor, it arrived in the wee hours of the morning so that the army van carrying it would not arouse controversy.

Aiken also had three arthritic DEC PDP-1s, good mostly for special graphics programs—such as Spacewar, the intergalactic video shoot-'em-up invented over a decade before by Bill's old C-Cubed mentor, Steve Russell, on a similar machine just down Mass Ave at MIT. Gates and his cronies spent hours in front of the PDP-1 screens annihilating each other's glowing spaceships.

As an independent study project, Gates decided to link the PDP-10 to a PDP-1 to create a video game of his own—baseball. Ideally, the pitcher would pitch, the batter would bat, a fielder would bend over and pick up the ball. By the end of the year about all that worked was the part where stick figures took the field. As Znaimer recalled it, "He took a simple end-of-term project and turned it into a monstrous endeavor."

Gates was known to be well off, but nobody accused him of flaunting it on campus. He wore rattier clothes than most, did his laundry as infrequently as possible, and rarely bothered using sheets on his bed—where Znaimer once found him slumbering, fully clothed, mumbling "One, comma, one, comma, one" as if dreaming mathematics.

Although the 1960s had run their course, the early '70s retained the flavor of sex and drugs and rock and roll. "I don't think I was unusual in any of those dimensions, plus or minus," Gates later recalled. But Gates was mostly indifferent to music; his record collection amounted to a bunch of albums by Seattle native Jimi Hendrix that had been urged upon him by guitar-playing rockhound Paul Allen with the catchphrase "Are you experienced?"

At Harvard, Gates was not known to have girlfriends, and didn't join his buddies for the social mixers that ended mostly in frustration when the girls refused to go home with them. He did, however, amass a fairly sizable collection of *Playboy* and *Penthouse* magazines, and was the subject of rumors for his visits to Boston's Combat Zone, notorious for porn films and prostitution and drug deals. "I used to hang out in the Zone for a little while, just watching what was going on," Bill related. "Mostly I just sat at this pizza place and read books." According to one tale, a mugger in Boston Common demanded and got Bill's wallet at gunpoint, somehow leaving him with a five-dollar bill. Gates jumped into a cab and asked to be taken five bucks' worth toward Harvard Square. With typical negotiating hustle, he then related his plight so movingly that the cabbie drove him all the way home. On his return, Gates regaled his friends with the narrative, right down to mimicking the robber's voice.

As for drugs—well, Gates was certainly not unusual there. Marijuana was the pharmaceutical of choice, but in Znaimer's words, "on a couple of well-planned isolated occasions we'd go off to the country and spend time contemplating the universe."

The ties to Seattle continued. Early in 1974, when Lakeside School discovered it was spending over $6,000 a year on computer time, the school consulted with Bill Gates about purchasing a computer of its own. An April Lakeside proposal pointed out that "In the process of doing assigned work, writing game programs, doing acceptance testing for one company or another, and even cracking codes to access the accounting files of one company, some students have become outstanding programmers." It sounded exactly like a biography of Bill Gates—or Paul Allen.

With all his extracurricular activities and "hardcore" work ethic, freshman Gates burned his candle at both ends. Just after final exams he suffered a case of ulcerative colitis serious enough to put him in the hospital for more than a week, fly home first class for the first time ever, and force him to continue a course of steroids into early summer. Although the disease is primarily genetic, friends believed the episode had been brought on by stress, overwork, and sheer Gatesian intensity. Some speculated that it had been linked to Bill's unhappiness at Harvard, the first place where he had been forced to confront his limitations. "I was under a lot of pressure," Gates later said, recalling his problems with the final exam in organic chemistry, a class he'd skipped "because I was nervous." He ended up with a C in the course, the lowest grade he would ever receive at Harvard.

The experience of discovering people who were every bit his intellectual equal was humbling and confusing. Even before the colitis attack, Gates had been getting "antsy." As he recalled it, "Paul and I were thinking we'd get a job, maybe take a year off and get a job together." So Bill had interviewed with a variety of companies, from a General Electric division in Kentucky to a school system on Long Island to ARAMCO oil looking for programmers to go to Saudi Arabia. Honeywell offered him a job in its Billerica, Massachusetts, facility—a job he accepted on the condition that his friend Paul Allen get to work with him. Honeywell interviewed Allen by phone and made him an offer, and must have been surprised when Allen accepted and Bill didn't.

Their Traf-O-Data enterprise, meanwhile, continued to roll down the highway of commerce like a Mercedes with three flat tires. Paul Gilbert's 8008 hardware was more or less finished, and so was Bill's software, but the company still had no viable device to read the traffic tapes automatically. An inventor Bill's dad knew had come up with an idea for what the company's young principals called "the squeeze reader," which would somehow sense the holes in the tapes by squeezing metallized rubber fingers through them, and Traf-O-Data, meaning Bill Gates, helped bankroll the prototype. The squeeze reader set the stage for a memorable scene in early summer 1974 in the Gates living room, where Bill had finally managed to lure a representative of the King County Engineering Department. The night before, Gilbert and Gates had made sure everything ran fine, right down to the brilliant graphical printout on the portable terminal Bill owned. At the actual demonstration, the squeeze reader failed dismally. Gates ran to get his mother: "Tell him, Mom! Tell him it worked last night!"

The squeeze reader had to go. Gilbert priced professional models. Gates bit the bullet and coughed up his own money, about $3,400 of it, to pay for an Enviro-Labs Model GS-311 Paper Tape Reader. By fall the partnership among Gates, Allen, and Gilbert was orally agreed to. By December Traf-O-Data had grossed a measly $252.67—probably from the District of Surrey, British Columbia, a municipality just south of Vancouver, B.C., that became Traf-O-Data's most dependable customer. It was Bill Gates's first brush with international trade.

But as usual, Gates was multitasking. His sister Kristi, a student officer at the University of Washington, helped hire him for the summer to computerize the class enrollment for the student government's freewheeling open-to-all Experimental College—a project he programmed on a DEC PDP-11 at Seattle Pacific College. It was a trivial task, far simpler than the Lakeside scheduler, but it familiarized him with the best version of BASIC he'd ever seen: a first-rate dialect called RSTS-11 BASIC-PLUS. The project would later serve as a hot potato when the campus newspaper hinted that the student government had been guilty of nepotism in giving Kristi's brother the $500 job.

In the fall Paul Allen was already in Boston, having driven with his girlfriend across the country to take the position at Honeywell. Back at Harvard, Gates and many of his cronies moved up to the Radcliffe campus and a dorm called Currier House. Geographically just outside the "social" whirl, Currier lured a motley parade of introverted "sciency people" with its low-pressure environment—and the theoretical promise of an almost one-to-one male-female ratio, significantly better than the dorms closer to Harvard Yard. Tipping the scales in Currier's favor, according to Gates: the availability of a hamburger for lunch each day.

At Currier, Bill found a new use for applied math: poker. In a sparsely furnished chamber that remains known today as the "poker room," the young scholars played for stakes connoted mathematically by fractional denominator. In the relatively rare and rarefied /1 game, pronounced "slash-one," chips were bought and sold at their full value: Red, for example, was worth a quarter. In the lower-stakes /20 game, known as the buffoon game, the chips would be worth one-twentieth of their nominal value. The fractions ranged as low as /100—known as the idiot game.

Math, socializing, arcane terminology, humor, and cutthroat competition —poker was a perfect package for the kid whose family nickname had come from the world of cardplaying. Initially Bill was found at the buffoon table, where his unorthodox dealing technique—distributing from his lap, a sort of under-the-table deal—was immortalized as "Gatesing the deck." Gates was "the Gator" to some, the "Gates gravy train" to others. He quickly graduated to high-stakes sessions with graduate students such as Brad Leithauser, who would later gain renown as a novelist and poet, and Scott Drill, who would eventually run a company specializing in office lettering systems. Floating from Currier House to other dorms to off-campus apartments, the games were mostly high-low variants, draw, stud, and, eventually, Texas hold 'em—and the pot limit table stakes could escalate to the point where a large kitty might run to $1,000. Winnings could amount to $500 over an evening—an evening that might begin late in the afternoon and end at noon the next day with the winners buying breakfast. By most accounts Gates, better at math than at bluffing, was a hit-and-miss player—as likely to lose $500 as to win $400.

The Gates theory of scholarship was "you kind of sign up for courses where you know you can learn it in reading period and then you can just audit different courses." During the fall of 1974, though, what Gates seemed to be auditing most was the poker colloquium—with an occasional visit to what was known to these math mavens as "the complex number seminar," where things went on in the "Z-plane"—sleep.

Another Gates obsession at the time was a video game called Breakout, a more abstract sort of super-Pong involving the destruction of bricks with a rectangular "ball." The game had been designed for Atari in four days by two young Silicon Valley engineers who would eventually cross Bill Gates's path. Steve Jobs, who was working for Atari, received the $5,000 check for the job, gave the trusting Steve Wozniak his "half"—$350—and pocketed the rest. They would later go on to collaborate on a computer called the Apple I.

Down the hall from Gates lived a math-science student who was as straight-arrow and outgoing as the typical Currier bunch was nerdy and introverted. Steve Ballmer, a big, bluff Detroiter with a high forehead and the mood swings of a manic-depressive, was the ultimate social guy, Mr. Extracurricular Activity, with fingers in every pie from the football team, which he eventually managed, to the literary magazine, of which he eventually became publisher. Yet somehow he and Gates got along, a Mutt and Jeff collaboration cemented by mutual tastes in movies and mutually snide, cynical senses of humor. That year they both competed in the prestigious Putnam national math prize competition. Harvard boasted twelve of the top one hundred competitors in the country, including Steve Ballmer. Bill finished out of the honors.

Meanwhile, the Gates and Allen collaboration was still hunting for a new venture. The two met on weekends and occasional weekday evenings, talking about what was going on in the computer world, brainstorming about what projects they might embark on next. The meager income for the fourth quarter of 1974 suggested strongly that Traf-O-Data still wasn't poised for takeoff, and an expression of vague interest from a consultant to the Brazilian National Highway Department was hardly enough to bolster their spirits. Allen's work on communications interfaces for Honeywell was not particularly rewarding.

In later years Gates would state flatly that "between 1970 and 1974 we pursued specialized applications. We programmed about half the elevators in the United States today. [They] have microcomputer programs that we developed that decide when the elevator should go up, when it should go down." This, as Gates would admit long after retailing this fiction, "never happened." The truth? Back when he had waited around for elevators as a congressional page, he had mentally toyed with some scheduling algorithms.

Gates would also come to claim that it was during this period that he and Allen came up with the phrase that he would eventually repeat ad infinitum as the Microsoft creed: "A computer on every desk and in every home, running Microsoft software." It was yet another Gatesian revision of history: Microsoft as a name did not yet exist, the slogan was not heard around the company until the mid-1980s, and it derived from a startling article the duo was about to see in print.

In early December, the January 1975 issue of *Popular Electronics* arrived at the newsstand in Harvard Square, and Paul Allen discovered it. "PROJECT BREAKTHROUGH!" screamed the headline. "World's First Minicomputer Kit to Rival Commercial Models . . . 'Altair 8800' SAVE OVER $1000." The cover boasted a sleek blue box whose front panel sported thirty-six LED indicator lights and twenty-five toggle switches and looked very much like a real minicomputer.

The article inside was headlined "EXCLUSIVE. ALTAIR 8800. The most powerful minicomputer project ever presented—can be built for under $400." Its text, appearing under the double byline of H. Edward Roberts and William Yates, began with a stirring and influential proclamation: "The era of the computer in every home—a favorite topic among science fiction writers—has arrived!"

This was it! Somebody had finally done it! Paul and Bill had already talked about Intel's advanced new 8080 chip, the brains of the Altair. They had even considered building a computer based on it. But the Traf-O-Data debacle had soured them on the idea of developing hardware. Now somebody out there had really done it.

Allen rushed to the dorm to find Bill Gates. They had to do a BASIC for this machine. They had to. If they didn't, the revolution would start without them!

What neither Paul nor Bill knew at the time was that like the Great Oz, the

Altair on the cover of *Popular Electronics* was a bit of a humbug. It was a mere mockup, a cardboard box whose front panel lights and switches were utterly inoperable. But like the unmasked Oz, the Altair definitely had the power to change lives. As for the yellow brick road, it would lead to the dusty flats of Albuquerque, New Mexico, where Messieurs Roberts and Yates, creators of the computer for every home, awaited someone to supply software for it.

5

HARDCORE!

The Altair was certainly not the first personal computer. You could argue that the earliest small IBM 600-series machines of the 1950s had been personal computers, because they were small by the standards of the day—about the size of a large desk—and unquestionably designed for one-person operation. You could argue that some of the smaller DEC units, such as the workhorse PDP-8, were personal computers, because most were used exclusively by a single individual. You could argue that Intel's development machines, systems intended for software and hardware gurus, were in truth personal computers, because they were generally used on a one-per-customer basis. Many still argue that the Alto, a far-reaching machine developed at Xerox's Palo Alto Research Center in 1973, was the first personal computer. But none of those units was marketed to the general public, none cost less than a luxury car of its day, and therefore none was personal in the important sense that an individual could easily find and afford one.

There had been cheap computers before the Altair. An obscure model known as the Kenbak dated to 1971, and had been based not on a microprocessor (which were not yet generally available), but on two discrete logic chips known as shift registers. An 8008-based unit, the Micral, was released in France in 1973. The following year, an 8008 machine called the Scelbi—for "SCientific, ELectronic, and BIological" was advertised to American ham radio enthusiasts. A couple hundred were sold in kit and assembled form, but at a price of $500, the unit was a money-loser.

Another kit, the Mark-8, had been featured on the cover of *Radio-Electronics* magazine's July 1974 issue. Building it was a matter of ordering manuals from the magazine, circuit boards from a designated supplier, and electronic components wherever you could find them, for a total of about $250. Still, 10,000 manuals and a couple of thousand boards were sold, and enough machines were put together to spawn user groups and newsletters exploring ways to do something with the machine other than making its LED indicators blink. The Scelbi and Mark-8 were considered successes: In the months to come you could get a $150 discount if you traded one in on an Altair.

The editors of *Popular Electronics* had been looking for a computer project as a response to the September 1973 issue of *Radio-Electronics* ("For Men with Ideas in Electronics"), which featured Don Lancaster's legendary "TV Typewriter," a low-cost video terminal design that let you display sixteen lines of thirty-two upper-case characters on a standard TV screen. The Mark-8 issue of *Radio-Electronics* raised the stakes.

Popular Electronics had been working with MITS and its president, Ed Roberts, since the days when the company was known as Micro Instrumentation and Telemetry Systems and it made radio transmitters for model rockets. Since then *Popular Electronics* had run articles touting other MITS electronics projects, culminating in an electronic calculator kit that was a runaway success. But when the calculator boom fell prey to a vicious round of price cutting, MITS had to sell its machines at a loss. By mid-1974 the company was over a quarter of a million bucks in hock to its bank.

Somehow Ed Roberts, a bearish six-foot-four former air force engineer, managed to borrow another $65,000 on the strength of a business plan he presented to the bankers. The plan was one of Roberts's longtime dreams: to build a full-fledged digital computer. Roberts figured he could break even if he sold 200 units; with luck he could move 800 a year.

Roberts and fellow air force veteran Bill Yates designed the machine around an advanced microprocessor: the new Intel 8080, which included lots of ways to manipulate data, could directly address a whopping 64K of memory—65,536 bytes, the equivalent of some thirty pages of text, four times more than the 8008 could handle, or about half as much as C-Cubed's PDP-10. The 8080 also solved most of the 8008's other shortcomings. So Roberts cut a deal with Intel: It would sell him the chip in bulk for a mere $75 each instead of the quantity-one price of $360.

Taking a page from DEC and other minicomputer manufacturers, Roberts and Yates designed the machine with what was known as open bus architecture —a design they borrowed from such minicomputer classics as the Data General Nova they used for their accounting. The bus was a set of circuits that carried all the important signals in the computer to and from simple connector slots. By plugging printed-circuit cards into the slots, you could expand your machine almost infinitely. The cabinet of the Altair was big enough to hold sixteen cards, so adding more memory, attaching a Teletype, or hooking up a radically expensive floppy disk drive would be—in theory, at least—a simple matter of plug and play.

Roberts shipped the first completed prototype to the *Popular Electronics* office and hopped a plane to New York to demonstrate it. The engineer arrived safely, but the machine did not: Somehow the express company had managed to lose it. Yates cobbled together a mockup in time to make the magazine's deadline for front-cover photography, and the machine was dubbed Altair— either for the star itself or the Enterprise's destination on an episode of "Star Trek."

The Altair was a hit from the start. Orders flooded in to the MITS Albuquerque headquarters. Two hundred machines in a year? MITS soon sold that many on one hectic Friday. Never mind that the magazine's laundry list of "Applications for the Altair 8800 computer" included such homey suggestions as "multichannel data acquisition system," "automatic IC tester," "digital signal generator," and "brain for a robot." Never mind that the $397 (plus postage) that you sent to MITS, Inc., got you merely a box stuffed with computer chips, capacitors, resistors, LEDs, ribbon cables, mounting boards, toggle switches, power supply, and metal case—though if you happened to have the last three items lying around the house, you could save an additional $99, and some solderheads actually did. Never mind that no matter how dexterous you were with a soldering gun, you'd probably screw something up somewhere and need expensive oscilloscopes and digital test meters to figure out what went wrong. Sure, you could cough up an extra $101 to have the company do the assembly, but who knew how much of an extra wait that might entail? And even if you did manage to get the machine up and running, there was virtually nothing you could do with it except painstakingly flip the tiny toggle switches—eight or sixteen per instruction—to enter dumb little programs that might make the lights blink on and off in some sort of way significant to those proficient in octal arithmetic.

But never mind. The Altair put it all together in a way that none of its predecessors had managed. The Altair was one-stop shopping. There was no hunting around for a manual here, boards there, chips somewhere else. With one letter, one phone call, one check, bang! You had bought it all, the whole enchilada kit. You could brag to your friends that you owned your own computer. You could show them every single part that you were going to put together some day when you got around to it. In 1975, when everybody knew that plain old regular people couldn't even begin to own their own computers, doctors and dentists and hackers and wireheads realized that owning your own computer was the ultimate status symbol.

In a sense the Altair was a genuine bargain. After all, the whole machine, kit and kaboodle, was selling for a few dollars more than Intel's price for a single 8080 chip. To price-wise soldering-iron savants who kept their eyes on integrated circuits, it was like getting most of a computer for free. And if you could get it put together, the Altair would look like a real computer, not a bunch of boards. Just as Paul Gilbert did in building the Traf-O-Data machine, Ed Roberts had fashioned the exterior design after a favorite minicomputer—

in this case the Data General Nova II. Although minicomputer prices had been dropping steadily, the Altair cost about half as much as an equivalent DEC machine.

Yet as exciting as this machine might be to the wire-and-solder crowd, from many standpoints it was a toy, a joke. Every time you turned the machine off, it would go utterly blank. Merely to get it to do anything after you powered it up, you had to "bootstrap," or "boot," it with half a hundred sequences of instructions entered by flipping switches. If one of those instructions had been entered incorrectly—one flip among hundreds—the machine would refuse to do anything at all.

Besides, the standard unit came with only 256 bytes of RAM—random-access memory, the fast, essential chips that temporarily store programs and data while the computer is using them. That much memory was enough to hold only the characters in a four-line paragraph or a very rudimentary computer program indeed. According to the price list, you could take the machine all the way up to 1024 bytes (1K)—a sixteen-line paragraph—for an extra $102. Four kilobytes would set you back $198.

But even with that whopping 4K of memory, you'd still have a machine that could do essentially nothing. The box would sit there and blink, but for more sensible means of communication than flipping switches and counting lights, you'd need some kind of terminal. The MITS catalog offered a couple of models based on a Burroughs "Self-Scan" neon display that could produce thirty-two characters at once, but neither unit was anywhere near ready, and the cheaper one would cost nearly $900. You could buy a Teletype, but even on the used market that would cost significantly more than the computer itself. And then you'd also need a special $148 input/output (I/O) card to hook the thing up, not to mention yet another $19 card that would give you a place to plug in the I/O card. You'd also have to figure out how to flip those tinny front-panel switches each and every time you turned the machine on in order to get your computer talking to your Teletype.

Still, as Roberts remembered years later, "People lusted after those machines. I don't know of any better way to describe it: They lusted after it. They wanted it. They had to have an Altair. It was an emotional reaction."

Bill Gates and Paul Allen shared the emotion. The Intel 8080 chip, they knew, worked much the same way as the 8008 in their Traf-O-Data machine, only much more flexibly, much more ably. Its vastly richer instruction set, its ability to take advantage of more memory, meant programmers could make the chip sing. If they wrote a BASIC for the MITS machine, they'd be able to translate, or "port," it to the other 8080 machines that would surely follow.

Their ace in the hole, they quickly realized, was the 8008 simulator Paul had designed so that Bill could program the Traf-O-Data machine. It wouldn't be trivial to convert that simulator to work for the 8080, but it wouldn't be insanely difficult, either. And it would give them a head start on the rest of the pack. While others might try to design 8080 software on the crappy MITS hardware, Bill and Paul would have the advantage of the speed and luxury of the PDP-10 environment.

Of course, the 8008 simulator could conceivably be construed as the property of the Traf-O-Data partnership. So over the Christmas vacation, Gates finally drew up a written agreement to formalize that august entity. The badly typewritten document that Gates signed on New Year's Day 1975 (though apparently neither Allen nor Gilbert got around to executing) theoretically reflected the money and labor each had put in thus far, leaving aside a loan of $200 from the company to Gilbert and a personal loan from Bill to Paul. Figuring it all in, Gates took 43 percent of the company and Allen 36 percent, leaving 21 percent for the long-suffering Gilbert—who was the only one actively involved in communicating with customers and had, after all, put the machine together. If there was any doubt that software was more important than hardware, this document would dispel it.

The agreement also covered work "any of the principals do in traffic tape processing, voltage measurement tapes, machine manufacture or converting of tapes to other medium, or any other closely related work." But the most important, if infelicitous, phrase followed: "Work such as developing software for microcomputers when the software is not related to data tapes would not be included under this." In other words, the work Bill and Paul knew they were about to commence, whatever it was, would be their own, even if it was based on the Traf-O-Data 8008 simulator—unless they happened to be so stupid as to focus on the tape-reading business. If the software business took off, too bad for the silent partner. Paul Gilbert, hardware guy, would have to stick to his soldering guns.

With that problem out of the way, Gates and Allen got moving. On official T-O-D stationery, Paul Allen, "president," offered time-sharing companies the 8008 simulator, along with the still-figmentitious 8080 version, for a paltry "$800 per copy" or under a royalty agreement. According to Gates and Allen, they also offered equally nonexistent BASIC, FORTRAN, and PL/I language cross-compilers. The idea was to have the time-sharing firms offer these software tools to others who might want to use PDP-10s to develop programs that would run on the Altair and other machines. Alas, none of the firms bothered to reply.

But Gates and Allen were still smitten with their original idea: the BASIC language that they'd cut their teeth on. To trained software engineers, BASIC was a "toy language." It was limited. It wouldn't let you do many of the things a real language would allow, such as linking prewritten program modules. And in most implementations it was interpreted—translated on the fly into machine code—rather than compiled—translated in an entirely separate process—which meant it was slow.

But Bill and Paul saw BASIC as the perfect complement to a simple computer. An interpreted version would be easy to fit into a limited-memory machine. It was easy to learn, easy to use—and, they knew from past experience, relatively easy to create. This time they wrote to MITS.

Precisely what they wrote remains in dispute. According to a 1982 *PC Magazine* article that Gates would later assail as inaccurate, the letter, dated January 2, read

> *We have available a BASIC language interpreter that runs on MCS-8080 series computers. We are interested in selling copies of this software to hobbyists through you. It could be supplied on cassettes or floppy disks to users of your Altair series microcomputers. We should anticipate charging you $.50, which you could then sell for somewhere between $75 and $100. If you are interested, please contact us.*

However the letter actually read, Ed Roberts was more than interested. He'd been hunting for a language, preferably BASIC, to sell with the machine, but to no avail. MITS was awash in a deluge of paper: checks for $298 and $397 and $498 and more—some people just wrote big checks and asked for "one of everything" in the catalog. What they got for their money was a long delay and then, maybe, a computer kit, but rarely more. The company was so swamped that it was way behind in fulfilling its computer orders; most of the other products in its catalog were either barely under development or a mere optimistic glimmer in someone's eye.

Software for the machine? As he watched his highly indebted company go from red ink to a sea of black overnight or at least overmonth, Ed Roberts knew he'd need it. He'd always liked the idea of BASIC, had even mentioned it in the initial *Popular Electronics* article. BASIC might open new markets for the Altair, because it could actually make the machines do something beside blink their lights. But nobody at MITS had time to even think about writing software.

Roberts called the number on the stationery. The phone rang at the official Traf-O-Data headquarters—the home of Paul Gilbert's mother. Gilbert wasn't there, and even if he had been, he would have been almost as puzzled as his mother was to hear about a BASIC language interpreter. The trail went dead.

It would shortly be revived. Back at Harvard, Gates and Allen argued about who should make the follow-up call to their letter. Each wanted the other to do it. Compromise: Bill would call, but use Paul's name, on the theory that the older, more mature-looking Allen would probably be the first to meet Roberts should any deal materialize.

Gates—"Allen"—told Roberts, "We've got this BASIC and can we come out and talk to you?" Allen recalled. "And Ed said, 'Well, we don't have enough memory cards for the machine yet. . . . Why don't you come out in a month?' So we hung up the phone and Bill was sort of jubilant about this, and Bill says, 'God, we gotta get going on this!' " Thus did William Gates and Paul Allen, principals of the august and highly reputed Seattle firm of Traf-O-Data, inaugurate the deal that eventually ushered in the personal computer software revolution. There was just one minor detail to be taken care of: The BASIC wasn't actually written yet.

But hey, no problem: Bill and Paul knew plenty of dialects of BASIC inside and out, had foraged around in their source code. It was time to kick ass!

Kick ass! Deep-down! Vigorous! These were the words of encouragement and approbation that fueled conversation among the math-science mavens at Currier House. Also, above all: hardcore! Forget classes: It was time to get hardcore!

Bill and Paul didn't bother with the obvious, such as sending for an Altair machine. Why deal with a boxful of cheap, flaky hardware—mere hardware—when you could simulate it all, every instruction, every blinking light, every finger-busting toggle switch, in solid, easy-to-use, dependable software?

Gates and Allen contacted an electronics parts distributor, got their hands on the Intel 8080 manuals they needed, and set to work. A much later version of the source code memorializes the date as February 9, 1975, but the project almost certainly began earlier—during Harvard's January "reading period" when classes were in recess.

Allen simply dusted off the old Traf-O-Data 8008 simulator and began—*Witness the transformation!*—turning it into a simulator for the 8080. After modifying his modified version of DEC's macro assembler, he moved on to adapt the debugger as well. The development tools Allen put together in this era would serve as the core of Microsoft's language efforts for years.

Gates focused on BASIC itself. What to put in and what to leave out was not trivial. There were dozens of dialects of BASIC out and about, from bare-bones versions to fancy ones that offered commands to perform just about any operation a programmer might think of. The instant you departed from the most basic BASIC, everything was up for grabs, from syntax to features. Would users have to type a space between **PRINT** and **X**? Would hobbyist programmers ever use transcendental math? Was it worthwhile including stuff nobody had ever used before? Hundreds of these agonizing decisions confronted the budding software artiste.

But Gates didn't agonize. Taking a shortcut, he simply adapted the feature set of the sexiest BASIC around—DEC's RSTS-11 BASIC-PLUS. Such free and easy borrowing of intellectual property was nothing new. Whereas the first version of BASIC, the Kemeny and Kurtz Dartmouth edition, had been an outright innovation, it had built on the platforms of the earlier FORTRAN and ALGOL languages. All of the original BASIC's successors—and there were already dozens—had built on, adapted, or outright swiped ideas from their predecessors. And when it came to computer programs, exactly what could be legally protected was, as it remains today, a matter of debate. It was generally believed that though actual program code could not be copied with impunity, a language's syntax and structure were fair game.

And DEC's BASIC-PLUS syntax and structure were terrific. This was the BASIC dialect Bill had used to write the UW Experimental College's enrollment program. It offered, as the manual claimed, "many features not found in standard Dartmouth BASIC or any other version of BASIC." BASIC-PLUS included fancy functions for manipulating "strings" of text (such as words), a variety of ways to format printed output (such as dollars and cents), special techniques for handling data files and hardware devices, and a nifty "immediate mode" that in effect let the user run a quickie one-line program without messing up the one already in memory. Gates decided to implement as much of it as he could.

In any art there are limitations. The question of what features Gates could put in and what to leave out was complicated by the question of how much memory the target machine might have. It was absolutely clear that a decent BASIC or anything else would not be possible in the el-cheapo low-end Altair's standard 256 bytes of RAM or even the additional low-cost 768 plug-in bytes. Four kilobytes—the size of the cheapest reasonable upgrade—seemed a sensible goal, even if that limited space would have to accommodate not only the program but all the data it manipulated.

Finished with the spec, Gates began writing assembly-language code on yellow legal pads late into the night, with occasional breaks for classes, meals, and poker. Allen juggled his day job at Honeywell with evenings at Harvard. Sleep was where they found it, and Gates was the master of the catnap. When forty winks were evidently needed, Bill would curl up on the floor behind the Aiken Lab PDP-10's rows of memory banks. When slumber sneaked up on him, he'd simply pass out at the keyboard, waking up to begin typing where he'd left off. Once Allen looked up and found his colleague standing in front of him with his arms crossed, asking about a club they'd supposedly visited together. Paul had no idea what Bill was talking about; when he woke up, Bill had no idea either. Apparently he had been sleepwalking at the time.

During a meal with the math-science gang at Currier House, Bill and Paul were debating an element they felt their BASIC needed but neither one wanted to write: floating-point math, the ability to represent and manipulate a wide range of numbers in scientific notation. A freshman eavesdropper interrupted them by piping "I've written those kinds of routines." The freshman was Monte Davidoff, an affable curly-haired Milwaukeean known as "Mad Dog" and "20/20," nicknames derived from Mogen David "Mad Dog" 20/20, the cheap fortified wine that shared his initials and ethnic heritage.

Davidoff, who'd cut his programming teeth in high school on a tiny PDP-8, found himself being grilled about his familiarity with floating-point code. Bill and Paul kept the details of their project close to the vest for another week, but finally they showed Monte the initial *Popular Electronics* article and the follow-up piece that had run in the February edition. Davidoff joined the secret project and set to work busting butt on code for BASIC's mathematical functions.

Soon afterward, Gates contacted MITS's Yates to inquire about some important specifics of the Altair that weren't clear from the documentation. "Wow," said Yates, "you guys must be serious. You're the first guys to ask us how to get characters in and out of the machine." What Yates didn't say was that although character input and output was theoretically possible, Altair machines went out the door—when they went out the door at all—without any actual way of doing it. As the orders began flooding in, Ed Roberts had decided to concentrate on shipping computers and nothing but computers— and not even computers, but bags of parts. The peripheral interfaces and memory cards that might make them useful would simply have to wait.

Deducing from the conversation that they had a head start, Gates urged Allen and Davidoff to pick up the pace. Once Allen had the simulator fine-tuned, he pitched in to help Gates on aspects of the interpreter itself. Davidoff plugged along doggedly on the math package. After a grueling month, the BASIC was doing most of what it was supposed to do—at least on Paul's 8080 simulator. It might have been prudent to try it on a real machine, and by now there might conceivably have been a MITS machine somewhere in Boston, but Gates and Allen didn't even consider hunting one up. Instead, the phone at MITS again rang with a call from Paul Allen, this time with his own voice attached. "We're not that far away," Paul told Ed Roberts. "Should we come out?"

Roberts replied that fifty guys had said their BASIC would be ready, but none of them had come out yet. "Well," Allen told him, "we're just putting the finishing touches on it."

The trip to Albuquerque was set. The code that was supposed to run in 4K of memory had now ballooned to need 6K, but that was okay. For the demo, MITS could set up a machine with extra memory and, if luck was with them, even get it to work.

Now that there was a deadline—Paul's trip to Albuquerque—the effort zoomed into hyperspace. The goal was by no means a flawless final version, perfectly debugged. What they needed was simply something that was good enough to demonstrate. They'd worry about fixing the rest later.

The night before Allen was supposed to leave for Albuquerque, Gates got nervous. "Jesus, Paul," he said, "if I've got one of these opcodes wrong, this thing is just not gonna work." If Bill's interpreter or Paul's 8080 simulator had even the tiniest error—a single bit set wrong somehow—their BASIC program probably wouldn't even start up. While Allen slept, Gates pored over the code and the documentation. Satisfied by morning that the program was what it was supposed to be, Gates cranked out a paper tape at Aiken on the PDP-10's high-speed tape punch. Early in the morning, he handed it to his partner and wished him good luck.

On the plane to Albuquerque, Paul Allen mentally reviewed the demonstration he had ahead of him. The program had never been run on an 8080 machine before, only on the simulator. It dawned on Allen that there was one detail he and Bill had forgotten. "Oh, my God, I didn't write a loader for this thing!" The loader was a program to get the Altair to listen to the Teletype and understand where to put the program it was about to receive. It wouldn't be a terribly complicated program—fifty simple instructions would do the trick—but without it, Allen's roll of tape might just as well be toilet paper.

First Allen wrote the loader in the standard mnemonic instructions he now knew by heart. But since he had no assembler handy, he took out the 8080 manual and translated opcodes like **PUSH A** and **POP B** into their machine-language patterns of ones and zeroes—hand-assembling, as it had come to be known. Fortunately when he was done he needn't hunt up some sort of data storage medium. To transfer the code from the paper to the Altair's memory, the basic entry device would be Paul Allen's hand-eye coordination—reading the ones and zeroes from the page and neurally transmitting them to his fingers on those tiny front panel switches.

Allen finished writing the short program by the time the plane touched down. At the curbside arrival area of the little Albuquerque airport, he looked around in vain for an executive in a business suit. Instead, Allen recalled, "there's this really big guy standing next to his pickup truck looking around, and nobody else was there." The beefy guy in slacks and shirtsleeves looked more like an oversize cab driver in search of a fare, but Allen walked over and inquired whether he might be Ed Roberts. "Yep," Roberts said without formalities of introduction. "Climb in the truck."

During the ride across town to MITS, Allen kept thinking "This is not quite what I expected." And where Roberts failed to initially impress, MITS itself nearly appalled. The word "unimposing" didn't begin to describe it. Just off once-fabled and now-fallen Route 66, the MITS headquarters, which the company had occupied since its initial days of glory in the calculator business, shared a nondescript storefront strip with an office supply shop and a massage parlor. Inside, the place was packed to the rafters with new hires weary from seven-day weeks of overtime and feverishly trying to catch up with a backlog of orders that seemed to grow worse, not better. "This is really a fly-by-night company," Allen thought.

Roberts led the dubious visitor to a small rear cubicle, where his co-bylinee and top hardware guy Bill Yates was bent over the first real Altair Paul Allen had ever seen. It was a squat sheet-metal box that looked one cut above military surplus, but nonetheless, Allen was in awe. The nondescript box held the most memory of any microcomputer in the world—seven boards of a single kilobyte each. Allen, thinking of his colleagues waiting anxiously for news back in Boston, was "antsy" to give the machine a whirl.

Roberts and Yates demurred. The front panel lights were blinking because the Altair was currently running a test program to see if all that memory and all the connectors that supported it would actually work reliably. Until the computer passed the test, there was no point even trying BASIC. After offering the grand tour of the facility, Roberts deposited Allen at the Hilton, Albuquerque's most expensive hotel. The tab: $40 more than Paul had brought with him. Apologizing that he was "a little short right now," Allen asked for a loan. Roberts magnanimously put the tab on his credit card, but the mutual confidence level was falling off the meter: Allen thought Roberts was "some kind of fly-by-night entrepreneur. And he's thinking 'Who's this guy selling software who can't even afford a room for the night?' "

Paul called Bill at Harvard and told him everything that had happened—what the machine looked like, how much memory it had. Gates cut to the chase: "Have you run the program yet?" Allen explained the delay and then tried, unsuccessfully, to get a good night's sleep.

At MITS that morning, there was good news: The 7K Altair had passed its memory test. So Allen threaded the punched tape through the Teletype's tape reader. Consulting the notes he'd written on the plane, he spent about five minutes awkwardly flipping switches on the Altair's front panel to enter the loader program. Looking on, Roberts and Yates exchanged glances and chuckled, not believing this thing had a prayer of actually working. Allen turned on the tape reader and pressed the Altair's RUN switch. For nearly fifteen minutes, tape streamed through the reader. When the last couple of inches fed through to the take-up spindle, Allen waited expectantly.

The Teletype clacked out the words **MEMORY SIZE?**

Allen was flabbergasted. "Oh, my God, it actually works on a real computer!" he thought to himself. "This is wonderful!"

"Hey, it typed something," said Bill Yates. "How should I answer this?"

"Oh, yeah, it typed something?" said an amazed Ed Roberts.

Still stunned that the program actually worked, Allen managed to type in the memory size—**7168**. He pressed the return key.

Clack-clack-clack-clack. **READY**, said the Teletype. Roberts knew enough about software to recognize the standard BASIC prompt—a prompt that during development had metamorphosed into such jokey phrases as **S'ALRIGHT BOSS**.

"S'alright boss," indeed! Allen typed in **PRINT 2 + 2** and pressed the return key. The Teletype spat back **4**. Allen knew things were looking good. **PRINT 2 + 2** was their standard test. It exercised about two-thirds of the code, so if it worked, the BASIC was in reasonably good shape.

Next they typed in the classic "Lunar Lander" program—a text-based space simulation in which the idea is to make a soft landing without running out of fuel. Roberts and Yates kept telling Allen how great this was, how amazed they were that all this worked. Paul thought to himself, "You're not half as amazed as I am."

One thing that blew him away was the little Altair's speed. When he ran BASIC back at Harvard on the DEC machine, the overhead of the simulator and debugger had slowed it to a crawl. Now, freed from the constraints of all that excess baggage, running as originally intended, this BASIC was lightning-fast— maybe five times swifter on this little desktop unit than on the PDP-10 that took up a room.

Eventually the program crapped out, but what he had seen was more than enough for Ed Roberts. Gates and Allen had a deal. They also had a computer of their own: Paul brought one back with him from MITS, and they acquired a Teletype to go with it in Bill's dorm room. Allen also had a new job. Within a month, he was winging back to Albuquerque with a fancy new title: Vice President and Director of Software at MITS.

6

UP AND RUNNING

ALTAIR BASIC—UP AND RUNNING. That was the banner headline across the top of the April 1975 issue of *Computer Notes,* the very first issue of the MITS Altair newsletter. The headline was literally true; you really could get Bill and Paul's BASIC running on an Altair. On the other hand, you'd have to find a very special Altair—for openers, one that worked.

Then you'd have to find one that had at least 6 working kilobytes of memory, which was what it now took to run BASIC. And that was highly unlikely because the 4K dynamic memory board kits that MITS was peddling at $264 were so flaky they were spawning a fledgling clone parts industry. Out in California, a company called Processor Technology was beginning to sell boards that did work. The open bus architecture did mean plug and play, after all, and there seemed to be no good reason why what you plugged in had to be some piece of crap that happened to have a MITS label.

And if the brain-dead memory boards were brewing discontent among Altair's customers, the MITS policy regarding what it was now calling Altair BASIC was getting people genuinely angry. According to that first issue of *Computer Notes,* you could get BASIC at two wildly different prices: $500 all by itself—more than the whole damned machine!—or a mere $75 when purchased with an Altair, an interface card that would hook up either a Teletype or an audiocassette player, and 8K of dubious MITS memory. The pricing policy looked exactly like what it was: a clever way to stick people with those forgetful memory boards.

Yet this was a new frontier. How do you come up with a price for something that's never been marketed before? In the world of minicomputer software—and the Altair was, after all, advertised as a minicomputer—$500 for a commercial version of BASIC would have been the steal of the decade. Mainframe languages were generally rented, not sold; a typical price might be $400 a month. On the other hand, people who worked with big computers or used time-sharing machines didn't give a thought about what the software cost; it just sort of came with the territory. So to many customers, even $75 seemed way out of line for something that was totally intangible—and without which the machine was all but worthless anyway. It was like buying a Volkswagen and discovering that the gas tank was an option.

As angry as that made people, there was something else that made them absolutely livid: Despite the headline, despite the ads, despite the fact that MITS would take your money for it, you actually couldn't get the BASIC at all, because the BASIC was still full of bugs, still at least a couple of months away from being ready for release. Between the modest demands of classwork, the alleviation of deadline pressure, and the departure of Paul Allen, work had slowed a bit back at Aiken. But Gates and Davidoff were still on the case.

At some point, Harvard caught on. An assistant professor whom Bill had managed to get on the wrong side of in a class had become responsible for maintaining the Aiken computer system. When he ran the statistics, one password in particular kept coming up: Bill Gates's.

Gates had some explaining to do. "When they looked at the percentage of time I'd used, I don't know what the percentage was, but it was the majority." But it wasn't as if a million people were trying to log on and he had been keeping them off. Most nights Gates, Allen, and Davidoff had been the only ones in the place. And the official regulations, such as there were, hadn't exactly included prohibitions against effectively turning the big PDP-10 into a dinky machine you could buy for 500 bucks.

On the other hand, although other people were writing résumés and even books on the computer, they weren't exactly monopolizing the machine. Nor were they using the PDP-10 for commercial projects. Nor were they inviting off-campus friends, nonstudents such as Paul Allen, to join them at all hours of the night in the computer center. Nor were they using the Defense Department's unclassified ARPANET, the first nationwide computer network, to store some of their commercial efforts on a machine hundreds of miles away at Pittsburgh's Carnegie-Mellon University. In Harvard's view, this was a serious matter.

The university launched an administrative action. Bill might well have to appear before the administrative board and put up a formal defense. It was not inconceivable that he could be expelled. It was not even beyond the realm of possibility that Bill Gates could be "expunged"—a special punishment that supposedly involved the obliteration of every trace of one's Harvard record.

As former roommate Sam Znaimer recalled, "Bill was taking it very seriously." He worked hard on an essay explaining and defending what he had done. He agreed to put his current version of BASIC in the public domain on the Aiken PDP-10. And in the end, he was given no real punishment other than a strong reprimand, particularly with regard to bringing in nonstudents to work on Harvard machines.

The free computer time—that most valuable commodity—at Aiken was over. For the rest of the semester at Harvard, Bill would continue developing BASIC on a public time-sharing service, using the Teletype in his room. But that arrangement didn't last long. For the summer he moved to Albuquerque, where the local school system just happened to have a PDP-10, the only one in town. Most of the time it was just sitting there. To the school district, somebody coming in and offering to pay for time on the machine looked like found money. Paul Allen managed to get MITS a time-sharing deal so favorable— virtually unlimited hours for a ridiculously low monthly rate, and computer printout paper on a cost basis—that computer time was essentially free.

Another thing was becoming essentially free in the world of microcomputer pioneers: an early version of Altair BASIC. Back in March, when Bill had gone down to Albuquerque for a visit to MITS and a stay with Paul Allen at the less-than-elegant Sundowner Motel across Route 66, a young Californian named Steve Dompier had been hanging around the office. He'd sent in an early order for "one of everything" in the MITS catalog, had received nothing but a partial refund check for a few of the most pie-in-the-sky products, and had taken the radical step of flying from the Bay Area down to New Mexico to see if he could talk his way into prying at least maybe his Altair kit out of the company. While waiting for something to happen, Dompier cadged a tape of the current bug-plagued version of BASIC from Bill. There wasn't much Dompier could do with it, considering he would go back home with little more than an incomplete bag of parts and nowhere near enough memory to run BASIC. But he would soon help popularize the Gates/Allen BASIC in a way its creators could not have foreseen.

Dompier, with the straight, shoulder-length hair of a late 1960s British rock promoter, was an early guru in a newly founded and fast-growing society known as the Homebrew Computer Club. Based in the section of the San Francisco peninsula already known as Silicon Valley among the cognoscenti, Homebrew was the hangout for a variety of high-tech chipheads who had that California change-the-world attitude. These were the kinds of guys (and, very, very rarely, gals) who would once have proclaimed that drugs would change the world, or composting toilets, or Earth Shoes, or strobe lights, or Eastern religions. Now they were all electronics engineers or minor-league toll-swiping phone phreaks or maybe, like Dompier, laid-back free-lance carpenters who had somehow stumbled into the world of programming. But they were beginning to realize, with almost religious fervor, that hey, the thing that would really change the world—or at least one's own personal slice of it, which amounted to the same thing—was the computer.

At a March Homebrew meeting, Dompier reported on his bizarre trip to MITS headquarters. At an April meeting in the decrepit Peninsula School, he demonstrated the first Altair program that actually did something. Dompier hooked his newly built Altair into an extension cord that ran down a flight of stairs, stuck an AM radio on top of it, spent five minutes flipping switches to enter his program, and suddenly saw all the lights go out on the front panel. The machine was playing dead, but that wasn't the neat trick he had programmed it to do. Two kids fooling around had knocked the cord out of the outlet.

Dompier tried again. As he neared the end of his five minutes of flippity-flipping, he raised his hand for silence. Fuzzy but identifiable tones began coming out of the radio's speaker—tones that the assembled throng quickly recognized as the plaintive opening bars of the Beatles' "Fool on the Hill." As an encore, the Altair went on to perform "Daisy" or "A Bicycle Built for Two"—the first tune ever played on a computer, back in 1957 at Bell Laboratories, and the swan song of HAL, the computer in the movie *2001*.

The crowd went nuts. Yes! You could do something with this cheap little machine! There was no doubt about it: Computers would—yes!—change the world!

Dompier went on to publish the program in *People's Computer Company*, a countercultural *Whole Earthy* tabloid that had been espousing the computers-changing-the-world ethic with minicomputers as the medium until the even-more-populist little Altair came along. In the second issue of MITS's *Computer Notes*, no less an authority than Bill Gates expressed unaccustomed puzzlement: "His article gives an explanation of how to output different notes, spaces and rests. He doesn't explain why it works and I don't see why. Does anyone know?"

The answer was that Dompier had taken advantage of one of the Altair's many little flaws. The Federal Communications Commission (FCC) watchdogs who later came to regulate computers' radio frequency interference were not yet in evidence, and when it came to spurious radio emissions, the Altair machine was a veritable top-forty station. Dompier's program, whose logic otherwise made no apparent sense, simply turned the emissions into musical tones.

It was also in April that MITS sent out its "unique marketing tool," the MITS-mobile—"a camper van equipped with an Altair BASIC-language system." It included "an Altair 8800, Comter 256 computer terminal, ASR-33 Teletype, Altair Line Printer, Altair Floppy Disk and BASIC language"—products that aside from the machine and the Teletype had not yet been released to the general public. The first swing was through Texas, and MITS knew it had a hit on its hands. As former MITS executive Eddie Currie recalled, "People would follow you from one town to another, just to see the demo again or just to touch the computer or just to talk to you. And if you'd allow them to sit in the MITS-mobile, well, that was like sitting in Queen Victoria's throne or something."

In late May the traveling road show rolled up the coast to the East Bay, where the first venue was the Emeryville Holiday Inn. There the van was met by a dedicated contingent of MITS customers, many of whom had sent in good money for things that had not yet been delivered—things like, say, BASIC. The customers were patient; they accepted the explanations for the hardware delays. They were also frustrated; those who'd actually suffered with the notorious 4K memory boards were fit to be tied.

But they, like voyagers elsewhere waiting in line for their passage to the land of Altair, were just blown away when they saw the **READY** prompt on the Teletype. When they pounded in a little program, it seemed to work. So why should they have to wait for a BASIC when this one, to all appearances, worked wondrously well and could be duplicated in a trice?

Well, they shouldn't, at least one of them thought. And then, mysteriously —the details are shrouded in murk, and the actual scene of the crime may have been down the valley in Palo Alto at Rickey's Hyatt House—one of the BASIC tapes disappeared. It next turned up in the hands of Steve Dompier. It passed into the clutches of a Homebrewer named Dan Sokol who had access to a high-speed tape punch where he worked. It then appeared, in the form of fifty identical copies, in a cardboard box at the front of the next Homebrew meeting.

When the contents were described, the ensuing stampede left the box empty in seconds. There was one stipulation: Anyone who took a tape was supposed to come back to the next meeting with two tapes. This pyramid scheme—and the advent of user groups like Homebrew here, there, and everywhere, spurred on by the arrival of the MITS-mobile—insured that identical copies of this paper tape of a buggy, not-yet-ready-for-prime-time BASIC would circle the globe and become the world's first and most pirated software.

And all this happened even before the ink was wet on the MITS contract for BASIC. By now the plan was to have three versions: a standard BASIC taking 8K, a stripped-down model for 4K machines, and a bells-and-whistles special for people who could afford 12K of memory. From their furnished college-minimalist two-bedroom apartment at an Albuquerque complex known as the Portals, Gates and Allen hired Davidoff as an independent contractor to finish work on the BASIC over the summer, putting him up (for $180 summer rent) on the couch. The typical daily schedule was reminiscent of the glory days at the RODS facility: bopping in at 2:00 P.M., lurching out at maybe 6:00 A.M. the next day, with dinner and sometimes a movie as a break. It went on seven days a week. For a summer of this and all his work since January, independent contractor Davidoff took down a grand total of $4,200—the same amount Bill had received for his Lakeside scheduling.

Bill obsessively pored over the code, trying to save a byte here, steal a byte there, speed things up somewhere else by such ruses as replacing the classic BASIC prompt—**READY**—with the three-bytes-shorter **OK**. But BASIC wasn't the only thing in the works. For MITS, Allen was overseeing a monitor, assembler, and program editor that could run on the Altair. Both he and Bill pitched in and wrote technical articles for *Computer Notes*.

The contract negotiations dragged on. Gates and Allen were using an attorney Bill's father had found at the Albuquerque firm of Poole, Tinnen and Martin, and in *Computer Notes* MITS had announced that the 4K and 8K versions of BASIC would ship beginning June 23. But Ed Roberts still hadn't managed to sign the agreement. At some point Gates got fed up and announced he would depart for Seattle and return only when the contract was signed; the agreement was finally inked on July 22.

Microsoft was not yet an official partnership. It was not even a name that had appeared anywhere in public. So the contract was a deal between Paul G. Allen and William Gates (with a Seattle address that was actually Paul's parents' house), thereinafter referred to as Licensors, and MITS, thereinafter referred to as the Company, regarding a BASIC interpreter software program thereinafter referred to as the Program. The Licensors granted the Company an exclusive worldwide license to the program (and improvements, variations, or refinements) for ten years. MITS also got the exclusive right to sublicense the program to third parties such as other companies, which meant that Bill and Paul would have to depend on MITS to rustle up new customers and sign them up. But MITS agreed to use its "best efforts" to license, promote, and commercialize the program.

Gates and Allen got $3,000 cash on signing. Additionally, they were due a royalty for every copy of BASIC that went out with hardware: $30 for the 4K version, $35 for the 8K, and $60 for the extended edition. They were due another $10 every time a hardware sale expanded a customer's machine past the 8K mark. If the software was licensed without hardware, or the source code was licensed to a third party, the Gates/Allen duo would knock down 50 percent of the gross. The deal had a cap of $180,000, with one exception—the licensing of source code to other parties, for which there was no limit on what Bill and Paul might take in. The effective date of the agreement was March 1, 1975—back when Allen and Roberts had initially agreed to a deal.

One of the Licensors would have to make himself available full time until the end of the year to support the program as long as royalties amounted to $2,500 a month. Both would be necessary if the royalties averaged $5,000 a month. What this contractual agreement meant in practice was that Bill would not be returning to Harvard in the fall.

MITS would supply the computer time necessary for development—the computer time that Paul had worked out with the Albuquerque schools. And, oh, yes: Everyone to whom MITS sold a copy of the program would have to sign a secrecy agreement.

This was the first in a long series of mostly futile efforts by Bill Gates to try to prevent theft of his intellectual property. He'd already gotten wind of the copying that was being done, particularly at user groups. They were stealing the stuff! They were taking money out of his pocket! At least people should be put on warning that the copy they were buying was for their sole use!

But the secrecy agreement—like copy-protected software in the future— was a pain in the butt for customers and for MITS. It meant that every time a customer ordered BASIC, MITS had to send out a form agreement and wait for it to be returned. It was a bookkeeping headache and essentially treated every customer as a potential thief. And although an article in *Computer Notes* warned "we will prosecute anyone who violates their license agreement," that was obviously sheer bluster. Eventually Roberts would unilaterally discontinue the secrecy agreements—over the bitter protest of young Bill Gates.

Yet people were willing to pay what they considered a fair price, and the bundled-with-hardware prices seemed fair enough. Besides, the royalty rate dictated the consumer price in a classic retail formula that became typical in the microcomputer industry: MITS simply took the cost of the item and marked it up roughly 100 percent. But over the next two years, fewer than forty copies would be sold at the outrageous $500 to $750 software-only rates. Given the choice between being a victim of what they considered extortion and swiping the software, people chose the latter.

In July Paul and Bill used the Data General Nova machine at MITS to crank out paper tapes. An Altair generated copies in the new medium that was fast becoming the low-cost "people's choice"—the tape format that turned an audiocassette player into a computer peripheral by turning data into sound and vice versa on the model of the modem. BASIC Version 2.0 became the first edition to ship officially, in both 4K and 8K editions, thereby beginning two microcomputer industry traditions—the integer-and-decimal version number and the avoidance of shipping versions beginning with "1."

Even as the first official BASIC headed out the door, Gates was working on performance improvements for the version 3.0 release, but delighted recipients of the initial edition were more than willing to overlook the bugs. By August users were submitting BASIC programs—notably blackjack games. Davidoff contributed a few simple BASIC demonstration programs to the newsletter. And Altair BASIC was beginning to receive strongly favorable reviews in such proudly independent journals as the longtime BASIC champion *People's Computer Company,* which pointed out that "A BASIC with the power of this one is a major achievement, there's a monstrous amount of work in it, and they have [previously] sold in the low kilobuck range for each copy."

To RSTS-11 BASIC, Paul and Bill added a few tricks of their own, particularly for those who knew their way around machine language. The **PEEK** command, lifted from some DEC operating systems, and its new companion **POKE**, allowed users to look at or modify specific memory addresses. A new function called **USR** allowed interfacing machine-language routines to the BASIC for greater speed or specialized control.

The Gates programming style was terse and tight, clever but hard for others to fathom. In *Computer Notes,* his "Software Notes" offered advice "for tricky programmers," including a byte-saving technique called "the LXI trick" and the suggestion that "Some tricks involve instruction sequences which at first sight seem meaningless." Trickster Bill had used a variety of these shortcuts in his BASIC. They would later cause untold hours of grief when hackers tried to disassemble the code in attempts to reverse-engineer it—and when Microsoft programmers tried to update and maintain it.

Although the informal partnership with Allen had initially been fifty/fifty, Bill Gates bargained for a change. The partnership was restructured on a sixty/forty basis—with Bill exacting the larger share by reminding Paul that he remained a full-time salaried employee of MITS. Their initial investments were $910 and $606 respectively. Though exactly when and in what orthography remains unclear, they christened the company Microsoft.

They hoped it would never suffer from the kinds of stupidity they saw at MITS. Though Gates and Allen had friends at the company, they viewed its management more as mismanagement. "Even from our TRW days we'd seen companies can get kind of screwed up," Gates recalled. For a confirming example, they needed to look no further than their other enterprise: Traf-O-Data. By now Paul Gilbert had found a few customers—the cities of Bellingham and Tukwila, Washington, and good old reliable Surrey—but income was still minuscule and Traf-O-Data was no closer to its goal of selling machines instead of services. Mismanagement? Well, somehow the tape containing the Traf-O-Data program had disappeared, which made things tough when customers asked for changes.

So for the month of August, Bill and Paul imported their willing longtime Traf-O-Data slave, the irrepressible Chris Larson, now about to enter the eleventh grade at Lakeside. His official job in Albuquerque was to retype the hundred pages of 8008 source code from a printout, for which he received unrestricted use of the second sofa in the Portals living room and was eventually paid the munificent sum of $182. His unofficial job was to lighten things up.

Whereas Paul was a dyed-in-the-Stratocaster rock guitarist who favored Santana and Trower and would one day offer Seattle a Jimi Hendrix museum, Bill was going through a Frank Sinatra phase. Early in the morning, emerging from a restaurant after a night of programming, he and Chris and Monte would get Paul's goat by crooning "My Way." What would rile Allen more severely was a venture to what came to be known as Cement Plant Road. Allen owned the only car among the bunch, a new Chevy Monza that he had barely begun to make payments on, and Gates and Larson often borrowed it for 3:00 A.M. hairpin-turn joyrides in the Sandia Mountains. During one of these speed-therapy sessions, Gates took a curve a little too fast and ended up heading into a barbed-wire fence. The graphic array of scratches on the front of the new Monza pleased Allen not at all, but Bill took care of the damage.

By this time, little more than half a year since the advent of the Altair, the beginnings of a MITS-driven industry infrastructure were clearly visible. The Computer Store—that was its entire name, The Computer Store—opened by consultant Dick Heiser in West Los Angeles was the first independent retail computer shop anywhere, and additional exclusive MITS outlets quickly followed. MITS developed a network of sales representatives to rustle up business customers. The MITS *Computer Notes* newsletter was required reading. The MITS-mobile's tour spawned Altair Users Clubs across the country. MITS was developing a Software Library from its users' contributions, offering the simple programs for a couple of bucks a pop—little more than what it cost MITS to type them up and copy them. The professional-looking MITS ads dominated new publications such as *Byte,* whose entire raison d'être was the industry the Altair had single-handedly created.

And there were signs of life elsewhere, especially around San Francisco Bay, where logic circuitry was almost a second language. The area became the hotbed of activity, the Mecca of garage-based startups, or "parasite companies" as Roberts called them in an October screed. An outfit called Cromemco developed a card called the TV Dazzler that let you hook the Altair up to a color TV set; Processor Technology made the similar VDM. Bill Godbout, like Processor Tech, was selling memory boards, and an outfit called Solid State Music was pushing input/output cards. By the end of the year there were enough "parasite" boards available, many of them hogging far more power than the official Altair low-power units, that a user might conceivably push the limits of the Altair's power supply. As one Altair owner put it, "You have to learn good things like how many boards can I use before blowing it up."

For an undisputed industry leader, MITS always seemed to be on the defensive. The front cover of *Computer Notes* would trumpet some grandiose new triumph, but inside there'd always be some rationale for why the printer or the low-cost terminal or the real-time clock was late and some irritable defense such as "we may not be perfect, but we have a pretty damned good track record."

Nowhere was MITS more defensive than on the matter of software. In his September column in *Computer Notes,* editor David Bunnell wrote:

> . . . one thing that bothers me is the fact that a few of our customers have been ripping off MITS software. In violation of their software license some people have been arrogantly, and I think foolishly, copying MITS BASIC for resale or to pass out to their freinds. [sic]
>
> I believe this practice is fostered by the contention that all software should be made part of the public domain.
>
> Now I ask you—does a musician have the right to collect the royalty on the sale of his records or does a writer have the right to collect the royalty on the sale of his books? Are people who copy software any different than those who copy records and books?
>
> Altair BASIC is one of the most advanced BASIC's ever written and it cost MITS a premium price to develop. Considering this and the price charged by many companies for software, $75 for Altair 8K BASIC is a near steal. And the price of $500 for people who haven't purchased a minimum 8800 system is more than reasonable.

The record-royalty argument fell on deaf ears. The same people who were copying software thought nothing of dubbing a tape of a record and passing it on to their friends, and too bad for Mick Jagger, who'd never miss it. Ed Roberts took a more businesslike approach. In his first "Letter from the President" in October, he reacted to the suggestion that "MITS should give BASIC to its customers" with the following prickly reply—the first known mention of Microsoft, in any spelling, ever to see its way to public print:

> Wrong. We made a $180,000 commitment to Micro Soft in order to have BASIC available to our customers. MITS makes essentially no profit on BASIC. It is done as a service to our customers. The BASIC we supply has universally been accepted as fantastic and has allowed Altair customers to be literally years ahead of where they would have been without this software. Contrary to some opinions, software developments are expensive and the people who do these developments feel that they should be paid for their efforts, I agree. It is irrelevent [sic] whether software is developed to run on a large IBM computer or the Altair, it costs money. We are selling the BASIC at 1/10 to 1/100 the price large computer companies would get for a similar package, but we are still taking gas. Anyone who would like to argue this point, should feel free to call me at MITS. Anyone who is using a stolen copy of MITS BASIC should identify himself for what he is, a thief.

Despite a few other intemperate outbursts, Roberts's piece was largely a *mea culpa*. He admitted that there was "an excessive failure rate for the 4K card," and offered fixes and even a $50 credit to those who'd purchased the beasts, along with a $69 price reduction to new customers. "The problem we have," he bemoaned, "is training people internally to respond to customer requirements, and frankly the number of customers have [sic] increased more than our ability to train." He summed it up with "please bear with us. We are trying!!!"

Trying it was, but MITS was also sorely tried, worried about competitive computers on the way—both independent designs and direct clones of the Altair. Almost on their doorstep in New Mexico, Don Lancaster, Mr. TV Typewriter, had designed a unit based on the Motorola 6800 chip for Southwest Technical Products (SWTP). In Bountiful, Utah, a startup company called Sphere was offering something truly radical: an integrated system based on the 6800—"integrated" meaning it came complete with a keyboard and video display. In Denver The Digital Group, which offered cards for the Altair, was developing a computer of its own. In California an outfit called IMSAI was advertising its first machines—Altair knockoffs made from sturdier parts.

So on the front page of the October 1975 issue of *Computer Notes,* despite all the problems MITS was having keeping its main business on course, the company announced a new computer, the Altair 680, a computer that would be significantly cheaper than even the 8800—a mere $293 in kit form if ordered by the end of the year. Physically smaller and harder to expand than the 8800, the 680 was mostly a protective strike against the SWTP machine. But because the instruction set and architecture of the Motorola 6800 chip in the 680 were significantly different from those of the 8080, the new machine would not run any of the current Altair software.

Bill Gates and Paul Allen saw that as a business opportunity.

7

►

THIEVES IN OUR MIDST!

Announcing a product that didn't exist, developing it on the model of the best version available elsewhere, demonstrating an edition that didn't fully work, and finally releasing the product in rather buggy form after a lengthy delay: The history of BASIC was one that would repeat itself at Microsoft again and again. In the fall Bill and Paul would begin another practice that would become standard operating procedure: reworking an existing product for new markets.

Back in Seattle after a junior year in England, uninspired by the prospect of returning to electrical engineering courses at Stanford University, Ric Weiland, the "silent partner" of the Lakeside Programmers Group, got a September phone call from Bill Gates. Bill still had his hands full finishing the promised Extended and Disk BASICs for the 8080. How would Ric like to come down to Albuquerque and work on a brand-new BASIC for the 6800 chip?

Weiland liked the idea. He and Bill the Parsimonious agreed to a price, the first portion of which would be a bonus for on-time completion by early January and the rest of which would be a 25 percent royalty on net sales. Next thing he knew, Weiland was installed in the palatial living room Davidoff and Larson had recently abandoned. Unlike them, he didn't bother traveling to the MITS offices to get work done. A DECwriter printing terminal was installed right there in the living room and linked by phone to the Albuquerque school district's PDP-10.

Paul Allen's role was getting to be routine. Just as he'd adapted his 8008 simulator for the 8080, Allen rewrote the 8080 simulator for the 6800. The two chips were different enough to make Weiland's job a lot more complicated than a simple mechanical translation: He was simply supposed to create as close a copy of Bill's BASIC as he could. There were no formal specifications: Bill's source code, the Altair BASIC manual, and the Motorola chip manual were Weiland's only guides. Between the pressure of the official contractual deadline and a desire to go back to Stanford in January, Weiland got "pretty hardcore" and, to hosannas from *Computer Notes,* delivered the language on time and in good shape.

It turned out not to matter. Announced in October, the Altair 680 was delayed way past its January release date for an engineering "upgrade," meaning the first version didn't work. Eventually it emerged as the 680b, the "b" signifying the new, improved—and only available—model.

In November Bill flew up to Kansas City in Ed Roberts's new plane—another of the MITS chief's longtime dreams—for the first standards conference in the new microcomputer industry. "Those in attendance," reported *Computer Notes,* "included representatives of *Byte* magazine, *Popular Electronics,* MITS, Processor Technology, SWTP, Godbout, *The Computer Hobbyist,* Pronetics, LGS, and Sphere"—in other words, virtually the entire known microcomputer universe of 1975. The conference managed to hammer out a single standard for storing data on audiocassette tapes so that data tapes could be swapped between different machines. But, like many other "standards" of the era—for disk drives, communications interfaces, terminal designs—this one quickly broke down in a maelstrom of competitive engineering egos and "better" ideas. The tiny industry would wrestle with incompatibility and fragmentation for years.

Hanging out at MITS, Gates felt he was "doing too much stuff that wasn't generating royalties"—"bullshit stuff," demo programs, "type in your birthday, tells you what sign you are"—and figured if he had to demean his skills, he might as well get paid for it. As Ed Roberts later remembered it, MITS paid Bill $10 an hour, but Bunnell recalled it as more like minimum wage. Gates has admitted he was paid, but has made it a point of pride and autonomy to insist that he was never an employee of MITS. "I don't remember him being an employee," Paul Allen said years later. "He would have worked for me."

Meanwhile, Bill was still tinkering with the 4K edition of BASIC, speeding up and fixing major bugs in version 2.0, fixing minor bugs in version 3.0, fixing tinier bugs in version 3.1, adding a feature here and there for version 3.2. He was finishing the 12K Extended BASIC, which included a bunch of RSTS features there hadn't been room for in the smaller versions, plus such first-time-ever commands as **TRON** and **TROFF**—short for **TRACE ON** and **TRACE OFF**—which aided programmers in the debugging process.

Yet Bill's parents were not entirely convinced of the wisdom of the enterprise. Mom was a university regent; her son had departed the hallowed halls of higher education. For their 1975 Christmas card, Bill and Mary Gates featured a group portrait of their kids on the cover and penned a short poem about each one inside. The verse about Bill ran:

Trey took time off this fall
in old Albuquerque

His own software business—
we hope not a turkey.
(The profits are murky.)

Murky, perhaps, but profits there were. The total royalties paid on BASIC —Microsoft's entire income for 1975—amounted to $16,005, including the initial $3,000 signing payment, but not $14,405 the company was owed for the final quarter.

But by January, when Weiland had finished the 6800 BASIC and headed back to school, Paul Allen was getting desperate. Despite the terms of the MITS contract, Gates had decided to return to Harvard for spring semester, but his version of BASIC for the forthcoming Altair floppy disk drives was still only a promise. Under Allen's prodding, Bill checked into the Albuquerque Hilton with a stack of legal pads. Emerging a few days later with a sheaf of handwritten notes, he went into hardcore mode for a nonstop typing session at the terminal and got the program running before boarding a plane for Boston. Bill's Altair Disk BASIC would become the mainstay of the MITS disk drives— whenever they actually hit the market. In *Computer Notes,* Gates proudly crowed about his earlier triumphs: "For a piece of software that's been running for nine months, with over a thousand copies in use and nine different versions, it's pretty respectable to have had only five bugs—none of them serious."

Bill wasn't exaggerating the number of copies that had been sold—provided you counted a few bootlegs. Roughly 900 copies had been accounted for between July and the year's end. And revenues were growing, albeit irregularly. In January the royalty stream would amount to about $6,000, in February $12,000, in March $8,000, in April $12,000 again.

Not bad at all for a college junior, yet as with Traf-O-Data, the get-rich-quick dream far outstripped the reality. It was crazy. Here MITS was shipping maybe a thousand machines a month, yet BASIC was selling in the low hundreds. Sure, not every Altair owner had the Teletype or terminal BASIC demanded, but even so the discrepancy was ridiculous—like selling thousands of cassette players but hardly any cassettes. In December Bill had put his finger on the reason: "If anyone is using BASIC version 1.1, you have a copy of a tape that was stolen back in March. No customers were ever shipped 1.1, as it was experimental and full of bugs!"

And, most galling, there were no other OEM customers—"Original Equipment Manufacturers," the common but misleading term for companies that would adapt a product like Altair BASIC and sell it under their own label. Despite the "best efforts" clause in the contract, MITS hadn't managed to license Altair BASIC to anyone else—and didn't seem to be trying very hard. Cheap and free BASICs were beginning to creep onto the market from other sources. Altair BASIC ran rings around the other versions, but technical superiority wasn't enough; price and availability were becoming a problem.

An announcement in the January issue of *Computer Notes* offered three flavors of Altair BASIC for Intel's development systems: Extended for $350, 8K for $200, 4K for $150. "Licenses for source listings and rights to distribute the binary are also available to OEM buyers," the ad stated optimistically. "Write or call Mr. Paul Allen at the MITS plant in Albuquerque for more detailed information." But virtually nobody actually did.

In February Gates wrote a letter intended to gain him fame and notoriety within the microcomputer community if not a few extra bucks besides. Called "An Open Letter to Hobbyists," the impassioned tirade was featured prominently in *Computer Notes*. To add impact, MITS media maven Bunnell sent it via special delivery mail to every major computer publication in the country:

> To me, the most critical thing in the hobby market right now is the lack of good software courses, books and software itself. Without good software and an owner who understands programming, a hobby computer is wasted. Will quality software be written for the hobby market?
>
> Almost a year ago, Paul Allen and myself, expecting the hobby market to expand, hired Monte Davidoff and developed Altair BASIC. Though the initial work took only two months, the three of us have spent most of the last year documenting, improving, and adding features to BASIC. Now we have 4K, 8K, EXTENDED, ROM, and Disk BASIC. The value of the computer time we have used exceeds $40,000.
>
> The feedback we have gotten from the hundreds of people who say they are using BASIC has all been positive. Two surprising things are apparent, however. 1) Most of these "users" never bought BASIC (less than 10 percent of all Altair owners have bought BASIC), and 2) The amount of royalties we have received from sales to hobbyists makes the time spent on Altair BASIC worth less than $2 an hour.
>
> Why is this? As the majority of hobbyists must be aware, most of you steal your software. Hardware must be paid for, but software is something to share. Who cares if the people who worked on it get paid?
>
> Is this fair? One thing you don't do by stealing software is get back at MITS for some problem you may have had. MITS doesn't make money selling software. The royalty paid to us, the manual, the tape and the overhead make it a break-even operation. One thing you do do is prevent good software from being written. Who can afford to do professional work for nothing? What hobbyist can put 3 man-years into programming, finding all bugs, documenting his product and distribute for free? The fact is, no one besides us has invested a lot of money in hobby software. We have written 6800 BASIC, and are writing 8080 APL

and 6800 APL, but there is very little incentive to make this software available to hobbyists. Most directly, the thing you do is theft.

What about the guys who re-sell Altair BASIC, aren't they making some money on hobby software? Yes, but those who have been reported to us may lose in the end. They are the ones who give hobbyists a bad name, and should be kicked out of any club meeting they show up at.

I would appreciate letters from anyone who wants to pay up, or has a suggestion or comment. Just write me at 1180 Alvarado SE, #114, Albuquerque, New Mexico, 87108. Nothing would please me more than being able to hire ten programmers and deluge the hobby market with good software.

In the *Homebrew Club Newsletter,* in *People's Computer Company,* in the *Micro-8 Computer User Group Newsletter,* the letter was reprinted in full, right down to the signature of Bill Gates, General Partner, Micro-Soft—the hyphenated spelling that was used for the first few months of 1976. Letters from people who wanted to pay up did not flood Bill's mailbox.

However, there were suggestions and comments aplenty—so many that within a month, the affair was widely known as "the software flap." Nobody, of course, wanted to condone piracy, but counterarguments suddenly seemed to be flying around like evils from Pandora's box. Wasn't the MITS official policy of requiring you to sign some sort of legal document just to get a copy of BASIC—something the hobbyists were unaware was a contractual demand from Gates and Allen—needlessly draconian? And how dare anyone connected with MITS complain about unethical practices, given the company's track record of what *Micro-8 Computer User Group Newsletter* termed "misleading advertising and failure to deliver mail order products as advertised in a reasonable time."

And what was it Ed Roberts had written about a "$180,000 royalty commitment to Micro Soft in order to have BASIC available to our customers?" As one programmer wrote, "I certainly wish I could have put in a bid on that project! A price tag like that to me indicates someone trying to get rich in a hurry . . . a top systems programmer in this neighborhood might make $18–20K a year, if he's really good."

And wasn't the $40,000 of computer time Gates mentioned a gross exaggeration? In fact, noted the editor of the *Micro-8 Newsletter,* "rumors have been circulating thru the hobby computer community that imply that developement [*sic*] of the BASIC referred to in Bill Gates's letter was done on a Harvard University computer provided at least in part with government funds and that there was some question as to the propriety if not the legality of selling the results."

Besides, what self-respecting hobbyist would use "black box" software, where you couldn't see and/or modify the source code unless you ponied up an exorbitant $3,000? *People's Computer Company* had been pioneering a "Tiny BASIC" you could get in five different versions for five bucks each, complete with annotated source code. Maybe it didn't have all the bells and whistles Bill Gates's version did, but there was nothing to stop a clever programmer from adding them.

In "An Open Letter to Bill Gates," one legal eagle called the original letter "defamatory and insulting" and went on to provide a short course in copyright, trade secret, and patent law. But some members of the dinky-computer community defended Gates. As "one of the 10 percent minority who paid for Altair 8K BASIC" pointed out, "We programmers have to eat, too!"

Gates loftily surveyed the hubbub from the ivory tower of Harvard, where he had returned for spring semester. The ever-conservative, ever-pessimistic Bill Gates hadn't been kidding in the letter, particularly the part about hiring ten programmers and flooding the market with software. He had once told Paul Allen that if the company was really successful, they might someday employ twenty people.

In late March Gates found himself back in Albuquerque, where MITS had another scheme to further the cause of its low-cost machines: the grandiosely named First Annual World Altair Computer Convention—WACC for short. This was a happening, a love-in, a Woodstock for virtually everyone connected with the little computers. Altair dealers, Altair owners, Altair programmers, computer society presidents, "crazed and determined individuals" all converged on the Airport Marina Hotel in Albuquerque on March 27, 1976, for the first confabulation of the microcomputer era.

Editors and publishers arrived from *Popular Electronics, Radio-Electronics, Byte, Interface, Creative Computing.* In the exhibit hall there were demonstrations of chess programs, backgammon programs, music programs, Bill Gates's "bullshit stuff." And upstairs in the penthouse suite—denied space in the exhibit hall, they had posted a sign out front that David Bunnell took down and the ever-genteel Ed Roberts put back up—were the principals of "parasite" Processor Technology (including Steve Dompier), selling their 4K plug-and-play-and-actually-work boards for the Altair.

There were a few negative vibes, particularly among the authorized Altair dealers. Other machines were coming along, most notably the Altair-clone IMSAI with its heftier power supply and sturdier front panel, and many Altair dealers wanted to be able to diversify into other brands—simply put a bunch of them up on the shelves, may the best one win. That did not sit well with Ed Roberts, who demanded that Altair Computer Centers, as they were known, sell Altairs exclusively. His policy would lead to major defections from the Altair fold and cost MITS dearly as computer retailing began to heat up.

But to most of the attendees, the dealers were a passing cloud on an otherwise sunny scene. Bob Wallace was a programmer, organizer, counterculture figure, and employee of Seattle's laid-back Retail Computer Store. Wallace knew about the theory propounded in 1964 by Intel's Gordon Moore, which basically boiled down to the idea that the cost of computing came down 25 percent every year, mainly because chipmakers kept finding new ways of cramming more transistors, meaning more information and power, onto every chip. To put Moore's Law another way, the power of computing doubled every two years—which meant that in two years, you'd be able to get 8K of memory for what 4K cost now, and 16K two years after that, and then 32K, and chips would get faster, and—well, just work out the Malthusian progression, and it was clear that there would be millions of cheap, fast, powerful computers everywhere, and the most important thing in the world, the most wonderful thing, would be writing software for them.

And here, right here, a few yards away, up behind the lectern, was the software session's opening speaker, Bill Gates, the author of MITS's hardcore "Software Notes," the genius behind Altair BASIC, which Wallace knew intimately from having used it to develop an inventory management system at the computer store. Wallace was "sort of in awe."

As Bill explained "why I think software makes the difference between a computer being a fascinating educational tool for years and being an exciting enigma for a few months and then gathering dust in a closet," there was something infectious about his energy, his enthusiasm, his charisma, even his squeaky-voiced awkwardness. Afterward, for the first time ever but by no means the last, people came up to ask questions, to complain, to argue, to hear pearls of Gatesian wisdom. Bill Gates was a star. And Paul Allen, MITS director of software? Far more diffident than Bill when it came to public speaking, he let his partner have the limelight.

Though it was the topic of heated conversation at WACC, the piracy problem had not yet been solved. Despite strong MITS sales, royalties from BASIC were leveling off at an average of $7,000, or less than 200 copies, per month. *Computer Notes* published "A SECOND AND FINAL LETTER" from Bill Gates.

In an unaccustomed gesture of humility, Bill admitted that "the majority" of computer hobbyists "are intelligent and honest individuals who share my concern for the future of software development." He fretted about some of the suggestions he'd received, such as providing software in ROM—Read-Only Memory, a chip that would be far more difficult to copy than a paper or cassette tape. ROM-based software, he noted, meant that "users will have to accept the bugs that inevitably turn up. Having a select trustworthy group do field testing for six months would mean that most of the bugs could be eliminated, but delaying the introduction of a product this long isn't feasible or desirable. In any event, software on ROM can be copied." But copying the contents of a ROM, whose code was embedded in silicon, was far more complicated than simply duplicating a paper tape or cassette and generally more trouble than it was worth, and Bill Gates, who could and would argue vehemently with almost anyone about almost anything, was willing to change his mind when convinced he was mistaken. He would soon become convinced about the desirability of ROM-based software.

Gates also had second thoughts about his rejection of the idea that "software should be sold for a flat fee to hardware companies who would then add the cost of the software to the price of their computer." Probably recalling IBM's 1969 decision to unbundle software from hardware under threat of antitrust action, Bill wondered "whether this is legal or not." But then he changed course and decided to let the hardware companies worry about that. For the agreement with MITS regarding 6800 BASIC, Gates and Allen took a new tack, one that would remove them entirely from worries about freebooters: They simply licensed the BASIC outright on a nonexclusive basis for a flat fee of $31,200, to be paid at $1,300 a month over the next two years.

In one fell swoop, this approach solved two problems. First, Micro-Soft retained control of its product. So far MITS hadn't come up with even a single third-party source code deal for the 8080 BASIC; how could Bill and Paul do worse? Second, Micro-Soft could ignore bootleggers. With the flat-fee deal, what MITS charged—or even *if* it charged—for BASIC would be up to MITS. Hell, they could even give it away. If MITS sold lots of copies, more power to 'em. If not, no skin off Micro-Soft's nose.

Except for the leftover arrangement on the 8080 BASIC, Micro-Soft had removed itself from the piracy fray. From now on, for years to come, most of its deals would be for flat fees. What generally ended up happening was what hobbyists really wanted anyway: BASIC would be built into or bundled with the hardware, making piracy unnecessary. Which was more or less the MITS policy for the Altair 680b: If you bought a 16K memory board, you would get BASIC absolutely free—though there was still some irritation that the price would otherwise be $200.

A committee of the American National Standards Institute (ANSI) had a standard for BASIC in the works under the mellifluous label of "X3J2/76-01." In April, after reading a draft, William Gates, Managing Partner of Micro-Soft, Inc.—a corporate status it would not actually attain until 1981—fired off a three-page letter regarding what he considered errors and omissions in the proposed standard. He enclosed the manual for Micro-Soft's Extended BASIC, brashly recommended the committee take a look at its features, and proudly mentioned the 1,000 copies in use and the variety of the company's corporate customers. To the irritation of many committee members, Micro-Soft eventually participated only tangentially in the official standard-making process—in part because its product would soon set a standard of its own.

And by the time Bill returned to Harvard for the rest of spring semester, Micro-Soft actually had found corporate customers—Motorola and Intel and other chipmakers were buying the BASIC, albeit in single-unit quantities. There was an even bigger customer—a California company called Data Terminal Corporation (DTC) that made printing terminals, a sort of combination daisy-wheel printer and keyboard with an 8080 chip built in. BASIC, it turned out, had a future outside the hobby market—but on 8080-based machines that were not truly computers at all.

In fact, that was BASIC's primary destiny for the next year or so. That was fine with Bill Gates, who never passed up an opportunity. If "smart terminals" were where the money was, others could change the world with their computers for a while. The third contract for 8080 BASIC was with NCR, the cash-register giant that was now one of the "seven dwarfs" competing with IBM in the big-computer market. NCR's 7200 series, a data-entry terminal based on the 8080 chip, had a built-in audiocassette drive for data storage. Micro-Soft agreed to adapt BASIC for it.

In drumming up business, Gates discovered one of the pitfalls of being an underage entrepreneur: On a trip to the headquarters of Applied Digital Data Systems (ADDS), a terminal manufacturer in Hauppauge, New York, Bill was refused a rental car. The reason: He was under twenty-one. The ADDS people had to come out and pick him up at the airport. Until he attained his majority, Bill arranged alternative transportation.

By now Micro-Soft actually had its first employee, Marc McDonald. Although Weiland and Davidoff had both worked on a contract basis, McDonald was the first to draw a salary. Another former Lakesider who had counted traffic tapes for Bill, the laid-back McDonald had spent a year studying computer science at the University of Washington but was ready for a change. He went to work converting 8080 BASIC for the NCR machine.

Ric Weiland became employee number two. After graduating early from Stanford, he returned to Albuquerque as Micro-Soft's general manager. His job was to set up such essentials as a checking account and bookkeeping, to register the company name, to act as a liaison with MITS, to work toward acquiring new customers—and, inevitably, to do some programming. The company was still headquartered at the Portals in Suite 114, otherwise known as Apartment 114. Weiland got the couch again; Allen still had his own bedroom, and McDonald had commandeered Bill's.

Although Weiland and McDonald had their hands full with programming chores, Gates insisted that the company make more of a promotional effort. Weiland embarked on a campaign of letter-writing, cold-calling, and publicity-seeking. He and Bill attended the annual National Computer Conference in New York, hanging around the MITS booth and trolling the exhibit floor in search of microprocessor-controlled devices—cash registers, terminals, they weren't particular—that might be suitable platforms for their BASICs. The computer on every desk and in every home could come later: Running Microsoft software came first.

A convention flyer became an ad—Microsoft's first ever—in the chiphead journal *Digital Design*. It was "The Legend of the Micro-Kid," a cartoon strip about a microprocessor pugilist. "The kid had power and he had speed, but he didn't have no training," related a stogie-chomping trainer in a derby. " 'Kid,' I told him when he came to, 'you have a great future, but what you need is a manager.' "

The ad's slogan, "Microsoft: What's a Microprocessor Without It?" was the pure expression of the very principle hobbyists had complained about regarding the high prices of BASIC—namely, that without software, hardware was utterly useless. The ad was professional: It included the first Microsoft logo (and the abandonment of the hyphen, though internal capitalization—MicroSoft—was the more common form of the name for the next year or so), an impressive list of products, and a proud claim—"Microsoft is the company that will efficiently produce and implement quality software for any microprocessor, in any amount, at any level of complexity. Why not contact them about your microsoftware needs?" Anyone reading it might reasonably expect that the company was far bigger than a four-man shop run out of an apartment living room.

Actually, by the time the ad ran, the Albuquerque operation was being run out of a sparsely furnished house that McDonald and Allen shared with Ric Weiland, who finally got his own bedroom. The DECWriter terminal occupied the living room. The job of maintaining the initially unmowed lawn quickly fell to the immediate neighbors, who feared dandelion contamination.

And Bill Gates? Early that summer in Albuquerque he had agreed to co-write a "Software Column" with Paul Allen for David Bunnell's forthcoming magazine *Personal Computing*. At a local watering hole to discuss the matter over lunch, the magazine's editor, Nelson Winkless, was "awe-stricken" when William Henry Gates introduced himself as president of Microsoft and ordered a Shirley Temple. Winkless pointed out that partnerships didn't officially have presidents. "I'm *styled* president," the underage executive confidently replied.

Later that summer Bill headed off to Seattle to work on a pet project he had casually mentioned in both open letters and the Micro-Kid ad had described as "Upcoming Bout: APL for the 8080." APL was the acronym for an offbeat programming language dubbed with terminal feyness "A Programming Language," and Bill had become infatuated with it. Languages often create cults around them, and APL had one of the most vociferous.

An interpreted language, APL was extremely condensed: In a couple of well-thought-out APL statements, you could do what would take line after line of code in other languages. APL used special symbols, its own goofy alphabet:

Full of arrows and deltas and squiggles, the code appeared to be written in hieroglyphics or Greek or something. All this gave APL high marks among mathematicians and scientists who liked its elegant, powerful solutions to complex vector and matrix problems. APL code was almost impossible to read and therefore hard for a third party to understand and maintain, but it was popular enough to be one of two languages (BASIC was the other) available for the IBM 5100, the first in the IBM series of small computers—some would later say personal computers—that eventually would lead to the IBM PC.

A year or so before, Gates had been introduced to the language by Mike Courtney, a Seattle APL specialist who had read about Altair BASIC, sent for the manual, and couldn't believe a version that good had actually been implemented on a microprocessor. A casual reference to APL in a phone call to Gates led to a meeting that summer in Seattle, where Courtney had fired up Bill's enthusiasm for the language. Over the following year, Gates delved deeper into APL, to the point of examining at least one version of its source code.

At least one person saw Bill's affection for the language as a hopeless crush. Back in Seattle for a visit, Paul Allen lunched with Courtney to discuss the possibility of his coming to work for MITS. The two had never met before, and, sensing Allen's coolness, Courtney asked what the problem was. The problem, Allen told him, was that Courtney had Bill working on this APL thing, and it was a bunch of crap. Allen wanted Gates to work on something real, like FORTRAN or COBOL—something they could actually sell.

But Weiland agreed with Bill. FORTRAN and COBOL seemed sort of passé; APL was avant-garde. Now all that was left was to write a version of it for the 8080. In Seattle for the summer of 1976, Gates seemed to be making headway, and by August he was telling the Northwest Computer Club that it ought to be finished in the fall. In the fall Bill returned to Harvard with APL uncompleted. By January the club newsletter was asking "Whatever happened to MicroSoft's 8080 APL?"

But if Bill wasn't going to do a FORTRAN, somebody else could. Weiland had just opened Microsoft's first real offices—temporary quarters in Albuquerque's One Park Central Tower. Next he hired two programmers from Stanford —Albert Chu and Steve Wood. Wood, Microsoft's first and, for more than a year, only married employee, had finished his master's degree, had experience with microprocessors, and had worked on a compiler for Pascal, a language that was becoming all the rage in academic circles. Using the 8080 simulator that Allen had developed for BASIC, he and Chu set to work on a FORTRAN based on a design by a consultant named Dick Wallman.

There was an even more obscure language called FOCAL that Bill and Paul and Ric liked—an interpreted language invented by Digital Equipment and used mainly to control scientific instruments. Designed to squeeze into a minimal amount of memory, FOCAL was more cryptic than BASIC and harder to use. Weiland had gotten wind of a version for the 8080 that Processor Technology had placed in the public domain and was giving away.

Weiland contacted its author, a Texas A & M computer science major named Bob Arnstein, to create versions for the 6800 processor and the new 6502. At the end of the summer, Arnstein came up to Albuquerque to finish the job. For a total of $3,000, Microsoft had two new products for its catalog and was impressed enough to offer the programmer a job. Arnstein returned to Texas and finished college instead.

FOCAL turned out to be the company's most colossal early flop. Two years later an internal memo from Bill Gates would announce that FOCAL was being discontinued as a product "as a result of the following: 1) We can't find it and 2) We can't sell it. All references to this product should be taken out of our literature." Not selling was an understatement; it is likely that no one ever bought a single copy of FOCAL. And given the lackadaisical internal controls of Microsoft's early years, the product's disappearance, like the Traf-O-Data code before it, was no surprise.

Still trying to expand the business, Weiland was contacting chip manufacturers to find out who was using their microprocessors. The latest, and certainly not the greatest, was the 6502 chip from a little outfit known as MOS Technology. The 6502 had been developed by an engineer named Chuck Peddle and in the right hands could be made to stand in for the competitive 8080 or 6800 chips, but programming it was tricky. The 6502 had only one overarching advantage: At about $25 per chip, it was cheap.

The 6502 was the foundation of more than one new computer. Steve Jobs and Steve Wozniak of Breakout fame were using it as the centerpiece of a one-board computer called the Apple I that they were building in Jobs's garage—in part because they couldn't afford an Altair. Somehow getting wind of this, Weiland phoned, reached Jobs's mother, and, after a couple of false starts, got through to Jobs himself. To Weiland's suggestion that maybe they'd be interested in a BASIC, Jobs responded that they already had a BASIC—Wozniak had written it even before he'd built the machine—and if they needed a better one, they could do it themselves over the weekend.

MOS Technology was peddling a one-board computer of its own—the KIM-1. A machine only a hobbyist could love, it actually included a keyboard and a display—although the keys allowed you only to punch in hexadecimal numbers (0 through F), and the display was a line of red alphanumeric calculator-style LEDs. But Peddle hinted he had plans for a more impressive new machine based on the 6502. He told Weiland he was holding a contest—first good BASIC for the 6502 would win.

The idea of writing a BASIC for the 6502 provoked considerable debate. Weiland argued that the 6502 was very much like the 6800 and that developing a simulator for it, and then a BASIC, wouldn't be much of a problem. Though Bill Gates apparently viewed it as a technically inadequate "dog processor" that might not catch on, he came around to the idea that the project was worth doing. McDonald, working primarily at a Teletype at MITS, modified the 6800 simulator for the 6502, and then Weiland cranked out a 6502 edition of BASIC. The whole project was essentially done on spec; no customers for the 6502 BASIC would appear until after the first version was completed.

But in October Commodore International—one of the calculator giants that a few years back had put Ed Roberts and MITS on the ropes—bought MOS Technology, including the 6502 chip and the KIM-1. It turned out Chuck Peddle did have a scheme for a new machine—one as different from the KIM as any computer could be. His vision was a computer you could use right out of the box. It would come complete in one unit with a display, a keyboard, a cassette deck, and BASIC in ROM. The combination meant that you could flip one switch, and—bingo!—the BASIC prompt would be right up there on your screen without having to wait to load from a cassette or a disk. That machine was to become the Commodore PET—Personal Electronic Transactor, officially, or Programmable Educational Terminal, or Peddle's Ego Trip—though Peddle claimed it had been named for the gift craze of the era, the wildly popular "Pet Rock."

"We were floored by the Commodore PET," one insider remembered. And no wonder: Peddle had craftily designed the machine to appeal to computer users who had already experienced the magic of time-sharing terminals. As Peddle would put it, "the last ten years of college graduates were the entire market for my product, because they were the ones who were BASIC-trained."

For Microsoft it marked a bunch of historic firsts. It was the first time every unit of a personal computer would include Microsoft BASIC in the ROM form that Bill Gates had once disdained. It was the first BASIC to control the bus known as IEEE-488, whose specifications were an offical standard of the Institute of Electrical and Electronics Engineers or "eye-triple-ee"—a design that had been developed primarily for scientific instrumentation but was included in the PET. It was the first BASIC to include special graphics characters —squares and triangles and such. Thanks to editor-whiz Weiland, it was also the first BASIC to include a built-in editor that allowed users to make changes simply by moving the cursor on the screen and retyping part of a line. And it was the first Microsoft BASIC (except for the original unreleased version from Altair) to use the **READY** prompt instead of Microsoft's standard byte-saving **OK**—a quirky tradition that remained at Commodore for years.

Yet by the end of 1976 things were tight at Microsoft, which had just moved next door, to the eighth floor of the new Two Park Central Tower. The Commodore project was pay on delivery, which meant no money until 1977, when the machine and its software were scheduled to be finished. The contracts with DTC and particularly NCR were fairly lucrative, but the proceeds were split fifty/fifty with MITS, causing a delay in the payments, and they would produce income only toward the end of the year. In fact, the NCR deal would initially be a loss leader, because it required customization work for which MITS refused to reimburse Microsoft.

Under the monikers DEVELOP-80, DEVELOP-68, and DEVELOP-65, Microsoft publicly offered the simulator/debugger/assembler packages it had been using to develop its languages, but found no takers. FOCAL didn't sell. APL and FORTRAN weren't ready. Still, the rent had to be paid, and so did the staff. As the year wound down, Microsoft was skating on the edge of solvency.

What saved the day was a windfall—a contract with General Electric that gave the giant company the unlimited right to use Microsoft's 8080 BASIC anywhere within its organization. Exactly how GE discovered Microsoft remains unclear, but according to Weiland, GE's internal budget for the purchase had to be used up before the end of the year. Microsoft's half of the $50,000 deal brought the books from just below the red to a solid pretax profit— $22,496 on income of $104,216. The continued existence of General Electric belies Bill Gates's oft-repeated claim that his first thirteen customers had gone bankrupt. "I made that up," Gates eventually admitted.

By the end of 1976 the personal computer market was beginning to look as if it could sustain a full-fledged industry. One estimate put the total at roughly $27 million, with MITS at 25 percent, IMSAI 17 percent, Processor Technology and SWTP about 8 percent each, and the rest divided among a motley crew including The Digital Group, Polymorphic, Ohio Scientific, Cromemco, and MOS Technology. What was striking as the year ended was that Microsoft BASIC (still known as "Altair BASIC") was available on machines from only one of these manufacturers—MITS. Having jumped aboard the personal computer wave, Gates and Allen seemed to have slipped off and been picked up by a different wave entirely—the wave of smart terminals.

But the microcomputer industry was beginning to attract attention from bigger players—companies such as Pertec Computer Corporation, with $100 million in revenues annually, mostly from such things as big hard disk drives for minicomputers. On December 3, 1976, Pertec signed a letter of intent to acquire MITS for $6 million worth of stock. Remembering what had happened when big players had moved in on the calculator business, Ed Roberts and his fellow shareholders were not hesitant to sell out. Roberts was to be kept on for five years as research director with a $250,000 annual budget. Pertec had grandiose plans for little MITS. It looked like a great deal all around.

With Gates at Harvard and Allen at MITS, Weiland was still minding the store, to the extent of stopping at Commodore in Silicon Valley as he made his way home to Seattle on the twenty-fourth of December. BASIC wasn't running yet on the PET prototype; the problem was a single bug that Weiland fixed in time to get back to Seattle for a family Christmas Eve. But that was simply the Microsoft Way. There was no concept of overtime. "We could work all the time," Steve Wood recalled. "It wasn't that anybody was sitting there saying you've got to work, you've got to come in. We just did it."

For the moment, Bill Gates was a peripheral figure at Microsoft's offices. For the fall term he had returned to Harvard, where he frequented ever-higher-stakes poker games, fourteen-hour marathons where $1,000 might be won or lost in a night. He had also sealed his friendship with nongambler Steve Ballmer, the social lion who had "punched" him—nominations took place at parties where punch was served—for the Fox Club, one of Harvard's exclusive fratlike "final clubs" for upperclassmen. Bill went through the whole ritual: a touch football game, some parties to "prove you can wear that tuxedo," and then, as an initiation, a drunken trip to MIT, where he was blindfolded and forced to give a stirring discourse about the Turing machine, the theoretical prototype of digital computers. Gates good-naturedly learned the secret songs and the secret handshakes and got drunk and signed his name in the book that demonstrated the wobbliness of his hand. To some, Bill may have been a nerd; to Ballmer and his colleagues, he was definitely a clubbable nerd.

Bill's official fall schedule included a math course, a course in Victorian history, and ECON 2010, a stone-tough graduate-level microeconomics course taught by Mike Spence, who would later become dean of the Stanford Business School. Since Gates had followed his tradition of attending only the first class meeting, reading period in January was somewhat intense. Ballmer, who "majored in extracurriculars," found himself in the same boat.

Gates and Ballmer embarked on a one-week late-night study program working on problems from the midterm exam—none of which, at the outset, they could solve. "We're just fucked in this course" was Bill's sober estimation. Ballmer shared the panic. "We're golden!" Ballmer would shout in his manic moods. "No, we're not!" he would mutter in depressed moments.

When the exam was handed out and it proved to be one page, Gates knew they had the Midas touch. The questions were all theoretical, and if Bill and Steve knew anything, it was the math, not the economics. Gates came in first, Ballmer came in second, and "it was kind of rude," but the head of Microsoft never returned to pick up his blue book. When he flew out of Boston at the end of his sixth semester of college, Bill Gates was gone from Harvard for good.

8

→

NEW MEXICAN STANDOFF

On his post-Harvard return to Microsoft's global headquarters in February 1977, the parsimonious Bill Gates discovered Ric Weiland sitting in an office decorated with furniture that seemed unnecessarily posh. After blowing his top about the needless extravagance, Gates confiscated the furniture and the office —for himself. Henceforth there would be no doubt at all about who was really running this company.

Despite Bill's characteristic worries over where the money was going to come from to pay him, Paul Allen had left MITS in November 1976 and joined Microsoft full time. Now Bill moved immediately to formalize their informal partnership deal. By the time they signed the official agreement on February 3, the existing sixty/forty split had changed to sixty-four/thirty-six—with Gates retaining the larger share. The arguments about Paul's full-time status had become moot, because he was now a full-time employee, but the ever-hustling Gates had added a new wrinkle to the debate: He deserved more money because he was about to end his college career. Yet Bill managed to hedge even that: Although the agreement legally set forth the new split and stated that both partners were to work full time, it included a special clause limiting the duties of any partner who happened to be a full-time student.

Still a Lakeside student, Chris Larson was down in Albuquerque for a high school senior-year job not unlike Bill's RODS stint. He and Gates found an apartment together not far from the infamous Portals, and immediately Bill bought his first car—a used dark-green Porsche 911. Finally he had a vehicle that liked to move as fast as he did—way beyond the speed limit.

Bill Gates may have dropped out of college, but college was the model at Microsoft. The offices resembled a dormitory minus beds: late hours, loud music, walls full of junk, anything-goes dress, Coke, adrenaline, unbuttoned behavior. Not that college was a prerequisite: Neither the company's partners nor its first employee had graduated, and Gates would try unsuccessfully to get his loyal Lakeside buddy Larson to quit Princeton and come work full time for Microsoft.

At twenty, Bill Gates did not know much about how to run a company, but he had plenty of experience in how not to. Exhibits A, B, and C: C-Cubed, RODS, and MITS. So Gates hired in his own image: young, smart, energetic, and outspoken—and usually white and male. If you were going to work for Bill Gates, you had to know your stuff and be willing to show it on a round-the-clock basis. One Albuquerquian recalled:

> The bit about working very long hours was always true right from the very beginning. One of the things that they really pushed on in my interview was whether or not I had ever worked really hard on a big project. And I dredged up some stuff I'd done . . . I'd probably worked incredible hours on the thing . . . and they liked that. It wasn't until later that I understood the meaning of that one. But I'm sure that they were looking for people who were workaholics to begin with, and they wanted evidence of being a workaholic.

At Microsoft work came first, and second, and third. Eating and sleeping were somewhere down the scale. Play, in the form of self-devised pranks, road rallies, or a movie, was catch as catch can. Microsoft life in Albuquerque adopted a software paradigm, the endless loop: work, eat, catch a flick, sleep, return to work. In Albuquerque there was plenty of work to do, and not much else. "We would just work until we dropped," Paul Allen said. "I used to joke that Albuquerque is a repeating pattern of a gas station, a 7-Eleven, and a movie theater."

Programmers would typically straggle in around noon and get cracking. About seven or eight it would be time for a break, usually pizza and Coke at the nearest hangout, often with some shoot-'em-up movie afterward. Then it was back to the office for nocturnal code hammering, occasionally followed by a wee-hours snack before heading home to crash. One bloodshot Albuquerquian recalled an early-morning encounter with a truck stop waitress who asked if the guys were doing speed. "No," came the response with nerdy pride. "We're programmers."

Salaries, in the neighborhood of $20,000, were slightly above the industry average. But so were the work hours. Employees got just two weeks' vacation, though they supposedly could take off any religious holiday of significance. The holy day was informally rescinded after one employee actually took it and the senior partner threw a fit.

"Microsoft," Gates wrote in one memo, "expects a level of dedication from its employees higher than most companies. Therefore, if some deadline or discussion or interesting piece of work causes you to work extra time some week it just goes with the job." But, Bill acknowledged, a prolonged stretch of specifically requested overtime work deserved special consideration. In that case, the employee was to record the extra hours and report them—and receive extra compensation at the "normal hourly rate." This overtime policy —at best skirting the letter of the law, at worst violating it outright—would eventually cause much unhappiness and some departures. Like all the employment policies, its model was the guy at the top, the guy whose 1978 salary of $16,000 was bettered by virtually every other employee's and who proudly and defiantly took a hardcore attitude toward work, work, work.

And then there was the "confrontational style" set by the senior partner. "That's the stupidest thing I ever heard," the classic Gates catchphrase, had survived from his childhood. As one Albuquerqian recalled, if the impatient Bill Gates told you something and you didn't understand his point, his Socratic method was to tell you the same thing, only "louder. You know, like 'You stupid idiot. This is what I said. Just listen to what I say.' " With Bill Gates, you learned quickly to stand your ground or do anything in your power to avoid incurring his wrath.

Microsoft was beginning to find customers. The 6502 BASIC for Commodore was almost finished, and an up-and-coming outfit (its computer was called the Challenger) known as Ohio Scientific had signed up for it as well. As for the 8080 version—well, if MITS wouldn't do the marketing, Bill would do it himself. Yet something weird seemed to be going on. The whole Pertec buyout was being performed as a reverse merger, in which a wholly owned Pertec subsidiary, MITS Acquisition Inc., created for the occasion, would actually be merged into MITS. Insiders at Microsoft had the distinct impression that this goofy structure might have something to do with the fact that MITS could not assign its contract for BASIC to a third party.

There was definitely something afoot. By mid-January 1977 Microsoft had steered toward MITS a raft of potential customers—representatives of terminal maker Rydacom, disk drive maker Icom, and chipmaker Zilog, whose new Z-80 chip, almost but not quite fully compatible with the Intel 8080, was destined to grab much of the market. But MITS had refused to deal with any of them. Bill argued, cajoled, and pleaded with Ed Roberts—and tried harder. By mid-April there were still more potential customers: Intel, ADDS, Delta Data, Intelligent Systems Corporation, and others. At roughly $35,000 per license, the total of the four deals for which Microsoft had received oral commitments would be over $140,000, and half of that would go to MITS.

The "best efforts" clause in the license agreement seemed to indicate that MITS had to license the 8080 BASIC to all comers. But MITS, apparently at Pertec's direction, flatly refused to license BASIC to anyone else, competitor or not. Worse, MITS told Microsoft to quit marketing BASIC to potential MITS competitors, claiming, with some validity, that Microsoft's marketing efforts were in violation of the agreement.

This stonewall policy was a body blow to Microsoft. Not only would it steal income; it would also help competitors who were developing BASIC versions of their own. The revenue stream from MITS was drying up—down to about $3,500 a month including the NCR payments. The "hardware royalty" of $10 for each machine 8K and over had never been paid and ended up being the subject of an oral agreement whereby MITS would pay $18,000 at a rate of $3,000 per month beginning in October and increase the royalty rate by 20 percent. And it didn't really matter: MITS hadn't bothered to pay.

But who could be pessimistic when there was a revolution in the works? Out in San Francisco, the entire microcomputer industry, with a singular exception, was converging upon the Civic Auditorium for an event even bigger than the World Altair Computer Convention. There had been other independent conventions, including one the previous fall in Atlantic City, but the First Annual West Coast Computer Faire scheduled for April 15 through 17, tapping into the fervor and energy of the Homebrew Computer Club and People's Computer Company and the entrepreneurial companies that were popping up like weeds in Silicon Valley, was—everybody knew it—The One. Lines ran all the way around the block and met at the back of the hall.

Inside, if you could elbow your way through the crowd to the booths, you'd hardly be disappointed. Of course MITS, with typical haughtiness and by now promulgating futile plans for its second World Altair Computer Convention the following month, skipped the show.

But so what? Nowadays machines came with keyboards attached, and sometimes even screens. In the booth of a Commodore outlet known as "Mr. Calculator," Chuck Peddle, Mr. 6502, gave the first public demonstrations of the Commodore PET and its built-in Microsoft BASIC. Processor Technology took a quadruple booth to show off the latest incarnation of its wood-paneled keyboard-and-cassette-deck-included Sol computer. IMSAI was there with its stylish Altair knockoffs. And in the fancy custom-designed booth at the center entrance, beneath a new multicolored logo that an infusion of venture capital had helped finance, Wozniak and Jobs and crew were giving the first public demonstrations anywhere of a do-it-all machine they called the Apple II.

Despite all the attention people were paying to hardware, they weren't overlooking the other half of the equation. Steve Dompier's Target game showed off the Sol, and so did the first real word processing program for microcomputers—Michael Shrayer's Electric Pencil. In microcomputer history, The Pencil, as it was colloquially known, was vitally important as one of the earliest application programs—programs that actually let regular people do something useful, as opposed to letting programmers do more programming.

This was an idea that had just begun to surface. In 1976 Alan Kay and Adele Goldberg of the Xerox Palo Alto Research Center (PARC) had publicly discussed a concept they called the Dynabook—"a personal dynamic medium the size of a notebook which could be owned by everyone and could have the power to handle virtually all of its owner's information-related needs." In a January 1977 *Personal Computing* software column, Paul Allen had aired similar views:

> *I expect the personal computer to become the kind of thing that people carry with them, a companion that takes notes, does accounting, gives reminders, handles a thousand personal tasks. Leaving everything to the computer opens the possibility of accidentally paying 20 years of insurance premiums in advance and things like that, but other kinds of accidents happen already and we learn to deal with them.*
>
> *New questions are raised. In addition to playing games, calculating income taxes and all that, what are the uses of the home computer? What will inexpensive computers* do?
>
> *These are chiefly software questions.*

But at this point in history Bill Gates approached those questions from an entirely different direction, remaining firmly uninterested in "novice users," people who didn't know how to program. In his *Personal Computing* column, Bill wrote primarily about tools for hardcore programmers, tools like those he had available on the DECsystem 10—utility programs, as they were known. Text editors for typing in and modifying programs; cross-reference programs that aided in the debugging process; diagnostic programs that helped you maintain your system—as Bill saw it, "The idea of using software that helps to write software . . . may be somewhat confusing to a novice user, but is key to bringing the computer to a level of usability that makes it attractive to people without a technical background."

In that techie vein, there were a couple of interesting items over at the Digital Research booth of the Computer Faire. DR, formerly Intergalactic Digital Research, was a company founded in Pacific Grove, California, by former Seattleite Gary Kildall, a Ph.D. computer scientist who taught at the Naval Postgraduate School near Monterey. Modeled after DEC's TOPS-10 for PDP-10 machines, his major product was a program called CP/M—Control Program for Microcomputers. CP/M was an operating system, or "OS"—a program that ran "underneath" other programs and took care of a lot of the dirty work.

An operating system is a sort of butler that takes care of software's demands on hardware. Without one, a programmer would personally have to worry about such niggling details as where the data would be stored on a disk, or precisely how a printer port or terminal worked. With one, the programmer could let the butler do the work by giving it a simple request, or "call":

Put that file on the disk, send these characters to the printer, whatever. Presto! —the OS would do the rest.

This was a concept Bill Gates had already been thinking about. "The best thing for users," Bill pointed out in *Personal Computing*, "would have been if all the manufacturers of personal computer hardware had got together years ago and decided on a standard OS. Every time a new device was introduced the driver needed in the standard OS would have to be included with the hardware. Software houses would write programs to run under the standard OS and wouldn't have to worry about multiple versions." This dream OS, in other words, would mean less work and more potential customers for developers such as Microsoft.

Kildall had similar ideas. He had just made his first major business deal for CP/M. IMSAI was aiming its machines toward well-heeled business customers rather than impecunious hobbyists, so its machines generally included floppy disk drives. After the deal with Kildall, CP/M came with every one. Now Gary was trying to expand the CP/M empire to other machines and make it that "standard operating system" Bill wrote about so longingly.

At the moment, Gates had no operating system of his own in the works. But he did have BASIC. And sharing the Digital Research booth at the Faire— the archaic spelling had been lifted from the locally popular Renaissance Faire —was Gordon Eubanks, a naval officer and one of Kildall's former students. Eubanks had written a version called BASIC-E and, bankrolled by IMSAI, was putting the finishing touches on what would come to be known as CBASIC.

The Eubanks BASIC had one great gimmick. Whereas Microsoft's version was interpreted, his was pseudocompiled. When you ran a Microsoft BASIC program, each line of source code would be translated on the fly to language the computer could understand. But CBASIC would first translate your program to a special intermediate code known as "pseudocode" or "p-code." Another program, known as the "translator" or "interpreter," would then decode it for the computer.

The extra step made programming and debugging somewhat clunky, but it had one great advantage: secrecy. If you sold someone a program written in Microsoft BASIC, anyone could simply list out the source code and rewrite or steal any part of it they liked. With CBASIC, you could distribute the intermediate code along with the translator, keeping your program safe from prying eyes. It was little wonder that the earliest versions of microcomputer accounting packages used the BASIC from Eubanks's Compiler Systems instead of the one from Microsoft. Still, as Steve Wood recalled, Microsoft had an effective strategic weapon against Eubanks and his BASIC: "We would go into a competitive situation and we'd say, 'Yeah. Okay. That's an okay product. But who are you going to call for tech support when he's out on his submarine?' "

Eubanks wasn't the only one besides Microsoft with a BASIC that worked. Processor Technology had its own version, and so did North Star and Polymorphic and The Digital Group and other hardware makers, including IBM, weighing in with a BASIC for its pricey model 5100 machine—a BASIC two to three times slower than the Microsoft editions. There were public domain "Tiny BASICs" all over the place, but they lacked floating-point math. Although Microsoft BASIC had competitors, particularly on 8080-based machines, there was no question that among the interpreted versions, it was the clear leader.

Yet because MITS refused to license Altair BASIC to others, the 8080 market was exactly where Microsoft was stymied. When it became clear that the ADDS agreement, which Gates had been working on for more than a year, was about to blow up because of MITS's refusal to deal, Bill did a little blowing up of his own.

On April 20, Gates and Allen sent Ed Roberts a letter outlining five problems, including overdue royalty payments and MITS's failure to live up to its obligation to "license, promote, and commercialize the program." It was bad enough that MITS was sitting on its hands: To add injury to insult, Microsoft had spent some $36,000 of its own money in marketing 8080 BASIC. If the matters were not remedied within ten days, the letter stated, Microsoft would terminate its agreement with MITS.

The following day an attorney for MITS denied all five charges in a letter that asserted MITS was up to date in its payments, called Microsoft's marketing expenses unauthorized, and claimed, among other things, that "Mits, Inc., does not believe that the agreement requires it to license the program to its competitors." The letter pointed out that if Microsoft disagreed, it could, as the agreement permitted, submit its demands to arbitration.

One week later the same attorney sent Microsoft a check for $14,526 to cover royalties dating back to December 1—rather tardy, considering the contractual stipulation of monthly payment. He also forwarded a bombshell: a copy of the Demand for Arbitration that MITS had sent to the American Arbitration Association asking for a decision that the contract was still valid. And for good measure, MITS filed suit in the District Court of the County of Bernalillo, State of New Mexico, on May 5, asking for a temporary restraining order to prevent Microsoft from disclosing the BASIC source code to any third party. On May 9, after hiding in a stairwell to avoid being served, Gates found a copy of the court summons posted on the door of his apartment at 4801 Gibson Street. On May 12 the judge issued the order: Microsoft was restrained from disclosing the 8080 source code to anyone until June 8 or the arbitrator's determination, whichever came first.

The effect on Microsoft was potentially disastrous. Income from MITS, whether from sales of Altair BASIC or the NCR and other deals, simply ceased. The pending deals for 8080 BASIC, worth at least $70,000 to Microsoft, were put on ice, with the possibility that competitors or internal development teams might snatch them away. Gates and Allen couldn't even cash the $14,526 check for fear that action might be taken as satisfaction with Pertec's claims. And as the total royalties MITS had paid Microsoft were nearing the $180,000 cap, Pertec had the gall to suggest that *all* the royalties came under this cap, including the third-party source code licenses that had been specifically excluded.

Worse, all this was happening just as Microsoft was ramping up for a new project, at $100,000 its biggest deal yet: an entirely new version of BASIC for a new machine from Texas Instruments, like Commodore one of the survivors of the calculator wars and therefore one of the expected winners of the coming battle of personal computers. The new machine, code-named the SP-70, would be a low-cost home unit using the proprietary Texas Instruments TMS 9900 chip. For it, TI was demanding a dialect of BASIC that would be compatible with the developing ANSI standard, which differed in significant respects from Microsoft's version. Much later TI would discover that its adherence to the "official" standard would make its BASIC the odd dialect out in a world that was actually standardizing on Microsoft's edition.

This project was going to be big, and it was getting to be costly. Allen would be working on the simulator for the new chip. Monte Davidoff was coming down for the summer to work on the project. Since Ric Weiland was about to depart for California to work for COBOL king Ryan-McFarland, Bill hired Bob Greenberg, a hotshot programmer he knew from Harvard, to do much of the TI work. Devoting all these resources to the TI project wouldn't come cheap. Hell, even the visit from the Texas Instruments representatives had cost money: The day before, someone from the office had to run out and invest in a couple of extra chairs, because every seat in the place was currently occupied.

However—and it was a very big "however"—TI wouldn't cough up a dime until Microsoft delivered the code. And although Microsoft had grossed roughly $65,000 for the first three months of 1977—largely from deals for the MITSless 6502 BASIC—cash was beginning to run low. The announcement in early April of FORTRAN-80 brought in some inquiries, but since FORTRAN was clearly a far more specialized language than BASIC, it would be unlikely to attract big upfront deals from OEMs or to set the world on fire at the single-copy price of $500.

More Microsoft cash dwindled on a company trip to Dallas for the 1977 National Computer Convention. Chaired by industry gadfly Portia Isaacson, it marked the first time a "big computer" conference included a special Personal

Computer Section. The little computers were tucked away downstairs in what Nelson Winkless remembered as a "hot, miserable, crowded hall"—crowded because that's where all the interesting stuff was.

In his appearance on the Personal Computing and Software panel alongside Gary Kildall and others, Bill made some salient points. Until now software had been primarily created by hardware manufacturers with their high margins. This led them to treat software as a loss leader, pricing it unrealistically low, which led to its general mediocrity. Bigger bucks and protection from piracy would give software creators more of an impetus to create. But "until stronger incentives to develop software are set up," according to Gates, "there is a danger that so many people will learn BASIC and so many programs will be written in it that it will become a de facto standard despite the fact that superior languages will be developed." It was typical Binary Bill: In one brash utterance, he had managed to suggest the possibility of unprecedented success for his lead product while subtly trashing it as a potential "danger."

Back in Albuquerque, the arbitration process seemed to drag on forever. First there was a problem finding a mutually agreeable arbitrator. When one was appointed, he couldn't schedule hearings until June 22.

Weiland, who had been the main conduit to MITS during Bill's absence, helped Bill and Paul prepare for the arbitration. At the hearings, a diary he'd kept over the past year proved invaluable as evidence. But after the hearings, the arbitrator kept delaying his decision. Again and again the judge extended the restraining order: through July 1, through July 25, through August 10, through August 20, through August 29.

Although Microsoft's attorney, Paull Mines of Poole, Tinnen and Martin, kept telling his clients they had a good chance of winning, salaries and rent had to be paid. Microsoft's coffers were dwindling, and Bill was beginning to worry. "We were in very close contact with him then," his mother remembered, "and we spent hours talking about it, what his strategy should be." In one phone call to his parents, he intimated that the company's funds were running so low he might have to settle the case. Though they offered him a loan, he found a different source of cash: In July Microsoft borrowed $7,000 from its new hire, Bob Greenberg.

In early August the company's savior was a $10,500 payment from Apple Computer for the first half of its flat-fee license to Microsoft's 6502 BASIC. Despite the bluster of Steve Jobs, Wozniak's primitive "Integer BASIC," built into every Apple II, turned out not to be good enough, and now that the Apple II was getting hot, a free weekend to write a new version was a luxury Woz didn't have. Apple licensed Microsoft's version, set a high school kid named Randy Wigginton to work on integrating some of Wozniak's graphics routines with it, and—after Wigginton managed to reconstruct six months' work that he had lost when the minicomputer tape with his only copy was accidentally erased—released it as Applesoft BASIC. Given the million-plus Apple II machines eventually sold with the program, Microsoft would have made out better with even a one-cent royalty, but who knew? Nearly a decade later, when it was about to expire, the Applesoft flat-fee deal would become the focus of one of Bill Gates's most notorious games of Business Poker.

Although finances were low, spirits remained high. Sometime after midnight, with funmeister Larson riding shotgun, Gates would fire up the Porsche and put pedal to the metal on a deserted three-mile stretch of freeway in an attempt to break the previous outing's record. During one visit to a mechanic, Gates was heard to complain that the manual stated the car's top speed was 126 miles an hour, but he had only been able to get the thing up to 121.

After the freeway came the grand prix course up twisty Cement Plant Road to the Sandia Crest at 60 or 70 miles an hour—at which speed a patch of gravel once got the better of Bill Gates and led to a noisy spinout against a rock wall. Except for a strip of rubber on the front bumper, the car was undamaged, but as Bill and Chris staggered out, an agitated resident ran up from a nearby house and demanded, "What happened? Did you hear that?" Bill Gates's response dripped with the same withering sarcasm he would employ in response to any other question he deemed stupid: "No. What?" It was in this era that Gates "noticed that other people could read signs farther away than I could" and first got a pair of the glasses that would become a smudged personal trademark.

The Cement Plant Road was also the site of another favorite sport of the summer of '77—"dozing." Having discovered earthmoving equipment at a road-construction site, Larson and Gates investigated further. Lo and behold, the machines had keys in them. Under cover of darkness, with the same curiosity that had led them to fool around with computers, Bill Gates and Chris Larson—known fondly in each other's company as "Ugliest" and "Pimpdog" —set about to learn how to run the machines. Slowly, methodically, over half a dozen sessions, they discovered the tricks. This is how you go forward. This is how you go backward. Oh, here's the blade. Here's how you scoop dirt.

Dozing continued with more fantastic variations. After mastering Heavy Machinery 101, Gates and Larson decided to "race" the machines. The whole event lasted about ten seconds, maybe 150 feet on a straight course, and ended with laughs of wild exhilaration. Although they joked about how much fun it would be to drive a huge dump truck from the site to town at four in the morning, dozing remained confined to the construction area. Eventually Bill learned about the perils of reverse gear when he nearly backed a 'dozer over his Porsche.

Where the bulldozer missed, Bill's own automotive insouciance succeeded. That fall, the 911's oil light kept coming on as he rounded curves. Gates ignored it until he couldn't ignore it anymore—when the engine seized. The Porsche with the unlubricated motor endured a long tow back to the shop for an engine rebuild. What Bill rued most after he got the car back was having to take it easy for the 600-mile break-in period.

During normal business hours Gates had to settle for more conventional grand-prix style sprints to the airport to pick up visitors and across town— leading an early Japanese customer, shivering and pale, to ask Paul Allen, "Mr. Gates—he always drive this fast?" Bill's driving skills, with dragstrip starts and panic traffic-light stops (and sometimes no stops at all), so stupefied some passengers that they refused to ride with him ever again.

Gates, Allen, and McDonald started an informal competition to see who could make it the fastest to or from a movie or the law firm. The races to Poole, Tinnen and Martin paid off. By the beginning of September, the arbitrator sent down word in no uncertain terms: MITS had violated the agreement in what Paul Allen remembered the arbitrator calling "one of the worst cases of corporate piracy I've ever seen." Although MITS could continue to sell Microsoft's 8080 BASIC for its own machines, its exclusive license was officially terminated. MITS would no longer share in future third-party royalties, and Microsoft was free to sell the product to all comers.

Winning the arbitration caused more relief than exhilaration around the office. "It was kind of like, whoossssshhhhh, that's over with," Steve Wood recalled. "Now let's get on the phone quick and . . . close these five deals that have been waiting in line and get some cash in here." And close they did. Not only was Microsoft now in control of its own destiny, it had effectively doubled the potential revenue from each deal. Henceforth it would keep the whole amount instead of just half.

The deals began to stream in. ADDS signed up at once. There were agreements pending with Ontel and the Warner and Swasey Company and MECA and TEI. There was even overseas interest from the hottest new Japanese startup, Sord.

And Bill was out rounding up more customers. Potentially the biggest was Radio Shack, which on August 3 had introduced its TRS-80 machine, the "TRS" an unfortunate acronym for "The Radio Shack" that within the industry quickly gained the affectionate pronunciation "Trash." Like the Commodore PET, the TRS-80 was a complete package (though not a single physical unit), with keyboard, video display, cassette recorder, 4K of RAM, and, built into ROM, a version of BASIC—all for $599. Initially 3,000 machines were built; the company figured that if they didn't sell, the 3,000 stores in the Radio Shack chain could find some use for them. The company quickly discovered it couldn't produce the machines fast enough to keep up with demand.

Unfortunately, the BASIC in ROM wasn't from Microsoft. It was a version that Steve Leininger, one of the machine's designers, had adapted from a public domain "Tiny" BASIC. In early reviews, the Radio Shack BASIC took a lot of flak for its inadequacies. Bill Gates kept pressing Radio Shack to switch to the real stuff.

When John Roach, the company's vice president in charge of manufacturing, finally agreed to a meeting, Bill was up in Seattle for the first wedding of his older sister, Kristi. During the bachelor party and the rest of the weekend, Gates obsessed about the deal. He sought advice from his father about the negotiation: how to price the product, how to sell it, how to make its advantages clear.

Then Bill met Paul Allen down in Texas to demonstrate their BASIC at Radio Shack's imposing Fort Worth headquarters. Roach, a tall, bluff no-nonsense Texan, seemed to like it, and Bill pulled out a two-page proposal. They went over it line by line, with Gates expanding on the features, the advantages, the value. Then they came to the price. "How much is this thing going to cost?" Roach asked.

"Fifty thousand dollars," Bill Gates said confidently.

"Horseshit," John Roach replied.

For once, Bill Gates was speechless. "My father hadn't coached me for that eventuality," he would recall a few years later.

Nonetheless, Roach and Radio Shack signed a flat-fee contract for Microsoft BASIC at Microsoft's price within a month. The Leininger BASIC fit into one 4K ROM chip, but the TRS-80 had sockets for two more. The version of BASIC that Gates came up with had to be shoehorned into a tight 12K—which meant he had to abandon some features that were now standard in other versions. But Gates cleverly left "hooks" in the code—software interfaces that would allow extra functions to be loaded from cassette or disk. Though they meant nothing at the time, Microsoft would eventually grab on to these hooks as a profit center—and as a model for a later BASIC for the most important machine in Microsoft's history.

Microcomputers were beginning to break out of their "hobbyist" world. *Parade* magazine had picked up the trend with a piece dubbed—that phrase again—"A Computer in Every Home." The *Wall Street Journal* covered the phenomenon. The September 1977 issue of *Scientific American* featured a chip design on its cover and was entirely devoted to "Microelectronics."

By late fall the Commodore PET, the Radio Shack TRS-80, and the Apple II were slugging it out in the low end of the marketplace. The PET already came with Microsoft BASIC, and the other two machines would soon. In less than a year, Microsoft BASIC had witnessed a transformation: Instead of being a captive of a single microcomputer company and a bunch of smart terminals, it was becoming the common denominator of microcomputer software.

In *Electronic Engineering Times,* with all the tact of a techie, Bill Gates made friends and influenced customers by airing a disagreement with designer Chuck Peddle and calling the PET's keyboard "totally wretched." Luckily, Microsoft's Bob Greenberg more diplomatically praised the machine's all-in-one design and character-based graphics. Besides, Microsoft was hardly blameless itself: The same article reported just the kind of problem Bill had anticipated ROM-based software would bring: "a bug in the ROM BASIC for the PET [that] will be fixed after 3500 units have been shipped." It was not the first widely reported bug in a Microsoft product. It would be far from the last.

Another deal that would prove important was the latest arrangement with NCR, which was updating its cassette-based 7200 terminal to the floppy-disk-based 8200. Although Bill's Altair Disk BASIC would have worked, the way it stored data on the disk caused performance bottlenecks. Marc McDonald understood the problems intimately, because he'd been involved in adapting BASIC for a variety of disk-based systems. In conversations with Gates, McDonald came up with a new format: a short table that would keep track of the entire sequence of data on the disk. Because the table would be read into memory the first time it was needed and stay there, finding information in it would be virtually instantaneous. This elegant scheme, which McDonald designed and coded for the NCR 8200, became known as the File Allocation Table—FAT for short. It would serve as the underpinning of what came to be known as Standalone BASIC and eventually find its way into far more sophisticated machines—including the IBM PC.

Despite the fact that microcomputer sales were beginning to kick into high gear, Microsoft continued to sell BASIC on a flat-fee, no-royalty basis. The Gatesian reasoning was simple. In theory, any customer could write its own BASIC; Radio Shack and others had actually done it. Customers always believed they could do programming projects far faster and cheaper than they actually could—hell, Microsoft usually believed that about its own projects. What Microsoft was really competing against, then, was not what it would cost for a customer to do a project itself, but rather what the customer *thought* it would cost.

There was another side of the equation. As Steve Smith, a sales executive who arrived later, recalled: "Even on a $3,000 license . . . if you lost that deal, it was a $6,000 loss because you gave your competitor $3,000 and you didn't get $3,000. So our bottom line was, you never lose a deal. And we never lost a deal." Microsoft kept its prices so low that the customer would be absolutely certain there was no way of beating them. For Microsoft the trick was to sell the same product—BASIC, FORTRAN, whatever—over and over again. After all, you only had to write it once.

At least, that was the theory. In those days of utterly nonstandard computers, there was always at least some customization work to be done. Microsoft tried to lay it off on the customer or negotiate a customization fee; often it had to eat the expense. The BASIC source code was beginning to cause problems: It had become one giant program with special sections for special purposes and special machines. When a programmer compiled it into machine code, he'd specify via a series of commands known as "switches" exactly what should be done: put graphics in, adapt for the Z-80 chip, leave out disk functions, whatever.

The advantage was that new versions could employ a vast amount of the code that had already been written. But as the code grew bigger, with special sections for every new machine, it got harder to understand, and somebody fiddling with the common parts—"improving" it—might make changes that would cause unexpected trouble.

Besides, some customers insisted on acquiring the source code, either so they could perform their own modifications or, as McDonald put it, "for comfort, a warm fuzzy feeling" of security. Microsoft wasn't about to distribute all the conditional code that applied to other machines but was totally useless to anyone else. McDonald came up with a program that would filter out all the unnecessary stuff—a program that became increasingly necessary as the customer list grew.

Still, there were virtually no controls on the process of software creation, no check-in and check-out procedure to insure that one person's work wouldn't negate another's. Program testing was rudimentary at best. In early 1978 Radio Shack's one-man software applications "group" Van Chandler recalled, he was "still finding one bug after another. It was so unstable and screwed up that John Roach finally told me, 'Go to Albuquerque and don't come back until you have the disk BASIC running.' It took three weeks, but we got it done." Chandler was far from alone.

The office protocols were equally lackadaisical. In September 1977 Steve Wood, who had taken over the reins as general manager from the departed Ric Weiland, was hunting for a new receptionist and secretary. One candidate was Miriam Lubow, a talkative mother-hen type in her forties whose real-estate business was feeling the pinch of a sluggish market. Her first surprise was the office demeanor: Wood greeted her in jeans. The second surprise was when Wood told her that "We write software." Lubow had never heard of the word, but she was hired anyway.

Lubow began keeping a notebook of terms she didn't understand and urging Wood to explain them. A week or so later a kid who appeared to be a teenager strolled in with messy hair and jeans, walked into the president's office, rummaged through the mail, and then headed for the room that held the terminals and various computers. Miriam ran into Wood's office and warned him that some kid had just gone into the room nobody was allowed into without permission. "Oh," said Wood. "That's Bill."

"Who?"

"Bill Gates. The president. He's your boss."

"How old is he?" Lubow asked suspiciously.

"Twenty-one," Wood replied.

A flabbergasted Miriam Lubow went home that night to explain to her husband that her boss was barely old enough to drink.

Miriam became a kind of den mother to the Microsoft clan. She managed the checkbook, ran the payroll, paid the taxes, and warned customers coming to the airport that the way to spot the president of the company at the gate was to look for a blond sixteen-year-old with glasses—which Bill, pushing them back up his nose via the lenses, would never manage to keep clean. She collected debts, made daily runs to the Albuquerque Public Schools computer facility to collect printouts. Her kids stuffed envelopes with Microsoft brochures to earn movie money. After arriving at the office in the morning, she'd type up the letters Bill had scrawled overnight on yellow legal pads, in complete agreement with the Gatesian theory that it was a waste of both people's time to be "standing there, one dictating, one writing." And she learned to fib about airplane departure times to keep Bill from engaging in his standard practice of leaving for the airport five minutes before his plane was due to take off. After all, it was she who had to ride with him to bring the car back from the airport.

Miriam adopted a motherly solicitousness toward her abstracted young boss, setting up barbering appointments, making sure his hair was combed, straightening his tie. She fretted over his erratic sleeping habits—arriving for work she would find him curled up on the floor after a hard night at the terminal—and his tendency to skip meals. "I would buzz him and say 'Bill, you know, it's way past one-thirty. I think your people would like to have lunch.' And he'd say oh, thank you, and they would traipse out to lunch. But he was oblivious to that."

When Gates asked her to get him an American Express card, Lubow discovered "they wouldn't give it to him. He didn't have a credit line. And I said we don't need it, he pays cash, he has $100,000 in the bank. They said they weren't interested." Eventually Bill managed to establish a credit record; from then on the big chore became keeping the card from getting lost.

Despite the company's motto, "We set the standard," Lubow did none of her daily chores with the help of a computer. Although the programmers had a printing terminal that could produce clean copy, Microsoft did not own a single word processor. For accounting, it used no software at all; everything was kept in ledger books.

And there was beginning to be something to account for. By November Microsoft was boasting that its BASIC for 8080 and Z-80 machines had "a user base of over 5000." By the end of 1977 Microsoft showed total revenues of $381,715, with a net pretax income of $112,471. Over and above that total Paul and Bill shared a total draw of $37,320, split roughly equally. This business was looking as if it might conceivably live up to the get-rich dreams of William Henry Gates.

9

▶

FAREWELL TO THE DESERT

By early 1978 the same crack Pertec team that had managed to deal itself out of half the profits of Altair BASIC was managing to keep MITS out of the limelight with a variety of plans and products that woefully failed to keep up with changes in the marketplace. The TRS-80 and the Apple and the Commodore PET and a rash of CP/M-based machines were getting all the play in the computer media; MITS products were all but forgotten. Under the influence of MITS's competitors and despite the bitter protests of Ed Roberts, the IEEE had anointed as "S-100" a standard that was essentially a clone of the Roberts/Yates Altair bus. Albuquerque, briefly the capital of the microcomputer revolution, had become at best the capital of green chile production, with its limited computer importance deriving almost entirely from the little software company in the eighth-floor offices at Two Park Central Tower.

Microsoft had grown sufficiently to need additional office space, and with its fortunes unchained from the MITS shackles, New Mexico had little left to offer. Paul Allen saw Albuquerque as a drag on recruiting: "People would fly out and they'd kind of look around and say, 'Geez, what do you do here at night?'" The only Microsoft employee from the area was former MITS technical writer and *Computer Notes* editor Andrea Lewis, and aside from Greenberg and a new hire, Texan Bob O'Rear, at thirty-five the "old man" of the bunch, the rest of the staff hailed from the Pacific Northwest. Paul Allen "was really tired of not having any water in sight for a thousand miles." But when it came to microcomputers, Seattle was almost as much of a backwater as Albuquerque.

Bill Gates found California more seductive. The indisputable center of the microcomputer world was California's Bay Area, the capital of microcomputer hardware from the chips of Intel and Motorola and Zilog and National Semiconductor right up to the machines from Apple and Commodore and IMSAI. And in Pacific Grove, a pleasant drive from Silicon Valley, was Gary Kildall's

Digital Research, with its CP/M that was beginning to become a standard comparable to Microsoft BASIC. In November 1977 Gates paid Kildall a visit. In many ways the two Seattle natives could not have been more different. Kildall, thirteen years Bill's senior, was the consummate computer academic, with a degree in computer science, years of teaching under his belt, and a love for the computer languages such as PL/I that were considered politically correct in academe. Kildall had written a BASIC compiler during his days at the University of Washington—and "just hated the language."

And here was Bill Gates, a self-taught computer hacker, a seat-of-the-pants programmer who wrote fast code full of neat but frowned-upon tricks. The brash kid knew a few things, but to the likes of a Kildall he hadn't paid his dues, which would probably explain why he was lame enough to promote a toy language as the future of computing.

Physically the two were like Woody Allen meets Gary Cooper—the nerdy, bespectacled Gates a perfect foil to the tall, bearded, infinitely hipper Kildall. There was also a difference in lifestyles. Whereas Gates, who had grown up in relative luxury, was, the Porsche aside, something of an ascetic, the churchmouse-poor academic Kildall, in the first flush of cash, began indulging himself with the better things of life: house, hot tub, car, airplanes, a restaurant. Microsoft's office was all business, with no real frills beyond an occasional view of spectacular desert thunderstorms; Digital Research would be housed in a Victorian building, a former doctor's abode complete with good-looking secretaries, a resident ghost, and crackling logs in the fireplace.

The immediate business problem facing Bill Gates was that unlike his Standalone BASIC, which had a minimal operating system built in and thus could handle disk drives all by itself, his FORTRAN language required the CP/M operating system—which meant that the user would have to buy CP/M before FORTRAN would be of any value at all. In Kildall's hot tub not far from Monterey Bay, Gates was investigating not only the idea of a California move for Microsoft but also the possibility of some sort of merger with Digital Research.

The merger talks never got past initial feelers. And although Bill was in favor of a move to California, with Dallas/Fort Worth in the land of Radio Shack as a distant second choice, Paul Allen increasingly argued for a move back to familiar Seattle turf. Hiring might be simpler in Silicon Valley, but keeping employees would clearly be harder, a major consideration in a business where the primary assets walk out the door every night or, in Microsoft's case, the wee hours of the morning. The tremendous demand for their services had made Bay Area engineers notoriously fickle; at the first sign of dissatisfaction, they would find a position across the street or check out a "job fair" brimming with offers. Then there were the high housing prices, which meant higher salaries.

Luring top talent to Seattle might be tougher, but the University of Washington provided a decent base of trained computer scientists, and the gray Seattle skies reinforced the Microsoft ethic of work till you drop. Software firms were few and far between in the Northwest, so the work force would be more stable. Silicon Valley was only a hour and a half away by air. Besides, Seattle was home. Paul Allen missed the trees and the water and fishing with his father. And Allen made sure that Bill's parents let him know how happy they'd be to see him return to his native Northwest. "I don't think Bill really cared," said O'Rear. "The people that drove the decision, I think, were Paul —and Bill and Mary Gates."

They drove it fast. The official memo about the relocation came on March 13, 1978. The move was to take place around the end of the year, and Microsoft would acquire its own minicomputer for the first time: a DECsystem 2020, successor to the venerable PDP-10. The early decision was intended to blunt the bitter dissent that inevitably arose over the wisdom of the relocation.

In the legend that would grow over the years, the move from Albuquerque was often cited incorrectly as a reaction to Bill's troubles with his New Mexico driver's license. Although the advance notice clearly invalidates that rumor, its origin is understandable. The impromptu drag races, mad dashes to the airport, and other hot-wheeled adventures in and around Albuquerque had provided plenty of paperwork for local police. Miriam Lubow recalled Gates accumulating tickets so fast, "I'd worry about seeing headlines in the *Albuquerque Journal:* 'Bill Gates, president of Microsoft, behind bars!' "

One midnight joyride did the job. In the wee hours of the morning Paul Allen got a call from Bill that began "Got arrested." After being bailed out of the local drunk tank, Gates revealed he'd "kind of had a disagreement" with a traffic cop who had stopped him and demanded his license, which Bill had left in the apartment along with all his other ID. "I kept saying, 'Why do you need my driver's license?' " Gates told Allen, "trying to joke around," but the officer didn't chuckle. Bill's sense of humor was sorely tried, too, when it came to his fellow detainees: "They're like six feet away from me throwing up! I'm so mad!" he told Allen.

In another incident, Gates was tracked down after eluding pursuing officers. This time he had enough money to post bail, but that raised suspicions: "People that young aren't supposed to have that much money—it must mean they're doing something wrong." From that point on Bill was on the hit list of an officer "who thought I must be a drug dealer because that had to be the only way I could afford a Porsche." It was getting harder and harder for a young software guy in a green Porsche to drive at 120 miles an hour unnoticed.

Hot dry nights were sparkled by bottle rockets launched from the Gates digs toward Kirtland Air Force Base, which apparently never confused the nocturnal pranks with a Soviet invasion. Bill's personal hobbyhorse was watch-

ough binoculars. If a blaze looked promising, Gates would hop in
to check it out.

For a time there was chess, with Steve Wood as a rotating third, but in
Albuquerque Gates and Allen finally abandoned their longstanding chess rivalry, with most observers giving the nod to Allen as the net winner. An
aggressive player, Gates would launch initial assaults that Allen had learned to
weather and turn against his foe. As Allen recalled it, "He'd say, 'If I hadn't
made that third move, I would've won.' And I'd say, 'Yeah, but I had a
countermove for that.' 'No, you didn't, you know you didn't, I would've won
that.' And it just wasn't worth it. After a while, we just stopped playing."

Despite the gains in its fortunes, Microsoft still had a long way to go in its
recruiting techniques. The same Bob Wallace who had attended the World
Altair Convention and was now about to finish his master's degree at the
University of Washington walked into the Retail Computer Store where he
worked and discovered a photocopied page that Paul Allen had dropped off on a
trip to Seattle. The notice said, in effect, "Programmer Wanted." Wallace
flew down to Albuquerque and got the job.

Fresh from academe, he loved the challenge. "It wasn't like there was
pressure to work twelve-hour days. It's like you were an astronaut or something. You just kind of loved working so much." Microsoft's young cadre had
the freedom to experiment, to take an interesting new wrinkle or idea and run
with it. "I put in a lot of extra time trying to get the TI BASIC to do funny
little things. . . . In BASIC, you could bring up a line and edit the line. So
. . . suppose you wanted the same line somewhere else. Why can't you just
edit the line numbers? And it didn't work that way, so I worked a lot to get it
to work that way."

It was sink or swim: You were hired, given a job, and expected to do it.
Sometimes you were even expected to define it. And this policy extended
beyond the programmers. Office manager Steve Wood's wife Marla, already
legendary for her pet python, pitched in to help with the files even though her
entire clerical training had been a high school typing course. She eventually
would inherit the bookkeeping chores for the entire company from Miriam
Lubow.

No matter how generously you interpreted the Traf-O-Data experience,
the truth was that neither Gates nor Allen had ever managed a company before,
which put them on equal footing with their employees. Even phone duties were
evenly distributed: Callers with questions about BASIC would often be asked,
"You want to talk to the guy who wrote it?" When his hectic travel schedule
permitted, Gates worked on BASIC, checked on projects, and reviewed code,
mainly making suggestions for improvements rather than rewriting. Occasionally there were contests to see who could write a routine in the fewest bytes,

the kind of intellectual gamesmanship Bill had learned so well in the Gates family and now worked on his equally competitive staff.

The lack of hierarchy and formality meant that differences of opinion got resolved on the spot, often by the person who could yell the loudest, in the tradition of Lakeside computer room arguments over who deserved the most time on the terminal. For all his slightness of build and puppy-dog innocence, Gates could bellow with the best of them, and the apparently mellower Paul Allen was up there in the hollering Hall of Fame. Emotionally drained after winning or losing these shouting matches, a disgusted Allen would sometimes stalk out of the office until he and his longtime buddy had cooled off. As Marla Wood recalled, "We actually kind of liked it when Bill was out of town. It was much quieter around the office. Paul would yell, but five minutes later everything would be back to normal. He didn't go into the ragings that Bill would."

The Gates motivational method: You yell, you holler, you point out how stupid something is; the chastened subject goes back and redoubles his efforts to do a better job. It wasn't the gospel according to Dale Carnegie, but it seemed to do the trick. "I could write this in BASIC over the weekend," Gates was fond of telling his disciples. The subtext: Prove to me you're better. The self-motivated, hardcore programmers Gates hired would take the bait again and again. Somehow, partly through personal charisma, partly through the power of the dare, Gates got his legions to stick with him through all the noise. "He always wanted you to argue back," said Wallace. "It wasn't like personal. He would say 'That's stupid!' or 'That's brain-damaged!' or something like that, but it wasn't like you were stupid or brain-damaged."

Bill's insistence on getting things done left his early charges with the impression that he was more the doer, the deal-maker, while Allen was more the visionary able to scope out trends, divine the future. Gates's contribution was to walk into a roomful of suits, ignore their skeptical looks at his scrawny frame and adolescent demeanor, and pin their ears back with his command of the technology and marketplace. "He could waltz into places and knew so much more about their needs than they did," an Albuquerque employee remembered. An offhand comment such as "By the way, if you put the floppy drive there it will overheat" would break whatever corporate resistance the whippersnapper encountered and prove "that he knew his stuff better than they did and that they would be well advised to listen to him."

Slaving over computers and shouting about them can be thirsty work. Gates eventually instructed Miriam Lubow to keep Microsoft supplied with Coca-Cola. When a six-pack disappeared inside of five minutes, Bill explained that he was thinking more in terms of a case. "I had no idea that a company would give employees free drinks," Lubow said, but she began ordering directly from Coca-Cola anyway. Thus was instituted Microsoft's free Coke policy, a cornerstone of corporate culture that evolved over the years to include virtually any soft drink short of labor-intensive espresso. Instead of running out of the office or hunting up change for vending machines, employees with a powerful thirst could hit the fridge with no more than a minor derailment of their train of thought. Soft-drink consumption kept escalating, but ironically, Miriam Lubow herself was unable to take advantage of the policy. After developing a mysterious skin rash, she received medical orders to cease her Coke-a-day habit.

Whether in Coke or java, caffeine was the drug of choice, although it was by no means the only one. At parties where most of the staff would gather to watch "Saturday Night Live" or the premiere of *Battlestar Galactica* on Paul Allen's big-screen TV, joints would be passed. "It was probably the only time that nobody was at the company office," one programmer recalled. But although some indulged as a means of reducing the constant stress, by all accounts Microsoft was never among what one Albuquerque veteran called "drug-based companies."

And by all accounts, Gates's killer schedule and corrosive social skills kept him out of whatever dating scene Albuquerque had to offer. In this era, Microsoft was his only mistress.

It could be a cruel one. Bill's APL continued to exist only in an incomplete state on yellow legal pads in a desk drawer somewhere. In August, *Computerworld* put it this way:

> A spokeswoman for Microsoft . . . vehemently denied rumors such a product is nearly available for delivery.
>
> There is "no way" anyone will see the product in the third quarter of this year, she said in reaction to one version of the rumors. "It's not close. He's still writing it," she said.
>
> She refused to identify the developer or put callers in touch with him or anyone else associated with the company. She explained there had been "many calls" and the developer "just doesn't have time to talk" about the project.

The lack of an APL was hardly a make-or-break issue. Bill Gates really was busy—not just programming, but making contacts with customers. Chipmakers came calling. Intel wanted BASIC. National Semiconductor took BASIC and FORTRAN for its development systems. And COBOL was finally ready. Based on a design by a California consultant named Ken Sidell and programming by Ric Weiland, who had returned in January when Microsoft made the high bid for his services—$35,000 a year, which made him the highest-paid Microsoft employee by about 20 percent—Microsoft COBOL for the CP/M and Intel ISIS-II operating systems went out the door by midyear.

The money kept on rolling in. By April Microsoft had $233,000 in savings in the bank, with no real liabilities—and the ever-conservative Bill Gates forecast an April-to-April gross of nearly $1 million and a projected net of about $350,000. Even the MITS license was still generating dribs and drabs of cash.

But a shakeout in the fledgling industry was beginning to produce a string of bad debts. The $60,000 IMSAI owed for FORTRAN and BASIC would become uncollectable when the company went bankrupt. Other high flyers were being brought down to earth. Bill's money-up-front, flat-fee policy was being vindicated.

Despite the onslaught of contracts, 1978 would turn out to be most important for the people it brought to the doorstep of Bill Gates. First was Vern Raburn, a former Byte Shop franchisee who had discovered that "being a retailer sucks." Raburn had formed a small company to develop a decent BASIC for Processor Technology's Sol, one of the few major machines left that did not offer Microsoft's version. Raburn was no programmer, and as it turned out, the developers of his BASIC weren't, either: Their coding efforts had consisted mostly of changing the copyright statement in a pirated edition of Bill Gates's pride and joy.

In April, when Microsoft's lawyers contacted the unwitting Raburn with a "cease-and-desist" letter, he phoned Bill Gates. "And in his normal, tactful way," Raburn recalled, Gates said essentially that " 'You're ripping us off, and if you don't quit, I'm going to kill you.' " A meeting in Albuquerque convinced Raburn to dissolve his relationship with the pirates.

A month or so later Raburn turned up at GRT—Great Records and Tapes, a record distributor that at his prodding was trying to extend its reach to the world of computer software with a division known as G2. Raburn's BASIC was supposed to have been the first product, but when that blew up, he went on the payroll and acquired other software—biorhythm programs, diet programs, blackjack programs. Although packaged software had begun to appear on the market, it remained largely a mail-order enterprise except at the captive outlets of Radio Shack. It was Raburn who sold Bill Gates on the idea of getting into the retail software business.

Raburn convinced Gates to supply G2 with two customized versions of BASIC—one for the Sol and one for the Southwest Technical Products machines. But GRT's top-selling Microsoft product would be the one that took advantage of the hooks Bill had left in his initial TRS-80 Level II BASIC. Level III BASIC, sold at retail on cassette tape, added a slew of classic Microsoft BASIC features that had to be left out of the 12K ROM; it was an instant hit with TRS-80 users. The GRT deal was Microsoft's first tiny step into the world of retail software—a form of marketing that eventually would become the company's primary source of income. Bill Gates owed that part of Microsoft's vision to Vern Raburn.

But the year's most fateful meeting was with a Japanese wild man named Kazuhiko Nishi, better known as Kay. A native of Kobe, where his parents ran a private school for girls, Nishi had begun his fledgling publishing empire as an engineering student at Tokyo's Waseda University, where he cranked out a mimeographed computer newsletter, then dropped out to start a computer magazine called *ASCII*. Short and stocky, brash and outgoing, Nishi was a visionary with boundless energy, enthusiasm, and persuasiveness. His small company still was only a magazine publisher, but if anything, Nishi's ambitions were even broader than Bill's.

In spring 1978 he called the overseas operator from his office in Japan and asked to be put through to Microsoft in the United States. "Where is it?" the operator inquired.

Nishi took a guess. He was familiar with the Altair, and he remembered where MITS was located. "New Mexico."

"What city?"

"The biggest city in New Mexico," Nishi replied.

Moments later Nishi was talking to the "president" of Microsoft. Adopting his supersalesman manner, Nishi said let's do something with BASIC, come on over, he'd send a first-class ticket. Bill Gates was already involved in reasonably lucrative negotiations with Sord, Ai Electronics, Ricoh, and Matsushita Communications Industries, so the potential of the Japanese market was hardly news to him. He replied that he was kind of busy at the moment, but eventually agreed to meet for an hour at the National Computer Conference in Anaheim in June.

The one-hour meeting turned into a free-form eight-hour marathon. The twenty-two-year-old Gates and the twenty-two-year-old Nishi hit it off immediately. "For a guy from Japan, Kay's more like me than probably anybody I've ever met," Gates would later say. "Whatever you think I am, that's what Kay is . . . thinking, futuristic, energetic." Two days later Nishi visited Albuquerque and signed a two-page preliminary deal that would be formalized in October and lead to his becoming Microsoft's exclusive agent in the Far East under the name of ASCII Microsoft—for a 30 percent commission. Like the meeting with Raburn, it was an encounter whose fruits would take some time to ripen but eventually would grace a full-fledged money tree.

A third major meeting of the minds took place in the unlikely setting of St. Joseph, Michigan, home of the Heathkit. Befitting its role as a haven for soldering-iron types, Heath was now marketing its own computers, including a Z-80 machine with a homegrown edition of BASIC instead of the Microsoft version.

As Bill Gates was in the process of attempting to correct this egregious error, he was introduced to a black-haired gnome by the name of Gordon Letwin, who proceeded to chew him out in front of a group of about fifteen people. Letwin, the author of Heath's BASIC, felt his turf was being violated—and by the purveyor of an inferior product to boot. Bill Gates nonetheless prevailed, selling Heath his BASIC and FORTRAN for H-DOS, a proprietary operating system Letwin had developed for Heath. But Letwin had instinctively understood how to win the favor of William Henry Gates: Stand up to the guy. By the end of the year Gordon Letwin would come to work for Microsoft and begin work on a BASIC compiler.

One more key project had its beginnings in late 1978, when Microsoft hired Jim Lane, a burly, bearded software engineer who had cut his teeth on microcomputers with The Digital Group, a pioneering but ultimately luckless Denver outfit. Lane's job was to write a DEC simulator for a new 16-bit chip: Intel's 8086. At the same time, Bob O'Rear set to work on a translator to turn the 8080 BASIC into 8086 code.

Sixteen-bit microprocessors were the wave of the future: Motorola announced its 68000, Zilog had its Z-8000, and Intel was pushing its 8086. Each would be a major leap from what had gone before. Not only were these chips faster than their predecessors, but they had significantly improved instruction sets and architectures. Beyond that was a more crucial point: Each of these chips could directly address vastly more memory than the old 8-bitters. Even the 8086, the worst in this regard, could handle 1 megabyte of memory—more than 1 million characters. The number seemed unimaginably huge in a day when the typical Apple II or Commodore PET or TRS-80 machine could handle no more than 64K and typically came with 4K or 16K. But Moore's Law was still working its inexorable magic; in fact, somewhere along the line Moore had updated it to state that now the density of computer chips doubled or prices halved every eighteen months.

At the time, none of the new-generation microprocessors was yet available. The 8086 seemed the reasonable candidate for the first new simulator because it seemed likely to be delivered first. But in fall 1978, not even the manuals were ready. Lane and O'Rear had to work from Xerox copies of notes from the Intel engineers who were designing the chip. There was no real hurry, since the chip itself was still a long way off, yet in the pressure-cooker atmosphere that prevailed at Microsoft, there was always a sense of urgency to get the job done. Like the original 6502 work, the 8086 project was done entirely on spec in an attempt to get ahead of the hardware curve. Like later similar projects, it was an educated gamble that would take much longer to pay dividends than anyone realized at the time—but would reap a fortune when it eventually did pay off.

To suitably immortalize the Albuquerque years, Bob Greenberg cut a deal with a photo studio for a group portrait on December 7. Pearl Harbor Day in Albuquerque featured a snowstorm, but only Miriam Lubow, who was stranded at home with her kids, and Ric Weiland, out of town on business, failed to make the sitting. All eleven of the employees in the Albuquerque picture, along with Weiland, were about to make the trip to Seattle. Only Miriam Lubow would stay behind—reluctantly. Gates offered to pay for her and her family's move to Seattle, but Miriam's husband demurred: "He said, 'Why are we going to follow this kid to Seattle? It always rains in Seattle.' " On a Concorde flight to Europe, Gates wrote her a thank-you note for her service to Microsoft. As it turned out, she was merely postponing the inevitable. Three years later Miriam would move to the Seattle area and work again for Microsoft, this time focusing more narrowly on a skill she had developed in Albuquerque: getting customers to pay up.

In December Microsoft finished its first million-dollar sales year— $1,355,665, to be exact. Then it was off to greener and wetter pastures in the great Northwest. "I was leaving Albuquerque and doing eighty," Bob Wallace recalled. "I remember looking in my rearview mirror and saw this little tiny green dot. It got bigger and bigger, and he passed me and he must have been going ninety or a hundred." It was Bill Gates, on his way to Seattle via at least three speeding tickets—including, as he would tell it, two from the same cop on the same day on his way to Silicon Valley to visit the makers of a computer called the Umtech Video Brain.

The first ticket on I-5 was a routine 110 miles an hour. The second time, "I handed him my license, and he said 'I don't need to see that.' I looked at the guy; they're all generic. And then I realized that this is the same guy, and he says, 'Come on, sit in the back of my car,' and he talked to me for a long time, saying that you know, double the national speed limit was a whole different thing than normal speeding." In Microsoft legend, where Bill Gates stories were beginning to acquire larger-than-life proportions, the incident would eventually come to include a third ticket from the same cop.

10

WE SELL PROMISES

In fast-growing Bellevue, a suburban city just east of Seattle across mile-wide Lake Washington, Microsoft settled into much larger quarters on the eighth floor of the relatively new Old National Bank building. Miriam Lubow had made sure the new suite was given the official number 819, in homage to the Albuquerque original. In another bit of historical whimsy, Bill Gates asked for the phone number 455-8080, the last four digits in tribute to the chip responsible for Microsoft's initial success. And Gates settled into a large corner office with a panoramic view of the mountains and the lake.

Bellevue was still on the sleepy side of a transition from cow pastures and horse trails to edge-city suburbanville, but none of its relaxed atmosphere rubbed off on the software soldiers from Albuquerque. After a welcome-to-the-Northwest party hosted by Bill's parents in Laurelhurst, it was nose to the grindstone. Led by the example of Bill the Indefatigable, who had an office couch where he'd curl up for catnaps, and with a DECsystem 2020 of their very own, the troops worked round the clock. Marla and Steve Wood defined the working couple of the 1980s before the decade even arrived, going to work so early and returning home so late that they rarely saw their new house in daylight. For lunch breaks Marla would run across the street to a hamburger joint for "gut bombs—real greasy hamburgers, on these little wax-paper kind of holders with the grease kind of dripping." Shakes and sundaes and the company-supplied sodas provided plenty of sucrose to keep the codesmiths cranking. The Northwest felt right.

The business was still pretty much what it always had been: selling mini-computer languages for microprocessors. By March Microsoft boasted forty-eight OEM customers for its 8080 BASIC and twenty-nine for FORTRAN, numbers that had more than doubled in less than a year. The new COBOL had a dozen takers. Increasingly the customers were making computers, but there were also chipmakers, terminal makers, and even makers of microprocessor-controlled machine tools and aluminum smelting equipment.

In the second corner office was Microsoft's new marketing director, a smooth, slick MBA named Steve Smith who had moved north from Portland's Tektronix, where he'd been responsible for getting Microsoft to develop a Pascal compiler. Surprise! "When I got to Microsoft from Tektronix, I discovered that they not only didn't have Pascal, they didn't even have the project really planned. So I had just experienced my first purchase of vaporware" —a term that had yet to be coined, and one in which Bill Gates would play a starring role—"and suddenly I became the person who now had to deliver vaporware to my former employer, who by the way had just fired me."

Smith quickly learned that it was just the way Bill Gates did business. "We could sell a promise and pull it off, because we had the money and the smart technical people and the commitment. And virtually everything that we sold was not a product when we sold it. We sold promises."

There were plenty of new promises in development, with McDonald working on a macro assembler, Letwin on the BASIC compiler, and Wallace on Pascal. The biggest customer, brought in just as Kay Nishi came on board, was Ricoh, which made a Z-80 based business computer for sale in Japan and essentially "bought everything"—BASIC, FORTRAN, and COBOL—for the biggest total deal thus far, $120,000. On April 4 Microsoft received its first corporate recognition from the industry. Its BASIC became the first microcomputer software product to win the Million Dollar Award given by International Computer Programs (ICP).

Smith came to realize the significance of the OEM business as the eyes and ears of the company. "In a sense what we were doing was integrating the information from all the OEM companies and trying to give them a common solution without telling them 'This guy said this and this guy said that.' So eventually we had more knowledge than anybody."

Bill Gates wasn't afraid to use it. Smith recalled customers "talking to me because I'd have a suit on or something and I was a little older, and frankly they really thought that Bill was my tech support guy. It wasn't until finally I'd toss a question to him and say 'What do you think of that, Bill?' And they'd either catch on at that point or when he'd just kind of open up and it was like drinking out of a fire hose." That phrase—"drinking out of a fire hose"— would eventually come to be a catchword at Microsoft, symbolizing both the CEO's "bandwidth" and the rigors of the company work ethic.

In Seattle Bill's driving habits finally caught up with him. Down in Albuquerque, his New Mexico license had come perilously close to revocation, and he had switched to his new Washington State card. But with a couple of leftover violations from Albuquerque, three from the trip north, and a bunch in his old hometown, Gates was nailed. "Now, *now* they decide they're gonna forward their stuff to Washington State," an exasperated Gates told Allen. "Just when I get tickets." According to Gates, he was restricted for ninety days to driving to and from work only—not much of a problem for a born workaholic. Chris Larson briefly ended up being his personal chauffeur—and, on one occasion, his personal scapegoat. As Gates remembered it, "An officer pulled me over, and we just traded seats, and that guy hadn't looked at what was going on. And Chris could afford the ticket and I couldn't."

At Microsoft, 1979 became the year of Japan. Back in Albuquerque, the first customer Nishi brought through the doors had been Kazuya "Ted" Watanabe, from the staid, giant Nippon Electric Company—NEC. Gates and Larson met him at the airport in Bill's Porsche; after a high-speed ride back to the offices, Gates and Allen convinced him they knew their stuff. Watanabe later said, "I always felt that only young people could develop software for personal computers—people with no tie, working with a Coke and a hamburger—only such people could make a personal computer adequate for other young people."

So this time Microsoft would not only write the software; it would have a hand in designing the machine as well. "Kay was very interested in getting involved with the customer's machine design, and he had lots of little suggestions," one Microsoftie remembered. "Kay was very instrumental in helping us really form design partnerships with these companies where we'd work together on the design of the machine."

In Japan the NEC PC-8001 "was the equivalent of sort of the Commodore PET and the Apple II and the TRS-80 all rolled into one." Whereas those three machines fought tooth and nail for market share in the United States, NEC "just kind of walked away with the marketplace." The head start NEC managed to get for its machine quickly led to the company's strong dominance of the personal computer business in Japan, with market share topping 50 percent.

This new kind of business relationship would set a pattern for the future, one that would soon come in handy with a big, staid American company that was also known by three letters:

> The Japanese always seemed to be much better at listening to our suggestions than the American companies were. We'd say, "Gee . . . put some graphics in there," and they'd do it. We'd suggest that to the American companies, and they'd say, "Oh, well, we already designed it, too late." Or "It's gonna be too expensive." And so in the case of the American companies it was more "Okay, here's the hardware, go do the BASIC for it." In the case of the Japanese companies, we were much more involved in actually shaping some of the hardware aspects of the machine.

Soon NEC's Japanese competitors came calling with deals at prices so elevated that even after Nishi's commission the licenses were typically more lucrative than American arrangements.

If Nishi and Japan and the international market set the stage for new revenue sources, so did a program that had one of its earliest incarnations as a demonstration written in Applesoft BASIC on an Apple II computer. Wiry, soft-spoken programmer and Harvard Business School student Dan Bricklin, and stocky, spiky Bob Frankston, the two principals of a fledgling attic-based firm called Software Arts, had developed a program they originally called Calculedger, because it was sort of a cross between a calculator and a ledger sheet. By the time they showed it publicly for the first time at the West Coast Computer Faire in May, they had renamed the program VisiCalc. Although there had been mainframe computer programs that could with great effort do similar things, VisiCalc was the first true computer spreadsheet—and the single biggest innovation in microcomputer software.

Although the initial reaction was moderately cool, VisiCalc was the kind of program that created enthusiasts, evangelists, even though it was still months away from being released. Nobody had ever seen anything like it. As an early beta tester—someone who tries out a prerelease version of a product—Vern Raburn had become fanatic about VisiCalc and was the first person to show it to Bill Gates. GRT's fiscal state had been far too dire for Raburn's $50,000 worth of monthly software revenues to save the company from bankruptcy, and Raburn was now out of work and urging Bill to get into end-user applications software in a big way—by buying Personal Software and installing him to run it. An enterprise headed by Dan Fylstra, a one-time student of Bricklin's, Personal Software was marketing the popular Micro Chess software and had acquired exclusive rights to the forthcoming VisiCalc. Gates and Fylstra engaged in serious discussions about the merger; at the last minute, negotiations fell apart.

Gates had succinctly summed up Microsoft's policy in an internal memo: ''We do not talk to any End Users.'' End users—the people who actually ended up working with software—had never been Bill Gates's favorite people. End users tied up the phone with stupid questions. End users stole software. Microsoft's flat-fee OEM deals minimized its exposure to piracy by those same questionable end users. Gates was far happier dealing with OEM customers and letting them handle the rabble.

Nonetheless, Raburn still believed he and Microsoft had a future selling software directly to end users. Over Memorial Day weekend Raburn visited Bill at his grandmother's house on Hood Canal, brought along a business plan, and proposed that Microsoft start publishing software. By the end of June 1979 Raburn was made president of Microsoft Consumer Products. Initially the plan was to make MCP—an unfortunate choice of acronym—a distinct organization under the Microsoft umbrella, with its own logo and its own facility, in part to avoid potential clashes with the OEM customers who were the lifeblood of the rest of the company. A lease was signed for space in Santa Clara, in the heart of Silicon Valley, near where Raburn was living. The buildout was begun, a sign was prepared—and then Bill Gates got cold feet. Gates told Raburn he was uncomfortable with the idea of managing a location 800 miles away, Microsoft scrambled to shed the lease, and MCP was installed in Bellevue. The logo, separate office space, and a separate checkbook were all that remained of the initial separation-of-powers doctrine. From then until now, virtually all product development at Microsoft would be done in Seattle under the watchful eye of the CEO who felt vaguely insecure about losing control of his products.

MCP's first release took place in December of 1979. Its initial product line included the TRS-80 Level III BASIC from Microsoft as well as the independently developed Typing Tutor, an instructional program that Raburn had been in on from the beginning when GRT had sold it. Unlike many entrepreneurs, Bill Gates had no objection to buying or licensing something when he didn't have the resources to build it. The only question was the price.

There was also Adventure, a game wherein the intrepid keyboard voyager could traverse a Tolkienesque virtual labyrinth known as Colossal Cave via such terse commands as GO NORTH, DROP GOLD, HIT TROLL. It had originated on Stanford minicomputers in the late 1960s and had been knocking around the computer world ever since. Microsoft programming wizard Gordon Letwin, who'd already tackled the BASIC compiler and was now wrestling with Pascal, had done his own adaptation of Adventure back in his Heath days. In Seattle Letwin had been teasing Paul Allen about his new car, and Allen shot back that if Letwin wanted to make some extra money, why not sell a version of Adventure?

Such moonlighting was against unofficial Microsoft policy—Gates, supposedly the computer-in-every-home guy, discouraged his own employees from that proposition, because they might be tempted to expend valuable brainpower on non-Microsoft projects. Letwin and Gates locked horns over Adventure; in the end, the program went out with Raburn's Microsoft Computer Products logo, and Letwin was paid a royalty on every copy. It was the first and last time in recorded history that Bill Gates ever paid any of his employees for a product they had created in their off hours. Among the other programmers, resentment festered.

Letwin and Raburn had taken an instant dislike to each other. The rift was exacerbated by the fact that both had been installed in the "400 building" offices a few blocks from Microsoft headquarters. Letwin, the consummate engineer, considered Raburn a nontechnical self-promoter and took offense at everything from his expensive furniture to the personal biographies he sent out. What particularly galled Letwin was Raburn's attempt to assign him to a smaller office than his own. "I argued that if Vern's butt was too good to sit in a regular-sized office, then mine was too." The Solomonic solution? The company "moved the interior wall over some small amount." Letwin paid for it.

Gates understood that technical guys weren't the only ones who had ideas to contribute. Raburn was a key figure in a project that began with the idea of offering Microsoft FORTRAN and COBOL for the Apple II computer and its underwhelming 6502 chip. As Raburn remembered it, "I was the only Apple user in the whole company. The view of people at Microsoft was that CP/M machines were real machines, the TRS-80 was an interesting toy machine, and the Apple II was a real toy." From the Memorial Day meeting onward, even before he joined the company in June, he kept pushing Gates and Allen to find a way to put FORTRAN and COBOL on the Apple II. "Paul and Bill were busy telling me how hard it was to write a compiler on the 6502 . . . and I kept saying 'Yeah, yeah, yeah, but we gotta get it onto this machine.' "

On the way to lunch with Bill one day, Paul Allen came up with the solution: hardware! Allen proposed a board that would plug into the Apple II and run the Z-80 editions of FORTRAN and COBOL that Microsoft already had. As Raburn recalled, "He said, 'I think what we can do is plug a processor on, and then we can just patch it into the Apple operating system, so that we're actually running on the Z-80, but it looks like you're running under Apple.' And I said, 'Sounds good to me.' "

In the process of doing yet another dull language derived from the mini-computer world, Allen had come up with a radical solution and an entirely new product. The SoftCard, as it would eventually be named, would be the first Microsoft product that wasn't a mere adaptation or extension of some mini-computer language or programming tool. The SoftCard was a different way to skin the cat: Instead of rewriting its compilers, Microsoft would offer hardware that let users run the compilers it had already written.

The SoftCard was one of Microsoft's rare wholly original ideas; Gates would later admit that it probably could and should have been patented. It was a double win: Not only would it likely save precious development time, it would provide a new source of revenue.

But that prospective income was way out in the future. As things turned out, the SoftCard project was anything but simple. For openers, Microsoft did not have a single hardware expert on staff. But there was one hardware engineer who had been hanging around the offices a lot and had developed some cards of his own.

Tim Paterson, an intense, elfin, bearded alumnus of the University of Washington and the Retail Computer Store, was an employee at Seattle Computer Products, a mom-and-pop outfit run out of suburban Tukwila by a jack-of-all-trades named Rod Brock and supplying mostly memory cards for S-100-

bus computers. In late 1978 a sales rep for the local Intel distributor had put a bug in Brock's ear about a seminar covering the forthcoming 8086 chip. The seminar convinced Brock to set Paterson to work on developing a CPU—central processing unit—card for the S-100 bus. The idea was that you could yank your tired old 8-bit 8080 or Z-80 CPU and replace it with Seattle Computer's state-of-the-art, high-speed 8086 model. But once Paterson had his two-card solution designed and built, there was no software to run on it except his own assembler, debugger, and monitor.

Paterson gave Microsoft a call. No one at Microsoft had ever seen an 8086, but they had a few things almost as important: a commitment to develop software for the chip, the DEC-based simulator of it—and an 8086 version of Standalone BASIC that Bob O'Rear had translated from the 8080 edition. Paterson drove up Lake Washington with a Cromemco Z-2 S-100 box in the backseat, and quite possibly the world's only 8086 CPU boardset inside it.

At Microsoft's offices, O'Rear brought his 8086 BASIC down to the 8-inch floppy drives of the Cromemco box and ran it on an actual 8086 chip for the very first time. A couple of minor bugs in his translation from the 8080 version —largely due to errors in the Intel documentation explaining the correspondences between 8080 code and 8086 code—initially kept the BASIC from running. With the help of Paterson's homebrewed debugger, the two solved the problems, and by the end of the day Microsoft BASIC was running on the 8086 machine. The feat earned Paterson a trip to the June National Computer Conference in New York.

For the 1979 convention, Microsoft shared a booth with Lifeboat Associates, the biggest vendor of CP/M software. CP/M, for all its claims of being a standard, was a standard only in the most charitable sense of the term. Machines were wildly incompatible—buses differed, disk formats differed, keyboards differed, printers differed—so there were in effect dozens of different flavors of CP/M, all requiring programs to be adapted in one way or another to get them to run. Microsoft offered CP/M versions of its languages and worked on customizations with its OEM customers, but that left plenty of machines it didn't support directly. Lifeboat licensed the languages from Microsoft and did the tweaking for those machines.

But in the Lifeboat booth that year, the most forward-looking product had nothing to do with CP/M. Microsoft's Standalone BASIC was running on Tim Paterson's 8086 Seattle Computer CPU. The cleanly engineered second prototype was displayed on top of the table, mainly because it didn't work yet. The original version, with gobs of unsightly wire-wrap all over it, actually did work, so it was tucked away inside the computer underneath the table. The demonstration was interesting but not dazzling; since the BASIC was a brute-force translation from 8-bit code, the 16-bit machine didn't appear to be much faster than competitive 8-bitters.

That conference was notable also for Microsoft's first corporate party, complete with bottle rockets being set off from the windows of the Plaza Hotel. Eventually Kay Nishi showed up in the hospitality suite with an assortment of customers from Japan who had not managed to find rooms. Chris Larson, temporary director of entertainment, suavely took charge and ordered seven rollaway beds that were eventually brought to the room by a procession of puzzled bellhops, each of whom Larson grandly gave a $10 bill. The accommodations were adequate, except for one Japanese gentleman carrying $20,000 in cash, who insisted on sleeping in the closet. Gates and Company then repaired across the street to the Playboy Club, where his money-saving practice of renewing his membership only in alternate years caught up with him when the doorkeepers noticed that the card had expired.

It was at that conference, over drinks, that Paterson learned about a project Marc McDonald had been working on since the Albuquerque days—an operating system called MIDAS. Strictly for 8-bit computers, it wasn't something Paterson could run on his 16-bit CPU, but it was designed to have all sorts of nifty features. What interested Paterson wasn't the operating system but its file system—a variant of McDonald's Standalone BASIC File Allocation Table (FAT) scheme. It interested Paterson because he knew that one of these days he'd need an operating system of his own for his cards. When he'd contacted Digital Research to find out when their version of CP/M for the 8086 chip was coming, he'd been told December.

While waiting for the 16-bit operating system to appear, Paterson had some time on his hands. So Paul Allen hired him as a consultant to develop Microsoft's new hardware product for the Apple II, then dubbed the Z-80 Card. The initial plan was to have the board run customized versions of Microsoft's Z-80 languages in the "background," while the Apple's 6502 chip managed the rest of the show, but when the limitations of Apple's primitive operating system became clear, Raburn came up with the better idea of having the Z-80 chip run CP/M.

Still, the project began as a comedy of errors. As Raburn remembered it: "We went through like 178 different revs [revisions], and we could never get the thing to work. It took us four revs to figure out that the 6502 was a dynamic device," one that would not retain its memory without constant "refresh" signals. "Tim didn't know that, so every time we would switch . . . you know, we'd put the 6502 to sleep, switch to the Z-80, and when we came back to the 6502, the system would crash." For Allen, the hardware enthusiast, it was an unpleasant reminder of the endless delays in the construction of the Traf-O-Data machine.

There was also the question of software; nobody at Microsoft had much experience with the Apple machine. But the answer had literally walked through the door a couple of months earlier in the form of Neil Konzen, a big, affable, goofy high school senior who had gotten deep enough into the mysteries of the Apple to have written a program editor for it that he was selling through the mail. When he read in *Byte* that Microsoft, the originators of the amazing Applesoft BASIC, had moved to his hometown of Bellevue, he got on his bike and rode right over.

Konzen was first handed to Mike Courtney: The man who had turned Bill on to APL was now working at Microsoft. Konzen explained that he was working on a project to enhance Applesoft BASIC and that he had disassembled the code—a task somewhat akin to taking a watch apart to see exactly how it works. He wanted to speed up his programs, so he requested a peek at the Applesoft source code, which would make things easier. Within minutes he had talked his way into audiences with Paul Allen, Ric Weiland, and Bill Gates.

Konzen was a curious character, but he clearly knew his stuff. Still, to Microsoft the source code was the family jewels. Gates agreed to show Konzen the listings provided he would swear not to give away any trade secrets. That evening Konzen was still high from the meeting. "Back then, nobody had heard of this computer stuff. I was beside myself—you know, just being able to go up there and check out these listings! . . . So, naturally I went back under more excuses and guises."

Konzen and Gates hit it off. Neil managed to impress Bill by pointing out such things as a bug in the line-drawing routine for the TRS-80 BASIC. And Konzen was captivated with the adolescent élan of the company and the man. Walking down the hallway or during a slow spot in a meeting, Bill would spontaneously leap in the air and try to touch the ceiling. Konzen and a friend once found Bill bouncing on a minitrampoline in Microsoft's lobby and warned him to be careful or he might hit his head. "I can hit my head if I want to," Bill said without missing a beat. "It's my company!"

Konzen kept going back: Eventually he was offered a part-time job working on the software side of Paul Allen's Apple II hardware venture. But because the hardware wasn't anywhere near ready, Konzen marked time on a variety of other projects. By the end of the year, when the hardware began to work at least some of the time, Konzen began adding enhancements to the rather barebones CP/M BASIC, putting in features and color graphics to make it competitive with Applesoft—and stepping on the toes of other variants being developed at the same time from the single gargantuan BASIC source file. "We would constantly screw each other over," Konzen remembered. "As a beginner, I screwed other people more than they screwed me."

The Z-80 SoftCard had its first public demonstration at Microsoft's booth at the West Coast Computer Faire in March 1980—leading Zilog to demand that its "Z-80" trademark be deleted from the name forthwith. Still, the booth attracted tremendous crowds despite the product's obvious failings. "The total marketing was one brochure . . . and we had one little round thing that was stuck on the wall. It said 'CP/M for the Apple,' " Raburn remembered. "We had this version that would work for an hour or so, and then it would crash, and we didn't know why. And I had gotten really frustrated . . . didn't feel like we were ever going to get something working."

Earlier Raburn had hired a California hardware wizard named Don Burtis to give an opinion on the design of the card. "He'd come back and told us this is the biggest piece of shit in the world. So Paul and I actually sat up in the seats there in Brooks Hall, the auditorium in San Francisco, looking down at this booth with hundreds of people crowded around it, and negotiated with this guy to do a complete new design of this card."

There was another problem. According to Raburn, getting a license for CP/M from Gary Kildall's Digital Research "was Bill's task on this project. He was supposed to get the license, and he never had. So we're announcing this thing at Computer Faire, and Bill's trying to track down Gary to get the license for this thing we're showing." Gates offered a royalty, but Kildall demanded a flat fee—$75,000 in time payments, or about $50,000 in cash. Gates took the cash deal. As with some of Microsoft's early contracts, the fully-paid up-front sure thing turned out to be a bad bet—in this case, for Digital Research, because the SoftCard would go on to sell more than 100,000 units after its 1980 release. Microsoft's one duty under the agreement was to send Digital Research the registration cards. According to Raburn, "they used to wait every month for those things to come in, because they were just looking for a way to break that contract."

But SoftCard was by no means the only Microsoft project in the works. During 1979, the company's work force had more than doubled. Bill Gates had developed a schedule worthy of the perpetual motion Kay Nishi machine— programming, traveling, evangelizing, and selling, selling, selling. On rare occasions he was even dealing with the remains of Traf-O-Data, which, by now mostly in the hands of Chris Larson, was gasping its last despite a new computer scavenged from Microsoft and entirely new Larson-designed software. By May Paul Gilbert was writing erstwhile clients, such as the Public Works Department of the city of Tukwila, that "sporadic business coupled with equipment reliability problems" had forced the partnership to "suspend business." Gates would later claim that Traf-O-Data had grossed $20,000 or $30,000 per year. Less than $10,000 over its lifetime was closer to the truth.

In the traffic world Bill was a bust; in the business world he was beginning to attract attention. Early in June 1979 ADDS, his longtime customer, had made overtures about a business merger. Later that month there were similar discussions with Seymour Rubinstein of MicroPro, which had just released a CP/M word processing program called WordStar that was about to become a supernova in the applications field.

In August Gates visited Dallas and the headquarters of Electronic Data

Systems, the giant computer service company headed by H. Ross Perot—in a sense the Mr. Software of mainframes—who had become interested in the fledgling microcomputer industry and its leading citizens. The year before, Perot had sent a lieutenant named Joe Glover on a scouting trip to Albuquerque and had also made overtures to Apple. Now EDS was contacting Bill Gates about the possibility of a buyout.

"He flew down to Dallas, got his hair cut at an airport barbershop, to go out and visit. And he came back with an offer to purchase this company. It was an amazing thing," Bill's mother recalled.

Gates met first with Glover and EDS president Mort Meyerson, the one EDS executive who had risen through the ranks from the technical side. Gates recalled, "We thought, 'Hey, these guys can help take micros into big corporations . . . and really get these guys to proliferate the micro-based idea.' " But after "some interesting talks," Gates was lukewarm about the deal. "I was very bowled over by their size and everything, but when we talked about the product vision it was just strange. They weren't really thinking about it."

In retrospect, Meyerson agreed. "I think Bill expected a lot more at that phase of the game, and I think we did not have the leap of faith. Nobody had the vision of where it would go."

Later in the day, Bill met with Perot. "It's this big office on top of this building," Gates recalled. "He had this kind of anteroom to this big office with very fancy stuff—an American eagle, the flag, and all these famous pictures." Then "this guy comes out, and he's this little tiny guy, [from] a special elevator." As Gates remembered it, Perot asked him, "If I buy this, will I make money? Why would you sell?"

As Perot remembered it years later, "There was no division at all in terms of our interest and our sense that he would build a great company, and our sense that he was absolutely on the right track with what he was doing." The division was over money; in Perot's opinion, Bill wanted too much of it—somewhere between $40 and $60 million in Perot's recollection, somewhere between $6 and $15 million in Bill's.

Perot wound up kicking himself over the deal. "I should have just said, now Bill, you set the price, and I'll take it," Perot said. "That's what I should have done, and I've always regretted that we didn't get together. . . I consider it one of the biggest business mistakes I've ever made." Gates "has never kidded me about that, but I think if the shoe were on the other foot, I'd probably needle him."

As for Bill, "I don't think he gave it any kind of serious thought at all," his mother recalled. "I gave it a *lot* of serious thought: 'Son, now let's talk about this again! Just think what you could do, the flexibility that you'd have in your life.' "

"I sent them a nice 'No' letter," Bill Gates pointed out.

Later that month Gates and Allen made a two-week trip to Japan, where Nishi hosted them in royal fashion, used them to drum up more business, and involved them in the public launch of the NEC PC-8001, featuring Microsoft BASIC in ROM. The highlights of the journey, as guitarist Paul Allen remembered them: meeting John Lennon and Yoko Ono in an elevator in the Hotel Okura and watching Bill Gates insist on showing off from a fifteen-foot diving tower in front of a gaggle of gigglers at the girls' school Nishi's parents owned in Osaka.

Before and after the trip Gates found himself involved in two of the odder projects in Microsoft history, under the intermittent direction of a counterculture figure and legitimate businessman named Blair Newman. The curly-haired, hyperactive Newman was a character who could have been bred only in California. He had scored his first success running an outfit called Amorphia, which sold Acapulco Gold rolling paper and plowed its profits into a drive to legalize marijuana. After a stint at Harvard Business School, he eventually hooked up with Shugart Associates, the developer of the 5¼-inch disk drive that made microcomputers more than a toy, and turned up later at Apple Computer. At both companies he was seen as a visionary with brilliant ideas and an utter inability to execute them. According to one associate, he was "one of the flakiest guys I've ever known; he had the attention span of a gnat." He was also a drug abuser, an abrasive personality, and, as one former roommate later put it, "combative and competitive."

Bill Gates was no stranger to drugs, combat, or competition. He and Newman met on the speaking circuit at one of the many conferences where America's corporate giants were paying big coin to try to figure out how they could make a few bucks off the burgeoning small-computer revolution. Gates was having trouble pulling together a speech, and Newman helped solve the problem. The two became fast friends.

Newman cut a wide swath in the computer industry; the way he told it, he seemed to know everybody. And he certainly shared and molded Bill's vision of home computers sneaking into every household any day now. But Newman claimed to know exactly how it would happen: disguised as typewriters. In his Shugart days Newman had somehow discovered a Kansas City inventor named Craig Rooney, who had patented designs for a printhead and keyboard. Newman was going to combine the new technologies in a unit called Microtype— an electronic typewriter/computer printer that could be expanded with a cornucopia of optional extras into a full-fledged personal computer. In an era when the choice was between dot-matrix printers that cost $750 and produced godawful copy that looked and sounded as if it had been hammered onto the page with tiny rivets, and humongous $3,000 state-of-the-art daisy-wheel printers that produced typewriter-quality output with the silence of a machine gun, Newman's $250 unit sounded attractive enough for Gates to kick $25,000 of Microsoft money into Microtype, Inc.

After reviewing the proposal, Japan's giant Matsushita ponied up $20,000 and then another $60,000 in exchange for exclusive rights to negotiate for the machine. Microtype was nonetheless woefully undercapitalized. Microsoft eventually kicked in a second $25,000 and loaned Kay Nishi $100,000 for a personal investment. Alas, the patents were less successful in reality than in concept, and the entire undertaking was headed directly for oblivion. The state of the project was eventually clarified when Newman tried to convince a board member that cocaine costs ought to be considered a legitimate business expense.

But Microtype was only one of Newman's big ideas. His other enthusiasm was something called the Home Bus. The idea, as expressed in an early document, was that "by the end of the 1980s, experts predict microprocessors will be a part of almost every electrical consumer product selling for more than $20." The logical extension of this prediction—which actually turned out to be more or less true—was that for virtually no additional cost, these microprocessors could be designed to communicate with each other, forming "a modular intelligent network . . . the central nervous system of the microcomputerized home of the future."

Shades of the 1962 Seattle World's Fair! "Energy Conservation . . . Personal Safety . . . Convenience." With Home Bus, you could remotely control everything from your blender to your hot tub. Newman's Home Bus Standards Association, in conjunction with the research firm SRI International, would develop a single home bus standard that everyone could agree on, and chipmakers and home computer makers would jump gleefully on board. Bill Gates was one of the Association's original three directors.

An outfit called 3Com, masterminded by Robert Metcalfe, who had invented the seminal Ethernet computer network in his Xerox days, was doing Home Bus consulting for General Electric. The idea was that GE would produce its own computer—code name Homer—that could via some sort of network—Home Bus!—control all the GE toasters and blenders and dishwashers in the house. At Newman's advice, Metcalfe brought Bill Gates to a meeting with top GE executives at the San Francisco airport, where Gates explained what his company had done with such firms as NEC and offered his design services for GE's new machine—a project the company ultimately killed.

All this led in mid-1980 to a briefing with top executives of Sears, Roebuck. The concept Newman was pitching was something called Sears Tech Centers, complete with satellite dishes on the roof, where America could shop for a Microtype and a computer or three. Bill Gates and Kay Nishi were along to suggest that Sears might be able to put its label on one of the Japanese personal machines they knew so well. Industry consultant and retail expert Portia Isaacson rang in with her perspective. Bob Metcalfe pitched the Home Bus story.

"It all boils down to this," Nishi said, writing his summation on an overhead projector. "Act quickly and make no mistakes." Each of the quick-acting, punctilious Sears executives took out a pen and copied this wisdom down. In the end, the Sears meeting led to a rejection of the ideas that were being pushed but an expressed desire to explore computer retailing—and somehow to work with Bill Gates.

The machine that Newman was pitching was probably the one Bill Gates and his crew had fallen in love with—the Oki IF-800. The Oki machine was another Gates/Nishi collaboration where the engineers had paid close attention. It included not only high-resolution color graphics but also a built-in printer that could copy the screen exactly, though in black and white. Oki BASIC, developed at Microsoft by Bill Gates and a programmer named Marc Wilson, included jazzy new features such as PAINT, DRAW, and CIRCLE graphics commands and "turtle graphics" derived from Seymour Papert's Logo teaching language. Under the rubric "Microsell," Newman was proposing to import the Oki machine for the American market; even though the idea never got past the proposal stage and the Oki was never imported, the machine's seminal influence would eventually reverberate throughout the PC world.

Newman was indirectly involved in a watershed Microsoft event: the hiring of Steve Ballmer, the old Harvard Fox Club crony of Bill Gates. Upon graduation, Ballmer had been accepted to the Stanford Business School but decided to defer his entry for a year or two and do a stint in the employ of Procter and Gamble in Cincinnati. While ironing out the test-market launch of something called Coldsnap Freezer Dessert Maker in Dallas and Denver in the fall of 1978, he paid a quick, unexceptional visit to Bill Gates in Albuquerque. Ballmer later worked on the marketing of Duncan Hines mixes: brownie and blueberry muffins and Moist 'n' Easy Snack Cake. It was the kind of position where a major achievement would be reorienting the boxes horizontally to command more shelf space.

In early 1979 Ballmer checked out the movie business. His efforts on a hologram project at Universal, parking cars at charity auctions, doing script evaluations for NBC, and kicking around for a few months convinced him that he didn't want to start in that business at the bottom. He headed for Stanford, found himself a place to live, and then visited Bill Gates in his tall-windowed $166,000 house-on-a-hill in Seattle's lakeside Leschi neighborhood, commanding a spectacular view of the Cascades, Lake Washington, and the traffic across the floating bridge toward Bellevue, and known to one and all as "the pad." It was in the pad that Gates began his tradition of live-in female housekeepers who would take care of shopping and bill-paying and other mundane aspects of his home life—and, in at least one instance, his romantic life as well.

Gates was surreptitiously courting Ballmer for an executive role at Microsoft. And an executive was sorely needed. When you looked at the company's organizational chart, which somebody finally had gotten around to drawing up for the first time, it became clear that Bill Gates was the sole head of everything, with seven of his twenty-six employees nominally, and far more actually, reporting directly to him. Middle managers were nowhere to be seen. The books of this high-tech multimillion-dollar company were kept not on some state-of-the-art computer system, but by hand in ledgers. And Microsoft was still a two-man partnership, governed by the same document Allen and Gates had signed in 1977.

By early 1980 Ballmer was beginning to worry about what to do for the summer, in part because he had won two competitive summer internships. Gates phoned and told Ballmer he needed a business guy; had he thought about maybe coming up to Seattle? Ballmer said he'd be available only for the summer. Gates said it was too bad; he really needed somebody full time.

When Ballmer called Bill a couple of days later to pursue the matter, he reached Paul Allen, who asked him when he was going to come work for Microsoft. Paul thought Bill might be at the pad, but when Ballmer tried there Kay Nishi picked up the phone and said, "You're coming to Microsoft, right?" Ballmer finally agreed to visit Seattle.

Gates went into his supersalesman mode. "Ballmer comes to visit me, and the whole idea is to hire the guy. . . . I'm saying to Ballmer, 'Do you know anybody who's as smart as you are? Jeez, I gotta get some help.' Then we go to dinner with my parents, and they're asking what he wants to do with his life. We're taking him around Seattle, all just working on him." In the end Bill came up with a formal offer that Ballmer agreed to ponder. Steve dropped him at the airport for his first real vacation in years—a bareboat charter in the British Virgin Islands with a short-term girlfriend from Microsoft and three other couples: the newlywed Mr. and Mrs. Kay Nishi, Blair Newman and his girlfriend, and Mr. and Mrs. Dan Thorne, a friend of Newman's who had recently been recruited to head up Microtype.

The deal with Ballmer had to be concluded via ship-to-shore phone from the sailboat *Doo-Wah,* with Bill punctuating each transmission with "*Doo-Wah Doo-Wah,* over" and spifflicated hecklers in the background punctuating the negotiations with cries of "Aw, give him what he wants, Bill!" In the end, Bill did give him the $50,000 a year he wanted, and Ballmer accepted the job of assistant to the president.

Ballmer arrived in June, as General Manager Steve Wood was about to leave for Datapoint. Ballmer was walking into a minefield. The job had no official responsibilities, so in theory he could step on anyone's toes. If Bill was confrontational, Ballmer was hyperconfrontational—and had a nasty habit of getting personal that Bill somehow managed to avoid. To the troops, Ballmer was a bright guy, but unlike Wood, he wasn't a technical guy, a programmer, and knowing about programming was the badge of respect at Microsoft. Besides, how much could Ballmer really know about business, anyway, after one whole year at Stanford? It all looked like a pure case of hiring one's friends.

What looked worse was Bill's letter confirming Ballmer's offer, which became a personnel disaster when some disgruntled soul copied it and tacked it on the office bulletin board. Along with his salary, high for Microsoft, Ballmer was to get a 5 to 10 percent cut of the company based on a formula involving the year's revenue growth. It sorely rankled loyalists who had been slaving for the company since the Albuquerque days without so much as a profit-sharing plan to show for it.

When it came to the clerical help, Gates had been tightfisted beyond the bounds of the law. Overtime had always been paid on a straight-time basis, and though the rules affecting programmers might be debatable, the rules affecting clerical workers were not. Marla Wood and other office staffers had checked into the labor regulations and discovered that they deserved time and a half for overtime—currently and retroactively. When Steve Wood approached Gates about it, he agreed to start paying time and a half but insisted that back pay was out of the question. If the secretaries wanted to file a complaint, well, let 'em.

They did. When the state notified Gates that the back pay was due, it wasn't long before Marla Wood got the news:

> *Bill comes storming into my office saying he just had a phone call from these people, just livid. This was the one time I was really on the receiving end of one of his rages—I mean, just screaming about this and how it was going to ruin his reputation. . . . This would be on his reports forever and ever. . . .*
>
> *I was saved by an overseas phone call which he proceeded to take at my desk, whereupon I ran out, went down to Steve's office and said "I'm quitting, I can't stand it here any more." And he said "That's all right; I'm seeing a headhunter tomorrow anyway."*

But before she and her husband departed Microsoft, Marla saw to it that the issue was settled. Although it amounted to only $100 or so for her and as little as $20 for the others, "It was just a matter of principle."

The overtime issue remained a *bête noir* for Gates and his new lieutenant Ballmer. With the crushing demands on the understaffed company, the programmers' pay was shooting through the roof even at the straight hourly overtime rates they were being paid. It wasn't long before a new plan came down from the executive suite: Overtime pay would be dropped altogether, replaced by straight salary and a 15 percent bonus at the end of the year. To inaugurate the new plan and soften the financial impact, most of the developers were given generous raises.

But you didn't fool programmers with sneaky math: 15 percent amounted to six hours a week. Some of them were putting in that much extra *a day*. Moreover, with the new plan, the Albuquerque practice of paying slightly above the going rate was trashed. Salaries would now be above-par only if the bonus was figured in.

"I was frustrated about it," recalled one of the Albuquerque transplants whose net pay went down. Response to the new bonus plan set the hallways humming. "It was conspicuously never explained as to where the bonuses came from, who decided them," said another member of the Albuquerque 11. "There was an official review when you got your bonus numbers, but it was never understood what they were based on."

Even without the overtime policy to enforce, Ballmer had his hands full. His attempt to formalize things—"to waltz in and just say your reimbursement had to be filed in triplicate," as one programmer put it—irritated the independent-minded troops in the trenches. His style of management by crisis proved unpopular. But for the first time, Microsoft had someone who was assigned to take care of operations—finance, legal, personnel. In order to delegate these things effectively, Gates needed someone he could trust—and he trusted Steve Ballmer.

Despite the ill will over Ballmer's arrival, despite the modest decline in the we're-all-in-this-together camaraderie that had accompanied the company's move to Bellevue and its expansion, the group remained relatively close-knit, with unofficial Friday night blowouts that Gates attended only sporadically. Still, Bill did make it to more formal parties. Alan Boyd, a longtime Microsoft executive, recalled Bill dancing barefoot on gravel, his feet bleeding, and nobody giving it a second thought "because everybody was working so hard the stress release was just something." At a housewarming for Paul Allen, a well-oiled Gates body-surfed headfirst down the staircase and threw someone's shoe off the deck, leaving one new recruit wondering "My God, this is the president of the company?" It was all in the name of blowing off steam from sixty- to eighty-hour work weeks. On Saturday morning, it was back to work.

For a time, Bill's pad, which eventually acquired a hot tub, was the scene of company Halloween parties, which, with the programmer's save-a-byte diligence for compression, were combined with Bill's October 28 birthday celebrations. At one he received a costume based on the "Saturday Night Live" character "Mr. Bill"—something his Japanese customers often called him. At another he arrived as Mickey Mouse.

A year or two later Gates showed up as Napoleon, who had fascinated him since adolescence, and whose life resonated with his own hopes, ambitions, and will. "How can an ugly little guy who isn't even really French manage to rise up and rewrite the laws of Europe so that even today the Code Napoleon is a big thing? And the way he recognized scientific and artistic leaders of the time: That's a pretty unusual thing." Yet with his customary pessimism, Gates didn't flinch from the downside of Napoleon's life: "At a time when there was no opportunity for leadership, most leaders were killed or overthrown, he put himself into such an incredible position and yet ruined his own success. The thing that's incredible about it is that at the end of his life he sat on an island and he dictated his thoughts. This is one smart guy." In the Gates argot, that was the ultimate compliment.

Among the regular partygoers was the golden couple of Andy Evans and Ann Llewellyn, two intensely driven stockbrokers who had joined the Gatesian inner circle. Gates had met Evans when he was trading in the stock of a "crazy company" called Solid State Technology that had licensed languages from Microsoft. Marketing a machine with a built-in printer, Solid State kept trying to get Gates to accept stock instead of cash and asked Evans to help convince Bill of the wisdom of this arrangement. No dice: Gates felt the company was "a little flaky," told Evans as much, and demanded and got the cash. Eventually they shorted Solid State and did well on the deal.

Gates was immediately attracted to Evans, a fanatic race-car buff for whom the terms "hard-driving" and "life in the fast lane" were literal as well as figurative. Evans would later declare that his motto was "Dare to stick your chin out. Never say die. Never quit." Like Steve Ballmer, this was a Bill Gates kind of guy.

Evans, a high school classmate of Steve Jobs, set up shop in an office he subleased from Microsoft, where he became legendary among Microsofties for cursing and for destroying telephones. Some did deals with him, particularly Bill Gates. "He and I shared ideas, and I went on a streak of investing that was unbelievable," Gates recalled. Going long on Mostek and AMD. Calling Amdahl "at the right time." Making "a ton of money" in Apple. In less than two years, Gates "like six-timesed our money."

In a 1987 interview Gates would boast that "When I was investing, I was able to have a fairly good sense of when things were peaking. In the case of VisiCorp I had an incredible amount of . . . information. I knew how good the relationship was with Software Arts. I knew when I first saw 1-2-3, I knew what I was looking at. So I'm not an outsider in that whole thing. In the things I invested in I didn't have that kind of total knowledge, but they were high tech." In later years Gates would deny he had any particular advantage. When it came to shorting Solid State, "Anybody should have known that they were flaky."

Microsoft was anything but flaky. If Bill Gates was as smart as he claimed to be, 16-bit chips would make the company grow even faster. The catch was which 16-bit chip to bet on. The Gator's bet on the 8086 had created a grand total of one license agreement—to tiny Seattle Computer Products for BASIC. He had a side bet on Zilog's Z-8000 chip, but that wasn't exactly setting sales records either. The Motorola 68000 chip was coming down the pike, and so was the National 16000. It was far from clear which one would turn out to be the winner—or even if there would be a winner.

So what he bet on was something called UNIX—an operating system that just might be for the 16-bit market that "standard OS" he had envisioned back in 1977 when he wrote of the possibility that "Software houses would write programs under the standard OS and wouldn't have to worry about multiple versions." If UNIX took off, not only would it reduce language development time—Microsoft could develop its languages for UNIX and not for each chip—but Microsoft would make money from selling the operating system itself.

UNIX had been created around 1969 at AT&T's Bell Labs in a language called C. Its gimmick, if there was one, was that it was "portable"—unlike proprietary operating systems that worked on a particular type of machine, UNIX could in theory run on almost anything. And since AT&T gave away educational licenses for free, it quickly became a standard at academic institutions around the world, where a cult of UNIX gurus sprang up.

But AT&T's commercial licensing practices gradually became more restrictive. By 1980 it was offering the product on a sliding scale: The more copies you bought, the lower the price. The scale was cumulative, so past sales counted: Once you'd bought a couple of million dollars' worth of UNIX, you hit the bottom of the price scale and stayed there.

To any individual purchaser, two million dollars' worth was a lot of UNIX. To Bill Gates, it didn't look like such a terribly big number. The way he saw it, he could license UNIX, modify it for various chips and machines, and sublicense it at the higher prices in the low-volume range of the AT&T curve. By generating enough volume to get quickly out to the high-volume, low-cost range, Microsoft would be able to maintain a comfortable profit margin.

One minor problem: Microsoft's product couldn't be called UNIX. AT&T licenses expressly forbade it. After considerable discussion, the high-tech sounding XENIX, pronounced "Zee-nicks," was adopted. *Microsoft Quarterly,* the publication that went out to OEM customers, articulated its advantages: "The system is versatile enough to be tailored to almost any application, and the system is highly portable because is it [*sic*] written in the C programming language." The *Quarterly* went further: "The XENIX system's inherent flexibility, along with this commitment from Microsoft, will make the XENIX OS the standard operating system for the computers of the eighties." Ads proclaimed "Microsoft is pleased to announce there will be no 16-bit software crisis."

No? XENIX was a resource hog, requiring copious amounts of memory and disk space, both quite expensive in this era. Besides, Microsoft had its hands so full customizing versions of BASIC and its other languages to the spate of new machines that kept coming through the door, particularly from Japan, that it was unwilling to divert precious resources to XENIX: At the outset, the XENIX team consisted entirely of Product Manager Bob Greenberg and Program Manager Gordon Letwin. The first version of XENIX, due in November 1980, would be for DEC's PDP-11 machines—which wouldn't be hard, since UNIX had been developed on those very machines, and adaptation was trivial. The harder ''ports''—adaptations for other machines—were to come later.

And eventually they did. But XENIX did not manage to become the 16-bit standard. What took that prize, what beat out the academic elegance of the UNIX derivative, was a rough-and-ready little operating system that wasn't portable, wasn't terribly versatile, didn't offer even a tenth of the ''abundance of auxiliary software that accompanies the XENIX OS,'' and by the standards of some computer purists wasn't really an operating system at all. It was an operating system known as QDOS, and not even Bill Gates knew about it. At the time the XENIX project began, you could count on the fingers of one hand the worldwide total of people who had ever heard of the Quick and Dirty Operating System.

11

▶

PLAYING CHESS

By early 1980 the personal computer business was unquestionably for real, more or less doubling annually, with pundits predicting a billion-dollar year for 1981. Radio Shack led the way with about 40 percent of the market, offering TRS-80 machines in a variety of sizes, flavors, and incompatibilities, from an $8,000 office system to a $500 bare-bones home unit. Number-two Apple, with its one-size-fits all Apple II priced from $1,000 to $3,000, was on its way to 1980 revenues of $117 million and a net profit of $11.7 million. Third-place Commodore, with an assortment of PETs, fared decently in the United States, better in Europe. The rest of the market, a motley variety of business-oriented computers with disk drives, coalesced around Digital Research's CP/M operating system.

By the end of the year, new machines that appeared at opposite price poles hinted strongly where the divergent market was headed. Commodore's VIC-20 (originally named "The Other Intellect" or, appropriately, "TOI") and Radio Shack's Color Computer, which sold for $399 each, were essentially keyboards with 4K computers built in: Hook one up to your TV and away you'd go, mostly with computer games. With Atari and Texas Instruments and others entering the home market, the downmarket competitors would shortly engage in the same sort of suicidal price-cutting that had marked the earlier calculator wars. That mattered hardly at all to the company that supplied the one standard common to virtually all the machines: Microsoft BASIC, in its various OEM flavors.

At the other end of the spectrum was the Apple III, Apple's $4,500 and up "business" machine, which came complete with a built-in floppy disk drive and a whopping 96K of memory expandable to 128K. This market, with the potential for applications from number-crunching to word processing, was far more interesting to traditional computer makers, and it was not going unnoticed. Hewlett-Packard, a leader in scientific machines, and Wang, the leader in word processors, and Xerox, the leader in copiers and unimplemented computer innovation, and Digital Equipment, the leader in minicomputers, all had microcomputer projects in the works by mid-1980. And so did IBM.

In 1978 and '79, secretive skunk works types at IBM's Boca Raton and Atlanta labs had fooled around with Altairs, IMSAIs, Sols, PETs, Apples. Their own plans for home computers had gone as far as prototypes—wild, goofy designs that looked great with kids in warm-and-fuzzy milk-and-cookie publicity shots. All that was missing was a way to turn the machines into a real business.

Around the Fourth of July 1980, Bill Lowe, the director of IBM's Boca Raton labs, got word of a proposal from Atari, king of the video game business, whose Model 800 was considered an up-and-comer in the home-computer market. Atari suggested that IBM should "OEM" the machine: Slap its logo on the box and market the unit as its own.

It was a variant of this proposal that Bill Lowe and his boss Jack Rogers took in mid-July to IBM's august CMC, the Corporate Management Committee that wielded life-and-death power over major projects. Frank Cary, chairman of the board, shot down the idea almost immediately. He wanted to know why the world's largest computer company couldn't design and market a low-end machine of its own.

This was no idle question. The low-end Datamaster project, underway for more than two years already, had consumed huge amounts of resources with no product and no end in sight. When Cary muttered something about projects taking 300 people three years, Lowe stuck his neck out and respectfully disagreed. "I said, 'No, sir. You're wrong. We can get a project out in a year.'" Next thing Lowe knew, he had been charged with assembling a small task force to consider the possibility of a crash program for an IBM personal computer. His report was due back to the CMC within a month.

Back in Boca, Lowe rounded up a dozen men he trusted, mostly from the Datamaster project, mostly mavericks known in IBM parlance as "wild ducks" ever since Chairman Tom Watson Jr. had used the phrase in a 1963 speech. What became clear at the weekend session was that to meet Lowe's one-year timetable, the new machine would have to be built from off-the-shelf parts—both hardware and software.

The task force became known unofficially as the Manhattan Project. Soft-spoken southerner Jack Sams, at the age of fifty-one a twenty-year IBM veteran with a strong background in operating systems, was chosen to head up the software effort. Sams was well aware of Microsoft's BASIC; months before, he'd recommended that IBM buy it for the Datamaster project. Instead IBM had decided that it had plenty of programmers that could do the job just fine, set a bunch of them to the task, and watched the cost for the in-house BASIC balloon far beyond any fee Microsoft might reasonably have exacted. It was a classic case of the kind of internal overoptimism that had led to the Gatesian lowball pricing strategy.

On Monday, July 21, 1980, Sams phoned Microsoft. He needed to see Bill Gates, and he needed to do it fast. Gates suggested the following week, but Sams was insistent: He wanted a meeting the next day. Bill agreed, then scurried to reschedule his previous commitment—a meeting, ironically, with Ray Kassar, the head of Atari, one of the very few companies that still hadn't committed to bundling some form of Microsoft BASIC with its computers.

In their straight-arrow-down-to-the-wingtips all-business uniforms, Jack Sams and IBM Contracts Administrator Pat Harrington arrived at the Microsoft offices on Tuesday, July 22, and were quickly introduced to a young fellow wearing an ill-fitting suit. "When he came out to bring us back to the office, I thought he was the office boy," Sams recalled. But Bill Gates quickly dispelled that notion. "He was obviously in control. He's one of the smartest men I've ever known."

Gates had Steve Ballmer join the meeting—because, said Ballmer, "I was a good suit-type guy." The first order of business was to sign a two-page IBM agreement stipulating that neither party would disclose any proprietary information, that either party would be free to disclose what was discussed without limitation, and that "IBM also wishes to make clear that no further activity is to be guaranteed as a result of this initial meeting." As Ballmer would put it later, "We're big boys; we can decide what we are going to tell them, and we're not going to tell them stuff we don't want to tell them. And there was nothing in particular we didn't want to tell them." He and Gates signed without hesitation.

To avoid tipping his hand, Sams dropped hints that IBM was considering some sort of experimental project—possibly a plug-in board not unlike Bill's SoftCard that might allow users to run 8-bit CP/M and BASIC on IBM's already released 16-bit 8086-based Displaywriter word processing system. Sams emphasized that as a planner, most of the projects he proposed never saw the light of day, but if this one got off the ground, it was going to be a rush job.

Sams had IBM intelligence on Microsoft and knew about some of its products from having played around with them. He was looking for reassurance. Could these guys meet deadlines? Did they have enough manpower and resources? Could their facilities be made secure enough to meet IBM standards? On most counts Microsoft passed the test. Sams had expected to find a much smaller company—fifteen employees instead of forty, rinky-dink offices instead of pleasant ones. As for deadlines, Gates pointed to a long roster of satisfied customers—nearly a hundred for BASIC alone—to whom Microsoft had delivered software more or less on schedule.

Security was a different story. Just outside Bill's office was a big open area full of unreleased machines, most of them Japanese. Gates and his staff made no attempts to conceal them, and nothing stood in the way of anyone who wanted to swipe an idea or two or even an entire design. For secrecy-obsessed IBM, other arrangements would obviously be required.

On the other hand, when Kay Nishi stepped in to demonstrate one of the machines—the beloved color-graphics Oki—it became clear that Gates and his crew knew quite a bit about hardware design as well. Sams "gave him sort of an open invitation to tell us what was needed" and got an earful: Gates pushed hard for color graphics, for a built-in serial-number chip that would help minimize his longtime bugaboo, software piracy—and, most important, for a 16-bit design instead of the outmoded 8-bit.

Sams and Harrington were impressed. The men in the dark suits flew home with a sense that this was something of a new world—this youthful, vital little company where the employees walked around in garb and hairstyles that were utterly taboo at IBM. Sams was energized by Bill's openness, his forthrightness, his interest in the inner workings of IBM. Big Blue could definitely do business with these guys.

As for Bill Gates, he was both appreciative of and amazed at the courtship from IBM. This was the ultimate client, potentially the coolest deal a little software company could dream of making, and Gates was fascinated by IBM's corporate politics. Besides, in his own way, Sams seemed like a Smart Guy. "We loved Jack Sams," Gates said. "We thought he was a cool guy, 'cause he was so nice to us and he always coached us. . . . In those early days he would always tell us before we went down to meetings what was going on, who was who, all that kind of stuff. He was our friend."

Elsewhere the rest of the IBM task force found candidates to supply other pieces of the hardware and software puzzle. The Manhattan Project reconvened in Boca, convinced that "open architecture" was the way to go. IBM's earlier small-systems efforts had failed in part because nobody was writing software or developing add-on hardware for them. By designing the PC around an open hardware bus not unlike the Altair's or the Apple II's and publishing the specifications, IBM would encourage third parties to add value to the new systems. By publishing the software specifications, IBM would stimulate outside developers to come up with new and different applications. Although in the MITS days third parties had been seen as "parasites," it had become increasingly clear that they were now the linchpins of a successful machine.

Lowe went to the CMC on August 6 with the group's presentation. The specs: 32K of ROS (read-only storage, IBM's unique acronym for what everyone else in the world called ROM—read-only memory), 16K of RAM, a six-slot open bus, and a variety of options: RAM up to 256K, a printer adapter, a choice of color or monochrome display, 8-inch disk drives and, as options, a floating-point processor to speed up math-intensive work, and an "auxiliary user interface," otherwise known as a joystick. The six slots eventually became five, and the 8-inch drives were supplanted by 5¼s, but otherwise the proposed machine was virtually identical to the one that would eventually become the IBM Personal Computer. The proposal claimed that IBM could sell 221,000 units between 1981 and 1984 in professional, commercial, home, and recreational markets. The figure was mostly guesswork, intended primarily to support what Lowe was proposing to do.

The chip meant to power all this was Intel's 16-bit 8088, the little brother of the 8086. Internally the two chips were identical, so they could run the same software; however, the 8088 used an 8-bit data path to the outside world, which would mean a tradeoff in a machine built around it: lower engineering costs at the expense of performance. Compared with other designs, compared even with its big brother, the 8088 was a dumpy chip: It performed little better than the popular 8-bit Z-80. Worse, Intel gave its 16-bit chips a uniquely convoluted memory-addressing scheme called "segmented architecture," which required programmers to master devilish computations that they quickly came to curse and detest. Still, the 8088 could directly access a megabyte of memory—a million characters, a book's worth of information—a sixteenfold advantage over the pamphlet-size 64,000-odd bytes of the 8-bit world. As Bill Gates was among the earliest to recognize, this huge expansion in memory capability would be perhaps the single most important factor in the IBM machine's success.

In later years Gates and Microsoft would claim credit for the selection of this chip, insisting that the IBM plan had initially been a lame 8-bit design that he convinced the company to abandon. The claim was understandable but wrong. At the first meeting Sams and Harrington played their chips close to the vest, disclosing no more than a general idea of what was being considered. Their mention of an 8-bit project was mainly to throw Microsoft off the scent. In that meeting Gates did push for a 16-bit design, and, as Sams put it, "I'm sure we nodded." But "it was redundant." IBM's engineers knew all about the horrors of 8-bit chips from their experience with the still-unreleased Datamaster. They weren't about to go through that nightmare again.

So it wasn't, as Bill would later insist, "our fault that it became a 16-bit machine." The 8088 chip was clearly specified in Bill Lowe's August 6 presentation to the CMC. Although the prototype wheeled in for the occasion had been surreptitiously based on the 8-bit 8085 and then refused to work, the 8088 proposal nonetheless earned the CMC's go-ahead for an expansion to a thirty-five-man team. Charts dated August 10 by Lew Eggebrecht, the engineer largely responsible for the PC's hardware design, clearly specified the 8088.

Jack Sams had told Gates not to expect anything. He might hear back from IBM; he might not. Bill heard back in early August; IBM wanted a meeting in Seattle on the twenty-first, and sent along a three-page formal document dated August 12 detailing the nondisclosure terms for the occasion. "IBM Confidential information," explicitly identified as such, might be disclosed during the meeting or afterward. If so, Microsoft could not reveal it to any third party. If it was supplied on paper, Microsoft would have to secure it in a locked file. Furthermore, "IBM does not wish to receive confidential information of the Seller"—Microsoft—"and any information disclosed by the Seller to IBM shall not be deemed confidential." IBM could drop in unannounced at any time to make sure Microsoft was living up to its part of the bargain. Despite the one-sidedness of the agreement, "President" William H. Gates signed it without modification at the start of the meeting. It set the pattern of Gates's relationship with the Blue Monster: Do what it takes to get the business and worry about refinements later.

This time there were four members of the IBM contingent—Sams and Harrington again, plus commercial relations specialist Phil Bailey and attorney Tom Galvin. To balance things out, Microsoft fielded a four-man team of its own: Gates, Ballmer, OEM sales chief Mark Ursino, and outside counsel Dale Roundy. IBM explained more fully what it was up to, revealing its general plans for the new machine and declaring that Microsoft was its first choice for computer languages—not just interpreted BASIC, but the whole product line: COBOL, FORTRAN, Pascal, and the BASIC compiler.

Thanks to an agreement with Convergent Technologies, a high-flying startup about to make 8086-based machines for a variety of OEM customers, Microsoft's 8086 language development effort was finally beginning to show some signs of life. After two years of effort, it looked as if Bill's bet on the 8086 might really pay off. "We were walking around like it was too good to be true," recalled Ursino, "because we'd essentially done a handshake deal on $600,000 of software." A follow-up letter from Steve Ballmer was dated August 26 and supplied prices exclusively for 16-bit versions of the languages —conclusive proof that the computer's design was already 8088-based at this first serious meeting.

But there was one missing item, one essential thing IBM would clearly need: an operating system. Sams asked Gates if Microsoft could simply sublicense the CP/M it had been selling with its SoftCard.

No, Microsoft could not. For one thing, the company had no rights to sublicense the product. For another, it wouldn't work on the 16-bit 8088 anyway; CP/M, Bill Gates explained, was an 8-bit operating system. But that was no problem. Microsoft and Digital Research had a close relationship of long standing, DR had a long-overdue 16-bit version of CP/M called CP/M-86 in the works, and Microsoft had a preliminary edition in house. Bill would be happy to phone the folks in Pacific Grove and see what was going on down there—after all, without an operating system for the machine, there was no way he could peddle his languages.

Gates first reached technical support representative Phil Nelson. When,

Bill asked, was CP/M-86 going to be ready? Nelson gave the standard answer —sometime next year. That, Gates replied, wasn't good enough. He demanded to speak to his old buddy Gary Kildall.

Gates told Kildall that he had some important customers in Seattle who needed an operating system—customers from IBM. Could they come down and visit the next day? Kildall said he'd arrange it. Bill's guests concluded their discussions at Microsoft and flew south to California.

The next day's events have become the Rashomon of microcomputer history, the industry's most-disputed, most-rehashed story. Bill Gates would later relish describing the situation as "Gary went flying." Kildall would put his own spin on it, which simply would not mesh with any of the other eyewitness accounts. What really happened? Something very much like this:

At the Victorian home on Lighthouse Street that served as the headquarters of Digital Research, four men in dark suits, white shirts, ties, and well-polished leather shoes stepped out of a dark Chevrolet sedan. To the laid-back, jeans-wearing, late-hippie Digital Research stalwarts, they looked like representatives of the hated FBI—or narcs.

Kildall was nowhere to be seen. He had gone flying, all right—on business. He flew every chance he got, and today he had previously scheduled engagements in the Bay Area. As far as Kildall was concerned, IBM was just another customer, a customer that was likely to screw up whatever it was plotting now just as badly as it had screwed up the 5100, its first effort on the personal computer scene.

Besides, Kildall was a technical guy who didn't much care for business. His wife, corporate vice president Dorothy McEwen, handled all the dealing, and she had plenty of experience handling big companies—none of which, in Kildall's view, had done much of anything right with personal computers. If the IBM people needed technical guys, there were plenty around the office. So Dorothy McEwen and Phil Nelson were the ones who ushered the IBM group into the "conference room" of the Victorian house, a former dining room where they all sat down around a big oak table.

The IBM attorney handed her a copy of the nondisclosure agreement Bill Gates had signed at his first meeting. McEwen knew her way around a contract, and she found this one ridiculously one-sided. The discussions, it said, would "not serve to impair the right of either party to make, procure, and market products or services now or in the future which may be competitive with those offered by the other." In other words, as McEwen saw it, we can tell you what we're doing, and you can go off and do it without us? Forget it! Refusing to sign, she excused Nelson; until the legal impasse was broken, technical services would not be necessary.

Dealing with a hippie software company that was infinitesimal by IBM standards, even if it happened to be the undisputed leader in personal computer operating systems, was not an area of particular IBM expertise. Sams and the other IBM emissaries cajoled, pleaded, tried to convince McEwen. Standing firm, she phoned attorney G. Gervaise "Gerry" Davis, who sat on the board and was a principal in Digital Research. He suggested alternative language that IBM's lawyer wouldn't accept. The atmosphere grew increasingly frosty.

To break the deadlock, the group recessed for lunch. McEwen met with Davis at his office and tried to come up with new language that would satisfy IBM. When the group reconvened, IBM's lawyer didn't break the ice: He froze it hard, asking whether McEwen was now ready to sign the original agreement. IBM wouldn't accept the modified wording McEwen and Davis had worked out; the stalemate continued. The IBM contingent tried to convince McEwen that their intentions were honorable, that it was in her best interest to sign. McEwen remained immovable.

In the end, a member of the IBM group came up with another approach merely to get something in motion: Digital Research would simply agree not to disclose for three years that the emissaries from IBM had ever visited. McEwen did sign that agreement; so did Nelson and everyone else who had met with the IBM representatives, however briefly. Enough discussion took place for IBM to get product information and a few manuals—which, because they were marked with copyright notices on each page, IBM considered confidential and later shipped back.

Leaving the scene in midafternoon, Sams was stunned and baffled, wondering "My God, what are we going to do now?" He phoned Bill Gates, asking him to get back in touch with Kildall and do a little groundwork, find out what the problem was. Gates checked with Gary and reported back to Sams that the deal didn't seem dead. But when Sams called Pacific Grove and finally talked with Kildall, he couldn't pin down a firm price or a firm date for CP/M-86— or a commitment to the secrecy pact.

The set of papers Bill Gates had signed without hesitation was only part of the story. What ultimately lost the IBM operating system deal for Kildall wasn't his absence at the first meeting but the lateness of CP/M-86. Had CP/M-86 been ready on time, IBM would have been able to license it. Besides, Kildall sensed that for him the IBM deal looked nowhere as good as it did for Bill Gates. Gates had a whole line of languages to offer; Kildall had his operating system, a version of the PL/I language, and not much else. The kinds of contracts IBM generally demanded, Kildall knew, with their ability to rewrite, change, and distort the code, might mean he'd be signing away his one commercial product forever for one lousy flat fee. And Kildall wasn't the only one who refused to play ball with IBM: Seymour Rubinstein of MicroPro had rebuffed IBM's overtures about licensing WordStar.

The following Thursday, August 28, a meeting at Microsoft included Jack

Sams, hardware guru Lew Eggebrecht, and a contingent of folks from IBM. As Gates would retell it with his typical flair for exaggeration:

> . . . They said, "We have a lot of things to do, so let's do them in parallel. We'll have our legal team meet with your legal team, we'll have the purchasing team meet with your purchasing team, we'll have our technical team meet with your technical team, so we can do four or five things at once." Well, that is fine, but that's me who is going to do those things and I can do only maybe two things at once, so we're not going to be able to have five simultaneous meetings.

One would have to do. Bill Gates signed a consulting agreement that paid Microsoft the sum of $15,000 for a month's work on "developing a more precise specification of the software requirements for [IBM's] system." For the first time, IBM fully disclosed to Microsoft all the technical minutiae of its plan.

But now one of the foundations of the plan—the use of a 16-bit processor —was being called into question. If IBM couldn't find an off-the-shelf 16-bit operating system, how could it build a 16-bit machine? Sams wondered if Gates knew of a 16-bit alternative. Well, there was XENIX, Gates suggested; unfortunately XENIX wouldn't even begin to run on a low-end machine like the one IBM had in mind. But the Gates luck, sometimes known as Paul Allen, held again. Allen happened to know of a computer engineer who was almost as frustrated with Digital Research as IBM was. Like giant IBM, this mom-and-pop-shop engineer had a 16-bit machine and had been thwarted in trying to buy an operating system for it. The engineer was Tim Paterson of Seattle Computer.

Once it had become clear that Seattle Computer had lost Microsoft's SoftCard business, Paterson had gone back to tinkering with his 16-bit boardset. By April 1980 Digital Research's promised delivery date for CP/M-86 had long since passed, so there was still only one major software product that could run on the Seattle Computer machine: Microsoft's Standalone BASIC with its rudimentary built-in operating system. Since that was kind of limited, Paterson set out to clone CP/M on his own. The result was what he called QDOS— Quick and Dirty Operating System.

QDOS wasn't an absolute clone of CP/M. Remembering his conversation at NCC with Marc McDonald about File Allocation Tables in his unfinished, large, and never-released 8-bit MIDAS operating system, Paterson decided that the FAT scheme was a better way to handle disk information than the way CP/M did it. Paterson also made modest improvements for users. With CP/M, copying a file from drive A to drive B required the goofy syntax Kildall had adopted from old DEC operating systems:

```
PIP B: A:FILENAME
```

With QDOS you simply typed

```
COPY A:FILENAME B:
```

Paterson also changed CP/M's classic **A>** prompt to **A:**, borrowed the idea of a command-line editor from North Star DOS, and added elements from CDOS, Cromemco's CP/M clone.

But for programmers' convenience, QDOS mimicked every last internal function call of CP/M, along with many other technical aspects. So close a clone was QDOS that the preliminary user's manual for its public unveiling as 86-DOS (Disk Operating System) carried this disclaimer:

> *SPECIAL NOTE: 86-DOS is not related to the popular CP/M operating system of Digital Research. Disk directory formatting and space allocation are completely different and incompatible. 86-DOS does, however, provide a utility called RDCPM which will transfer files from CP/M disks to 86-DOS disks. Further, operating system calls and calling conventions have been provided which make possible automatic translation of Z80 programs written for CP/M into 8086 programs that run under 86-DOS.*

In fact, translating old programs or writing them from scratch with Paterson's bare-bones assembler were the only ways to get software running on his new DOS.

Languages were clearly called for, and in early August Paterson wrote Bob O'Rear about adapting Microsoft BASIC for the new operating system. Seattle Computer's general manager, the well-traveled former Boeing sales rep, newspaper editor, and real estate salesman Rod Brock, then wrote Paul Allen to propose a cross-licensing arrangement. Seattle Computer was offering to swap the right to license 86-DOS for the right to license Microsoft's languages. Result: When the IBM emissaries at the August 28 meeting asked about 16-bit operating systems, Bill Gates hinted he might just be able to find one.

Over the next few weeks, in intermittent meetings with IBMers, particularly Eggebrecht, the Microsoft consultants, primarily Gates, Nishi, and O'Rear, forcefully expressed their opinions of what the IBM machine ought to be. With typical wild panache, Nishi grandly pushed for everything he could get: more memory in the box, more colors on the screen, more keys on the keyboard. Gates essentially plumped for a 16-bit version of the Oki machine, minus the built-in printer, plus rudimentary sound capabilities.

On occasion Gates would put in a pitch for the faster 8086 chip, the more elegant Motorola 68000 chip, extra memory, a floppy disk drive, or his anti-piracy hardware scheme as standard equipment. Eggebrecht, charged with meeting a price point, would swat each suggestion down as a budget-buster. Still, as one IBM insider remembered it, "Every time I talked to Bill, he gave me the impression I was his most important customer. He even gave us free advice."

Advice? Gates and Nishi gave it gladly. In their view, even 48K machines were underpowered for business purposes, so a 16K system was silly. At a time when disk drives had become virtual standards—though not on the Apple II that was the clear target of IBM's machine—making them mere options was ridiculous. And the built-in cassette port was utterly ludicrous.

Eggebrecht wasn't happy about the compromises. Their primary reason, he kept reminding Gates and Nishi, was so that a diskless machine could be advertised at an attractive price. Eggebrecht finally came up with the line that stopped Bill's nagging: "I'm putting in fifty cents' worth of parts for the cassette port; you put in fifty cents' worth of software."

Gates and Nishi urged changes in the keyboard design, but given IBM's off-the-shelf concept, the keyboard had to use designs already in place at IBM's manufacturing facility. And an IBM committee insisted the keyboard had to be good for three things: programming, word processing, and spreadsheets. Still, many of Microsoft's suggestions were adopted. The result would be roundly criticized, yet the keyboard was better than virtually any other that existed at the time. The Apple II of the day didn't even have cursor keys.

Nishi and Gates also had some luck in pushing for improvements in the machine's graphics—at their prodding, Eggebrecht finally added a chip that allowed switching among color palettes. Although the IBM BASIC would be based almost entirely on the Oki version, IBM's graphics were inferior, and the cheap, popular monochrome screens couldn't even display them. But unlike the off-the-shelf Apple II, any IBM machine could display lines of 80 characters, upper and lower case, plus special characters that were strongly influenced by Gates and Nishi. As fans of the Wang word processing system, they fought hard for and eventually won a complete set of special Wanglike on-screen characters —paragraph and section markers for legal documents and a collection of arcane arrows.

Their secret scheme was to do a clone of the Wang word processor for the IBM machine—another Gates leveraging of hardware to further his own software designs. But this time it would backfire. By the end of the year, Bill Gates would fall in love with a whole different kind of word processing and abandon his Wang-clone efforts. Competitors would soon ride to success on the screen characters he had proposed and jilted.

The IBM operating system could not be ignored much longer. By the end of September Microsoft would have to deliver a formal proposal in Boca Raton.

To Gates, the fatherly Sams, with a son the same age as Bill, was a mentor, a guide to IBM's endlessly fascinating protocols, personalities, and politics—politics that were about to remove Sams and his boss Jan Winston from the project. Frustrated by Digital Research's inability to come up with dates or terms or secrecy agreements, Sams strongly recommended that Bill include in his proposal the 16-bit operating system they had been talking about.

At a late-night powwow Sunday, September 21, Allen, Gates, Ballmer, and Nishi looked at the angles. The company was insanely busy, overcommitted, bursting at the seams, with more business than it could handle, programmers doubling up in offices, and engineers from Japanese companies sleeping on mats in the hallways, taking sponge baths in the men's room, wolfing down cases of Cup o' Noodles. Among their machines was a unit code-named Go—an 8-bit computer from Matsushita that another wing of IBM was considering as an OEM slap-the-label-on quickie.

But all that was trivial compared to the Boca Raton IBM project, for which Microsoft was already committing to a tremendous amount of new code on a backbreaking schedule. Yet when you looked at it that way, tossing in an operating system, particularly one that already seemed technically sound and would be developed mostly elsewhere, didn't seem such a big deal. It was a small increment over the rest of the code. It offered control over the way things would be done. It meant independence from an outside software vendor who might be late with essential deliveries. And ultimately it might just mean the deal. By all accounts it was Kay Nishi who danced around and sounded the battle cry: "Gotta do it! Gotta do it!"

Paul Allen phoned Rod Brock of Seattle Computer in the morning. A customer was interested in sublicensing DOS, Allen said, but secrecy agreements prevented him from saying who. Brock and Allen reached a verbal agreement the next day—the same day that, in a preliminary proposal to Jack Sams, Steve Ballmer first set in writing Microsoft's willingness to supply an operating system along with a complete specification for BASIC and the other languages.

Brock confirmed the 86-DOS deal the following day. For an upfront fee of $10,000, Microsoft would have the right to distribute 86-DOS to an unlimited number of end users. For an additional fee of $10,000 per company, or $15,000 if source code was included, Microsoft could sublicense 86-DOS to OEM customers. The deal was nonexclusive; Seattle Computer could cut similar deals on its own. But Seattle Computer agreed to "work in a diligent manner to improve and update 86-DOS during the next year with a substantial effort being expended in the next several weeks." All that was left was to translate the terms into a formal contract within sixty days.

Negotiated by Paul Allen, the deal was a masterstroke that even Bill Gates could be proud of. Microsoft hadn't signed anything; if for some reason IBM backed out at next week's meeting in Boca, Bill Gates could likely wriggle out of the Seattle Computer deal without spending a cent. If IBM dropped out somewhere farther down the line—it was always possible, since IBM was known to sponsor competing products such as that Go machine, many of which never saw the light of day—Microsoft would be out a mere ten grand. And if the project went through to completion—well, there was no way the crafty Bill Gates would let IBM steal an entire operating system for anything like $15,000.

The Boca powwow was scheduled for September 30. Late the night before, in typical Microsoft fashion, Bob O'Rear finished incorporating Jack Sams's suggestions into the final proposal, ripped it from the Wang word processor, jumped into Bill's Porsche, and closed his eyes. It was time for one of the patented Gatesian high-speed can-we-make-it races to the airport to meet Steve Ballmer and the red-eye to the sun.

Upon arriving in Miami, the trio stepped into a men's room, changed into their suits, and discovered that Bill Gates had forgotten to pack a tie. As they drove north—a lot farther north than they'd imagined—for their 10:00 A.M. appointment, the tie became the primary subject of discussion. They were already going to be late; the tie would make them even later. Still, this was IBM, and IBM was the land of suits. The trio pulled into a shopping center, waited for a Burdine's to open, and dashed in to find a neckpiece for the president.

The tie was probably unnecessary. At the all-day round of meetings, the boyish Chairman Bill initially puzzled the IBM group. To software engineer Ed Kiser, he looked like a "kid that had chased somebody around the block and stolen a suit off him and the suit was way too big for him. His collar stuck up and he looked like some punk kid, and I said, 'Who the hell is this?' " Sams and Eggebrecht were already in Microsoft's corner; eventually Bill won over the rest of the group with his calm, matter-of-fact presentation and ready answers to almost everything. Kiser was the toughest nut to crack: A user of Microsoft's TRS-80 assembler, he had firsthand experience with Microsoft's commitment to quality. "If you ever try to sell IBM that piece of crap you call a linker," he told Gates, "it will be over my dead body."

But even before the meeting, Bill Gates had been in the mind of Philip D. "Don" Estridge, an easygoing but decisive maverick IBM engineer who wore cowboy boots around the office, reminded people of Fred MacMurray, and had just taken over the reins of what was now known officially within IBM as Project Chess. As Estridge explained to his visitors over lunch, Bill had support from a higher authority.

Days before, Estridge had mentioned something to IBM's president, John

Opel, about buying software from a little company named Microsoft in Belle-vue, Washington. "Oh, that's run by Bill Gates, Mary Gates's son," Opel had replied. He knew Bill's mom from the national board of the United Way.

Estridge smiled at Bill. "You take your bluebirds where you can get them, I guess."

After dinner with Sams, the Microsoft contingent flew back to Seattle with no deal, no commitment. But negotiations began almost at once with attorney Galvin and a fast-talking Philadelphian named Sandy Meade, who had replaced Sams as the head of the software effort at Boca.

In Boca, Gates and Ballmer had told IBM that the initial flat-fee price quote no longer applied. Because IBM wanted the rights to use the code on a variety of future machines, not just one, it would have to pay more and pay royalties. Meade was taken aback at Microsoft's boldness. The other software companies he'd been dealing with had been pushovers. With Microsoft, Meade remem-bered, "I never felt that they needed the money." So Meade pushed hard on the concept of a "long-term relationship with the potential for big business."

The agreement between IBM and Microsoft later became public record in a court case, so the terms are clear; unfortunately, the numbers were obliter-ated. Sources close to the negotiations said Microsoft received an advance of roughly $100,000 against a royalty of about $50 per copy for each of four language compilers—Pascal, COBOL, FORTRAN, BASIC. It received a fee of roughly $200,000 for all its "adaptation" work to get everything to run on the IBM system. And it got a combined advance of roughly $400,000 for DOS and interpreted BASIC, against a royalty of $1 (or $10 or $15, depending on the source) for each copy of DOS and/or that BASIC.

That particular royalty, however, was unimportant. Under the terms of the agreement, as long as BASIC remained in ROM on the initial machine and its descendants (making Microsoft BASIC the undisputed IBM standard), no roy-alty would be due for BASIC—or for DOS. There might be additional pay-ments for enhancements and fixes, but as long as BASIC remained in ROM, the price for BASIC and DOS was essentially the initial flat fee. Whether that aspect of the contract was ever amended remains unclear, but to this day, every IBM Personal Computer has the original BASIC—intended primarily for use with a cassette recorder that is no longer even an option—stored in a ROM chip within the machine.

There was another wrinkle in the agreement. IBM could in theory sell copies of the programs to third parties; what it could not do was "publish or disseminate the SOURCE CODE for a period of seven (7) years from the effective date of this Agreement." Further, IBM's liability for violating this clause was theoretically unlimited. What this meant in practice was that IBM could not license Microsoft's programs to third parties. But the contract was nonexclusive, so Microsoft could—and would.

Finally there were the schedules: brutal ones. IBM was to deliver a prototype machine by December 1. DOS and all of the ROM-based work on interfaces and BASIC were to be done within 96 days of the delivery of the prototype in Bellevue. Delivery time for the compilers ranged from 145 days for Pascal to 257 days for FORTRAN. The schedule also partitioned out the crucial ROM software work: Except for BASIC, most of it was IBM's responsibility.

Meade vividly remembered Bill's unorthodox way of contemplating contract terms. "Gates went into his office at ten-thirty at night, lay down on the floor, and was tossing and turning, moaning 'Should I do this? I don't know. It's a good relationship. I don't know.'" After talking with Ballmer, Gates decided he wanted to renegotiate. Meade reminded him that this could be a long relationship and stood firm.

In the end, the final papers were brought to Seattle by Ed Kiser and Glenn Dardick, two IBM programmers who negotiated the final points with Gates and Ballmer and, in those pre-fax days, commuted across Lake Washington to IBM's Seattle offices to receive a succession of revised versions from the New York lawyers. On the day the contract was signed, November 6, 1980, Steve Ballmer was wearing a suit. Not Bill Gates. Sporting a sweatshirt with the emphasis on sweat, he looked as if he needed a shave.

Gates did much of the final negotiating from a reclining position on the sofa. When the papers were finally complete, he got up, walked over to the window cabinet, borrowed an IBM standard-issue pen from Kiser, and signed the contract. In his sole concession to IBM awe, he affixed the accurate title "Partner" beneath his name rather than his usual inflated "President."

Handing back the pen, Gates looked at Ballmer and said, "Well, Steve, now we can get to work."

It was just two days after Ronald Reagan had trounced Jimmy Carter in the presidential election, ushering in a new era of national conservatism. The deal with IBM was about to usher in a new era of its own. "I felt there should have been a fanfare of trumpets, or at least a gong," Kiser said. "But we just gathered up the papers, shook hands, and walked out the door."

12

DOS CAPITAL

Venture capitalists were getting a lot of use out of Microsoft's door, in both directions. Since the days of the Pertec suit, Microsoft had never been short on cash. What it was short on was business experience, though Bill Gates's improvisational management and master salesmanship helped conceal that imperfection. Yet as one of the hottest properties in the software business, Bill Gates was constantly being wooed by venture capitalists telling him how they'd take the company public and make him rich.

That was not the way to get to Bill Gates. Gates was already rich. With the upper-crust kid's professed disdain for mere lucre—not that he'd ever turned it down or given much of it away—Gates saw himself as a mover, a shaker, a builder, a leader, the smartest of the Smart Guys. The company was his brainchild, and he was the mastermind. There was no rush to divide it up among mere end users.

In October 1980 David Marquardt, a dashing, genial former mechanical engineer and Homebrew clubber who had become a partner in Menlo Park's Technology Venture Investors (TVI), took a different route after being tipped off to Microsoft by none other than Blair Newman. On a dank, blustery autumn day, Marquardt joined Bill and his family in the Gates box for a University of Washington football game. Even though being cold was one of his personal aversions, the clothes-unconscious Gates showed up in a tennis shirt. Marquardt scored a touchdown by lending Bill his blazer, then added an extra point by *not* talking about going public. "We didn't really watch much of the football game," Marquardt recalled. "We were talking about compiler architectures. . . . He drew out his whole strategy on the back of a football program." And Marquardt understood it.

A venture capitalist who was a Smart Guy! Gates invited Marquardt to bring his partners to Seattle in November for a presentation. Impressed, Bill proposed a six-month trial: "Pretend you own part of our company and see how you add value." Where they added value, it turned out, was in their business experience and contacts in Silicon Valley circles. Steve Ballmer liked Marquardt's hands-on talents. Marquardt became a trusted confidant and helped Ballmer put together a plan for turning the partnership into a corporation. He did not yet get the opportunity to buy in.

A couple of weeks before the IBM deal was signed, Charles Simonyi, a slender, intense Hungarian bearing an uncanny resemblance to pictures of the young Napoleon, had walked through the door. At thirty-one, seven years older than Bill Gates, Simonyi was already a senior citizen of desktop computing, his roots as convincingly hardcore as Bill's. As a teenager in the mid-sixties he had honed his programming skills in machine language on an archaic Russian vacuum-tube computer, the Ural II. Eventually he had advanced to a Danish transistor-based machine and had escaped his homeland at the age of seventeen with the help of a Danish computer repairman.

After studying in Denmark and at Berkeley and Stanford, Simonyi began working at Xerox PARC. Housed in the golden California hills near the Stanford campus, PARC was the Valhalla of computerdom, an idea factory spawning the industry's present and future software Hall of Famers. But Xerox PARC was like the nutty professor who never makes a dime off his brilliant inventions. To this day some hackers claim that PARC's Alto, initially demonstrated in 1973, was the first true "personal computer." The Alto was never released commercially; to call it "perhaps the most important unannounced computer product of the 1970s" was hardly stretching the point.

Charles Simonyi had personally developed Bravo, the Alto's writing software, the first word processor to remotely approach the screen-as-paper goal of WYSIWYG—"what you see is what you get," a phrase filched from comedian Flip Wilson's drag lady of the night, Geraldine. The Alto's 8½ - by 11-inch black-on-white display showed a full page of text with typefaces that looked the way they would on paper. A technique called bit-mapping, in which each of the screen's 489,648 tiny dots, known as pixels, could be individually turned on or off, allowed for the on-screen type variations—as well as the display of monochrome images from architectural drawings to photos.

WYSIWYG was just the beginning. The Alto had a mouse. It had a 2.5 megabyte removable cartridge disk. It could link up to other Altos and a shared laser printer via a network called Ethernet. The Alto of 1973 was a machine whose features would not stack up poorly against the desktop computers of 1990, yet only 1,200 saw the light of day. The biggest problem was cost— $15,000 just to produce the unit, not to mention maintenance, which required specially trained technicians.

Alan Kay, PARC's philosopher king, considered the Alto an interim system, a stopgap until his dream could be realized. The dream was still Dynabook, a flat one-piece keyboard and screen about the size and weight of a typical notebook. Dynabook would feature screen resolution better than newsprint and animation almost as good as the movies, not to mention high-fidelity audio. It would include useful software and give access to a huge assortment of data. It would, in short, be something of a do-all, be-all metamedium.

And it would be wildly beyond the capabilities of the hardware of the time, so the Alto would have to do. Or the Xerox Star, the first general-market computer to feature a fully integrated graphics-based system incorporating a mouse and bit-mapped windows technology. The Star was a bigger and better Alto, featuring higher resolution on a larger and less flickery screen, a 10-megabyte hard drive, convenient 8-inch floppy disks, and half again as much memory as the Alto—a whopping 192K. The Star also offered a laser printer and Ethernet compatibility. Charles Simonyi knew all about it.

He also knew that when it was finally released, it would be prohibitively expensive. The machine that got him excited was a secret project built around an off-the-shelf Intel 8086 chip: the Cub, put together in a garage by Bob Belleville, a conservative, button-down PARC hardware whiz. The Cub had a bit-mapped display, a mouse, and sound capabilities: It was the Alto and Star in off-the-rack Intel clothing.

Simonyi was revved. "Let's go into business," he told Belleville. "You build the machine . . . I'll write an editor for it."

Belleville wasn't ready to make the move. "The honest answer is neither of us was that keen on starting a company," he recalled.

By 1980, four years after Simonyi had moved from PARC to Xerox's more product-oriented Systems Development Division (SDD), he had acquired a reputation as a maverick. He had even programmed Bravo in a dialect of his own, impishly called "Butte," that was seen as subverting Xerox's officially sanctioned Mesa language. "It was kind of this hopeless, hopeless rebellion—a crew of one person without any support." Simonyi felt he had done a great job at Xerox, yet "all the accumulated work would come to nothing."

His friend Bob Metcalfe had been telling him about "this crazy guy in Seattle" that he absolutely had to meet. So on a trip to look after some Altos at the Boeing Company in the fall of 1980, Simonyi dropped by Microsoft's Bellevue headquarters with a portfolio of his work, much of which had never been outside the walls of the Xerox labs.

Gates was occupied with Japanese customers, so Simonyi met with Steve Ballmer. Ten minutes into the interview Ballmer erupted from his chair and exclaimed, "Bill has to see this!" Gates cut off the Japanese meeting, paged through Simonyi's work, and offered him a ride back to Sea-Tac. It was one of the rare occasions that Gates took his time getting to an airport.

Bill and Charles were soulmates from the outset:

We were saying everything at the same time, Bill and I. And he said, you know, we're going to do C and we're going to do interfaces and laser printing, applications, you know—we'll be dominant! . . . The guy was high energy and really animated and—wow! . . . I was superimpressed. I mean, this guy knew the future like anything!

If Simonyi wasn't sure what to do next, a courtesy call on the Xerox top brass convinced him: "The impression I got after talking with them was these guys don't know beans. And there was this crazy kid, and he knows everything!" Xerox was the comfortable but circumscribed option, Microsoft the risky choice with more potential. "I realized that it's a big linear thing or a small exponential thing."

In mid-November, just after Bill had signed the IBM deal, Simonyi flew back to Bellevue to reveal a detailed business plan prepared with the help of Bravo X, the final version of his word processor. The plan was printed on both sides of a standard sheet of paper and folded like a pamphlet. It used an impressive collection of typographic fonts—heady stuff in the days when laser printers were expensive rarities. And as stunning as the form was, the content was even better: The plan was nothing less than a scheme for global domination of applications software under the Microsoft brand name.

Microsoft would do VisiCalc—well, not VisiCalc exactly, but something an awful lot like it, possibly with a database and graphics built in. Microsoft would do Bravo—well, not Bravo exactly, but a word processing program as much like it as possible given the restrictions of the hardware. Microsoft would do database software, electronic mail software, software for computer-assisted design, for robots, for voice recognition. It would do software that took advantage of advanced hardware like hard disks, mouse pointers, voice synthesizers, bit-mapped screens, networks. Simonyi hinted that some of this advanced hardware would be found in something he called the Apple IV.

Bill Gates was blown away. Simonyi had just proposed nothing less than a global extension of the classic Microsoft strategy: Take software from other platforms and popularize it for new ones. For applications, this business plan was the logical extension of what Bill had been doing so successfully with his languages.

Charles Simonyi would later describe himself as "the messenger RNA of the PARC virus." The following week he gave Bill a tour of PARC, along with a personal demonstration of the Alto and Bravo X. Even though it was the first time Gates had laid eyes on the machine, Simonyi remembered, "He knew everything about it." Bill had "one of those reactions like when you first see the Eiffel Tower and it's just like in the pictures. It's nice to see it, but it's not like he was impressed."

But Gates was impressed with the Mad Hungarian. In early February 1981,

Gates greeted him as Microsoft's new director of advanced product development and offered to show him the Chess machine. Simonyi shook his head in disgust. He hadn't joined the company to fool around with games. "Bill, give me a break! This is serious business. Chess is a fad. We should look farther into the future."

"No, no," Gates said with a grin, then led the way down a long hallway and opened a door. Inside a tiny closet were two guys working on the prototype for the IBM PC.

In the months since Simonyi's first visit, a lot had changed around Microsoft. On top of the usual insanity was all the extra work for IBM. Unlike most OEMs, IBM was testing the products as they went along, howling about bugs early and often, placing demands on Microsoft that no one else had done before. Gates, whose growing propensity for looking on the dark side was being fed by the maniacal IBM pace, had his doubts about whether the project was going to be all that hot.

"Paul believed it more than Bill," said Bob O'Rear, recalling a "big argument" at a corporate retreat. The question was whether the company should "hire another guy for the IBM project," or hire someone for one of the language products. In the end the language got the extra man, and the IBM work was done entirely with staffers already in place. Allen, who lost the battle, would again be right about the war.

As one Microsoft insider would later put it, "IBM is schedule-driven." The prototype units were contractually due at Microsoft on December 1, 1980. IBM's Dave Bradley was a software guy, but he celebrated the end of his Thanksgiving holiday, Sunday, November 30, by putting nine big boxes of hardware on a plane headed west and accompanying them to Seattle. As December began, Bradley went back to writing the ROM BIOS (Basic Input/Output System) code that provided the basic interface between the software and the hardware.

IBM's draconian security clashed with the insouciant Microsoft style. By IBM fiat, the equipment was installed in a tiny windowless storage closet at the end of a long corridor. The room was to be locked at all times, whether someone was inside or not. Access was supposedly limited to a select few. But with computers and humans radiating heat, the airless closet invariably became a sweatbox, and the giant fan installed to cool things off simply stirred the sultriness around. Eventually the door was kept open except during visits from IBM. On those occasions, Steve Ballmer's voice would be heard booming down the hall: "Clean it up, guys!"

As the year wound down, there was a less-technical matter that had to be dealt with: the contract with Seattle Computer. Still in the dark about the mystery customer, Brock submitted his proposed agreement on November 7—the day *after* Bill had signed his agreement with IBM committing him to deliver

86-DOS. But there was still no formal deal even after the initial sixty-day agreement period had passed, and the redrafted contract Ballmer sent Brock later in the month omitted the $10,000 front money that had been originally agreed to. With the restoration of that clause and a few other modifications, the license agreement was signed early in January. On that one, William H. Gates reverted to "style" as president.

From the relative calm of Seattle Computer, Tim Paterson dutifully supplied fix after fix to DOS—such things as better error messages and a change in his **A:** prompt to the CP/M-like **A>**—for transmission to the unknown customer and the unseen machine. The only early inkling of the customer's identity came when Rod Brock fielded a question about 86-DOS from someone at IBM. When Brock inquired where the caller had gotten a copy of the program—at the time there were only seventy or eighty in the hands of customers, and Brock didn't recall any having gone out to the Armonk behemoth—the caller hemmed, hawed, and hung up.

At Microsoft, Bob O'Rear methodically adapted 86-DOS to the Chess machine. Every time he got new code from Paterson, he would move it to the prototype machine via a wildly kludgy multistep process that involved a stroll from one end of the building to the other and the use of three different machines, not counting the IBM prototype. But by the beginning of 1981—a month after it had been delivered—the prototype still refused to work reliably. In the heat of the storage room, wires on the circuit boards would randomly disconnect, creating intermittent problems. As O'Rear wrote IBM, "it sometimes takes days to ascertain whether the problem lies with the hardware or the software," and "to prove the hardware is actually failing takes days of our time." The color video cards refused to work, and in the dark some of the components of the power supply actually glowed—before the unit failed entirely.

The phone lines between Bellevue and Boca burned with endless questions, complaints, fixes. The already tight schedules were beginning to slip. It wasn't until late January that O'Rear was able to bring up DOS and BASIC on the prototype machine. By February 2 he asked IBM to take on the responsibility of testing some of the software in order to keep as close to schedule as possible.

A bailout clause in the contract expired on March 1. When that date passed, it became clear to Microsoft that IBM was not likely to abandon the project. On March 12, after a series of troubleshooting visits from IBM staffers, Ballmer wrote IBM's Harrington reminding him of the sixty days lost before the prototype actually worked and confirming a revised schedule for software delivery.

One of the saviors of the project was Microsoft's set of minicomputer development tools—especially the 8086 simulator that had been begun on spec back in Albuquerque. Those tools allowed programmers to keep cranking code on the DEC mini while the hardware wrinkles were being ironed out of the IBM prototype. Using software to emulate hardware, Microsoft's advantage since the MITS days, was proving crucial yet again.

Software exchanges took place daily. Every afternoon around five o'clock, someone from Microsoft would round up the disks and drive down the freeway to Sea-Tac Airport and the Delta DASH package delivery service. Eventually modems were set up to speed transfers even further. And then there were the human transfers. Bill and other Microsofties would grab the red-eye for the bone-numbing cross-country trek that, if you timed it right, could be done in less than twenty-four hours round trip. A procession of IBMers would make the same trip beginning at the other coast.

IBM's top priority was the ROM BASIC; because it had to be "burned" into the hardware before machines could go into production, it had to be finished first. Mike Courtney of APL fame worked overtime, double time, triple time, to get the thing done, while Allen toiled over the advanced disk-based versions. Gates pitched in wherever he could. Charged on one trip with bringing the latest version of BASIC back to Boca, IBM's Bradley found Bill on the floor at five-thirty in the morning, making changes to the code. Gates himself was supposed to put "hooks" in the ROM BASIC for the advanced versions, just as he had for the original TRS-80, but somehow he never found time to do them all. The job fell to Courtney—who accidentally left one out at the mid-March deadline. It was by no means the only bug that would be immortalized in the ROM.

For the final weekend of the ROM BASIC acceptance testing, Courtney recalled, IBM went as hardcore as Microsoft:

> As far as I know, it's the only time that IBM ever worked all day, all night, all weekend. They had a speakerphone down there—IBM loves speakerphones. And there was all this kind of noise going on, and I said, "What's going on?" and they said, "We're having pizza." And so I was imagining all these people with their ties undone, and they're actually having a party. . . . They got a flavor of what it was like to be where we were.

With Courtney's BASIC and Bradley's BIOS ready, IBM burned ROMs in late March and delivered a production model of the Chess machine to Microsoft shortly thereafter. The ROM work was finished—though a bug in the BIOS required another pass—but all the disk-based language work still hung fire. By April at least twenty-five of Microsoft's sixty employees were spending at least some of their time on the IBM project.

Outside of maintaining the relationship, Bill Gates's main involvement with the IBM machine was with his first love, BASIC—refining the specs, coding and reviewing, teaching Neil Konzen the "right" way to put the IBM logo on the screen, getting pissed off when a self-described "random little grit" like Konzen came up with a better algorithm for a graphics routine.

Gates and Konzen were responsible for one of the oddest programs IBM ever released: DONKEY, a game in which the player's car tries to avoid hitting the eponymous animals—one of the few real-life driving experiences Bill Gates seems to have missed. "Sunday afternoon it was the two of us in that sweaty room," Konzen recalled. "I drew the thing. It was supposed to be a cow, and it was a feeble little cow, and we figured, 'Okay, it's a donkey.' " Avoiding the beast was no thrill; hitting it, however, blew a raspberry from the speaker and displayed the message "BOOM! Donkey loses!"

The general weirdness of the program was not lost on the IBM wild ducks, who threw it on the DOS disk anyway. IBM wasn't all that particular about what it sent out to its entry-level customers. With DOS, it would also toss in a rudimentary text editor called EDLIN, written by Tim Paterson back in the Quick and Dirty days and initially unintended for public consumption. It would survive for more than ten years.

IBM was of two minds about Microsoft. On one hand, this outlaw band was clearly violating the cherished security protocols. The IBM cops had already fretted about a possible security gap involving the hotbox closet's false ceiling. At their direction, chicken wire had been installed above it in order to prevent untoward attacks.

But a surprise visit April 9 from Big Blue's security troops revealed more shocking lapses. Parts of the prototype were found outside the locked room; programmers were cavalierly handling IBM confidential information rather than logging it in and out to their offices; the door locks were appallingly flimsy.

And that was just what the IBM police found out about. In truth, virtually everybody in the place knew about the "secret" machine, kids like Neil Konzen were bringing their girlfriends and pals by to see it, and on one occasion, the delay between the time Eggebrecht arrived and the time he actually got to work on the machine led him to suspect that Bill had taken it home.

Yet on the same April day Ballmer was writing IBM to smooth over the security snafus, he sent another letter to sell the company even more software. Typing Tutor II, Time Manager, and Olympic Decathlon were all developed elsewhere but published by Microsoft Computer Products for other machines, and then there was Letwin's Adventure. A fifth product was little more than an idea: a low-end database that could handle Japanese Kanji characters as well as English. Finally, there was Electronic Paper, a VisiCalc knockoff discussed for months but barely off the drawing board.

Ballmer's initial quote for the low-end products was a per-copy royalty on the order of $3 to $5, with adaptation fees from $9,000 to $30,000. For Electronic Paper, he thought bigger—a royalty of $20 per copy, with a minimum of $1 million over two years, plus an adaptation fee of roughly $50,000 —all for a product that existed solely as a design prototype. IBM said yes to everything. Good old American salesmanship had scored again.

In May, after a falling-out with Rod Brock over Seattle Computer's marketing strategy, Tim Paterson strolled through the door as an employee of Microsoft. Old Retail Computer Store cohort and current Microsoft Pascal wizard Bob Wallace greeted him at the reception desk, had him sign the standard nondisclosure agreement, and ushered him down the hall to a hot little closet. It was there that Paterson got his first glimpse of the machine whose operating system he had been fine-tuning for months and was now virtually complete. Indeed, much of IBM's DOS technical documentation had been lifted directly from Paterson's 86-DOS manuals for Seattle Computer.

At IBM, marketing considerations, not technical ones, were becoming dominant as the machine turned real. One faction wanted to call the machine "Freedom," but the name that stuck was classically simple: the IBM Personal Computer. It would be the first IBM computer marketed without a number, although it had one—5150—discreetly on the back. And it would be the flagship product of the new Business Centers of Sears that were not all that different from the Tech Centers Blair Newman had proposed.

Word of the PC was beginning to leak out to the world at large. The code name was changed from Chess to Acorn, but except on official correspondence, no one paid much attention; at Microsoft, the machine was commonly known as HAL, after the computer in the film *2001*.

In May Bill Gates wrote IBM's Estridge proclaiming his enthusiasm for the project and making two requests. First, he and Paul asked to be invited to the official rollout of the machine—a request that Estridge denied. The second request was pure tightwad Bill Gates hustle: He asked for a special group-purchase price on Chess machines—and apparently got turned down on that too.

The news leaks increased. Gates and Ballmer grew frantic about the possibility that IBM might trace the leaks back to Microsoft—which, given their cavalier security precautions, was far from impossible. They had already spilled the beans to venture capitalist and mentor David Marquardt, and he clearly wasn't the only one. By early June an *InfoWorld* report described the machine reasonably accurately. *Electronics* correctly added the fact that "its disk operating system, developed by Microsoft Inc. of Bellevue, Washington is similar to CP/M and will be called IBM Personal Computer DOS." The report was on target: IBM had rechristened 86-DOS to its own taste. Although the IBM Personal Computer Disk Operating System would soon become known familiarly as PC-DOS, neither Microsoft nor IBM ever trademarked or officially used the term.

Suddenly there was a lot of interest in that mysterious DOS. Japanese customers began contacting Microsoft about the possibility of licensing it—something Microsoft was eminently permitted to do under the terms of its agreements with Seattle Computer and IBM. In June Rod Brock began getting calls too—from Eddie Currie of Lifeboat Associates, the leading independent distributor of CP/M and CP/M software. Currie was offering to make 86-DOS Lifeboat's 16-bit standard, and he was prepared to back the offer with money—a couple of hundred thousand dollars of it.

News of Lifeboat's offer woke Bill Gates up to what he was sitting on. Originally he had looked at this cheesy little operating system as just another way to sell his languages. Now—*Witness the transformation!*—this cheesy little operating system was supporting Microsoft's fledgling applications business too. And if the Japanese clamor was any indication, this cheesy little operating system might just be able to make some money on its own.

This would piss off Gary Kildall, who had for about a year been peddling his true language love, PL/I. Bill Gates viewed that as violating an unstated agreement that Microsoft would stick to languages and Digital Research would stick to operating systems—an agreement he himself had long since breached with XENIX. But it was beginning to be clear that any "agreement" had long since died. Bill was doing DOS; rumors were flying that Gary was planning to buy Gordon Eubanks's Compiler Systems, whose main product was CBASIC. If you messed with BASIC, you were messing where Bill Gates lived.

But now Bill Gates was clanking around in Kildall's operating system garage, and although CP/M-86 was still late, Kildall was not about to concede defeat. Having gotten wind of Microsoft's DOS deal and seen a copy of 86-DOS, he and attorney Gerry Davis were pointing out to IBM's legal department and Don Estridge and anyone else who might listen that there were suspicious similarities between DOS and CP/M—similarities so substantial that they skirted the edges and possibly even breached the bounds of legality.

Under similar circumstances, Digital Research had convinced earlier CP/M clones, such as Cromemco's CDOS, to acquire licenses. The hint of some sort of court action—a delightful little California injunction, perhaps, something that might cast a pall over the initial product rollout, caught the attention of the litigation-shy IBM.

Still, Kildall had little stomach for suing a behemoth whose legal department probably had a bigger payroll than his entire company's. When he and his crew met with Don Estridge, IBM's laid-back engineer confronted them point-blank. What did they *really* want?

Kildall said he wanted CP/M-86 to be offered on the IBM machine. That was fine with Estridge. In exchange for an agreement to drop any thought of injunctive relief, he struck the deal. Bill Gates would shortly find himself sharing the IBM machine with a competitor he thought had disappeared. He would later charge that IBM was "blackmailed into it."

It was time to take off the gloves. On June 25 Paul Allen took the first step to acquire Seattle Computer's 86-DOS outright. In a letter to Rod Brock, Allen proposed that Microsoft buy all rights to 86-DOS for $30,000, plus a free license to Microsoft's 8086 macro assembler and linker. Microsoft would take over the chore of supporting and revising the product, and SCP would get whatever enhancements Microsoft might make, free of charge. As Allen wrote, "You would be releived [sic] of the support of SCP DOS and have extra cash to potentially expand your hardware efforts, while we would be able to try to take CP/M-86 to the mat."

On July 10, two days after receiving the $15,000 payment due from Microsoft for its sublicensing of 86-DOS source and object code to one unnamed customer, Brock made a counterproposal. Tony Gold of Lifeboat, Brock wrote, was offering "a substantial up-front payment, with the guarantee of several $20,000 royalty payments," for the right to sell 86-DOS. "His interest is also the reason the exclusivity portion of the proposed agreement has such a high price tag." Brock suggested a fee of $150,000, plus the right to license Microsoft languages at a discount. In return, Microsoft would get the exclusive right to license 86-DOS to all OEM customers except those purchasing SCP's hardware.

Gates, Ballmer, and Allen met to discuss the proposal. High price tag? As Ballmer remembered it, "the $150,000 number we all agreed was just this mighty grab for gold." Bill saw this whole Lifeboat thing as out of control. The $150,000 figure would, in typical Gatesian exaggeration, "bankrupt the company"—this from the same Bill Gates who reportedly made $1 million and paid $500,000 in federal income tax that very year.

Allen thought something like $50,000 might get the deal done. That number was fine with Bill. But he insisted that the deal be an outright purchase, not a mere license. He reminded Paul about the hassles involved in their original license with MITS and what had happened when that agreement hadn't worked out. It was better, cleaner, to own a product outright.

"At this stage of the game," according to Ballmer, "we were trying to put together a business arrangement which would allow us to feel comfortable about being aggressive in terms of moving forward with our DOS plans with IBM and with other customers. And in that context, Bill's judgment and gut told him that the best thing is for this to be something that's clearly ours and clearly unencumbered and something where we could have flexibility to do whatever we wanted to do with it."

Gates knew the deal had to be done fast. By now the new IBM machine was an open secret, and Brock was sure to have guessed who the unnamed customer was. Still, Brock hadn't yet seen the machine and couldn't possibly understand just how important it was likely to be. Ballmer rushed the deal through, personally delivering the papers to Seattle Computer's offices. "I went down there . . . as part of the process to get the license signed, get the license signed, get the license signed. Bill had been pushing on me. . . . We knew the IBM Personal Computer and MS-DOS, not 86-DOS, but MS-DOS, would be announced sometime in the not-too-distant future from the end of July. And I wanted to have this agreement signed before the IBM PC was introduced.''

The final agreement, signed on July 27, sold 86-DOS outright to Microsoft for an additional payment of $50,000. In return, Seattle Computer got a royalty-free license back, permitting it to license the use of the software to ''purchasers of hardware manufactured by Seller.'' Seattle Computer would also get ''updates and enhancements,'' half its development costs for a projected multiuser DOS, and licenses to Microsoft's languages at roughly half the usual price.

If Gates was worried about Kildall's legal saber-rattling, he didn't show it. The still-evolving laws continued to indicate that you could sue someone who swiped portions of your source code, but not someone who reverse-engineered it. Microsoft agreed that if DOS somehow infringed on someone's copyright, Seattle Computer would be liable for no more than the amount of the deal.

Brock felt it was a reasonable arrangement. He was in the hardware business, and now he could afford to give his operating system away. ''Cash was important. . . . We visualized that we would have a tremendous advantage over any other OEM because we didn't have to pay for the license,'' and the sweetheart deal for the languages meant he could price those low too. Tim Paterson, still a shareholder and director of Seattle Computer, did know what was going on with IBM, though his nondisclosure agreement as a Microsoft employee kept him from telling Brock. He read the contract and ''thought it was a fair deal.''

It wasn't just a fair deal for Microsoft. It was the deal of the century. For a grand total of $75,000—$25,000 on the first agreement, $50,000 on the second—the company now owned DOS lock, stock, and barrel—or thought it did. Bill Gates would go on to make DOS the foundation of his empire. But he had not heard the last from Rod Brock.

Gates and Company were beginning to reach an audience outside the computer industry. In June 1981 *Fortune* ran a piece on leading industry figures, including Gates and Allen, pictured with their glasses sardonically perched halfway down their noses. Although still officially a Harvard undergrad, the article noted, ''Gates doesn't think he can go back. 'The pace in school,' he says, 'is a little bit different.' '' The article was a hit with Steve Ballmer, who distributed a companywide memo pointing out ''As slow as progress may seem, some times [*sic*] we are having an impact.''

Ballmer was definitely having an impact. A partnership since its inception, Microsoft finally became a Washington State corporation on July 1, 1981, thanks largely to his efforts and David Marquardt's. Initial stock went to a very few insiders. Gates and Allen held 53 and 31 percent of the shares respectively; Ballmer got about 8 percent, Raburn about 4; Simonyi and Letwin drew roughly 1½ percent each. In September Marquardt's TVI bought 5 percent of the company for a cool million dollars, diluting the other stockholders. As usual, Microsoft didn't need the money; the cash went straight into the bank.

Many veterans saw the stock partition as yet another slap in the face. They'd been responsible for the company's success, and yet stock was going only to Gates's closest pals—such as Chris Larson, who as a freshly minted Princeton graduate was cut in when he became the manager of OEM planning and the public advocate for DOS.

An option plan shortly put in place was only partly successful at muffling the complaints, in part because not everybody got stock. For those who did, the plan called for a one-year waiting period, then eight equal disbursements over four years. The initial stock price was 95 cents; a typical grant to a newly hired programmer might be 2,500 shares, and those who'd been with the company longer might get more. By early 1992 one of those initial shares would be worth $1,500, and a programmer with the foresight to have held all 2,500 would be a millionaire nearly four times over.

But as long as the company remained private, there was no telling how much the options eventually would be worth. "My stock options were like a standing joke in my family for years," one programmer recalled. Another remembered "a lot of cynicism around the company" because "the scale of the options was seen as being pretty minor compared to people's overtime work. It didn't even look like it paid the overtime."

Like the bonus-instead-of-overtime plan, stock options were a typically Gatesian low-risk way of offering rewards. Since the bonuses weren't guaranteed, they let Microsoft maintain control over its personnel expenditures. In a bad year the bonuses could be suspended temporarily. And at a firm paying average or even below-average wages, the stock option plan gave employees a sense of ownership, tying them to the company with golden handcuffs, keeping them from fleeing to greener pastures. Still, the core workers, especially the ex-Albuquerquians, continued to consider themselves grossly underpaid.

There was no doubt that the company was grossly understaffed and over-worked. Bill Gates deputized Steve Ballmer as Mr. Recruiting. Ballmer had understood the shortage of human resources ever since he'd begun to under-stand the company, and he had three surefire solutions: Hire, hire, and hire. To "straighten the place out," Ballmer asked Gates to approve the hiring of "about fifty people."

"I said no," Gates recalled. "I wasn't going to preauthorize fifty people. And he never got ahead of my willingness to hire people."

As Ballmer remembered it, the situation was yet another replay of Bill's gloom-and-doom attitude. "Even Paul wants me to add more people. Bill is afraid I'm going to bankrupt the company. . . . 'I brought you in to make sure that we be responsible and not hire a bunch of people and you're going to bankrupt us and you're going to bankrupt us and how could you do this?'"

Still, Ballmer moved fast. "I hire everybody. Nobody gets hired without my interviewing them and liking them. I make every offer and I close everybody and I decide the money on every candidate."

"He wasn't really interviewing you to see if you could do the job. He was interviewing you to see if you were a jerk or not," recalled Mike Slade, who went through the process successfully. "He would say, don't talk about work, just talk. . . . Then he'd decide if he liked you or not."

On their first official college recruiting trip, Ballmer and Paul Allen snared Doug Klunder, a slight, long-haired, fine-featured ascetic who refused on personal principle to drive cars or carry identification. Klunder photographed like a mild young Jesus but could program like the devil. About to graduate early from MIT with a degree in computer science, he was invited out to Seattle for a long weekend of interviewing and hanging around. After talking with several programmers, he eventually worked his way up to Bill Gates, who argued for the future of interpreted languages such as BASIC. Klunder, innocently using the tactic that would serve so many so well in their initial meetings with Bill Gates, stood up to him and ridiculed interpreted languages as too slow.

On Saturday Gates and Ballmer took him to lunch—at the local branch of Shakey's Pizza. "It just seemed—incorrectly—that [Microsoft] was a pretty laid-back place. . . . On the surface, stuff is very casual and, you know, you wear whatever you want. . . . Back then you certainly only worked whenever you wanted. But what was obvious from a brief interview was the intensity that underlies that: the amount of work you do and the pressure."

Even though the pay was "about the minimum I would accept," Klunder took the job and, as employee number sixty, became Microsoft's first official recruit. His observation about the intensity turned out to be intensely accurate. "From the top you saw Bill working really hard, and there was kind of an expectation. And a lot of it was just we had deadlines, and we needed to ship, and if you cared about your project, you worked on it. So it's not like I can ever recall anyone ever saying 'Well, you need to show up this weekend, all day and all night.' But it came to the point that you did." Klunder was yet another in a long line of brilliant young Smart Guys who had been and would be the company's technical backbone. As one executive would succinctly put it: "We hire little Bills."

Charles Simonyi, Ballmer's recruiting partner, rationalized the policy: "We were really looking for the inexperienced people," who were "easier to get, or more predictable to get. . . . We could actually depend on a flow of such people. . . . There was a supply and we had a mining operation."

There was another advantage to hiring green kids: "They were easier to motivate."

Simonyi's doctoral dissertation had been a study of programmer productivity, pushing the concept of a "meta-programmer"—say, Simonyi—who would write detailed specifications that "technicians" would simply code into a program. That didn't begin to work in Bellevue: The high-bandwidth young hotshots Microsoft hired couldn't possibly imagine themselves as mere "technicians." The way to motivate them, the company discovered from the outset, was just the opposite: Give them "ownership," a sizable say in the way their programs looked and worked. At Microsoft the primary legacy of Simonyi's dissertation was a style of naming program elements that was soon dubbed "Hungarian" in honor of its perpetrator.

The hiring continued, but even with people who worked fourteen-hour days and seven-day weeks, the company was chronically understaffed. And underequipped: One visitor had to deliver his presentation to Bill by holding 35-millimeter slides up to the light because Microsoft did not yet own a slide projector.

Despite the corporate growth, the unusual relationship between Bill Gates and Paul Allen remained at the core of the company. Within the hallways of Microsoft and among industry cognoscenti, Allen was gaining increasing respect as the ideas guy behind Microsoft. BASIC, SoftCard, DOS, and *not* APL —Allen had a sixth sense about new products. "That was in fact what made the partnership between Bill and Paul so brilliant," Vern Raburn observed. "Paul is very intuitive in his thinking. . . . And yet it was Bill's kind of just almost anal-retentive, pure-logic approach to things that would take Paul's sometimes random ideas and turn 'em into brilliant products."

At the time, Gates himself acknowledged, "I guess you could call me the doer and Paul the idea man. I'm more aggressive and crazily competitive, the front man in running the business day-to-day, while Paul keeps us out front in research and development."

Gates's explosive confrontational style was the diametrical opposite of Allen's subdued thoughtfulness and empathy. Even in Bellevue, with the constant pressure to work and produce, Allen, whose shaggy ZZ Top beard, soulful eyes, and gentle demeanor gave him an avuncular charm, seemed to be more rooted in real life than Binary Bill. Paul threw more parties, opened his doors to visitors, and—the cardinal sin to workaholics Ballmer and Gates—kept a looser schedule. "Paul always seemed closer to life than Bill," one former employee said. "Bill was wrapped up in the company and really in a sense is a victim of the company. I mean, the company owns him, not the other way around."

Allen could withstand and even rebuff Gates's withering attacks, but it extracted an increasingly debilitating toll. "You'd see Paul go home after one of these marathon screaming sessions that was five hours long, and he wouldn't show up at work for three or four days," Raburn recalled. "He was just physically wrung out."

Mike Courtney remembered one late evening when he followed the voices of Gates and Allen, arguing back and forth, "all the way out in the lobby, all the way out in the hall." After the two boarded the elevator the shouting slowly faded away. Moments later, when they emerged in the parking lot eight floors down, Courtney could hear them again, "and it went on for about another half an hour."

David Marquardt thought the friction between the two was as natural as flint and stone:

> Bill was this kind of wild, crazy young kid who would do almost anything on a dare, and Paul in the early days was the darer: "Aw, this can't be done." And Bill would go, "Oh, yeah? I'll show you," and he'd stay up all night. . . .
>
> Paul had an incredible amount of the initial vision of the company and kept kind of pushing Bill around . . . by daring him into things and kind of goading him. And then Bill would come back, and they used to have these incredible fights all the time, just tantrums, and a lot of the tantrums and arguments resulted in very good decisions, where Bill would think one thing, like "We'll just give it to everybody for free," and Paul would go, "Wait a minute, no, we should be charging money for this." "No, no, just think, if we give it to everybody for free, then we'll own the market," and "Yeah, but then we won't have any money to do anything with it." And so they'd get into these incredible arguments, and as a result, I think, very good decisions got made.

Over time, Marquardt believed, Paul "got tired of the arguing." But there were plenty of combatants left. "Steve would fight with him occasionally. I'd come in and fight with Bill occasionally."

And there were always plenty of underlings to fight with. Gates's combative style went back to the days of family games, of fighting for his rights as the scrawniest kid way back in the days of "soak 'em" and scouting. But it was also a survival tactic, former vice president Ida Cole suggested:

> My theory about it is that when Bill was nineteen years old and looked like a little owl and was starting a company, that the only way you get taken seriously in a situation like that is by being very confrontational. That's really how you make your point, because if you try to do it in another way, just being smart is not going to be enough. I mean, you've really got to make some noise about it if you're under the gun that way. And it worked for him, and he kept doing it. And it kept working for him.

Gates expended some of his energy on fast driving. With his green 911 on its last wheels and speeding tickets piling up, the software speedster found himself the proud possessor of a Mercedes 300D Diesel, the fastest slow car in the world. Gates purchased the car to slow himself down, but airport-bound passengers recall screaming along in freeway ditches, passing on the right in an attempt to make the twenty-minute drive in fifteen minutes. Traffic records from the era indicate tickets of 68 mph in a 50 mph zone, 60 in a 45 zone, 49 in a 30 zone, and another violation with speeds unspecified. But some of the more flagrant violations were expunged from the record by Bill's attendance at traffic school.

As with the 911 before it, Gates took lousy care of the Mercedes. Not that he discriminated against his own cars. When the Mercedes was in the shop after Gates ripped out its oil pan, Gates borrowed pal Andy Evans's Porsche 928. As Bill recalled it, the narrow road was curvy and wet, the guy coming toward him had wandered out of his lane, and Gates swerved. "There's this big cement block there that hit the side of the car, and then the car kind of spins. . . . The axle was broken. The mobility was highly reduced"—so reduced that the Porsche factory rep from San Francisco came up for a personal inspection and the Porsche was laid up for months. Gates walked away unscathed.

Gary Kildall liked to go fast too. The first weekend in August, he had flown his personal jet up for Seafair, an annual Seattle ritual celebrating things that go fast and make loud noises, culminating in hydroplane races on Lake Washington and an intermission show by the navy's Blue Angel aerobatic team. From his hillside pad, Bill and friends could see the whole production. A few hours after the race, Gates, Ballmer, and Allen met Kildall and Digital Research marketing director John Katsaros for a strange session at the Blue Max, a deserted restaurant near Boeing Field, where both sides tiptoed around the important issues.

As Ballmer recalled it, "They had been threatening IBM, and we knew they'd been threatening IBM, and they knew we knew, and nobody talked about it." As Katsaros recalled it, Gates was "offended" by Kildall's move into languages, but neither side was particularly forthcoming about its complaints. Though Kildall knew about DOS and Gates knew about DR's impending deal for CBASIC, the discussion centered instead around such delicate topics as format compatibility.

Just three days later, on August 12, 1981, IBM announced the IBM Personal Computer. Although no one realized it at the time, this announcement really would change the world.

13

THE REALITY DISTORTION FIELD

At that moment another machine was aborning that promised to have a few world-changing powers of its own. It was emerging not from some renegade mainframers in IBM clothing but from a few genuine Silicon Valley Homebrew change-the-world types now subscribing to one of the sects of the persuasion known as Apple Computer.

In late summer 1981, just after the IBM PC was announced, Apple's chairman, mercurial wunderkind and media genius Steve Jobs, brought a small entourage to pay a call on Bill Gates. Jobs was personal computing's golden boy, the barefoot, T-shirted prodigy of Silicon Valley. In December 1980, just six years after he had made a find-yourself pilgrimage to India, Apple's public stock offering had made him a millionaire two hundred times over, at twenty-five the youngest person ever to reach the Forbes 400 list. Within a few months his moustachioed, brooding intensity would grace the cover of *Time*. Jobs and Joan Baez would briefly be an item, and his dashing good looks and suave style made him the focus of attention wherever he went—including Microsoft head-quarters.

The man he was visiting was barely known to the general public—in part because compared to Jobs, Bill Gates had all the sex appeal of a floppy disk. True, within the industry he was an established figure, if not from the Altair BASIC piracy letters then through Microsoft's language development and ag-gressive business style. But if you looked at the past-performance sheets, Jobs genuinely deserved all the public attention. In 1981 Apple had total sales of $334 million and profits of $39.4 million. Microsoft, with its puny $15 million gross and $1.5 million net, wasn't in the same ballpark.

Still, Bill Gates had a few aces up his sleeve. As Ida Cole, who worked at both companies, would put it, Microsoft was "a technological company. And it's run by a technoid. Apple was very much a marketing company. Steve Jobs was the most prominent person at Apple, and he was not a technology guy."

Unlike Steve, Bill had listening posts in every far-flung corner of the hardware world, giving him a sweeping, global vision of the future. And Bill, in the July reorganization that had finally turned Microsoft into a corporation, still held a majority of his own company's stock, with virtually all the rest in the hands of such pals as Allen and Ballmer. By contrast Jobs was a mere pawn in the hands of venture capitalists; although the single biggest Apple shareholder, he held only 15 percent of the firm he treated as if it were his own.

Yet on the August day in 1981 when he came to Microsoft to present the latest revision of his vision, Jobs thought he had the future in his pocket. He chortled over Apple's latest coup: a full-page ad in the *Wall Street Journal,* headlined "Welcome, IBM. Seriously." In it, Apple reiterated its classic over-blown claim to have "invented the first personal computer system," talked about "increasing social capital by enhancing individual productivity," and declared "We look forward to responsible competition in the massive effort to distribute this American technology to the world." Jobs thought it was perfect; on the plane north to Microsoft, he gleefully passed the ad around to the Apple team traveling with him.

Little did the group realize, as young Applesoft developer Randy Wiggin-ton would recall, that "We were signing our own death warrant." Blinded by his own tunnel vision, Jobs was blissfully unaware that the clunky machine that had first sprung to life in a closet down the hall from Bill's office was about to push personal computing into new realms of popularity and power—and give Apple fits. Jobs could think only about the far more dazzling state-of-the-art Apple computers he had up his sleeve.

Back in 1979, on a tour of Xerox PARC, Jobs had seen the graphical-based stuff Simonyi and his colleagues had been working on. It utterly knocked his socks off: Steve Jobs became an instant convert to the religion of the GUI—the graphical user interface with its icons and fonts and mouse that let users manipulate their computers the way they did their desktops. It was the wave of the future, Jobs was sure, and he would ride it for all it was worth.

First out of the chutes with a commercial product, however, was Xerox with its Star, announced in mid-1981. The Star's vision was so complete that a decade later the PC workplace still would be struggling to put all its elements together. But the Star was expensive—over $16,000 per workstation, not counting the pricey printer and other peripherals. The Star was slow. Worst of all—fatal, actually—the Star was a closed system. It would run only the software it came with, and that software didn't even include a spreadsheet. Without software or any easy way to create it, the Star was at bottom a very expensive word processing system. As such, it was dead on arrival.

But if you were an acolyte of the GUI religion, the Star was an essential shrine. Microsoft sank tens of thousands of dollars into a Star system complete with printer. Gates liked to tinker with it, but otherwise it was used mostly to design clever party invitations. Still, at least one Microsoft executive divined the power of good-looking output. Challenged by the tight-as-a-tick Gates over his expense reports, Alan Boyd began printing them out with the Star's slick fonts and rules and headings. Bill never questioned his expenses again.

The Lisa, Apple's maiden GUI entry, was still under development. At one time it had been Steve Jobs's pet. Initially referred to as the Apple IV, it was eventually named for a real person, most likely the girl for whom Jobs was paying $385 a month in child support despite his dismissive proclamation that "28 percent of the male population of the United States could have been the father." Designed by former PARC stars like Larry Tesler, Lisa was turning out a lot like the Star—expensive, slow, and closed. By committing to ship it with a collection of internally developed software, Apple had cut independent developers such as Microsoft and VisiCorp out of the loop. And Jobs's personality had abraded the development team's nerves—to the point where Apple president Mike Scott, in a corporate reorganization, relieved him of the project. Stung at first, Jobs merely switched his always fickle allegiance to another developing machine, one that he recast as the new change-the-worlder. It was called the Macintosh.

Certain that the high-powered Lisa would eat this dirtball machine for lunch, Jobs had opposed the Mac for nearly two years after its originator, a bearded, balding artificial intelligence scholar, composer, and university professor named Jef Raskin, had put the project together. "He said it was one of the dumbest ideas he'd ever heard of," Raskin recalled. Dumbest, stupidest: The terms were interchangeable depending on whether you were in Cupertino or Bellevue, revealing Steve Jobs and Bill Gates as brothers of invective.

Raskin himself had been at PARC in the early 1970s. He had tried to convince Jobs and Apple co-founder Steve Wozniak of the joys of GUI computing while they were still garage monkeys. It was Raskin who wrote the bulk of the enabling blueprint called "The Book of Macintosh," who assembled the original team to work on the project, and who named the computer for his favorite apple. After Jobs seized control of the design, the disenchanted Raskin became largely forgotten in Macintosh legend.

But Raskin was still involved in the project when Jobs made initial overtures to Bill Gates in the spring of 1981, just before Xerox announced the Star. If the Star was a Rolls-Royce, the Mac would be a Volkswagen: a machine nearly as functional, but without all the chrome, for a price of $1,000.

Gates, Jobs, and Raskin had initially met on June 5. Two key issues were emerging: Which applications should Microsoft develop for the Mac, and should they be bundled—included free—with every machine? The PC universe was changing. Users cared less and less about languages and more and more about applications. The applications they wanted most were word processors and spreadsheets.

Spreadsheets had been a sore point for Jobs. VisiCalc had almost single-handedly turned the Apple II from a hobbyist toy into a business machine. Customers would beat a path to their local computer store to buy an Apple II just so they could run VisiCalc. The program had sold 200,000 copies within two years, making it by far the best-selling computer application. For the Apple III version, bundled with the machine, VisiCorp was getting a royalty of $75 per copy—a royalty Jobs considered exorbitant. And Bill Gates just happened to have a spreadsheet project called Electronic Paper, which the master of the lowball had successfully peddled to IBM at no more than $20 per copy.

Years later Gates would admit that "I should have hired people faster and gotten into the applications business sooner" when asked about his greatest mistakes. Electronic Paper had dragged on and on at Microsoft with little support until the coming of Charles Simonyi. Vern Raburn, the VisiCalc fanatic, had been pushing for Microsoft to do a spreadsheet even before he had arrived. He and Bob Greenberg had cobbled together a specification back in 1979, but Bill wasn't willing to devote manpower to the project. The first time Raburn showed him VisiCalc, Gates had shrugged and said, "With two or three primitives, I can do this in BASIC." He was not about to commit precious resources to mere applications when a ton of language business was coming through the door.

In May 1980 Paul Heckel, yet another PARC alumnus, had been brought in as a consultant and recommended that Microsoft produce a clone of VisiCalc with a better user interface. Since VisiCalc had a lock on the retail market, Heckel suggested Microsoft court OEM customers. "Basic Strategy: The IBM Strategy. Don't be the first to introduce a new technology. Be second, and make money on it." Near the end of 1980, programmer Mark Mathews was commissioned to put together a working prototype. He had it up and running by the time Charles Simonyi became a Microsoft employee.

It was a rude awakening for the Mad Hungarian. The character-based program "was all junk" compared to the elegant-looking stuff he'd become accustomed to at Xerox. But the customers loved it. Heckel's "OEMs first" strategy had been adopted, and when Simonyi went out on sales calls, the Mathews demo got companies excited enough to reach for their checkbooks. At least Electronic Paper had on-screen menus, which made it easier to use than VisiCalc. Simonyi realized that he'd gained a reputation at Xerox for not being a team player, so he was "very reluctant to come in and start by cleaning house." His proposed fancy VisiCalc follow-on with graphics and database would have to wait. Simonyi had a better idea—an idea he dubbed "the revenue bomb."

Originally developed for the Apple II, VisiCalc was taking forever to appear on other machines. In Simonyi's view the trick for Microsoft was to get its applications running quickly on as many machines as possible. The fastest way was a one-size-fits-all approach. Instead of writing code for a particular computer, programmers would write pseudocode (p-code) for a software pseudomachine (p-machine) that could interpret it for the real machine. The concept of Paul Allen's 8008 emulator was back once more: Use software to behave like hardware.

The beauty of this scheme was that in theory the program code would have to be written only once. For each new computer, all you'd need would be a new p-code interpreter. And you wouldn't even have to write that. Instead, you'd give your OEM customer the specifications for the interpreter, and let the customer worry about writing it. As programmer Doug Klunder remembered the gist of Simonyi's "revenue bomb" speech at a companywide meeting, "We invest a little effort, and then everyone else writes interpreters, and then we just keep getting the money."

It seemed pure genius. These p-coded programs would run on almost anything. P-coded programs saved memory, one thing the 8-bit machines of the day were woefully short on. And Simonyi designed the user interface to be as flexible as possible. Dubbed the Multi-Tool Interface, a handle only Black and Decker could love, it was meant to work on everything from spreadsheets to DOS. Menus appeared at the bottom of the screen as lines of one-word instructions such as "Copy" or "Delete." It worked with character-based systems, but Simonyi and Gates knew it would be perfect for the point-and-click mouse-based machines that had to be coming soon.

Electronic Paper was renamed Multiplan and became the first Multi-Tool program. At the urging of Bill Gates, who loved neat features and plenty of them, Multiplan had features that no competitor had yet matched. Multiplan made educated guesses at some of your intentions, offered "windows" that showed you multiple areas of the spreadsheet at once, and allowed you to link spreadsheets so that three divisions of a company could maintain separate ledgers and easily combine them into one. Named ranges let you write formulas such as "Profit = Sales − Costs" if you chose to, instead of "R1C2 = R4C5 − R6C7." Help screens, unusual for the day, assisted the confused. Recalculations were performed automatically.

One interface, one core code, one menu structure. It looked great on paper. On the computer, it wasn't quite as impressive. Multiplan was slow. Very slow. In computing as in life, there are no free lunches, and compared with compiled applications, the p-code technique cut performance by at least 50 percent, sometimes more. The Multi-Tool Interface, though far more accommodating than the baffling VisiCalc model, featured such puzzling commands as "Alpha" and "Transfer." And that "R1C1" format, the R standing for "row" and the C for "column," seemed hopelessly clunky and typing-intensive compared with the VisiStandard "A1" scheme. But Multiplan, like the Macintosh, was still a mere infant; Doug Klunder was still busy coding it.

In the promise-selling world of computerdom, the slow, awkward, pudgy baby is invariably guaranteed to grow up a Jesse Owens.

So OEMs were signing up for Multiplan in droves. In the end, Multiplan may well have run on more different platforms than any other application program ever. It first ran on Datapoint machines, with their proprietary processors. It ran on XENIX. It ran on Texas Instruments' 99/4A and the Commodore 64, essentially toy computers. As Simonyi remembered it, "At one point there were more than a hundred OEMs for Multiplan. . . . We were delivering like a Multiplan a day, like Liberty ships in World War II."

Why not the Mac? That was the idea of the visit from Jobs and Company in August on the heels of the IBM rollout. During a day-long session at Microsoft headquarters, Charles Simonyi gave the group a demo of Multiplan and talked about the whole Multi-Tool vision—ease of use, consistent interface, mouse manipulation.

That evening, Bill hosted a summit meeting at the Seattle Tennis Club on the shores of Lake Washington. Jobs brought along Randy Wigginton, the Applesoft master who had become one of the mainstays of the new Raskinless Mac team, programming wizards Andy Hertzfeld and Bud Tribble, and Joanna Hoffman, creator of the initial Macintosh User Interface Guidelines. Along with Paul Allen and Charles Simonyi, Bill's high-octane entourage included Multiplan programmer Mark Mathews, Multiplan IBM account manager Jeff Harbers, and boy-wonder Apple magician Neil Konzen. Months before, Konzen had actually been recruited for the Mac team and rejected for inexperience; as a dyed-in-the-peel Apple fanatic and the only Microsoftie who had actually seen a prototype Mac, he was the most enthusiastic of the lot.

Jobs gave a mesmerizing performance. He was going to build a factory where sand, the silicon that computer chips were based on, would go in one end and emerge at the other as an "information appliance," a term he'd borrowed from Raskin. The new computer would be as easy to use and functionally indispensable as a toaster. "We were incredibly excited," Harbers recalled. "It was exactly the hardware we wanted, and he was going to ship it at low cost, in these high volumes. This was incredible. This was the machine that we had all been dying for."

To hear Jobs tell it, the Macintosh would offer exponentially greater value than anything on the market. It would be so childishly simple that it would need no manual. It would include all the basic software anyone could ask for. And he would deliver it incredibly fast, by late 1982, just over a year away. "We thought it would be great to be bundled on this platform and he was going to sell 25 million of them," Harbers remembered. "It was my first encounter with Steve Jobs and the reality distortion field."

Reality distortion field: That three-word phrase would soon become synonymous with Jobs's ability to convince perfectly reasonable people of totally unrealizable notions. But at the time, Jobs's enthusiasm was infectious. The wizards of Microsoft had caught a bad case of Macintosh fever.

For the poker-savvy Gator, the Macintosh was a calculated side bet to hedge against the still-uncertain fortunes of the IBM PC. Although it clearly showed a lot of potential, the IBM machine brought no great technological advances to the party and was certain to draw a raft of me-too competitors. The IBM PC was a step up from the Apple II, but the Macintosh Jobs promised would be a major leap beyond them both. It might not succeed, but if it turned out to be the wave of the future, as Gates and Simonyi genuinely believed, Microsoft would be there to capitalize on it.

In October Jobs invited the Microsoft applications team down to a demonstration in Cupertino. Here was a computer that not only did real-life work but was almost as much fun as a video game. Even though the hardware was a breadboard prototype hooked up to a cheap Apple II disk drive, the panache of Andy Hertzfeld's whimsical animated "bouncing icons" demo dazzled the emissaries from Bellevue.

Microsoft still had a lot to learn about this graphics stuff. Bill Gates himself was green enough in the ways of the Mac to ask what Hertzfeld considered a stupid question about how the hardware displayed the mouse cursor—which, Gates knew, was the way the Star handled it.

Hardware? Hardware wasn't the issue, Hertzfeld informed him with true nerdy pride; the cursor stuff had all been done with software magic, which he then began haughtily to explain. Steve Jobs said "Shut up!" and cut him off. No sense giving away the family jewels.

Hertzfeld was not particularly impressed with Gates. Upon the release of the IBM PC, the gang at Apple had gotten hold of a machine immediately, cracked the cover, looked inside, and laughed. Everything about the computer was kludgy—it had limited graphics, an almost nonexistent user interface, no mouse, no network capability, minimal sound facilities. And talk about lame engineering! The circuitry just to control the disk drive used as many chips as the entire Macintosh.

But the real revelation was on the DOS disk. There was this terminally stupid BASIC game called DONKEY that used brute-force animation and blocky, ugly graphics. The sheer bozosity of it had the Macintosh gang in stitches. They laughed even louder when they learned that the code had been written by none other than Bill Gates.

By January 1982 the deal with Apple was nearly complete. Aboard a flight to the Valley, Mathews, Allen, and Harbers shook their heads as the plane backed away from the gate. Gates had dragged Simonyi along on one of his patented last-minute airport runs, and this time it hadn't worked.

And then, to the utter amazement of the Microsoft contingent, the plane stopped, reversed, and returned to the gate. Somehow the fast-talking Bill Gates had convinced the agents this was a life-and-death matter.

As the flabbergasted Microsofties marveled once again at their chief's leadership talents, Gates stepped aboard and magically reverted to the awkward twelve-year-old nerd. Fumbling with the combination on his briefcase, he couldn't manage to open it and produce his boarding pass. Fortunately, Charles Simonyi was having the same problem. The two eventually realized that in the confusion they had swapped their identical cases.

On their return, the team brought home Microsoft's first Mac prototype, a collection of circuit boards in a carrying case. "It was like we were sneaking through the airport," remembered Harbers, who would shortly become Microsoft's development manager for the Mac. "And we were part of the inner circle of the greatest technological breakthrough that was going to change the world. I was just totally jazzed by the stuff." At Microsoft, Harbers installed the breadboard machine in an isolated room that featured a little sandbox; in honor of the silicon-to-machine concept that Jobs had pitched so successfully, Harbers had given the machine the Microsoft code name SAND—which also stood for Steve's Amazing New Device. "People would say, 'I'm going down to the beach,'" Harbers recalled, "and we would just smile."

It was time to deal. In a contract dated January 22, 1982, Apple agreed to supply Microsoft four prototypes of the Macintosh, which the company would use to produce three software applications: a spreadsheet, a business graphics program, and a database. No word processor, no BASIC, to Bill's great chagrin; Jobs already had those products in development. Left open-ended was the issue of bundling Microsoft's programs. The agreement gave Jobs a choice: Either include the applications with the machine and pay Microsoft $5 per program (with a limit of $1 million per program per year), or sell them separately and pay Microsoft $10 a copy or 10 percent of the suggested retail price, whichever was greater. Apple promised a $50,000 advance on signing, with another $50,000 due on acceptance of the apps.

Wary of Gates using his Mac experience to produce competing software, Jobs dictated that Microsoft could not "undertake in any way to sell, lease, license, publish or otherwise distribute . . . any financial modeling, business graphics or database program which utilizes a mouse or tracking ball for any computer not manufactured by Apple." The intent was to give the Mac a head start by keeping Microsoft from releasing similar GUI programs for the IBM PC world before the Mac came out. But blinded by his impossible production schedule, Jobs limited the exclusivity clause to twelve months after the earlier of two dates: the initial shipment of the Macintosh or January 1, 1983. Bill Gates would soon take advantage of the fact that Steve Jobs had tripped over his own reality distortion field.

Gates had clearly bought the bit-mapped GUI dream. In May 1981 he had touted it as a featured speaker at the Rosen Research Personal Computer Forum, a high-level confab held that year in Lake Geneva, Wisconsin, at the Playboy Resort and Country Club in tacit homage to the testicularity of the industry.

Gates pointed out to the 370 conferees that "Software today does define the solution. . . . The reason that people pay $8,000 or $9,000 to buy a Wang word processor is because of the software that's inside there.

"The key thing that's going on with software right now is we're trying to make the machines easier to use"—a goal that was apparently a long way off. "Today there's incredible innovation in the hardware area. . . . People are really unable to take advantage of that technology because the software's really lagging behind and bottlenecking the use of that technology.

"Today we've essentially lifted up what existed on the minicomputer and mainframe world and thrown it onto a micro," Gates noted, succinctly describing the policy that had made Microsoft's success. But most people, he knew, "want things to be user-friendly. They want a way of understanding how information is represented in their terms. Drawers, files, folders—whatever terminology you pick, it's got to somehow tie into something the user had used before."

An example? The Xerox Star. "If you're waiting for an operation to proceed, you see a timeglass sitting there. The amount of sand in the top of the timeglass actually shows you how far along the operation is. You watch as it drains down; when it completes, the operation is over. And that may sound like a cute technique, but a number of those things put together in a uniform manner really reach the threshold level where you no longer view the machine as a computer."

At the same forum two years later, enthusiasm would give way to reality when Gates would point out that "The hourglass cursor has a bad reputation because the speed of the Xerox Star forces you to stare at that hourglass about 75 percent of the time." But no matter: In these interim versions of Dynabook, the vision of Xerox's grand dreamer Alan Kay was alive and well. Bill Gates had bought the dream, and he would do something the grand dreamer could not.

He would sell it.

14

A COMPETITIVE PERSON

Initial press for the IBM Personal Computer was mixed. From techies, the standard response was a bored snicker. The 16-bit design was nice, but the 8088 was the lamest 16-bit chip around. And how dare IBM charge a premium price for a machine with no disk drives, a paltry 16K of memory, and a BASIC that tested barely faster than the Apple II's?

But the August 1981 release clearly rocked the industry. An *InfoWorld* reporter discovered that "On the morning of the announcement, phone calls to IBM's competitors revealed that almost everyone was having an 'executive meeting' involving the high-level officials who might be in a position to publicly react to the IBM announcement." In a *New York Times* article headlined "Next, a Computer on Every Desk"—that phrase again—reporter Andrew Pollack got the essential point: "I.B.M.'s entry erased any lingering doubts that personal computers are serious business."

The industry understood quite well that the low-end $1,265 cassette-only 16K IBM PC and even the $2,235 48K single-disk unit were simply bait-and-switch marketing devices much like a stripped-down "deluxe" model car. If an adamant bargain hunter wanted to take one out the door without armrests or a clock, fine. Most buyers would end up configuring their machines with the "options" that were in fact essentials—disk drives, extra memory, a monitor. Viewed that way, the IBM PC cost about the same as comparable machines and, despite its vaunted 16-bit power, offered only slightly better performance.

But the combination of the 16-bit design, open architecture, and IBM's business presence meant there really were no comparable machines. In a remarkably prescient interview in the charter issue of *PC Magazine,* Bill Gates predicted IBM would sell 200,000 machines in 1982 and explained precisely why the IBM PC was important:

I think 16-bits is extremely important, and it is not because of speed. . . .

The main reason for the 16-bit micro being advantageous is its increased address space. That sounds like a technical issue, but what it boils down to for the end-user is that we can do more complex software, with a better end-user interface. . . .

. . . the logical address space limit is for all practical purposes gone away. The chip is designed to address up to a megabyte (1 million characters). . . . that factor will make all the difference in terms of quality end-user interface integrated software.

The hardware, in other words, was simply making possible the triumph of software. What was important about the IBM PC was its potential to plug in all that wonderful memory in the service of greater software glory. On opening day, most IBM PCs might be going out the door with no more than the traditional 64K of RAM that 8-bit machines could handle. But on 8-bit machines, some of that 64K had to be dedicated to the screen and housekeeping chores; on the IBM PC, you could use every bit of that 64K for programs and data. And tomorrow, with Moore's Law ensuring inexorably cheaper memory, people would add lots of it to their machines and programmers would take advantage of it.

Gates went on to look at the future with twenty/twenty vision, derived in part from what he already knew about the Macintosh:

Hardware in effect will be a lot less interesting. The total job will be in the software, and we'll be able to write big fat programs. We can let them run somewhat inefficiently because there will be so much horsepower that just sits there. The real focus won't be who can cram it down in, or who can do it in the machine language. It will be who can define the right end-user interface and properly integrate the main packages.

I think five years from now the amount of software and the quality of the software on this machine will be incredible. It will dwarf what is available on mainframes, minicomputers, and other machines.

"We're still not at the stage where I'd tell my mother, or some naive person, just to go out and buy one of these machines," Bill admitted in a reprise of his "Don't *you* ever think?" attitude. "In a couple of years we'll achieve that real peak—to fill that gap and feel like it's a real tool."

Although it was by no means universally recognized at the time, the IBM deal had given Microsoft an enormous head start in the race to fill that gap. Puzzled observers seemed to think IBM had screwed up yet again by developing its own operating system instead of the "industry standard" CP/M.

What few seemed to notice was that even though three operating systems had been announced for the IBM PC, IBM had thrown all its weight behind the IBM Personal Computer DOS—the one from Microsoft. Operating System option number two, Softech's Pascal-based p-system, was never a threat. Digital Research's CP/M-86 was another matter. Analysts expected CP/M-86 to knock DOS off the moment it became available—despite the fact that it would not ship for months.

But from Day One of the PC, IBM was at best ignoring CP/M-86, at worst trying to make it go away. Microsoft's suite of computer languages ran only under DOS and produced only DOS programs, assuring that at least initially, most applications would be developed for DOS. Indeed, every single software application sold under the official IBM label ran under DOS and only DOS. The IBM Personal Computer DOS came with two separate advanced versions of BASIC, ran virtually all the software available for the machine, and cost a mere $40. In the spring, when CP/M-86 was finally ready to ship, IBM would slap a premium price on it: $240 for an operating system that didn't include BASIC and could run virtually nothing. On the IBM PC, CP/M-86 was dead before arrival. For a time the point was lost on the pundits, but it was utterly obvious to independent software developers. They were writing a flood of new DOS programs and virtually none for CP/M-86.

Yet as late as August 6, a few days before the IBM PC announcement, Gates was still testing the waters, still debating what to do with the operating system he'd acquired the week before. He had been down to Intel to get its endorsement, but had been turned away by engineers who considered DOS a crude hack and believed CP/M-86 was technically superior when it came to such features as memory management.

Facing a competitor whose leader, Gary Kildall, would publicly admit "I'm not a competitive person," Bill and Company were about to Gates the deck and grease the skids under CP/M-86. To gain additional credibility, Bill cut a deal with CP/M vendor Lifeboat Associates.

Having lost his bid for rights to Seattle Computer's 86-DOS, Lifeboat's Eddie Currie, a buddy of Bill's from their MITS days, approached him with the idea of some sort of collaboration. In the end, Gates proposed that Lifeboat might get a percentage of the revenue from OEM sales it referred to Microsoft. In a New York press conference, Lifeboat announced its policy toward the 16-bit world: It would cast its fate with Microsoft, selling DOS under the name Software Bus-86 (SB-86). Tony Gold, Lifeboat's chief, also bankrolled *PC Magazine,* which swiftly became one of the most successful business publications in history. CP/M-86 was out of the Lifeboat and thrashing in the water.

Microsoft itself was roiling the waters by pushing DOS aggressively under the name MS-DOS. Although the initial plethora of names—MS-DOS, PC-DOS, SB-86, anything any customer wanted to call it—caused confusion, interest began to surface as the meaning of the IBM PC sank in. Computer makers in the United States and abroad suddenly awakened to the idea that 16-bit machines were the future of microcomputing. Industry guru Portia Isaacson, who had initially dubbed the IBM PC "the CP/M record player," quickly reversed herself and declared that "CP/M-86 will not be the operating system of choice for most buyers of the IBM personal computer." In *Microsoft Quarterly,* Bill Gates predicted that "16-bit microprocessors will sweep the microcomputer market." Within weeks of the IBM PC announcement, dozens of 16-bit machines were on the drawing boards. Bill Gates intended to put Microsoft's DOS on every one of them.

The initial license was the free one to Seattle Computer, the first company to offer the product under the MS-DOS name. The second customer was Cleveland's Tecmar, which was developing an 8086 computer of its own but put it on the back burner when it decided to become a major player in the burgeoning IBM PC add-on business. Lomas Data Products and Compu-Systems, direct competitors of Seattle Computer, were next to sign. But the big guys were not yet aboard, and they were the ones Bill Gates needed.

The Microsoft sales pitch was simple. MS-DOS had been endorsed by IBM and Lifeboat. There were already plenty of applications that ran under it, and more were coming along every day. Translating old CP/M programs to MS-DOS would be a breeze. And even though Microsoft did sign agreements to deliver CP/M-86 versions of its languages, a March 1982 Gates memo revealed how little effort the company planned to expend on CP/M-86. Only Pascal, FORTRAN, and the BASIC interpreter were on the schedule, and the BASIC was an inferior "standard" edition without the graphics of the IBM version. For the CP/M-86 compilers, moreover, Microsoft would charge a premium of 50 percent over the MS-DOS language price, ostensibly for "what CP/M lacks"—utility software such as a linker. This technique of using one product to leverage another became one of the prized tactics in Microsoft's strategic arsenal.

DOS benefited from the classic Gates lowball pricing that had made Microsoft BASIC a global standard. In the early going, Gates virtually gave MS-DOS away. The official price was $95,000, flat fee—but for a limited time only, OEMs could get the first version of DOS for half that. The sales argument was potent: CP/M-86 didn't even exist yet. Even if you'd already committed to it, even if you thought it would win in the end, wasn't it worth a lousy fifty or a hundred grand to clear your bet?

But BASIC was still the cash machine. In November, at the annual Las Vegas ritual known as Fall Comdex, Hitachi got on board for the graphics-oriented BASIC first released in the Oki and IBM machines and now known as GW-BASIC—the mysterious GW standing officially for Gee Whiz, though Golly Wow, Gates William, and Graphics With were often guessed. It was

Microsoft's first single-product million-dollar deal; to celebrate, Bill and the Microsoft higher-ups went out drinking and casino-hopping. The exuberant Bill, feeling no pain, hopped other things as well, including the hoods of taxicabs, in rare public displays of his legendary jumping ability.

The next morning or the morning after—memories are understandably fuzzy—on the heels of a late-night casino poker session, another document needed Bill's signature: Microsoft's first major DOS deal. Chuck Peddle, father of the 6502 chip and the Commodore PET, had a new startup company called Sirius whose forthcoming Victor was among the first in a long line of 16-bit computers that were similar to and better than the IBM PC, but incompatible with it. Peddle needed languages and an operating system, and the contract negotiations with Microsoft had dragged for weeks. Peddle and an entourage from Victor Business Products went to Bill's hotel room for an 8:00 A.M. meeting and pulled out the contract. Tired and nursing a bad hangover, Gates took a look at it, excused himself, and, as he remembered it, "I actually got sick during a brief intermission" of upchucking.

Although Peddle also had a deal for CP/M-86, the flat-fee contract for MS-DOS and per-machine fee for BASIC made it inevitable that they would be bundled with the computer—relegating CP/M-86 to the status of optional extra. In fact, the deal was so favorable to Victor—a long-term license to DOS, BASIC, and all the languages for any machine Victor might choose to make, with a cap on the royalty—that the contract became one of its most valuable assets when the company went through Chapter 11 proceedings a few years later. Gates would later tell one executive that he had agreed to such terms only because Peddle and Microsoft sales manager Steve Smith had ganged up on him while he was busy inspecting the porcelain.

By the end of the year, *InfoWorld* was reporting that "a healthy and diverse cottage industry is springing up around the newly released IBM Personal Computer," even though IBM had badly underestimated demand and its machines were in short supply. In 1981 Apple had sold roughly 150,000 machines; in its first year on the market, IBM would sell more than 200,000. Bill Lowe's forecast had been wildly pessimistic; Bill Gates's had been right on.

The future looked rosy. In mid-November 1981, three weeks after welcoming its hundredth employee, Microsoft moved a mile north to the top floor of a new two-story building on Bellevue's Northup Way. Other companies coasted during such periods; not Microsoft. Computer downtime was minimized to a single day by juggling the DEC 20's move and the PDP-11's. A company memo cheerily suggested that the doors would be open Sunday "for those wishing to reorganize their new offices to be ready for business as usual Monday morning."

The move continued several Microsoft traditions and started a new one: dining at Burgermaster, the drive-in restaurant right next door, whose cheeseburgers and shakes quickly became a longstanding Bill Gates lunch ritual. By April Burgermaster had become such an essential aspect of Microsoft that a path had been cut between it and the offices, and it had acquired the "speed dialing" number of 611 on the Microsoft phone system.

Among the old traditions, the two longest running were free soft drinks and windowed offices. At Microsoft, nobody believed in the "open office" maze of cubicles; this was one company where you got your own office with a door you could close and a window you could look out of—although sometimes only into the hallway via a pane of glass known as a "relight."

Tradition number three was electronic mail—e-mail—to which everyone in the company would eventually be attached. Part corporate roundtable, part hallway gossip, part instant postal service, e-mail was quick, direct, convenient, democratic. Eventually anybody anywhere in the company could communicate with anybody else—or everybody else—without intervention of secretary or answering machine. It quickly became a major underpinning of the Microsoft corporate culture. In typical in-house conversation employees would almost invariably refer to themselves and others by their e-mail "handles"—first name and as much of the last name as it took for uniqueness, all lowercase, Gates as billg (pronounced "bill-gee" or, less flatteringly, "bilge")—an odd quirk outsiders found reminiscent of cult groups.

Tradition number four was the hiring of "Bill Clones" and "Golden Boys." In July Carl Stork had arrived fresh from Harvard to become Gates's personal "technical assistant." With his glasses, boyish looks, and abstracted mien, Stork seemed to be a dead ringer for Bill Gates.

Until the real ringer came along. With his sandy hair, blue eyes, glasses, and high cheekbones, Nebraska-born farm boy Jeff Raikes soon had the patented Gates mannerisms down pat. Pushing glasses up his nose, pursing his lips when making a point, even rocking impatiently in his chair, Raikes was quickly dubbed "Clone Number One" in Microsoft circles. A Stanford BA, Raikes had migrated from Cupertino, where he had headed up the software effort on the ill-fated Apple III and had gained a reputation as a "firefighter" for taking on tough software assignments.

The Golden Boys tended to be technical types looking for worlds to conquer. The Clones were managers who knew enough about the nuts and bolts to elevate to a higher plane. The standard line on the Clones and the Golden Boys—in fact, on almost anybody—was binary: You were either golden or fucked, a god or a waste. Once you'd fallen from favor, you weren't smart, you had lost, you were not a contender—worst of all, you were dumb. "Once someone was called dumb," said a former Softie, "they weren't going to go anywhere"—though only rarely did they get sacked.

It was a variation of the Bozo Bit first defined by Steve Jobs at Apple. The Bozo Bit categorized all humans as Ones or Zeros. Once a Zero Bit got turned on, it could never be turned off again. "There were so many managers in Microsoft like that: 'He's great!' 'He sucks!' There was no middle ground," former executive Mike Slade recalled.

But beyond the Clones and the Golden Boys, the force that was really going to drive Microsoft to the top was the Smart Guys. IBM had its wild ducks, Apple had its Pirates, and Microsoft had its Smart Guys—the Letwins, Simonyis, Klunders, Konzens, Harberses, maverick programmers who took gas from no one, who churned out code in crazed frenzies like digital Mozarts and Kerouacs, who worked hard and drove fast and had the kind of rocket-sled no-limits mentality that billg and steveb loved to see. So dominant would their impact be that whenever Bill Gates was asked the secret to his company's success, he would unhesitatingly answer with a variant of the phrase, "We hire smart guys." Young mostly, white mostly, male mostly—as at other high-tech companies—but smart always. The smartest? By general consensus, William Henry Gates, secure enough to hire egos even bigger than his own.

Witness the transformation! At the end of 1979, Microsoft had been a part-nership with twenty-eight employees and sales of roughly $2.4 million. It had offered a variety of programming languages, mostly for OEM customers, and a tiny assortment of lowball packages for end users. Just two years later Microsoft was a corporation with venture capital funding, sales of $16 million, 130 employees, over $1 million in the bank, and the broadest product line in the microcomputer software business: languages, operating systems, applica-tion programs, even hardware. The IBM deal and MS-DOS had completed Microsoft's transformation from a little language house to that "one-stop shopping" center Blair Newman had envisioned. And Bill Gates was publicly predicting the company would reach $100 million in sales within five years.

15

NATURAL MONOPOLY

Microsoft was growing; now it needed to grow up. Budgeting and planning were nonexistent. Product pricing was seat-of-the-pants. The company didn't even have a clear idea how many computers it owned. Until mid-1981 the entire accounting system had amounted to some handwritten ledgers and two checkbooks, one for Consumer Products and one for the rest of the company. Now, at least, the accounts were managed via computer—a clunky Radio Shack TRS-80 Model 2.

Some of the free-form, improvisatory environment was unquestionably a spur to creativity. Some of it was hindering the company's ability to do business. In a dark mood, Steve Ballmer said, he "was giving Marquardt a bad time, and things were kind of screwed up, and I was yelling at him about how screwed up things were." Ballmer was supposed to be the business guy, but he knew he wasn't really running the business. Bill was a leader, not a manager, and was spending far more time on products and deals than on the day-to-day stuff. Marquardt, Ballmer, and Gates finally agreed: It was time the company hired itself a president.

A Silicon Valley headhunter recruited by Marquardt delivered a sober opinion: Nice growth, guys, but a $16 million company on its way to $35 million was still puny, and unlikely to lure anybody north to obscurity from the sun and go-go atmosphere of the Valley. Gates and Company ought to set their sights on candidates from the Northwest.

Aside from Boeing, the biggest, most visible high-tech outfit in the Northwest was the company with "tech" in its name: Tektronix of Beaverton, Oregon, a $1.1 billion maker of oscilloscopes, test equipment, and other forms of electronic instrumentation. Jim Towne, a Northwest native, had been there thirteen years and had the reputation of being a good general manager with a knack for turning troubled divisions around. But with thirteen jobs in those thirteen years, and current responsibility for a division with $700 million in sales, he was beginning to feel exploited.

Towne flew up to Seattle on a June Saturday and interviewed with Gates, Allen, and Ballmer. Towne was an Eagle Scout, an Army Intelligence veteran, a Stanford MBA, a straight arrow, a married man with two kids, a good guy. His experience as a manager at a high-tech company seemed to fit the company's needs. At thirty-nine, he had a degree of maturity that most of Microsoft's employees utterly lacked. He looked distinguished, he had polish, he seemed presidential. He wasn't a technical guy, and he didn't know much about software, but weren't professional managers supposed to be able to run anything?

On July 6, 1982, Towne became president of Microsoft, responsible for day-to-day operations. Bill Gates became executive vice president, taking over all product-related activities, while remaining chairman and CEO. As he told Towne, he was trying to grow up, and he expected the guys around him to grow up too.

Immensely well liked among the rank and file, Towne was "a populist president." A first-rate racquetball player, he deliberately started at the bottom of Microsoft's ladder strictly for the chance to meet everybody as he played his way up. Dubbed "the suit" in the Microsoft corridors, Towne enjoyed the sobriquet so much he took to mentioning it in press interviews. Bill, in high dudgeon, proclaimed that he disliked the term, tried to find out who had initiated it, and eventually accused Towne of inventing it. It was the sort of exchange that would come to characterize their relationship.

What was seen as Towne's major failing was his general lack of interest in the company's products. "He had no passion for software. He didn't use it, he didn't play around with it, and he didn't think about it," one insider said. That was not the Microsoft Way. And Microsoft management was hands-on: Here's a crisis, roll up your sleeves, fix this now. Towne, accustomed to the support and administrative systems of a large outfit like Tektronix, didn't seem to mesh with the dirty-hands style at his new company.

So almost from the outset, Binary Bill set Jim Towne's Bozo Bit. To Gates, Towne was hopelessly untechnical. Faced with someone who failed to understand something, the typical Gates response was to repeat it, louder. But as Charles Simonyi would say, "Bill doesn't like to explain things more than twice."

It all came down to bandwidth, a technical term dating back to the days of radio. In the computer world it referred to how much information you could transfer at once and was anthropomorphized among techies. Low bandwidth was like sipping from a water fountain; high bandwidth was like drinking from a fire hose. For years, "bandwidth" would be the recurring term used to explain the difference between success and failure at Microsoft. It was taken for granted that Bill Gates had the highest bandwidth of all.

But to Towne, Gates could definitely do with some of that growing up he'd promised. Bill was like one of the kids on the playground who hated to lose. "He'd throw an intellectual fit if somebody was doing well," one observer noted. "I think it just drove him to working harder to beat other people." And Towne didn't know how to handle Bill's patented confrontational style; rather than argue with the smartest man he'd ever met, he would back off—sending Gates the message that he could get away with even more winning by intimidation.

Conclusion: Microsoft had hired the wrong guy. Towne personally objected to some of the ways Microsoft ran its business. And as far as Gates was concerned, this Boy Scout wasn't organizing the jamboree. According to Bill, "[He] couldn't get the phone system to work, and he didn't ask for the power cord for the computer he took home. It just wasn't a good match." Less than nine months after Towne started, Bill Gates would be hunting for another president.

A more fortuitous hire was an outgoing Indian-born Britisher from Surrey, late of Xerox PARC, named Estelle Mathers. After seeing an ad for an administrative assistant to the chairman of Microsoft, Mathers had called up her former Xerox colleague Charles Simonyi. "Go for it!" he told her.

In her "funny" initial interview, Gates asked if she took lunches. She didn't. What did she like to do least? "Filing," she said. "I don't do filing." Gates went down to personnel and said, "Hire her."

"I ran his life," Mathers said. Night owl Bill liked to sleep in, so she called and roused him from bed for early-morning appointments. She drove him to the airport. She advised him on what to wear for photo sessions and "told him to comb his hair." Snowbound in New York with time on his hands, Gates had Mathers read him his indispensable e-mail over the phone. She even monitored his speeding tickets. "Getting Bill to court was like pulling teeth. We were always deferring court cases." And to the Gatesian lexicon that already included "awesome," "cool," and "random," Mathers made the permanent contribution of the British "super."

To Mathers, as to Towne and dozens of others who would cross Bill's path, her boss was "the most intelligent human being I've ever met." But when it came to money—whether in the form of cash, credit cards, or traveler's checks—Gates was nonchalant to the point of being cavalier. "He would leave his desk covered with money and walk away from it," Mathers said. After the chairman returned from one trip to Australia, American Express phoned, asking if someone named Bill Gates worked there—and had perhaps misplaced a fairly large number of traveler's checks. "Well, yes, I guess I did," Gates mumbled sheepishly. It was nothing new to Mathers; Gates had lost his Master-Card so often, canceling it had become routine.

"Bill is moody," and Mathers understood him. "He told somebody once that one of the things he loved so much about me was that I knew when to leave him alone. If you tended to interrupt him at a bad time, you could get hurt." Mathers also grasped Rule Number One of dealing with Bill. "He liked it when you stood up to him. I remember banging my fist on the desk one day, and he banged back, and I banged back. If you backed down from Bill, he wouldn't have respect for you."

Social life? "Can you imagine being married to Microsoft? No woman could be as important," said Mathers. It was important to Bill to find someone well matched and well suited to be the only woman in his life. After years of kidding him that "thirty-seven is the magic age," she began to change her tune to "Bill, it's not long now."

"In some ways I haven't mixed around," Gates admitted in a 1982 interview. "Coming back to the Northwest, part of the idea was we'd be able to see our families, friends, and take advantage of the wonderful outdoor opportunities. But we've surprised ourselves with how hardcore we've remained."

Gates spent some time hanging out at a local bar, he said, but felt shy with new people, preferring those he knew. "We spend a lot of time at work. Because you have customers you want to do business with, and then you want to relax with. So you go out with them." As for potential nonindustry dates, Gates joked, "Send the young ones to me and the old ones to Paul."

That was yet another reason Jim Towne was an ill fit with Microsoft: He was a devoted family man. From his first week on the job he made a point of talking about his wife and two kids, two and seven years old, and their three dogs. For Bill, who once pointed at a two-month-old at a party and muttered, "That scares me," there was room for only one child: the growing baby called Microsoft.

Although it might not have been an era of good feeling around the executive offices, the Towne period was as active as any in the history of the company. Microsoft was doing well by selling software to hardware manufacturers. It wasn't doing badly selling hardware of its own.

Microsoft's new RamCard added 16K to the 48K Apple II+, allowing it to run CP/M applications that required a 64K machine—provided you also had Microsoft's SoftCard. By the end of 1981 the SoftCard had become a masterpiece of irony. Here was Microsoft, a software company, and yet its first retail home run had turned out to be hardware—hardware used mostly to run competitors' products, most notably WordStar, the CP/M word processor that had become the industry standard.

SoftCard was teaching the company valuable lessons about the retail market. At a time when many of its competitors sold their products in three-ring binders, in envelopes, in Ziploc bags, Microsoft's consumer products, packaged in attractive full-color boxes designed by MCP's Dottie Hall, *looked* like consumer products. Microsoft was also discovering how much effort and expense it took to support nontechnical consumers. Eventually the SoftCard would become the single most popular platform ever to run CP/M.

The SoftCard was such a hit that Bill Gates found it necessary to fire what *InfoWorld* called a "public broadside" across the bow of pirates: On the eve of the 1982 West Coast Computer Faire in San Francisco, Microsoft sued Advanced Logic Systems (ALS) for copyright infringement. ALS's Z-Card had purportedly copied the SoftCard's BIOS and boot code software—a claim bolstered by the fact that Neil Konzen had stuck his initials in it and they appeared in the competing product. The suit was propelled by the fact that ALS was offering a package called "The Synergizer," including its SoftCard clone, a card with 16K of RAM, and an 80-column card—a package that competed directly with Microsoft's recently released SoftCard Plus package.

"It is clearly piracy when a company takes our code and puts us in the position of competing against ourselves," Gates told *InfoWorld*, adding that Microsoft wanted to set a legal precedent regarding piracy. Claiming it had made an inadvertent error, ALS quickly changed its software. That wasn't good enough for Bill. To *InfoWorld*'s reporter "Gates claimed that ALS sold 1186 cards prior to the changing of the code," and was continuing his suit. In the view of one ALS executive, it was an attempt to "litigate a competitor out of the market." The case was settled out of court in an agreement that remains under seal.

Still smarting from the DOS affair, which he continued to believe was a shameless ripoff of his concept and maybe his code, Gary Kildall chided Microsoft for the suit: "My personal feeling is, if you're suing people all the time, the people doing business with you start to wonder if you're going to start suing them. And they'll start reading those contracts really carefully." Eventually Digital Research, in yet another of its many star-crossed moves to compete with Microsoft, ended up collaborating with ALS on an Apple card— which, unfortunately, ran the less-than-popular CP/M Version 3.

As for DOS, Microsoft was out there pushing it by any means available— including polite exaggeration. The first 1982 issue of *Microsoft Quarterly,* published around April, boasted that "Microsoft currently has 35 OEMs signed for the product, 11 of whom are from Japan." In fact, as late as July, Microsoft had signed no more than eight Japanese and twenty American deals. And although Microsoft's promotional literature touted "Easy Conversion from 8080 to 8086," Bill Gates pointed out in his own *Quarterly* that "the value of machine translation has been vastly overrated."

Yet another item was promised for the next release of DOS: a "Visual Shell" known in-house as MUSH—the Microsoft User Shell, an extension of

Simonyi's Multi-Tool interface. Via Multiplan-style menus instead of cryptic commands, users would be able to do such things as copy files and delete them. Unfortunately, since virtually everyone responsible had a different idea of what such a shell should do, the designers threw in everything but a "Kitchensink" command. The shell ended up being so big, cumbersome, and slow that IBM decided to pass on it. Since Microsoft's sales pitch to other customers was based on giving them precisely what IBM got, memorizing and typing commands, instead of picking them from menus, became the much-cursed standard.

"Why do we need standards?" Gates had asked the previous year at the Rosen Forum. "It's only through volume that you can offer reasonable software at a low price. Standards increase the basic machine we can sell into." And the standard he was pushing now was DOS.

"I really shouldn't say this, but in some ways it leads, in an individual product category, to a natural monopoly: where somebody properly documents, properly trains, properly promotes a particular package and through momentum, user loyalty, reputation, sales force, and prices builds a very strong position within that product."

Natural monopoly? That sounded fine to Bill Gates. The way to get there in operating systems, clearly, was to use the IBM deal as the fulcrum for enormous leverage. But a decade later, the "M" word would come back to haunt him. As usual, Gates was right: He shouldn't have said it.

Sixteen bits was where it was happening, and hardware manufacturers without the three magic initials thought they knew exactly how to make their machines competitive. The answer seemed simple: Make them better. Offer the user some technological advantage—higher-capacity disk drives as NEC did, a higher-resolution screen as Victor did, more colors as Texas Instruments did, a touch-screen user interface as HP did, dual processors as DEC did, something, anything, to make you stand out from the pack. From a classical business perspective, it made perfect sense: Add value, don't imitate.

But there was a fatal bug in that program: software incompatibility. A program that ran on an IBM PC was virtually guaranteed dead on arrival on any "improved" machine. If the display was different, the screen would be garbled. If the disk drives were different, the program would effectively be invisible to the machine.

In theory, developers could write their programs to be "DOS compatible." In practice, if you wanted your program not to crawl, you'd have it sneak underneath DOS and talk directly with the hardware. In which case you'd have to rewrite your program for every new computer that came along.

But what if a computer was functionally identical to The Big One, the IBM PC? Forget better: Particularly while IBM was struggling to keep up with its backlog of orders, the sensible thing might well be to make your computer *just like* IBM's, able to take advantage of the burgeoning variety of IBM PC software right out of the box without waiting, possibly forever, for developers to make conversions.

At Fall Comdex 1981, according to Gates, "We wanted people to do compatible machines. We were chicken when Hitachi came to us to do a compatible machine. Because even during the IBM PC development project we got a sense of IBM's attitude toward Japan. So we talked Hitachi out of doing a compatible machine."

There were a couple of roads to compatibility: The easy way was simply to swipe the code from IBM's ROM BIOS chip. The hard way was to put some engineers in a "clean room," tell them exactly what the chip was supposed to do, and then wait until they emerged with a design that was functionally, but not physically, identical to the original. The first PC-compatible, the Compaq Portable, did things the second way, the noble way, and Compaq almost instantly became one of the fastest-growing companies in history.

And it came to Microsoft for DOS early in 1982. Pete Dyer, Microsoft's laconic, tenacious OEM sales chief, had known Gary Stimac, Steve Flanagan, and Rod Canion before they left Texas Instruments to form what was then known as Gateway Technology and would shortly become Compaq. On a hectic Texas swing, Dyer squeezed them in for a 6:00 A.M. breakfast meeting to do the DOS deal. As Gates recalled it, "Here's some clean-cut Texas boys gonna do a compatible. Let's see what patents or any bullshit comes out of this. This is great."

Eventually the relationship with Compaq would become one of Microsoft's closest. The situation was delicate: By giving Compaq the source code to the generic version of MS-DOS along with the code to IBM's DOS, Microsoft gave Compaq a head start on the road to compatibility. BASIC was trickier, because the IBM version had been divided into two parts, one in ROM and one on disk. In order to assure compatibility with the IBM version without stepping on IBM toes, Gates assigned a separate team to work with Compaq. As the Compaq engineers fed back changes and requirements, Microsoft incorporated them into its generic DOS and BASIC. Eventually the changes would find their way into future editions of the IBM versions to further tighten the compatibility loop.

The result benefited both companies: Compaq ended up with an IBM-compatible BASIC for its machine; Microsoft got an IBM-compatible BASIC it could sell to other customers. "Bill has a tremendous way of leveraging," Gary Stimac would say years later. "Dealing with Bill is being willing to return technology to him. You give it to Bill, and then you buy it back." It was the kind of strategic partnership that Microsoft would participate in again and again over the years.

But in the early going, incompatible machines were the only machines, and

DOS was gathering momentum on them, thanks to the swashbuckling sales tactics of Bill and crew. The company might entrust programming to green kids, but when it came to the sales side, it hired veterans like Dyer from companies like Data General. When Dyer heard that Hewlett-Packard was about to close a deal with Digital Research to put CP/M-86 on its new 16-bit computer, he flew Gates and Ballmer down to the Valley to plead their case. They put it bluntly: Were you really going to bet on some operating system that second-raters used, or were you going to bet on the one endorsed by IBM? HP thought it over and climbed aboard the DOS bandwagon.

Years afterward, Digital Research stalwarts would swear that Bill Gates had an intelligence network. And he did: The relationships Microsoft had developed over years of OEM dealings had given him thousands of connections in the industry. The Microsoft OEM sales force was the company's eyes and ears, its CIA, the instrument that enabled Bill Gates to see the future as clearly as anyone in the business and to make alliances with the most important players.

DEC was a more equivocal conquest. The pioneer of the minicomputer, DEC was fumbling the personal computer era badly with an internal competition among four machines that were utterly incompatible with each other and everything else in the universe. A DEC engineer named Barry James Folsom was in charge of an oddball machine that along with its 8088 had a Z-80 processor to run old CP/M programs. Folsom was trying to get VisiCalc customized for the machine, but VisiCorp had snubbed him. Realizing the folly of releasing a machine without a spreadsheet, Folsom met with Bill Gates in Bellevue on a Sunday early in 1982 to try to license Multiplan.

Multiplan? When Gates heard about Folsom's machine, he said he wanted to see DOS on it. If DEC, the number-two computer maker, left DOS off its machine, he told Folsom, "You're going to torpedo us."

Gates was not yet aware of the internal battle at DEC over what to name the machine. Folsom was pushing for "Rainbow," a name Ken Olsen, Digital's founder and president, personally detested. Olsen had a better idea: Call it the "CP/M." Folsom hated that name, but dutifully approached Digital Research, hoping the company would refuse to license the name. Wrong: DR's new president, John Rowley, was taken with the idea. Talk about sticking it to Microsoft and Bill Gates!

Folsom had one last card to play. "I told Gates we were going to call the product 'CP/M,'" Folsom said, "and he went nonlinear." It was just the reaction Folsom had hoped for. He invited Bill Gates to Digital's headquarters in Maynard, Massachusetts, to meet with Ken Olsen.

Olsen was an industry legend. He had put together Digital Equipment, the company that had led the first wave toward downsizing computers, making them cheaper, making them accessible and understandable to hackers like the young Bill Gates. In a sense, Olsen was DEC, and DEC had been the company most responsible for Bill's early success. And Olsen was sticking adamantly to the CP/M name.

None of that fazed Bill Gates. He was there to do a sales job, and he did it. CP/M still wasn't running on IBM machines, he reminded Olsen. DEC might well be betting on the wrong operating system. MS-DOS had momentum and bid fair to become the standard. On the way out of the office, Ken Olsen turned to Barry Folsom and said, "I think we ought to change the name." Folsom changed it to Rainbow.

DEC signed the customary $95,000 DOS flat-fee contract in May, just before the machine was announced. When the Rainbow eventually went out to the public after months of delay, it still featured CP/M and CP/M-86. But DOS was offered as an optional extra, and in its own small way the Rainbow— a dud so incompatible it could use only special expensive floppy disks from DEC—helped maintain the credibility of DOS.

The credibility of BASIC was another matter when a front-page story in the April 5, 1982, issue of the *New York Times* revealed that IBM did not know how to count. A Minneapolis consultant named David S. Walonick had discovered that IBM's BASIC—Microsoft's name was nowhere in evidence—would give the wrong answer when you asked it to divide .1, and possibly other numbers as well, by 10. The culprit: a bug in Bob O'Rear's floating-point math routines, burned into the ROM chip in each and every IBM PC.

Gates was terrified that this would unravel the deal with Don Estridge and Boca. But once again, Gates's luck and foresight were about to pay off. The "hooks" he'd designed into BASIC meant that for disk-based machines, the problem could be solved merely by papering over the offending ROM code with a fix from a floppy. As for no-disk machines—well, just as Gates had predicted, hardly anybody was buying those, except for clever individuals who'd discovered they could install their own disk drives for far less than IBM was charging. For adamant cassette users, Microsoft provided and IBM published a quick and dirty workaround, and that was that. Don Estridge told Bill Gates not to worry.

As far as IBM was concerned, a few minor changes in DOS were all that were needed for the next release. The primary goal of DOS 2.0 was support for the hard disk in IBM's forthcoming PC XT, and by all accounts IBM—and Bill Gates—would have been satisfied with just that.

Paul Allen pushed to do more. Allen believed, and DOS programmers Mark Zbikowski and Aaron Reynolds agreed, that the operating system needed a rewrite virtually from the ground up, not to mention a raft of new UNIX-like features—as much for the benefit of programmers as for users. IBM came up with a bare-bones specification; Allen and his team worked to extend it and proposed a raft of features that had never been specified by "the customer"— as Gates referred to IBM. The original delivery date of June 1, 1982, had come and gone, the new version of DOS was getting later and later, and Bill was getting heavy heat from the Boca band, particularly Joe Sarubbi, the 280-pound, six-foot-four hard disk guru who would make a weekly pilgrimage to Seattle to growl, "You're going to have DOS 2.0 *when?*"

When Reynolds or Zbikowski would go to Bill about a problem with IBM, his first reaction was to take IBM's side; he had to be convinced that his programmers weren't just being difficult. In Zbikowski's office early one evening, Bill, just back from Boca, screamed at Paul Allen about one feature after another that "the customer" found totally unnecessary, not to mention that the code was unacceptable.

"Bill and Paul got a micron apart and were just screaming at each other," Zbikowski recalled. Paul took the technical line: We have to push the envelope. The new features were great, and they had to stay in. "This played out for about an hour and a half. . . . Both of them got red, and they were just like yelling and screaming." It was just like chess: Weather Bill's attack, attack, attack and eventually you'd come out on top. In the end, Allen prevailed. The features stayed in, and most have survived to this day.

To go with DOS 2.0, IBM would need new versions of the disk-based BASICs. IBM was getting bad press over the fact that its BASIC wasn't much faster than the one for the Apple II, largely because the IBM version was based on the same 8-bit code and had never been optimized for a 16-bit machine. But to Bill, "There was no incentive to improve BASIC when they wouldn't ship a non-ROM version of BASIC," since Microsoft wouldn't get a royalty for it. The contractually obligated revisions were minimal—not much more than making sure IBM got versions that wouldn't actually crash under the new DOS. That was enough for Bill Gates, and that was what he asked programmer Mike Courtney to do.

About a week into the work, Paul Allen visited Courtney's office and asked him how things were going. What Courtney showed him, in Allen's view, was utterly lame. There was virtually no support for any of the neat new features of the new DOS. Allen returned with a two-page list of features to be added— maybe twenty in all. "Did you talk to Bill about these?" Courtney asked suspiciously.

"Don't worry about that," Paul told him.

Courtney rolled up his sleeves and set to work.

"You're doing *what?*" Gates howled when he met with Courtney a week later. The subsequent executive powwow was a classic.

"They're both in my office screaming at each other," Courtney recalled, "and I'm trying to leave, sort of like a little animal trying to slip underneath the door, and just as I'm about to make it, the giant puts his foot in the door. . . . I was trying desperately to get out of the room, and I think actually succeeded. They kept saying 'Come back! Come back!' "

Next morning, an unhappy Bill Gates grumbled at Courtney that he was busy, to work with Paul on this. Courtney returned to his office for a crash-out schedule. He had "signed up" for the project, which at Microsoft meant you'd do what it took to get the job done right and done on time. If his deadline now seemed impossible—well, he might just have to make it possible with twenty-hour days, seven days a week, and lots and lots of coffee.

In the middle of one long programming night, Courtney went for a java fix, thought he was having a heart attack, and ended up in the hospital. Exhausted and strung out on caffeine, he was put on medication to stabilize his heart rate. Yet he'd signed up for the project. Loaded up with medication, suffering from caffeine withdrawal, barely able to sleep at night, Courtney finished the job. When his work later flashed on the screen at a company meeting, he was astonished to discover how much he'd accomplished in so short a time.

Sick leave? "It didn't occur to me. I was still doing stuff." Courtney switched to a different product, but still debilitated, he was down to working three hours a day. Not the Microsoft Way: Without warning, his immediate superior called him into the office and told him he was fired. Courtney was shattered. He discussed the situation with a supervisor, who suggested he take the matter to Bill Gates.

Courtney sat down in Bill's office and told him he'd been fired. "I understand you haven't been feeling well," Gates said. Surprised that Bill had even heard about his illness, Courtney explained the situation. He was flabbergasted when Gates, perhaps recalling his bout with colitis, told him, "Mike, why don't you just take a month off and look around the company and find something easy to do. I don't want you to die on me."

"I thought that was really great," Courtney recalled. "It was a personal side of Bill I hadn't really seen before."

Late but feature-packed, DOS 2.0 and the new BASIC were introduced in March 1983 with the announcement of IBM's hard-disk PC XT. Bill Gates and crew were still hyping the 16-bit future, pushing DOS, and occasionally the more powerful XENIX, to anyone who'd listen. But there was life in the 8-bit world yet. Although the old 8-bit desktop computers were fast becoming relics, classic 8-bit chips had dropped drastically in price and were becoming the mainstays of cheap home units. The older chip designs were also being reworked to require significantly less power—just the thing for machines powered by batteries. Kay Nishi, Microsoft's vice president of planning, unpaid except from ASCII's lucrative 30 percent commissions, would do his best to see that these 8-bit chips too would run Microsoft software.

Nishi had been fascinated by tiny computers for years. In 1979 he'd sent Bill a memo about what he called "Hand Top Computers," listing twenty-four applications—everything from "Language Translator" to "Mahjong Helper," from "Astronomical Fortune Telling" to "Barth [sic] Control"—that might be available with a change of plug-in ROM chips. Nothing much came of it.

In 1981 Microsoft did a version of BASIC for a little Japanese unit Bill Gates "was not enthused about"—Epson's HX-20. Perhaps the first "notebook computer," it weighed less than four pounds and included a full-size keyboard, an adding-machine-tape printer, and a microcassette data recorder. The drawback was the tiny screen—a liquid-crystal display (LCD) with 4 dim lines of 20 characters each. Released in 1982, the HX-20 was not good for much of anything—except to show how small a computer could be.

But Kay Nishi was on the case. As profligate as Coach Class Bill was ascetic, Kay always traveled first cabin. Settling in up front on Japan Airlines Flight 001 from San Francisco to Tokyo, Nishi discovered his seatmate was Kazuo Inamori, president of Kyocera, a company whose specialty was ceramics—including shoehorning multiple computer chips onto a single ceramic substrate. Like MITS years before, Kyocera had fallen on hard times with its involvement in the electronic calculator business. Nishi decided he and Inamori ought to work together somehow.

What jump-started the relationship was a single electronic part—a dim, black-on-gray, 8-line by 40-character LCD from Hitachi that Inamori showed off during Nishi's visit to the company. That display was the missing link, Nishi instantly realized, in putting together a general-purpose portable computer.

Kay and Bill developed a spec for the machine. In a sense, it was a throwback to the MITS days: limited memory, limited display, no real operating system. Yet tucked away in ROM would be a rudimentary but serviceable word processor, a communications program, an address book, and a telephone dialer—not to mention a powerful version of good old Microsoft BASIC. Using a special Kyocera package of power-saving RAM, the machine would run for hours and hours on four AA batteries. With a full-size keyboard and the serviceable if not thrilling display, Gates and Nishi were sure the unit would be a dazzler.

By early 1982 all that was left was to sell the machine. Nishi was ready with a plan worthy of ancient conquistadors: Divide the world in three parts. Japan's NEC would market its version in the Orient. Olivetti would sell a European model. In the Americas, the vendor would be Radio Shack. Microsoft would get a royalty on every unit sold.

Gates took Nishi down to Fort Worth to pitch Tandy's Jon Shirley on the idea. In multiple meetings the three hammered out refinements. In the end, the three vendors came up with three slightly different designs. Radio Shack's machine, though by far the least stylish, managed to pack a 300-baud modem into the box—a crucial consideration that led it to become a standard among journalists who could fire stories up the phone line to their editors.

1. Bill Gates between planes, 1986.

2. Great-granddad J. W. Maxwell at age eighty-three, 1947.

3. Grandparents Adelle ("Gam") and Willard Maxwell before a 1957 trip to Tokyo.

4. Parents Bill Jr. and Mary Gates, circa 1990.

5. Bill Gates (lower right), Cub Scout, circa 1965.

6. Gates (top row, center), linebacker, circa 1966.

7. Gates with sisters Kristi and Libby, 1971.

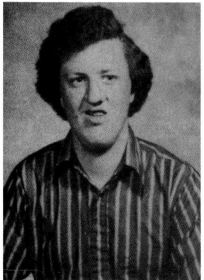

8. Hendrix fan Paul Allen with Bill Gates at the Lakeside computer room Teletype, circa 1968.

9. Kent Evans, Gates's Lakeside Programmers Group comrade, 1972.

10. Lakeside graduation, 1973: father and son.

11 Flathead Lake, Montana: Bill Gates attempts tower waterski start.

Traf-O-Data

12. Traf-O-Data letterhead.

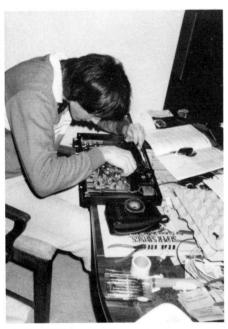

13. Paul Gilbert, Traf-O-Data hardware guy, circa 1973.

14. Traf-O-Data report graphically depicting traffic flow at fifteen-minute intervals.

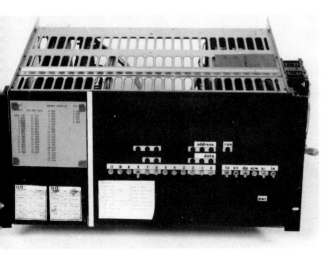

15. The amazing Traf-O-Data computer.

16. *Popular Electronics* cover, January 1975, featuring Altair mockup.

For cost sensitive applications, the Altair 8800 and most Altair options come in kit form. Already, thousands of Altair computer kits have been assembled and are in full operating order.

Altair 8800 kit builders include individuals, companies and industrial users.

At MITS, we have been successfully marketing electronic kits for years. We take the extra pain to write accurate, straight-forward assembly manuals. (We leave nothing to the imagination.)

At MITS, we're quite serious about making computer power available at a price most everyone can afford.

17. A box of parts: the Altair 8800 in kit form.

18. Cover of first Altair catalog: the assembled Altair 8800.

19. The first Microsoft product: paper tape of the initial Gates/Allen/Davidoff BASIC.

20. Monte Davidoff, BASIC "math package" guy, circa 1973.

21. Front-page news: the first issue of MITS *Computer Notes,* April 7, 1975.

ALTAIR BASIC - UP AND RUNNING

In January, when Popular Electronics featured the Altair Computer on its front cover, we knew that we had a great product. But no one could have predicted the enormous flood of inquiries and phone calls and orders that started hitting us about mid-January.

Partly because the Altair has generated such a huge volume of business, we have been able to speed up our Altair development program and broaden our horizons somewhat. Undoubtedly the most newsworthy of these developments is the introduction of a BASIC programming language for the Altair Computer.

That's right. We've got BASIC and it's up and running!

People who are familiar with programming and BASIC language will most likely understand why we're making such a big deal out of this. For those who aren't familiar, we offer the following explanation.

A few years back, realizing that computers needn't be so darn complicated, a group of professors at Dartmouth College developed a revolutionary, new computer language called BASIC language. This language was designed so that people with little or no computer knowledge could learn how to program.

BASIC language works because it is just what it says--it is, namely, BASIC. For example, when you want to instruct the computer to

PRINT something and you are using BASIC language, you simply type the word PRINT on your terminal or tele-type keyboard followed by whatever it is you want the computer to print. BASIC is BASIC. It is simple and understandable.

To illustrate this further, let's take a look at this sample BASIC program, designed to calculate a simple interest problem.

```
SCRATCH ↵

10 LET P=650 ↵

20 LET T=18 ↵

30 LET R=.065 ↵

40 LET I=P*T*R/12 ↵

50 LET P1=P+I ↵

60 LET M=P1/T ↵

70 PRINT "TOTAL INTEREST IS";I ↵

80 PRINT "TOTAL MONEY OWED IS";P1 ↵

90 PRINT "MONTHLY PAYMENTS ARE";M ↵

    RUN ↵
```

COMPUTER NOTES

APRIL 7, 1975

© MITS, INC. 1975

A PUBLICATION OF THE ALTAIR USERS GROUP   VOLUME ONE ISSUE ONE

22. Bill Gates at World Altair Computer Convention, 1976.

23. Gates after presentation to Northwest Computer Club, 1976, conversing with Mike Courtney, APL guru and future Softie.

24. Ric Weiland and Gates at Waldorf-Astoria during 1976 National Computer Conference. Bill's drink: a Shirley Temple.

Squirreled away in Bellevue, the lead programmers were three ASCII Microsoft employees from Japan: Jey Suzuki, Rick Yamashita, and Jun Hayashi, whose names later turned up in the ROM. But there was also the handiwork of William Henry Gates, who designed the machine's data structures and some of its user interface.

Later, Bill became impatient with the lame line-oriented text editor that had been developed for the machine. The programmers insisted a change was impossible; with all the other goodies in the 32K ROM, there just wouldn't be room enough for a full-screen text editor. The next morning Gates had delivered the "impossible" editor in the same amount of code as the rudimentary one. It would be the last time Gates wrote a program that shipped as a Microsoft product. The demands of business had inexorably become more compelling than mere codesmithing.

Released in March 1983, the four-pound Radio Shack Model 100 was the first full-function lightweight computer, a totally integrated machine with everything you needed, hardware and software, right in the box. You could even get a plug-in ROM chip with Multiplan on it. Although it had a somewhat awkward user interface, lacked a built-in disk drive, and was incompatible with virtually everything else on the market, the machine was a marvel of its day and wildly popular for a time. Although the lightweight-computer market would cool off and plod along listlessly until the advent of DOS-compatible units, the Model 100 was a genuine innovation in which Kay Nishi, Bill Gates, and Microsoft played a decisive role.

Although there were increasing rumblings about Nishi's unreliability when it came to follow-through, there was no question that "the incredible madman" had almost single-handedly made Microsoft a power in the Japanese market. In Europe business was tougher. Microsoft's European connection had been a Belgian-based outfit known as Vector International, which also represented Digital Research. That was no problem when the two companies were complementary, but once they began going head to head over just about everything but applications, it was time for a change.

At the beginning of 1982, Bill Gates and Steve Ballmer, then head of international operations, cut Vector out of the picture, hired a British chip marketeer named Chris Gare, and dispatched Bob O'Rear to England to start Microsoft's European operation. The UK office opened in spring of 1982 with the mission of bringing DOS and the rest of the Microsoft line to the disparate machines of the Old World.

But in many ways Digital Research was better served in Europe than on its home turf. Europe was always slightly behind the American times, which tied in well with DR's routine lateness. Particularly in Germany, CP/M was a far more entrenched standard outside the United States than in it. And there were other quirks to the European market: Unable to make machines fast enough to satisfy the demand at home, IBM delayed its European entry, enabling Chuck Peddle's Sirius machine (known stateside as Victor) to become a European powerhouse, primarily on CP/M-86 rather than DOS. Without the IBM machine and its shelfful of software in the picture, CP/M-86 found its way onto machines from Philips, ICL, and others. After six months and exactly two European DOS licensees—Bull Micral and Axel Micro-ordinateur—it became clear that Microsoft's English base, in the Hertfordshire countryside sixty miles from London, was not winning the battle for Europe.

Scott Oki, a Seattle native in Microsoft's short, wiry, curt mold, was a trained accountant and MBA who'd spent time at Hewlett-Packard and as a Silicon Valley consultant. After joining Microsoft in March 1982, he began to focus on the flailing international business. Oki decided the solution was to divide all Europe into three parts, servicing them from offices in Paris, Munich, and London. Soon after arriving he "just did the typical MBA thing and wrote a business plan" for global domination.

Oki pleaded with Gates and Ballmer to ditch the recently hired European chief and reorganize Europe. "Steve and Bill weren't in the mood to hear me say that someone they had just hired wasn't any good. So they were jumping up and down and bouncing off the walls saying 'You're crazy. You don't know anything about what this guy can do.' " It was Oki's baptismal encounter with Microsoft's confrontational style, the precise opposite of HP's decorous consensus-building. He left the meeting "literally trembling," wondering "What did I get myself into?"

When Towne came aboard, Oki enlisted his support. In late September 1982 Towne appointed Oki Microsoft's director of international operations, responsible for the European subsidiary as well as relations with Nishi's ASCII Microsoft. As Towne accurately predicted at the time, "How effective we are in Europe, especially during the next year, will largely determine how successful we will eventually be."

Oki's mission was simple: "Go conquer the world." The post of European chief was eliminated. By the middle of 1983 Oki had hired Frenchman Bernard Vergnes, German Joachim Kempin, and Scotsman David Fraser to head up offices in their respective countries. In Bellevue there began a push to "internationalize" products with foreign menus, help screens, and manuals under the direction of former wunderkind Carl Stork, who had begun to spin out from the Gatesian inner circle. The first big win was one of the great explosions of Simonyi's revenue bomb: Multiplan in French. On the Apple II, it was strongly endorsed by Apple's French chief Jean-Louis Gassée; on the IBM PC, it was pushed by IBM France; on CP/M-86 machines such as the Victor and the still-popular 8-bit CP/M machines, it was pushed by Microsoft itself. DOS 2.0, which had been designed for easy internationalization, was also beginning to find some converts.

Kay and Bill held sway over Japan, where the challenges were somewhat different. In the early 1980s the problem hadn't been finding customers; the problem had been finding products they hadn't already bought. Take Ricoh: As Gates put it, "There was this incredibly famous meeting where they were coming to see us, and they'd already bought BASIC, FORTRAN, COBOL, everything we had. So Nishi called up beforehand and said they've got a huge budget; you have to sell them stuff."

"Literally, we had customers who would come over with bags full of money," Oki recalled, "and Bill would simply make up products." Or buy them. To satisfy the demand, Bill found a Philadelphia outfit called International Database Systems, licensed its minicomputer database called Micro-SEED, and offered it mostly to Japanese companies, along with a report generator called Harvest. The Japanese needed a word processor? Bill found one called Quill down in New Orleans.

As for delivering working versions of these and other products, Oki recalled, "We danced. The number of undeliverables to Japanese customers in the early days—I mean, boy, that's a real long list. The number of missed product dates: It's incredible. We missed everything. But the Japanese, being very patient and very long-term-oriented, kind of lived with that. . . . . There were some very embarrassing moments." But Oki knew how the game worked: "You make new promises and you miss those promised dates, and you go back and you dance some more."

In the Microsoft tradition of twenty-four-hour days and eighty-hour weeks, Oki soon found himself globe-trotting, spending the better part of his life aboard airplanes. "It was just pathetic watching him come back from trips sometimes," remembered one executive. "He was so tired, so exhausted."

Tired and exhausted? Just part of the corporate culture. Oki adjusted by learning how to sleep standing up. But at least fatigue wasn't potentially terminal. In September 1982, on a European speaking trip with Bill Gates, Paul Allen noticed some lumps on his neck and "started feeling real crummy in Munich. And then I went to Paris, and I had to give a speech, and I felt really crummy and ended up coming back home and going straight to the hospital for a biopsy and getting diagnosed." He checked into Swedish Hospital, birthplace of Bill Gates.

"Well, Mr. Allen," a doctor told him somberly, "you've got lymphoma."

"And so what does this mean?" Allen wanted to know.

"Well, the outlook is not good. We won't know for sure what the details are."

The next day the doctors returned and informed Allen he had the eminently treatable Hodgkin's disease. "They're smiling, and they're going, 'Hey, you're going to live! No problem!' "

No problem, that is, if you didn't mind two five-week courses of X-ray therapy, after which "you go home and throw up for about four hours straight."

But Paul Allen was a Microsoft trouper, even if only on a half-time basis. "I worked through that period. I worked just to keep going."

By March of 1983, with DOS 2.0 out the door, Allen was gone, resigning from Microsoft to travel in Europe and "think about the kinds of things I wanted to do—things I didn't have time to do before." According to one friend of Bill's, it was a crushing blow to him:

> I think Bill had a hard time relating to it. I don't think that he understood it. I don't think he understood what Paul was going through: Paul could have died.
>
> And I think it hurt Bill a lot. Number one because it was happening, and number two, there was just a distance there at that time between the two of them. Because Bill didn't understand it. Bill wanted him next to him at the company, he wanted him there bad. He was all by himself, you know. It was a tough time for the company. Bill was miserable.

There was another, unspoken, reason for Bill's reaction. It would be hinted at some years later when a friend, aghast at his speeding, remarked, "I hope your life insurance is paid up," and Gates turned the idle remark into a serious matter, explaining that he had no life insurance because he had a lot of assets and no dependents. What Gates believed but did not explain was that he was probably uninsurable. Episodes of childhood-onset colitis are strong predictors of future colon cancer.

Allen's illness and departure coalesced uneasiness within the ranks of the remaining Albuquerquians—the core group that had helped establish Microsoft early, had followed their leader to Bellevue, had stuck with the company through some tumultuous years, and now found themselves being middle-managed into oblivion. In March 1983 Bob Wallace, in the best Microsoft tradition, got into a heated dispute with his supervisor over a technical point. The supervisor told him "there's nothing you can do about it, and you can't talk to Bill about it. . . . I'm the only one who can talk to Bill."

For Wallace, being barred from talking with Bill was not just a shock but an insult. He told his supervisor as much, half expecting Gates to intercede. When it didn't happen, he resigned.

The departures of Allen and Wallace signaled the end of whatever impact the Albuquerque group still had on Microsoft. Gone were four of the photographed eleven—Wallace, Bob Greenberg, and Steve and Marla Wood. Paul Allen did some consulting but by late 1984 was putting together his own company. By early 1985 Andrea Lewis, Marc McDonald, and Jim Lane would be gone. Having returned in 1981, Miriam Lubow left once more, returned, and finally departed in 1990 to work with Allen. Only three of the Albuquerquians would stick with the company into the 1990s: Bob O'Rear, Gordon Letwin, and the chairman himself. Albuquerque part-timer Chris Larson also remained.

Although not the first, Wallace may have been the most prominent personification of a new term floating around the company: Microsoft Syndrome. One of the early group described the process:

> . . . *They come to Microsoft, and it has this magic ring to it. It's the* crême de la crême *of software companies, they have that attitude about it, and they get there and they're all excited and all hepped up and ready to give their all for this company. And after a while, they realize they're being used.*
>
> *It takes a year or two, but you can see it happen. All of a sudden, over a span of a short time, either a few weeks to a few months, they go from working sixty-hour weeks normally—with eighty-hour weeks on special pushes—down to working a straight forty hours every week. And their attitude suffers a lot, they get very cynical, they realize that a lot of the very short time schedules are very short because Microsoft is looking to push people to work very hard. This is never official policy, of course, but a lot of people came to the same conclusion after having been with the company for a certain period of time.*

Within a couple of years, though, Jeff Raikes would publicly state that it was official policy to keep the company thinly staffed. "Gates is a hero (one who models a company's cultural values); he creates the elemental intensity," Raikes told a seminar on corporate culture. "Why don't we have enough people?" Raikes asked rhetorically. Because Bill Gates and his executives were "conscious about maintaining momentum," and you couldn't do that by hiring and firing on the whim of the moment.

Still, there was a lot more hiring than firing. By the end of 1982 the company had doubled again, to 200 employees and sales of $32 million, as the industry burgeoned to the point where *Time* would laud not a man but a machine of the year: the personal computer. But as always, Bill Gates could find reason to fret. In November, the annual Comdex convention in Las Vegas had dropped a couple of unlikely bombshells that managed to surprise and unnerve Microsoft's Chief Executive Worrier.

16

THE SMART GUYS

Since January 1982 the Macintosh team at Microsoft had been programming like madmen. Secrecy called for the Mac prototypes to be kept under wraps in a separate room, but the boys from Bellevue twisted Apple marketing manager Mike Boich's arm into letting them keep the machines in their offices, provided they stuck them behind a bookshelf or some other camouflage. At Microsoft, they loved their Macs.

At Apple, where the Lisa was seen as the politically correct project and the Mac some crazy idea to keep Jobs out of everyone else's hair, Jobs told his team "It's better to be a pirate than to join the navy"; from then on, the Macintoshen were known as the Pirates. But there was just as much piratical fervor in Bellevue. Aside from the buccaneers in Cupertino, Microsoft's Smart Guys were virtually the only ones programming for the Mac. Which wasn't easy, since the Macintosh was still a work in progress. Not even the "look and feel" were entirely clear; every demo program—and there were some dazzlers —had a different user interface.

The Macintosh itself was nowhere near ready to use as a development tool. Apple programmers used Apple IIs and IIIs and eventually got Lisas. Microsoft didn't get Lisas; Apple was writing its own software for that machine and was not about to let a competitor horn in. So at Microsoft, with its hallowed tradition of software as hardware, most of the development took place first on DEC VAX and then high-powered Sun UNIX systems, using homebrewed software tools that could compile code for the Mac and, eventually, communicate with it for debugging.

First goal: to get a p-code interpreter running on the Mac, one place where Simonyi's "revenue bomb" would actually explode. Given all the extra code involved in graphics programming, the Mac's memory space was tiny. On this machine, the size advantage in using p-code far outweighed the speed curbs.

Microsoft's team was in virtually daily contact with the Mac group, ironing out scores of programming guidelines, interfaces, standards. Jobs's Pirates and Simonyi's Smart Guys seemed mirror images, young, iconoclastic, pizza-fed, Coke-drenched, fuck-you rock 'n' rollers of the digital world. At one point Microsoft had as many programmers assigned to the project as Apple. This was the computer of the future, everyone was sure of it, and the teams worked with all stops out. "It was the highlight of our career to work with that bunch, and we were like *this*," Simonyi remembered, crossing his fingers emphatically. "We bet everything on graphical interfaces—everything."

But the Macintosh hardware kept changing, complicating the job. The initial 64K of memory was quickly upped to 128K. Then the screen resolution was increased from its initial grainy level, stealing back some of the memory that had been added. Then the disk drive was changed from the Lisa's disastrously unreliable "Twiggy" model to Sony's new $3\frac{1}{2}$-inch hard-cased design.

Microsoft managed to make numerous contributions to the Mac's final software design—although their exact nature is a matter of debate. "We helped them debug their operating system, and we suggested changes and additions," Neil Konzen remembered. "We had ideas for the ROMs and the interfaces and the 'toolbox,' as they called it. We also argued about the user interface guidelines—although we didn't have as much impact on that as we did on the code or the technical stuff."

The Macintosh's developers today downplay Microsoft's role, acknowledging that the Bellevue team suggested improvements, refinements, and fixes, but maintaining that it rarely proposed specific elements. Microsoft programmers proudly rattle off a short list of items to which they claim joint creative ownership—items such as the terms "radio button" and "dialog box," the arrangement and display of some of the pull-down menus, the double-bordering of default selections, the way windows were zoomed to fill the screen. According to Andy Hertzfeld, at least one essential contribution came from the chairman himself: During early discussions in mid-1981, when the Mac was still without a file system, Gates suggested the file allocation table (FAT) scheme he and McDonald had devised for Standalone BASIC and Paterson had adapted for DOS. The Pirates quickly commandeered it for the Mac.

Mike Boich, the original Mac "software evangelist," admitted that the Microsofties "were the first guys trying to do really ambitious applications on top of the operating system, and the operating system was in a very rudimentary state when they first saw it, so they certainly got to say, 'Look, we could do things a lot better if you did X, Y, or Z.' . . . If there's a theme to those discussions, it's that the Microsoft guys were always looking for more power and features; the Apple guys were always looking to keep the stuff just as simple and conceptually pure as possible."

Microsoft was not sitting on its hands with the technological tutorial from

Apple. On Valentine's Day 1982, less than three weeks after Bill Gates signed the agreement to develop applications for the Mac, the *Seattle Times* ran a photo of Gates and Paul Allen in Microsoft headquarters. Behind them was a whiteboard with seemingly random scribbles of numbers and symbols. In the upper right-hand corner were jotted two strategic words: *Window manager*. To the world at large they seemed to mean nothing in particular; within a couple of years they would take on almost cosmic significance.

Back in the spring of 1977, Gates had written about the need for operating system standardization. A key element, in Bill's view, was "device-independent I/O"—the use of software called "device drivers" to take over the job of communicating between programs and peripherals. The goal was that any program would work no matter what kinds of disks or displays or printers happened to be hooked up. "Anyone who thinks it isn't too late to do something along these lines has my enthusiastic support," Gates wrote.

It was too late. Even in 1977, the market was so fragmented and parochial, with small computers totally unable to work with one another except on the most rudimentary levels, that any hope for an across-the-board operating system seemed ludicrous.

Or maybe not. At 1982's annual Fall Comdex convention where 50,000 PC pilgrims journeyed to Las Vegas, Microsoft got its loudest, clearest wakeup call ever—in the form of a new integrated software system called VisiOn. It was the hit of the show, not least because it was a total surprise. Nothing in the dweeby character-based world of green-on-black monitors and baffling A> prompts had prepared the assembled gathering for VisiOn's what-you-see-is-what-you-get, high-resolution graphics. VisiOn used a mouse. VisiOn did windows. And, to the horror of Bill Gates, VisiOn came with its own collection of application software.

Ironically, the Mac folks had already dismissed VisiOn. In a meeting with Jobs and Macintosh evangelists, VisiCorp chiefs had made a pitch to adapt the system to the Mac hardware. Jobs was so unimpressed he did not even bother to call the VisiFolk back. When they finally got through on the phone, Apple's chairman more or less told them not to bother.

The house that VisiCalc built, VisiCorp (formerly Personal Software) was the number-one software company in the personal computer industry, riding high on royalties from its flagship spreadsheet product. Now its Comdex booth was the place you absolutely positively had to see. Among the more obsessive onlookers was an alternately admiring and apoplectic Bill Gates, whose Microsoft booth was only a couple of yards away.

"He came and grabbed me out of the booth, screaming 'Come see this! Come see this!' " a former executive recalled. Gates was so blown away by the VisiOn demo that he called Charles Simonyi in Seattle and told him to catch the next flight down. VisiOn was new, it was exciting, it was great. It wasn't as refined as the Macintosh, but it was close enough. Code-named Quasar, VisiOn had somehow been two years in the making without the incredibly well-connected Bill Gates ever getting wind of it.

Most depressing of all, it was there, actually running—well, demoing—on an IBM PC, the platform Gates thought he owned. It was all there, everything he'd dreamed about putting on the PC himself. The Apple Lisa hadn't been introduced, the Macintosh was over a year away, and yet there was VisiCorp chairman Dan Fylstra grinning broadly, calling this thing the "metaphor of the desktop," crowing that this "operating environment" sitting between the operating system and applications would offer what "no operating system has provided" before—"a machine-independent way of interacting with the user." Machine independence; device independence. One of Gates's pet concepts had been purloined right from under his nose.

And that wasn't the only excitement at Fall Comdex. Unwittingly financed in part by VisiCorp when it had bought Mitch Kapor's VisiPlot and VisiTrend programs (derived from something called Tiny Troll) for $1.2 million back in October 1981, the startup Lotus Development Corporation was demonstrating a new product, a spreadsheet that also included database and graphic functions. It was called 1-2-3.

In the tiny industry of a couple of years before, in the era when you could get away with calling your product Tiny Troll, just about everybody knew everybody else. The pudgy, laid-back, onetime disk jockey and Transcendental Meditation teacher Kapor had saved Microsoft from untoward embarrassment a couple of years back, when as a beta tester for SoftCard he had discovered a nearly fatal bug. For a time he and Microsoft's Alan Boyd had engaged in discussions about Kapor's doing some sort of charting program that Microsoft would publish. More recently Vern Raburn had become excited enough about Kapor to sign on with Lotus and walk away from a huge number of Microsoft stock options.

So the program was no surprise in the halls of Microsoft. It was precisely the program Charles Simonyi had proposed in his initial business plan. It was the big-memory program that Bill Gates himself had forecast in the very first issue of *PC Magazine*. It was, in short, just radical enough that Microsoft hadn't done it first.

Lotus 1-2-3 wouldn't run on a standard 64K IBM PC. To run the program, you had to have at least 128K of memory, which required an add-in card. The advantage? The program flew like a bat out of hell. Although 1-2-3 lacked Multiplan's consolidation features, it could take advantage of far more memory, allowing much bigger spreadsheets. And Lotus tossed in the ability to produce graphs, handle rudimentary databases, and give a computer-based tutorial that got users up and running.

Lotus 1-2-3 took exactly the opposite approach from the revenue bomb: It was written and optimized specifically for one machine, the IBM PC, and an extra-memory version at that. It used DOS, but snuck around it to get better performance. Other machines would have to wait for adaptations, unless they happened to be fully IBM-compatible—such as the Compaq Portable, which was also announced at that Comdex.

A synergy was at work here. Lotus 1-2-3 was about to become the "killer program" that made the IBM PC, the way VisiCalc had made the Apple II, the way WordStar had made the CP/M machines. The Compaq was the only non-IBM machine that could run it. Eventually Lotus would get around to adapting 1-2-3 to twenty-seven different machines, but in this industry, as hardware makers were beginning to realize, "eventually" was as good as forever. By being so machine-dependent, by going around DOS, Lotus helped launch a wave of IBM-only software and a wave of IBM clone machines that would slowly but inexorably inundate the market.

In this market, "better" was worse. The way to move machines was to be exactly like IBM. Industry consultant Portia Isaacson defined a series of "levels of compatibility" and tested machines in her Future Computing lab, funded in part by Sears. At the highest level, a machine could run the IBM version of Flight Simulator—a product Microsoft had licensed from outsiders as the first in a never-completed line of high-quality game programs intended to make computers more accessible to the uninitiated. Flight Simulator, an on-screen rendition of a Cessna 182, remains a mainstay of Microsoft's product line to this day. Ironically, it was the consummate compatibility test precisely because programming whiz Bruce Artwick had devised his own swift, purposive built-in operating system rather than using clunky old DOS.

It would take the big companies a long while to learn the lesson of compatibility. A year or so later Barry James Folsom would tell Bill Gates that he was finally recommending that DEC, one of the last of the go-your-own-way holdouts, build a compatible machine. Bill "sort of said 'Oh, shit,' and sank back in his chair." As long as machines were incompatible, Microsoft would remain in control of the true standard—DOS. Once the world went to clones, the theme song was "Anything Goes."

Over the short term, compatibles looked great for Microsoft, because being just like IBM meant running DOS. Long term? Less great. For openers, compatibles made the "revenue bomb" applications strategy look stupid. Not only would Microsoft lose its edge in being able to customize special versions for incompatible machines, but in head-to-head comparisons with barnburners like 1-2-3, p-code–based programs such as the lethargic Multiplan wouldn't even get out of the starting blocks.

And if IBM changed directions and abandoned DOS for something better —and there had been rumors about this since Day One of the IBM PC—the clones would probably be able to run that something better too. What if—no, it was too gruesome to contemplate—what if that something was VisiOn? For Bill, it was a cruel way to return from one of his rare vacations—a week of R&R with sister Libby at John Gardiner's Tennis Ranch in Scottsdale, Arizona. The gods had punished him for taking time off! If VisiOn really was machine independent and device independent, no one would care about IBM PC compatibility. And who'd need DOS? If the VisiFolk were capable of writing something as complicated as a graphical windowing system, they'd certainly have no trouble producing an operating system of their own.

There was only one good thing about this: VisiOn was still only a demo. By tipping their hand before they had a product, the VisiFolks had given Bill Gates a window of opportunity.

Make that an Interface Manager of opportunity. Dispatching his lieutenants to take notes at the booth, Gates went into hardcore planning mode. First step: Assemble a team to put together a spec for something that had been hastily dubbed Interface Manager. Even on the plane home, Gates was bending the ears of his top managers to talk up the new project. Next step: Get the word out fast that Microsoft was working on something as good as, no, better than, anything VisiCorp could ever hope to accomplish. Bill himself would take care of large clients, including IBM. The sales force would have Interface Manager tumbling from their lips every time they made an OEM call. Final step: Get dotted-line commitments to support a windowing environment from Microsoft.

Gates knew he could handle some of it, but not all of it. His OEM guys were smart, but he needed a genius—someone who knew the industry, knew the players, and could sweet-talk a pit bull into kissing a cat. He needed a smart-ass, congenial, fast-talking marketing guy by the name of Jim Harris.

Harris was marketing manager for the software distribution and support operation of chipmaker Intel. A rugged individualist, he was getting restless in a software slot at a company so savvy about software that it had let Gary Kildall walk out the door with CP/M. After listening to Harris blow steam one day, a breathless headhunter told him about a job at a little software company in Seattle. Harris asked how things were at Microsoft.

Next thing he knew, he was the beneficiary of one of Steve Ballmer's patented airport pickups, this one enhanced by piles of laundry in the back of the Mustang and a nagging hangover from the Microsoft annual company party the night before. At the Northup Building, Gates had to come downstairs and let them in. Ballmer had forgotten his key.

On January 10, 1983, Harris was hired with a simple mission: Sell MS-DOS to everybody in the world. Version 2.0 was due out soon, but the DOS battle had not yet been won. CP/M-86 was still in the initial convulsions of its protracted death throes, and Digital Research had something in the works called Concurrent CP/M-86 that boasted multitasking—the ability to let you run more than one program at once.

Multitasking was still the great grail of programmers, primarily because a lot of them had worked on old minicomputers that could do it—"machines a lot less powerful than this one on my desk," they would always say, failing to account for the sophisticated hardware that did much of the difficult internal bookkeeping on the minis. Multitasking was important to programmers because they spent a lot of their time staring at blank screens or going for coffee while they waited for their programs to compile. With multitasking, they could continue typing on the screen while the compiler churned silently away in the "background." In the real world, multitasking was a lot less useful: If you were working on a letter to your customers, you weren't likely to need to have your computer run some goofy game at the same time. Still, the ever-competitive Bill Gates was about to put a couple of his programmers on a multitasking project of his own, known for the moment as Multitasking DOS, and a long, long way from reality.

But though broadening the spread of DOS was foremost when Harris came on board, it was not the only system software Microsoft needed to sell. Interface Manager, whatever it was—and at the moment it wasn't even a spec —needed to tag along for the ride. Gates had been on the phone almost constantly since Comdex, urging OEM customers to wait, just wait, till they could see what Microsoft had to offer before inking any deals with VisiCorp. "Bill called around saying ours is coming," one insider remembered. "VisiOn was too close to a product for comfort." It wasn't an easy sell for Gates— particularly when he had nothing to sell but a concept. But in 1983 the graphical interface revolution was the software equivalent of the PC revolution that Paul Allen had insisted must not pass them by. Gates wasn't going to let this one happen without him either.

Graphical and windowing software systems were suddenly coming out of the woodwork. Throughout 1983 you could hear rumors that VisiOn would be released any day now. In January, to amazingly positive reaction from a dazzled, gushing press, Apple revealed its Lisa, though it would not be delivered until June. Waiting in the wings was the Macintosh, as Steve Jobs frequently and painfully reminded Gates every time he phoned to demand why Microsoft was working so hard on DOS and so sluggishly on the Mac. In Santa Monica a tiny outfit by the name of Quarterdeck Office Systems was at work on a windowing system called DESQ that could multitask regular DOS programs but didn't offer graphics. And Digital Research had under development something called GEM, Graphics Environment Manager, which offered graphics and a Macintosh-like interface but didn't do multitasking.

Microsoft's first-pass reply to these competitors came in April, in the form of one of the most illusive demonstrations of all time. Hastily assembled by a programmer named Rao Remala, the Interface Manager demo consisted largely of a screenful of overlapping windows apparently running simultaneous programs, none of which actually did anything. Remala had cobbled the thing together by borrowing from graphics routines Microsoft had done for its Macintosh Chart application. In the estimation of one senior programmer, it was simply a series of "Mac knockoffs." At Microsoft it quickly became known as the "smoke-and-mirrors" demo. Still, if it had worked with Ed Roberts at MITS, it could certainly work again: Demo first, contract second, finish code later.

Throughout 1983 Gates publicly pushed the concept, stating flatly that "what the new graphics technology represents is a revolution in user interface. The bottom line is that graphics are going to be a standard part of all computers." What he didn't say was that Interface Manager's device independence could put Microsoft in control of that new standard. Device independence meant manufacturers would once more feel free to make their machines incompatible again—and better—because software developers would write to Interface Manager instead of to DOS or the hardware. "The revolution is here," Gates said, "and it is soft."

But Gates had some hardware leverage in the works. By the time of the momentous 1982 Comdex, Paul Allen had brought in engineer Raleigh Roark to head up a new hardware department. But Allen's health had deteriorated, and Bill Gates had no particular interest in the hardware business, except for one product: the mouse.

The mouse pointing device, along with many other key concepts of graphical computing, had been invented by computer visionary Doug Engelbart at Stanford Research Institute in 1963. As the linchpin of the graphical user interface at Xerox and then with the Lisa, Mac, and VisiOn, the mouse was essential to Microsoft's strategies. So once more, as with SoftCard, Microsoft executed what it considered a strategic move: Make hardware that would help sell software, while incidentally making a few bucks on the hardware as well.

Work on the mouse moved fast. The design project was handed to Seattle designer David Strong, who had recently come up with Microsoft's new logo and dark-green packaging. Strong put together a series of clay models with thumbtacks in the bottoms for sliders. In a typical model of meticulous, scientific Microsoft research, Gates, Roark, Simonyi, and others slid these lumps of clay around a table and came to tentative conclusions about which design would be best.

Within a week Roark found himself on a plane to Tokyo with Kay Nishi. Two train rides later they arrived at an Alps Electric factory in the Japanese countryside for a high-level meeting. Nishi handed over the clay models and explained that the electronics had to fit inside. The executives called in the engineers. The engineers made faces. "Our engineers say they probably can't do it," Roark was informed, "but they wonder if they can make it a little bigger."

Nishi stuck to his guns. The leader of the Alps team announced, "Our engineers will now leave the room for exactly one hour, and when they return they will have a solution to this problem." In June 1983 Microsoft released its first mouse—the so-called bus mouse, powered from a special add-on board.

An important variant came from an idle remark by Bill Gates as he and Roark toured the floor of a 1983 computer show, looking at the mice already on the market, including the one that came with VisiOn. "It's really too bad," Bill said, "you can't just stick a mouse on a serial port"—an outlet that was standard on every new PC XT unit.

"Yeah, it's too bad you can't do that," Roark replied. "They just draw too much power."

And then Roark figured out that by adopting a low-power chip technology from the Model 100, the mouse could indeed be powered by the serial port. Roark turned the idea over to engineer John Hall, who did the actual design work. Microsoft eventually patented the concept.

When the Microsoft Mouse was introduced, there was virtually nothing you could do with it except run the demonstration programs that came in the box or, if you were an excellent programmer, write your own interfaces to the thing. By the end of the year Microsoft was supplying software menus that would work with popular programs—Multiplan, VisiCalc, 1-2-3, WordStar—and make them somewhat mouseable. Yet still the little beast wasn't selling. But while waiting for Interface Manager, Microsoft was about to leverage the mouse hardware with another piece of software—a word processor from Bravo master Charles Simonyi.

By this time computer printers, both dot matrix and daisy-wheel, had improved markedly in quality and dropped markedly in price, making word processing in general, and WordStar in particular, the growing thing in software, to the point where MicroPro had become the country's top microcomputer software company, with sales of $60 million in fiscal 1983, edging out Microsoft by $5 million. The up-and-coming program was MultiMate, Softword Systems' Wang clone, which capitalized on the special characters Nishi and Gates had stuck into the IBM PC display. Another strong contender was Displaywrite, IBM's only remotely successful attempt to develop its own application software for the PC.

But with the hiring of Simonyi, Gates had abandoned the outmoded Wang model and cast his fate with WYSIWYG—the what-you-see-is-what-you-get word processing that Simonyi had implemented in Bravo. It had been the first project in Simonyi's master plan, but it had been delayed—in part because of the common Microsoft complaint, "lack of resources," meaning not enough programmers to do the job and Bill's unwillingness to hire more.

For this project, conceived as the follow-on to Multiplan in a planned Multi-Tool line, Simonyi's programming protégé was Richard Brodie, an ambitious, cocky, quirky Harvard computer jock and one of the original Golden Boys. Brodie had taken a couple of years off from college to work for Simonyi at Xerox, and at Microsoft in the summer of 1981 he had worked on the language compiler for Multiplan and the p-coded revenue bomb projects. As Simonyi would put it, "The bandwidth between us was just tremendous."

In the summer of 1982 Brodie had checked in to write the code for what was then known as Multi-Tool Word. Word had features aplenty. It offered support for the Microsoft Mouse; in the early days, it came boxed with one. Like Multiplan, Word let the user open multiple windows on a document, and added the ability to work on multiple documents at once—all in a neatly "tiled" side-by-side layout. It included elaborate formatting options via a mystifying technique called style sheets. With the right hardware, Word could display boldface, italics, underlines, superscripts, and subscripts on the screen —something most of its competitors indicated by clunky indicators such as ∧B. Word could even format output with the precision of typesetting machines, down to fractions of an inch, down to picas—measurements that were utterly useless and utterly baffling to users of dot-matrix and daisy-wheel printers in an age when affordable laser printers were still far off. It was, in short, a distillation of Simonyi's experience—and Brodie's—with Bravo and the high-end systems they'd used at Xerox.

But the IBM PC was no Alto. Although Word moved closer toward a graphical interface than anything available at the time, the program, stuck with the clunky IBM hardware, was hard to learn and not particularly easy to use. The p-code technique made it exceptionally slow on machines that lacked a hard disk, which meant most of them. Word was copy-protected to avoid piracy, making it still more awkward to use. Unlike the freely copyable Word-Star, Word offered no spelling checker or mailing-list program, which had come to be regarded as essential. And bundling Word with the mouse gave keyboard jocks the mistaken idea you had to use a mouse with the program, like it or not. Most didn't.

But once the project got underway, Brodie had moved it out the door fast. Word shipped in November 1983, making Brodie a god at Microsoft. For a time he would succeed Carl Stork as the personal protégé of Bill Gates, the Golden Boy sitting at the feet of the master. On his next assignment Brodie would not be so fortunate.

But what about the Mac? That was what Steve Jobs kept wondering. Throughout the Mac's development cycle, Jobs kept reading Gates the riot act, both in person and over the phone. "Steve would pick up the phone and he'd call up Bill and he'd say, 'Bill, I hear that you're doing this and you're doing this and you're doing this and that isn't what you told me in our last meeting!' " recalled Mike Murray, the Macintosh's original marketing manager. " 'You've gone back on your word, and you get down here right now. I don't care what your schedule says. I want you down here tomorrow morning at eight-thirty and I want you to tell me exactly what you're doing at Microsoft.' "

At the time, Gates had little choice but to oblige. Jobs was the industry's top dog, Microsoft needed to get a foothold in applications software, and Gates was telling everyone within earshot that the graphical interface was the heart of God for personal computing. When Steve talked, Bill listened.

In the Picasso Room at Apple's Bandley 3 building, the Mac nerve center, Gates would saunter up to the whiteboard and outline Microsoft's progress. Murray, at least, believed Gates: "I could just tell by reading the guy, because it was total stream of consciousness, no notes or anything, that this guy isn't lying. He's just telling us everything he's doing. Everything! He'd lay it all out. Hell, I'd actually be a little amazed by how open he was."

Jobs and Bob Belleville—who had jumped from PARC when Jobs called him "and said everything you've ever done in your life is terrible, so why don't you come and work with me?"—held a different view. "They wouldn't have happy faces," Murray recalled, "because they thought this guy was just twisting his words a little bit. Gates would leave, and immediately Steve and Bob would say, 'I'm not sure. I don't think this was really what they're really doing.' "

Looking back, Belleville said, "I wouldn't read paranoia into this. I think the model of really tough competitors applied. Steve was dependent on Bill and Bill dependent on Steve, but Steve's dependency was growing."

Apple, Jobs knew, was heading for trouble. The Apple II was still selling well but had peaked and was losing market share to the IBM PC. The Apple III, plagued by manufacturing defects and a dearth of software, was sputtering along on the road to nowhere. The failing Lisa was so slow it generated a popular "Knock Knock" joke wherein the response to "Who's there?" was a fifteen-second pause followed by the word "Lisa." The Pirates believed the company had to "bet the ranch on the Macintosh."

"Steve had appropriate paranoia," Murray recalled. "Microsoft wasn't the enemy, but IBM was. If IBM could come out with a friendly user interface and revolutionize this whole thing, then where is our competitive advantage?"

Murray had become an Apple confidant of sorts for Gates. In the spring of 1981 Microsoft had recruited Murray fresh out of Stanford Business School, where he had gotten to know Steve Ballmer. After a Saturday interview with Gates at Microsoft headquarters, the three ended up in Ballmer's living room.

Gates began his characteristic rocking motion, elbows at his hips, looking like a waif freezing in an unheated room. Ballmer started doing it. After a while Murray found himself rocking back and forth too. "It just seemed to be the thing to do." But Murray didn't get a job at Microsoft until 1987. The company already had a nontechnical guy in Ballmer; at the time it wasn't entirely clear what a second one would bring to the party.

So after his Apple briefings, Gates would call Murray from Seattle in a distressed state, wanting to know what he was doing wrong, whether the Macintosh strategy had changed. "You guys don't believe me," Gates would say, reminding Murray that Microsoft had committed a third of its programming resources to this project.

"No, Bill, nothing has changed," Murray would tell him soothingly.

These guys get a little excited. What I want you to do is nothing different than what you were doing the day before yesterday.

Six weeks later, Steve would pick up the phone. "Bill, I don't know what's going on up there, but here's what I'll tell you I'm hearing. You're doing this, and you're doing this, and you're doing this. So I want you to stop everything and I want you down here tomorrow morning and I want you to tell me personally what you're doing." Bill would be down the next morning and I would sit in on all these meetings, and it would just be a repeat. Bill would fly home, and the phone would ring. "Mike, what should we do?"

At one point, Jobs tried to give Bill Gates a lesson in business, to convince him that too much of his resources were being squandered on low-profit operating systems when they'd be better spent on high-profit applications. "It's not that I don't trust you," Jobs added, "but I can't get my people to trust your people, and that makes it hard for us to really give you all the information we'd like to. If your big brother punched my big brother in the nose, people wouldn't say your big brother punched my big brother. They'd say the Gateses are beating up on the Jobses."

"No, Steve," Gates instantly shot back, "I think it's more like we both have this rich neighbor named Xerox, and you broke in to steal the TV set, and you found out I'd been there first and you said, 'Hey, that's no fair! I wanted to steal the TV set!' "

The things Jobs was hearing were no doubt derived in part from Microsoft puffery. When it came to DOS and Interface Manager, the old never-lose-a-deal philosophy was very much in evidence. As the bluff, charming Harris began making the rounds, Bill was often along for the ride. Gates "was very aggressive in doing things to sign you up," recalled Barry James Folsom.

Whenever an OEM sounded dubious at the prospect of a multitasking, windowing, graphics-based system running on a measly 8088, Microsoft trotted out the smoke-and-mirrors demo, which for sales purposes one account rep had taken to calling "Magic." It wasn't much, but it held its own against the other stuff out there: Lisa was late, priced at a sky-high $10,000, and unavailable to OEM customers. VisiOn kept getting delayed further into the future. DESQ was looking good but not fully functional. The Macintosh, GEM, and something IBM was rumored to have up its sleeve were still rumor fodder on the bytevine.

Although Microsoft did not have Interface Manager even close to working, it had something the other vendors didn't: DOS. OEM customers engaged in DOS negotiations would find Interface Manager promoted with evangelistic zeal that would make a TV preacher blush. The theme: If you like DOS, you're gonna love Interface Manager. If you like DOS, this is the only 100 percent guaranteed compatible windowing program. If you like DOS and BASIC, we'll turn the deal into a hat trick that gives you Interface Manager. Oh, and you'll probably need a mouse. We've got that too. It's easy: Sign here.

Also hinted was that IBM had pretty much given its blessing to the young program—even though it hadn't and wouldn't. Despite wheedling, cajoling, and pleading from Gates, IBM staunchly refused to throw its weight behind Interface Manager. To the contrary, it was leaning toward VisiOn and, from all appearances, trying to develop something similar of its own—an intention it had from the very beginning, with the ultimate goal of taking back the system for its own purposes, to somehow leverage what IBM always considered its real business—the business of selling big mainframe computers.

Still, you never knew. Maybe IBM would get religion. Meantime, there was no harm in playing the IBM card. "There was that kind of implied understanding that we're IBM's partner and IBM is certainly going to come in on this," pioneer Windows developer George Grayson recalled. And this time you could join the party at the very beginning.

Microsoft wasn't just leveraging DOS and IBM. Every feature of Interface Manager was aimed at undercutting the competition. VisiOn required a hard disk, an expensive commodity in 1983; Interface Manager could do its magic with the two floppy drives everybody had. Other systems required 350K or more of memory. Interface Manager could get by on 192K. And Microsoft's product was cheaper. VisiOn was going to cost over $1,000; DESQ debuted at $199. With OEM DOS deals, Interface Manager was thrown in for peanuts—loss leadership at its finest, another Gatesway to significant market share.

Software marketing circa 1983 was still a new and largely legally unmapped province. From newspaper key scams as a kid to self-appropriated on-line time at Harvard, Gates had never been one to cleave to the rules. With DOS, Gates knew he had leverage—and used it to help to sign up commitments for Interface Manager, soon to be known as Windows.

Tying the purchase of one dominant product to the purchase of another is prohibited under antitrust law. Microsoft executives said the company assiduously avoided trouble. As one former OEM sales executive put it:

> I kept a gun in my desk, which I promised to use on any account manager who ever tried that. In front of an audience. And it never happened. Not on my watch. First of all it's illegal, just simply flat illegal. And second of all it's unethical. Even if you could get away with it. And we just didn't do it.

Yet OEM customers recalled other strongarm tactics from the Bellevueites. Barry James Folsom, the DEC Rainbow manager, said Gates "wanted us to do some business practices that weren't right" but wouldn't elaborate. Phil Nelson, who had left Digital Research for Victor, remembered: "When VisiOn was coming out and Windows was in its infancy, Microsoft sent a letter to its MS-DOS OEMs and others stating that we will give you a beta of Windows 1.0 only if you agree not to do any development on any competing product"—say, a product like VisiOn. Victor refused to sign the agreement. The word was out: Gates was selling Interface Manager like "a Chinese warlord."

One high-ranking Microsoft executive of the era put the early tactics in focus, recalling some things Microsoft did that he didn't like, things that "I wouldn't want the law to hear about." He surmised they happened mostly "because it was an inexperienced bunch of guys trying to win."

One of the warlords put it another way:

> We had a price list. And I remember a few times when we followed it. We did business.
>
> . . . we got this great new product, here are the nineteen reasons we think it's a great one, and anything after two is probably bullshit. They looked at it, they talked about it, we told them what we were going to do and how we were going to roll it out, how important it was going to be. They wondered if IBM had licensed it. We told them they knew we couldn't tell them anything about what other OEMs were doing. And they probably wondered how their refusal to play with us on that would affect the relationship in the future.
>
> But that was their wondering. I never told anybody they weren't going to get DOS if they didn't license Windows or something. And they never said they were afraid they weren't going to get it. But their thinking is influenced by the whole relationship. So is ours. These people you took in and explained what Windows was, you showed them the demo, tried to miss the bugs, they said "Right, where do I sign?"—you treat them differently than the guys who waited until two days before the show in New York and then decided they wanted their names on the list.

At Apple, the one place besides Xerox where windowed software was something more than smoke, Steve Jobs was not amused. Interface Manager was clearly diverting more of Microsoft's attention away from Mac development and could ultimately compete with the forthcoming Macintosh. Jobs called Bill in for another official upbraiding.

Jobs reminded Gates of their original January 1982 agreement. Having gained its inside knowledge of the Mac from Apple's generosity in sharing system information, Microsoft should not turn around and use that knowledge to produce competing products for the IBM PC market. Jobs maintained that the agreement implicitly prohibited Microsoft from doing a program like Windows.

No, Gates argued, that was not what the contract said. The wording applied only to the three applications mentioned, not to an overall operating environment. The letter of the contract left his company free to proceed.

And, he pointed out, there was also the expiration date: The restriction applied only to the first twelve months after January 1, 1983 or initial shipment of the Mac, whichever came first. Although Microsoft was selling Windows, it certainly wasn't selling the proscribed applications—and wouldn't consider doing so before New Year's Day 1984.

"Bill had to defend himself against a vehement, steaming-mad Steve Jobs," Andy Hertzfeld recalled. "And he did a pretty good job of representing his point of view."

The entreprenurial sword-crossing made for Lincoln-Douglas debates and Ali-Frazier battles of will, but at its base the relationship between Jobs and Gates was by all accounts friendly. The two got together frequently at trade shows, conferences, and visits to each other's domains for hours-long discussions on the future of the industry. "Bill didn't like some of the things we were doing and we didn't like some of the things he was doing," Belleville said. "There was really no personal animosity that I ever detected." Ross Perot, who would bankroll a later Jobs venture, went further: "I'll tell you Steve absolutely is a Bill Gates fan. I've just heard him bring it up too often: No jealousy, no resentment, all those things that could be there."

Gates found Jobs's roller-coaster mood swings somewhat amusing: "Whenever we have these two-day meetings he'll start off, he'll be superaggressive at the start of the meeting 'cause his guys are there, and he's kind of got to posture, he says everything is incredible, it's all ahead of schedule," Gates recounted. "Then after you've been talking with him, after three or four hours, he gets into this solicitous mode where he says, 'Do you think we're doing anything right here? Do you think this will ever sell?' "

▼ While Gates was working on both 16-bit platforms, Kay Nishi was keeping the 8-bit world alive with a Microsoft standard announced in June 1983 in

Tokyo as MSX. MSX was designed for the bottom of the market—home computers costing less than $300. An MSX machine would include a Z-80 processor, specified sound and graphics chips, a joystick, a slot for a ROM cartridge, color-TV output, and 32K of ROM that included Microsoft BASIC and some special subroutines. The idea was to offer a standard in the 8-bit world much like the one DOS and the IBM PC presented in the 16-bit arena, and to leapfrog Digital Research's CP/M by including all the bells and whistles it lacked. Under MSX, based in part on technology from a Hong Kong outfit called Spectravideo, software developers could develop their game, entertainment, and educational software and be assured that it would run on a variety of machines without reworking.

This was mostly a Nishi enterprise—ASCII's longtime hacker-king Rick Yamashita was the technical wizard behind it—and Bill Gates saw it as a sweet deal. Companies could license MSX from Microsoft for $100,000 in advance, plus a minimum royalty commitment of $150,000 against royalties ranging from $3 down to $2 per machine depending on volume. In return, they'd get little more than a set of hardware specifications and the code for Microsoft's ROM BASIC interpreter. If they wanted to offer a disk drive, they could pony up an additional fee of $50,000 against $5 per copy for something called MSX-DOS, essentially an 8-bit version of MS-DOS that would be written by DOS creator Tim Paterson, who by this time was working as a consultant to Microsoft. It was the old Albuquerque technique: Write it once, sell it often.

In *Microsoft Quarterly*, Bill Gates hailed MSX for allowing "Microsoft to deliver a single form of BASIC to all the newcomers in the low-end market, leaving us free to focus on the office market"—a typically tactful Gatesian hint that MSX customers were not exactly Microsoft's top priority. Still, fifteen Japanese companies, including Matsushita, Hitachi, Sony, Toshiba, and Yamaha, signed up for MSX, giving Microsoft and Nishi's ASCII an instant $1.5 million cash windfall. In the early going the singular absentee was NEC; its commanding lead in the Japanese arena gave it no incentive to join a me-too consortium. One boost came after the midyear Consumer Electronics Show, where Philips, the Dutch electronics behemoth, joined the bandwagon. At that show, Nishi held up a single-chip integrated version of the MSX hardware   one of his first ventures into chip design, which would become an ASCII specialty and one of his personal hobbyhorses.

Nishi had plenty of those. As a publisher of magazines, he had diversified into becoming a publisher of software. Now he was urging Bill Gates to take the opposite tack—in part to help pave the way for Microsoft's increasingly retail business to get a foothold in outlets it had never reached before. The first venture that looked appealing was *PC Magazine*, which founder Tony Gold had put on the block late in 1982. Seeing himself about to be squeezed out, Bill's old MITS pal David Bunnell, the magazine's editor and publisher, appealed to

Gates "as a sort of savior." After a brief flirtation, Bill scuttled the idea when David Marquardt and others questioned the value of a magazine that would lack, or appear to lack, independence and objectivity.

Even without buying in, Gates saw his golden luck hold yet again. After its purchase by Ziff-Davis, *PC Magazine* went on to spawn a whole family of successful computer publications that helped fuel interest in computers in general and Microsoft products in particular. Bunnell went on to start his own magazine, *PC World*, which would give Microsoft reams of coverage over the years.

In 1982 Nishi was interviewed for an article by an American writer named Nahum Stiskin, a free-lancer who had just sold his publishing company and was noodling around the fringes of computerdom in Japan. Stiskin, a fast-talking little guy with the glib personal hustle of a Hollywood producer, had once headed up Autumn Press, a tiny English-language publishing house headquartered in Tokyo and later Boston. Its volumes on yoga and Zen took advantage of the countercultural interest in things Oriental, preferably spiritual or edible, and the company had made its biggest splash with the *Book of Tofu*.

Impressed with Stiskin, Nishi turned the interview around and hired him as a consultant. Two weeks later, in March 1983, Stiskin presented Gates a business plan "right down to the wastebaskets" for a Microsoft book publishing arm. Shortly thereafter he became manager of Microsoft Press.

Stiskin announced that the books "must set new standards for editorial and graphic quality in the book publishing business," and by computer-book standards, the books and their promotion were lavish. Like so many other Microsoft products, the books were intended to have a strategic value beyond their intrinsic value. Not only would classy volumes be potential moneymakers, they would spread the Microsoft name and gospel out in the world, offer gilt by association, beat the drum for Microsoft products, and provide a profitable means of customer support.

They could even be used to help cement OEM relationships: Apple, for example, provided its wholehearted cooperation for Microsoft's *The Apple Macintosh Book*. Chairman Bill, the hands-on CEO, had his hands on even here: Gates personally buttonholed author Cary Lu at a Microsoft convention event and "pitched me very hard about doing the book." Lu later encountered a singular act of censorship: The editors requested that he remove any mention of the names of Microsoft's Macintosh developers. In a business where the assets walked out the door at night, there was no sense giving headhunters and competitors a handy reference tool.

Those assets had their hands full. As an unsigned internal memo reported years before, "The CMERGE project is unique amoung [sic] the major Microsoft efforts in that it is not directly tied to a short-term goal, i.e., shipping a product to meet a contract deadline. As we're all aware, Microsoft typically suffers from a form of software 'gridlock.' We can't take the long-term view because we're too pressed to deliver commitments; we're pressed so hard because we couldn't take a long-term view." Nothing much had changed since, except the arrival of Charles Simonyi and a long-term view that saw GUI, GUI, GUI.

The CMERGE project had been in the works since back when languages were the company's primary business. An attempt to streamline Microsoft's language development efforts by using a common-code strategy akin to Simonyi's revenue bomb, it was behind schedule and failing dismally.

And CMERGE was just the tip of the mismanagement iceberg. At an off-site technical retreat in May 1983, Gates got an earful of just how bad the situation was. Even though Microsoft preached the gospel of the microcomputer, it certainly didn't practice it. The marketing/communications and technical publications people were using the DEC-20 minicomputer for word processing, slowing it down horribly for the programmers who absolutely depended on it. The XENIX systems the company was using for development were woefully overloaded.

As Gates admitted in a memo, "the Company is short of hardware resources. . . . We view this as a crisis since your productivity on machine is our most valuable resource. Please bear with us through this desperate situation." The solution Gates chose focused not on the microcomputers he was pushing to the rest of the world but on minicomputers—two more PDP-11s—and a dozen UNIX workstations. A measly eight PC XTs were the only microcomputers to be added to the company's arsenal.

There were other ways to gain personal productivity. "We have considered asking people to intentionally work off hours until these fixes help," Gates wrote. "If desperation persists, [we] will meet with relevant users and seek their cooperation."

The retreat also focused on the question of "systems assurance and testing"—something that had been given virtually no attention in the past. Testing had been fobbed off on the OEM customers, but that didn't always work—as the IBM BASIC flap and many unpublicized incidents, such as a data-corrupting FORTRAN bug, had conclusively proven. Now, with increasing sales at retail, Gates proposed hiring staff to develop test methodology. But the idea of methodical testing was only a trial balloon. It would remain full of hot air for years to come.

In the summer of 1983 Tricia McGinnis, Microsoft's director of design and production services, held a party at her place on the lake. Her beau, Bill Clone Jeff Raikes, was there, and so were the Original Bill, his loyal lieutenant Steve Ballmer, and a Prime Computer sales rep named Jill Bennett. Tall, blond, and self-assured, Bennett was first introduced to the outgoing Ballmer and then to Microsoft's chief. Her first question to Gates: Why didn't he develop software for 32-bit minicomputers? It was a lower volume business, certainly, but it would produce much higher per-unit returns. "He laughed pretty hard and nicknamed me '32-bit,' " Bennett recalled. Confrontation was the way to Bill's heart.

Born a day apart in the same Seattle hospital, the two had much in common: tennis, computers, friends. "We even look a little alike," Bennett said, though she more strongly resembled Bill's younger sister Libby. It was techie love at first sight.

Given his "hardcore exterior" of intellectual and business aggressiveness, Bennett was surprised to discover Bill's personal diffidence. "I think he always wanted to belong to a fraternity and be a major force on campus, but his shyness kept him from being a part of 'the' group."

But if Bill Gates was shy, he was also focused. So focused, Bennett discovered, that he had disconnected the radio in his Mercedes and refused to own a television set. Since his youth, he told her, he had organized his mind into "a huge bank of drawers," divided into subjects and topics. "Everything that comes in goes into a drawer, so his whole mind is structured." It made Gates a formidable opponent when it came to games like Trivial Pursuit. "We used to give him a bad time: What if one of the drawers gets stuck?"

Bill brooded constantly. "He feels so committed and he's so hung up on setting such an extreme good example for his people, being there, being there late, working hard, setting the pace," Bennett said. "He was always worried about stuff." It translated to insomnia. "Just worried about everything," he would have "a real hard time sleeping at night, and then during the day he could sleep instantly. He'd crawl under a desk. He'd crawl under chairs at the airport and fall asleep. People would lose him."

Yet the Gates focus went soft when it came to the mundane—money, clothing, credit cards, wallets. Fixed on corporate problems, Bill paid little attention to himself: "He doesn't get enough sleep, and he doesn't exercise, and he doesn't eat right." Gates would leave clothes in hotel rooms, leave money in clothes sent out for cleaning. On dates with Jill, he'd often discover he was short of cash and had forgotten his credit cards; Bennett would pay for the date. But when he wasn't flush out, Gates was flush: "He would just go to the bank and get $2,000 cash."

Driving was another bone of contention. "He's just not a good driver," Bennett declared, adding "he will dispute that." Bill loved speed and did fine at 100 miles an hour on the open road down a straightaway, but Bennett found herself in one too many close calls on narrow highways, and in city traffic Gates, focused elsewhere, was "the absent-minded professor."

In early 1983 Gates focused on a house for sale in Laurelhurst, half a mile from the home he'd grown up in and his parents still occupied. With typical decisiveness, Gates went for it—to the tune of $889,000. The money for the house came largely from the proceeds of stock deals with the high-flying Andy Evans.

Unassuming from the street, the 4,400-square-foot 1946-vintage house was much like his parents' place, taking advantage of a sloping lot and lake view with common rooms on the entry level and bedrooms in a lower level that led to the backyard. It also had extra amenities: forty-eight feet of Lake Washington waterfront, a dock, and, most important, a view of the floating bridge so that Gates could scope out commuter backups before heading across the lake to Microsoft. Even so, it was not a surefire deal. There had been serious talk about his simply moving into the Ramada Inn just down the road from Microsoft headquarters.

Bill's mother and grandmother took charge of the interior decorating and had his furniture and belongings moved while he was away on a trip to Japan. Back in town with a case of jet-lag confusion, he called Mathers from the airport and asked, "Estelle, which house do I go to?"

When he arrived at the new house, he found everything neatly in place. The resourceful Gam had gone so far as to label Bill's dresser drawers with yellow Post-it notes designating their contents.

Gates eventually installed an enclosed thirty-foot swimming pool but immediately ordered a bigger bathtub. Bill preferred baths to showers so he could multitask, doing things while the water was running, and then reading while soaking in the tub. But he often omitted sudsing his hair, leading to reams of copy over the years about his "greasy locks" and "dandruff." According to Bennett, she and his mother were "always after him" to shampoo. But what else could you possibly do while you were doing that?

17

THE SOFTWARE FACTORY

Jim Towne hadn't worked out, and Bill Gates knew it. This time no executive search firm need apply. After batting it around with Ballmer and Marquardt, Gates knew exactly who he wanted: Jon Shirley, a slight, wiry fellow who looked like the unassuming engineer he had once intended to become but was tough as cheap steak when it got down to business. A veteran of twenty-four years at Radio Shack, Shirley had been in the microcomputer industry almost as long as Bill Gates, knew retailing as well as anyone around, and had worked with Gates and Microsoft on a variety of projects from the earliest BASICs to the Model 100. Like Gates, Shirley had dropped out of a famous Massachusetts college, in his case MIT. And there was absolutely no question of Shirley's standing up to Bill: He'd done that plenty of times across the bargaining table.

In the dog-eat-dog consumer electronics business, Radio Shack was the acknowledged master of wheedling suppliers down on their prices by nickels, dimes, and pennies; Microsoft considered the Texans, from John "Horseshit" Roach on down, the hardest-nosed negotiators in the industry. Just the year before, Bill had gone down to Fort Worth to sell Radio Shack on XENIX for its multiuser Model 16 computer, based on the same Motorola 68000 chip that would power the Macintosh. This time Gates found the door closed. Radio Shack had already contracted with a Massachusetts company to adapt UNIX for the machine. But Bill Gates, consummate salesman, knew better than to let a little problem like that stand in his way.

Shirley was unmovable. Burned in the past by late deliveries on other projects, he guessed that Bill's XENIX might not be entirely "real" and told him so in no uncertain terms. Gates insisted his product was a lot better than the one Shirley had signed up for. After tromping off together to Roach's office, they came up with a deal: If Microsoft could give a successful demonstration within ninety days, Radio Shack would do the deal.

The very day the offer was due to expire, Microsoft's XENIX marketeer,

Mark Ursino, showed up in Fort Worth, gave the promised demo, and saved the day. Though the finished product would barely be ready on time, that mattered less; Microsoft's competitor for the Model 16 business had gotten so far behind that Radio Shack canceled its contract. Microsoft received a royalty of $50 for every Model 16 sold; it became by far the company's biggest XENIX contract. In Shirley's words, "It was a pretty amazing demonstration of what they could do when you really held their feet to the fire."

At the May 1983 National Computer Conference in Anaheim, "real" computer companies such as IBM basked in air-conditioned comfort while many microcomputer firms, including Microsoft, were relegated to oppressively hot, airless tents in the convention center's parking lot. Evenings were a refreshing change. At the posh Balboa Bay Club, Microsoft held a lavish party complete with oysters, crab, roast beef, melons, a twenty-six-foot sloop hoisted via crane into the swimming pool, and a huge power yacht cruising the harbor with an open bar. This was the beginning of the computerdom-as-Hollywood era, complete with flashy parties, stars, gossip columnists. To Young America, it was no longer nerdy to be involved with computers: It was cool, it was hip, and better still, in the Reagan years, it was where the money was.

Bill did not utter the word "decadent," a favorite in future years, but he may have thought it. The biggest Microsoft party yet, the festivities attracted all the industry's major figures—everyone from Lotus's Mitch Kapor to Radio Shack's Jon Shirley. Just back from two weeks in Japan, Shirley was suffering from intense jet lag and planning to call it an early evening so he could get some sleep before a morning meeting he'd scheduled with Bill Gates about the successors to the Model 100.

David Marquardt, Microsoft's venture capitalist board member, cornered Bill and Ballmer and suggested it was time to pop the question. "I can't do it! I can't do it!" Bill shrieked. "What if he says no? What am I going to say?"

"I don't even know the guy!" Ballmer said, drawing back.

That left Marquardt to do the deed. Bill was kind of having a hard time about how to bring this up, he told Shirley. Had he ever thought about leaving Tandy?

Flabbergasted, Radio Shack's vice president of computer merchandising muttered, "Are you kidding?"

Marquardt insisted he was absolutely serious. Would Shirley consider being president of Microsoft?

Marquardt thought Shirley might fall over backward. "Why would you be interested in me?" Shirley said. "I'm just a guy who sells things over the counter."

But Shirley was definitely interested. A navy brat, he loved the water and was itching to get back to the West Coast where he'd been born. A year before, he and his wife had spent weeks enjoying the Northwest, where his son had just graduated from Lewis and Clark College in Portland, Oregon. A reorganization of Radio Shack's computer business had left it, he felt, without much direction at the upper end of the product line—where he had just committed the company to a mistake called the Model 2000, the first in a planned series of PC-incompatibles with high-resolution graphics that would be perfect for running the Interface Manager that was supposed to be delivered Real Soon Now. On a Radio Shack pretext, Shirley came up to Seattle for interviews in May and June, and later thrashed out his financial deal with Steve Ballmer in a lounge at the Dallas airport. Towne was gone by June 16; Shirley moved in six weeks later.

Shirley's initial mission was to free Bill Gates to do the two things he did best: work on product development and maintain personal contact with the major OEM customers. The retail business, where Shirley's years of experience were invaluable, would be under the new president's wing. So would manufacturing and merchandising and finance.

Microsoft's business was changing. Its major thrust had long been to round up OEM customers and sell them code. That high-margin business was still essential, but now the company was also trying to sell products directly to the public via retail channels. Although the OEM sales force was experienced, as Shirley saw it, the retail marketing department consisted of MBAs barely out of school—kids such as Jeff Raikes, the Bill Clone from Apple, and Pete Higgins, another of the Stanford Mafia. They were green, but at least they had potential.

Steve Ballmer, in Shirley's eyes, was a loose cannon—responsible for everything from personnel to accounting to the IBM business. Shirley aimed the cannon, putting Ballmer in charge of marketing—an effort that would increase enormously during Shirley's regime.

But even though the company gave the public illusion of high-speed sleekness, in many ways it was dropping pieces along the highway. When Shirley arrived, order entry was done on a time-sharing system out of San Francisco that didn't work reliably during the day. The general ledger was still being kept on that venerable Radio Shack Model 2—even given Shirley's history, not exactly what he'd choose for a $50 million company on its way to $100 million. The MIS (Management Information Systems) department amounted to exactly two employees.

Manufacturing was a disaster. The ongoing transition from a purely OEM business, where inventory amounted to little more than a disk or two full of code, to a company that produced a variety of retail products that had to be manufactured, warehoused, and shipped was extremely rocky. The warehouse and manufacturing facility in Totem Lake north of Bellevue was out of room, and most of the work was being jobbed out to expensive vendors.

When Mark Rolsing, the burly angler who had run Tandy's software assembly plant, followed Shirley to a similar post at Microsoft, he had only the vaguest idea of what he was getting into. When Rolsing asked what the P & Ls looked like, Shirley explained that profit-and-loss statements, the numbers by which Tandy lived and died, were not yet a part of the picture at Microsoft. Diskettes were copied on a personal computer instead of a high-speed duplicator. Manuals were assembled by hand. The day Rolsing bought half a dozen electric label dispensers, he became an instant hero around the warehouse.

Microsoft's clear plastic "easel" boxes, for which the company had actually acquired a patent, were considered part of the Microsoft quality image. From a manufacturing standpoint, they were an unmitigated disaster. They broke. They got scratched. And since they couldn't be folded flat like cardboard boxes, they occupied vast amounts of precious warehouse space. Eventually, space limitations got so tight that some assembly work was farmed out to an outfit best known for putting labels on cans of salmon.

Inventory maintenance? What was that? Some 30,000 Microsoft Mice infested the warehouse—at the current sales rate, a seven-year supply. Production was geared to monthly forecasts, and when demand outstripped guess— and in a company with Microsoft's phenomenal growth rate, this happened all the time—the manufacturing plant would struggle to catch up. Shirley decreed that a sixty-day stock would be kept on hand at all times—causing short-term chaos for Rolsing's loyal troops, who by then had just undergone a move to more capacious quarters. Still, Shirley was beginning to make headway on problems no one else had tackled or even recognized.

At Shirley's suggestion, Microsoft began matching employee contributions to United Way dollar for dollar. The matching-funds strategy had "resulted in very high participation" at Tandy, Shirley noted, and there was a practical side as well: "Frankly, it makes it awfully easy then to not have to deal with every single entity that comes in the door looking for money. You say, look, we support this one major entity in a major way."

Given Mary Gates's longtime role with United Way, Shirley didn't have to do too much arm-twisting. But Bill wasn't openly thrilled about the potential demands on his increasingly precious time. When he grumbled to Shirley that IBM's chief John Akers "has told me I've got to join the United Way national board," Shirley replied, "Look, Bill: At least that gives you the chance to meet with John" when the board convened.

Gates thought it over. "Yeah," he admitted. "I guess it's worth it for that."

Shirley was Gates's kind of administrator: He didn't need to be told what to do or how to do it. He just did it. Around the office, neither was long on warm fuzziness—"If you put Bill and Jon in the same room they couldn't melt an ice cube," former vice president Ida Cole cracked—but Shirley's unflappable hand was seen in every aspect of the company, from employee guidelines down to the purchase of pricey newsletter subscriptions. Marquardt laughed at the difference in organizational styles: Bill's office had "piles on the floor, up on the desk, just crap everywhere. And you go into Jon's office, and it was just perfect. Jon is the kind of guy who could tell you how many number-two pencils they consumed in the U.K. branch office in the third quarter of 1982."

Under Shirley there was also a new push in marketing, spearheaded by Ballmer. The most visible mastermind was a new recruit who dated back to the waning days of the Towne era. A thirty-one-year-old marketeer on his way up, tall, dapper, sun-loving Rowland Hanson was a veteran of Betty Crocker and Contadina and was currently making his mark at Neutrogena. He knew absolutely nothing about personal computers, he had absolutely no interest in them, he was getting ready to start his own business, and he was not about to listen to a headhunter's suggestion that he take a day off to go up to rainy Seattle on a wild-goose chase. But somehow he found himself in the office of Bill Gates.

Hanson asked why Gates had any interest in him at all, considering he knew nothing about computers or software. "You know," Gates told him, "the only difference between a dollar-an-ounce moisturizer and a forty-dollar-an-ounce moisturizer is in the consumer's mind. There is no technical difference between the moisturizers."

Hanson was impressed.

"Well," Gates went on, "I know that we will have the reality of the software. We will technically be the best software. But if people don't believe it or people don't recognize it, it won't matter. While we're on the leading edge of technology, we also have to be creating the right perception about our products and our company, the right image. And right now I don't think we're doing that."

On the way up to Seattle, Hanson had been thinking "NFW. No way am I going to take this job." On the way back, he was thinking "You know, I believe these guys are on to something." His conversation with the master convincer had Hanson hooked.

Hanson's courtship remarkably paralleled that of another marketing maven, John Sculley. Toward the end of 1982 Steve Jobs was beginning to recognize that to be successful, the Mac would have to appeal to people who didn't already use computers and understand them. Apple would have to sell Macs like—well, like soft drinks. Sculley, a career Pepsi executive being groomed for chairman, was contacted by a headhunter about a search for a new chief executive at Apple. Sculley knew virtually nothing about computers—he had an Apple II+ but found it "more work to use than it was worth." But he had liked to tinker with electronics as a kid. When he mentioned offhandedly he was going to meet with Steve Jobs, his nineteen-year-old daughter's mouth dropped open: "You're going to meet Steve Jobs?" she exclaimed. Sculley took note.

In a cat-and-mouse courtship over the next few months the two hit it off, the analytical, Ivy League, corporate Sculley providing a perfect foil to Reed College dropout Jobs's quicksilver intemperateness and excitability. Still, despite millions of dollars on the table, Sculley was not convinced he wanted to work for Apple—until Jobs zinged him with the line "Do you want to spend the rest of your life selling sugared water or do you want a chance to change the world?" It summed up the forty-two-year-old Sculley's midlife crisis in one sentence; by May of 1983—a month and a half before Towne was being shown the door at Microsoft—Sculley was at the helm of Apple.

Sugared water, scented water . . . Bill Gates didn't want to change the world, he wanted to rule it. As vice president, corporate communications, Hanson saw his job as positioning Microsoft and its products in the marketplace —as the $40-an-ounce brand. Hanson embarked on market research and discovered that influential core users relied far more heavily on editorial coverage in computer magazines than on advertisements. So while competitors such as Lotus and Ashton-Tate squandered resources on television ads—something Hanson rejected as too wasteful—Microsoft painstakingly went to work rebuilding its corporate image.

Hanson understood the value of public relations as well as anyone. His mentor at Neutrogena, Lloyd Cotsen, had built the company on a policy of influencing "opinion leaders"—dermatologists, beauty editors, people who wrote about skin care. Another of Hanson's research studies was aimed at finding out how Microsoft was perceived among magazine editors—who were then carefully cultivated in the months that followed.

Not long after the redesign of the Microsoft corporate "look" to forest green packaging and the "blibbet" logo whose horizontal lines vaguely suggested IBM's, Hanson discovered the look wasn't working. On the strength of focus group research, Hanson switched to "friendlier" boxes, emphasizing people rather than merely the name of the product and coding by color—red for Apple, blue for IBM.

It was Hanson who killed the "Multi-Tool" name and cut a deal with David Bunnell's *PC World* to enclose a sample disk of Microsoft Word in every subscription copy of the October 1983 issue—just the way cosmetics companies hawked their wares in women's magazines. It was Hanson who pushed to make Microsoft a brand name by putting the corporate identity first and using a generic name for virtually every product. It wasn't Word, it was Microsoft Word. It wasn't Chart, but Microsoft Chart. Had he been on board earlier, Multiplan would have been Microsoft Spreadsheet, and MS-DOS would have been Microsoft DOS, but it was too late for that. Hanson had to settle for ads reminding customers that Microsoft "designed the MS-DOS operating system that tells the IBM PC how to think."

Hanson's marketing efforts were about to culminate in an amazing crescendo. Interface Manager was dead; in its place was Windows. Although a strong contingent in the company actually preferred the name Interface Manager, Hanson tirelessly hammered away on the subject in e-mail to Gates. A product name should communicate a product feature, Hanson insisted: Windows was logical because windows were what you saw on the computer screen. An interface manager—come on, what was that? Bill Gates finally gave Windows the green light, barely in time to revise the PR material.

For Gates, selling Windows was just the tip of the iceberg. Although far and away the leader in systems software, the company ranked only sixth in applications. If it could establish Windows as the standard that everybody wrote for, it would have another shot at the applications opportunities it had missed on plain old DOS. It could use the knowledge it was gaining from its development on the Mac to get an inside track on GUI application development for Windows. And Microsoft, not IBM, would control the platform.

At least by now there was actually something—though not much—more than smoke. In June of '83 Simonyi had begun recruiting a balding, wispy programmer and Stanford grad named Scott McGregor whom he had known of at Xerox. McGregor, now working on software for an "ultimate environment for programmers" known as Cedar, had "only vaguely heard of" Microsoft. He met with Gates in Palo Alto, then visited Seattle for an interview session that included a wild helicopter ride with the Mad Hungarian, a fledgling pilot, at the controls.

McGregor shared what he saw as Bill's belief "that this was the future of the PC industry, and that Microsoft had to play in this environment, that it was destiny. . . . And we decided Microsoft absolutely had to be the champion of all this." In the fall he was hired to head Microsoft's Interactive Systems Group. His goal: Figure out what Windows ought to be and deliver it to the world.

McGregor was surprised to discover that there was not yet so much as a completed spec for the thing; over the next two years, there never would be one. And he was aghast that Bill and his salesfolk were promising the product for April 1984. McGregor thought the chairman didn't understand the complexity of the project: "He had no idea of what a windowing system was. He thought of it as a collection of subroutines that applications would incorporate to do windowing stuff, as opposed to a windowing environment."

When McGregor arrived, the Windows team was tiny—little more than the Dukes of Demo, long on drama, short on code. By Fall Comdex the crew had cobbled together a new demo showing multiple programs—Multiplan here, Word there, Chart somewhere else—running at once, still with the Multi-Tool Interface. It was about as convincing as the other demos out there, though a whole lot uglier than VisiOn.

And Gates was determined that the VisiOn blindside job of the previous

Comdex would never happen again. VisiCorp's announcement that it would start shipping VisiOn was scheduled for the week before Comdex. The week before that, Windows was everywhere.

It was Microsoft's most scintillating use of a page from The Book of IBM, a tactic known as the preemptive strike. Figure out what the competition is going to do and beat them to the punch with an announcement, press conference, news leak, whatever—as long as word gets out. Some twenty-years before, IBM had used the technique so effectively against Control Data that it found itself in court, accused of anticompetitive practices, denounced for selling "paper machines and phantom computers." One year before, VisiCorp had performed the same stunt with VisiOn. Now, as Scott McGregor would put it, Microsoft "basically announced the product when we hadn't even designed it yet."

At New York's Plaza Hotel on November 10, 1983, Microsoft sponsored the biggest software splash since Lotus had arrived on the scene. It trotted out twenty-three DOS hardware licensees who had pledged to support Windows, including most of the biggest names in the business—Compaq, Convergent, Data General, Digital, Hewlett-Packard, Radio Shack, Zenith—along with some current high flyers that would one day end up in bankruptcy court—Columbia Data, Eagle, Seequa, Wang. Bill Gates, Jim Harris, and their warlords had done a yeoman job of rounding up the vassals.

The rollout press release gave a partial hint of how they'd done it. "Microsoft Windows is an OEM product and each OEM is expected to set its own pricing," it stated. "Microsoft Windows will be sold like MS-DOS, adding little or no cost to the system. . . . We have no plans [to sell a retail version] at this time." Microsoft was offering Windows to its biggest customers for as little as $8 a system or $24 a copy. The truly skeptical could buy in for as little as a $20,000 commitment, but the $90 per-copy wholesale price made such deals impractical. Step up to the $60,000 commitment level, and you could have Windows for a more reasonable $48.

Exactly how far the OEMs' support went beyond flag-waving symbolism was subject to question, since several had already pledged to back Windows archfoe VisiOn. The day before the announcement, Quarterdeck had signed up NCR and DEC for DESQ. But the real salt in the wound came from Boca Raton, where the great powers of IBM were about to signal their allegiance to a different windowing system: VisiOn. At the Plaza, the vendors who had signed up on the basis of the veiled hints of IBM's interest must have looked around and wondered: Where are those guys?

It wasn't the only snub from IBM. Just before Comdex, IBM introduced a new combination PC and terminal, the 3270 PC, intended to link mainframe data with DOS applications. Lotus, VisiCorp, and Ashton-Tate had received 3270 PCs to adapt their software. Microsoft had not. Suspicions grew about that homegrown IBM operating system supposedly in the works. Perhaps Big Blue felt the participation of the Bellevue gang would not be required.

In public, the Windows drumbeat crescendoed: trade stories, magazine features, newspaper articles. An early-deadline full-page story in *Popular Computing* quoted Jim Harris extensively and referred to Microsoft's program as the "interface manager," lower case. Gates told *PC Week* that Microsoft's goal was to put Windows on 80 percent of the installed base of PCs. Industry pundit Esther Dyson considered that a bit ambitious, but opined that sales would come close: "Microsoft is running for president."

Then came Fall Comdex '83. Passengers arriving at the Las Vegas airport saw Windows banners the moment they stepped off the plane. Taxicabs had Windows ad plates. Budget and Avis handed out Windows keychains.

Slipped under the door of every hotel room in Sin City was a plastic bag with Windows flackery. Pam Edstrom, the petite take-charge dynamo who headed Microsoft's public relations, just happened to be there when the bellboy knocked on the door of VisiCorp's suite and handed its occupants the Windows materials. "You could sort of hear" the reaction, she recalled with a snicker.

Windows was unavoidable. The Las Vegas entertainment guide listed eighteen pages of hardware manufacturers showing Windows, every one of their booths trumpeting the Microsoft product. Cocktail napkins inscribed "Look Through the Microsoft Windows" contained $1 discounts when presented at any of twenty-five restaurants. A contest that required matching your Microsoft button with the ones worn by OEMs had half the convention staring at the other half's lapels. "You couldn't take a leak in Vegas without seeing a Windows sticker that year," one Microsoft executive recalled.

All this for a product that was not going to be sold retail? A seismic shift in philosophy had overtaken Microsoft somewhere between New York and Nevada. A retail version of Windows, it was announced, would be priced at less than $100 when it was released the following April. The reason? IBM had stopped "sitting there farting and farting and not knowing what to do." Now IBM had decided what to do: Show Windows the back of its hand. Without a retail version, Microsoft would be frozen out of the IBM platform.

As one Microsoft executive recalled, "It was clear that IBM was not going to endorse Windows, and so a lot of people who had already signed contracts with us for it said, 'You're going to get that much out of me because my lawyers tell me I have to pay you, but I'll be fucked if I'll give you any more.' " Still, not everybody felt that way, and the Comdex hoopla created good feeling for Windows among most of the OEMs who had signed up for it.

Gates gave the Comdex keynote address, recruiting his dad to show his glass-mounted slides manually when the union projectionist could not find an appropriate tray. Afterward he was encircled by the admiring attentions of several young women and backstage was heard to exclaim "The chicks love it!'' For a celebration in Caesars Palace, Hanson's contacts wrangled the Rhine-stone Cowboy, country music star Glen Campbell, into showing up and shaking hands with his good buddy Bill Gates. Neither had the foggiest notion who the other was.

It didn't matter. Inebriated with all the attention and a few drinks, forgetting Jill Bennett back in Seattle, Gates danced the night away with a computer journalist, eventually becoming uninhibited enough to start shouting "I want to get laid!"

The Windows hype was having an effect: How much more graphical could Bill's interface get?

18

GROWING PANES

Everyone in the computer business, it seemed, was doing windows—or talking about it. Some were not convinced. In the real world, the grueling task of graphics-based programming was giving DOS developers at least as many fits as it produced in Jobs's Macintosh team.

All the talk and no action got to Ann Winblad, a brainy, articulate programmer and entrepreneur who had co-founded a Minneapolis accounting-software firm called Open Systems. She began "commercializing" a new term describing the smoke-and-mirrors set that she had actually heard first from Microsoftie Mark Ursino: vaporware. Esther Dyson, editor of *RELease 1.0* and a sort of Rona Barrett of the PC industry, picked up the term for her November newsletter, and a previously undefined category was suddenly put into sharp focus. Before long Microsoft would become its best-known purveyor, with Bill Gates himself the reigning Viscount of Vapor. When he and Winblad began dating the following year, it would somehow seem manifest destiny.

VisiOn wasn't vapor, but it was VisiOff. Although it shipped a month after Comdex and continued to gain major OEM endorsements, the program was on the downslide. So was VisiCorp. Despite having sold 600,000 copies, VisiCalc, worn around the edges, was swiftly losing market share to Lotus 1-2-3 and even Multiplan. In September 1983 VisiCorp sued Software Arts, from whom it licensed VisiCalc, for failing to update the spreadsheet. Software Arts countersued with claims of its own. The bitter litigation paralyzed both companies.

Besides, VisiOn couldn't run DOS applications, so it cried out for the whole VisiOn package: VisiOn Calc, VisiOn Graph, VisiOn Word, and the VisiOn mouse, for a total of $1,765. The program was horrendously slow and buggy. To develop applications for it required a DEC VAX minicomputer, wiping out any hope of attracting garage-based independent developers.

Desperation surfaced. Prices were slashed. A floppy disk version was announced for September, an MS-DOS compatibility window for October. In August Control Data bought VisiOn. Virtually nothing was heard of it again until April 1986 when a *Byte* headline declared "VisiOn is Back On." Actually it was dead, despite claims that Control Data "has been busy retooling the product and now is almost ready to release it."

Where had users heard that line before? Once more a Microsoft competitor apparently speeding along on the inside track to success would discover its tires were off the pavement and spin out in flames, clearing the way for the Billmobile. As Vern Raburn would put it, "Microsoft has been the single greatest beneficiary of inept competition of any company in the world."

Yet on the Macintosh, where Microsoft seemed to have the inside track, things were coming unglued, with rumblings from Cupertino escalating even beyond their usual thunderous intensity. Although the Comdex Windows slam dunk was seen largely as a preemptive move against VisiOn, it also riveted the microcomputer world on the IBM platform at the worst possible time for the reality field of a certain darkly intense impresario from the Valley.

Windows this, Windows that . . . the machine with *real* windows was finally ready for the market, and Bill Gates had spoiled the party. Even *Byte* had declared, "Barring a surprise product introduction from another company, Microsoft Windows will be the first large-scale test of the desktop metaphor in the hands of its intended users." It was time for Steve Jobs to fire up the hotline to Bill Gates.

Why wasn't Microsoft working on getting Multiplan, Chart, and File out the door on schedule instead of all this Windows hoo-ha? When Microsoft wasn't close to shipping the products it had agreed to back in January 1982, why was it expending resources on Mac versions of BASIC and Word, direct competitors with Apple's own products?

"They pimped us on Word and BASIC," Bill later complained. In the initial dealings, Gates had pushed hard to get his personal pet Microsoft language onto the Mac—and lost out to an all-Apple product called MacBASIC. Over the years, at Apple briefings, Gates had listened attentively as Donn Denman, MacBASIC's lead programmer, described the latest set of features he was adding to the language. Gates said little, but thought the BASIC was a "pretty nice" adaptation, with "ambitious ideas."

At one of the meetings with Microsoft, Denman described something called streams, a methodology adapted from UNIX. No good, said the Microsoft team: The concept would be too hard for BASIC novices to master. Denman thought a more sophisticated BASIC would appeal to forward-looking Mac users. He left the feature in.

It was the kind of thing he may have done once too often. Confident that his BASIC would win Mac users over, Denman took his time finishing it. The product kept getting stronger, but its ship date kept slipping back. Seeing that

Denman clearly wouldn't be ready for the January Macintosh rollout, Bill Gates seized the opportunity and ordered a crash project that resulted in a BASIC in what one developer called "an incredibly fast amount of time"—six months by Bill's reckoning.

It was quick, it was dirty, and it showed. Denman and the other Mac programmers considered it a joke. The Mac version of Microsoft BASIC had a screen editor far less powerful than the IBM version, offered no way to tap most of the Mac's special graphics routines, and in general didn't even conform to the Macintosh interface guidelines. But for months after the Mac shipped, Microsoft's product sold well, primarily because it was the only one on the shelves.

As for the Macintosh version of Word, it was a direct response to the obvious limitations of Apple's Wigginton-developed MacWrite, which could not handle documents bigger than about ten pages. The Mac version of Word under development was an adaptation of the PC Word code, which had no such restrictions. It was another wide-open opportunity for Gates, the master opportunist.

But as Gates said admiringly of Jobs: "He never turns it off. He's always pushing." Annoyed as Jobs was about the development of those programs, the entire Apple-Microsoft relationship was undermined by his contrary suspicion that because Microsoft controlled the operating system on the PC side, the Gator was only marginally interested in supporting the Macintosh as a side bet. On January 15, 1984, exactly one week before a Super Bowl Sunday TV ad for the Macintosh would rock the computer universe, Jobs and Gates signed a one-page, seven-paragraph agreement rescinding the original applications contract for reasons of "mutual convenience." Everything was back at square one. Microsoft could market its own programs. Apple had no rights or financial stake in them.

Only two points of the original agreement remained. First, Microsoft got to keep the $50,000 Apple had already advanced. Second, the confidentiality agreement the two companies had entered into even before the applications contract remained in force. By the time the Macintosh Girl tossed her famous antiestablishment hammer in Apple's startling "1984" Super Bowl commercial, the Microsoft-Apple relationship was in the same sort of shards as Big Brother's telescreen.

The Apple ad, as dramatic as anything that happened on the football field that day, was actually aimed at IBM, which had earlier in the game run a cutesy "bright little addition to the family" commercial for its new PCjr computer— a miserably colicky baby soon to suffer Sudden Infant Death Syndrome, and one in which Microsoft had invested considerable resources. Two years had changed Jobs's "Welcome IBM" attitude 180 degrees; now Big Blue was the enemy, the monolith, the Orwellian promulgator of a digital Newspeak based on C>

and `dir *.*` and `cd\util\bat` commands. Every hero needs an archfoe, and IBM was the convenient CIA to Macintosh's little band of campus protesters. By extension, Microsoft, DOS capitalist, the company responsible for the `C>` and `dir *.*` and `cd\util\bat`s of the IBM universe, had, with the introduction of Windows and the Apple contract rescission, become the enemy as well—or at least a partner in crime.

Yet in public, everything looked fine. Bill Gates was telling anyone who asked that the Mac, unlike the original IBM PC, was the personal computer he would give his long-suffering mom—and eventually, he made good on the promise. Back in October 1983, Bill had been one of the featured players in Apple's national sales conference in Honolulu, which, under the expert guidance of Steve Jobs, took on the aura of an old-time tent meeting. The theme, set to the breathless score of *Flashdance,* was "Leading the Way." As Jeff Harbers described it:

> *Bill says, "This is Steve Jobs at his best." An incredibly stirring speech. These are Apple sales people who have been getting the shit kicked out of them by IBM, and they're seeing their livelihood just going down the drain—Apple, you know, it's going to die any second. How are we going to survive? And seeing this [the Mac] and seeing that they were going to win—it all dawned on them! And Steve ended it with the "1984" commercial. . . . Everybody was up on their chairs screaming. It was the best revival meeting that I have ever been to. It just shook you to the bone. People would have done anything for Steve Jobs at that moment.*

Then it was Bill Gates's turn, in a version of "The Dating Game" with Lotus's Mitch Kapor and Software Publishing's Fred Gibbons. Emcee Steve Jobs asked Bachelor Number Three what he was going to do to make the Mac a success. Bill Gates, clad in a Macintosh T-shirt, replied that 50 percent of Microsoft's applications revenues would come from Macintosh sales; that was his company's projection for the coming year. The crowd went crazy.

To Gates, sharing the limelight with Kapor at this meeting was a little unsettling, since Lotus didn't have a Macintosh product even remotely near ready. But by this time, Lotus Development Corporation was riding high. Its 1-2-3, the leading software application, had become a phenomenon, propelling Lotus toward a $157 million 1984 sales year that would swipe the software lead from Microsoft and make Lotus the new *bête noir* of William Henry Gates.

Kapor was the latest Boy Wonder Turned Multimillionaire. 1-2-3 was whipping Multiplan soundly in the PC arena. 1-2-3 on the Macintosh seemed like a can't-lose proposition. Mitch Kapor had "wanted to do a version of 1-2-3 concurrently with the IBM version. But they wouldn't give us a Mac." In fact, at the time Apple *couldn't* give Lotus a Mac. Bill had cleverly Gatesed the deck. In its contract with Microsoft, Apple expressly agreed that during the exclusivity period, it would not "sell, lease, license, publish or otherwise distribute, or solicit others" to do likewise with regard to any Macintosh program "which the marketplace would consider to be competitive" with Microsoft's Mac offerings. But once the exclusivity period no longer seemed to matter, Apple had gone calling on both Lotus and Software Publishing.

By this time Kapor had been smitten with a better idea: integrated software, a single program that could do it all, spreadsheet, business graphics, word processor, database manager, and telecommunications rolled into one big, powerful, irresistible package. In February 1984 Lotus announced just such a package for the IBM platform under the name Symphony—although in terms of ease, lightness, and grace it bore a far closer resemblance to Bruckner than to Mozart. Bill Gates immediately went on the attack, publicly discoursing on why integrated software was no match for separate programs that ran in an integrated environment—such as Windows or the Mac.

But for the Mac, Lotus had another integrated product in development: Jazz. As its name suggested, Jazz was designed to be the cool, sexy be-all and end-all of Macintosh software applications, everything that Symphony was only simpler, a 1-2-3 and 4-5-6. Jazz was going to blow everything else out of the water.

Not if Bill Gates had anything to say about it. He first learned of Lotus's plans to develop Jazz in February 1984, just weeks after the Macintosh shipped, and he knew full well what it meant. Jazz threatened not just Multiplan, but the whole floundering triad of Microsoft's Mac applications. Chart had been announced but would not be released until August. File had been announced but would not be ready until December.

And Multiplan? Multiplan, like BASIC, was pronounced ready to ship the same day as the Mac. At the public rollout of the Macintosh in San Francisco on January 24, Bill Gates held up a box of each product. But neither one had been thoroughly tested.

Testing was something Microsoft had never paid much attention to. Traditionally a product would go out the door, an OEM would find bugs and bitch about them, and Microsoft would supply fixes. Despite SoftCard and Multiplan and Word, nobody had quite gotten the picture that retail products were different. "Steve Ballmer had this belief that for testing, just hire some high school guys. You know, guys after school can test this stuff for us," said Jeff Harbers, who knew how complex this graphics stuff was and started "bootlegging people in to start testing." Eventually Harbers insisted on hiring the consulting firm of Arthur Andersen to test the code, really beat on it. But exercising all the kinks of the Mac's complex architecture was a challenge even for them. As a result, Multiplan was bug city until the day came to "freeze" the code for production. Harbers found what he thought was the last bug at a typical programmer's hour: six in the morning.

Multiplan was shipped to great fanfare and sold 20,000 copies in its first three months on the stands. But from the outset, reports had begun trickling in of a bug—not a minor irritant, but a destructive data mangler so elusive that Harbers and Company "didn't believe it for three months." Even when they did pinpoint the bug, its origins remained puzzling: "All you knew is that one morning you came in and you tried to load this file and it would crash." Finally, through trial and error, the Mac team pieced together enough steps to pinpoint the problem. The bug was real, all right.

Now it was up to Microsoft to ship a fix update to Multiplan's 20,000 buyers. Harbers calculated the cost at $10 a disk—a $200,000 goof, not the kind of budget adjustment you like to bring up with the boss.

Harbers called a meeting with Gates, who listened patiently while rocking back and forth, back and forth. Bill wanted to know all the details. Harbers explained that most users would probably never encounter the bug, but that it did corrupt data and should be fixed. Back and forth Bill rocked, back and forth. Harbers dropped the $200,000 on the table. Bill stopped rocking.

"He just kind of sat there and he said, 'Two hundred thousand dollars, huh? Well, I guess you get up in the morning, you come into work, you lose $200,000, you go home, and you try to do better the next time.' And that was it."

To this day the story, sometimes ballooning to the half-million-dollar mark, is legend around Microsoft headquarters, where Gates retains the image of an emotional springcoil likely to pop at any moment. "The great thing was that he didn't make us feel like we were the world's worst idiots or something," Harbers said. "He really did understand." If it held any lesson, the incident showed that Gates played his "stupidest thing I've ever heard" card mostly when it could do some good—before a product shipped, not after.

And the "stupidest thing" outbursts played little part in the public image of Bill Gates. Here it was the Year of the Mac, but after the initial Macinsplash, Steve Jobs seemed to have used up his Warholian fifteen minutes of fame. Somehow Bill Gates had moved to the forefront in the public prints.

Much of this was the doing of tough, diminutive, flashy-shoed Pam Edstrom, who had worked with Jim Towne at Tektronix and had been hired as Microsoft's public relations manager in September 1982. As Microsoft increasingly turned its business toward the public, Edstrom launched a PR campaign to turn Bill Gates into the personification of the company. Though awkward at public speaking and somewhat shy around new acquaintances, Bill could wax romantic about the future of computing. As the "boy genius" and "computer nerd" whose life came packaged as a legend, Gates was the perfect mouthpiece to spread the Microsoft message to the rest of the world. It would, he knew, be at the expense of his hotly defended personal privacy, but it would be good for the company. Besides, all the attention over Steve Jobs got Bill's competitive dander up. No way had Apple "invented the first personal computer system"; when Bill had started with the Altair, he liked to point out, "Jobs was still contemplating his navel in India."

In November 1982, just after Edstrom had started, Gates had made the cover of *Money* magazine, though the actual coverage of Microsoft and its chairman had been perfunctory. But during the following year Edstrom began spending over $300,000 polishing the Nerd Makes Good theme. Surprise! Along with Ronald Reagan, Fidel Castro, Debra Winger, and Mr. T, Gates turned up in—though not on the cover of—*People* magazine's 1983 end-of-year "25 Most Intriguing People" issue, photographed on a giant pillow in the shape of a computer. "Dropping out of Harvard pays off for a computer whiz kid who's making hard cash from software," the first national general-interest profile of Gates, set the standard for all to follow.

The article repeated Bill's claim about writing "slick, tight code" three times at a point when Microsoft was being creamed in the industry press for its slow p-coded applications and was a few months away from recalling Mac Multiplan. It stated "His MSX software is preeminent in Japan" when in fact it had only been announced in midyear and had barely gained a toehold against the NEC standard. The story recast his TRW stint from twelfth grade to a much-more-startling ninth, promoted him to full-fledged Eagle Scout, floated the wild McGovern-Eagleton button tale, and inflated his company's first eighteen months' earnings from a hundred-odd thousand dollars to "a few hundred thousand." The article's description of Gates as an "Andy Hardy in his boyish grin and unruly cowlick" would over the years be reworked in the dozens of rip-and-clip articles that followed. As a spokesman for himself and Microsoft, Bill Gates did just fine, especially if you didn't bother to check the facts.

In January 1984 *Fortune* covered "Microsoft's Drive to Dominate Software" with the requisite full-page photo of Bill Gates. "William H. Gates III wants to make Microsoft the General Motors of the industry," it claimed, portraying the "monstrously competitive" Gates as "a remarkable piece of software in his own right. He is childishly awkward at times, throws things when angry and fidgets uncontrollably when he speaks."

In March Gates appeared on the "Today" show, answering Jane Pauley's inane questions—"You are a computer whiz. Are you a business genius too?" —with the same gawky impatience he would later display when confronted on the witness stand. To Pauley's query, "At what age did you yourself become a millionaire?" he replied, "Well, Microsoft is a company owned primarily by its employees, and it's not easy to put a value on it." Huddled around a TV set in the Northup building, a group of stockless Microsoft laborers howled with gales of sardonic laughter.

In April, wearing thick-framed glasses, balancing a floppy disk on his finger in a photo taken the same day as the Pauley interview, Bill appeared on the cover of *Time*. Take that, Steve Jobs! In the space of half a year, Bill Gates had performed the Time Incorporated hat trick—*People, Fortune, Time*—though *Sports Illustrated* never allowed him to hit for the cycle. Actually the *Time* cover story was about software, not Gates, but a sidebar covered Bill and Paul, Bill and Jill, Bill and bull, such as the $20,000 annual Traf-O-Data gross and the McGovern-Eagleton buttons.

In August Gates received the Vollum Award for achievements in science and technology from Portland's Reed College—the alma mater of none other than fellow dropout Steve Jobs. At the end of the year, *Esquire* chose Gates as one of the "Best of the New Generation." To crown it all, in February 1985, Bill made *Good Housekeeping*'s list of the fifty most eligible bachelors that included Warren Beatty, Michael Jackson, Burt Reynolds, and Tom Selleck. "They are all wealthy and charming," the article cooed, "and waiting for the right woman to come along!"

In the industry, the twist in early 1984 was that—as a story in *Micro Market World* trumpeted—"Microsoft Aims to be the IBM of Software." On ESPN's "Business Times" program, Gates was asked about it. "We want to be the number-one company in the microcomputer software business," he replied with typical tact, "but I wouldn't say we want to be exactly like IBM."

If "the IBM of Software" wasn't quite the phrase Bill wanted to communicate, "softer software" might do. Gates coined the expression to characterize programs that would record and interpret the actions of the user, then adjust accordingly. A free-lance writer might enter a command to double-space a document; the program would deduce that the writer was readying a manuscript for submission and automatically set up the page. It wasn't exactly "artificial intelligence," a computer chimera Gates had been intrigued with since Harvard, but in a period where "AI" was becoming a marketing tool, it would do. In reality, Microsoft would take years to include even rudimentary implementations of "softer" in its software, but it was pretty to think about.

The more universal mantra was "A computer on every desk and in every home," the battle cry that supposedly dated back to 1974. It didn't, but no one would wear the phrase—or wear it out—like Bill Gates. In 1984 he used it in a talk to Apple programmers. The 1986 Microsoft annual report would state that the corporate mission was "to create software that makes the microcomputer a valuable tool on every desk and in every home." During the late 1980s the phrase "A computer on every desk and in every home," ultimately appended with "running Microsoft software," would become so synonymous with Bill Gates that even he would admit, "If you've been around here a lot the computer on every desk thing would really drive you crazy." But he insisted, "That's the way these things go. If you want to get a message out to the broad public, you've got to be pretty damn consistent and really believe your message."

Other aspects of Bill's life didn't make the PR cut. In the Miriam Lubow tradition of fretting over Bill's erratic slumbers, Estelle Mathers offered Bill a Ramada Inn one-night-free coupon she had won at a party there, suggesting he might need it sometime. "Who would *want* to stay at the Ramada Inn?" Bill sniffed, perhaps articulating the very thoughts of some clients whom Microsoft had put up there. Fine, said Mathers, I'll leave it in my desk drawer just in case.

In the wee hours of the morning in the dead of winter, Gates ran out of gas on the freeway not far from Microsoft. Ditching the Mercedes on the side of the road, he hoofed it back to the Ramada and asked for a room. Asked for ID and a deposit, Gates discovered his wallet was missing. Don't worry, he told the desk clerk. He was Bill Gates, he worked at Microsoft, and his assistant would pay in the morning. The clerk smiled sweetly and told him she was sorry, sir, but without cash or credit card, she couldn't give him a room.

Gates trudged over to his office. As he was about to sack out on his couch, he suddenly remembered the infamous coupon. He raided the desk, walked back to the motel, and waved the coupon under the desk clerk's nose. *Now* would she give him a room? After the Bellevue police found the Mercedes and notified a frantic Mary Gates, the story eventually came to a happy ending with mother and son reunited at the Ramada.

And Mary Gates soon had more to worry about. Bill's friends and brokers Andy Evans and Ann Llewellyn had put together Evans Llewellyn Securities complete with their own three-story downtown Bellevue building, soared to the top of the high-flying '80s-yuppie financial heap, and tumbled back down again amid massive losses in 1983 and Evans's subsequent Securities and Exchange Commission sanctions for alleged violations. The drama would come to a close late in 1985 when they would plead guilty to bank fraud and be sentenced to six months in federal prison. "This tragedy," said Judge John Coughenour, "is not atypical of what can happen to young people consumed with ambition."

In the midst of the troubles, Evans rustled up some fast cash by selling Bill his dark metallic blue Porsche 930 Turbo. Known with Gatesian understatement as The Rocket, it was the fastest model Porsche had yet built, capable of 0 to 60 in 5.3 seconds and 0 to 120 in 19.1 seconds. To Mathers it sounded like an airplane taking off.

By now Jill Bennett was out of the picture, a victim of Gates's inattention, including "seven-hour turnarounds" from the time he left Microsoft till he was back at the office the next morning. The mutual parting had taken place at a nondescript restaurant in Seattle's International District, where Gates drowned his sorrows in sake.

Gates soon had a new romantic interest: Ann Winblad, the pixyish blonde "commercializer" of the word "vaporware," whom he had met in spring 1984 at the speaker's dinner of Esther Dyson's exclusive EDventure conference. Winblad was also a self-made millionaire. Three months before, for $15.5 million, she had sold the Open Systems company she had co-founded in the mid-1970s with $500. When she and Bill met, she recalled, "I would like to think he thought, 'What a great little company in Minneapolis! Gee, this must be a really talented woman running this!' But I don't think that's true."

Besides, Winblad was intent on bending Bill's ear about a recent encounter with his best friend, who had stiffed her months earlier at a scheduled meeting to discuss the rumored rocky future of XENIX. Steve Ballmer, in the throes of "Crisis! Crisis! Crisis!" had insisted Winblad, who had flown halfway across the country for this meeting, would have to come back another day. When Gates waxed rhapsodic on Ballmer's virtues, Winblad disagreed: "I said, 'I think we might have a difference of opinion about Steve.' And he goes, 'Oh?' And I said, 'Yeah. I think Steve is the biggest jerk that I've ever met.' "

Winblad had unwittingly worked the Stand-Up-to-Bill magic. The two continued to cross paths on the rubber chicken circuit and began dating; she even found reasons to patch things up with Ballmer. Winblad, a "heavyweight in the gray matter," as one senior Softie put it, provided a perfect counterpoint to Gates's quirky intellectual gamesmanship—neither awed nor underwhelmed by what she and other computerists called his "massive parallelism," after supercomputer designs that could do a myriad of computations at once. In her Open Systems days, Winblad had decided against Microsoft's "lackluster" languages in favor of competitive versions. Microsoft "wrote dumb languages as far as we were concerned, and they had a nonusable BASIC and a nonusable COBOL."

More worldly than her beau, and an abstainer from red meat since college, Winblad weaned Gates off hamburgers and Coke to the more healthful, more vegetarian Thai and Indian cuisines. In a paroxysm of high-tech romanticism, the two would even have "virtual dates": They would go to the same movie simultaneously in different cities, and discuss it on their car phones on their way to and from the theater. So that they could watch and discuss old movies when they were together, Ann bought Bill a VCR and monitor. But at Bill's insistence, both lacked the tempting broadcast tuner that he viewed as "decadent."

▼ Windows wasn't decadent: It was barely real. The problem with Windows was that Gates had fallen victim to his own reality distortion field. But the existence of Windows as little more than a demo did not keep Bill Gates from promoting it. For a Windows product manager Gates had once again dipped into the Xerox pool. This time he rescued Leo Nikora, a soft-spoken, gentle family man with dark, earnest eyes. These attributes supremely qualified him for his job at Microsoft, which was essentially to apologize for Windows.

An engineer by training, the bushy-browed, serene Nikora knew little about marketing except that Xerox couldn't do it. Gates didn't care. When he brought Nikora on in mid-1983, he told him he'd rather hire a technical person and train him to do marketing than hire a marketing person and train him in technology. Not that there was ever much training at Microsoft, where management philosophy was still basically sink or swim. No one had ever trained Bill or Paul or any of the others in how to run a company; why should Microsoft start now?

Nikora's job was to get the word out about Windows. The problem was, there wasn't much word to get out. Nikora did not realize it until later, he said, but he and McGregor had been hired as the "great white saviors" for Windows. McGregor had loftier ideas: He told one colleague that he viewed himself as Prometheus, bringing fire from the gods of PARC to the mere mortals of Microsoft.

The McGregor demo unveiled in November was not the smoke and mirrors of the original announcement, but it was not quite ready for prime time either. In one configuration, it showed a "paint" application—an evergreen tree with the Microsoft logo emblazoned in the sky—in the top left window. A DOS window with the prompt, date, and time appeared in the pane below, a calendar occupied the lower right window, and above it a text window displayed Microsoft Word. As delays kept pushing Windows farther into the future, the text in the Word pane gained Delphic proportions:

Heuristic reasoning is reasoning not regarded as final and strict but as provisional and plausible only, whose purpose is to discover the solution of the present problem. We are often obliged to use heuristic reasoning. We shall attain complete certainty when we shall have obtained the complete solution, but before obtaining certainty we must often be satisfied with a more or less plausible guess. We may need the provisional before we attain the final.

By that definition, Windows circa 1984 was nothing if not heuristic.

At least the Bellevue lads had begun working in earnest on turning smoke into fire and mirrors into Windows. Still, the Windows development team was a random shop from the start, as might be expected from a maverick collection of Smart Guys full of conflicting visions about the one true path to righteousness. No Prometheus, McGregor, though a charismatic ideas guy, was seen as uncommunicative and aloof, constantly saying "We did it this way at PARC."

His big-systems orientation was seen as out of step with the circumscribed 8088 environment. More of an Ivory Tower type than Microsoft was used to, McGregor was a poor cultural fit. "He did not have a very hands-on approach," said one senior developer. "He came in and told people kind of roughly what he wanted them to do and they did it." That was not the Microsoft Way.

Neither was the magnitude of the Windows project. Microsoft was used to tiny development teams, with its ten-man XENIX team the absolute top. McGregor suspected "Bill didn't really understand a project that took a couple people more than a couple weekends." Bringing together a staff of maybe twenty engineers and coordinating them would require a whole new process of management and communication. Not even the programming tools available at Microsoft were yet up to the task.

From PARC, McGregor brought what was called the "push" paradigm. Under a "push" environment, the system handles "events"—a key being pressed, a mouse button being clicked—processes them, and "pushes" the results to an application like a word processor or spreadsheet. The Macintosh used the "pull" model, in which the application itself handles the events, and the system "pulls" them in. In a multitasking system, which Windows was and the Mac was not, the push model seemed clearly superior, because it gave the system greater control.

Then there were tiled windows, which McGregor brought with him from a Xerox prototype known as Tioga. Tiled windows were easier to read and manipulate, McGregor argued. With overlapping windows, data got hidden, windows got lost. With tiling, all the windows were visible at once. It made sense, as long as the screen had copious real estate—as the big Xerox systems did.

On the little screen of what Neil Konzen called "a little shitbox 8088," it was a different ballgame—as Bill Gates noticed. The early popularity of the Macintosh, with overlapping windows on a downright tiny display, suggested that users found its system workable. And a Mac-like system would make it easier to port Microsoft's Mac applications to Windows—code, documentation, and all. So, according to Neil Konzen, "Bill really championed this Macintosh compatibility thing."

Leo Nikora remembered it too:

My personal opinion is that Bill wanted Mac on a PC. He said that direct statement to me several, several times. And one of the biggest religious arguments raging at Microsoft at that time, that poor Scott McGregor was involved in, was tiling versus overlapping. And Scott was trying to make arguments as to why tiling was a more efficient use of the screen, and could be executed faster, and would make a more efficient system, and he had a whole bunch of other arguments. And Bill just said, "That's not what a Mac does. I want Mac on the PC, I want Mac on the PC."

Amid the hoopla of November '83, Windows had been promised for release the following April, at about the same time that DESQ was due to appear. DESQ made it; Windows did not. The Windows release was postponed a month to May. May arrived; Windows didn't. In May President Jon Shirley baldly—and badly—adopted Bill's forecast that by year's end 80 percent of DOS computers would run Windows—an amazing act of chutzpah, considering that a majority of DOS computers didn't have the graphics card that Windows would require. No matter: In June Shirley promised Windows for September. No go.

As McGregor saw it, the delays fed upon themselves. "You told your customers dates you couldn't meet, and then of course you didn't meet them. And since it's late, you say, well, the market conditions have changed a little bit, so let's make this change." The spec kept evolving; every change made the product later and later.

The Windows delays meant that the music from the Kapor keyboard had absolutely no charms to soothe the savage breast of a certain CEO in Bellevue, Washington. Lotus Symphony, the integrated be-all, end-all, had been designed to allow third-party developers to write add-in programs, and Gloomy Gates was positive that programmers would write for it instead of Windows. Despite all Bill's speeches and interviews about how all-in-one Swiss Army knife software was the wrong idea, an integrated software boomlet had preoccupied the computer magazines with talk of Symphony and Framework and Enable and Ovation and Jazz.

Despite all Bill's bluster, Microsoft actually had such products in development—primarily for a forthcoming series of portable machines from Japan. Unfortunately, that undertaking, known for a time as Works, had already become a nightmare of missed deadlines and broken commitments.

But back in June, Gates and Ballmer had co-written an internal "APPLI-CATIONS STRATEGY" memo that had articulated unambiguously the depth of the company's commitment to the graphical user interface. The piece had even been written on a Mac:

> *Microsoft believes in mouse and graphics as invaluable to the man-machine interface. We will bet on that belief by focusing new development on the two new environments with mouse and graphics . . . Macintosh and Windows.*
>
> *This also makes sense from a marketing perspective. Our focus will be on the business user, a customer who can afford the extra hardware expense of a mouse and high resolution screen, and who will pay premium prices for quality easy-to-learn software.*

Microsoft will not invest significant development resources in new Apple II, MSX, CP/M-80 or character-based IBM PC applications. We will finish development and do a few enhancements to existing products.

. . . Over the foreseeable future our plan is to implement products first for the Mac and then to port them to Windows. We are taking care in the design of the Windows user interface to make this as easy as possible.

There it was: Gates was betting the company on GUIs. He wanted Microsoft products to be "the standard" and intended to "achieve very high market share on the Mac." Microsoft would start a project called Mac Library to acquire Mac applications from sources outside the company. Contrary to anything Steve Jobs might think, the Mac was no side bet for Bill Gates.

Neither was Windows. According to the June memo, "it goes far beyond Mac in several areas including support for multiple active applications, and variable resolution. Over time Windows systems will dominate since they will have more software than any other. It is crucial to our future to establish Windows as THE STANDARD graphics interface for microprocessor software development by the end of 1984."

If there had been any doubt about Gates's commitment to Windows, the still amorphous and ill-defined Cashmere would dispel it. Cashmere, named for Bill's preppy sweaters, was a pet project he'd been working on with Golden Boy Brodie for nearly six months. Actually, Brodie was platinum by now, having repeated his bravado performance on Word by taking only a couple of weeks to crank out a PCjr adaptation that could even play music. At Bill's urging, Brodie had finally abandoned Harvard for good in favor of Microsoft. In return he had been handed the prize applications project.

"We will use an approach that allows many of our stand-alone products to 'fit into' our integrated product without change," Bill said in his June memo. Cashmere "will be the glue that allows integrated usage of the stand-alone products . . . it will, itself, be an integrated product that provides table management with rich documents, and a strong programmatic interface. It merges pieces of File, Word, and BASIC."

So once again—it had become a tradition—Bill Gates was reacting to products already on the market. Cashmere, initially, was a response to the dreaded integrated products with add-in capabilities: Symphony, most importantly, but also the more fluent Framework, which had a powerful built-in language called FRED. But whereas both those programs were based on a spreadsheet model, Cashmere would at bottom be a word processor—and would have that all-important graphical user interface to boot.

Assigned to the product along with Brodie was word processing marketeer Jonathan Prusky, who had been the product manager for the PC version of Microsoft Word. According to Prusky, Gates was mesmerized with the idea of tables. "He would read the *World Almanac* for pleasure. I remember him rocking back and forth and saying 'Look at these pages. How are we gonna do this stuff?' " Cashmere was going to be a home run, a package that would be the king of word processors and do tables brilliantly. It was also going to be the first application for Windows.

But Windows wasn't ready, and Microsoft needed some way of responding to the ominous rumblings from Lotus. What Microsoft had was a project that had been set in motion the previous August in the basement of the less-than-decadent Red Lion Hotel in Bellevue during a three-day retreat. Multiplan was doing well on some platforms and in some markets, especially in Europe, where internationalized versions were released early. Domestically 1-2-3 was going off the charts and Multiplan was nowhere. Gates decided something had to be done before Lotus exterminated Microsoft in the spreadsheet arena. To hash out a strategy, he assembled the finest spreadsheet minds in the company: Simonyi, Harbers, Jabe Blumenthal, Jeff Raikes, Doug Klunder. From the discussion, argument, debate, and wish-listing, a specification for a "dream spreadsheet" emerged—for the IBM PC platform. At the time Microsoft was still contractually committed to Multiplan on the Macintosh, and Jazz was not even a rumor. The PC was where Lotus was eating Microsoft's lunch.

To put together the spreadsheet, Gates tapped one of his best developers, Microsoft's original college recruit, the brilliant, willfully ascetic Doug Klunder, who had worked on the original version of Multiplan. Honest and forthright to a fault, Klunder refused to play corporate politics but had acquired the binary ethic: With Doug, a colleague once said, everything is black or white.

Before the super spreadsheet was dangled in front of him, Klunder had been thinking of leaving the company—"just the little wanderlust hitting." When he was spotted on a plane to San Jose and word got back to Gates, the company offered him stock "sweeteners" and the spreadsheet project. Program manager and Lakeside alumnus Jabe Blumenthal, Klunder's best friend, christened it "Odyssey," because it promised to be a Lotus-eater, and to reflect his "skepticism about the schedule and how it was going to be a seven-year voyage."

Klunder immediately took a parochial and paternalistic attitude toward "my baby," Odyssey. "Our mission was do everything 1-2-3 does and do it better. Plus intelligent recalc." If you changed a single entry in 1-2-3, every cell in the entire spreadsheet would have to be recalculated; Odyssey's "intelligent recalc" would refigure only the numbers that were affected by the change. It promised to be a major speedup, and speed was what 1-2-3 had been all about. But Odyssey was still going to use p-code and the creaky old Multi-Tool Interface.

The biggest argument was over what the macro language should be.

Macros, little programs that let you play back a series of keystrokes and special functions at the touch of a key, were considered a very big deal in 1-2-3. Klunder demanded that Odyssey's macros be "learnable," allowing users to simply enter a set of keystrokes and play them back. That was a feature 1-2-3 lacked, and that was fine with Bill Gates. But Klunder also wanted his macros to use a special language unique to his program. Gates wanted it to be BASIC. Klunder argued and argued, but Bill was adamant. BASIC was, after all, *his* baby.

Klunder prevailed nonetheless. "You argue long enough, hard enough," he explained, "particularly if you're the one doing the code!" Klunder had learned well the secret of dealing with the chairman: "Bill will be very argumentative and call you on stuff. But you can also tell him he's full of shit and get him to back down. Most people are too scared to do that, but I think actually what he respects most is if they call him on his random claims."

With roughly six months to get the project done before summer 1984, Klunder literally started living at Microsoft. He kept a big bean bag in the office. "Got a blind to put on my relight, pull it down, go to sleep, get up a few hours later, and get back to work." As part of his deal to lead the project, Klunder was supposed to get one of the company's top programmers; instead he was given a good programmer but a green one, fresh out of college. The project began to slip.

Around January Klunder received a fateful screenful of e-mail, a note from the technical writer on the project, who reported "I've been told Odyssey is now a Windows app. What am I supposed to do for the documentation?"

It was the first Klunder had heard of it. He went to Bill Gates, told him he'd been hearing all these rumors, and demanded to know what was going on. Gates hedged. He'd just been kind of idly voicing thoughts about changing, he said, but nothing had really been decided. It was a classic Gates maneuver: Despite his tradition of confrontation, there were times he found it wiser to defer a difficult battle.

A summit session was called. Paul Allen, in the waning days of his tenure at Microsoft, tried to mollify Klunder with the line that the mouse was the future of personal computing. Allen could raise his voice a notch or two when conviction called, but he was no match for the eruptive charms of Klunder, who "basically screamed at Allen, 'This *is* a mouse-based app! What is this crap?' "

By the end of the meeting, the Windows idea was scrapped—and so was the idea of doing Odyssey for the PC. The project had now been redirected to the Macintosh. Klunder believed that, "scared to take on Lotus," Microsoft was foolishly conceding the PC spreadsheet market.

But Gates had come up with an end-run strategy to stop Lotus on the Mac. If Mitch Kapor was abandoning a 1-2-3 spreadsheet approach in favor of the all-in-one Jazz, why shouldn't Microsoft pick up his fumble? Concede the integrated apps market to Lotus, and focus on the killer spreadsheet. Since early 1983, when he began flogging Windows, Gates had been telling the world that the integrated applications approach was the wrong one, primarily because each individual component would be underpowered. Microsoft's integrated applications approach sure wasn't working on the laptop platform. The right approach, Gates had been telling anyone who'd listen, was integration at the system level. He might as well play his hunch, bet on a power spreadsheet, and let the Mac do the integrating.

Klunder "was really feeling screwed." For one thing, the stock "sweeteners" were tied to the date of his completion of Odyssey, and Gates hadn't even mentioned what he was going to do about that. The day after the summit meeting, Klunder returned to Microsoft with resignation in hand.

When Ballmer stopped him in the hall to discuss how well the meeting had gone, Klunder told him he was quitting. We need to talk, Ballmer said. Klunder hollered first at Ballmer, the company's dean of decibels, then ranted at the more placid Simonyi, to the point where, Klunder admitted, "I don't think a lot of people in my wing got a lot done that day."

Word, perhaps aftershock, of the discussions reached Gates. At about 8:00 P.M. he brought Klunder in and entered avoidance mode, spending more than an hour going over the minutest questions about Odyssey and its future. This program, Gates told Klunder, was a real problem.

"Well, Bill," Klunder shot back, "you know, there are actually two problems here."

"Oh, yeah," said Gates, as if suddenly waking up.

The session ran until three in the morning. Gates wanted Klunder to stay, appealed to his guilt, told him he shouldn't just run out on the project. Klunder spewed out the problems he thought Bill really ought to be concerned about: "We weren't as innovative as we claimed. The atmosphere was getting worse—more corporate and less technically driven. Our not delivering on promises."

In the end, Gates convinced Klunder to stay nine months. But the young programmer managed to attach some stringent conditions. For one thing, he wouldn't kill himself anymore; he'd work a straight forty-hour week. For another, Klunder renegotiated his stock deal. Furthermore, "They had to agree that they would not try to talk me into staying beyond [nine months]. That just drove Ballmer nuts. I think it's probably true that if I had given him the opportunity he probably would have talked me into sticking around." Klunder and Charles Simonyi went off and wrote a thirty-page spec for the new program. Klunder, "the one doing the code," would eventually add some controversial features over the protests of product manager Jabe Blumenthal. And for his own programming convenience, Klunder retained the "segmented memory'' model that was required on the IBM PC and most Mac programmers considered impossible to write for. Eventually it would cause problems when users began filling their Macs with more than a megabyte of memory. But Klunder had started the program on the PC. Why throw out perfectly good code?

▼ In the competitive world of software, Bill Gates knew, there was one important lesson: Be first or play catch-up. First to market with BASIC, Microsoft had quickly taken a commanding lead. First to market as a low-end 16-bit operating system, MS-DOS had become the company's cash cow. Microsoft had been first with most of the 16-bit languages it offered, and was still in the lead with them. In many foreign markets, it had been first with a spreadsheet whose menus and commands appeared in the native language; Multiplan had become the leader in Germany, France, and elsewhere, and Word seemed destined to follow. On the Mac, Microsoft's early applications had virtually sewed up the market. But on the PC platform in America, where it had not been first to offer a spreadsheet or a word processor, Microsoft's applications lagged badly. And there were entire areas such as databases where Microsoft's products would be doomed to confront an entrenched market leader, assuming they could ever get off the ground.

Once he'd won a market, Bill Gates had never lost it, had never really had any serious competition. Now, from laid-back Scotts Valley, California, hard by the hippie haven of Santa Cruz, came a radical, unexpected salvo from a company named Borland International. Its leader was a big, exuberant, food-loving, sax-blowing, yacht-sailing Frenchman, a self-styled ''Barbarian'' named Philippe Kahn who had given his company its name ''because Borland International sounded more important than Kahn International.'' His first product was aimed right at Microsoft's traditional foundation—the languages business. Turbo Pascal, first arriving on the scene late in 1983, was a triumph in many ways, not least in terms of marketing.

The attention-getting ploy was price: At $49.95, Turbo Pascal sold for one-sixth the price of Microsoft's Pascal compiler. Kahn's particular marketing gimmick was to sell the product through the mail via a media blitz in computer magazines. Gates and Microsoft had never tried this approach, and at Radio Shack Jon Shirley had learned a time-honored retail rule: Once you cut your prices, they never go up again.

But price was only part of the equation: Turbo Pascal added real innovation, real value. Though it didn't offer every last bell and whistle of Microsoft's version and was less attractive if you were planning to write a really big commercial program, Turbo Pascal offered not just a compiler but what became known as an integrated programming environment.

If you were a programmer using a typical compiler—say Microsoft's—

you'd actually spend most of your time writing source code with a separate program called a text editor. After saving the code, you'd exit the editor and run the code through a program called a compiler. If you were lucky and the compiler discovered no egregious errors, you'd run its output through a program called a linker. Finally you'd run the program itself and test it—and undoubtedly discover it wouldn't work because of some annoying little bug. Back to square one and the editor again.

There had to be a better way—and once Turbo Pascal came along, there was. What Turbo Pascal let you do, essentially, was live in your editor, which was built right in, no extra charge. When your code was done, you didn't have to waste time exiting the editor and loading the compiler. You simply issued a compile command from right where you were in the editor. If the compiler ran across a syntax error, you wouldn't get some obscure message that would force you to search your text for what had gone wrong. Turbo Pascal would put the offending code up there on the screen right under your nose so you could edit it and try again. Once the errors were fixed, you ran the program and tested it from Turbo Pascal too.

Programmers had never seen anything like it. There were minor technical drawbacks, but who could argue with the price? In fact, the price initially raised suspicions as one of those deals too good to be true. A year or two earlier JRT Pascal, another widely advertised lowball product, garnered a lot of attention before users discovered it simply didn't work. More than a few suspicious hackers thought Turbo Pascal might just be a repackaged version of the JRT fiasco, but once Borland overcame that stigma the program simply marched in and stole the Pascal market—burgeoning in the education field as the language of choice now that BASIC had fallen out of academic favor—right out from under Microsoft's nose.

For Bill Gates it was bad enough that Turbo Pascal was challenging Microsoft Pascal head to head, but Borland was also challenging the whole price structure of the software industry. Gates was beside himself: If this thing started a trend, it could cut the astounding margins on software down to merely comfortable. Aside from operating expenses, such as development, administration, and sales, Microsoft's cost of revenues was around 20 percent for retail software products, and—it was almost embarrassing—less than 1 percent for OEM stuff. In fiscal 1984, although Microsoft had some dismal clunkers, such as a Multiplan budgeting template, not one of Microsoft's software or hardware products made less money than it cost to produce. Only Microsoft Press, with low margins and high costs, operated at a loss. Surely this indicated a large amount of wiggle room for Philippe—or some other upstart —to slash prices.

And Kahn, in his muumuu-size Hawaiian shirts, was as flamboyant as Gates was ascetic, keeping up a flow of outrageous rhetoric, self-promotion, anything to flog the product. As Turbo Pascal was ramping up, Borland launched another innovative salvo: SideKick, the first important program to take advantage of what was known as the Terminate-and-Stay-Resident feature of DOS—TSR for short. Once you loaded a TSR program, it "hid" in memory, ready to "pop up" instantly over another program at the touch of a key or two.

There had been earlier TSRs, but SideKick was by far the most ambitious attempt, a semi-integrated package that popped up over the program you were running. It included a calculator, a phone dialer, a WordStar-compatible text editor that could steal characters right off the screen, a calendar, and other goodies, any and all of which you could display on the screen at once. Despite its weird and seemingly endless program bugs, which could crash not only the program itself but the one it had popped up over, SideKick became an instant cult classic. In a sense, it was really the first successful integrated windowed environment for the IBM PC, albeit a modest one. It was the kind of innovation Microsoft rarely seemed to come up with.

Around the Microsoft campus, Philippe became the newest *bête noire,* a goofy bear of a man who somehow knew exactly how to push Bill's buttons. Over the years at Microsoft, the mere mention of Kahn, as the leader of the forces of evil, could be counted on to rally the troops. There were PR crisis meetings, Borland War Councils. One version of Microsoft's QuickBASIC was code-named "PK"—Philippe Killer. The phrase "stick it to Philippe" turned up in a 1986 language group briefing, and "Kick Borland's butt!" was penciled in on a product manager's personal evaluation form. One group even passed out "Delete Philippe" T-shirts.

The warfare opened out to the public in September 1985 when Microsoft offered Turbo Pascal users a $40 rebate if they traded up to the $300 Microsoft Pascal. "I think it's a compliment and I appreciate it," Kahn declared. "This is the way Bill Gates says Turbo Pascal is a decent product."

▼ Meanwhile DOS, the cash cow, was still producing milk, cream, butter, cheese. The days of the flat fee for DOS were long gone, and Microsoft was beginning to insist that the product be called MS-DOS, not Compaq DOS or Zenith DOS or any bright idea some customer came up with. Except for the lucky few who had bought DOS in the early days and had managed to get Microsoft to throw in revisions, OEM customers were paying significant fees, both up front and on a per-machine basis. Except for the tiniest vendors, per-copy deals were strongly discouraged. Per-machine deals were far easier to audit—just send us your sales figures and multiply. Better still, per-machine deals made it virtually impossible for competitors to crack the DOS monopoly. If you were already paying a royalty for DOS on every machine you made, you weren't likely to offer a different operating system except as a high-priced option.

The deals were structured to include as many limitations as possible, in the hope that in one way or another the contract would expire and the licensee would be back at Microsoft's doorstep for a new one. Typical licenses lasted two years, were limited to a single machine, and did not extend to any version number with a new digit to the left of the decimal point. So if you had a deal for version 2.1 on your Model F machine, you'd be saying hello to your friendly Microsoft representative whenever DOS version 3.0 or your Model G came out.

The business was coming in faster than the company could handle it. At one point, as an insider remembered it, "The only way of getting an appointment with anybody at Microsoft was to call them up and threaten them. There were four salespeople handling the world. They were just overwhelmed. There was more business than they could do."

Two representatives of a Finnish company once sat in the lobby for an entire day waiting to meet an account manager with whom they had no appointment. "The next morning, there they were, sitting right in the same spot." Eventually a member of the sales team took pity on them and ushered them in. It turned out they had been talking with friends at a Swedish company that had done its own DOS deal. "And they were told, 'Don't send a letter. Don't call on the phone. Get the money, U.S. dollars. Go there and stay there until they talk to you and give you the software so you can go home, because otherwise you'll never hear from them.' And . . . they were absolutely right!" Without DOS, your machine might as well be a doorstop.

As DOS became mandatory, the price kept going up, though the sales force had tremendous discretion in structuring deals. In general, the more you were willing to commit to up front, the better deal you got. In January 1983 Televideo guaranteed a minimum of $300,000 over four years, which enabled it to license DOS for $10 per machine—$5 after the commitment level was reached. Less well fixed outfits, such as Pronto Computer, that could commit only to a two-year total of $20,000, would get DOS for $31 per machine and BASIC for $45.

In the early days, BASIC cost significantly more than DOS. In the eyes of Bill Gates, "That was where the value was." In order to get a two-year flat-fee deal for DOS at $105,000, Seequa Computer, an early maker of IBM compatibles, committed to $240,000 worth of BASIC at $30 per machine. Tiny clone vendor Amqute's two-year commitment for DOS was $40,000 at $30 per machine; for BASIC it was $120,000 and another $30 per unit.

As packaged products rather than homegrown programming became the order of the day and BASIC declined in importance, it eventually became part of DOS, not broken out separately. But the sliding-scale pricing remained, craftily encouraging manufacturers to err on the side of overoptimism to get what looked like a better deal. As Intel's William Davidow wrote, "Each of twenty PC companies was planning to capture an impossible 20 percent of the market."

Such overoptimism led to overcommitment. When the DOS version changed, or a new product cycle turned a hot machine into just another turkey, customers often had to go back to Microsoft for another contract while still owing thousands and thousands of dollars of "overhang" in commitments for machines that would never be shipped. Sometimes the "overhang" could be worked off with a subsequent commitment; sometimes it couldn't. So although it was obvious that Microsoft collected a bounty, a tax virtually every time anybody bought a DOS machine from someone other than IBM, what was less well known was that Microsoft profited even from machines that had just been figments of sales directors' overheated imaginations.

It was a hell of a business. By 1984 hardware manufacturers were shipping 5 million machines a year domestically, the foreign market was almost as big, MS-DOS went out with the vast majority of units, and its market share was growing inexorably. In fiscal 1984 more than half of Microsoft's $97 million in revenues came from its systems business—operating systems and languages. BASIC, with revenues of nearly $25 million, amounted to nearly one-quarter of the company's revenues. At $9 million, DOS actually took third place to Multiplan's $19 million.

And the business was changing. The second wave of IBM-compatible machines, computers from Eagle and Corona, had broken on the shore—and headed back out to sea. Unlike Compaq, those companies had done things the easy way—simply copying the all-important code in IBM's BIOS chips. In early 1984 IBM hauled them into court and got them to repent.

But by then it hardly mattered. In May 1984 an outfit called Phoenix Software Associates announced it had used "a TI-9900 programmer"—an expert who had no knowledge of the workings of the IBM PC or the Intel chip inside it—to reverse-engineer an IBM-compatible ROM BIOS that Phoenix would sell to all comers. Its advertisements to hardware manufacturers touted an insurance policy against copyright-infringement suits.

There were similar products, but Phoenix's marketing made it the brand to reckon with. The off-the-shelf ROM BIOS chip was the missing link that made the IBM-compatible market explode. Now building a fully compatible IBM PC was little more than a matter of hiring engineers and assembling parts.

For Microsoft, this was good news and bad news. PC clones, as they were dubbed, brought price competition to hardware, drove prices down, and vastly increased the number of machines that ran DOS and other Microsoft software. Clones meant that instead of stocking separate software packages for each machine, retailers could stock a single IBM edition, simplifying software production, inventory, sales. The cloud? If IBM decided on a standard other than DOS, the rest of the compatible world might stampede to follow it.

So Bill Gates committed to a scheme of operating systems for the future, successors to DOS. Microsoft already had prototypes of IBM's newest machine in house—the model destined to become the PC AT, known at IBM as "Bigtop" and at Microsoft as "Salmon." Its forthcoming network software, "Ringmaster" to IBM, was "Octopus" to Microsoft. "IBM at this point was just totally in love with code names," said DOS programmer Mark Zbikowski. Microsoft kept its unit under lock and key in what the DOS gurus called "the Aquarium."

The AT's 80286 chip, 286 for short, offered something new, something called "protected mode," with which it could address a whopping 16 megabytes of memory, a sixteenfold increase over the old 8088 standard—paralleling that chip's sixteenfold increase over the old 8-bitters. To a limited extent, protected mode could help keep multiple programs from getting in each other's way. It seemed like just the thing for a multitasking operating system, and if nothing else, it offered the potential to break the dreaded "640K barrier," the limitation on memory built into the original IBM PC design. Although Bill Gates had predicted in 1981 that the PC's sixteenfold increase in memory meant that the "logical address space limit is for all practical purposes gone away," programs had quickly expanded to fill the space available and were now chafing at the limits.

And all that might be bad news for Microsoft. Where the bad news began was the upper right-hand corner of the redesigned keyboard, where users found a puzzling key labeled SysRq—for System Request. It was an entirely new label in the IBM PC world, and users hadn't a clue about what it was supposed to do. What it was supposed to do, if the software engineers at IBM on the "Mermaid" project (known to Microsoft as "Fish Magic") had anything to say about it, was to switch the AT from DOS into a higher plane of consciousness, a "virtual machine" or "hypervisor" mode that would allow you to run multiple programs simultaneously. And they didn't even have to be DOS programs: At a touch of the SysRq key, this software—a homegrown IBM version of something in the works at Digital Research called Concurrent PC-DOS—could actually run DOS programs and CP/M-86 programs and other programs, all at the same time.

Then there was TopView. "TopView," Gates would later contend, "was one of many attempts to design us out of existence." Earlier IBM had hired Gates "to come in and tell them what I thought about TopView, how it could or could not work with DOS." Gates was not terribly equivocal. "I said, 'This is bullshit.' And they said, 'No, we want to know what you really think. Seriously!' "

TopView was typical IBM code: slow, ungainly, character-based. But it symbolized IBM's attempt to distance itself from Microsoft. TopView—or Topheavy, as it was quickly nicknamed—offered character-based windows and multitasking: the ability to run, not just switch between, several programs at once, say, recalculating a spreadsheet while printing out a text file. But it had severe limitations, in part because it was something of a memory hog.

But IBM, as Bill himself once remarked, is a pretty big company. Waiting in the wings behind TopView was a flotilla of nautically themed operating systems: Nina, Pinta, and Santa Maria. Exactly which was which wasn't entirely clear, but they had something to do with variants of the 3270 PC Control Program, a windowing technology out of Kingston, New York, and a display technology out of Hursley, England. Eventually the Columbian operating systems would coalesce into something known as CP-DOS.

TopView! Nina! Pinta! Santa Maria! Fish Magic! Gates must have felt as if he were drowning. What about good old DOS and Windows, guys? Bill Gates went down to Boca to make his pitch, to toss Microsoft's next-generation operating systems into the ring, avoiding any mention that they were about as tangible as mermaids.

First would come DOS 4, a multitasking system that would work on any old PC you happened to have around. Next up: DOS 5, a multitasking system that would take advantage of the 286 chip's memory-friendly protected mode. And finally, the real operating system everybody was waiting for: DOS 6, which would finally make good on past claims of easy migration from DOS to UNIX. DOS 6 would be a better UNIX than UNIX, not only because it would have all sorts of neat DOS stuff, but also because it would be rewritten totally from scratch, thereby avoiding all those expensive royalties to AT&T. And, oh yes: They'd all need a graphical user interface, and Windows would run on top of every one of them. Pretty cool, huh?

IBM's Bocans told Bill they'd let him know. For the moment they'd be happy to get their hands on the next version of plain-vanilla DOS, now dubbed 3.0. They were writing much of the networking software that would link DOS with IBM's new network hardware and had expected Microsoft to deliver the new DOS by the end of May 1984.

Not quite. To accomplish everything IBM wanted, Mark Zbikowski and Aaron Reynolds "just broke DOS and pulled it apart, and it didn't recover until like November or so of '83," Zbikowski said. "So there's a long period here where IBM was really upset because we weren't shipping them anything." Early in 1984, with Gates, Ballmer, and account manager Steve Snyder hovering over them, Zbikowski and Reynolds made a fateful call. To a group huddled around a speakerphone in Boca, Zbikowski pointed out that the promised network support was at least half a year away. "For a good fifteen minutes there was silence on the speakerphone." It was as if IBM's phone had gone dead. What had actually gone dead was the release schedule for the PC AT.

As Zbikowski later admitted, his five-man team "believed we understood all the problems involved in making DOS a networking product. [But] as time progressed, we realized that we didn't fully understand it, either from a compatibility standpoint or from an operating-system standpoint." In the end, adding networking support to DOS proved so complicated that Microsoft didn't even meet its revised schedule.

So the AT rolled out in August 1984 with a DOS called 3.0 that supported the special features of the new machine but omitted the network stuff. Actually, the crashed-out 3.0 included a significant amount of network code that did absolutely nothing, along with a plethora of bugs. According to Zbikowski, "the product was not ready for us to ship when IBM said, 'Fine, we'll take it.' "

The networking problems earned Zbikowski and Reynolds a series of unwanted midwinter sojourns in sunny Florida. Zbikowski "left the day after Christmas, was gone until the day before New Year's, spent New Year's Day at home, left," and spent seven more intermittent weeks in Boca trying to get the problems resolved. He complained to Bill Gates about having to red-eye across the country at a moment's notice. The response: "Whatever it takes to get the customer happy, we've got to do it."

What it took was code, code, code, but cooperation with IBM wasn't easy. The IBM programmers weren't allowed to show anyone from Microsoft the source code to their network program, and because of the disclosure restrictions in the original DOS contract, IBM was mortally afraid of peeking at Microsoft's source. Solutions could depend on interpersonal relationships. At one point Zbikowski and an IBMer "were just banging our heads against a problem, and he said, 'This is ridiculous.' We walked into his office, he shut the door, and he just pulled the source out, and he said 'Let's find the problem.' "

The networkable 3.1 version of DOS hit the stands in spring 1985, along with The IBM PC Network, as Big Blue called its software. MS-NET, Microsoft's networking counterpart, went out to OEM customers around the same time. The main difference between it and IBM's networking package was that Microsoft's software had to be run on a machine, or "server," earmarked, or "dedicated," for that purpose, whereas IBM's edition let an individual user work—at a crawl—on the same machine that serviced the network. Although Microsoft's OEM customers sold adaptations of MS-NET under a variety of names, the software was rudimentary at best. Gates wasn't paying close attention to a little Utah company called Novell, whose software worked with a wide range of third-party network cards and would shortly manage to steal the market out from under his nose. "We should have gotten serious earlier about networking," Gates would say years later when enumerating Microsoft's biggest mistakes.

But that was all in the future. On August 14, 1984, Bill Gates sent an outwardly euphoric memo to all 600 Microsoft employees: IBM's PC AT, based on Intel's 80286 chip, had been released. Gates called it "the most significant personal computer announcement since the introduction of the PC just three years ago"—as if the Apple Macintosh had been little more than a computerized Etch-a-Sketch.

Along with the announcement of DOS 3.0, there was other good news: The AT would run XENIX 286, a new version of Microsoft's forgotten solution to the 16-bit software crisis, which Bill Gates had managed to sell IBM at the last minute when Boca suddenly realized it had nothing at all to show off the new chip's protected mode. The machine would support a new graphics standard known as EGA (Extended Graphics Adapter), on which Gates and Microsoft had consulted, and which would allow Windows to run in color, assuming it ever managed to reach the market. The AT's data bus was 16 bits wide, which meant the machine could move information faster.

But Gates took great pains to point out that "some people may view the TopView window manager developed at IBM and announced for [first quarter] availability as a competitor to our Windows product. Actually TopView is very different from Windows since it does not provide a graphical user interface." Actually, TopView was very similar to Windows—late, bloated, and underpowered—but why bother with technicalities?

Still, IBM was selling TopView hard. It was pushing software developers to forget about DOS, forget about Windows, and write directly for TopView and its API—Applications Program Interface. If the operating system is a sort of butler, an API is a sort of footman, assisting programmers in doing a variety of odd jobs. Instead of writing code to put a box or a circle on the screen, the programmer would "call" the API to do it.

Since APIs, like operating systems, were typically incompatible with one another, which one you wrote for—or whether you'd bother writing for one at all—was a crucial question. There were millions more DOS machines out there than TopView machines, but IBM was behind this thing and not behind Windows, so software developers were initially willing to at least listen to the IBM pitch. It was the first shot in the great PC API war that would rage on for years with Windows as the pivotal combatant.

As sorry as TopView was—and it wouldn't even be released until February 1985—it had a stultifying impact on the windowing market. "TopView was announced in August 1984 as the most strategic software product from IBM," recalled president Therese Myers of Quarterdeck, the maker of DESQ. "Our sales stopped. We practically went bankrupt."

With TopView in the works, there was no way Big Blue was going to endorse Windows. Not that it had ever intended to. IBM's Mike Maples, a Jackie Gleason–size, lightning-witted Oklahoma good ol' boy, was just one of the many IBMers Bill Gates had visited in hopes of making the sale. Microsoft was continually sending prerelease copies of Windows to every nook and cranny of IBM, hoping someone would bite on the thing. Gates gave Maples his demo on the woefully underpowered IBM PCjr. No go: As Maples remembered it, "We thought it was more hope than not."

"In the early days losing was something Bill took in a really bad way. I mean, I've seen Bill cry over something that he thought was just disastrous for the company," Jon Shirley remembered. It was 1984ish, Shirley said, and involved an operating system product. At the time it seemed a real disaster. "What it was was immaterial," Shirley said. "It was the reaction."

19

ACTUALLY IN HELL

By 1984 Microsoft had become the second-fastest-growing company in the state of Washington, outstripped only by an outfit—no relation—called Weathervane Window. By July the company was six times as big as when it had moved to Northup, spilling across the freeway from Burgermaster to buildings 2, 3, and 4 in what was dubbed Corporate Campus East. And the new environs were merely a safety valve. On August 14 Jon Shirley sent out a companywide memo alerting everyone not to get comfortably ensconced: Within a year Microsoft would need far more space, and Shirley was soliciting ideas about it.

Microsoft had grown so big it was experiencing a computer-age phenomenon: junk e-mail. Systems guru Gordon Letwin urged that e-mail addicts sending companywide messages "stop to consider the amount of system resources you are tying up, and whether your message warrants such extensive distribution." Global messages went to nearly 500 folks and cost the company "about a man-day in mail-reading overhead." It was time to clean up the e-mail act: By September the company would be linked internationally by e-mail with direct links to all subsidiaries, and global messages would truly be global. It wasn't long before messages to "all" regarding charitable events or deals on used cars finally became so pervasive that global messaging was restricted to the upper echelons.

For the fiscal year through July 1984, Microsoft had reported sales of $100 million, twice as much as the year before, and trumpeted that it was the first microcomputer software company ever to reach that level. The company had reached this milestone in a little over half the time Bill had predicted, largely because of the unprecedented growth of the personal computer industry.

Yet recomputed under a different accounting method two years later, the sales figures would be revised down to $97.5 million. And despite the incoming stream of dollars, the financial side of Microsoft's business was at best screwed up, at worst simply ignored. Acutely aware of the problem, Jon Shirley had embarked on a national search for a chief financial officer almost a year before. In September 1984 he finally found his man—a street fighter, Korean war paratrooper, and feisty Irish Catholic fireplug who seemed an unlikely candidate for the WASPy Microsoft culture. Frank Gaudette had grown up on the streets of Astoria, Queens, still had his New York accent and man-of-the-people demeanor, and at forty-nine was old enough to be the father of Bill Gates.

Although there was considerable internal discussion about how this street–Smart Guy would mesh with Microsoft's honors-class atmosphere, Gaudette got extra points for his experience in taking companies public, most recently a defense-contracting outfit called C3—shades of the C-Cubed days!—which stood for Command, Control, and Computers. Gaudette had read the *Time* article about Bill Gates and expected to find a "techie nerd." But he was "amazed at how well he knew finance, how well he knew the company I was with, how well he knew the workings of the public marketplace, the competition, and people I knew." Gaudette was hired within days and charged with fixing what he viewed as "close to uncontrollable chaos in finance" and taking the company from its mom-and-pop financial style to business maturity with financial controls. One of the things most desperately needed on the fiscal end: computers.

Meanwhile Jon Shirley had gotten a feel for the company and had reorganized it again. This time he divided development, product marketing, user education, and testing into two groups: systems software, under Steve Ballmer; and applications, under Bill Gates until a suitable successor could be found. "As soon as we hire someone," Shirley wrote in an August 7 memo, "Bill will spend full time as chairman—representing the Company, selling to key customers, and, most importantly, formulating strategy, designing and providing design guidance and review. Bill will continue to review systems design issues."

Ballmer, the newly crowned Mr. Systems, was not the most technical person around. Microsoft's Smart Guys wondered how someone with so little programming knowledge could head the division. But Ballmer was renowned for his motivational capabilities, even if it sometimes meant beating up on people. Given Ballmer's True Believer nature and the True Believer nature of Windows chief Scott McGregor, it was inevitable that the two would clash bigtime.

McGregor, a polished and articulate academic, just didn't samba with Ballmer's roll-up-the-shirtsleeves rah-rahism. Whereas McGregor found Gates a "technical visionary" whose ideas dovetailed with his own, he considered Ballmer a "nontech cheerleader." About all Ballmer had in common with McGregor was premature hair loss. And now he was supposed to be the Windows messiah.

25. Microsoft's first advertisement, 1976.

26. Microsoft's first real offices: Two Park Central Building, Albuquerque.

27. Miriam Lubow, 1978.

28. Albuquerque farewell, 1978. Top row: Steve Wood, Bob Wallace, Jim Lane. Second row: Bob O'Rear, Bob Greenberg, Marc McDonald, Gordon Letwin. Front row: Bill Gates, Andrea Lewis, Marla Wood, Paul Allen.

29. Executive suite at Bellevue offices, 1979: Bill Gates, Paul Allen, Andrea Lewis.

Plaza Hotel revels, National Computer Conference, 1979:

30. Chris Larson and a weary Gates.

31. Gates and Kay Nishi.

32. Gates and the Tandy men: John "Horseshit" Roach and future Microsoft president Jon Shirley.

33. Portrait of the young executive, circa 1979.

West Coast Computer Faire, 1980:

34. Neil Konzen and Kay Nishi in Microsoft booth.

35. Vern Raburn, Dottie Hall, and Paul Allen with Microsoft's first hardware product: SoftCard.

36. Jack Sams, IBM emissary and "cool guy."

38. Tim Paterson, father of DOS, 1992.

40. Charles Simonyi, messenger from Xerox PARC, 1986.

<table>
<tbody></tbody>
</table>

ORDER FORM 7a 7-27-81

Bil'ing Address: MICROSOFT
10800 NE 8th Suite 819
Bellevue, WA 98004

Shipping Address:

Delivered
UPS OK? _____ Phone: _____ Contact: _____

Quantity	Description	Unit	Total
	8 BIT RAMS - Model_____ nsec		
	8/16 Ram - 200 nsec.		
	8086 SET - Eprom:_____		
	CPU SUPPORT - No Eprom		
	86-DOS - Format:_____		
	BASIC-86 - Format:_____		
	MISC. SOFTWARE - Format:_____		
	MULTI-PORT SERIAL - 2 port____ 4 port____		
	CABLES - Male___ Female___ 14"__18"__28"__		
	86-DOS SALES RIGHTS		50,000.00

(X)Prepaid CB7610 ( )COD ( ) Open Acct____
MC VISA Number:_____ Exp:___ Auth:____
Purchase Order Number:_____ Desired Shipping:____
Scheduled Ship Date _delivered_ Order Number:____ Serial Numbers:____
Date Shipped:_____ Via:____
Special Instructions:_____

9003057

Order Taken By: Rod   Name: MICROSOFT   State: WA

37. Seattle Computer order form confirming the deal for DOS.

39. Bill Gates and Paul Allen consider windows 1982.

41. Bill Gates and "32-bit" Jill Bennett, circa 1983.

42. Systems operators, 1984: VisiCorp's Dan Fylstra, Gates, Digital Research's Gary Kildall.

43. Jon Shirley, president of Microsoft, 1986.

44. Borland's Philippe Kahn in a dour mood, 1990.

45. IBM's Bill Lowe, 1988.

46. Apple's John Sculley (plaid shirt) and Steve Jobs (bow tie), 1984.

47. Bill Gates talks, Lotus's Mitchell Kapor listens, 1988.

48. Ann Winblad, longtime friend of Gates, 1984.

. Paul Allen and Bill Gates laugh
out old times, 1987.

50. Steve Ballmer will do anything to get the
business, get the business, get the business,
1987.

51. Contemplating the Microsoft relationship?
IBM's Jim Cannavino, 1992.

52. Melinda French and Bill Gates, 1993.

53. Serious work: Gordon Letwin in Bill
Gates's office, 1988.

54. Serious fun: organized confusion at
Microgames, 1989.

55. Bill Gates with his Office of the President: Mike Maples, Frank Gaudette, Steve Ballmer, 1992.

56. Bill Gates's home territory:
1 Microsoft campus
2 parents' house
3 first house
4 current house
5 new house (under construction)
6 Microsoft's first Bellevue headquarters
7 Microsoft's Northup headquarters
8 site of C-Cubed headquarters

To get things rolling, Ballmer had held a meeting to fire up the troops about how great the product was going to be. The response: laughter. "You don't believe in this?" Ballmer asked. The reply was a chorus of noes. Ballmer, the take-charge guy, was suddenly "in McGregor's shorts."

Into the thick of the fray, somewhat unwillingly, marched Neil Konzen. Bill Gates had asked his leading Macintosh wizard to take a look at the idea of porting Multiplan from the Mac to Windows. By that time Konzen could recite Mac Multiplan code in his sleep. He had worked on the initial bug-plagued version, and he had just finished rewriting it twice.

Gates wasn't the only CEO with high esteem for Konzen's skills. Steve Jobs himself had recently given him a call inviting him to Cupertino. But Konzen had found out that the Mac Pirates, burned out and feeling unappreciated, were jumping ship, and rumors that Jobs was about to walk the plank didn't help any. Passed over once before, Konzen decided to return the favor.

When Konzen strolled into the Windows fracas, it was not a magic moment. Windows, as he charitably viewed it, was "a piece of crap." The project was "actually in hell." McGregor wasn't communicating with the developers; the developers weren't working together. What code existed was a joke.

Diplomacy was not one of Neil Konzen's strong suits. Although he "felt kind of funny about this because we had started Windows back before the Mac had shipped and I sort of felt like there was a lot of cross-pollination," Konzen, an avowed "Apple bigot," decided to tear into the whole damned program. His mission to port Multiplan "turned into kind of critiquing Windows and scoffing at it and jumping up and down about how it should change."

Better than virtually anyone else at Microsoft, Konzen knew how this graphical user interface stuff was supposed to work. He'd spent too long helping make it right on the Mac to accept the shortcomings of Windows. Besides, "Bill was very concerned. Bill rammed down everybody's throats this Macintosh compatibility. He didn't want everybody to have to redo the manuals and redesign the user interface. We had just learned how hard it was to do that."

So Ballmer drafted Konzen onto the Windows team and convened a meeting in the new boardroom. Gates listened as Konzen told him, "Bill, this is what I want to do, and this is what I think we should do. . . . It was a really tough time and really politically charged for me, because I was this guy who came in and said we should change all this stuff. And it was running counter to what Scott McGregor wanted to do." But what Konzen was saying made sense to Gates, the technical guy. So Ballmer, the nontechnical guy, put on his coach cap. "He just came right out and said, 'Look, I'm depending on you. You've got to do this thing. You're the one that can do it. There's nothing I can do. So do a good job.' "

Over a six-week period, Konzen feverishly rewrote much of the Windows code from the push model to the Mac's pull model, with totally new code to manage the windows, to handle memory. It was an amazing hack. "And it was really hard, because I was a real prick to McGregor and he hated my guts, and I didn't like him very much, and I was pretty intimidated, and I was like twenty." It was the self-described twenty-year-old snot-nosed kid versus the erudite PARC software engineer. Push versus pull.

And tiled versus overlapping. McGregor won that one. According to Konzen, "Windows at the time was just a total disaster. We were just way behind and shitty. We had already done a bunch of work to figure out it would be really hard to port our apps to it. And so we didn't fix it."

But everything else about Windows shouted Neil Konzen's influence, so much so that Mac partisans recognized his imprint immediately. "The internal structure of Windows came through Neil Konzen almost directly," said former PARC and Mac wizard Bob Belleville, a self-described Windows user from Day One. "They can tell all the stories you want to hear about it, but that was a very strong intellectual derivative of the Mac. It had the same internal structure . . . in fact, some of the same errors were carried across."

The political fallout was taking its toll on Windows ship dates, every single one of them. Windows was turning Winblad's term "vaporware" into a household word. In June 1984, Jon Shirley said that Microsoft had made Windows "extremely Mac-like in appearance in the hope that many vendors will be able to write a product for Apple's machine that can be ported to MS-Windows, or vice versa, with little change in documentation."

Now it was Leo Nikora's turn to apologize. October 23: "We set goals that were awfully ambitious for the 8088 processor." November 16: "[Windows is] the triumph of good product over haste." November 19: "We announced it last November because, as an extension to the operating system, it needs a lot of lead time."

In a November 19, 1984, *InfoWorld* editorial entitled "There You Go Again," Stewart Alsop wrote that Microsoft "seems to have fallen into a bad habit with Windows. Announce, show, promise and delay. Then delay some more." Back in Bellevue, a cartoon was posted showing a Middle East terrorist lining people up against a wall and shooting them. The terrorist was identified as Ballmer.

By Fall Comdex '84, with nearly every news organ in the PC universe questioning the status of Windows, a new strategy was called for. No more predictions of vapor-ridden ship dates. It was *mea culpa* time. "We were trying to figure out how to put the best face on," said PR director Marty Taucher, who had succeeded Pam Edstrom after she joined Microsoft's outside PR firm headed by Melissa Waggener. The standard line: "We were wrong, and it's going to take longer than we thought."

Diversionary tactics helped. At Comdex onlookers trooped by the thousands through an interactive theater Microsoft had set up to show off its new Mac apps. You want windows? Microsoft can do windows—just not on a PC.

Microsoft Syndrome had struck the Windows team. McGregor, burned out on Ballmer, a lack of California sunshine, and IBM's increasingly anti-Microsoft strategy, was about to head back to Palo Alto—this time to DEC. Nikora, tired of "this confrontational thing" and of being the fall guy, was packing it in as well. The post-Xerox "great white saviors" were now in yellowed tatters.

Once the hot project for up-and-coming Golden Boys, Windows had earned an in-house reputation as the last stop to Margaritaville. "Well, God, they're giving me this project so I'll fail and this is the easy way of easing me out of the company," thought Tandy Trower when offered the frightening position of Windows program manager in January 1985.

By then many of the OEM customers had jumped ship. IBM had not the slightest iota of interest in the project. "This is the point that nobody wanted to touch Windows," Trower said. "It was like the death project."

▼ In October 1984 Steve Jobs and the Apple sales force returned to the scene of their Hawaiian punch of the year before. The mood was still upbeat. The 1985 Super Bowl commercial, "Lemmings," though not as subtle as and considerably less well received than its predecessor, would twit IBM directly with blue-suited executives marching blindly over a cliff. And Apple was about to unveil The Macintosh Office, a whole vision of new-generation 512K "Fat Macs" networked to each other and to laser printers, looking surprisingly like the Xerox Star, only much, much cheaper. The sales presentations conveniently ignored the fact that with a dearth of apps, Mac sales were on the shaky side; only 20,000 a month were going out the door, but the top brass was sure that would all change soon.

The mood was bleaker for Bill Gates. His Macintosh product-for-everything strategy had just begun to surface from a sea of woes. Odyssey was clearly not going to be ready before Doug Klunder's nine-month grace period expired, and nothing much was being done about training a successor. Things had gotten so bad with Mac File that Jeff Harbers had moved into the office, taking showers in the men's room, grabbing naps in his sleeping bag, munching boxes of Wheat Thins. Charles Simonyi had set up a "War Room" to manage the campaign against bugs in Chart and Word. Program code and optimization goals bedecked the walls, and the Mad Hungarian would blow a powerful air horn every time some significant milestone was accomplished, driving everyone else in the building nuts.

Now Chart was finally shipping, and Word and File were ready to demo at the Apple sales meeting. But in Hawaii, Lotus trotted out an early version of Jazz. It wasn't yet ready for public consumption, but it was enough to make Bill Gates "go 'Oh shit, this thing looks really good.' "

Steve Jobs thought so too. His tendency to play favorites was in full force: Microsoft was not getting the job done, and Lotus was the new savior. While Jobs, Sculley, and Apple's marketing whiz kids lavished attention on Lotus, they virtually snubbed Bill Gates. Jazz would do for the Mac what 1-2-3 was doing for the PC.

"We were terrified! Absolutely terrified!" recalled Mike Slade, an intense, sardonic northwesterner from Stanford Business School who was Microsoft's marketing manager for Mac products. He and Gates went for a long contemplative walk on the beach at Hilton Hawaiian Village at Waikiki, mulling what Microsoft's next step should be. Maybe Word and Odyssey should be combined to make a product that would at least sell half as well as Jazz. "God, this is bad, this is bad," Bill Gates kept muttering.

In the end, he went with a radically different idea. Jeff Harbers had heard somehow that Andy Hertzfeld, one of the original Macintosh Pirates who'd left Apple, was working on something called Switcher. If you had enough memory in your Mac—as the forthcoming 512K Fat Macs would—Switcher would let you load a bunch of programs all at once and flip between them at the touch of a key. Since each of the Microsoft programs would run in 128K, they would all fit nicely—not quite the integration Jazz was promising, but close enough.

According to Hertzfeld, Bill Gates met with him to discuss buying the program. "I felt Gates basically treated me like an idiot lacking any kind of business sense. He wanted me to accept a very low amount of money for the work I was doing, and what he said was 'Well, you're a really good programmer, aren't you, and a really good programmer could write this really fast, couldn't he?' Sort of trying to play off my ego in this adolescent way. He offered me a flat fee of forty thousand dollars to do the program." The lowball strategy didn't work with Hertzfeld: "Eventually I got $150,000 for the program" from Apple.

Bill Gates lost Switcher, but it would nonetheless become one part of the strategy to nail Jazz. The other part was Odyssey, by now renamed, less poetically, Excel—to the chagrin of Rowland Hanson. The renaming had become one of the company's great bugaboos, with everyone favoring a different choice. Blumenthal and Klunder liked Number Buddy and Mr. Spreadsheet. Jon Shirley favored Sigma. The ever-consistent Hanson backed Microsoft Plansheet. Slade even took a thesaurus, a dictionary, and *Bartlett's Familiar Quotations* to the beach in search of the perfect name. Finally a district manager suggested Excel: Bingo!

Upon the program's release, Microsoft was promptly sued by Manufacturers Hanover Trust, which offered a computerized banking service under the same name. A settlement stipulated that use of the word was okay—as long as it was preceded by Microsoft. Rowland Hanson's revenge was complete.

In January 1985 Gates, Slade, and a huge group of colleagues took an early version of the program down to Cupertino. The software was still far from stable, Slade had worked until 4:00 A.M. the morning before the trip to make sure the demo wouldn't crash, and the session at Apple was "a long, fucked-up meeting" at which Steve Jobs swore his love for Jazz.

Slade and fellow product manager Pete Higgins were assigned to get Bill home. Late for their plane, the three argued frantically about the best way to get to the San Francisco airport. The miles, the distance, the terminals— everything was subject to minute intellectual scrutiny. Gates was on his way home from a Hawaiian vacation, so, loaded down with his luggage and a ton of Macintosh gear, the trio lumbered through the terminal—to discover their flight had been grounded because of fog in Seattle. "Portland!" Bill exclaimed, and the three tore off for the farthest reaches of the terminal.

Portland was fogged in too. After three hours and a hamburger, the trio boarded a plane for Seattle via Portland. Bill sat in the middle between Slade and Higgins, who were both "just draggin'."

But Gates was just getting his second wind. At the airport newsstand he had found a copy of *Scientific American* and had become absolutely enthralled with an article on the history of the crossbow. "Pete is just like faking he's asleep—he just can't handle it. And Bill's like—'This is amazing!' And he's going on and on, like he's just discovered the crossbow and da Vinci. 'This guy da Vinci was really smart! Look at this!' " That evening Mike Slade learned "more about this fucking thing than I'll ever want to know" from the utterly indefatigable William Henry Gates.

Meanwhile Doug Klunder, to the absolute amazement of everyone at Microsoft, was sticking to his promise to leave, and Microsoft, to the absolute amazement of Doug Klunder, was sticking to its promise not to try to change his mind about it. In January 1985 he spent some twenty hours videotaping an Excel-according-to-Doug explanation of all the program's data structures and coding conventions because, as Slade put it, no one knew what the hell he was doing.

Then Klunder took off. "I'm totally burned out. I think technology sucks. I get rid of everything I own except what I carry around in a backpack. Go down to California and find work there as a migrant farmer." He wound up in the lettuce fields near Oxnard. "I only actually managed to do a few days of farm labor, but since I was putting up my tent, my expenses were pretty low, and I was surviving." After about six weeks, "my pack got stolen, and so I was left down in California, basically with the shirt on my back and not a whole lot else. At which point, having the need to eat, I said, 'Gee, I bet I know where I can get money fast. I can go back to Microsoft.' "

He called up and was offered plane fare back but took the bus instead. "I originally intended to come back for just a few weeks to get a little money so I could head off. I ended up sticking around to ship Excel." Forevermore there would be an expression at Microsoft for employees, especially headstrong programmers with momentary wanderlust, who come and go and come back again. The term: "lettuce pickers."

To preempt Jazz, Microsoft unveiled Excel in an all-stops-out press conference at Tavern on the Green in New York's Central Park in May 1985. The night before, at the rehearsal in a hotel room, the demo kept crashing, and, according to Jabe Blumenthal, "Bill was getting like really, really pissed." After a yelling match where Blumenthal told Gates to shut up and be constructive, plus some last-minute phone calls to Klunder, the demo came together about two in the morning. Approaching the rocky section at the rollout, Gates slowed down his speech in anticipation of disaster, but the demonstration came off fine.

Excel, said Steve Jobs from the podium, is "the fastest, largest, and most full-function spreadsheet available in the world," though it would not actually be available until late September. But he added that "There is a war brewing between Lotus and Microsoft if you haven't noticed," deliberately goading the two software combatants. "Gates got tremendously upset," said Mike Murray, which was a step toward the intended result: more aggressive competition for Mac software.

But Jobs still worried about Microsoft's doings apart from the Mac. On a visit with Belleville to Japan after the Mac came out, Jobs saw a Mac-like Paint program running on an NEC computer and, according to Belleville, "really got wrapped around the axle on that one." Upon returning, Jobs immediately contacted Gates to complain that he had fed NEC the program. As Belleville recalled it:

> Steve got real real angry and called Bill and said "You and Jon Shirley get down here." Bill and Jon got on a flight, came down, we sat at one of our famous round conference tables. And Steve just read him the riot act. He just hollered and screamed. And they just sat, especially Jon Shirley. He was wonderful, he just sat and smiled. And they apologized and went away, and that was that. They kind of understood Steve in a business way in that if you let him dance you'll probably be better off in the end.

Then the term "horsetrading" came to characterize a major deal involving the horse Bill backed hardest: BASIC. Unlike every other machine of the early days, the Apple II design was still alive and well. Descendants of the original Apple II—the Apple IIc and Apple IIe—were still providing the company with significant revenues, particularly from the educational market. But now the

1977 license for Applesoft BASIC, an absolutely essential part of every Apple II machine, was about to expire. Bill Gates was in the driver's seat. It was time to deal.

What Apple wanted was a renewal of the Applesoft license. What Gates wanted—or thought he wanted—was an end to the threat of Donn Denman's MacBASIC, still beta after all these years. During its development, MacBASIC had managed to gain an underground following. Widely distributed for testing, it had found its way to Dartmouth College, birthplace of the original BASIC. Even in prerelease, MacBASIC was used for an introductory programming course at Dartmouth and made the university rounds through various channels. Books were published about it. A sort of cult had formed around it even before it officially existed. Denman was a change-the-world type, a perfectionist who fiddled with his program while Gates burned.

Bill Gates didn't want to change the world; he wanted to rule it. Jobs had little choice but to make the swap: In return for a renewal of Applesoft BASIC, Jobs agreed to deep-six MacBASIC and turn the program over to Microsoft, which later incorporated some of Denman's code into its own version. Nobody bothered to tell Donn Denman—at least not Steve Jobs, whom Gates, despite his own shortcomings in the bad-news messenger department, would describe as "a chickenshit guy" for avoiding the situation. In a reprise of the Klunder-Excel incident, Denman got the word when a writer working on the program's tutorial manual called to tell him that the book had been dropped because there would no longer be a program to go with it. Denman, who felt as if his two-year-old baby had been torn from his arms, jumped on his motorcycle and headed for the hills. Coming back down he took a turn too fast and wiped out. The bike and its rider were scraped up, but not as much as Denman's pride.

The MacBASIC horsetrade also sent shivers through the rest of the Mac team, which had always held lofty notions about controlling its own destiny. Even so, some Apple insiders felt their side got the best of a something-for-nothing deal. BASIC was absolutely crucial to the Apple II; on the Macintosh, it was little more than a toy. "If you ask me, that's one where Bill Gates got snookered," former Apple executive Guy Kawasaki opined. Bill Gates would concur: In his view, it was "one of the stupidest deals I have ever done."

And it was Gates whose reputation absorbed the worst damage from the swap session. Nobody would make it official, but word got around that Gates had driven the deal with a threat—as Gates snidely put it, "Later to be printed in the [Wall Street] *Journal* as I threatened to cut off Apple BASIC—similar to if you don't pay for your subscription, they threaten not to deliver it. How capitalism works. My BASIC I threatened!"

In an early instance of what came to be called "Bill-bashing," rumblings of "ruthlessness" and "blackmail" began to emanate from the Mac's Bandley 3 headquarters whenever Bill's name was mentioned. "He insisted that Apple withdraw what was an exceptional product,'' Apple Macintosh braintruster Bill Atkinson told the *Wall Street Journal*. ''He held a gun to our head.'' Deservedly or not, Gates and Microsoft had become the enemy.

And on September 17, so had Steve Jobs. On that day, Jobs resigned, taking five of Apple's top people with him to start a new venture. Six days later the company sued him. It was a portent of things to come for Bill Gates.

20

SLOW BURN

IBM finally got back to Bill Gates. Despite their general unhappiness over the delays in DOS 3.0 and the networking software, the Boca folks were still willing to consider future versions of DOS, particularly versions that would show off their new machines. By the end of 1984, a task force commissioned by IBM's Bob Markell, vice president of software and communications products for IBM's Entry Systems Division, had finally tossed all the contenders into the ring and decided what to do about them. For openers, Bill's DOS 6 UNIX clone was lopped off the charts; IBM's Boca group had divined correctly that it was mostly smoke. XENIX was out too. IBM would continue to offer it in a halfhearted way but would not develop it further.

That was okay with Gates. XENIX wasn't doing all that well in the marketplace anyhow, and it was sucking up more programmer resources than DOS. Worse, it carried one piece of baggage that was the ultimate sin in the eyes of Bill Gates: He had to pay a royalty to AT&T for every single copy.

After breakup and deregulation, AT&T was now selling its own flavors of UNIX competitively, and, according to Gates, "had reset the [pricing] curve on the next version on us." So at a Microsoft retreat in 1984, it became clear to just about everyone that XENIX was not the product that would propel the company into the future—DOS was, with Windows in the wings. Eventually Microsoft gave most of the XENIX work to a California UNIX shop called the Santa Cruz Operation (SCO).

Microsoft's XENIX wizard, Gordon Letwin, went to work on the multitasking version of DOS. Known at the time as DOS 4, the project had been plodding along at Microsoft since early in 1983 under First Employee Marc McDonald. Taming all the "ill-behaved" programs that snuck "under" DOS for greater speed was a challenge, but McDonald had managed to get a DOS 4 prototype up and running by the end of the year. With Letwin's arrival, the project headed in a different direction not unlike that of IBM's Pinta: an all-new operating system that could take advantage of the 286 chip's "protected mode," allowing access to vast stores of memory and helping ensure that one program couldn't step on the toes of another. By using some wizardry that Microsoft would later patent, that same operating system would cleverly be able to multitask in "real mode," meaning it would work on old 8088 and 8086 machines too. The catch: New from the ground up, this operating system wouldn't run old DOS programs. But in theory it would be so simple to convert those programs that everybody would do it, and customers could get their improved-OS versions of 1-2-3 or MultiMate or whatever as upgrades.

IBM was still working on its own all-new operating system, CP-DOS. As design team leader Ed Iacobucci later observed, a sizable faction at IBM urged saying "the hell with Microsoft," but in the end, Boca proposed a merger of its CP-DOS ideas with Letwin's multitasking DOS efforts. Letwin and colleague Anthony Short soon found themselves in a huge conference room in Boca as forty IBMers shot random questions at them about everything from minute technical issues to what the manual would look like. Iacobucci, fresh from IBM's defunct XENIX group, took one look and decreed that henceforth all design meetings would be four on four. Months of small-group sessions followed—a feasibility study to see if IBM and Microsoft could make a go of this. Conclusion: They could and would. There was just one ominous joker in the deck: IBM insisted on calling the project CP-DOS.

Bill Gates kept pushing for two things: integration of networking, something the Microsofties had little experience with, and integration of Windows, which they had more than enough experience with. IBM was vaguely interested in the networking idea but remained utterly skeptical about the still-unborn Windows.

At least that "death project" was beginning to show stirrings of life. Bill Gates and Steve Ballmer insisted to product manager Tandy Trower that this could be a great product: Just apply your skills, see what you can do, and figure out how to sell it at retail now that the OEM customers had mostly jumped ship.

One idea that immediately occurred to Trower when he arrived in January 1985 was to change the windowing system from tiled back to overlapping. Don't monkey with that, he was told; just get the thing out the door by the end of the year—*this* year.

At the time, there was no software for Windows. But every Mac came bundled with MacWrite and MacPaint right in the box, along with Clock, Puzzle, Notepad, and a utility program called Control Panel. So Trower took the hint. Write, an elementary WYSIWYG word processor cannibalized from the code for Mac Word, had originally been intended as a separate product, but Trower took it under his wing to bundle with Windows. The same thing happened with Paint, a basic free-form graphics program. Then came a rudimentary calendar, a clock, a game, a control panel. You could almost hear the chairman saying "All I want is Mac on the PC." According to Gates, when Steve Jobs saw the Windows Puzzle, "he said that was another thing he was pissed off about. But I said, 'Hey, it's in color!' " The Puzzle never made it out the door; a game called Reversi did.

The Mac did not have cursor keys. Steve Jobs was a purist: If you wanted to move the cursor, you had to move the mouse. But the pragmatic Gates pushed hard for keyboard equivalents. There were people in odd places—manufacturing plants, army combat zones—where a mouse might be inappropriate. And plenty of customers, DEC among them, just plain didn't think mice were the animals of the future. Besides, Gates realized, "mice weren't selling very well."

So Bill insisted that "this thing has got to have a keyboard interface. And we said, 'No, no, no!' Because we were idiots, we were Apple bigots, a lot of us," Konzen admitted. "The other reason we were against it—we being pretty much everybody in Windows—was that it was going to be hell." Despite what Konzen called "this wrench thrown at us," Gates prevailed, causing no end of programming grief in a project that was already insanely late and not insanely great. But, Konzen later said, Bill "was totally right."

The other issue was the ability to run "ill-behaved" DOS applications—in other words, most of them. For help with that, Microsoft swiped a concept from IBM: Program Information Files (PIF). PIFs had been developed for TopView to let the program understand quirks of various DOS applications. Microsoft's adaptation of PIFs would remain long after TopView had withered and died.

And then there were dozens of other questions to resolve, as Gates, the hands-on chairman, would ruefully recall years later:

> Things like getting fifty-nine printer drivers done, and the vendor out in Massachusetts isn't getting them done: Now we're talking! Making this thing fit into a small system: Now we're talking! . . . All the features that the Word guys wanted to do in an advanced word processor. Should we do the Kanji version in the first version?
>
> What about the differences in hardware, because IBM compatibility is becoming popular? . . . What about the fact that these character sets are different? DEC has a different character set from IBM, which is different from ANSI: What are we gonna do about these goddamn character sets?
>
> Should we do the font metrics the same way as Apple? . . . That's typographically completely stupid, but people know the way Apple does it. Should we do it that weird way? . . .
>
> And people can argue and argue about this—not "argue," that's not the right word—but there's just so many decisions to be made.

And even if VisiOn was gone, Windows wasn't the only graphical user interface on the market. Microsoft's hapless nemesis, Digital Research, was finally getting ready to ship GEM, a product that had become a virtual dead ringer for the Macintosh. Graphics guru Lee Lorenzen, DR's requisite Man From PARC, had put GEM together so it could emulate Windows, VisiOn, Lisa—whichever windowing system might eventually "win." When the Mac came out, the battle was over. DR's Darrell Miller took his wife to an early demo of the Mac, and "Her eyes got big and round, and she hates computers." Miller knew what it meant: "If the Macintosh gets that kind of reaction out of her, this is powerful." The next day he told Lorenzen to go for the Mac: "We copied it exactly."

Actually, they could copy only the look. They had intended to clone the Mac's internals too, for a real "Mac on the PC," but someone in DR's languages group had signed an Apple nondisclosure agreement that virtually guaranteed litigation if they tried it. The look would have to do.

Steve Jobs and John Sculley saw a demo of GEM at Fall Comdex in 1984. "You did a great job! I can't believe this thing is running on a floppy!" Jobs told Miller. DR had signed up a moderately impressive list of OEMs for the program. Pointedly noting that unlike Microsoft, it didn't sell applications of its own, DR had even lined up a dozen independent developers to create software that ran under GEM.

DR was also working on a potential CP-DOS killer called Concurrent DOS 86, which promised to multitask DOS applications on 286-based machines. Though bugs in early versions of the 286 chip would send Concurrent DOS to the same watery grave as IBM's Mermaid, DR insiders believed IBM was on the verge of signing up for their advanced operating system and graphical interface.

Microsoft was not standing idly by. Word leaked out to the industry that a multitasking DOS 4.0 was on its way. And in July something called the "premiere edition" of Windows, more or less a beta-test version, went out to software developers, OEM customers, and selected members of the press so at least they could play around with it and Microsoft could crow that it had finally shipped something—anything!—called Windows. In Neil Konzen's humble estimation, "It was just a bag and we knew it, but we wanted to get it out and we wanted people to see this. . . . And then we put in the real work and a couple of months getting it all to work."

Down in Pacific Grove, Kildall and Company could name this tune in three notes. CP/M-86 gets preempted by MS-DOS 1.0. Concurrent DOS 86 gets preempted by DOS 4.0. GEM gets preempted by Windows.

And then, in a single magic moment, the GEM diamond briefly turned to coal. In the summer of 1985, Apple took DR out to the woodshed, where, as Apple attorney Irv Rappaport put it, DR was told "in excruciating detail what we see as the similarities" between it and the Mac. When it returned in

September, GEM had changed. Most obvious: No more trash can icon. Less obvious: Some menu alterations. GEM still looked a lot like the Mac, but Apple had made its point—a point it would one day take up with DR's good friends in Bellevue, Washington.

At IBM, the personal computer effort was undergoing a sea change, symbolized by the ouster of Don Estridge and his succession by his original patron, Bill Lowe, an IBM lifer who looked and spoke like Walter Mondale. Estridge had brilliantly masterminded the initial release of the PC and its follow-on XT, but he was seen as having screwed up twice: first with the disastrous PCjr and now with the PC AT's defective hard disks. For IBM, that was one screwup too many, particularly from an engineer who had successfully challenged corporate convention to the point where he had developed something of a Gates-like personality cult within the company and the industry. In March Estridge was shunted off to a new position as vice president of manufacturing. By August he would be dead along with 129 others in a tragic Delta Airlines crash in Dallas.

What Bill Lowe found when he took over the reins was grim: Other than the feckless XENIX, there was still no operating system that could take advantage of the AT's protected-mode architecture and address lots of memory. The IBM-Microsoft feasibility studies for a new DOS were still underway.

TopView had just been released to overwhelming yawns, but Microsoft still viewed it as a threat. In May an *InfoWorld* cartoon depicted gunslinger Bill Lowe aiming a gun called TopView at a cowboy named Bill Gates. Bellevue's master of opportunism used it as an opening to meet with Lowe and cement the deal for a new DOS.

IBM was still chafing under the restrictions of the original DOS contract, which made the company liable without limitation for damages if somehow the DOS source code got out to third parties. "That was very bad," Ballmer said. "They didn't like that we might sue them for fifty billion dollars. That didn't feel right."

Lowe agreed: "We had such a large business that was dependent upon that operating system, we felt uncomfortable not having a legal right to the source code."

Gates, Ballmer, and Shirley met with Lowe, vice president of programming Dick Hanrahan, and other IBMers to hammer out a momentous deal known as the Joint Development Agreement (JDA). The pact was signed on June 10 but not announced until August 22; according to Gates, the delay was to make sure Microsoft could explain the delicate situation to its other customers. "In a sense, a hardware manufacturer in the kitchen—it's dirty pool. What is Compaq supposed to think?" Gates had little trouble convincing the other customers that the new DOS, now dubbed DOS 5 at Microsoft, would be no less open and available than the old one. It would be the original DOS strategy all over again: Sell it to IBM, then sell it to everybody else.

Set up on a two-year basis with options to renew, the JDA eliminated IBM's DOS source code worries. It also went much farther, describing a new business relationship between the two companies, specifying generally what would happen in various situations. There would be IBM code, there would be Microsoft code, there would be joint code, and how it could be marketed would differ in each case. Would IBM be able to sell Microsoft's programming tools—its assembler and compiler? Would Microsoft be able to use IBM's compilers but not sell them? The JDA spelled it all out.

Yet to some at Microsoft, the JDA was only "a framework," "a set of namby-pamby documents." The details for individual cases would appear in what were known as Phase One and Phase Two documents. And Phase Two Document One, signed concurrently with the JDA, spelled out the specifics of the deal for the new multitasking DOS. This time there were royalties involved and substantial amounts of cash. Bill Gates called it "by far the biggest contract we've ever signed."

For a graphical user interface, Gates was selling Windows. IBM wasn't buying. "Bill is a determined individual. I don't think I ever had a session with him when he didn't bring up Windows," Bob Markell recalled. Markell thought Windows was improving slowly, but he was already saddled with TopView. "I already have one failure," he would tell Bill. "Why do I want to put out another?"

The announcement of the JDA swiftly put an end to all the rumors of a Microsoft-IBM rift. With speculation rampant about Microsoft going public and its initial public offering (IPO) already under intense discussion internally, it didn't hurt to have a public vote of confidence from Microsoft's number-one customer.

But when it came to Windows, not even picking up the tab for a sumptuous dinner at the La Reserve Hotel in White Plains could sway the men in blue. IBM's software leaders, mainframers down to their toes, put little stock in the need for graphical user interfaces. For years computer users had done just fine with monospaced characters on green screens, thank you, and now they were working the same way with DOS. If they needed windows, TopView's character-based windows would do just fine. Why slow down development with this graphical stuff?

Yet TopView was going virtually nowhere. By fall IBM had started giving away free copies with some of its hard-disk-based machines. Except in a few true-Blue corporate circles where companies were putting together their own systems, TopView was recognized as a clunker, and independent software developers were giving it a wide berth.

Microsoft wasn't making many new friends with Windows either. "Competing with Bill Gates is like putting your head in a vise and turning the handle. He doesn't take no for an answer, and he keeps coming back," said Mitch

Kapor of Lotus, who was beginning to believe that "Windows was not a serious product" and that he had originally endorsed it only because he "couldn't resist Bill's hypnotic will and didn't have the character to shut the door." Complaints were also cropping up about the way the Bellevue warlords were leveraging Windows. Microsoft actually told some independent developers that if they refused to provide information on their Windows products—business plans, pricing, distribution, and release dates—they would not receive support.

As far back as 1983, Ballmer had stated that "We have shown in the past that there is a very clean separation between our operating system business and our applications software. It's like the separation between church and state. And if you don't play it straight, you can't expect to get the business." But except for Ballmer's favorite phrase, "Get the business," it was hard to swallow. There had been no formal division between systems and apps until mid-1984. For the last half of that year, Bill Gates personally headed up Microsoft's applications efforts, with his best friend Ballmer as head of systems. If it was church and state, the government seemed to be showing up regularly at the confession box.

Besides, "Microsoft kept changing the product substantially," recalled independent Windows developer George Grayson. "That was the story from Day One: People who, like Lotus and others, said they were going to support [Windows] started writing code. And Microsoft sent us all a letter and said, 'Sorry. We decided to start over. We've taken the wrong approach, so everything you've done you need to trash and start over.' "

So almost no one was betting on Windows. The one true believer was a little outfit down in Richardson, Texas, known as Micrografx, which had been selling a program called PC Draw. Back in 1984, at a Windows developers' conference in downtown Seattle, brothers Paul and George Grayson waylaid Bill Gates in a hallway and "sort of grabbed him and held onto him and said . . . we want to do a drawing program for Windows and we don't want you to." Gates was looking for a free-form paint program, he said, but when the Graysons expressed no interest in doing one, he said, "Well, I guess that's okay. I'll do the paint program and if you guys do a good drawing program, I won't have to do one." On the way back home, in a Dallas nightclub, the Graysons met and recruited a fellow programmer named Lyle Griffin. He would eventually become the world's first Windows developer outside the halls of Microsoft.

Yet the computer world was hardly clamoring for graphical user interfaces, and if you wanted one there was always the Mac. The immediate problem, the one everybody worried about, was memory. The big, memory-hungry programs that Bill had predicted in the initial days of the IBM PC were here, and now they were straining at the bounds of the PC's 640K memory limit. To get beyond it, Intel had come up with a standard first called Above Board and later the Expanded Memory Specification (EMS), but it was an obvious hack, a short-term solution. In its initial form, the standard wouldn't do much but permit bigger 1-2-3 spreadsheets—which was enough to get Lotus to sign up. At the time it was unclear what advantage Microsoft might derive from this scheme, but Mitch Kapor got Bill Gates to agree at least not to stomp on it. After some jockeying for position, Gates gave the scheme this ringing endorsement: "It's garbage! It's a kludge! . . . But we're going to do it." That was enough to ensure that the spec would become known as LIM—for Lotus, Intel, and Microsoft—and eventually help Windows overcome some of its severe memory problems.

IBM ignored this stopgap measure. How could it possibly compete with the new operating system that could handle all 16 megabytes of memory that you could throw into a PC AT and multitask besides? CP-DOS was going to be something that, as Bill Lowe said with wild IBM hyperbole, you could "become accustomed to."

▼ After its initial flash of lightning, the Macintosh had fallen on hard times in the marketplace, thunking along at 20,000 units a month in 1985—frighteningly below the early forecasts of 80,000 to 100,000 units a month, as Apple endured its worst year ever. Bill Gates had a remedy for that. In a position paper dated June 25, 1985, he and his lieutenant Jeff Raikes, formerly of Apple, made a startling proposition to Sculley and his redoubtable marketing guru, Jean-Louis Gassée. If Apple would consider licensing its technology to outside vendors, Microsoft would help convince them about the wonders of the Mac. Gates had in mind such companies as AT&T, Sony, Kyocera, Texas Instruments, Digital Equipment, Xerox, Hewlett-Packard—in short, all the heavy hitters of computer hardware except the one with three initials. It would help, of course, that they were all Microsoft customers.

A month later Gates followed up with a letter to Sculley focusing on three hot prospects for Mac technology: Northern Telecom, a "first-class" Canadian company; Motorola, chipmaker for the Macintosh ("They aren't doing well. Their direct sales force is good but not so large that it will threaten the retail channel"); and AT&T, whose 68000-based UNIX PC was "not selling." Gates even offered friendly advice about sales strategy: AT&T, for example, would "try to confuse things by trying to involve UNIX in the discussion."

The letter went on to suggest a detente with DOS. "We recently sent Chris Larson down to discuss making your 3.5-inch disk compatible with MS-DOS. Unfortunately the people he talked to didn't agree with us on the importance." But then, in Bill's eyes, IBM wasn't a land of princes either: "Ironically, IBM is viewed as being a technological innovator. This is because compatible manufacturers are afraid to innovate too much and stray from the standard.''

Perhaps a shade too obviously this time, Gates was once again working both sides of the street, not to mention the sidewalk and the center divider. If the Mac interface was licensed to other vendors, Gates could sell his incredibly successful Mac applications on their machines. If you could read DOS disks on a Mac—which would actually happen years later—you could swap data between Microsoft's Mac applications and the versions Gates intended to develop for Windows. And there was another angle, an acute one in light of the unpleasantness over GEM: If Apple licensed Mac technology to the world at large, perhaps it would license it to Microsoft as well.

No dice. In fact, Apple's lawyers were ready to tackle the big fish of Puget Sound. Written all over Windows was the influence of Neil Konzen, the maverick programmer who had been so closely involved with development of the Mac apps for Microsoft. Much of Konzen's work was recognizable by a superficial glance at the screen. Gone was the unwieldy Multi-Tool interface, with its ugly pick-and-click menus. In its place was a Mac-like top-of-screen command bar with Mac-like pull-down menus. And then there were the additions Trower had pushed for—the Mac-like Calculator, Mac-like Control Panel, Mac-like icons. About all that was missing was a Mac-like trash can.

The way Apple's attorneys saw it, that kind of cross-pollination wasn't supposed to happen—not, at least, under their interpretation of the still-standing confidentiality agreement Gates had signed with Jobs. In the Apple view, Gates had violated the confidentiality agreement and competed unfairly. No way, Chairman Bill retorted. Hadn't he demoed Windows the previous fall in Cupertino? Hadn't he gone out of his way to supervise the Mac development effort and make sure Microsoft used only visual displays ''that we had created or otherwise had the right to use''? At no time had Apple given him ''reason to believe that Apple considered any of our Windows visual display technology to infringe any Apple copyright.'' His company had never even seen the Mac's source code, Gates told Apple attorneys Al Eisenstat and Jack Brown at a mid-October meeting at Microsoft. ''That was news to them,'' Gates observed. '' 'I've tried more trade secret lawsuits than any lawyer in this country, and I sure haven't lost many,' '' he recalled Brown saying.

Times had changed from the blow up and blow over days of Jobs. Ex-Pepsi guy Sculley was not long removed from the cola wars, where secret ingredients were guarded like the Hope diamond. No less a Microsoft light than Jon Shirley had stressed in public that the new, improved Windows looked remarkably like the Mac. The message Apple delivered via its lawyers was the same one it had handed to Digital Research: Change the offending stuff or defend it in court.

After the Brown-Eisenstat session, Gates called Sculley, demanding to know what was going on. Microsoft was set to release Windows 1.01 in a few weeks, a mere two years after first ballyhooing it at the Plaza. If Apple was going to sue, Gates said, it had better tell him now. Sculley acknowledged "problems" and said the company was ready to take action to protect its technology. Gates found that too noncommittal: Call off the hounds, he told Sculley, or I'll stop development on Macintosh products.

"I hope we can find a way to settle this thing," Gates said, emphasizing the Mac's importance to Microsoft. Sculley was noncommittal, saying Apple intended to do whatever was necessary to protect its technology. The two set a meeting for the following week in Cupertino—just four days before Bill would turn thirty.

From a technical standpoint, Sculley was no Smart Guy. But Sculley did know marketing. He was the guy who as company president had spearheaded the "Pepsi Challenge," the famous TV commercial series where blindfolded middle Americans discovered they liked Pepsi better than Coke. He knew that people would continue to buy the Macintosh only if they perceived it was better. If Windows and every other graphical interface that ever saw the light of a screen ended up looking like the Macintosh, people wouldn't be able to tell the difference.

Before meeting with Gates, Sculley polled his inner circle. The consensus: Stand up to the guy, he's bluffing, we need to safeguard the family jewels. Seeing the Mac market as easy pickings for new applications dominance, Microsoft wouldn't dare pull its software off the shelves. But the Gator had the better hand: He could do without Apple; it was unclear whether Apple could do without him.

Sculley promised to "represent Apple's best interests," but told his team, "I'm not ready to bloody the company." The only bloodshed was of the piscine variety: "They ordered sushi for thirty people and two of us show up, and the sushi is just sitting there," Gates recalled. "Nobody ever eats it, it's just sitting there in this huge fancy conference room." Luxurious conference rooms, food going to waste: To Gates they symbolized the kind of "decadence," like flying first class, that Apple indulged in all the time and Microsoft fastidiously avoided.

Sculley was conciliatory. As Gates recalled it, Sculley told him, "What I'm really asking for, Bill, is a good relationship." What that meant was an agreement from Microsoft to hold off shipping a Windows version of Excel for a while, giving the Mac version a chance in the business community. "I'm glad to give you the rights to this stuff," Sculley said. He and Eisenstat and Gates and Neukom worked out a compromise that would enable Microsoft to use Mac technology in Windows. Exactly how much technology and what it could be used for awaited formal documentation. Happy birthday, thirty-year-old!

The 1985 Halloween/birthday celebration was particularly notable: Windows was two years old and almost potty-trained, the company was ten and about to go public, Bill was thirty and about to become a gazillionaire. The Apple lawyers were breathing down his neck, but hey, the situation was in hand. It was time to party! At the Kamber warehouse, employees gathered for a tribute to Golden Gates, presenting him with a mockup of the *Time* cover with *Bill* in place of the logo and the headline, "Microsoft Releases Gates 30.0." After a round of jokes from some of the Smart Guys, Bill stepped up to address the gathering. Although most of his message was positive—"I have to say that reaching thirty for me is really exciting because working with the people here I've had a chance to do all the things I've wanted to do"—the pessimist within Gates could not quite contain himself. "I'm hoping that my thirtieth year is not as exciting as it has been for Steve Jobs"—who had just been sued by Apple. The party moved to a Bellevue roller rink, where Bill showed up as Jay Gatsby.

Two weeks later Apple attorney Irving Rappaport sent Microsoft a proposed draft agreement, granting Microsoft a nonexclusive, worldwide, and nontransferable license to Lisa and Mac technology for use in Windows, as long as Microsoft made a number of alterations to the interface to make it less Mac-like and prominently displayed a notice reading "Copyright 1981–1985 Apple Computer, Inc." on startup of Windows and sublicensed products. In effect, that would be free advertising for the Mac on every competitive Windows machine, not to mention an admission that Microsoft was not the innovator it claimed to be. If the changes were made, Microsoft could develop additional applications for Windows under the agreement after November 1, 1986, but "at no time shall this grant extend to any appearance, look, feel, visual feature or operation other than that incorporated in Microsoft Windows as it shall exist after completion of the changes set forth."

Gates was appalled. What was this "look and feel" garbage? "It didn't give us what we needed," he recalled. "It was just baloney." Gates rejected the draft in part "because that draft does actually have an attempt to constrain our activities to be no more Mac-like. . . . And we completely and explicitly and in a documented fashion reject the notion that that's a meaningful or livable concept."

Neukom and Gates hammered out a revised draft in less than a week. Gone was the startup copyright notice. Instead Microsoft would privately acknowledge that its Mac applications (Plan, Chart, File, Excel, Word) and Windows were "derivative works of the visual displays generated by Apple's Lisa and Macintosh." Gates also agreed to revise Windows, change the Paint and Terminal programs by August 31, 1986, and delay the release of Excel for Windows until October 1, 1986. And he would commit to deliver a new version of Mac Word by July 31, 1986.

End of Round Two. Back in Cupertino, Rappaport wanted to add a few more tiny wrinkles—at least, they seemed tiny at the time. In a memo to Apple attorney Edwin Taylor, he stated the license as drafted by Microsoft was "broader than we intend; we intend to license only their current version of Windows." Taylor changed the key mentions of Windows in the agreement to read "Windows Version 1.0" and later told Neukom that he did not want Microsoft to change future versions of Windows to appear more like the Macintosh. But Neukom later said of Taylor's request, "It was not something Microsoft thought of doing [or] agreeing to."

On November 20 Neukom flew to Cupertino to meet with Eisenstat and go over the Microsoft draft. The same day in Las Vegas, Microsoft announced at Comdex that it was shipping Windows to dealers and distributors, and issued a press release stating that Windows had been licensed by Apple under its visual copyrights.

Two days later Gates and Sculley signed the final version of the three-page agreement, which granted Microsoft a "non-exclusive, worldwide, royalty-free, perpetual, nontransferable license to use these derivative works in present and future software programs, and to license them to and through third parties for use in their software programs." No further alterations to Windows were required.

On Sunday, November 24, 1985, at 5:37 P.M., workaholic Bill Gates was at his computer, excitedly pounding out electronic mail on the deal. Microsoft, Gates wrote to eleven corporate bigwigs, had "received a release from Apple for any possible copyright, trade secret or patent issues relation [sic] to our products including Windows." Microsoft did not have rights to specific Mac applications, Gates noted, "so we have to be careful not to take additional things from Apple screens when we make enhancements." However, "everything we do today is fine."

The arrangement would be kept confidential, and no press release would be issued. "Although we put a lot of time into this agreement, there was never any danger of this becoming a major issue because of our strong legal position," he added. "However it is nice to have it totally behind us." Totally behind him? Although Steve Jobs was out of the picture, a reality distortion field remained.

Yet at first the deal looked like one more example of the golden Gates touch. Apple seemed to have turned over the keys to its kingdom, yet all it got was a Word upgrade, an Excel delay, and an acknowledgment that Windows and related applications were visually indebted to the Macintosh. Microsoft was going to come out with an upgraded version of Word whether it signed an agreement with Apple or not: It was just good business, and Microsoft was bent on sinking MacWrite. And Gates knew it was unlikely that Excel for Windows would ship before October 1, 1986, agreement or no. The October date, he stated in the e-mail, "is not a problem for us since we can announce, test, give to particular customers, etc., before that date." But it was also not a problem because the product probably wouldn't be ready before then anyway: "We will be doing everything to make" the October date, he wrote, "and I believe we can make that." In fact, Excel for Windows would not ship until late October 1987, more than a full year after the agreed-to "postponement." Gates was giving up nothing, it seemed, to get everything.

But Sculley remained convinced that the agreement, as he later observed, "protected the integrity of our Macintosh technology" at a time when "if we sued our most important software customer, our business customers would think we'd lost our minds." Excel was going to be a strategic product for the Macintosh as Sculley repositioned the machine to attract the crucial business market. When Sculley soon afterward told Gates of his 50-50-50 plan for the Mac—50,000 units a month sold, 50 percent gross margins, and a stock price over $50, Bill Gates actually smiled. "I think that may work," he said.

The signing of the Apple agreement was not the only joyful Las Vegas event. An industry columnist had said that Windows would ship when pigs had wings, and the Windows developers had hung toy pigs from their ceilings in the last-minute crunch. Microsoft had finally shoved Windows out the door, primarily as a retail package listing for $99. But the company was using the term "slow burn" as its mantra, hinting strongly that the product wouldn't set the world on fire.

In honor of finally getting the product out, Microsoft sponsored the "Windows Roast," a little bit of decadence of its own. Media and opinionmakers were invited, even paraded, to the dais, in the hope they'd somehow forgive Windows for being two years late. It was another masterful PR stroke from Pam Edstrom and company. How do you keep someone else from making fun of you? Make fun of yourself first.

With buckets of dry ice onstage doing a poor job of simulating vapor, Gates and Ballmer were in form unseen since their Harvard Fox Club days. Joking about each other and Windows, dishing it out and taking it, the two offered up an unusually self-mocking tribute to Microsoft's own ineptitude. Industry gadfly Stewart Alsop presented Gates with the Golden Vaporware Award. Columnist John C. Dvorak, hired by Microsoft to emcee the event, observed that when Windows was first announced, Ballmer still had hair. Gates joked that Ballmer had kept insisting "we just gotta cut features. He came up with this idea that we could rename this thing Microsoft Window, and we would have shipped that thing a long time ago."

Ballmer took the mike to recount how the program had grown from a single diskette and six man-years to five floppies and eighty man-years—"so they moved me into a new job!" At one point Gates, having discovered yet another bug, supposedly threatened to fire him unless the project shaped up. "He starts screaming at me—this is like Bill's ninety-ninth Windows bug he had discovered—and I tried to explain to him, hey, Bill . . . most people don't hit the A, D, G, K, and S keys simultaneously at two in the afternoon." Gates told him, "Ship this thing before the snow falls, or you'll end your career here doing Windows!" Snow seldom fell in rainy Bellevue, and Gates would later call the firing threat a joke, something he would never think of doing to the man he considered his best friend. But it made almost as good a story as the McGovern buttons. For a climax Gates and Ballmer duetted on "The Impossible Dream."

Missing was OEM sales chief Jim Harris, who around the office twitted Ballmer by pointing out that some of the contracts for Windows had expired before the product shipped, but never mind. Microsoft preemption struck pay dirt again, and Windows got a tremendous amount of favorable early press. *InfoWorld* trumpeted "Windows Arrives: The Wait is Over." *PC Magazine* called the program "impressive," its price/performance ratio "remarkable." Only later, after fuller tests, would more reasoned judgments be rendered: *InfoWorld*'s reviewer decreed a "poor" rating on performance, decried a lack of support for all but the most common printers, and declared the product worth a mere 4.5 points out of a possible ten. Microsoft's product support woman, the reviewer pointed out, "was knowledgeable about the program and aware of its shortcomings." A few months later Microsoft would tacitly admit Windows was too slow for PC and XT machines by releasing yet another of its hardware-to-leverage-software products, the Mach 10 speedup board, but even that hardware was too lethargic to give Windows the oomph it needed.

And even if it did run fast enough, there was another crucial question: Where would you find software to run on it? Microsoft's own Windows projects—Excel, Cashmere, a database called Omega—were nowhere near ready, and neither was anything else. Aside from the mini-applications included with the product, there was Micrografx's In*A*Vision, a professional design program that had actually shipped before Windows by including an early, cut-down, "run-time" version of it in the box. And that was all.

Steve Ballmer told Paul and George Grayson that Bill Gates was upset about In*A*Vision. What happened to the low-end Draw program Micrografx had promised? The Graysons replied that people weren't exactly buying Windows in droves, that they needed to be motivated by a high-end application. Ballmer disagreed, thought a mass-market Draw program would sell. "We said, okay, we're tapped out. We've put everything into In*A*Vision. If you really want us to do that, you're going to have to help us," Grayson recalled. "And they said okay and made some promises that they didn't keep but they also did some things they did keep. Steve Ballmer told me he'd buy 4,000 copies of Windows Draw, he'd guarantee a purchase order for us. They never bought one. They also did, though, lend us $100,000 to cover the marketing expenses . . . on very favorable terms." And Microsoft agreed to adapt and market the product abroad for three years, and did so successfully.

One way or another, Gates knew, applications would come. One way or another, Windows would improve. What Windows needed now was a boost from computerdom's biggest player. And in the middle of Microsoft's big Windows shipping party—another little smattering of decadence—Windows gurus Neil Konzen and Steve Wood (a different Steve Wood, a Lakeside and Yale graduate who had joined Microsoft in 1983) were called away to meet with IBM. IBM was beginning to get interested in Windows after all, particularly if Microsoft could somehow meld it with—the programmers from Bellevue had to suppress their giggles—TopView.

If there was one place on earth that programmers knew about TopView compatibility, it was Santa Monica, California, at the headquarters of tiny Quarterdeck, which had undergone a revival of sorts. Staring bankruptcy in the face, the company had frantically rewritten its DESQ program to be TopView-compatible and renamed it DESQview to reflect the change.

Enter Gates and Ballmer. Shortly before Christmas the two visited Quarterdeck with an eye toward purchasing the company and its TopView-knowledgeable software engineers. "They met all the technical team," recalled Therese Myers, Quarterdeck's president. "They were buying people; they did not want the product."

An offer for $3 million was made and accepted with handshakes. Marketing director Stanton Kaye, a former wunderkind of experimental filmmaking who had become wise in the ways of the software business, asked the visitors to sign a simple document: If for some reason the deal fell through, Microsoft would agree not to hire Quarterdeck's people away. With that formality completed, Kaye invited the Washingtonians to the company Christmas party. Bill danced, Bill drank, Bill held court. A good time was had.

Next morning, Myers got the bad news: Gates and Ballmer had decided the price was too high. Myers said thanks; no deal. Bill Gates and Steve Ballmer would have to look elsewhere for TopView compatibility. Not that they really wanted it in the first place, but when it came to IBM, you had to get the business, get the business, get the business.

21

▶

SHARK FRENZY

"Bill Gates is the leader of the parade," said one industry veteran, "because he sees where the parade is going and gets in front of it." But Gates had been leading one parade longer than anyone else: the campaign against software piracy. Bitterly remembering his initial experience with BASIC, Gates was not about to get screwed again. In the OEM market, where the deals were still mostly flat fee or per machine, illicit copying wasn't an issue. In the retail software business, Gates saw copying as a major problem.

Which, depending on how you looked at it, it was. As more and more computers appeared on people's desks, more and more people needed software, and copying a disk was easier and faster than copying an audio or video tape. Most software vendors simply looked the other way, reasoning that people who would stoop to filch their product wouldn't buy it no matter what. And copying could be viewed as a form of free advertising that could help make your software a de facto standard. After trying a bootleg, people might order an upgrade to get the latest version and the manual.

Still, copy protection was universal in the computer game business. Gordon Letwin's original copy-protection scheme for Adventure may have set a record for complexity: IBM demanded modifications when the company discovered it took twenty minutes to duplicate each disk. The sharing ethic among young gamers created a cottage industry of companies developing hardware and software to "break" copy-protection stratagems.

In the business world, copy protection was less common, and it caused no end of irritation. It turned the essential process of making security copies of master disks into an obstacle, annoyed hard-disk users, and outraged honest citizens who disliked being treated as thieves. Nonetheless Microsoft, VisiCorp, Lotus, and others used a variety of methods of copy protection, most involving clever modifications of the original disk that would deter average users but not clever programmers.

Firmly in the copy-protection camp, Gates joined Lotus's Mitch Kapor in May 1984 to announce a two-pronged industrywide attack on software piracy. Prong one would be an ad campaign "to raise public awareness that software piracy is not littering, it's stealing"—just as Bill had insisted back in 1976. Prong two would be the idea Gates had struck out on during the development of the PC: convincing hardware manufacturers to get behind a device that contained an electronic serial number and plugged into a standard port. Gates hoped computer makers might build the code into every machine—though he grudgingly admitted "Manufacturers, as with all standards, will say, 'Why should we add even a dime to our cost?' " The ad campaign eventually got off the ground; except in very special situations, the hardware didn't.

So disk-based copy protection bumped along at Microsoft, to the great irritation of users. And worse: Late in 1985, Sheldon Richman of the *Washington Times* reported that his brand-new copy of Microsoft Access had displayed a message that went something like this: "Internal security violation. The tree of evil bears bitter fruit; crime does not pay. The Shadow knows. Trashing program disk." What followed was a horrendous racket from the disk drive.

Spin control time: Microsoft's Jeff Raikes told the press that a programmer had slipped the "idle threat" into the program unbeknownst to his superiors and that it had been excised. End of story.

Well, not quite. Clever computerists suddenly began hunting for and finding such messages in most of their Microsoft applications—and revealing their discoveries to the press. "How can a $70 million company like Microsoft tolerate this idiocy?" *InfoWorld*'s John Dvorak fulminated. Years later developer Jeff Harbers would admit that the racket—harmless though scary—had been his design, a general feature of the applications copy-protection code that wasn't supposed to show up except when snoops and crackers ran debuggers to sneak a look at it. The message itself had been the work of a summer intern from Caltech.

In the face of a growing attack on copy protection in general and the company's version of it in particular, the incident was the beginning of the end of the practice with regard to Microsoft's domestic products. In November Raikes announced that protection had been removed from Access and Chart. By mid-1986 copy protection remained only on Flight Simulator, and eventually it disappeared even from that. Copy protection for Microsoft products persists to this day only in foreign markets where piracy runs rampant—although even in America, illicit copying is a software industry bugaboo. Microsoft remains one of the driving forces behind the Software Publishers Association, which plays a major role in antipiracy efforts—including raids on businesses suspected of using illicit copies.

With copy protection or without it, Microsoft's applications programs were beginning to take off. Virtually every Mac sold eventually ran either Excel or Word or both. On various platforms, Multiplan had become a leader abroad. PC Word, which offered support for laser printers from the beginning, got a big boost from a strategic alliance with Hewlett-Packard, which had begun delivering laser printers normal users could actually afford. Yet there were problem products, such as Access, a communications package that had been developed outside the halls of Microsoft but still had the typical Microsoft mix: tons of features and no speed at all. The Windows projects, Cashmere and Omega, were still in their larval stages, since it wasn't easy to develop for Windows under the best of circumstances, and not having the product was not the best of circumstances.

In February 1985 Ida Cole had replaced Bill himself as Microsoft's applications chief, becoming the first female vice president in Microsoft's history and heading up an increasingly important division on its way to a $50 million year. An outgoing, empathic people person who'd been a professional programmer when Bill was pounding the Teletypes at C-Cubed, Cole had nearly five years' managerial experience at Apple, which was known for its outrageous TV commercials, designer T-shirts, Friday afternoon pizza-and-beer blasts, and trips to exotic locales to celebrate product releases. When Cole left, Apple was going through one of its periodic psychodramas, but it was still the Silicon Valley version of the Merry Pranksters.

Microsoft was more like a northwestern Paul Bunyan. "It's a culture of work," Cole recalled. "Bill would hate it when the weather got good in Seattle. People would leave early. They weren't going to put in their twelve hours that day or sixteen hours that day." But the Pirates and just about everyone else at Apple worked long hours too. "The huge difference at Microsoft was nobody was having fun. People worked hard, all the smart, smart, smart people. But very few people were having any fun. They were grinding out the work."

Bill, Cole observed,

> cares so much, and his way of motivating of people is through shame and intimidation. And some people are motivated that way. I mean, all of us to a certain extent are motivated by shame and disgust. People lose weight before they go to their high school reunions, and before they have to get into a bathing suit for summer . . .
>
> It is motivating. But it's not motivating for all people in all situations. And that was in fact the only trick in the bag.

Bill's going nonlinear could be more theatrical than effective. "There was always all of this thunder, all of this confrontation and all of this yelling and all of this screaming going on. But in fact, it wasn't really followed up by what needed to happen in order to have the situation change." Gates had his inner circle, his personal favorites, and given his vaunted loyalty, it could be virtually impossible to dislodge them. Cole, "way past the age to sit at the feet of the master," never cracked that circle. When she threatened three people with dismissal, they ended up staying on. On Saturday mornings, "These guys would go in and they would have their relationship with Bill and it didn't seem to matter that they weren't doing the work."

It was a culture that came straight from the top. Gates was notorious for prowling the halls on Saturdays and Sundays and calling key people at home, asking "What's the matter? Why haven't I seen you around?" But the company was growing so fast that there was little time for training or traditional management. Gates's rule of sink or swim still applied: You were expected to learn your job and do it. If you didn't, find something else or take off.

"Ida said it very succinctly at the last meeting: Management cannot force you to work long hours, only YOU can do that," Charles Simonyi wrote in an April 1985 e-mail. "So why do otherwise intelligent people CHOOSE to come here at night and during the weekend?" Personal convenience, for one thing (if you happened to be a night owl); the bonus, for another. "We do reward outstanding contributions with a bonus. The most straightforward way to make an outstanding contribution is by working longer."

Then there was

the clincher. We live in a competitive world in a landscape littered with visible corpses. Do you think our schedules are tight? Too many features to write and test? Our competition will be happy to hear it. . . . If they work day and night and sleep under their desks, we may have to. I, for one, do not want to lose, not just because of pride, but also because it is very unpleasant.

The average age at Microsoft was something like twenty-six. In Cole's view, "It was kids at camp without adult supervision." Managers with technical know-how knew nothing about management; managers who knew how to manage "just got beat up" for not knowing the technology. Clerical workers were given no training; as one former employee put it, "sink or swim is fine if you're a genius, but not if you're an average Joe or Jill." Protocol was nonexistent; with a strict assurance of confidentiality, one employee complained about her boss to the personnel director—who told the boss anyway. Seven months' pregnant, the employee was fired, given a three-month pregnancy leave with salary and medical benefits, and told that if she fought the dismissal, both salary and benefits would be terminated immediately.

"There was a rule around the office," said Tandy Trower, "that you could not play games, because if Bill sees you playing games in your office, he'll get plenty mad." Yet the adolescent spirit often blossomed, especially among the software developers. One of the longer running jokes in Microsoft corporate history involved garishly colored ultra-bouncy balls that began mysteriously turning up in mailboxes, interoffice packages, equipment, desks.

Rumor had it that a Windows team member had purchased a railroad car full of the things and was distributing them as a sendup of the Mac's legendary bouncing icons demo. Then word got out that the powers that be, especially a bald-headed guy with the lungs of a moose, were trying to find out whodunit. While Ballmer was away on a weeklong business trip, an ad hoc team erected a large partition just behind his door and relight and filled the gap with bouncy balls. When Ballmer returned, it looked as though his office had been stuffed to the rafters with the very items he had been trying to ban from the premises. Ballmer's reaction could be heard in an office a hundred yards down the hall.

Ballmer's ultimate taboo, and Bill's, was developing software on your own. One developer who wrote Windows device drivers in his spare time at Microsoft and sold them to outside customers was roundly chastised, hounded by the legal department—and then told to finish one of the jobs because it was important to the acceptance of Windows. In later years, Microsoft's "Company Store" sold employees most software at bargain prices—typically less than $35. But to get a Software Development Kit required special authorization. Wasting time outside the office with your own projects was not something the company chose to encourage.

Gates took vacations, but they were widely spaced and never more than a week long. So why should anyone else expect more? Employees got just two weeks of vacation until they had put in five years of service, three weeks thereafter. The ten holidays included one floater. Sick leave was unspecified, but the Exempt Employee Handbook cheerfully noted: "We work hard at Microsoft, and we want you to be in great shape. Past records show that we are a pretty healthy company, and we want to keep it that way."

Long hours, little vacation, low pay: a perfect combination for youthful high achievers driven by Bill-infested visions of ruling the world. And a perfect prescription for Microsoft Syndrome. Or worse: having your body give out on you. The annals of Microsoft were to become littered with the physical wrecks of high achievers whose bodies finally told them what their brains would not: *no mas*. Chairman Bill could and did endow his minions with the enthusiasm, commitment, work ethic, and drive he himself possessed. What he could not give them was his indefatigable pep. Some projects, like Cashmere and Omega, became Death Marches, grinding up project managers and programmers and spitting them out like sawdust.

In a company that was always short of headcount, Bill Gates's selective hiring practices, tolerance for quirkiness, and personal loyalty meant that dismissal was a rarely employed last resort. "No one gets fired," said former executive Mike Slade. "You cannot get fired unless you are a complete fuckup!"

Still, in May 1985 a Manager's Handbook offered guidelines for evaluating and terminating employees. "Although we reserve the right to discharge an employee at any time for poor performance or misconduct, according to the company's sole discretion, we recommend that you review problems with employees and try to work out solutions within a reasonable timetable and not resort to firing as a first measure." The steps were: Discuss problem with employee. Discuss solution. If terms are not met, "the employee may at this point be terminated without further review." According to the handbook, no severance pay was required.

With perks few, the issue of stock became extremely dear to the hearts of the employees. Sooner or later the company was going to go public. It was inevitable. The press had been asking about it since 1981, when Gates declared, "If Paul and I wanted to get rich quick, we'd issue a bunch of stock to the public. But we want to continue to grow and advance the state of computer software art more than we want to get rich." By May of 1984 it had become obvious that a public offering was necessary to keep the troops from mutinying: Paul Allen told the *Seattle Times* that Microsoft would go public in 1986 in part because the employees "at some point . . . will want to see some value" for the shares.

Gates viewed a public offering as a distraction. There were products to attend to, particularly Windows, Excel, and the new operating system. There was the whole matter of the delicate relationship with IBM. And Bill was uncomfortable with the idea of stock analysts grilling the CEO: "The ball bearings shouldn't be asking the driver about the grease."

Besides, the last thing the company needed was more money; it was generating a pretax profit margin of over 34 percent—a profit of $30 million in the last half of calendar 1985 alone. It had no long-term debt and was sitting on $38 million in cash—about the amount a public offering might deliver to the corporate coffers. And once they could cash in their stock, his most important lieutenants might well jump ship.

But more and more employees had stock and nowhere to trade it, and they were getting irritated about it. In an engineering magazine, Raleigh Roark had read that not even 5 percent of engineers who enrolled in stock option programs ever made a dime from them. "The company goes down the tube, or you change jobs or whatever, but they rarely pay off." Roark nearly sold his shares to Gordon Letwin for the equivalent of a year's salary, but Letwin got cold feet after discussing the transaction with Bill Gates.

The way things were going, there would be over 500 shareholders by 1987, at which point the SEC would require that the stock be registered officially. If you were going to do it anyway, you might as well control your own destiny. As Jon Shirley put it, "We decided to do it when we wanted to, not when we had to."

One Goldman, Sachs vice president told Gates and his crew that Microsoft could have the "most visible initial public offering of 1986—or ever." This was a virtual certainty: With their unerring flair for publicity, the PR wizards of Microsoft had cut a deal with *Fortune* magazine. "We actually negotiated more on that article than we did for the whole public offering," said Frank Gaudette. By agreeing to hold the story until the expiration of the ninety-day postdeal "quiet period," the magazine was able to assign reporter Bro Uttal to the initial public offering dealings. His story, "Inside the Deal that Made Bill Gates $350,000,000," was a rare glimpse into the process of a public offering —compelling reading that would thrust Gates and Microsoft further into the public limelight.

Uttal accurately analyzed the issue that made this offering unique: "Instead of deferring to the priesthood of Wall Street underwriters, it took charge of the process from the start." Just as with the IBM deal, just as with many of its customers, Microsoft was dealing from a fuck-you position of strength.

Street-smart New Yorker Frank Gaudette had orchestrated public offerings before. In those, he recalled, the companies "were going to the market saying 'Please? May I? Will you?' " He saw underwriters as "dictators. And they're spoiled. They're used to it." So Gaudette did things differently, conducting a "beauty contest," orchestrating auditions with underwriters, grilling them, putting them through hoops. In the end, Microsoft anointed Goldman, Sachs and Alex. Brown. The latter had been courting Microsoft so long that Shirley put it succinctly: "Better the whore you know than the whore you don't."

The "due diligence" examination by analysts and attorneys evoked the typical Bill Gates gloominess, the worst-case "We're fucked!" scenario. It was not unlike what Ballmer would half sarcastically fret about in an interview a few months later:

> *Windows flops. Novell rises to pre-eminence in networking. A lot of things combine to hurt us in operating systems. Philippe wipes us out in the low end of the language business, while other competitors potshot us to death in the high end.*
>
> *On the application side, Word fails to gain market share, Excel doesn't amount to anything on the PC, and the Macintosh drifts into oblivion.*
>
> *There you go. We're belly up.*

Bill could match Ballmer worry for worry. Going public meant an even bigger globe for the software Atlas to shoulder—not just his lieutenants, not just the employees, but all those outside shareholders. Winblad understood Gates's typically binary feelings: "The willingness to take risks I think is high in Bill, both professionally and personally. . . . But I think that Bill's kind of a worrywart. . . . I think he feels a strong sense of responsibility to what he's created, and as it's gotten bigger and bigger, he feels the expectations of everyone else have gotten correspondingly bigger.''

The carefully drafted, conservative prospectus provided a revealing snapshot of Microsoft's financial fortunes—and its anxieties. The first was a nasty tax consideration, the possibility that Microsoft might be subject to something called the Personal Holding Company tax that could amount to $30 million plus interest—Microsoft's entire nest egg. Heavy lobbying by the high-tech industry would eventually make that problem go away.

Next was the ever-present IBM worry. ''A decision by IBM not to offer MS-DOS or to indicate a preference for another operating system on its current or future microcomputers would have an adverse impact on the Company's revenues . . . [and] the Company's relationships with its customers.'' Despite the Joint Development Agreement, that worry was still far more than mere paranoia.

Then came what might have been dubbed the Philippe Kahn scenario: ''It seems likely to management . . . that price competition, with its attendant reduced profit margins, will emerge in the next few years as a significant consideration.'' It would remain one of Bill Gates's greatest nightmare scenarios for years.

There was also a ''change in marketing structure in Japan,'' which had been providing about 12 percent of Microsoft's net revenues. But a rift between Bill Gates and Kay Nishi had grown into a chasm. Nishi kept pushing Bill to branch out into chip design, but Gates had seen quite enough of that. ASCII had already worked with Yamaha on chips for the MSX machine, and Microsoft had become embroiled in an ill-starred project to build a fancier version of IBM's EGA graphics chip.

''Telephones enhanced humans' hearing. TV enhanced humans' vision. For the brain, it's going to be the computer—my MSX,'' Nishi told the *Wall Street Journal*. ''I want MSX to be the general 'pronoun' for home computers.'' At one point, said Raleigh Roark, ''even Hello Kitty almost came out with an MSX machine.'' Nishi was even pushing MSX as the controller for ''intelligent appliances''—shades of Home Bus! Yet at the Consumer Electronics Show in January 1985, Nishi claimed half a million MSX machines had been sold in Japan and a hundred thousand in Europe—not bad, but hardly thrilling.

In the end, what ultimately broke things up was the way Nishi put Microsoft's money where his mouth was. There had already been a loan of $100,000 for a fruitless investment in Blair Newman's Microtype. With $275,000 borrowed from Microsoft back in 1983, Nishi had bought stock in Spectravideo, which was then about to introduce an MSX machine in the United States. ''Sell!'' Bill kept telling his Japanese counterpart as the stock kept climbing higher and higher. Not Kay Nishi: He rode the stock all the way to the top—and back down to the bottom. At 12 percent interest, the two unpaid loans represented a debt to Microsoft of over $500,000, and the company prepared to write it off.

Finally Nishi spent more than half a million dollars on an enormous robotic dinosaur in Tokyo's Shinjuku district—tied in some way to an ad campaign involving a boy dreaming about designing such a thing with the help of his MSX machine. By all accounts, it neatly wiped out most of the MSX profits.

On top of all that, Gates—and particularly international chief Scott Oki—believed the flamboyant Nishi was paying more attention to the other aspects of his business than to minding the Microsoft store. Oki kept leaning on Bill to take some action, but Gates's intense personal loyalty kept getting in the way: "It would be almost like a broken record—things aren't going great, these guys aren't doing the job, it's becoming increasingly difficult to get anything done through ASCII. . . . Bill and Kay, their relationship precedes me, so again it's 'Who is this Oki guy saying we should end the relationship?' "

Oki kept pushing, setting forth a plan. "I knew we could pull over some key ASCII personnel to actually form a nucleus of a Japanese subsidiary, and finally Bill accepted that." Gates revoked ASCII's agency and set up a wholly owned subsidiary, Microsoft K.K., to handle Japanese business. Nishi was out in the cold and found many of his best employees walking off to Microsoft—including Susumu "Sam" Furukawa, who headed up the new office.

Nishi was bitter: "We can see an example of how some foreign companies entering the Japanese market tend to behave. They first find Japanese partners and request them to sell more and to make more profits. When they become aware that Japan is a treasure island, they cut off their partnership with Japanese companies and landed [sic] the island for themselves."

One island that had sunk beneath the waves was a Gatesian side bet called Human Engineered Software, a distributor of software for the cheesy Commodore 64 machine. At David Marquardt's urging, Microsoft had invested $1.5 million in the company. Within six months, it began showing negative revenues on returned shipments and, in Marquardt's words, "was just a disaster." As the IPO prospectus pointed out, the entire investment had to be written off in fiscal 1984.

But of the "Certain Factors" in the prospectus, there was none more certain than the one marked "reliance on key officer":

> *William H. Gates III . . . plays an important role in the technical development and management efforts of the Company. Mr. Gates participates actively in significant operating decisions, leads deliberations concerning strategic decisions, and meets with OEM customers. Mr. Gates also has overall supervisory responsibility for the Company's research and development work. The loss of his services could have a material adverse effect on the Company's position in the microcomputer software industry and on its new product develop-*

*ment efforts. There is no employment agreement between Mr. Gates and the
company.*

For such a valuable player, Gates was woefully underpaid, taking down a
salary of just $133,000, far less than Jon Shirley's $228,000. But when it came
to money, Gates was parsimonious on principle. For the public offering, he
initially argued for a lower price range than the underwriters suggested—in
part to assure sales and maintain the public image of success, in part because he
was uncomfortable with the idea of a company with a market value of over half
a billion dollars.

Long before the IPO, Bill had discussed a different half-billion mark with
Ann Winblad: "Ann, I think I can get this company to half a billion dollars in
sales. I think. And everyone's counting on me to do that. Now in my mind, if I
really stretch my mind, I can get the company to half a billion dollars in sales.
Then everybody will expect more, and I don't have a clue how we'll ever get
past half a billion dollars in sales."

In public, it was no problem: In January 1984 Gates had predicted that
"it's possible that we'll be a billion-dollar company. Oh, it'll probably be in
about five or six years." In private, it was a different story. David Marquardt
recalled Bill's personal conservatism:

> *The company when I first got going up there was doing about three and a
> half million [dollars] in sales, and we kind of mapped it out, and over five or
> six years we were expecting that the company might get up to fifteen million in
> sales. And I can remember Bill saying, "You can't build a software company
> that's bigger than ten million in sales. It's impossible. There isn't a big enough
> market. You can't get that many people together on a project. You can't have a
> software company bigger than ten million. . . .*
>
> *When the IBM deal came together, Bill really got on the rocket sled. . . .
> Then he said, "A hundred million. You cannot build a software company bigger
> than a hundred million. And I will prove it to you.*

But now he was intent on proving something else. The IPO road trip
commenced with a dog-and-pony show in Phoenix and a typically Gatesian
schedule of eight cities in ten days. Even though the underwriters were supposedly picking up the tab, Gates refused to fly first class. The underwriters tried
to convince him that he was now the product, that he should fly front cabin to
be fresh and alert on arrival. Gates grudgingly gave in. Frank Gaudette recalled
a particularly enjoyable flight to Europe: "Bill figures out the difference in the
prices, and he goes to the underwriters and he wakes them up every hour and
asks them for $200. And they say why? And he says, 'Is it worth $200 every
hour to fly up here?' "

Limousines? Gates hated them. And even amid the pomp and circumstance for the royal investors of London gathered in the Guildhall to learn about the IPO, Gates engaged in his own form of rebellion. As colored light filtered in through huge stained-glass windows, Gates took his place between Frank Gaudette and Jon Shirley in the largest of three thrones, then slouched down as if he were slumping on his office couch. It was like "the king holding his court," Gaudette remembered, the investors listening raptly to the slumped Gates, a "little guy in a big chair," seemingly swallowed by the seat.

As the public offering neared, the market heated up, and the price clearly had to be raised. Educated guesses put the stock at about $25 under current conditions; Goldman, Sachs was suggesting an initial value of $20 to $21 per share. Now, as Gates saw it, he and Microsoft were getting screwed. "These guys who happen to be in good with Goldman and get some stock will make an instant profit of $4. Why are we handing millions of the company's money to Goldman's favorite clients?"

The experienced Gaudette mollified Gates; leaving more than crumbs on the table for the rich was all part of the game. Still, there was no harm in trying; after all, they didn't need the money. In the end, Gaudette cajoled Goldman into pushing hard for the $21 figure as a floor rather than a ceiling.

Gates put the deal in the hands of Gaudette, Shirley, and Marquardt and flew to Australia in pursuit of business and pleasure. On March 12, 1986, at the Goldman, Sachs office in New York, Gaudette took care of the final details. Everything went smoothly until he brought up the matter of the "spread"— the underwriters' commission on the deal. Gaudette was trying for a record low in the high-tech arena and came within a whisker of getting it. In a virtuoso display of Microsoft macho, the feisty chief financial officer threatened to walk out over a difference of three cents a share—$93,000 out of a total fee of $4 million.

Gaudette refused to be intimidated by people he didn't consider "two-sewer guys"—a Brooklyn stickball reference to heavy hitters: "I said, 'Thank you, I'm going over to see me sainted mother in Astoria' . . . And they couldn't believe that. Most of the time they have the ball and the bat. In this whole process the key thing is that we had the ball and the bat. All of their usual pressurized practices wouldn't work with us. . . . I also knew they had the whole selling force, hundreds of people at desks, ready to go." In the end, Gaudette reached Shirley by telephone at a restaurant and got the authority to give up one penny per share—$31,000. Goldman cut its price by two cents, later immortalized in a plaque the firm gave Gaudette.

The stock went out the next morning to what Gaudette remembered as "a shark frenzy. The phones were ringing at such a dramatic pace only for one subject—Microsoft stock." The first public over-the-counter trades went for

$25.75. By day's end the price was $27.75, and 2.5 million shares were in public hands.

At the initial price of $21, Gates took down nearly $1.7 million for the shares he sold—and still held another 45 percent of the firm, with a value of more than $311 million by the end of its first day as a public company. Gates celebrated the coup and his first trip Down Under with a four-day sailing excursion with two female employees and one of their boyfriends—a trip that Bill would later insist had "nothing at all decadent" about it.

Jon Shirley cashed $1.2 million of stock in the initial round, retaining over $7 million worth. Steve Ballmer cashed $630,000 and kept $35 million. David Marquardt's $1 million venture capital investment less than five years before had mushroomed to a value of $23 million on offering day. And for mere programmers, albeit brilliant ones, Charles Simonyi and Gordon Letwin were doing all right too. Each was sitting on stock worth over $6 million.

There was jubilation in the trenches too. Programmers with, say, 2,500 original shares of stock—which had split before the IPO but were still effectively worthless—now saw a hundred-grand cash windfall, soon to be a hundred-fifty grand—somewhat better than the "down payment on a house" that Steve Ballmer had originally intended. A programmer who held on to that stock until, say, January 1992 would be able to buy a house outright—a house worth nearly $4 million. In the loose wear-anything, do-anything, say-anything atmosphere of Microsoft, where numbers were stock in trade, it was inevitable that stock itself would become a topic of conversation. A popular button appeared with the initials FYIFV: Fuck You, I'm Fully Vested. And when the no longer golden Richard Brodie left in June 1986 amid rumors that he had cashed in his stock, a new metric was begun: the "Brodie," representing the difference between the current stock price and the price upon his departure, a reminder of what a mistake it would have been to sell off early. In the halls of Microsoft, not long after the offering, Gates wondered aloud, "Is this a distraction?"

In another low-downtime military-precision maneuver, those halls had moved again, along with more than 700 employees who during the five-day process were given one day off, asked to take their floating holiday, and discovered that Presidents' Day had been moved up a couple of weeks. "One guy wrote a piece of e-mail to Jon Shirley," an ex-Softie recalled, saying "wasn't it great that Microsoft could move holidays, and what did it have in mind for Thanksgiving and July 4, and was Pope Gregory a good friend of his in terms of calendar reform?"

Within a couple of hours the chorus had grown dissonant enough that Shirley announced Presidents' Day would stay put. After all, it was Shirley himself who most proudly promoted Microsoft's e-mail system as the great

democratizer of corporate infrastructure. "To me the thing that most epito-
mizes the culture of Microsoft is electronic mail," he said. "It flattens an
organization, makes it very very horizontal. . . . There's no secretaries, no
hierarchy you have to wade through. Everybody knows everybody's e-mail
name." And still used it even in conversation.

In February 1986 Microsoft took up quarters in suburban Redmond, Washington's forested 400-acre Evergreen Place, hard by a development known as
Sherwood Forest. Just far enough from major retail centers that they posed no
immediate temptation to Bill's band of merry men, the site was close enough
to the cross-lake freeway that commuters wouldn't waste much downtime
getting there. If the wooded locale was perfect, the buildings themselves
were the finest physical expression yet of the Gatesian ethic of work, work,
work.

The four X-shaped buildings were sleek, low-slung, muted two-story affairs with plenty of windows. It was a consciously egalitarian layout. Once
again, virtually everyone got a private office—a real office with a door and,
more often than not, a view. Most of the offices were the same size, though
Gates's and Shirley's were slightly larger but no more ostentatious. Trees had
been left standing wherever possible, so the vistas were pretty much the same
no matter where you sat. Once you knew your way around one building, you
could find your way around another. There would be no pecking order, no
fighting for privileged locations. You could decorate your office any way you
liked—typically college-style with pizza boxes, Coke can pyramids, stuffed
animals. And during the constant expansion, requiring entire groups to move
every three to six months, changing offices would be no big deal. The standing
joke was that your office resembled Seattle's weather: If you didn't like it, wait
a minute.

The constant movement led to its own brand of merry prankstering. One
favorite ploy: plastering a false wall over a door to make it look as if the office
no longer existed. Another: "grassing" offices with rolls of sod left by land-
scapers. One manager who had been complaining about the late arrival of
spring found his office completely landscaped with flowers, a miniature golf
course, and vernal music on the stereo. "To understand Microsoft," said one
developer, "you have to understand that we're all adolescents."

Hard-working adolescents: Although they eventually gained an eclectic
collection of artwork, the buildings were sleek, no-nonsense steel and glass
with industrial carpeting and subdued lighting. The walls lacked clocks, a
disincentive to the timecard mentality. The long narrow hallways were flanked
by offices on both sides, with easily accessible copy-and-supply rooms, plus
canteens stocked with what had by now become a full range of free soft drinks,
from sparkling water to natural fruit juices, one cooler from the Pepsi distributor, the other from Coke. Candy and snacks were available cheap. To discour-

age unproductive loitering, the canteens had room to stand and read the bulletin board but nowhere to sit. Security was tight—key cards were required for nonpublic entryways—but not suffocating. Parking slots were unnumbered —Bill's way of rewarding early arrivals. A night owl, Gates himself generally showed up late, prompting a question at one companywide meeting about why he always parked in the handicapped space—and, eventually, prompting his getting a space of his own, in part for security.

Things were comfortable but not fancy, pleasant but not cushy. One place where the company was absolutely unstinting was in its selection of office chairs—top-of-the-line ergonomic beauties from the likes of Herman Miller. After all, you were going to be using them a lot. Ditto for computers. Elite software developers got the hot boxes—usually more than one—which trickled down the organization chart whenever an upgrade was in order. On the Microsoft campus, half the Bill maxim was at last fulfilled: At Microsoft there was at least a computer on every desk and often two or three. And thanks in part to Jon Shirley, who had pushed the company to adopt Microsoft Word instead of Wang word processors, most of those computers were actually running Microsoft software.

As buildings were added—by the time of the move into the first four, work was already underway on building five—new cafeterias sprang up dispensing low-cost fare from around the Marriott institutional food globe—Mexican, Thai, Italian, vegetarian, hardcore carnivore. No need to waste valuable time going off campus for lunch: Everything you need is right on campus—except, often, a place to sit. As one former employee pointed out, "I don't know if this is by design, but the seating areas are real small. So you go in and you buy your food and there's nowhere to sit. So where do you go? You're not going to put the food back; you paid for it. You go back to your office."

But in good weather, you could eat outside. Basketball hoops were installed, a soccer field, a softball field. On rare sunny days the place resembled a cross between Camp Runamuck and a courtyard in Venice: People played guitar, banjo, recorder, flute. Programmers juggled, unicyclists jousted, impromptu volleyball games were started. Grassy knolls invited small groups to chat, benches invited weary developers and tech writers to snooze in the sun. The woods resembled the ones outside Bonneville Power's RODS facility. Or was it Cheerio, where young Bill had spent his summers? Or Lakeside—where in a matter of months ground would be broken on a science building funded by a $2.2 million donation from the Microsoft co-founders and named—after the Gator bet the wrong way in a coin flip—Allen-Gates Hall?

Yet in the end, the physical ambience hardly mattered. By far the more important part of the atmosphere was the agglomeration of Smart Guys. To the youth culture of Microsoft, joining the company simply meant exchanging one campus for another.

▼ Elsewhere in the region was a headquarters in far less fortunate circumstances. Rod Brock's Seattle Computer Products had fallen on hard times. Its multifunction add-on boards for the IBM PC, initially designed by Tim Paterson of DOS fame, did well for a time, but by 1985 Taiwanese boards were selling at retail for about what it cost Seattle Computer to make its own. Brock's Gazelle machine had become a casualty of the push toward IBM compatibility, "a computer that nothing would run on." After a major fire at the headquarters in 1984, Brock began actively looking to unload the company.

Among Seattle Computer's few remaining assets was its free right to license MS-DOS and "updates and enhancements" to purchasers of its hardware. To a clonemaker, that license would mean a chance to undercut the competition by not having to figure Microsoft's DOS license fee into the price. But by pulling such an end run, a clonemaker might piss Microsoft off, which might mean no BASIC, no Windows, no fancy new DOS. Brock offered a finder's fee to peddle the DOS license, but no buyers came forward.

The agreement limited the free license to one copy of DOS per "CPU" purchased. CPU meant "central processing unit"; in the industry it could mean either the main computer—say, an IBM PC—or the chip that ran it. In desperation, Brock decided to "see how far the language would stretch" and offered a tiny board that contained an 8088 chip—a "CPU"—and a bit of circuitry that let users switch between separate banks of memory. Since the chip duplicated the one in a user's machine, and since no packaged software would work with the memory-bank scheme, the board was essentially a ruse to have something with which to bundle a cheap copy of DOS. As Brock recalled, "Microsoft didn't like that."

So maybe, Brock suggested, Microsoft could buy Seattle Computer. On August 14, 1985, Brock wrote Jon Shirley guessing that the MS-DOS license would be worth, about, oh, say $20 million—and to a reporter from *Information Week* publicly floated his interest in selling. Shirley responded two weeks later in high indignation: "We were shocked to learn of your exaggerated interpretation of SCP's rights under the agreement and the astronomical value you have suggested." In Microsoft's view, he stated, the license was limited to "purchasers of SCP manufactured 8086 chip machines; and it does not authorize any use of Microsoft's trademark 'MS-DOS' "—and besides all that, it was nontransferable.

That was Microsoft's interpretation, though the terms "8086" and "nontransferable" were nowhere in the contract language concerning SCP's rights to license DOS. Moreover, Seattle Computer had in fact been the first company in the world to publicly promote the operating system under the name MS-DOS, with no gripes from Microsoft.

Negotiations went nowhere. In Bill's view, he had already bought the product; he was not about to buy it twice. So in early February 1986, Seattle Computer filed suit in King County Superior Court, demanding either that Microsoft acknowledge SCP's right to transfer its MS-DOS license or that Microsoft turn over most of the DOS revenues it had earned and declare the agreement null and void. Damages were set at over $20 million and could conceivably be trebled. For once, contractual language had caught up with Bill Gates.

The timing was exquisite; the existence of the suit had to be disclosed in the public offering prospectus. "The company," Microsoft sniffed, "believes that SCP's interpretation of the agreement is erroneous and intends to vigorously defend this action."

Yet there was another royalty-free license out and about in the world, one that had the potential to do even more damage to the Microsoft empire. Its existence was omitted from the IPO papers even though Bill Gates had discussed it with the license holder just five days before the stock rolled out to an expectant public. The agreement had been negotiated by Paul Allen back in December 1983 and signed by Bill Gates the following March. It was with an outfit called Falcon Technology.

Falcon Technology was, in effect, DOSmeister Tim Paterson, who had started a company to sell hard disk drives and other peripherals. By early 1986 Falcon was on the ropes, its debts amounting to over $700,000. The company did have a couple of assets—designs for a hard disk controller and a ROM BIOS. It also had a very interesting DOS license.

The agreement had been part of Paterson's consulting fee for developing MSX-DOS. It included free licenses to DOS 2.0 and 2.5 (soon renumbered 3.0), Multitasking DOS, and MS-NET—and free updates through December 1985. The licenses clearly extended to packaging DOS with hardware products based on just about anything in the Intel 8086-compatible chip family and were explicitly transferable to "any purchaser of substantially all the assets of COMPANY's computer system products business." So when a Taiwanese hardware firm came calling, it was time to see if Mr. Bill might up the ante.

Receiving no satisfaction from a telephone conversation, Paterson sent Gates a contractually required letter on March 17, indicating his intention to sell DOS with a variety of disk controllers. This got Microsoft's attention. House counsel Bill Neukom met with Paterson the following week and disputed his interpretation of the agreement. In a carefully worded letter, Neukom indicated Microsoft's willingness to "reach an understanding"—an entirely different face from the stonewall the company was presenting to Seattle Computer and Rod Brock.

Gates and Allen met with Paterson toward the end of April. In an earlier agreement for MSX-DOS signed by Steve Ballmer, Gates reminded Paterson, there had been a $300 minimum requirement on hardware to be shipped with

DOS. "Bill Gates got pretty pissed at me when we first started talking about this: Like 'What are you doing? We think the $300 value is still in there!' " Paterson stood firm and reminded Bill that the later agreement explicitly "merges all prior and contemporaneous communications."

"He's huffing and puffing," Paterson recalled. And bluffing. Gates snidely wondered where it would all end, suggesting that Falcon might ship DOS with its ROM BIOS—after all, that was hardware, right? No, Paterson shot back: A ROM chip probably wouldn't be covered under the agreement, since the BIOS was software, the ROM just the container. "So I'm going to try and have some integrity here. I'll ship it with things that are real hardware products. But floppy disk controllers are $17."

Paterson had called Bill's bluff, faced him down, and won. Microsoft agreed to acquire the assets of Falcon Technology for approximately $1 million. Paterson entered into a two-year employment agreement with Microsoft at $50,000 a year and ended up with 10 percent of a new entity known as Falcon International and, later, Paterson Labs. For $500,000, repayable to Microsoft on easy terms, the new company acquired Paterson's BIOS software and disk controller design, as well as a favorable DOS license and Paterson's paid-by-Microsoft services one day a week. Eventually the company was sold outright for about $10 million worth of stock in BIOS vendor Phoenix Software Associates.

For Bill Gates, it was one license down, one to go. The Seattle Computer case was plodding through the courts, and at first the Gates luck seemed to be holding. The judge who initially drew the case was one Gary Little, a social lion who traveled in Gatesian circles and happened to have been Bill's constitutional law instructor at Lakeside where, he later said, "Trey was one of my best students." Somehow that fact did not bother Little enough for him to recuse himself from the case. Seattle Computer's lawyer Kelly Corr, unaware of the connection and acting on hunch, demanded and got another judge—along with a blistering dressing-down from the imperious Little, who would blow his brains out in his chambers just two years later when his abuses of the law and adolescent males surfaced in the local press.

As readily as it had settled the Falcon license, Microsoft seemed absolutely adamant about taking the Seattle Computer suit to the bitter end. Motions, countermotions, discoveries, and depositions dragged on and on. The Gates deposition in particular was like pulling teeth. Directing a superior smirk at the admittedly untechnical Kelly Corr, the deponent answered with smug sarcasm and petulant sophism.

Asked why the word "hardware" was used in the agreement with Seattle Computer, Gates shot back, "You mean leaving the rest of the sentence alone, like if you put the word 'clown' in there? I don't know what you mean."

"You could put 'board' in there," Corr pointed out in exasperation, "you could put 'sets,' you could put 'memory enhancers.' "

"We understood what their hardware was," sneered Bill Gates.

That turned out to be a major issue. Judge Gerard Shellan ruled that the agreement applied only to Seattle Computer's original, long-outmoded hardware. As Tim Paterson remembered it, that "wasn't what anybody had in mind when they wrote it. And I told the Seattle Computer side to ask for my opinion, and they tried to, but the Microsoft side, who of course was my employer, objected and was able to say that my opinion was not relevant because I wasn't one of the parties. . . . Microsoft knew they would be in trouble if I said something." Having Paterson back at Microsoft was turning out to be even better than Gates had imagined.

Despite the judge's restrictive ruling, Microsoft wasn't entirely out of the woods. When the case finally went to trial in late November, the jury was essentially charged with deciding one question: Were recent versions of MS-DOS "versions, updates, or enhancements" of Paterson's original?

Yes, indeed, said many of the witnesses. Not really, others declared. But the balance seemed to be tipping Seattle Computer's way. Corr had found an untechnical analogy to drive home for the jury why upgrades of DOS were covered by the deal. It was as though, he said, Microsoft had promised SCP it could have the pick of the litter every time DOS had puppies. Now it was saying that the DOS upgrades were some other animal entirely. Thereafter, whenever a Microsoft attorney or witness would begin talking about how later DOSes weren't covered by the agreement, Corr would wordlessly haul out a statue of a dog he kept under the table and place it in full view of the jury.

Microsoft, which before the trial had made only token offers to settle, began upping the ante. Gradually, day by day, hundreds of thousands were appearing on the table. But Rod Brock had a number in mind: one million dollars. Rumor would later have it that was Bill's number too.

Taking the witness stand, a smug, cocky Bill Gates came girded for battle. When Corr referred to "your company," Gates asked if Corr meant Microsoft.

Didn't, Corr asked, Gates own about half the company's stock? About 40 percent, Bill said.

"You own about 11 million shares, don't you?"

"Yes."

"The last time I looked, it was about $50 a share, right?"

"I don't look," Gates declared.

"It's nice to have that luxury, I guess," Corr said pointedly. The jury seemed to get the message.

On December 12 the jury got the case. Microsoft's offers continued to escalate. Three days later, when they reached $925,000, Brock folded his hand. He too had called the Gator's bluff and won.

The jury was thanked for its services and went home. Seattle Computer was no longer a problem. As the year 1986 came to a close Microsoft finally controlled the destiny of MS-DOS once and for all—except for IBM's say in it.

When the trial was over, Kelly Corr went out and bought Microsoft stock.

22

"WE DAMN WELL CAN!"

On April 16, 1986, fresh from his Australian trip and the initial public offering, Gates flew to Boca with Steve Ballmer to make yet another pitch. What they proposed once more to the men in blue was that Windows be the standard graphical user interface for the new DOS—CP-DOS to IBM, 286DOS or DOS 5 to Microsoft.

Since the signing of the Joint Development Agreement months before, work on CP-DOS had moved along quickly, though the idea of joint development chafed both parties. Gordon Letwin, in charge of Microsoft's end of the project, had little patience for end users, and managing people was not one of his greatest skills. As he would later put it: "This is engineering, not politics. In politics, the goal is to convince the other guy you're right. In engineering, the goal is to find out what's right."

Letwin had been used to running the show. Before the JDA, he had been masterminding most of the design and much of the code for what was then known as DOS 4 and DOS 5. Shortly after the signing of the JDA, he received a rude awakening about the operating system he thought was his: "Something that Steve and Bill didn't bother to tell me was that IBM had artistic control."

This was at a meeting with some IBM guys down at Boca, and we were debating something which I thought was particularly stupid, and I'm saying "We can't do this!"—I don't remember what it was, but it was really screwed up. And they're saying "Well, we're going to do it. That's tough!" And we're saying they can't do this. And they say, "Well, we damn well can. We have the final say, and that's what we say, so fuck you."

And I said, "Oh, yeah?" So I went out into the hallway and called back here and . . . yeah. I wasn't too happy about it.

Steve claims that Bill doesn't like to deal with those kinds of situations, and sometimes he'll just procrastinate and just not deal with it and hope that maybe it goes away or something. And I always say, "Bullshit. Bill never makes mistakes like that."

Letwin soon discovered that IBM and Microsoft had very different ways of working. At Microsoft, "you make sure that a smart guy is doing the implementation, and you—if it's not you—meet with him a lot, and you see to it that this happens." At IBM, "they've got designers and implementers." The designer produces a spec. "That's it, he's done. And then the documents are taken by the implementers. They just code it up."

> *If the implementation's not going right, the implementers will say, "We don't care, that's what it says." And you go to the designers, and they say, "We don't care what the implementation is. That's not our problem." And so you end up with a piece of garbage!*
> *. . . I wasn't aware that they were going to sort of toss this over the wall to a bunch of trained monkeys and then abandon it. And the monkeys don't give a damn about anything. Except getting the lines of code out.*

Lines of code, lines of code. IBM lived and died by that mantra. At IBM, "there were good people," said design manager Ed Iacobucci. "There were a lot of not-so-good people also. That's not Microsoft's model. Microsoft's model is *only* good people. If you're not good, you don't stick around. At IBM, we used to call ours 'masses-of-asses programming.' "

And in early 1986, around the time the operating system first ran in its most rudimentary form, those masses escalated from roughly twenty to perhaps seventy developers at Boca. "At IBM," Iacobucci recalled, "it seemed like we were basically hiring anybody off the docks."

> *The developers were very, very green. And that created a lot of problems, because we could plan a lot of interesting things, but when it came down to actually doing them, it was very difficult to execute them. . . . In terms of the Microsoft view of the world, all they saw was masses of people that were growing rapidly. It didn't follow their culture of taking the top 1 percent of computer scientists. . . . So we had a real mismatch in the works there.*

In Iacobucci's view, "Microsoft programmers thought of themselves more as artists"—an insight confirmed by Gordon Letwin's "creative control" concept. IBM was more into "big development tools" and viewed such things as the way Microsoft kept track of program changes as hopelessly primitive. And then there was RAS—"Reliability, Availability, Serviceability"—the ability to document everything within an inch of its life so that IBM's customer service people could solve the inevitable problems. Unlike IBM, Microsoft didn't sell contracts to customers guaranteeing almost immediate fixes or workarounds to software problems, so it didn't see the need for special code for the purpose. Gordon Letwin would shake his head and wonder "Why does every secretary in America need this bullshit in the machine?" The answer: An IBM service technician might one day have to trace the secretary's problem.

"IBM was really fragmented groups," said Iacobucci. Boca had many masters to serve, from the division responsible for that secretary's machine to the architects of the most gargantuan mainframes. So Bill Gates made numerous "evangelizing" pilgrimages, listening to special concerns, trying to position the new DOS as the operating system panacea for the IBM empire.

Meanwhile, Letwin was getting increasingly frustrated. At IBM, he was beginning to feel, "The image is real, and the politics is real, and the code doesn't really matter":

> *If we look at it and we think there's a problem, there's nothing we can do. We tell them that the code is too big: Tough. It's too slow: Tough. We get more specific about what changes they should make: Tough. We rewrite a portion of it to show that it's much faster and smaller now: They throw that away. They have final cut, so we can't force them to take it.*

Even without IBM's problems, Letwin had plenty to worry about. The project was beginning to suffer from what IBM's System 360 designer Fred Brooks, in his classic volume *The Mythical Man-Month*, had called "the second-system effect." Quoting Ovid's maxim, "Add little to little and there will be a big pile," Brooks wrote that "The general tendency is to over-design the second system, using all the ideas and frills that were cautiously sidetracked on the first one."

Letwin and his IBM counterparts were trying to implement all sorts of neat ideas and frills comprehensible only to programmers, things like threads and semaphores and queues and named pipes and dynamic linking and interprocess communication that might someday be helpful to users but were from an intellectual standpoint the height of sexiness to computer-sciency Smart Guys weaned on UNIX. On top of that, they were trying to implement them on more than one microprocessor architecture.

In early 1986 the IBM group was beginning to realize that "this is way too complicated"; up in Seattle, Bill Gates was having similar thoughts. A time-out was called. Thus began what became known as the Great Simplification. "When it became clear that in our initial design we had bit off more than we could chew, there was a series of meetings, and we pruned things back quite a bit," said Letwin.

The real-mode version—the devilishly tricky part that would let people

run the new operating system on the millions of early-model PCs in the world
—was scrapped in the name of simplification. But in its place was added a
"DOS compatibility box"—a way of running good old DOS applications on
the all-new operating system. Even on a 286-class machine that would be a
tough hack. Net simplification: Not much.

Had CP-DOS been developed for the 80386 microprocessor coming soon
from Intel and known as the 386, vastly simpler solutions would have been
possible. The 286 had been devised back before the turn of the decade, and it
had frustrating design flaws that would lead Steve Ballmer to dub it "brain-
damaged." But Intel had designed the new chip expressly for microcomputers
and had solicited suggestions from the software industry, including Microsoft
and Gordon Letwin. The 386 was a true 32-bit chip, meaning it could address
gigabytes of memory, billions of characters, amounts imaginable only to programmers. Its special features, including advanced memory protection and
support for "virtual machines," meant that writing an advanced operating
system with even multiple "DOS boxes" would be a relative snap. And any
software that ran on the older 16-bit Intel chips would run on the 386.

Still, betting on the 386 seemed an unreasonable gamble. Given Intel's
bug-plagued record with the 286, it took a leap of faith to believe that the
vastly more complex 386 would be ready on time, in quantity, bug-free. In a
break with tradition, Intel had not licensed "second sources" to produce the
chip (aside from IBM), creating a monopoly position that would translate into
high prices. IBM believed that it had to offer a 286-based operating system to
keep a promise it had made to many PC AT customers. And IBM, which had a
huge chipmaking arm of its own, had a variety of in-house designs in the wings,
including a superfast low-power version of the 286. Decision: Develop for the
286 now, the 386 later.

The Great Simplification had been completed when Gates and Ballmer
went to Boca and made their pitch for Windows. What about the schedule? one
of the IBM group asked. No problem, Bill blithely assured them. Windows was
already in release. The code was in great shape. It wouldn't take much longer
to bring it over to CP-DOS. Markell, the Windows naysayer, was still skeptical: "I thought it was going to be an absolute disaster."

What about TopView compatibility? someone inquired. Ballmer groaned
silently: TopView was dying, but these guys refused to bury it. Markell pointed
out that IBM had made a commitment to TopView. A big IBM–Merrill Lynch
venture called Imnet ran on it, and other top Wall Street firms had signed up
for similar projects. IBM couldn't just abandon its customers, tell them their
stuff wouldn't run on the new DOS.

When it came to IBM, the customer was always right. Ballmer and Gates
promised they'd revise Windows to include the TopView API. Somebody on

the IBM side joked that a little company out in Berkeley had come down to Boca and demonstrated a TopView clone a quarter of the size and four to ten times faster. Maybe Microsoft ought to go out and buy it.

Ballmer tried. The company wouldn't sell the code without selling itself. So within two weeks, Microsoft signed a letter of intent to acquire the firm "lock, barrel, and stock options," as one employee later joked, for a total of $1.5 million in Microsoft stock. Its name: Dynamical Systems Research, Inc. Its product: the mystically christened Mondrian, a faster, smaller, better TopView. TopView compatibility for Windows? Sold.

DSR's six programmers included a bunch of Princeton physicists led by twenty-five-year-old Nathan Myhrvold, an excitable, wild-haired, frizzy-bearded elf who had studied with Stephen Hawking at Cambridge University. Within eight weeks they would be safely ensconced in the confines of Microsoft's new Redmond campus. Culturally, Microsoft and DSR were a perfect fit. At their initial meeting, Bill and Myhrvold had discussed chip architectures and their effect on program speed. Ballmer told anyone who would listen that the DSR crew were "our kind of guys" for managing to write a TopView clone far faster and far smaller. DSR's David Weise, himself a clone of the nerdier roles of Rick Moranis, had seen a copy of Windows 1.01 and noticed the date stamp: 3:05 A.M. the day before Fall Comdex began. "We said, this is a company we can like." Windows they were less impressed with. As Weise put it: "Pardon me for using technical terms, but it was dorky."

Dorky it was, particularly if you had anything less than a top-flight machine of the time, an AT-class unit with mouse, EGA card, and high-resolution monitor. Besides, there were still only two independent Windows applications: Micrografx's In*A*Vision and Palantir's Filer.

Steve Ballmer was working on that problem. In early June he and the gang held a Windows Development Seminar in New York City. The goal: to rustle up software, any software, for Windows. In his seminar introduction, Ballmer offered a tantalizing bonus:

> It's fairly well-known from the press, et cetera, that Microsoft is working on a future version of DOS that supports the 286 in its so-called protected mode, where you have the full 16 megabytes of address space and you get access to the memory-management features of the 286.
>
> We have committed to make sure that the Windows API exists in a completely compatible fashion between real mode or today's Windows and this new protected mode OS. We've also told people, and I'll tell you again today, that it'll be a fairly transparent process to take an application that runs on Windows today on top of DOS 3 and move it to a new version of Windows that runs on top of this new 286 protected mode version of DOS.

Succinctly: Develop for Windows, and you'd be developing for the operating system of the future. These words would come back to haunt Ballmer and Microsoft like the most horrible of ghosts. In the sunny spring of June 1986, they were as true as good intentions can be.

One month later, in the heat of July, they would wither and die. The first hint: Myhrvold's demonstration of Mondrian in Boca to "a bunch of CP-DOS guys" who "were stone-faced. We couldn't get anything at all out of them." IBM seemed to be up to something.

It was. With the burgeoning clone market, as IBM knew well, there were plenty of reasons for buying cheap machines and skipping IBM's high-priced boxes. At IBM, Markell recalled, "Everybody was searching for a silver bullet" with which to slay the doppelgangers, and a new line of machines was secretly being designed with that goal in mind. But there was something else at IBM that was intended to differentiate its machines from the low-priced clones, a monkey wrench that was about to knock Bill Gates upside the head just as he seemed to have TopView and the Windows deal in hand. The monkey wrench was still looking for a name, but it would eventually come to be called SAA.

The latest in the tradition of obscure acronymic constructs, SAA—Systems Application Architecture—was a grand concept that was part reality, part snake oil, and all IBM. The company would eventually describe it as "a set of software interfaces, conventions, and protocols—a framework for productively designing and developing applications with cross-system consistency." People at Microsoft and elsewhere would soon come to describe it in pithier, less flattering terms.

True, IBM made little rinky-dink machines that anybody could clone, but its real business, or so it believed, was "big iron"—expensive mainframes and minicomputers, most of them wildly incompatible with each other. IBM was also in the software business, selling thousands of dull but solid business programs that ran on these big computers—accounting, banking, order entry, you name it. And Earl Wheeler, corporate vice president, programming, had figured out that IBM's software designers were duplicating their efforts: They would design, say, an order-entry system for the IBM System 370 mainframes, and they'd have to start from scratch to do the exact same program over for the totally incompatible System/3X minicomputers.

If IBM could figure out a way to have the programmers write to one API across all the machines, it would save a tremendous amount of money in program development. Let the hardware be as incompatible as Dobermans and tabbies: All the programmer would see would be special software that would make it all seem identical. In effect, it was Paul Allen's 8008 simulator—or Windows—in a slightly different guise: Use a layer of lookalike software to insulate the programmer from whatever hardware it happened to be running on.

In the 1960s, IBM's wildly successful System 360 line had implemented a hardware version of that very strategy, but the company had long since strayed from that path. Now DEC was making hay with it: the VAX hardware architecture on everything, up and down the line, under the slogan "Digital has it now." As your company grows, DEC's salesmen could tell their customers, you can move up to bigger systems and your programs will all run fine: no need for retraining, no need to rejigger the data. The SAA scheme would let IBM salesmen once again tell their customers more or less the same thing.

SAA went farther. A standard called Common User Access (CUA) would define a consistent user interface, making such things as menus and function keys identical across a wide range of programs and machines—not unlike the set of guidelines that made a new Macintosh program seem so familiar so quickly. And SAA included communications standards so that machines could access data from one another. But above all, SAA was proprietary, totally for the benefit of IBM, no outsiders need apply.

In July 1986 the winds of SAA—which had not yet acquired those initials —were blowing harder than ever. In a meeting with Bill Lowe, Dick Hanrahan, and Information Systems and Communications Group executive Ed Kfoury, at IBM's Armonk, New York, headquarters, Bill Gates and Steve Ballmer walked right into the gale.

For openers, they were informed, strong gusts had blown TopView right off the table. TopView hadn't been part of SAA, and now it never would be. There was no need to discuss it further. Gates and Ballmer were flabbergasted: The deal with Dynamical Systems hadn't even been completed, and the entire reason for it was history!

And, according to Lowe, so was Windows. SAA dictated that everything would have to work in one compatible way. To support the graphics terminals that linked users to IBM mainframes, the only way—at least as IBM saw it— was to use an API called GDDM (Graphical Data Display Manager), code name Hawthorne, that was under development in IBM's labs at Hursley, England. Unfortunately, Hawthorne worked in a way that was almost entirely antithetical to the GDI (Graphics Device Interface) model that Windows used. So, Lowe told Bill Gates, Hawthorne and not Windows would be the graphical interface for CP-DOS. Lowe wanted Gates to know before his scheduled lunch with IBM's chairman John Akers the next day.

It was time for never-lose-a-deal, never-take-no-for-an-answer Gates to get creative, to vault into his supersalesman mode. No problem, he told Lowe. The operating system could have two graphical interfaces: instead of just Hawthorne, Windows *and* Hawthorne.

Hanrahan adamantly insisted it wouldn't work. If you put in two interfaces, one for the PC platform and one only for mainframes, the mainframe interface would die, and so would SAA.

"Test our flexibility," Gates insisted. His guys could work with IBM's Hursley guys. They would figure out a way to integrate Windows and Hawthorne. That way, everybody would be happy. Lowe was surprised, recognizing that what Gates was suggesting was a major compromise on Microsoft's part. By the end of the meeting, Lowe had granted Gates a reprieve: a few weeks to study whether Microsoft could work with Hursley on the graphical system. Bill's lunch with IBM's chairman Akers the following day was cordial.

On the way home, Gates and Ballmer were bushed but ecstatic. At the airport they ran into Mike Slade. They had saved the deal with IBM, they told him. They had been there all day, and they had saved it!

Slade had just read the *Fortune* article about the IPO, and on the flight home he began grilling Bill about other companies and their CEOs' holdings. "And Bill, unprompted, rattled off the percentages of every entrepreneur in the computer or high-tech industry you could ever want to know! You know, like to the decimal point! And guess who had the highest percentage?" It was a trait Slade found endearing, "just pure boyish competitiveness. . . . He just wants to win! At anything!"

But Bill's percentage might be far less meaningful if the IBM Windows deal fell through, and that deal was nowhere near done yet. "Get the business, get the business," Ballmer had been saying. "We'll bend over, we'll do what it takes." Back home, among the Smart Guys, the term "BOGU" came into vogue: Bend Over, Grease Up.

Led by Bill Gates and Nathan Myhrvold, a team from Microsoft hurried down to Boca for a powwow with Hanrahan and the chief of the Hawthorne project, IBM veteran Colin Powell. According to Myhrvold, he and Gates "managed to raise enough doubts" about Hawthorne to earn a rendezvous with a task force in Hursley. There, in a two-week series of daily meetings with the difficult goal of convincing IBM to change its decided course, Myhrvold and a cast of six challenged a thirty-person team from IBM. As Myhrvold put it, "We knew we had them outnumbered."

By the end of the session, in a marvel of amity, the new graphical user interface project would be dubbed "Winthorne"—a combination of Windows and Hawthorne. To Myhrvold:

> We thought we had won bigtime. We had snatched one out of the fire, gone over and gotten the business. And we knew that we'd made some compromises in doing so. We knew that there would be a few changes in Windows that would be likely as a part of this. We knew that we'd also have this additional piece of crap, this GDDM layer.

But the way Myhrvold envisioned things, the GDDM layer would virtually go away:

At one of these meetings at Hursley, I offered to put my home phone number in a dialogue box, so the first time [GDDM] was ever used it would pop up and say "Call Nathan collect!" We were kind of open the whole time that we were not convinced. . . . We thought, hey, all we've done is we've added this tumor that'll sit there on the disk.

The "tumor," unfortunately, proved to be malignant, slowly eating away at the Windows interface. The "Win" was fast fading out of Winthorne, which would utterly nullify Steve Ballmer's claim about "compatibility" between the GUI for the old DOS and the GUI for the new DOS. Winthorne would eventually become known as Presentation Manager, and as one Microsoft wag would put it, "In general Windows and Presentation Manager are very similar. They only differ in every single applicable detail." By October Ballmer would admit privately that despite what Microsoft had "committed" to do in June, Windows applications for DOS probably wouldn't run "transparently under 286DOS" and might have to be recompiled. His June declaration had now been sabotaged, in part by his ready acquiescence to IBM's demands.

Within Microsoft, there was still an illusion that the new DOS would repeat the success of the old one. Mark Mackaman, a new hire who became product manager for what Microsoft had begun to call "New DOS," was assigned to put together a business plan for it. With long experience at IBM and elsewhere, the newcomer was well aware how long it took to get corporate customers to adopt new technologies. His conclusion: By 1990 New DOS would be running on roughly 35 percent of all 286 and 386 machines. "And Bill sent flame mail back to me saying 'If that's the best you can do, then you're in the wrong job.' " Mackaman "was so intimidated" that he "toed the line, which was by 1990 we'll have 100 percent of the market. They actually believed that."

But if the graphical interface stuff was bad, things were not much better on the rest of the project. "They're always threatening us that the relationship is going to be over, the relationship is going to be over," Ballmer recalled. There were heated debates over what Microsoft called "sizzling" the code, fine-tuning it for performance, something that IBM's strict methodology didn't include. Worse, IBM wanted to rework the business deal. Still worse, in mid-1986 IBM finally decided what direction its forthcoming line of machines should take. "They don't want to talk to us about certain things, and we basically go into the mid-'86 Black Hole," Ballmer said. "And they do development and we do development separately during that period."

It was during that period that Bill Gates appeared at a Microsoft applications retreat and offered the pithy summary that "IBM is fucked and we all know that they're fucked. What we're gonna do for the next couple of years is play rats in a maze," going down blind alleys and backing off, trying one unsuccessful strategy and trying another. As the years would show, it was a brilliant analysis, but Gates was unwilling to cut himself loose from the head-strong rodent.

IBM's new hardware line, it turned out, would be its move to take back the standard from the clones. Most of the new machines would have a bus called the Micro Channel, which IBM was protecting with patents and any other legal means it could think of. Instead of the original BIOS chips, clones of which had by now become about as common as potato chips, they would have the new ABIOS—Advanced Basic Input/Output System. "Basically this was nonsense," said one former IBMer. "It was just there to create confusion, by not publishing the BIOS. . . . It was gonna take them so long to clone it, it would slow down all the cloning." More important, from the Redmond perspective, "There's all this activity going on on OS/2 1.1 that Microsoft knows nothing about."

Microsoft had been marching toward a December release of New DOS. But when the Black Hole period ended, CP-DOS 1.0 was dead as far as IBM was concerned. "Now," Ballmer recalled, "the whole project is thrown out and they start working on what they called CP-DOS 1.1," which supported the new machines. Microsoft was staggered. Such OEM customers as Zenith and Compaq had been working closely with the company to adapt their computers to the first version of CP-DOS—286DOS, New DOS, official name to come—so that they could make their public announcements the same day as IBM. Now the project had been scrapped, rolled back to square one. The OEMs' reaction? As Mackaman would soberly state it: "Pissed!"

Ballmer still believed IBM was essential, do what it takes, get the business, get the business. But in mid-September Chairman Bill, the eternal bet-hedger, turned up on the front page of *InfoWorld,* beaming with Compaq chairman Ben Rosen and president Rod Canion as they introduced Compaq's hot new industry-leading machine, the Deskpro 386.

Based on Intel's 80386 chip, and including special memory-management software developed with Microsoft, the Compaq machine was a shot across IBM's slow-moving bow. "Compaq Introduces 386 PC, Challenges IBM to Match It," the headline read. The story reported that "Canion warned that if IBM doesn't respond with its own 80386-based machine within six months, the Deskpro 386 will become the industry's 32-bit personal computer standard."

But there was another headline just to the right: "Microsoft Developing 80386-Based Windows." Whichever way the market went—IBM or Compaq and compatibles—Microsoft was positioned to take advantage. The Gator had covered himself again: IBM to show, Compaq to place, Microsoft to win, as in Windows.

In October, despite the best efforts of the sales force to "unsell" it and get Microsoft out from under its contractual commitments, the long-awaited original Multitasking DOS, MS-DOS 4.0—not to be confused with the IBM-developed single-tasking DOS 4.0 that would appear in late 1988—sneaked out the door to Wang in the United States, ICL abroad, and virtually nobody else. More than three years in the making, DOS 4 could run a single old-style DOS program in the foreground while running specially written programs in the background, but everything had to wedge into the 640K address space of the IBM PC. In essence it was Windows without the graphical user interface, and the Windows team had long tried to kill it as redundant. By the time it was ready, virtually nobody cared.

Philippe Kahn unintentionally delivered the epitaph, though he intended it more broadly: "The biggest fluff was all this bull about Windows and new versions of DOS. None of it is useful, none of it works, and none of it will change the way people work."

23

STORMING THE GATES

By 1986 Microsoft was losing much of its Pascal market to the dazzling Turbo version from Borland's Philippe Kahn. The Gates response? Fight back with a new, improved version of his first love, good old BASIC. In mid-1986 Microsoft released QuickBASIC 2.0, which transmogrified BASIC into a "structured" language very much like Pascal—and tossed in an integrated programming environment very much like the one Turbo Pascal had pioneered.

"I can program in this faster than even Philippe can in his stupid languages," Gates boasted to language group product marketing manager Rob Dickerson via e-mail, giving rise to the idea of a public head-to-head challenge that was eventually rejected. "Too confrontational," as Gates would later characterize it with tongue firmly in cheek.

So as part of an all-day press seminar at his Redmond headquarters, William Henry III issued a more general programming challenge called "Storm the Gates." Chairman Bill would use his new BASIC to take on whatever tools the members of the techie press might bring. It was as if Lee Iacocca had agreed to race in a Chrysler New Yorker against any car an automotive journalist might show up with. Gates was "nervous" about the idea, since he had done virtually no coding in years, and he certainly hadn't fooled around much with the new QuickBASIC. He spent the night before the event boning up.

Solicited for problems that could be completed in half an hour or so, the members of the press dropped them into a hat—and plucked out one designed by *PC Magazine*'s Bill Wong. It specified a simulation of a windowed environment with a different display in each of four windows—a simulation, come to think of it, not unlike the infamous Windows "smoke-and-mirrors" demonstration. The first three on-screen windows were to display various specified sequences of numbers. The fourth had to display circles of random radii. And the user had to be able to exit the program with the Escape key.

In a trice there was an apparent victory for the archenemy: Jeff Duntemann from *PC Tech Journal* finished first, using Borland's hated Turbo Pascal. Or he would have, except for one small problem: A glitch in Turbo Pascal made it impossible to use a single press of the Escape key to end the program as specified. Try as he would, Duntemann simply could not find a way around this problem. He finished out of the money.

Programming frantically in Microsoft C—which, unlike BASIC and Pascal, had no built-in graphics capabilities—*PC Magazine*'s Charles Petzold came in second. The Gates luck had held again: The problem was absolutely ideal for BASIC. Furiously coding, compiling, and cussing, Bill Gates kept running afoul of the odd terminology of BASIC's X-Y graphics coordinate system, but once he mastered it, there was no contest. QuickBASIC's built-in windowing and graphics commands made it easy for him to finish first—twice as fast as the runner-up.

Afterward, emcee Dickerson announced that since every program had at least one bug in it—a truism that Microsoft had never come close to violating —Bill's program would be distributed to the assembled throng. The first person who found a bug would win a plaque. Alas, a hasty conference with a representative from the Waggener PR agency put an end to that idea. The Gatesian triumph was duly trumpeted to nerds throughout the world, but if you wanted one of Bill's program bugs, you'd just have to buy it.

It seemed like a great victory. At Fall Comdex in November 1986, however, Philippe Kahn dared to tread directly on Microsoft's language turf and threaten to stomp all over it. Borland announced the soon-to-be-ready Turbo BASIC—a preemptive strike worthy of the master. But Microsoft knew all about preemptive strikes. For an internal presentation on the subject, a slide entitled "BORLAND'S BIG MISTAKE" succinctly summed up the response:

> They told us what they are going to do next.
> They gave us time to respond.
> This gives us the opportunity to build a winning product.

Winning? It was the only thing. Obsessed by the Borland threat, Gates reviewed the promotion plans for Microsoft's next version of QuickBASIC with Dickerson. This was war. The impending version of QuickBASIC that had been known as version 2.5 until Philippe's bombshell was suddenly renumbered version 3—"in order to make the release sound more significant"—and preannounced. Ads for the current version stressed that buyers would get a free upgrade to the next one when it hit the stands. Features were added. The sales force pushed the current version hard, since a retailer with a heavy stock of QuickBASIC would be unlikely to order a huge volume of what Microsoft took to calling "a cheap imitation." A program of "spiffs," the industry's polite term for "bribes"—payments to retail salespeople for pushing the product—was inaugurated. And Dickerson worked masterfully at manipulating the computer press, convincing editors to delay publishing head-to-head comparisons with the Borland product until QuickBASIC 3.0 shipped—thereby not only avoiding adverse publicity but also delaying coverage for Philippe.

Yet the Microsoft languages effort was floundering. In a meeting to discuss QuickC, Microsoft's response to Borland's $99.95 integrated-environment TurboC, Gates, Ballmer, and Shirley were less worried about their new product than—shades of IBM!—schemes to protect Microsoft's high-end, high-profit C compiler. Dickerson had returned from a 1987 languages strategy retreat with the realization that "we had absolutely no product plans." In some ways this was understandable: In an era where the "language" most computer users learned was something like Lotus 1-2-3 or WordPerfect, few bothered even learning BASIC. Selling languages, the foundation of the Gates empire, had become significantly less important.

The applications situation was better—particularly abroad, and domestically on the Mac. Excel was doing its job well: giving the Mac what Gates called a "depth" product and trouncing Jazz. Still needed: a "breadth" product. Gates and Company had discovered that they had been half right about integrated software: As they had claimed, it was no good for power users, who would inevitably complain about the features that had been left out. But for novices who didn't want the power and featuritis, not to mention the expense, of the top-shelf apps, integrated software could work just fine. The Apple II was being carried by such a program, called Appleworks, selling some 40,000 copies a month—even more than Lotus 1-2-3 on the PC.

Apple alumnus Don Williams was planning a similar program, called Mouseworks, for the Mac. Enter Bill Gates and lieutenant Alan Boyd, the smooth-talking Scotsman in charge of Microsoft's product acquisition. Boyd flew to Santa Cruz, spent three days in nonstop negotiations with Williams, and emerged with Microsoft Works for the Mac. The word-processor-spreadsheet-database-communications program was buggy and late—it did, after all, have the Microsoft logo on it—but made it out the door by September 1986, to favorable reviews.

Gates, who initially opposed the acquisition, never forgave himself for one aspect of the deal: Having to pay royalties on every copy of the product. When Works rolled out on the PC a year later, it contained a graphics program along with the other four modules, and it was a different beast entirely from Mac Works: built from scratch (in part by Ric Weiland as his final project for Microsoft), home-grown, developed in a royalty-free zone.

Gates's affection for the Mac was being tested in other ways as well. Under Lessons Not Learned the First Time Around file Mac Word 3.0, actually the second major release but renamed to conform with the current edition of Word on the PC. Promised for July 1986 in the Windows licensing agreement with Apple, Word 3.0 did not ship till February 1987, was found to be riddled with a mere 700 bugs (several of them fatal), and had to be fixed with a free upgrade to 70,000 users—at a cost to the company of more than $1 million— within two months of release. Mac Multiplan no longer had sole claim to being Microsoft's worst fuckup ever. "It was Simonyi's fault," said Mike Slade. "Simonyi didn't believe in testing. The guy wrote buggy code. He was a Smart Guy. He believed in the field beta test"—meaning let the customers find the bugs.

"That's where I screwed up royally," Simonyi admitted. "It was just a bad, bad, bad decision."

But on the IBM front things were looking better, with relations undergoing one of their periodic thaws. The day after Christmas 1986, the two companies signed a new set of Phase Two agreements, the ones that covered the money, primarily regarding the Winthorne graphical user interface for the new operating system. And although IBM wasn't giving Windows a ringing endorsement, at least its direct sales force would now officially sell it—along with the struggling GEM and TopView.

In early March 1987 IBM gave its strongest pseudoendorsement of Windows yet when its new Publishing Systems independent business unit announced it had settled on DOS, Windows, and Adobe PostScript as its standards. In public, Gates was happy, calling the move an important boost for Windows—while cautioning anyone from reading anything into it beyond desktop publishing.

The caution was wise. The atmosphere suddenly grew chilly when IBM told Microsoft the new DOS was going to be called Operating System/2— OS/2 for short. Worse, the graphical user interface would not be called Windows, but Presentation Manager—PM for short. And, come to think of it, Bill Gates, who had long pushed the idea of a GUI bundled with the operating system, had been right after all: Once PM was ready, it would be bundled with OS/2. However, because of time constraints, the first version of OS/2 would be released without graphics support.

Microsoft howled. The names were lame. And IBM's crack marketeers had somehow managed a stunning preemptive strike—against themselves! Preannouncing the version with built-in graphical support would all but guarantee that the initial character-only edition would fall on its butt. But, as was said in the halls of Microsoft, when you're dancing with the bear, he leads. On Steve Ballmer's birthday in March, his crew celebrated by giving him a jar of Vaseline. BOGU had been personalized to BOGUS: Bend Over, Grease Up, Steve. There was even an abortive attempt to have his administrative assistant order him a vanity license plate with that very logo.

On Saint Patrick's day, IBM went public with its plans for SAA. In an exciting-as-dishwater press release, the company delivered little more than a promise to deliver some documents later in the year. The rest of the world may have snored; at Microsoft this SAA thing was driving people crazy.

CUA, Common User Access, the display standard, was supposed to be more or less the same for screens that had graphics and screens that didn't. IBMers who came to be known as "the CUA police" were promulgating standards for Presentation Manager that the Microsofties genuinely hated. Character-based screens couldn't show icons: Forget 'em! One insider recalled a standard that "Bill used to fly off into rages about: Every menu and dialog box was always supposed to have 'OK = Enter; Esc = Cancel.' . . . It was like all this huge extra verbiage, and it used to drive him crazy." In the end, IBM agreed that graphics screens shouldn't be constrained by what character-based screens couldn't do, and the CUA standard began evolving into something that looked suspiciously like the Macintosh. To maintain some sort of consistency—and chance of eventually selling the product to IBM—the Microsofties decided that Windows should adopt an almost identical look.

Look was one thing; feel was another. Presentation Manager was careening out of control. At one point IBM decreed that the names of API calls—relatively clear names such as WinRegisterClass—had to be reduced to six letters each, because IBM's FORTRAN compiler couldn't handle more. Myhrvold swatted that one down, but recalled "there would be thousands" of DCRs—design change requests from the far-flung divisions of the Blue Behemoth—"per month." IBM and Microsoft programmers would team up for "DCR parties," where they'd conduct hearings—"it would be like a court case"—on how to dispose of the issues. "Over the first year and a half, we cleared so many DCRs, we had to keep renumbering the system. It would only go up to like 10,000, and so we'd recycle the numbers and start back with DCR 1. . . . It was like a big win when we took our three senior guys and we said, 'You only have to spend half of your time on DCRs. Write code the other half.' "

According to Myhrvold, change ran rampant in "every part of the product. The shell changed. Printing: My God, we went from this very simple printing model to this incredibly elaborate baroque thing." The Softies had tried for Windows compatibility, but now it was irrevocably out of the loop. "At a number of points in there, we'd have these meetings where we'd caucus back here at Microsoft and we'd say, 'Look, we've really broken the connection to Windows. This isn't Windows anymore.' "

The "kernel," the basic operating system, was going through IBMitis too, getting fatter and slower with each passing day, in part with support for the new machines, in part with support for every two-bit division in the IBM empire. When Mackaman discovered that source code on the video system alone had ballooned past a megabyte, his boss Adrian King first refused to believe it. But after taking it home, King understood Mackaman's judgment that "This thing is totally out of control. The code is just gross."

If there was bitterness before, there were agonies on April 2, when IBM released its new machines under the name Personal System/2. PS/2 and OS/2: They kind of went together. Maybe you even needed one to run the other, or so people might think. Imagine how that was going to play with Microsoft's OEM customers.

Bad as that looked, another item was even more galling. The OS/2 that IBM shared with Microsoft would be sold in IBM boxes labeled "Standard Edition"—evidently a stripped-down model. IBM would really push something it called "Extended Edition," communications and database software that would tie machines running OS/2 into IBM mainframes. And tell this one to your clone customers, Bill: You don't own any part of Extended Edition, and it will run only on IBM hardware.

This looked like the silver bullet, all right, the secret weapon against clones. A major portion of the software was proprietary and incompatible, and so was the hardware: All but the low-end machines used the new proprietary Micro Channel bus, and IBM pointedly put manufacturers on notice that if they cloned it without a license, they would end up in court. IBM was about to enforce its patents on standard-bus clones as well, requiring clonesters to pay for licenses or endure litigation. About the only good news for Microsoft was VGA (Video Graphics Array), a new color graphics standard that looked clone-able and would finally let programmers paint their graphical interfaces with the lipstick and rouge of typefaces and color.

Still, much of the IBM announcement was mere promise. OS/2 1.0—the one that had initially been known as 1.1, the one without any graphics at all—wouldn't be available until the beginning of 1988. No dates were announced for the new 1.1 version, which would include Presentation Manager.

This gave Bill Gates a golden opportunity to muddy the waters. In an opaque six-page press release, Microsoft announced Windows version 2.0, which boasted "visual fidelity" to something called the Microsoft Operating System/2 Windows presentation manager. This was a handy way of pretending that Windows and Presentation Manager were still almost the same thing, which they no longer were and never would be. Ballmer would now publicly mutter something about a "mechanical recompilation step" to translate Windows programs to the new graphical interface—a wild oversimplification. By this time, the links between Windows and Presentation Manager had been irrevocably broken.

Bill Gates felt forsaken.

We'd decided that we were working together to have a common center for the industry. It isn't really true because they're really promoting Extended Edition and they don't really think Standard Edition is gonna sell at all, so that kind of feels like a betrayal. They tie the software name to their hardware name, which is tied to a proprietary bus that they're charging huge fees for, so that doesn't feel too good. But hey, it's still IBM.

Somehow IBM still "viewed Microsoft as a subcontractor. You know: We're IBM and you're the small guy," Mackaman recalled. "About this time is when Microsoft really started to get hacked at IBM."

At IBM, more than a few people were starting to get hacked about how well a certain subcontractor was doing for itself. According to Lowe, "There was a real problem of controlling your destiny, and there was another problem. I don't know: You might call it manhood." The *Wall Street Journal* of March 20, 1987, didn't help any: It had crowned Microsoft's chairman as a billionaire, the youngest self-made one in history. Gates, who should have known as well as anyone, claimed that something like 10 million PCs were running DOS, and other industry sources said there were even more. Microsoft stock was about to reach its new high of $100, a fourfold increase over the space of a year. Wage slaves at IBM, where software engineers traditionally received far less respect and remuneration than their counterparts on the hardware side, began to wonder, "Why am I making this other guy successful?"

Nonetheless, IBM's endorsement of OS/2 translated to a bonanza for Microsoft. As Mackaman saw it, "OEMs don't care what's in the product. They just say 'Gimme what IBM has.' " The Microsoft sales force was busily signing up customers, collecting fat checks from them, and sitting on their money.

The deals were typically bigger than the ones for DOS. For example, Televideo had relicensed DOS in 1985 for $500,000 a year against $40 per machine. For OS/2, it committed in 1987 to $690,000 per year and $115 per copy—and by then Televideo was a bit player, barely in the game. Once again Microsoft aggressively pushed a sliding scale—the more you committed to up front, the less you'd pay per unit, so come on, think big, pony up. Small players need not apply, in part because adapting Microsoft's code to your machine was a far more complicated process than it had been in the days of DOS.

Witness the transformation! Instead of selling the first version cheap and making it indispensable, this time Microsoft was grabbing for the gold right from the outset. The fact that big OEM customers did plunk down big advances obscured a few potential problems. Bill Gates didn't have the Extended Edition that IBM had—"Own it or clone it," some OEMs demanded—and that became a minor sticking point. By their absence from the fold, the dozens of smaller computer makers, who refused to cough up huge cash advances for an unproven product, made the new system seem less than universal, less than necessary. And the high royalty translated to a high retail price when an adequate if not stunning competitor—DOS—was available for peanuts. In short, the sales strategy that Microsoft adopted for OS/2 was diametrically opposite to the one that had made DOS a success.

Yet it just might have worked. There was no question that times in the computer business had changed, nowhere more obviously than in IBM's ads. The original IBM PC had been symbolized by Charlie Chaplin, the lone individual and small businessman empowered by the computer to help create order from the chaos of modern times. The original DOS had been a quick and dirty one-man improvisation, rough but lovable, with adaptations by a team you could count on the fingers of one hand.

Now IBM's PS/2 was flacked by the cast of TV's "M*A*S*H"—minus, briefly, its star, Alan Alda, formerly a pitchman for Atari. The resurrected veterans of a dead sitcom now portrayed mere cogs in the wheel of a big corporation not unlike IBM. The metaphor was apt: OS/2 was a monstrous corporate effort involving hundreds and hundreds of programmers spread across the country and around the world. When it finally arrived, it was guaranteed to have all the soul, personality, and swiftness of a bureaucrat.

24

IN EVERY HOME

A computer on every desktop and in every home, running Microsoft software! That was the manifesto, and in the war for the desktop, Bill Gates was doing pretty damned well.

But the home—well, the home had been trickier. True, Microsoft BASIC came with virtually all the el cheapo home computers, the VIC-20s and Commodore 64s and their ilk, as well as such slightly more prestigious models as the Apple II and PCjr. But the home computer world, like the rest of the world, had moved past BASIC to the realm of packaged applications that eliminated the need for programming knowledge. Although a few frugal souls captained small businesses with their Commodores, the home market was mostly about education, which generally meant stupefying drill and practice, and entertainment, which generally meant games. Microsoft's Flight Simulator actually straddled the categories, yet even its success didn't prod Bill Gates into trying to repeat it.

But for years his minions, particularly the omnipresent Kay Nishi and hardware guru Raleigh Roark, had been giving Gates reports about interesting emerging technologies, most of them tied to cheap consumer electronics. One was the videodisc, a medium that IBM and others had long sensed could be used to produce a form of "interactive" television where the viewer would be in command. Movies with user-selectable endings, training films that repeated only what the viewer didn't already know, medical dictionaries with full-color movies of human cardiac arrest—the possibilities seemed endless.

But because the videodisc didn't store information digitally—as ones and zeros—it was less than ideal for a computer-related solution. East and west of Seattle, Sony and Philips had joined forces on a digital approach. In fall 1982 they had introduced the Compact Disc music system, which stored audio as digital data—hundreds of millions of bytes on each silver platter, as much as the text of an entire encyclopedia. So instead of using data for music, why not simply use it as data? In 1983 Sony and Philips announced CD-ROM—Compact Disc Read-Only Memory, a standard for physically arranging mountains of data on compact discs that could be pressed by the same production lines as Michael Jackson's.

CD-ROM was slightly more complicated than CD audio. If the laser misread a single one or zero on that Michael Jackson disc, an audio player would gracefully cover up the error by fudging it. In the computer world, a single-bit error could bring the system to a halt. Among the most important matters the CD-ROM standard resolved was a method of correcting the frequent errors that compact discs would otherwise produce.

But CD-ROM was more or less limited to text and pictures. For the consumer market, Dr. Richard Bruno of Philips began work on the next product, a do-it-all machine that would allow for audio/video extravaganzas under the absolute control of the user. It was dubbed CD-I for Compact Disc Interactive—"interactive" being one of the great buzzwords of the computer business at the time. Television was passive; CD-I was interactive! Of course, so were video games, and one of the things that had killed their first incarnation had been something utterly passive—MTV—but never mind. Sony joined the CD-I project in late 1984.

Raleigh Roark, of Microsoft Mouse fame, headed up a four-man CD-ROM team at Microsoft. Audio and video just happened to be part of the specification for MSX machines, and in 1984 the MSX spec was about to undergo a new revision, dubbed MSX-III—which, if Bill could swing it, would be developed stateside instead of in Japan, since the relationship with Kay Nishi had begun to sour. Sony and Philips were both producing MSX computers, and Gates believed that somehow the CD-I standard could be tied into the new MSX standard.

This was a hard sell. As far as the Philips and Sony representatives were concerned, the first two versions of MSX had not been rousing successes. In their view, the blame rested firmly on Microsoft, which hadn't promoted the concept aggressively enough to the general public. But Gates was becoming obsessive about CD-I and turned on the hard sell. If MSX wouldn't work, how about DOS? After all, there were more programmers who understood DOS than any other operating system, so lots of new software titles could be developed in a hurry. And software, as usual, would be the key to success. "There were like at least twenty-two meetings," Gates recalled. "Raleigh Roark and I were just totally burned out on meeting with guys that speak Dutch for the rest of our lives."

CD-I plodded along, but CD-ROM was moving ahead—particularly as a medium for distributing big collections of text. Since the CD-ROM standard offered little more than the bare bones of the data structure, Roark's group and its consultants developed a disc format called MS-CD—the idea being a single disc that would be compatible in all machines, or at least DOS machines and Macintoshes. But this was just one of many possible formats. DEC, for one, was dabbling in the concept—for openers, it seemed a promising way to distribute voluminous manuals. And the dozens of startups included a company that was developing the first encyclopedia on CD-ROM, a company known as Activenture and later KnowledgeSet. Its head: Gary Kildall.

On a visit to hometown Seattle, Kildall idly told Bill Gates that he was considering holding a conference on CD-ROM in the Asilomar center near his Pacific Grove headquarters. Shortly thereafter Kildall was dumbfounded to find himself being asked to give the keynote address at the first annual Microsoft CD-ROM conference, to be held in Seattle in March 1986. Considering that Microsoft did not have a single CD-ROM product yet in the works, it was Bill Gates deploying yet a new model of preemptive strike: positioning by association. Gates sent a flurry of internal e-mail to the conference organizers insisting that Kildall be heavily involved: No sense antagonizing the guy.

At the time, every CD-ROM maker had to organize the data on the disc its own way; there were no standards except at the very lowest level. In November 1985, near Lake Tahoe, a group of CD-ROM movers and shakers met to consider a standard format for organizing data on the disc into logical units such as files. Microsoft upheld the DOS standard. Apple defended the Mac. DEC demanded its VAX/VMS operating system be included. Others pushed for UNIX compatibility. In the end they were virtually all tossed in under the rubric of the High Sierra Proposal—which with minor modifications was adopted by the industry and eventually became approved by the International Organization for Standardization (ISO) as ISO standard 9660.

At the time, a two-man San Francisco outfit called Cytation was working under contract from Microsoft on a demonstration project for the conference, a hoked-up project that Kildall must have found yet another strange "coincidence": Multimedia Encyclopedia. But whereas Kildall's project was text only, the Microsoft demo let you put up a picture of John F. Kennedy, click on it, and actually hear him utter the immortal phrase about asking not what your country could do for you.

Cytation was also working on a project of its own, something called Bookshelf that would be a collection of reference works—dictionary, thesaurus, ZIP code directory, Bill's beloved World Almanac—on a single disc. In early January 1986 Microsoft took the Bookshelf project under its wing, bought Cytation outright, and installed its chief, Tom Lopez, as the head of Microsoft's new CD-ROM division.

Meanwhile, Microsoft's participation in CD-I was disintegrating. "We have more meetings in more random places throughout the world, ranging from an Alaskan airport to the Netherlands to Japan," Gates said, but it was a lot of effort for not much reward. Philips and Sony were clearly pushing for CD-I to be driven by a version of the Motorola 68000 chip—for which Microsoft had no operating system to offer. Microsoft insiders began to suspect Philips and Sony were stringing them along to delay the development of MSX-III.

By this time the relationship with Nishi had virtually disintegrated, and MSX was about to go to ASCII as part of the divorce agreement preceding Microsoft's initial public offering. About a month before the Microsoft conference, Philips chose to adapt an operating system known as OS-9, best known in industrial circles and as an add-on for the low-rent Tandy Color Computer. Unfortunately for Bill Gates, the Microsoft CD-ROM conference was where Philips chose to announce this fact—an embarrassing nine days before Microsoft was to take its stock public. Though one impressionable columnist wrote about CD-I as if it might drop a bombshell in the lap of the home computer business, the thing wasn't even an official standard yet.

Although the CD-I preannouncement was a minor black eye, Bill's conference strategy had worked brilliantly. As Stewart Alsop wrote, "Kildall started working on optical storage products three years ago. . . . But already people perceive Microsoft as the company with the most to say about the future of CD-ROMs, even though it has no products to sell yet." It was as though Gary Kildall was destined to have two words carved on his tombstone: Preempted again.

Preempted himself on the CD-I platform, Gates was still scheming to get aboard. Initial ploy: an offer to buy out Microware, developer of OS-9. The offer was spurned.

Shut out of CD-I for the time being, the new CD-ROM division at Microsoft worked on a variety of angles: developing Bookshelf, investigating new titles, writing software that would let DOS handle High Sierra discs. Yet within Microsoft, the CD-ROM division was seen as a bunch of losers, misfits, and aging wunderkinder who had made enemies elsewhere in the company. "It's a classic problem of it being a pet project of Bill's, but nobody else believing in it or caring about it or understanding it," said one former member of the group.

If Philips wouldn't play—well, maybe somebody else would. Lopez and Gates and Roark had been following some interesting work going on in Princeton, New Jersey, at RCA's David Sarnoff Labs. In the early 1980s, wizards there had developed the SelectaVision CED (capacitance electronic disc) videodisc system that RCA had promoted heavily in the face of crushing competition from the growing VCR market. Compared to the Philips/MCA LaserDisc system, SelectaVision was relatively cheap. It was considered hopelessly low-tech—it used a stylus, for godsake!—but the Princeton experts knew that with a little tweaking the system could store lots of digital data. More tweaking and the system might be able to spit that data out amazingly fast. It was one step away from pure digital television. And once you turned television digital, the viewer could go hog wild with it—change colors, shapes, you name it. In other words, it would be—that buzzword again—*interactive*.

In 1984 Art Kaiman, the short, feisty middle-age RCA veteran in charge of the project, got a phone call that began with the words "Are you sitting down?" RCA was waving the white flag and dropping its videodisc business. The VCR had won.

Desperate, Kaiman convinced the RCA brass to let his team transfer its technology to the more difficult Compact Disc platform. By the end of 1986 he had committed to giving the first public demonstration at the March 1987 Microsoft CD-ROM conference.

After a disastrous night of rehearsals, a haggard Kaiman stood at the conference podium as a huge TV screen lit up behind him with the initials DVI— Digital Video Interactive. Airplanes soared in full-color, full-screen motion; a Mozart divertimento floated from the speakers in high-fidelity sound; interactive applications manipulated computer-generated images. It absolutely astounded the ballroom full of hardened insiders who knew everything there was to know about CD-ROM, who knew the medium was just too underpowered, too low-bandwidth, to do what they had just seen. And yet they had seen it. They rose to their feet to give Kaiman a roaring ovation. Beefy Dutch burghers from Philips stumbled out of the ballroom looking as though they had just contracted the plague. DVI had just demonstrated more than CD-I was promising.

In the exhibit hall there was more. Under joystick control, a DVI disc let you walk through the Mayan ruins of Palenque, stop and look around. Another program let you choose wallpaper, carpets, and furniture and see what your room would look like. The DVI prototype hardware was so big and unwieldy that the cover had to be left off the machine it was plugged into, but the RCA team promised vast size reductions. And from Microsoft's point of view, the best part was precisely that uncovered machine: a standard IBM PC AT, a machine with an Intel chip, a machine running DOS. Screw CD-I and OS-9 and the Motorola 68000! Now here was a platform Bill Gates could support!

Microsoft had a couple of debuts of its own at the conference: its CD-ROM extensions for DOS, which let PC users access High Sierra discs, and the Bookshelf product that it had bought from Lopez and refined. But instead of being wildly acclaimed, the software revealed some of the failings of CD-ROM. True, you could put a whole mess of books on one tiny disc, but often the books were faster to use. Designed for the sequential data of music rather than the random data of text, CD-ROM players were slow to begin with; Microsoft's traditionally torpid software didn't help.

Then there was the price. Even though Bookshelf at $295 cost about the same as the bound volumes it contained, adding $900 more for a CD-ROM player made it significantly less attractive. Microsoft's mass-market strategy was based on the certainty that player prices would sink like a stone. It had happened with floppy drives and hard drives and printers and computers— and even audio CD players. There was no reason to think it wouldn't happen again.

But it didn't happen. At the precise moment the CD-ROM business seemed poised for takeoff, the Japanese yen took off instead. In just two years, a dollar that had been worth 260 yen was worth 150, nearly doubling American prices for Japanese goods. Worse, consumer products, cranked out with massive economies of scale, didn't reflect the dollar's drop. To the average consumer, there seemed to be something vitally wrong about having to pay $900 for a CD-ROM player when what looked like the same thing went for $99 at Crazy Eddie's. Actually, a CD-ROM player, designed to run from dawn to dusk for years with much back-and-forthing of the laser beam, required heavier-duty mechanisms than a Discman, but how could you expect the average consumer to figure that out?

And the very concept of the CD-ROM player suffered from the same problem that doomed the videodisc: If you bought a CD-ROM drive, you couldn't use it to store your own data. You could only play expensive prerecorded discs. Read-only media were a tough sell. Consumers preferred flexible, writeable media such as audio tape, videotape, or floppy and hard disks. Besides, CD-ROM still had to compete with paper. Publishers were not about to structure their licensing fees so that a CD-ROM encyclopedia or a vast storehouse of financial data would sell for the price of a Madonna CD.

So CD-ROM made its early inroads in niche markets. Lotus produced a product known as One Source, a subscription series carrying massive amounts of historical business and investment data. Libraries were willing to buy drives to access the databases and indexes that were becoming available on CD-ROM at prices that undercut the on-line versions. For the moment, Microsoft was a peripheral player, and the computer for every home was as distant as ever.

But Gates had begun developing another form of home entertainment, beginning with a small circle of friends who came for an intimate summer barbecue in 1986. Bill's longtime friend and employee Chris Larson manned the coals, a band was invited, and Estelle Mathers, who had helped organize the soiree, danced until she couldn't walk.

From those humble beginnings sprang Microgames, a grown-up version of the Cheerio Olympics held each summer for an ever-larger group of employees, family and friends. Hosted by Clan Gates, who judged but never competed, Microgames quickly became the exemplar of Gates family competitiveness. Divided into teams, guests would compete in a series of complex mental and physical contests for which the judges—the Gateses—awarded points. The format evolved into a tradition: puzzle-solving, singing, some sort of race, some sort of water event, some variation on a treasure or scavenger hunt.

"It's a bunch of grown-up people doing rather silly things," Ida Cole said. "Whenever I go there I think, good Lord, here's this whole place full of interesting people that I would really like to talk to and what am I doing? . . . Making a pyramid and sinking a boat."

In the middle of the 1987 pageant, a boat with two drunken men and a woman pulled up to Gates's dock. The crew began behaving obnoxiously, with one man claiming to be an old buddy of Gates from way back when. The incident occurred just as Bill Sr. was trying to convey the rules for the next event to the assembled guests, who were somewhat spooked by the intruders' rowdy behavior. Things got a little heated. Bill got involved. One of the troublemakers was tossed into the lake. "And then," Charles Simonyi recalled, "Mr. Gates says . . . 'Okay, number one . . . Which of the Shakespeare plays was it an allusion to, the second insult?' " The interlopers had been actors, their disruption a skit on which the Microgamers would now be tested.

The following year's goofiest event, called "Let It Blow!" involved matching letters on plastic balls and building pyramids of them. A shortage of the balls caused great consternation among the contestants until Simonyi's helicopter arrived and dropped thousands more all over the lawn. "People were just swimming in those balls," Simonyi said, "and of course, everything was blown to hell, all the little pyramids."

Think Smart! It might have been the motto for Microgames. "There's such a metamessage there, and it's not very subtle either," Simonyi noted. "The kinds of skills that you need are so varied. So basically what you learn is that you are around these incredibly talented people who have this incredible range of talents. I mean, it's just that random people can show off in really random ways. You find out that some of these guys are incredible athletes and some of them are great hams."

One of the random people was software entrepreneur J. A. Heidi Roizen, a striking blonde known universally as Heidi. Roizen had first spotted Bill in person wandering the floor with Steve Jobs at the insufferably hot 1983 National Computer Conference, and actually tailed the pair, hoping in vain to pick up some pearls of competitive wisdom. Gates and Roizen were later introduced at the wedding of Vern Raburn and Dottie Hall and were together enough to raise speculation that they were dating.

Roizen, a close friend of both Bill and Ann Winblad, said she and Gates never dated, but admitted that being seen dancing with him at Macworld in Boston and gambling with him at Comdex in Vegas did little to squelch the rumors. She even spent the night at his home once during a Microsoft CD-ROM conference—"probably a big mistake on my part."

Roizen would later become part of a post-Microgames group hanging out at Jeff Raikes's house. At one point in the evening, someone spilled a few drops of the Dom Perignon that Roizen had brought. "That's like a five-dollar puddle right there,'' said Bill Gates, who understood what decadence was all about. Later Roizen turned the tables:

> It's a long night, we're all sitting around and we decided we're just famished. . . . We called up Domino's and they'd just closed. . . . We said, "Tell them you're Bill Gates and pay them a lot of money to deliver a pizza." And he said, "Well . . ." And we said "Bill, what's it worth to you to have a pizza?" And he said like $240. And he said "Okay," and I got on the phone and said, "Okay, I'm Bill Gates and I'll pay you $240 to bring this pizza."

They got the pizza, but Domino's turned down the after-hours surcharge. According to Roizen, Bill "probably gave them a really good tip." In countless retellings the pizza story would get mangled to read that Gates had actually come up with the idea of the exorbitant sum and actually paid it. Neither were in character for the frugal Chairman Bill.

Fun-loving, loquacious, a storyteller and dynamo who could hold her own with Bill, Roizen had the right stuff to push his buttons, especially considering she was his only major female competitor in the testosterone-dominated software biz. Her company T/Maker, named after her brother Peter's pioneering spreadsheet, had published a popular word processor called Write Now for the Macintosh. At Microgames Gates gloated to Heidi that Microsoft's new Write program was about to appear and would blow Write Now "out of the water, 'cause it's the same thing you have, but it's our name on it and it's the same price."

Microsoft Write was not a wonderful product—"little more than a pale shadow of Word," *Macworld* reported. Later in the year Roizen ran into Gates at Comdex and told him she was coming out with a Write Now upgrade that would blow Microsoft Write out of the water. "And he said, 'Heidi, it's gotta be *in* the water before you can blow it out of the water.' "

Roizen had suggested that to eliminate the competition, Gates could simply buy her out. When he stayed at her place one night and left his vagrant American Express card on the coffee table, opportunity knocked. Roizen took the card to T/Maker's headquarters, ran it through her imprinter, entered the item as "one software company," and filled in the price as $2 million. When she presented the slip and the card to him at a meeting later that day, Gates deadpanned, "Hey, you overcharged me!"

In 1989 the Microgames moved to "Gateaway," the Hood Canal complex Bill had built on property his beloved Gam had discovered. After her death in 1987, Mary Gates recalled, the family had gathered in the Gates living room, where her son had spoken movingly of his grandmother: "I haven't forgotten that he described her as being the most principled person he had ever known.

And I think that her standards and values were great five-point star inspirations for him.''

An hour and a half by car from Seattle, the Hood Canal ''had a real spiritual impact on'' Gam, Bill's father said. According to Mary Gates, ''The idea was really a tribute to her, being that she was the glue that kept our family together. And that we wanted to preserve that very special opportunity for us to find times to be together even though everyone's life was moving off in different directions.'' So at a cost of roughly $650,000, Bill bought the three and a half acres of waterfront property and erected a tennis court, a spa, and four woodsy Northwest contemporary houses on it: three of identical size for each of the siblings, and, for his parents, a much larger building—which could double when necessary as a site for corporate retreats.

By then the Microgames had grown to upward of 120 guests in six teams and increasing levels of elaboration. Mike Slade remembered, ''I go to the Fauntleroy ferry terminal, and there's a guy with a sandwich board, walking up and down, and it says 'Bill says' and some cryptic saying. Sure enough, it was in the scavenger hunt two hours later! We're talking attention to detail here.'' A down-by-the-seashore theme included all sorts of nautical activities; six tons of sand had been trucked in for the sandcastle-building event.

In 1990 the Microgames theme was African Safari. The invitation was a little cargo box containing an African wildlife scene with lions and tigers by a lake. On a long drive to the Oregon coast, Bill and Melinda French, the female Microsoftie he had been dating for a couple of years, prepped themselves by memorizing all the countries and capitals of the continent. The ringer: Mike Slade, who had just returned from an African vacation. Slade picked himself to represent his squad in the last event, where a team could wager as many of its points as it wanted. Slade bet big.

''You're going to like this!'' Bill told him. The contest: Fill in a map of Africa in two minutes. Slade's heroic efforts failed to bring home the trophy. His team's earlier shortcomings had kept him from being able to bet big enough to win. ''We had a shitty sandcastle,'' he recalled ruefully.

''They spend tons of money and untold hours organizing this thing,'' Slade said. ''I got an evaluation form from Mrs. Gates in the mail. Like when you go to a seminar and they say, 'What did you like? Who was the best speaker? What would you change?' '' Among the Gateses, fun was serious business.

In 1991 the ''Showdown at the Gateaway Corral'' Microgames featured a Western theme, complete with a makeshift saloon erected on Gateaway's tennis court. The closing event was a smoke-signal contest, which involved communicating an assigned message from one member of the team to another using a theatrical smoke-making device—duck soup for Microsoft's masters of data communications. Among the attendees was Bill's Laurelhurst neighbor, ''Far Side'' cartoonist Gary Larson. For entertainment there was Kris Kristofferson.

To the Rhodes Scholar turned New Hollywood troubadour, Simonyi thought, it must have seemed pretty weird. "Like, who are these guys?"

These guys were young, smart, creative millionaires and billionaires, making and selling billions of dollars' worth of software to people around the world. These guys were the *new* New Hollywood.

25

"WE WERE PACKAGES"

In July 1987 Microsoft purchased Forethought, Inc., for $12 million in cash. In the words of Vern Raburn, the deal has "clearly been controversial ever since."

Cash from Bill Gates? Not very often, before or since: Most deals, like the Dynamical Systems acquisition the year before, involved stock. And Forethought got to stay in Sunnyvale, California, instead of moving under Bill's watchful gaze to Redmond, site of virtually all of Microsoft's development outside Japan.

What Gates got was PowerPoint, a desktop presentation program introduced on the Mac just five months earlier. The idea was to give Microsoft instant leadership in a rare Mac application area where it wasn't already number one. And Microsoft could port the code to Windows too.

If the deal broke the Gates mold, he quickly glued it back together. It's "lore in the company about how they'll never do that again," said Raburn. The deal, which never amounted to as much as Gates had hoped, confirmed the wisdom of his unique version of the Not Invented Here Syndrome: Seeing others' nascent development efforts, Gates would believe "We can do better" —an extension of his "I could do that in BASIC over the weekend" line.

Microsoft was eminently willing to buy technology on the cheap. "I've done all kinds of deals in acquiring code and whatever," said Nathan Myhrvold. "I learned that early on, when I first got to Microsoft: how to be . . . parsimonious, shall we say." But when it came to corporate acquisitions, a variety of deals would almost happen, and then, as with the Quarterdeck busted play and others, Microsoft would back off with the complaint that the code was not up to par or the price was too high.

This didn't occur just at Microsoft. Mitch Kapor likened it to his days at Yale, when the college went coed. "Every single guy thought about sleeping with every single girl, and all possibilities were examined, and it almost never

happened.'' Same thing with companies in the microcomputer business: ''Everybody talked about merging with everybody else. . . . It was titillation.
. . . Name me a pair of companies that didn't have discussions.''

One deal that didn't pan out was a Lotus-Microsoft merger back in 1986.
''We wanted to merge fifty/fifty,'' Gates claimed. ''We had it all figured out who was gonna do what. I was vice chairman, Mitch was chairman, Jon was president, [Lotus President Jim] Manzi ran the apps division, Steve ran the systems division.'' Had it happened, he said later, he would have developed a series of applications with the 1-2-3 interface.

How serious was the deal? According to Kapor, ''Not very. It only looked serious. There were a couple of two- or three-hour meetings. Nobody looked at anybody else's books. There were no discussions other than among the top two or three people from each side. There was only preliminary discussion of what the organizational structure might be.''

Manzi didn't want to do it, Kapor said, ''and I knew it didn't make sense.
There were geography problems of a major sort. I really didn't expect Bill and me to be able to coexist well within the same firm.'' The deal was scuttled.

''Bill doesn't like to deal with people he doesn't know,'' Raburn said, adding that ''Microsoft just won't pay a premium for any acquisition.'' The fact that Gates did pay a premium in the PowerPoint case was evidence of Microsoft's growing applications strategy, particularly for the Mac and Windows graphical platforms. The year 1987 would be a watershed for apps, with many upgrade releases. By 1988 applications would amount to a 40 percent slice of the company's revenues piechart.

But when it came to advanced operating systems, 1987 was more like pie in the face. The OS/2 project was a downright resource sink, swallowing up twenty, thirty, forty programmers at a time in Redmond and hundreds in Boca and Hursley as more and more resources were thrown at the project. And the meetings! Meetings in England! Meetings in Redmond! Meetings in Florida!
''We called it Delta DASH because we were packages,'' Gates said of the twenty-four-hour round trips to Boca. ''There was a period of at least a year and a half where I did that more than once a month, and Steve did it more than twice a month.''

OS/2 was where Ballmer was putting all his top talent. Among the Smart Guys, the word was out that OS/2 was beginning to be a pain in the butt. ''We were off in IBM Land,'' Konzen recalled. ''I mean, this was Ballmer's thing.
And Steve worked IBM and cut the deals and told us what to do and cracked the whip and everything.

''It was total hell,'' Konzen said. ''I was kind of a manager, and I wasn't much of a manager. I would spend every other week in England. That is not a job I like.'' But this was the future of the company. So BOGU!

Windows was the poor relation, the cereal premium of the industry, tossed in the box with computers, mice, video cards, turbo cards, who knew, maybe baseball cards. Although Microsoft claimed more than 500,000 copies of Windows sold as of March 1987, a huge proportion of those had been freebies or bundles, and only about 20 percent, if that, had been installed on users' hard drives. Besides, DOS was creaky, DOS was stunted, and DOS, alas, was the foundation for Windows.

"Frankly, we thought that Windows was dead," Konzen recalled. "But what the hell, let's keep shipping it because there are people out there that want it." After all, considerable work had been done on the second edition of Windows, much of it back in the days when it seemed to have the inside track as the graphical user interface for OS/2. It would run, after a fashion, on memory-hungry low-end machines that couldn't begin to consider OS/2. The Windows work continued with a skeleton crew while OS/2 sucked up the resources.

Despite Microsoft's attempts to blur the distinction between Windows and Presentation Manager, the industry understood clearly that IBM wasn't really supporting Windows except in the most backhanded of ways. Tandy Trower recalled "begging on our knees to people like Lotus and WordPerfect saying 'Please develop for Windows, please develop for Windows' . . . and they said, 'Nope, sorry, guys. Until you get IBM's blessing on this thing, we're not really interested.' " If Gates wanted a killer app for Windows, he would have to do it himself.

But within Microsoft the Windows vs. Presentation Manager battle had split the company. At a 1987 retreat Jon Shirley and Steve Ballmer argued in favor of developing Excel first for PM. Lotus had announced its 1-2-3/G for PM only weeks after the PS/2 rollout. If it won out on that platform of the future, Excel would be doomed.

Jeff Harbers had a team working on a Windows version of Excel, and he was as happy about changing the platform as Klunder had been the last time around. "Ballmer just tells us how stupid we were and that PM was the most important thing in the world." Harbers stuck to his guns: Windows first, PM later.

On October 6, 1987, Windows 2.0 and a 386-specific version called Windows 386 were officially announced. The second edition of Windows was a considerably changed beast from the tiled, clunky bastardization IBM and the independent developers had been complaining about: It was an overlapping, clunky bastardization. "They just whacked this thing together," Neil Konzen said.

As unimpressive as it was, Win 2 had one big thing Win 1 hadn't: Excel version 2.0, actually the first Windows version but cleverly numbered to correspond with the new Windows release. And Excel initially had something no other program on the market had: Windows 2, a special version of which shipped with the spreadsheet in October, three months before the official version of Win 2 appeared. Competitors groused about apps cozying up to systems at Microsoft. Church and state? More like church and steeple. But as one of the Excel Smart Guys put it, "We wanted to get it out the door. We didn't want to have to wait" for the Win 2 team.

Excel's release led to speculation about its potential impact on 1-2-3, which commanded roughly 90 percent of the PC-compatible market. The consensus: not much, in part because of the limitations of Windows.

To help Windows work better, the Expanded Memory Specification Bill had characterized as "It's garbage! It's a kludge!" was reborn as EMS 4.0. A joint effort with Lotus, Intel, and AST, the new version let DOS machines use up to 32 megabytes of memory in a way that was a boon to Windows. Microsoft followed up with yet another hardware helper, the Mach 20 board, designed to give your tired old 8088 machine a second life as a high-speed 286 and make Windows tolerable. Unfortunately, it was based on a slower version of the 286 than its competitors, arrived at a time when the 386 was becoming the hot chip, and became the latest in a long line of hardware failures that had included the Mac Enhancer and the PCjr Booster. It did not help Windows, Excel, or the bottom line in the slightest.

Neither did Jim Manzi, Mitch Kapor's successor. Just before Excel's release, Lotus dropped its hated copy protection from 1-2-3, although Manzi vigorously denied there was any connection. To steal some thunder from the Excel rollout, Lotus preannounced 1-2-3 for the Macintosh even though it was little more than a glimmer in someone's press kit.

The rivalry had been inflamed by the fact that during the third quarter of 1987 Microsoft had passed Lotus as the top PC software vendor—this time for good. When the fiscal 1987 tally sheet came out that summer, Gates's horses were pulling away, leading in revenues ($345.9 million, up 75 percent), profits ($71.9 million, up 83 percent), units shipped, number of employees (more · than 1,800 worldwide), and industry recognition. A particularly key figure was international revenue. At $146.2 million, it represented an increase of 83 percent over the previous year, amounting to 42.3 percent of overall sales, by far the largest international presence of any microcomputer software company.

Within the company there had been unaccustomed excitement about the good news, but Gates didn't think his employees should focus on such things. On a flight to Apple with Macintosh managers Mike Slade and Valerie Houtchens, Gates put things in perspective. As Slade recalled it, Houtchens asked Bill about a rumor that he was going to split the stock. "So Bill just sort of rolls his eyes and says, 'Give me a pencil.' So she does. And he breaks it in two and he gives it back to her. And he goes 'There: I just split the stock.' That's classic

Bill Gates. It's a putdown, you learn something from it, and you're a dumb shit and I'm not.''

The stock split was announced August 1. On August 16 Gates celebrated with an unrestrained memo pointing out that ''as conservative as we are about self-congratulation and celebrating our achievements,'' he did ''get a real kick out of the fight [sic] that their big distinction of being the largest is being taken away BEFORE WE HAVE EVEN BEGUN TO REALLY COMPETE WITH THEM'' [emphasis Gates's]. Not that the chairman had tucked away his worry beads: Microsoft could slip to second place again, he warned. It was time to get back to work.

▼ Compaq and IBM were locked in mortal combat for control of the desktop: During 1987 Compaq's market share rose from 16.5 to 22.8 percent, while IBM's dropped from 44.3 to 39.2 percent. More than a third of Compaq's gain had been in the 386 arena, where IBM had been late in producing a machine. By dropping a hint here and a rumor there while making deftly timed product announcements trumpeted in the trades, Gates shrewdly played the two off each other.

Windows 386, developed in close conjunction with Compaq, was a somewhat more interesting version of the flagship product, taking advantage of the 386 chip's capabilities to allow users to run bigger applications and switch among them faster and more effectively. But it required a top-of-the-line machine and was mostly a way of placating Compaq until the new operating system came along. Microsoft's switch-hitting talents were gaining renown; speculation soon drizzled out that Microsoft was using Win 386 as leverage against any attempt by IBM to make OS/2 any more proprietary than it already was. It did not escape the attention of Bill Gates that he was able to sell some of his best OEM customers twice: first on Windows 386 and Windows 2 and then on OS/2 and PM.

And the Windows partisans were beginning to hear some good news. Aldus, the Seattle inventor of desktop publishing, was porting its PageMaker from the Mac. Micrografx was still doing Windows apps, and beginning to do well. What helped, according to Paul Grayson, was, of all things, the announcement of Presentation Manager:

> Everybody predicted when IBM announced OS/2 and PM it was death for Windows developers. It was the exact opposite: Sales doubled the next month. . . . Everybody all of a sudden knew that graphical user interfaces were critical to the future of the PC, and they said, "How can I get one?" . . . [IBM] also started building the graphics card in. For us, we were in graphics heaven when they did that.

His brother George pointed to a "confluence of things":

> *You had better graphics, you had faster computers, you had kind of the acknowledgment that graphical user interfaces were in your future, you had the Macintosh being very successful. So you had this thing, this phenomenon called Mac envy, beginning to occur where people had PCs and they'd look at their DOS-based graphics program and say, "Boy, did I get ripped off." . . . And mice were becoming popular. People wanted a way to use mice. All these things just kind of happened at one moment in time, and it was like hitting the accelerator.*

So the question of the year 1987 for independent developers was "Windows or Presentation Manager?" Developing for either was a major undertaking, and few companies had the manpower to attempt both at once. Borland International's vice president of research and development Brad Silverberg succinctly stated the problem: "Microsoft had been saying 'If you code for Windows, you code for OS/2,' but that just isn't true. You shouldn't underestimate the effort of porting a Windows application."

Borland wouldn't do Windows. "People are afraid Microsoft is going to take control of the operating system," said the increasingly nettlesome Philippe Kahn. Ashton-Tate wouldn't do Windows. Neither would Lotus. "The first graphical applications that we're going to be introducing will be for the Presentation Manager," declared Jim Manzi. Gates and Ballmer had to be wondering whether BOGU had been a wise strategy.

There were howls about problems with OS/2 as well. Independent developers were irritated about the lack of support for the hot and hot-selling 386 chip. Maverick programmer Paul Mace recited a litany of technical woes and dubbed the DOS "compatibility box" the "Chernobyl Box." The penultimate slap in the face was the Software Development Kit (SDK). It included early releases of OS/2, a C compiler, an assembler, a linker, a subscription to Microsoft's on-line technical support bulletin board, free admission to a technical seminar, updates and fixes until the actual program was released, and ream upon ream of documentation. All that was fine. What wasn't fine was the price: $3,000. Despite Microsoft's insistence that it lost money on every copy, small developers considered the package a shameless ripoff.

But the ultimate worry about OS/2 was more insidious. *InfoWorld* columnist Michael Miller reported that "several developers I've talked to recently believe that Microsoft has an unfair advantage in developing applications that will run under OS/2. One has even whispered the ugly word 'antitrust.' After all, Microsoft will be competing with other firms in applications that will run under its operating system. Doesn't that give it a head start writing applications . . . ?'' It was the same "church and state" issue that had bothered Windows developers from the start.

"If we have some major advantage in applications because we develop the operating system, I want to know why we don't have dominant market share in applications," President Jon Shirley retorted. Microsoft's Adrian King insisted that "There are no undocumented interfaces in OS/2," then retreated to the position that "If there are any undocumented interfaces in OS/2, they are for operating system enhancement." Finally King admitted what was patently obvious: There were no official rules that truly separated the applications and systems sides of the company.

In later years that claimed separation would be roundly derided and the "ugly word" increasingly spoken. "There is kind of a wall but there is not a watertight wall, basically," a former Windows developer said. "It leaks when you get to Bill. . . . [And] when push comes to shove you're always going to be a little bit friendlier to the guy down in the next building than the guy off in Boston." If a Microsoft apps developer walked down the hall to a Windows developer and asked for a favor to make Excel run better, was that antitrust?

Besides, in the ego-dominated world of Microsoft, just asking for something didn't mean you'd get it. Windows developer Steve Wood—the second Steve Wood—kept begging the languages group to give its C compiler some features he felt were desperately missing for Windows developers both in-house and out. The languages guys didn't care, and it was years before his wish list was implemented.

Still, independent developers were crying foul to whomever would listen. On September 25, 1987, the *Wall Street Journal* published a story headlined "Software Hardball" describing the MacBASIC horsetrading incident and abrading the gloss from the carefully constructed Boy Nerd Makes Good image. Philippe Kahn weighed in with: "He has everyone—even enemies like IBM, Apple, Tandy and Compaq—believing he's their biggest ally. Of course he's the one that's the biggest winner." WordPerfect's Pete Peterson compared Microsoft to "the fox that takes you across the river and then eats you."

The sport of Bill-bashing had spread from Cupertino to the industry at large. All of a sudden the skinny naïf with oversized glasses had become the PC equivalent of a cigar-chomping railroad or oil baron, cutting deals, forging alliances, manipulating the market. How else could he have become the microcomputer industry's first billionaire? How else could Microsoft have marshalled such control over both major platforms—the operating system for IBM and compatibles, applications for the Macintosh? There was the suggestion that Bill had somehow broken the rules, played unfairly, Gatesed the deck.

Or was it sour grapes? The *Journal* article portrayed the MacBASIC deal as a Bill-takes-all affair, with no mention that Apple, which had already made millions off Applesoft BASIC, got to keep it for a song. Same thing on the

Windows licensing deal: The article alleged that Gates extracted "virtually a blank check to borrow many Macintosh ideas." Shelf upon shelf of documents in the San Francisco Federal District Court building would soon argue that if anyone got a blank check, it was the lawyers.

The unreported stories were darker and more substantial. Particularly in its dealings with OEM customers, Microsoft was beginning to be seen as more than just aggressive, engaging in practices that might well be one step over the antitrust line. When AST, a maker of add-on PC boards, began to make computers as well, Microsoft fought hard to get the company to stop bundling its boards with DESQview, a Windows competitor. Bob Kutnick, a former executive of AST, recalled "a letter from Microsoft stating that they would give us a better price on DOS if we would take DESQview out of the box." AST didn't respond to these strongarm tactics, but it worried about them. Microsoft's position, as Kutnick put it, was that "We work with certain vendors. It was a good old boy's network. And the question is how you become one of those certain vendors."

According to former Microsoft sales executive Mark Ursino, "We never published an OEM price list. It was for internal consumption only. And if anybody had ever been caught sending it out to an OEM, they would've been terminated. . . . We would talk to OEMs about what they wanted to do . . . and based on that put together a proposal." Besides,

> the standard price list was generally not something that most of the larger OEMs could live with. We'd have to come up with a custom deal to line up our pricing with their marketing plans. . . . Usually you could come up with some wrinkle that would be unique enough to allow you to come off the standard price list: It might be a little bit of joint development. . . . It might be a special promotional deal. . . . It could be just a mixing and matching of products.

But, Ursino added, "We were very careful to be aboveboard about the whole thing. There wasn't any unfair pricing involved. We would've offered the same deal to anybody. . . . Would we give this deal on the same terms to somebody else? If the answer was no, Bill wouldn't sign the deal." Of course, a Compaq could certainly offer more in the way of joint development, technology sharing, or promotional clout than some NoName. Preferential treatment was virtually guaranteed.

Still, few OEM customers were about to spill their guts to the press or the law. Microsoft had too much power to make their lives miserable. "We felt people who'd signed up with the enemy had pretty much given up their right to any sort of prerelease work product," Ursino said. "We're gonna reserve our best relationship for the people who are doing a solid Microsoft line. If you're playing games with VisiCorp or Digital Research with GEM, then, hey, you'll get Windows when the rest of the world gets Windows. For most of the OEMs, that was a pretty good competitive lever for us, because they knew that if they didn't get their hands on it before first release, there'd be no hope for them to release it in timely fashion.''

Bill's competitors were growing more media-savvy, and there was real resentment and envy of Gates's growing prominence in the industry—and his money. But on October 19, 1987, just over a month after Microsoft's first two-for-one stock split had been distributed, Black Monday brought the stock market's biggest dive since the Crash of '29. Microsoft stock nosedived, Gates's Microsoft holdings plummeted more than half a billion dollars—to a mere $971 million—and Bill-bashing settled back down to an armchair pastime. *Playboy* canceled an article featuring Gates. As an ex-billionaire, he was just not interesting enough.

Philippe Kahn was never uninteresting, and he was getting to be a downright pain. Borland's languages strategy had given Microsoft fits. Its unreleased Quattro spreadsheet was poised to compete against both 1-2-3 and Excel. And Kahn was about to swipe languages marketeer Rob Dickerson out from under the nose of Bill Gates. That kind of thing happened all the time in Silicon Valley. It had never happened before in the Silicon Forest.

The deal went down at Fall Comdex '87 the first week of November. Dickerson had been spearheading Microsoft's campaign against Borland's TurboC with aggressive comparison ads for QuickC, touting a vast array of features and claiming "No one else is truly 100 percent compatible with Microsoft C 5.0." Philippe knew his kind of guy when he saw him. In a "Battle of the Bands" at Comdex in Atlanta the previous spring, Philippe's Turbo Jazz combo had competed against Dickerson's Microsoft group, QuickRock.

At a private meeting with Kahn and his top brass at Caesars Palace, Dickerson found Philippe "selling Borland. He was describing how excellent the products were, how, while he couldn't discuss them, there were new products on the way that he thought were very exciting." Borland's marketing group was relatively tiny; Dickerson was offered the chance to head it, running the show not just for languages but for the whole Borland line, everything from databases to the new spreadsheet, in a vice-presidential slot that reported directly to Kahn.

Within a week, Dickerson visited Scotts Valley and liked what he saw. The Borland offer was better than he could have dreamed: $90,000 a year—almost double what he was making at Microsoft—plus moving expenses, a $25,000 signing bonus to help with relocation costs, and options on 150,000 shares of stock worth roughly half a million dollars. Borland even agreed to make him whole on the 3,000 shares of Microsoft options—early, valuable options exercisable at $1.75 and salable at about $50—he would forgo by leaving Seattle.

It was an offer he couldn't refuse. On Wednesday, November 11, Dickerson told his Microsoft superiors he would be leaving by the weekend. The response from Steve Ballmer was immediate: He threatened to sue.

On his first day of work at the company in July 1984, Dickerson, like all new hires, had been handed Microsoft's standard nondisclosure agreement and told to sign it. The new employee agreed not to "solicit, divert, or take away any customer or any supplier of Employer or otherwise compete with the business of the Employer as defined above"—the definition being "the development and sale of microcomputer software"—for a year after terminating employment.

Employees were rarely told about this document before they arrived, and they couldn't modify its wording once it was handed to them. "I talked to legal," one said, "and you know, they don't waver: This is the policy, take it or leave it." In theory, it meant that upon departing Microsoft, you might have to leave the software industry for a year—though the company had never before enforced it in a court of law.

"Would you like for me to get out of the office now?" Dickerson asked.

"No, no, no. I want you to stay here," Ballmer told him. "I believe you're an honorable man." They would meet the next day and talk to Bill.

"There was a lot of discussion of: The job is too big for me. The job is too small for me. Philippe hoards decisions," Dickerson stated in a sworn deposition. And then there was what in the eyes of Bill Gates must have been the most scurrilous charge imaginable: "Philippe is never at the office."

According to Dickerson, Bill told him " 'Microsoft has the leading-edge technology and will carry ahead into the future,' and was essentially kind of selling the benefits of Microsoft and questioning the value of the Borland job offer."

Ballmer made a counteroffer. He would split the languages group in two, with Dickerson getting total oversight—not merely marketing—of everything but BASIC and COBOL. He would give Rob 12,000 more shares of stock options. And he would raise his salary—to a magnanimous $56,000 a year.

But the money was less of an issue than the position. At Microsoft, he'd be one more module in the code; at Borland, he'd be a vice president running the show. Dickerson told Steve and Bill no deal. He had already spoken with Borland's legal department and extracted one final condition: Borland's agreement to defend him from any suits brought by Microsoft.

Dickerson left for California the following Monday, began househunting, and started work at Borland the next day. Wednesday night his wife phoned to tell him that she'd just been handed a summons; Microsoft was suing. The next day Microsoft got a fourteen-day temporary restraining order keeping Dickerson from working in any way for Borland or disclosing Microsoft plans to anyone. On December 2 Borland's chief put his own spin on the situation:

Solicited by a Hare Krishna member in Sea-Tac Airport, Le Grand Philippe forked over a $100 bill with the promise of $900 more if the supplicant could deliver a message to Bill Gates: "Philippe Kahn donated $1,000 for hot meals in case anyone in your legal department is out of a job soon." Gates was not amused, but after a flurry of filings, the parties came to an agreement: Dickerson could work for Borland, but not, for nine months, on its versions of BASIC or C. The two companies also agreed not to hire each other's employees for six months.

Bill Gates would later say, "Dickerson's a good guy, but who was Dickerson? Dickerson was a guy who worked for the guy who's in charge of marketing who worked for the guy who's in charge of the language business unit. I mean, Dickerson was offered so much money at Borland, there was no *way*, no *way* he wasn't going to go." But Rob Dickerson had become the latest in a distinguished line to prove that you could stand up to the Great Gates and survive.

Dickerson's was hardly the most important departure in Bill's life. Over the past few years, Gates and Ann Winblad, who in 1985 moved to the Bay Area to do consulting and would eventually head her own venture capital firm, had been seeing each other on weekends, holidays, whenever their paths crossed. Winblad even convinced Bill to take a vacation now and then by coming up with "reading themes . . . We had a physics vacation once, a biotech vacation once, and we had an F. Scott Fitzgerald vacation." Winblad was responsible for picking and packing all the reading material.

It was at the end of a 1987 business trip to Brazil, whose government prohibited imports of DOS and was considering a total ban on foreign software, that Winblad introduced Gates to a subject that would eventually fascinate him almost as much as software code: biological code, the elemental structure of life itself. Among other works he and Ann read on this trip: the classic 1,150-page text, *Molecular Biology of the Gene*, by Nobel Prize winner and DNA co-modeler James D. Watson. "We were going everywhere with these huge big stacks of books," she recalled. It was their idea of fun.

Winblad understood Gates as well as any woman he'd ever met. She dragged him to the Tacoma Boat Show, where he bought a sleek Mirage skiboat in which he would later get speeding tickets—just as he did when he drove her car in California. She gave him a letter written by Napoleon. She led him to adopt a no-red-meat diet—"just for the heck of it," he said later with typical defensiveness, after being quoted repeatedly that he had done it as a test of will. She sympathized when his Mercedes "ran out of oil or something" and he switched to a brown Jaguar XJ6. Most of all, she got him to think about something besides work: "When he takes a vacation he does not answer the phone. He will not return calls, he will not take calls, he is gone," she said. "And then he's a really fun guy. . . . Most of the time he has to be the trusted general, with thousands of soldiers marching around. So it's good that he can periodically take some kind of break."

Winblad and Gates seemed the perfect couple, dispassionately intellectual, practical, business-savvy, self-driven titans of the digital world. The rumor—and hope—around Microsoft and among friends and family was that they were going to get married.

Winblad had a beach house on the Outer Banks of North Carolina. On one visit she and Bill took hang-gliding lessons at Kitty Hawk. At first, she recalled, "They tell you, 'You're going to do this several times to get the feel of the glider. Whatever you do, do not turn.' " After the initial practice run, fearless Bill Gates figured, as Winblad put it, " 'I've already learned step one, I'm not going to do this three times,' " tried a turn, "and landed in a bramble bush facedown."

"Ann was very interested in getting Bill motivated to settle down and start a family," said Mitch Kapor. Unfortunately, Winblad met with no success when she invited Kapor and his wife and year-old infant to the Outer Banks for a weekend of what Kapor called "an inspiring domestic example" of familial bliss on the dunes. Despite the Kapor family's best efforts, Gates ignored the child in favor of a biography or two of Henry Ford. "It had zero impact on him," Kapor recalled. "We were working really hard to be charming, and playing with the baby. It had no visible impact whatsoever. He was hardcore."

Eventually Winblad grew tired of dropping such hints. For her, the subject had become like the heist in *The Thomas Crown Affair*—a constant strategic presence that she, like Faye Dunaway, refused to back down from, but that Gates, like Steve McQueen, refused to acknowledge. Both Bill and Ann knew he wanted to get married, knew he wanted to have kids, but a mistress called Microsoft stood squarely in the path. "I think it's a scary thing for him to think about making a commitment to another entity," Winblad said. "It used to be kind of bachelor heaven up here. No one was married. It was kind of like visiting the Lost Boys."

Bill "wasn't ready to spend any energy on other things," said T/Maker's Heidi Roizen, who, like other friends, had been hoping the two would stay together. "Bill and Ann had a really tremendous relationship on a lot of levels because they're so much alike at the intellectual level. And I think that Bill just wasn't really ready to get married and have a family and all that." Six years older than Bill, Winblad's biological clock was an issue too, Roizen noted: "You say, 'Okay, is there going to be a continuation of this or am I supposed to just sit there and just twiddle my fingers? I probably want to think about my other options.' "

In the end, like Dunaway, Ann called Bill's bluff, and like McQueen he stood pat. The two officially broke off in December 1987 at the wedding of Bill's older sister. "I don't know why they decided to do that at my wedding,"

Kristi recalled. "Neither of them was smiling in any of the pictures." Her reaction was the same as most of their friends: "It was very sad."

But that same month, there was some happiness at Microsoft: OS/2 version 1.0 went out the door early in all its dull character-based glory. Still, IBM's enthusiasm was rather restrained. "No one will really use OS/2 1.0," Bill Lowe declared to the press. "I view it as a tool for large-account customers or software developers who want to begin writing OS/2 applications." What Lowe really wanted to talk about was something else. "Our Extended Edition will be designed to work with our PS/2s better than any other hardware and software combination in the business."

So how come, Lowe was asked, you didn't invite Microsoft to participate in the development of that communications and database program? "Frankly," he said, "those are very complex subjects to master, and we alone had the skills to do those jobs."

Bill Gates would see about that.

26

LOOK AND FEEL

Saint Patrick's Day 1987 had been the day IBM announced the glories of SAA to an indifferent world—indifferent, that is, except for the Microsofties who had to live with it. On Saint Patrick's Day 1988 the rain on Bill Gates's parade would blow in from Cupertino, California.

A stream of reporters suddenly began calling Microsoft for comment on a lawsuit filed by Apple. Microsoft's attorneys had not previously been notified. Nor had Bill Gates, who just two days earlier had talked with John Sculley and received no indication of a pending legal action. Instead the first to receive word of the action had been the news media, contacted by Apple public relations representatives and sending the national e-mail network and Silicon Valley grapevine into hyperspace. Word soon spread throughout the Redmond campus that Apple had gone to court. Gates put it down to rumormongering and ignored it. But he got confirmation in a late-afternoon phone message from Apple general counsel Al Eisenstat that he would later characterize as "the most out-of-the-blue thing I ever experienced."

Gates returned Eisenstat's call that evening and got his first official news of the suit. The chairman went ballistic. The agreement he had negotiated with Sculley and Eisenstat more than two years earlier had been designed specifically to, as he had expressed to his inner circle, put the issue "totally behind us." Visual displays, future versions, even Apple's right to use Microsoft technology in the Mac were all covered. Gates thought he had bargained in good faith with Sculley, and now the Sugared Water Man was turning around and stabbing him in the back. And Sculley's knives were also out for Hewlett-Packard. Apple was also suing HP, whose New Wave software ran on top of Windows.

Gates got on the horn and demanded to know what was going on, later recalling Sculley's response in vivid mimicry of a confuddled drawl: "I don't know, the lawyer, I don't know much about it, my lawyer's, he got it . . . it's New Wave, isn't it? New Wave, yeah, New Wave. . . ." Other than the usual gossip-column rumblings, there'd been no recent indication that Apple had been even thinking of suing—although the 1985 Comdex agreement had not quite put an end to the bickering.

In an interview published in the June 1986 issue of *Computer Language,* Gates had made the revisionist statement that "Every microcomputer company we worked with in the first five years, they're gone." Apparently Apple had been the farthest thing from his mind. Yet on July 23, 1986, Apple's ubiquitous Irv Rappaport wrote Microsoft's house counsel Bill Neukom inquiring about a company called Data Pacific that was talking with Apple about a product called MacCartridge that would let Atari computers run Macintosh software. The Data Pacific attorney had mentioned that his company was negotiating with Microsoft "for some kind of license on the Macintosh interface," Rappaport reported. "That seemed very odd to us." Rappaport went on to state that the 1985 agreement did not permit Microsoft to grant such a license and was limited to version 1.0 of Windows.

Neukom's letter of September 2 denied any such negotiations. Besides, Neukom hinted, Microsoft thought Rappaport was generally all wet: "Apparently we do not have any pending controversy and the record now reads: you interpret the Agreement to include certain limitations and we utterly disagree with that interpretation."

In mid-October 1986 rumors of potential Apple litigation against Microsoft hit the press and provided one more black eye for the credibility of Windows. Independent developers began to worry that they might be liable in a suit against Windows or even get sued themselves—hardly an inducement to write applications for Microsoft's interface.

To counteract that notion, Microsoft contacted Eisenstat in December with a proposed press release claiming, among other things, that "The agreement eliminates uncertainty over visual copyrights without restricting either party or its developers." Eisenstat objected, but Microsoft put out its "clarification" anyway in early January 1987. A letter from Rappaport followed, claiming "there are limitations in our Agreement" and that Microsoft's unilateral press release violated the agreement's confidentiality clause.

And Apple wasn't the only place the press release was being read. On January 15, 1987, Hewlett-Packard attorney Robert Booth wrote to Microsoft's OEM sales chief Jim Harris inquiring "Specifically, does the Apple-MS agreement include or exclude modifications and extensions which HP may add to Windows?" If Microsoft had supplied HP "a product which may be infringing, we need to know this immediately." Reason: HP was finishing up work on New Wave.

HP had initially approached Apple for a license to its technology and had been turned down cold. Now New Wave was running under Windows and a license from Microsoft for its technology. HP was beginning to wonder if Microsoft actually had the right to grant the license.

Harris wrote back more than a month later that he could not disclose terms of the visual copyright agreement with Apple. "However, let me assure you that Windows 1.0, the version of Windows you are presently licensed to distribute, does not infringe Apple's proprietary rights. Notwithstanding the above, the nature of visual copyrights is such that it is conceivable Hewlett-Packard could create software, which would run in conjunction with any operating system, that Apple would consider infringing." So the answer was: Yes and no. If HP was looking for a green light on New Wave, it was not going to come from Microsoft.

And things were getting testy between the Apple and Microsoft camps. At Esther Dyson's Personal Computer Forum in the spring of 1987, Gates locked horns with Apple's Larry Tesler, another former PARC wizard who had worked on the Macintosh. When Tesler defended the notion of licensing the "look and feel" of a system, Gates jumped in: "Apple doesn't license any 'look and feel' to my developers. Nobody has to sign any license to do Macintosh applications."

"Well, that's not correct," Tesler said.

"We never signed any," Gates retorted. "There's no control of 'look and feel.' You leave the wrong impression if you say that."

"There's a court reporter down there," joked Robert Carr, the author of Framework.

"Good," Bill Gates declared.

On December 16, 1987, two months after the official announcement of Windows 2.0, Apple's peripatetic Rappaport visited HP's personal software division in Santa Clara for a prerelease demonstration of New Wave. According to Rappaport's sworn declaration, HP's New Wave product manager Bill Crow explained that the new product was designed to run in tandem with Win 2.03. Rappaport asked Crow if Microsoft had been involved in the development of New Wave. Filed under things he probably wished he hadn't said, Crow's response: Yes, Microsoft had participated in the design and development of the program. HP later acknowledged that New Wave had been designed to run with Windows and that Microsoft had licensed it, but denied other aspects of Rappaport's account.

Significantly, when Microsoft had released Windows 2.01 in October 1987 as part of Excel, Apple had taken no action, despite the new version's use of overlapping windows, movable icons, and other changes to the Windows 1.0 interface. When HP announced New Wave in November and Microsoft issued its retail edition, Windows 2.03, in January 1988, Apple's attorneys got busy.

Now here in Federal Court was Apple alleging a whole laundry list of violations of copyrights on the Lisa and Macintosh, which it termed "audiovisual works." Here was Apple claiming that the "visual displays and images" contained in Windows 2.03 were "illegal and infringing copies" of the Macintosh audiovisual works. Here was Apple asking for damages of $50,000 per infringement, as well as for the "impoundment and destruction of all computer programs known as New Wave and Windows 2.03." This was gratitude for the Smart Guys' contributions to the Mac? This was Apple's way of thanking Microsoft for developing the early apps that kept the company afloat when there was little else to run on the Mac?

"There's nothing that's happened in Windows to move it closer to the Mac," said Gates in an Alexandria, Virginia, press conference, adding presciently: "The suit will just be there for years." For good measure of moral outrage, he had Microsoft's attorneys countersue, charging Apple with slander and with "the intent of wrongfully inhibiting" Windows development.

Ironically, the last time Apple had taken a copyright case to court, it had walked away smelling like a rose—with the help of an *amicus* brief from Microsoft. In 1983 Apple had sued Franklin Computer Corporation for copying its ROM code in order to sell Apple II clones. Apple won, and the clones were history. Ecstatic about Apple's victory was a young DOS merchant named Bill Gates, under whose byline an opinion piece appeared in the business section of the *New York Times*. The ruling "may have saved the future of the United States computer software industry," Gates observed, adding: "Imagine the disincentive to software development if after months of work another company could come along and copy your work and market it under its own name. . . . Without legal restraints on such copying, companies like Apple could not afford to advance the state of the art." Imagine indeed: Four and a half years later Apple would use a virtually identical argument in suing Microsoft over Windows.

But this time nobody was claiming there had been any filching of actual code. This was a whole new realm of the law, where the precedents had more to do with the design of stuffed toys, jewelry, and clown costumes than with computers. Filed over a year before, the still-pending Lotus vs. Paperback Software "look-and-feel" case over a "clone" of 1-2-3 had muddied the waters and galvanized the industry over the issues of copyright protection and intellectual property. Now the Apple-Microsoft suit would become a study in trial by media. Rivers of ink flowed from the word processors of outraged columnists, angry software developers, querulous partisans on both sides. Few bothered to notice that it was a contract dispute as much as a copyright issue, and few bothered to notice the crucial importance of New Wave.

The problem with New Wave was that its enhancements were a closer imitation of the Mac than Windows had ever been. Instead of the lame Windows MS-DOS Executive, which listed files the way they appeared in DOS only worse, New Wave organized documents in folders—just like the Mac. It had file folder just like the Mac's, document icons just like the Mac's, and a Waste Basket that strongly resembled the Macintosh trash can. Look? Feel? There hadn't been such a direct visual knockoff of the Mac since the early days of GEM.

Apple did not ask for a temporary injunction, a move initially interpreted as evidence that it felt its case was weak. Gates tested Apple's resolve almost immediately, announcing a joint development project with HP on Excel for New Wave. It was the classic Gatesian chess game: attack, attack, attack.

Apple could afford to take a more leisurely course, stretching out the process over months, years, forcing HP and Microsoft to spend millions on the process, keeping the classic industry FUD factor—Fear, Uncertainty, and Doubt—foremost in the PC community's mind. Software developers from Sunnyvale to Boston were quoted as being nervous about developing for Windows. Philippe Kahn, who had publicly dubbed OS/2 "BS/2," said Apple's allegations, after longstanding reassurances from Microsoft that Windows was safe, were like "waking up and finding out that your partner might have AIDS."

Steve Jobs, now developing a graphical user interface of his own, had a different view. "When we were developing the Macintosh we kept in mind a famous quote of Picasso: 'Good artists copy, great artists steal.' " Actually, the quote almost certainly wasn't Picasso's, unless he stole it, but never mind. "What do I think of the suit? I personally don't understand it. . . . Can I copyright gravity? No!"

As for Gates himself, the warlord went on the warpath. The visual displays weren't copyrightable, he argued. Even if they were, they didn't originate with Apple but at Xerox PARC. And if some didn't originate at Xerox, Apple had developed them with Microsoft's help: "We're not trying to claim some of the credit, but yes, the original applications were written by us—take various techniques, like the zooming and window drop-down and the way the controls work, stuff like that. We had more people working on Macintosh software than Apple did, so we had some influence." Gates would get plenty of challenges to those assertions. Former Apple executive Trip Hawkins, acknowledging Microsoft had some input, pointed out on what basis: "If Gates had ever said he wanted a piece of the copyright, Apple would have told him to go jump in the lake."

In a sworn declaration a month after the suit was filed, the lawyer's son kept up the attack. Apple had been told and understood all along that Microsoft would "bring to market new versions of Windows," Gates stated. "Throughout the negotiations, we made it plain to Apple and Apple agreed that this settlement was to be a full and final resolution of these issues." But one of Bill's statements threw up red flags all over Cupertino: "From a user's perspective, the visual displays which appear in Windows 2.03 are virtually identical to those which appear in Windows 1.0."

Apple jumped on that one: "This assertion . . . is contradicted by even the most casual observation of the screen displays of the two products, and by the literature Microsoft itself published," Apple's manager of competitive analysis Paul Norris pointed out in a sworn declaration. In a February 1988 *Windows Reviewer's Handbook* published by Microsoft, the Redmond gang had described 2.0 as a "second-generation Windows product" offering "numerous advantages" over DOS and previous versions of Windows—including overlapping windows.

To illustrate its argument, Apple invoked its Happy Face demonstration, comparing Windows 1.0 and its tiling with the overlapping approach of Windows 2.03 and the Macintosh. In each instance, the graphics window displayed a circle with Mr. Smiley in it. It was one of the rare moments of humor the suit would see.

Apple's position was that the license to Microsoft for Windows permitted use of visual displays as long as Windows or any other Windows product did not become "more similar to the Macintosh than the version Windows 1.0," Eisenstat said in a sworn deposition. The overlapping windows of New Wave and Windows 2.03, and New Wave's familiar icons, were obviously more like the Macintosh, the suit alleged. And that was what Apple had been fighting all along. Apple attorneys cited Neukom's handwritten note from the negotiations: "Don't want MS to create Mac look!" Neukom countered that he had merely been recording what Apple's Edwin Taylor had told him, and had made no response to Taylor's admonition.

More like the Mac, more like the Mac. It became Apple's mantra in the trial. Apple's John Sculley stated in his sworn deposition: "It was my understanding that they could not add something that would make it look more like the Macintosh." Backing Sculley up was Jean-Louis Gassée, Apple's president, who asserted that Win 2 was closer to the Mac because "when you see it, you know it." See it? Know it? That seemed awfully close to "look and feel," the words that Bill Gates had specifically deleted from the draft agreement. The Microsoft side would later ridicule Gassée's comments as the "gestalt" theory.

Gates found particularly rankling the notion that Microsoft had somehow agreed to future restrictions, *any* future restrictions, on use of the Mac displays. The one thing he had hammered on in his negotiations with Apple, he repeated, was that Microsoft "would accept *no* restrictions on the use of the visual displays." It was a particularly sore point in that Gates had been negotiating the agreement right after Apple's saber-rattling over GEM, in which Digital

Research had agreed to let Apple review future versions to ensure they were not "substantially similar" to the Mac. The chairman had never accepted those kinds of limitations from Apple.

Henry Ford himself, Gates knew, had been plagued by a similar suit from a group owning what it claimed was a patent on the horseless carriage. For six frustrating years Ford had fought the suit, but in 1909 a judge upheld the patent. Nonetheless, Ford declared that "There will be no let up in the legal fight" and that the patent was "worthless as a patent and worthless as a device." Two years later the appeals court found for Ford. With his victory, one biographer noted, "a new American folk hero was beginning to stand revealed."

So the Henry Ford of software was not about to roll over either. Microsoft immediately moved to bifurcate the case into two separate phases, the first deciding whether Microsoft had been licensed to use Macintosh features in Windows 2.03 and the second, if necessary, determining whether Microsoft had violated Apple's copyrights. On May 20 Judge Robert Aguilar granted the bifurcation. Apple later moved to have Aguilar removed on the ground that his son worked for HP; on September 23, 1988, he refused to step down. A month later, however, the case was moved from Aguilar's San Jose court to San Francisco and the court of Judge William W. Schwarzer. Three years and one more judge later the case would still await trial.

In all the hoopla following the lawsuit, the biggest question nearly got missed: Where was Big Blue? Wasn't Presentation Manager promised to look, even feel, just like Windows? How did IBM manage to escape Apple's legal fishnet?

Up in Armonk, the guy who'd been there from the start, Bill Lowe himself, was playing it cool in public. PM was clean, there was no problem at all:

> As we entered into the joint development arrangement with Microsoft, and as we developed our own contributions to the Presentation Manager, we made every effort to ensure that both the work contributed by Microsoft and contributed by us was based on original development, or took advantage of development that either Microsoft or IBM has available through its copyright or patent arrangements. So my anticipation is that our products will be free of any accusation.

But in private, Lowe recalled, "IBM was worried about the potential threat," and had talks with Microsoft to "assess the damage." Lowe believed Apple was avoiding confrontation with IBM's huge legal staff in hopes of winning a precedent it could enforce at a later date.

After all, Gates and Gassée and Rappaport and Neukom could argue all they wanted about what the licensing agreement meant. Apple was betting that to Joe Sixpack's eyes the two operating environments would look pretty much alike and that it could show some untoward borrowing had been going on. For Microsoft and HP, the horror of horrors in the Apple lawsuit was a tiny mark on the cover sheet of the original complaint. In a section labeled JURY DEMAND, Apple attorney Martin L. Lagod had checked the box marked YES.

27

▶

YOU CAN MAKE IT HAPPEN!

OS/2 1.0 shipped in December 1987, and Bill Lowe's prediction instantly came true: Nobody used it. A handful of applications such as WordPerfect shipped for it, and that was all. Besides the dearth of software, another factor would stall acceptance of OS/2: For the first time since the advent of the microprocessor, Moore's Law had been broken.

Ever since the advent of Simonyi's revenue bomb, Microsoft's application programs always needed a little more power, a little more memory to run well. Fast, tight code could only take you so far, particularly when the boss engaged in "feature nymphomania." As Richard Brodie put it, "If you sit on your butt for a year and a half, you get speed automatically: The computer gets twice as fast. But if you sit on your butt for a year and a half, you don't get features."

Microsoft's products tended to be state-of-next-year's art, gambling that the hardware would eventually catch up. It was a pretty safe bet. As long as Moore's Law remained inexorable, machines would keep getting faster, and memory would keep getting cheaper.

But now, for a variety of reasons—lack of manufacturing capacity, an upgrade in chip technology, an antidumping agreement between Japan and the United States—chips were in short supply and the price of memory was not declining according to the classic curve. For the first time in memory, memory prices were actually going up! This put a bit of a crimp in plans to sell an operating system that required tons of memory, heaps of it, megabyte upon megabyte.

Eventually that would get sorted out. For now, it was time to get as hardcore as anyone at Microsoft had ever been. IBM had promised October 31, 1988, as the date for shipping Presentation Manager, and IBM was a schedule-driven company. On the Microsoft side, Steve Ballmer was in command: "We have to go on a death march. And nothing will stand in my way. *Nothing!* I'll rape any project! I mean, I'm almost a mad dog!''

The Smart Guys, the fast-trackers with the hot cars and ultralight planes and rock guitars who had hammered Windows together against all odds, were marching. Letwin was flying down to Boca, negotiating with Gates before every excruciating trip. Konzen was flying over to Hursley, renting the fastest car on the lot and screaming down the wrong side of country roads. Ballmer had swiped virtually all the Smart Guys for his OS/2 team.

''We had a great team,'' Gates boasted. ''If you look at our technical ratings, we put a more experienced team by a *large* amount over there on OS/2 . . . but don't think that they were enjoying it!'' Konzen, remembering the lackluster party for the initial Windows rollout, conned Steve Ballmer into promising an unaccustomed and slightly ''decadent'' fringe benefit for on-time delivery: a trip to Hawaii for the whole OS/2 gang. T-shirts, posters, and even office routing slips suddenly carried the battle cry: ''You Can Make It Happen! October '88.''

To Microsoft programmers, the working relationship with IBM was a distinct clash of cultures. Microsoft's typical way of approaching a project was to have a small group of developers put together enough specifications to get started and then let them dive in, changing things as they went along. It had worked for Bill Gates since the Altair BASIC days and before. But, as Windows and Cashmere and a host of other projects showed, the process had its own built-in inefficiencies, including ship dates of purest slime.

IBM's priority was to meet the ship date, hell or high water, and it had layer upon layer of rules for planning and implementing software code. At IBM, you documented your code with plenty of comments or ''remarks'' explaining what each portion did, and you started out with a ''prologue''—a paragraph or so of plain English describing the code's function. Crusty Ed Kiser, the man whose pen Bill Gates had used to sign the original IBM licensing agreement, found himself on IBM's OS/2 team. The only prologue in Microsoft code, he discovered, tended to be its copyright notice, and he once offered ''a prize for the guy who finds the first remark.''

There was another cultural clash: IBM was not big on programming in the C language. In the increasingly irrelevant world of IBM, the classical languages were COBOL, PL/I, and BAL (Basic Assembly Language). But C, originally developed at Bell Labs, had now become the language of choice among university-trained software developers, most of whom had been weaned on UNIX systems. Microsoft developed almost exclusively in C for Presentation Manager and considered IBM's C programmers rank amateurs.

The OS/2 kernel had been developed, and was now being modified, in assembly language. But IBM did even that differently. Much of the code was first written in a macro language known as STRUCT that produced big, ugly assembly code that the Smart Guys gleefully derided and "deSTRUCTed."

Gordon Letwin took to calling the project a "Mexican school bus." For IBM, this was going to be the low-end system for everything from cash registers to robots. As Iacobucci saw it, "There was so much different design input from various parts of the IBM universe that it wound up losing its purity and identity."

Bill Gates was getting increasingly irritated himself. As he had said back in mid-1986:

It would be so wrong to tell a guy it would be good if he wrote 2,000 lines [of code] a day. To apply some weird metric other than whether you can make it load and save really fast without speeding up any other attributes would be pretty artificial. We do have a customer who asked us to measure ourselves that way, so we have those kinds of statistics, but I'm not even aware of the numbers.

He wasn't then; he was now. There was no doubt about who that particular customer was. IBM measured progress by "K-LOCS"—thousands of lines of code. Bill Gates didn't think that measured much of anything:

There was a six-month period where we called it "sizzle." Zbikowski and Letwin just went to work; things were way too slow, way too big, so they just took modules—they took like this one IBM 5000-line module and replaced it with a 400-line module. Our net work over a six-month period: We wrote a negative number of lines of code. It was a scandal! Our percentage of the work had dropped!

Gates came up with a metaphor for IBM's vision: "Building the world's heaviest airplane." Adrian King understood Bill's frustration: "The project was so big, there were so many people involved, there were so few ways you could actually control, that his ability to give input and actually steer the project in any sense was incredibly limited. And that used to frustrate him immensely, I believe. So he just didn't know as much about OS/2, technically speaking, as he did about basically every other product Microsoft was doing."

In April 1988 Steve Ballmer tried to recapture the magic of the 1983 Windows announcement with a New York press conference for Microsoft's OS/2-based LAN Manager, the successor to MS-NET in Microsoft's networking strategy. The event featured thirty-three big-name OEM customers—just about everybody but independent network software vendors Novell and Banyan. The world seemed headed in Microsoft's direction.

It didn't help Bill's mood. Walking into the penthouse suite of the Marriott

Marquis hotel, he turned to an underling and demanded, "Who got this room? What are we paying for this room?" The suite included a huge bedroom, two living rooms, a kitchen, and a grand piano. To Bill Gates, it looked like decadence.

No, it was all part of a package deal, he was told, a bundle that included the ballroom and other rooms for the conference. The extra space in the suite would serve as a sort of staging area for interviews, meetings, and the like.

Only mildly relieved, Gates went to the window and looked out pensively. "Windows," he reflected. "Why can't the world just accept and understand Windows? Why can't they just buy Windows?"

Why couldn't they? Why couldn't they? Back on October 18, 1987, the day before the stock market crash, Dave Marquardt got married in Napa Valley. Bill Gates was one of the ushers; so was Scott McNealy of Sun Microsystems. Sun was another one of Marquardt's smart investments, right behind Compaq on the list of history's fastest-growing companies. Sun's business was workstations—high-powered desktop computers typically used by engineers and scientists and even, for a time, by some of Microsoft's programmers.

Under perfect California skies, Marquardt's wedding reception moved to a broad lawn, where a dance floor had been set up. As the band began to play, Gates and McNealy huddled in one corner of the grass, very obviously hammering out some high-powered deal. As one witness put it, "There's nothing more fun for these people than their business. So why not? Why waste a minute?"

The deal they were discussing was one that Nathan Myhrvold had been trying to put together. Sun machines ran on UNIX, which Microsoft perceived as a threat to OS/2. Myhrvold's idea was to make Presentation Manager the user interface for UNIX rather than one of the many alternatives, such as Sun's NeWS or the X Window system from MIT. As Myhrvold recalled: "We would work together to create it, then we would've licensed it to the UNIX community. And it would've been a standard window environment for UNIX which would've been Presentation Manager UNIX. . . . It was very reasonable financially to Microsoft and to Sun. This would've been perfect."

Microsoft and Sun even made "a bunch of presentations" to AT&T, the masters of the UNIX domain. But "There was this one week when we had a deal, and then they [Sun] backed off because they did their deal with AT&T, and they said, 'We don't need you anymore. We are now the Microsoft of the UNIX community. Fuck you'—more or less."

At Marquardt's wedding, Gates recognized that the negotiations "were actually kind of dying out." McNealy later said it was because Bill was demanding a $60 royalty per machine when McNealy considered even $6 "outrageous." And unbeknownst to Gates, AT&T was in the midst of negotiating a complicated agreement estimated to be worth $320 million to buy upward of

$7\frac{1}{2}$ percent of Sun. Announced in January 1988, the Sun-AT&T alliance intended to set its own standards for UNIX. Sun would call the tune; competitors would have to fall into line.

That was the idea, anyway. But the competitors were formidable, including the likes of DEC and Hewlett-Packard, companies that did not enjoy being dictated to by a Silicon Valley upstart and a phone company. And another big firm saw AT&T as a dangerous rival. So in May 1988 a consortium of seven companies, eventually growing to thirty-nine, announced the formation of the Open Software Foundation (OSF), which would develop its own UNIX standards. The leader of the pack? IBM.

"Boy, that was a big deal in terms of our relationship," Bill Lowe said, recalling how Bill Gates reacted to the news:

> At IBM we would always call somebody ahead of time and say you're gonna read about this. . . . And it exploded. He was very upset. He said, "This may not be betting the company for IBM, but it may be betting the company for Microsoft, in terms of the size of its investment. And you guys, if you're gonna push UNIX in addition to pushing OS/2, this is a real problem."
>
> . . . You have to remember that when OSF was introduced, they were pursuing AIX, the IBM version of UNIX. . . . That may have looked like more of a threat because it was based on an IBM operating system.
>
> . . . We were still working together, we were still merchandising OS/2, but my feeling at the time was that it impacted our relationship. . . . I think the real breakup began when IBM got into OSF. It was the right thing for IBM to do. IBM had to cover multiple bets. It was understandable that he got upset, because the bet he was covering on OS/2 represented for him a substantial part of his company. And, boy he got upset!

Gates tried to go over Lowe's head to IBM's executive vice president Jack Kuehler, but the answer was the same: IBM was in this thing for good. "It did piss us off," said Nathan Myhrvold, "because we saw it as a direct way of challenging OS/2." In "a hell of a weekend" of inner-circle phone calls, Microsoft considered joining OSF itself and finally decided not to. In March 1989 Gates would hedge his bet: Microsoft would buy just under 20 percent of the Santa Cruz Operation, an OSF member and longtime Microsoft XENIX partner, for a reported $25 million.

At Spring Comdex '88, independent software vendors showed a hundred less-than-thrilling OS/2 applications, few of them customer-ready, and a grand total of two PM apps: Aldus PageMaker and Micrografx Draw—both of which were a long way from being completed. And what was the big deal anyhow? If you wanted either program, you could already get a version that was ready to run—under Windows.

At long last, Windows was actually gaining momentum. And despite Ballmer's rah-rah for Presentation Manager, Microsoft was clearly pushing Windows development first. "They're focusing on Windows being the bridge to OS/2," said one developer. "I think we'll support Windows on DOS and wait awhile before going to OS/2," said another.

That's what Microsoft was doing internally, and it wasn't easy. By mid-1988 things were slipping badly on the applications side. Ida Cole's captaincy of the applications division had been doomed from the start. She quickly realized that she and Bill "didn't get on. He had a lot of respect for my abilities and talents, but they weren't his, and so he had a hard time talking to me. I had a real hard time with him mainly because I was older." Cole and Gates recognized the problem early in 1986, just before her first anniversary with the company. "I had gone in to Jon to tell him that he needed to find me another job. Bill had gone in to see Jon to say . . . 'This isn't going to work.' " Within months Cole took over international products, and Gates recaptured nominal control of the applications division that he had really never relinquished.

By early 1988, under Bill's personal guidance, many of the strategic applications efforts were in shambles. Revisions of the existing products were moving along, but aside from Excel, none of the major new products for Windows were going anywhere. The Windows database program, code-named Omega, was still nowhere near ready. Project for Windows was also rumored to be lost in Betaville. But the exemplary program, the one that would become so notorious as to be written up as a Harvard Business School case, was the project that had begun as Cashmere and had as many mothholes as one of Bill's vintage pullovers.

Back in 1984, Bill Gates had every reason to believe the do-it-all word processor with add-in functionality would be ready in a year under the swift coding fingers of Richard Brodie. Given the problems with Windows and the uncertainty about how much all-in-one integrated capability to give the product, what got finished by late 1985 was little more than the spec—a common problem at Microsoft, where the boss loved features but didn't give much input into implementing them. When Brodie left in 1986, it became clear that even the Cashmere spec was incomplete. The project was renamed Opus and restarted from scratch with a plan that omitted many of the advanced features—rudimentary spreadsheet capabilities, electronic mail, table orientation—originally intended for it. This Great Simplification didn't help any more than the one on OS/2.

At no time from the inception of the project did anyone ever see the ship date as more than a year away. In January 1987 the product was scheduled for a December rollout. In June 1987 it was scheduled for the following February. In February the project was presented to Bill Gates, who demanded a series of additional features and sent the programmers back to their keyboards. Still, by June 1988 the developers were sure it would ship that October.

Schedule pressure and inexperienced programmers had combined to create an atmosphere that one developer dubbed "Infinite Defects." Summer interns were hired and their code left unexamined until long after they were gone. In school, said Jeff Harbers, "they've been rewarded for writing incomplete programs and getting them done on time." When pressed, these green programmers would get code running, ignore trivial details such as major bugs, and move on to new tasks, leaving a trail of trouble in their wake.

Under the intense pressure, the development leader had developed a viral disease resembling chronic fatigue syndrome and had to take medical leave. Other managers burned out. In mid-1988, even though Microsoft actually demonstrated Opus in public under the WinWord name, the project looked grim. And so did the rest of the Windows applications development, except for Excel. "Products ship because you have people who make them ship," Harbers was coming to understand. Bill Gates was beginning to realize he desperately needed someone like that at the top. Once again he turned to the technique that had worked so well with Jon Shirley: Hire somebody you already know and respect.

Mike Maples, a spherical blue-eyed Oklahoman, had been with IBM for twenty-three years, and Bill Gates had been badgering him about Windows for five of them. As IBM's head of software strategy and business evaluation, Maples not only had key inside knowledge of Big Blue and the industry at large, but was a central figure in OS/2 and PM development. "I told Bill the first time that the thing was going to be called Presentation Manager and he about croaked because he wanted Windows so bad."

In their evangelizing for the new operating system, Gates and Maples kept bumping into each other on podiums across the country. At IBM, Maples recalled, there was a feeling that Microsoft would "say anything to anybody depending on the audience and what they thought they might want to hear." What irked Maples about Gates was his chameleon talent for changing his colors:

> You know, he'd go to an IBM forum and stand up and say, "Yeah, Micro Channel is great and [the] 8514 [IBM video standard] is the best thing that we've ever had in the business." And then he'd go to some user group in Peoria and say, "Gosh, I can't imagine anybody buying a Micro Channel machine." And one time I remember doing like an eight-week survey of all the places that he was quoted, that he was saying good things about IBM or not saying good things about IBM, and I gave it to him. I said, "Look, here are ninety-five times you are quoted, and sixty-three times you are saying bad things about IBM."

Standing up to Bill Gates: It was the perfect path to job happiness at Microsoft.

Steve Ballmer was the first to broach the idea of having Maples head up Microsoft's applications division. Maples passed: He was happy where he was, and it was hardly right for partners to hire each other's guys away. Asked a second time, Maples mulled it over and said he would think about it if IBM said okay. Bill Gates personally talked with the higher-ups and got the nod. Maples took a week to think about it: "It was really hard. It's kind of like a divorce." The offer letter spelled out one of the differences: two weeks vacation a year for the first five years, three weeks thereafter. At IBM Maples was getting six.

But Gates and Ballmer had been their usual convincing selves. When Maples broke the news to IBM, he expected to stick around for a week and fulfill some speaking commitments; instead his ID badge was taken, his desk was cleaned out, he was escorted everywhere he went, "and you know, by two o'clock, I was out." After twenty-three-and-a-half years, Maples felt like a foreigner. Early the next morning, Maples found he could log on to the e-mail system from home and "wrote a bunch of friends good-bye." An hour or so later, when he tried to get back on to the system to write some people he had forgotten, he was locked out. "We sort of risked pissing off IBM, and in fact they were pissed off when we hired him," Gates said.

Maples arrived in July 1988 and was met with the usual skepticism among the rank and file, who weren't sure anyone from Big Blue could possibly fathom Microsoft's ways. "Everybody thought, you know, 'Oh, jeez, this guy's going to come over from IBM and screw everything up,' " Mike Slade recalled. But Microsoft's results-oriented youth culture was willing to give him the benefit of the doubt.

Gates was sour on the way applications were coming out—or not coming out. One of Maples's first assignments was to analyze why the products were falling so far behind, especially Word: Word 4 for the Mac was late, PC Word 5 was late, Word for Windows was not just late but nearly terminal. As for Omega, the Windows database, it was an unmitigated botch. "We're not going to be in the database market for a long time," Gates had said presciently more than a year earlier.

Maples's most important finding: We're not bad programmers, we're just bad schedulers. The bright, fast-track high achievers tended to overestimate how much they could do but went ahead and tried anyway. There was more new code in Word 5 than in all of Word 1. "No wonder it takes longer!" he told his assembled apps throngs.

As one developer put it, "We always think we're good, and we always underestimate, and we're always like banging our heads for a long time." Schedules were purported to be ruthlessly accurate, yet each week a product "eighteen months away" would supposedly slip by three days, and Maples would say, "How do you know that?"

They didn't know that. In 1988 Microsoft confidently announced that PC and Mac updates of Word would ship by the end of the year, stopped producing the old versions, and allowed inventory to run dry. Next the release date was moved back to March 1989. When March rolled around, Microsoft announced yet another delay—sending its stock price down by more than 13 percent. Since Word typically accounted for more than 20 percent of sales, its unavailability led to poor third-quarter earnings, precipitating a shareholders' suit alleging that Microsoft had concealed its prior knowledge of the importance of the delay. Microsoft settled the suit in December 1990 for $1.5 million.

But that wasn't the only applications software snafu. When Maples arrived, estimates of the Word for Windows ship date had shrunk to half a year. In fact, a year and a half was more like it. Omega had even more wildly optimistic handlers. When Maples arrived, the thing was supposedly three months away from shipment, and field technicians and a beta test program had been put in place. A year and a half later, the product was finally scuttled.

Maples could see that a change was needed. Far from bringing a bloated, big-systems approach, he sensed that smaller, tighter groups targeting a specific competitor would provide more motivation and control over individual projects. After a series of sessions reviewing proposals with Bill, he reorganized the division into five business units: Office, Analysis, Graphics, Data Access, and Entry. Since Microsoft was not number one in any domestic applications market (except, depending on how you figured it, entry-level multifunction packages with Works), each unit would target the leader in its field: WordPerfect, 1-2-3, Harvard Graphics, dBASE IV.

The units were in essence businesses of their own, each with a product manager for marketing and program manager for development, each its own profit and loss center. It was focus, focus, focus. The Word group didn't have to worry about Lotus, the Excel group didn't have to worry about dBASE. It was exactly the kind of focus that in the past had led Jeff Raikes, at the time managing Microsoft Word, to memorize the names and birthdays of WordPerfect chief Pete Peterson's kids. When one of Peterson's sons turned sixteen, Raikes sent the boy a Microsoft key chain with the hint that he should hit Dad up for a new car.

And Maples meshed surprisingly well with the Microsoft culture. To dramatize the companywide United Way campaign, Maples's Apps guys squared off against Ballmer's Systems team to see who could raise more money—loser takes a swim in Lake Bill, the campus's tiny artificial pond. When both sides laid claim to statistical victory, the obvious solution was for both Maples and Ballmer to take a dive in the four-foot-deep megapuddle. With great ceremony at high noon on a chilly October day the stocky, athletic Ballmer stripped down to white boxer shorts and expertly splooshed his way to the opposite end, avoiding large chunks of dry ice dumped into Lake Bill to ensure a bracing dip.

Maples, agile despite his bulk, dived in fully clothed, his neatly pressed white shirt clinging to a wetsuit underneath. The event capped a United Way drive that generated more than half a million dollars in employee and Microsoft matching contributions. For good measure, the chairman tossed in $100,000 of his own, reportedly the largest personal contribution ever made to the local United Way, and pledged $1 million over the ensuing six to eight years. He could afford it: Although the stock had become mired in doldrums that would last for another year, his Microsoft holdings were worth more than $1.1 billion.

▼ With IBM's usual keen marketing savvy, OS/2 1.1, with Presentation Manager, was scheduled to ship on Halloween. Down in Boca, the Death March meant doing things IBM had never done before: establishing a nursery, bringing in dinners, putting employees up in nearby hotel rooms so they wouldn't have to drive home exhausted. A large IBM contingent flew in from Hursley. Forty Microsofties were airlifted down to Boca for what one called "the month in hell." After three days without sleep, one Microsoft programmer on assignment in Boca wondered "What is a week? A week is a long day."

But the Smart Guys made Halloween happen, and now they were on Broadway, appearing at the Marriott Marquis for the official announcement, complete with "PM" carved into pumpkins. When the programmers were asked to take bows, the Softies stood up in their T-shirts, sweatshirts, torn jeans. The more appropriately dressed IBM programmers looked as though they were attending a funeral. The Redmondians flew off to Maui. The Bocans went home to a luau in Boynton Beach, paid for out of the pockets of some of the managers.

Trick or tweak! At first glance, PM was better than anyone might have guessed. The graphical interface was cleaner and more subtle than Windows, with proportional fonts and pastel colors. There were Mac-like icons for disk drives and file folders, though the trash can was nowhere to be found. The system even had on-line help—something both the Macintosh and Windows lacked.

What didn't it have? Device drivers! The software that would let you use such arcane devices as printers and monitors was virtually nonexistent. If you had a nonstandard monitor or a printer from anyone other than IBM, you were out of luck—unless you happened to possess the considerable skills necessary to write your own driver. Chairman Bill's vaunted device independence was turning out to mean that the system would be independent of devices that worked.

Which joint partner was supposed to be responsible for the drivers? "Hursley," said Gates, quickly adding "it's complicated." Hursley was responsible for the IBM drivers, but the rest of the plan had been to shove the responsibility for the drivers off to the hardware manufacturers—who discovered that programming them was just short of impossible and threw up their hands. Gates quickly announced that Bauer Enterprises of San Jose would cobble together a one-size-fits-all printer driver for OEMs by the following quarter. It didn't happen.

Then there was the memory problem. The official minimum was a mere 2.5 megabytes, but getting anything done required 5 megs, and things went better with more. Unfortunately, prices were still defying the Law of Moore. A megabyte of memory that had cost $265 at the beginning of the year would now set you back nearly $350, and some of the fancier memory packages for new machines cost upward of $500 per megabyte. Users had been complaining about IBM's $340 list price for OS/2, but when they realized a usable version would actually cost more like $2,340, they decided that their good old DOS machines worked fine.

Except for DOS applications, which often had trouble using OS/2's flaky "compatibility box," about all a user could run on the new system was the slim assortment of character-based OS/2 applications that had crept to market. Not a single Presentation Manager application was ready on the day of the PM announcement—yet another marked and depressing difference from the original IBM PC and DOS rollout. In fact, there was a notable similarity to the original Windows rollout, right down to a very familiar term: "slow burn." At least the Microsoft OEM version of PM came with Bricks, a jazzed-up version of the Jobs-Wozniak Breakout game that Gates had mastered at Harvard. For a couple of grand you could turn your machine into the equivalent of a second-rate game arcade while waiting for programs that actually did something.

But what made PM look particularly lame was the return of Steve Jobs with his NeXT machine in October 1988. Introduced with customary Jobsian decadence at a dazzling black-tie invitation-only rollout to the Silicon Valley faithful, NeXT was a sleek, black, aesthetically pleasing $10,000 workstation. Its black-and-white high-resolution 17-inch screen had plenty of room for lots and lots of windows, and the UNIX-based NeXTStep operating system used Display PostScript to clearly show even the tiniest typefaces. The unit came with 8 megs of RAM, built-in Ethernet, sound, and a big but slow 256-megabyte read-write optical disc drive containing the complete works of Shakespeare. It did not come with anything so mundane as a floppy drive, because Jobs saw that as too low tech.

And if Gates had been upset about OSF, he went into orbit when the IBM brass told him they'd licensed rights to Jobs's NeXTStep, his windowing environment for UNIX. For now it ran only on the NeXT machine. Later on it could conceivably be adapted to run on OS/2. The deal with IBM had been cut in secret in the offices of Bill's might-have-been patron Ross Perot, one of NeXT's primary investors.

Gates couldn't believe it. After all this work, IBM would actually bet on NeXTStep? "Which one is more modern?" he asked a *Fortune* reporter. "Presentation Manager is color and his is black and white. Is compatibility with existing standards important? OS/2 and Presentation Manager will run all the old IBM PC programs. NeXTStep isn't compatible with anything." Actually, Presentation Manager wasn't turning out to be all that compatible either. Why, why, couldn't they just use Windows?

When Jobs declared the machine would be sold only to educational markets, at least at first, Chairman Bill announced that Microsoft would abstain from developing for a machine incompatible with everything but another NeXT. "I give him credit," Gates told an industry gathering, "but hey, if you want black, I'll sell you a can of paint." Jobs's response: "He'll come around sooner or later." Instead it was Jobs who eventually came around, later rather than sooner, to begin offering a DOS drive with NeXT machines.

To the puzzlement and astonishment of the rest of the industry, IBM did not do much of anything with its license to NeXTStep. IBM did, however, begin to make waves with an outfit called Metaphor Computer Systems, hinting that perhaps its object-oriented designs would serve as the real user interface for Presentation Manager—yet another unpleasant addition to Bill's woes.

And Microsoft's networking efforts remained a quagmire. Pursuing a strategy of software that would run on any network hardware from any vendor, and pushing it hard through a distribution network of loyal resellers, some of which it owned, Novell, Inc. of Provo, Utah, had trounced Microsoft's wimpy MS-NET and a variety of other competitors. Now it was about to go head to head with Microsoft's LAN Manager and win again. Microsoft had designed LAN Manager to run on top of OS/2, just as MS-NET had run on top of DOS. Novell designed its systems from the ground up to operate networks. They weren't perfect, but they beat Microsoft's versions soundly with more tools, more flexibility, greater stability, greater speed.

As usual with its system software, Microsoft's primary strategy was to sell through OEM channels. But installing networks was tricky. OEMs had rarely developed what came to be known as Novell's "infrastructure": strong working relationships with consultants and other resellers. Novell offered service, including training for the people who sold its products. Customers could make one call, and a Novell-certified technician would come out, install the software, plug in the hardware, wire up even incompatible machines, do whatever it took. Bill Gates sold technology, not service: In his view, the kind of expensive support effort Novell had mastered was the OEM's problem. Unfortunately, OEMs were bad at it.

Network vendor 3Com, founded by Ethernet inventor Bob Metcalfe, was getting beaten badly by Novell's network software and by cheap network hardware clones. Metcalfe would eventually put it this way: "3Com was very naive, so we had decided in 1987 or 1988 to bet on OS/2, to bet on LAN Manager, and to bet on Microsoft," by signing up for a joint development deal. "OS/2 didn't happen, LAN Manager was not delivered the way it was supposed to, and Microsoft is a rapacious partner. 3Com was not guileless, 3Com was just stupid. Partnering with Microsoft is like black widow spiders mating."

Stupid? Metcalfe would later add, "Everything that 3Com had to do was in the contract and everything Microsoft had to do wasn't." And Metcalfe would accuse Microsoft of unmitigated arrogance: "Here's Microsoft, which has had success squared. They've become the Hitler Youth. They think people who don't work there are assholes and bureaucratic jerks. There's probably some truth in that, but it's just unbearable." Although 3Com believed it had an exclusive right to sell the product at retail without associated hardware, eventually "Microsoft double-crossed 3Com by going to the same channels"—which the contract evidently permitted the Redmondians to do.

IBM threw a further monkey wrench into the works by modifying its version of the code just enough to make it incompatible with LAN Manager— and then calling its product LAN Server, again snubbing Microsoft with nomenclature. OEMs released the product under their own names—3Com called its version 3+Open LAN Manager—further diluting its impact. And Microsoft's efforts to come up with a surrogate for IBM's proprietary Extended Edition were not much more successful—in part because Extended Edition was no great shakes itself.

For OS/2 and PM, it was rivers of ink everywhere, except on the bottom line. One industry-tracking firm estimated that in 1988 only 4 percent of 286 and 16 percent of 386 users were purchasing OS/2. Meanwhile, Windows was selling 50,000 copies a month, Gates claimed in a speech to the Chicago Association of Microcomputer Professionals in mid-November. Still, a lot of those copies were sitting on shelves around the globe. A Dataquest survey at the close of 1988 found only 150,000 sales of Excel, dwarfed by 1-2-3 sales of 900,000. With an installed base of some 40 million machines, it was a DOS, DOS, DOS, DOS world.

"Why can't they just buy Windows?" Bill wondered. Well, maybe they could. For now, as Ballmer put it, "Excel single-handedly was giving mouth-to-mouth to Windows," and PageMaker was offering a jolt of adrenaline. A new plan in the works was about to give Windows a heart transplant and plastic surgery.

28

HOW THE SUNSHINE WORKS

At Microsoft, hiring Smart Guys had been honed to a science, a "mining operation," as Simonyi put it, focusing on Harvard, Yale, Caltech, MIT, and also such mother lodes as the New Mexico Institute of Mining and Technology and Ontario's University of Waterloo. With typical emphasis on economy and efficiency, the company would schedule a prospect for an all-day whirlwind of one-on-one meetings, including a lunch session, with members of the team he or she would be joining. "Part of it," one ex-Softie recalled, "was to see are these guys going to fit in, are these real aggressive guys who will fight for their project?"

Part of it, as dictated by Steve Ballmer's longstanding tradition, was to see how smart these guys really were. Questions requiring analytical skills were the norm: How many people were dying in Seattle every day? Estimate the volume of water flowing out of the Mississippi River. And then came the open-enders: What have you done wrong and how would you change it today if you could? Say you're working here: Tell me what you're going to do today. If you managed to stay on the case, you might just be a Smart Guy.

Between the end of one session and the beginning of the next, the interviewer would send e-mail to all his counterparts, offering impressions, observations, ideas for follow-up questions. Can't take the pressure? Think this process is dumb? You're probably not our kind of person.

Besides, if you couldn't take the interview, you certainly wouldn't last long in front of Bill. About two minutes into one presentation, Gates had stood up, looked around the room, scowled at the newly arrived product manager, and said, "Where the fuck did we hire you from?" The manager left the meeting in tears and within a week had left the company. But Mike Slade saw it as a strategy. "It may not be charitable, but it's efficient. In a meeting you challenge the integrity of the guy presenting. . . . Good people know their shit and don't take any shit from anybody, including Bill. I've seen guys stand on the table in the conference room and start yelling at him. . . . And they're done, and Bill goes 'Okay.' ''

And if you couldn't take the interview, you certainly couldn't take the pace. As former Word product manager Jonathan Prusky recalled, "The last six months I was there, I probably more often than not worked eighty to one hundred hours a week. Which is basically meaning you work, you go home and you get a little sleep, and you come back. I mean, you don't do anything else. During one period, I think it was from October to December, I traveled about thirty-thousand miles in the air."

As for pay—well, the recruiter would explain, Microsoft certainly couldn't match your current salary or your current vacation schedule. A Princeton science Ph.D., for example, might command $40,000—50 percent less than he or she might get elsewhere. But, the recruiter would point out, there were bennies. All the free soda you could drink. Fully paid moving expenses. The biannual bonus of up to 15 percent, assuming you did a good job and your boss agreed.

And stock, stock, stock! On signing up, you'd get a fixed number of options whose exercise price would be the lowest market price during the first thirty days of your employment. After your first eighteen months, you could exercise 25 percent of those options, and every six months thereafter you could cash in another eighth of the pie. But you didn't have to: You could exercise anytime within ten years.

More stock! Golden Handcuffs! Every July, after your first two reviews, you'd be eligible for another round of options. If your work kept your boss happy, you'd get another set of options on top of the first set. Play your cards right, and you could have four of these things working at once, at no cost to you until you decided to cash in, and then only the cost of the taxes on the difference between your option price and your selling price. Want more stock? Take advantage of a payroll deduction plan to put up to 10 percent of your salary into Microsoft shares at 85 percent of market value.

Of course, if the stock didn't go up, you were underpaid. But if you didn't believe in the yeasty rising power of Microsoft stock, there was always someone else who would. "There's like 10,000 unsolicited résumés a month that come in there," an ex-Softie said in 1991. "I mean, I saw the stacks—mailbags would come in full of résumés."

One young Yalie who'd been recruited by Microsoft happened to sit next to Ann Winblad on an airplane flight. "I made it to the final interview!" he told her proudly. "I didn't get hired. But I was a finalist!" Had he made it, he probably would have stuck around awhile. Of 106 employees on the payroll in 1981, 50 remained ten years later—a turnover rate even lower than the officially announced figure of 8 percent per year.

But there had been plenty of internal turnover on the Windows project. In

1988 the Windows group had become a skeleton crew once Mad Dog Ballmer began dragging people out the door to work on OS/2. Version 2 of Windows had been a death march of its own, but the Windows gang was still plugging away. Slowly but surely, a collection of Windows apps was beginning to turn up. Still, exactly what the next version of Windows should be, or even *if* it should be, remained unclear.

Then in June David Weise, one of the Smart Guys from the Dynamical Systems Research acquisition, ran into an old friend at a party for the grand opening of Microsoft's new manufacturing facility in Canyon Park northwest of Redmond—a brand-new building intended to end Microsoft's longtime manufacturing woes by automating and simplifying the process. If Microsoft's headquarters, as Frank Gaudette and others would cheerfully admit, was at bottom "a software factory," the Canyon Park facility was the packing plant.

Weise's old friend was Murray Sargent, "a world-renowned laser jock who happens to like to grope around computers." A physics professor from the University of Arizona, Sargent was up for the summer to adapt Microsoft's CodeView debugger to a kludge known as "DOS extension" that allowed specially written programs to use extended memory on 286 and 386 machines. He had recently added Windows support and a DOS extender to his own debugger, a program called SST that happened to be Weise's personal favorite.

In Weise's view, the three big problems with Windows were "memory, memory, memory." You were always bumping up against the memory limits one way or another, and it compromised every aspect of the program. There had been steps to change it: Windows 2 and Windows 386 allowed access to EMS memory, one of the things Weise had worked on and received industry awards for. But Bill Gates had been right about EMS being a kludge. The extended memory available by using the protected mode of 286 and 386 chips would make everything so much simpler.

So Weise brought Sargent back to his office, fired up the new debugger, and starting with line one began stepping through Windows to make it run under protected mode, thereby accessing extended memory. "We're not gonna ask anybody, and then if we're done and they shoot it down, they shoot it down." Weise began working on it at home, then moved to the office for three months of night and weekend work. The good news: "It turned out Steve Wood who I'd inherited the kernel from had structured the whole thing to wanna be" in protected mode. Actually, Wood had pushed hard for the concept before he'd been dragged off into the morass of Presentation Manager.

Weise, a one-time professional blackjack player, recalled it as if it were a trip through some Nintendo game:

> There are all these little gotchas throughout it, but basically you just work
> through the gotchas one at a time, you just close your eyes, and you just charge

ahead. You don't think of the problems, or you're not gonna do it. . . . It's
fun. Piece by piece, it's coming. Okay, here come the keyboard drivers, here
come the display drivers, here comes GDI—Oh, oh, look, here's USER!

Without that debugger running in protected mode with the DOS extender I
could not have done it.

A few weeks before a scheduled design review with the whole staff, including Bill, Weise let Ballmer know how close he was to getting Windows to run in protected mode. "This is interesting," Ballmer said.

Weise upped the ante at a group retreat in the basement of the nondecadent La Quinta motel in Kirkland. Product manager Russ Werner had been given his mission for Windows 3 by none other than Bill Gates: "Just make it great." What, Werner kept asking his troops, would make it great? An interface that could be custom-configured by the user, said some. A cleaner look, said another. "Using protected mode," said David Weise.

"How would that help?" Werner asked.

Without revealing how far along he was already, Weise rattled off a couple of dozen reasons. Werner told him to go ahead and give it a try.

The night before the design review, Weise told Ballmer to meet him in his office the next morning at eight. Weise stayed up until 3:00 A.M. getting the Windows desktop programs to run in protected mode and left the machine on when he walked out the door. When he came in to work a few minutes late, his machine had crashed. He knew who had to have done it. He ran down to Ballmer's office and asked, "Did you see it?"

"Yes," Ballmer told him. "Where do we go from here?"

"Steve, it's totally up to you."

"Let's go for it," Ballmer said.

Going into the meeting, Weise was ecstatic. "It's like [George] Gamow," he recalled, referring to the Russian-born physicist who had developed theories of stellar evolution. "His girlfriend says 'What are you thinking?' and he goes, 'I'm the only person in the world right now who knows how the sunshine works.' "

And what Weise was about to reveal might well be some sunshine in the middle of the Presentation Manager gloom. In a fashion, he was about to vindicate Steve Ballmer's pledge of 1985: Write your app for Windows and you'll be able to run it in protected mode without any trouble at all.

Others gave their presentations, and then Weise dropped his bombshell. Everything that had been discussed suddenly changed. "Half the people in my group," Weise recalled, "had no clue what was going on yet. You could tell Steve was excited." After the OSF thing—the NeXTStep announcement was still in the future—a little side bet against IBM might well be in order. "Okay, let's do it," Gates said.

Ballmer turned to Bill. "What do we tell IBM?"

A smile spread across the face of Bill Gates. "That's your problem, Steve."

▼ And a problem it was. IBM had seen Windows as an intermediate step between DOS and PM, and not much of one at that. Now, by overcoming the inbuilt limitations of DOS, Windows was positioning itself to undercut OS/2 and Presentation Manager. The only thing it was missing was ship dates.

Work on Windows 3 began to hum along. New features were added for programmers and users. In-house designer Virginia Thornton redid the colors and the fonts and added a spiffy new 3-D look with buttons that seemed to "depress" when you clicked on them. Designer Susan Kare, largely responsible for the look of the Macintosh, was brought in to work on the cute little icons. Mac on the PC!

Word went out to independent developers: Take another look at Windows. You might be surprised. It doesn't have OS/2's computer-sciency threads and semaphores and named pipes, and its multitasking isn't quite as sexy. But: It'll do what most users want. It'll run on machines with a lot less memory than PM needs. It'll cost a third of what OS/2 does. It'll look better than PM too. And it's coming soon, certainly by Fall Comdex 1989, maybe even earlier.

Independent developers began climbing aboard the Windows bandwagon. Suddenly Windows was picking up momentum, and PM was falling behind. Not even IBM could ignore the Windows buzz in the industry. "We finally get Hanrahan to see, the end of '88, there's a space below OS/2," said Ballmer. IBM "wants to learn more about it, compare the two products, understand the differences, I mean sort of endless studies. He must have spent all of 1989 preparing reports about which performs better. . . . There were meetings, comparisons, presentations, them trying to understand the differences in the technology, blah, blah, blah."

And then there were a few things Microsoft wasn't yet telling IBM. Nathan Myhrvold had become the head of a skunk works within Microsoft, looking at new technologies on the sly. One project he had been overseeing was a "portable" operating system designed to run on the new RISC (Reduced Instruction Set Computing) chips, touted by some as the next big wave in microprocessors. Simpler than older designs, RISC technology gave programmers fewer instructions to work with but executed the remaining ones faster. RISC chips, so the theory went, were faster and cheaper to produce and offered major speed advantages, but required new and more complex software to accomplish tasks previously fobbed off on hardware. It was unclear that RISC would inherit the desktop—Bill had in fact opposed it for years—but the Gator in him would not let a side bet slide by.

Myhrvold couched the issue of portability in horseracing terms. "We were the world's best jockeys, but our horse was getting old. We had to make sure that we were going to have some fresh blood, or we were going to get the shit beaten out of us by stupider jockeys riding younger horses." After the Sun deal broke down, Myhrvold licensed Mach, a UNIX-kernel clone developed at Carnegie-Mellon University, and the very thing that Jobs's NeXTStep ran on.

Next step for Myhrvold: Having Mach rewritten with the goal of using it as the basis for a future version of OS/2 that would be "portable"—able to ride RISC horses and traditional Intel horses and even multiprocessors, where the horsepower would be divided among a collection of chips. "The project was called 'Psycho,' in part because people thought we were crazy and in part because there's this Talking Heads song we like. Psycho kernel, *qu'est-ce que c'est?*"

In the fall of 1988, as the Death March on OS/2 1.1 was coming to an end, there were rumblings up the road in Bellevue at DEC West. Fed up with DEC politics that had just scuttled his longtime RISC development project, operating systems guru David Cutler was shopping around. A tough, muscular macho type who had been known to put his fist through walls and in a "miffed" mood had officially dubbed one project "Frigate," Cutler had been one of the designers of the immensely popular VMS operating system for DEC's VAX machines.

Cutler was looking to do something more than just another operating system, and he was no aficionado of personal computers. But he had seen how the initially constrained 32-bit VAX design had exploded when people realized how much memory they could add, and he sensed history might repeat itself. His goal: a high-integrity system, which meant input into hardware design as well as software.

Cutler joined Microsoft that fateful Halloween. His project, dubbed "NT" for "New Technology," initially began by designing hardware built around Intel's i860 RISC chip and software to run on it. Unfortunately, the 860 didn't work as advertised, creating political problems with Intel, a longtime partner, when Microsoft decided to switch to the R4000 chip from competitor MIPS.

Elsewhere on the Microsoft campus, OS/2 1.3 and 2.0, code-named Tiger and Cruiser, continued down the large-team joint-development path with the detested IBM. But to Cutler's tiny band of Smart Guys, OS/2 was a loser, a bloated stiff lacking desperately needed networking and security facilities. They had their own vision of the operating system for the future, and if things broke right, they might just make it stick.

Meanwhile, there was a lawsuit to fight. On March 21, 1989, a year after the St. Patrick's Day Massacre, San Francisco Federal District Court was abuzz again with the Apple look-and-feel business. Microsoft's license for Windows, Judge Schwarzer decided, did not give it the right "to develop future versions of Windows as it pleases. . . . What Microsoft received was a license to use the visual displays in the named software products as they appeared to the user in November, 1985." Bad news for Microsoft: In Schwarzer's view, "the displays of the two programs''—Windows 1 and Windows 2.03—''are funda-mentally different.''

The opinion sent Microsoft stock into a nosedive. Swashbuckling Steve Ballmer bet his faith. During the last ten days of March 1989, he plunked down $46.2 million to buy 945,000 shares at an average of $48.91 per share—''a gutsy thing,'' in the estimation of Frank Gaudette and many other Microsofties. Three years later, following two-for-one and three-for-two splits, the stock would be worth more than $350 million, a sixfold profit, and with his other holdings Ballmer would become the third Microsoft billionaire, after Gates and Allen.

Microsoft's lawyers kept nibbling away at Apple's look-and-feel concept. On July 25, 1989, Schwarzer in effect threw out 179 ''similarities in particular features'' between the Mac and Windows 2.03, stating that the license covered them. But certain ''changes in the appearance and use of icons are not covered by the 1985 license,'' Schwarzer ruled, nor were the use of overlapping win-dows and certain methods of moving and displaying them. In Windows 1, for example, icons appeared only at the bottom of the screen with their names immediately above. In Windows 2.03, icons could be put anywhere on the screen and with their names below—as on a Mac. The next step: to determine if the ''similarities'' violated Apple's copyrights.

Tiled vs. overlapping. Movable icons. Reel back to the days of yesteryear: If the overlapping guys had won out, there might have been no suit. And the guy who gave tiling the green light, Chairman Bill himself, now saw it coming back to haunt him. Before McGregor's arrival ''we'd never heard of fucking tiled windows; we'd never seen them or heard of them,'' Gates would later say, despite the fact that they previously existed in both Word and Multiplan.

Regardless, he maintained, the issue was trivial: ''Believe me, Windows 1 supported overlapping,'' Gates said, asserting that ''It's a lot of extra code, a moderate amount of extra code to go tiled.'' McGregor agreed: Making Win-dows overlapping instead of tiled was the simple matter of a ''minor change in the user interface, which is to delete some of the tiled code so that it only has overlap code.''

It was 179 down, 10 to go. The lawyers' fees had only begun to mount up.

▼ And yet Bill Gates would not let a mere lawsuit stand in the way of doing business. In September 1989 he and John Warnock, yet another Xerox PARC refugee, clashed in an epic battle of wills that came to be known as Font Wars. Fonts—the various typeface families that with a Macintosh, laser printer, and PageMaker had helped put a printing press on the desktop—had been very good to Warnock, head of the Silicon Valley firm of Adobe Systems, whose revenues had escalated from $4.8 million in 1985 to $83.5 million in 1988. Adobe's font technology, PostScript, had distinguished itself with device independence, allowing the drawing of virtually identical characters on printers and typesetting machines despite the differences in their resolution. But only the code that programs produced was device independent; what translated that code for a particular device was a PostScript interpreter custom-written for it. Writing interpreters for printers and typesetting machines—and selling fonts —was how Adobe made its money.

PostScript was derived from technology Warnock had developed at the University of Utah and refined at PARC. Adobe Systems, the company he and fellow PARC alumnus Charles Geschke had founded in 1982, had done a good job of hanging onto it, keeping aspects of the font technology encrypted and proprietary and difficult to clone. With the advent of the graphical user interface and low-cost laser printers, which turned even word processors into small-scale publishing systems, fonts started to look like big money. And where there was big money, there was Bill Gates. In 1989 Microsoft had a golden opportunity to land Adobe's technology for Windows and make it more Mac on the PC than ever.

The big Adobe booster was Apple, which had a PostScript interpreter built into every one of its laser printers. Apple and Adobe had been closely aligned ever since the Mac folks had bought 3.4 million shares of Adobe stock in November 1984. Considered a boneheaded Steve Jobs deal at the time—$2.5 million for 15 percent of the company—it looked brilliant by the time Apple unloaded the stock for nearly $82 million in July 1989. But in March 1988 Apple had announced that it would develop its own font technology for its next Mac operating system, System 7. One reason: Adobe was charging stratospheric royalties to printer vendors such as Apple—$50 to $100 a unit—and managing to get away with it because the PostScript clones on the market still had trouble handling Adobe's encrypted and proprietary fonts.

In March 1989 Microsoft announced it would put an existing open font technology in Windows, and Nathan Myhrvold conducted the search. Adobe was in the running, but it demanded its traditional high royalty on every copy of the operating system. Gates refused. His longstanding policy, learned in part from the lessons of DOS and XENIX: "We don't pay royalties on our system software." Asked if that meant he wanted PostScript for free, under the theory that Adobe would gain market share and sell more fonts because of the Microsoft association, Gates said "We pay people money, but not royalties"— even though, as in the Sun deal, he wasn't shy about asking for them when the shoe was on the other foot.

According to Myhrvold, Microsoft and Adobe actually worked out a large cash, no-royalty agreement, but the deal hung up on Microsoft's insistence that the font technology be made public: "They believed that basically we would have to suck eggs or come back with them."

In May Apple announced its font technology project would be code-named

Royal and would include technology for displaying fonts on computer monitors. Adobe announced its Type Manager program (ATM), which would generate font displays on Macintosh screens, thereby helping to blunt the effect of Royal. And in Redmond, Microsoft purchased Bauer Enterprises of San Jose. Cal Bauer and his team had worked with Microsoft on the desperately needed printer drivers for Windows and OS/2 and on something called PM/Script, which in effect would put Presentation Manager's screen graphics model into printers. That idea, like Presentation Manager, was going nowhere fast, but Bauer had also developed a PostScript clone for printers.

Part of the Gates strategy was to derail Adobe's Display PostScript, which happened to be the screen font system used by Jobs's—and, who knew, maybe IBM's—NeXTStep. So at the September 1989 Seybold Desktop Publishing Conference, Bill dropped a bombshell. Microsoft and Apple—the same two companies going toe to toe over Windows in San Francisco Federal District Court—had cut a deal to swap technology. Microsoft would get Apple's TrueType (formerly Royal) font technology; Apple would get Microsoft's TrueImage (formerly Bauer) printer technology. PostScript would be neatly shut out.

Warnock was beside himself. Described as on the verge of tears, he announced Adobe would for the first time publish the PostScript specs. Not that he was giving up much; by this time PostScript's encryption methodology was in the process of being deciphered by several cloners. Though apparently crushed, Warnock remained defiant: "What I heard today is the biggest bunch of garbage and mumbo-jumbo I've ever heard in my life," Warnock told the thousand Seybold conventioneers. "The desktop publishing industry has been built by the people in this room. It certainly hasn't been built by Bill Gates."

But it was on the verge of being revamped by Bill Gates. Adobe's stock plummeted on the news. Opening the standard meant diminished royalties and, presumably, diminished profits for PostScript. Suddenly Microsoft found itself besmirched in the press for beating up on the little guy: "We made John Warnock cry," as Bill Gates sarcastically put it. The same people who had been complaining about Adobe's proprietary high-handedness now considered it an underdog.

Adobe fought back. Within six months it had signed a deal with IBM to put PostScript into its printers and ATM into Presentation Manager. By April 1991 Apple and Adobe were back together again. For its low-end systems, Apple would retain the TrueType technology, which Mac fanatics disdained. For high-end systems, PostScript would be the primary offering.

For Gates, things did not work out quite the way he'd anticipated. By mid-1991 Bauer was out, the printer business unit was disbanded, and the TrueImage printer technology was sold. TrueType would not see the light of screen on PCs until April 1992, with the release of Windows 3.1 and the beginnings of what appeared to be a potentially big business for Microsoft in selling fonts.

Yet even earlier Gates believed the strategy had been successful: "We did everybody an incredible favor. If the goal was to open ATM, we did it. If the goal was to drop the price of PostScript by a third of what it was back then, we did it. We changed that printer business. Everybody should send us thank-you letters."

Buying Bauer "turned out to be a mistake," he admitted, adding that it was one of the few deals he'd ever made "that I didn't feel comfortable with doing and I went ahead and did." Nevertheless, he predicted in early 1992, "You'll see. Within a year from now we will make a lot of money in the printer business." The new plan? A Windows version of the PM/Script idea: putting much of the Windows graphics model into printers.

▼ In the weeks preceding Fall Comdex 1989, the trade press was in a dither about a new IBM project dubbed PM Lite. Hursley was supposedly in on it, and so was a Dutch outfit called Cyco that sold an add-on product for AutoCAD, and so was a Berkeley company called GeoWorks, which had constructed a windowing system that ran on machines with as little horsepower as the original IBM PC. The idea was to take the Presentation Manager API and put it on top of DOS. Apparently Hanrahan and crew had done a pretty good job of studying Windows. What they were now proposing was precisely the scheme Bill Gates had been pitching all along—except with PM, not Windows, as the link between DOS and OS/2. You could almost hear IBM's Ballmerian pitch to programmers: "Develop for OS/2 PM and you're developing for DOS PM."

Bill Gates could almost hear Windows slamming shut. After all the work, time, and money that had gone into Windows 3.0, he was not about to let it get blindsided by a DOS version of PM. In New York for nearly a month, Gates met "day and night" with IBM to head it off and stabilize the relationship:

> We were talking about when was the 386 version [of OS/2] coming along? Did we want to shrink the 286 version? What was our relationship gonna be? What would happen with Extended Edition? Would we commit not to do anything new to Windows—oops, they're not supposed to ask us to do that—would all of our resources be tied up doing all this OS/2 stuff, so we wouldn't have any time to do any more stuff for Windows? If not, what features were we willing to commit we'd never—might not put into Windows. It was a confusing deal. . . .

What came out of the meetings was a guarded, four-page press release—"Every word was negotiated over," said Marty Taucher—stating that as "the platform for the '90s," IBM and Microsoft were endorsing 386 and 486 systems with 4 megabytes of RAM and 60 megs of hard disk space running OS/2 and Presentation Manager. "Beginning in the second half of 1990, IBM and Microsoft plan to make their graphical applications available first on OS/2," the statement said. Both companies were "making a concerted effort" to pack OS/2 into 2 megs of RAM, and recommended Windows for machines with less. The distinction was significant, since virtually all PCs with less than 2 megs of RAM had just 1 meg—barely enough to run the forthcoming version of Windows at all.

Moreover, "Microsoft stated that Windows is not intended to be used as a [network] server, nor will future releases contain advanced OS/2 features such as distributed processing, the 32-bit flat memory model, threads or long file names." With each new paragraph the press release contained some new disrespect, indignity, or slur against Windows. You could almost hear the Windows Smart Guys back in Redmond gagging on their Vaseline.

But at least PM Lite was dead. At a Comdex press conference, IBM Entry Systems Division vice president Jim Cannavino said as much and hailed the agreement as a new show of cooperation between the two PC superpowers. Cooperation? About as much as in a heavyweight championship fight. Cannavino, a stocky up-from-the-ranks streetfighter who could be mistaken for a Chicago detective, seemed haggard and stoic; the lanky, preppyish Gates appeared ashen and wan.

Was it really the broadening, strengthening, renewing, and affirming of a relationship, as claimed, or the beginning of the end of a relationship that had for years been touch-and-go at best? Industry insiders were sure they knew. The Windows 3.0 rollout had been scheduled for Comdex, but the ship date had slipped half a year—sorely irking all the independent Windows developers who had frantically whipped their own rollout plans into shape and seen them crumble into dust. They knew exactly what the new version of Windows was, and it wasn't the cripple that was being reported.

At an exclusive banquet the night before the announcement, independent developer Mark Zachmann sat with Cannavino and heard him insist that Windows and DOS weren't going anywhere. Zachmann, whose Paintbrush program had become an integral part of the Windows 3.0 package, respectfully disagreed. During a question-and-answer session later in the evening, Zachmann impishly stood up and faced Steve Ballmer:

> I say, "Steve, let me ask you something. I've got an early copy of Win 3, and I think it's a really good operating system. Can you explain to me why my customers are gonna be convinced to switch to OS/2?"
> . . . And he says, "The reason is that everybody in the world is gonna be writing applications for this, and this operating system is gonna fly. Face it: In the future, everyone's gonna run Windows."

Oops! It was a Freudian slip, and Ballmer fell all over himself correcting it, but many in the crowd agreed. Gordon Eubanks, now head of Symantec, felt Gates "really stuck it to IBM." Big Blue may have believed in a 2-meg OS/2 and defanged Windows, but "Bill knew damn well it wasn't going to work." At the banquet Eubanks asked Ballmer, "Steve, is this for real?" and got a noncommittal response. Walking back to the hotel with IBM's Fernand Sarrat, Eubanks called it: "Do you really believe this bullshit?"

One week later, in response to a claim by Lotus's Jim Manzi that Microsoft had "neutered" Windows at IBM's behest, Jon Shirley picked up where Eubanks had left off. "That's a lot of crap," Shirley said at a conference in New York. "There has not been one change made to the next version of Windows, nor have there been any changes to the others that will follow." The whole drama had been little more than IBM throwing its weight around while Microsoft bowed and scraped and bought time to derail PM Lite. Fall Comdex '89 was where the relationship between IBM and Microsoft died. They would stay together temporarily for the sake of the business, a marriage of convenience glued together by sheer inertia.

All in all, it was not one of Gates's better Comdexes. At the annual everybody-wants-in John Dvorak party held that year at the garish, closely guarded Liberace mansion, Gates was initially refused entry by bouncers known as the Dragon Ladies. The next evening, at the user-group bash sponsored by Microsoft, dweeby chipheads corralled him to demand answers to tough questions such as why the Microsoft mouse didn't have three buttons. For more than an hour Gates and a small circle of combatants argued about everything from why Microsoft didn't make a trackball to why it didn't do more market-specific software such as computer-aided design tools.

Gates, who knew his products as well as any top executive in America, was probably the most visible, most accessible CEO in the world, appearing at industry conferences, lunch forums, charity functions, product promotions, user group meetings. At company meetings, he would good-naturedly don pointy ears as Mr. Spock or make a dramatic entrance on a Roman chariot or a Harley. At corporate seminars, Mike Slade recalled, Gates would field questions for half an hour: "Some guy would ask him some really specific thing, and he'd just rattle it off! People were going, 'That guy's smart!'" But all the Smartest Guy got this time around was a bunch of stupid questions from lame ungrateful hackers.

On Thursday, dog-tired and looking it, Gates left Comdex early on an afternoon all-coach flight back to Seattle. Gates sat down, read through a few papers, and pulled the airline-issue blanket over his head. He slept the whole way home.

29

A DATE WITH BILL

"Computer wizard needs a date, but warns that he's a nerd—and proud of it!" trumpeted the ever-reliable *Star* tabloid in October 1989, purveying a compendium of misinformation even more inaccurate than usual. Apparently it had gotten belated word of Bill's 1987 breakup with Ann Winblad.

Gates still kept Winblad's picture in his office and invited her to the summer Microgames. "We still are very good friends," she would say of their relationship. And her influence still resonated in Bill's latest intellectual passion, one she had kindled: biotech.

"Incredible book! Incredible book!" Gates raved over Eric Drexler's *Engines of Creation*, "about how the information revolution and biotechnology in combination are just part of a trend, and he extrapolates that trend somewhat in a very plausible way over the next fifty to a hundred years." In Drexler's realm, "nanotechnology," unthinkably tiny computers could repair DNA, retrieve the world's books from a speck of sand, and reinvent the way humans understood themselves.

Gates was also taken with *The Selfish Gene* by Oxford zoologist Richard Dawkins. Trenchantly Darwinistic, the book proposed the notion of memes— "tunes, ideas, catch phrases, clothes fashions, ways of making pots or of building arches"—that get replicated and elaborated to survive through the ages simply because they are better than run-of-the-mill thinking. It was survival of the smartest, Smart Guyism triumphant—as Gates enthused, "the idea of ideas, that the human mind is sort of the host for those ideas and there's a competition for which ideas work well, are effective, and so those ideas contain within them the seeds that allow them to be passed along to other humans and therefore survive." Memes were just like "programs, and eventually self-learning and self-organizing programs," Bill believed. They could speed up and improve the rate of understanding who we are—a kind of biological dynamic debugger.

On another biological front, the truth was that Gates didn't need a date. He was already involved in what would become an on-and-off relationship, one made more problematic than usual by the fact that his latest girlfriend, Melinda French, was also one of his employees, a Microsoft product manager nine years his junior. Although she often appeared with Bill in public, she craved anonymity—perhaps from the lesson of Jill Bennett, who had moved to Boston in part to escape the nuisance of being known as Bill's ex. Dark-haired, smart, a runner and MBA, his latest flame was also a hit with his mom, who had long been hoping for a Hangman birth announcement from her son. But friends still mourned the breakup with Winblad and considered the new relationship far less magical—in part because Bill kept playing the field. In particular, as one of his former companions had learned, "When he was out of town, all bets were off." Bill was out of town a lot.

In theory, at least, Gates was making plans for a family. At the end of 1988 he acquired the first parcels of land for a new house in the swank little community of Medina—four lots totaling roughly 3.3 acres, including 415 feet of lakefront and views of Seattle, the Olympic Mountains, and his parents' home, the house where he'd grown up, two miles across Lake Washington. The total deal cost $3.6 million, but included one two-year-old 7,000-square-foot mock-Tudor house that had been built on spec but never occupied and was appraised by the county assessor at over half a million dollars. The house had no part in the plans; Bill rented it to his outside PR flack Melissa Waggener until he could figure out what to do with it. In December 1989 Gates would add three-fifths of an acre for $450,000 and, a month later, another seven-tenths acre for $1 million more. The site now amounted to more than four and a half acres at a total cost of over $5 million.

For the future garage, Gates picked up a road machine that knew what performance was all about. Paul Allen "calls me up," Gates recalled, "and says, hey, he'll do all the stuff and I'll just write a check"—for $380,000. "All the stuff" included arranging for a German citizen to lend Gates and Allen two uncertified vehicles: a silver one for Bill, a white one for Paul.

Built in 1985 and 1986, the 200 Porsche 959s initially sold at the deutschmark equivalent of $159,138 each, shot up over $1 million in late 1980s' speculation, and plunged in value when the 1990 recession hit. For much of 1989 Gates drove his car, cranking it up above 170 mph, 27 mph short of the rated top speed. But by January 1990 the foreign citizen exemption expired. The car had to be sent back to Germany, purchased from the original owner, and shipped back to the United States at a cost of $30,000 each way. Then it had to be approved for American roads.

That wasn't likely to happen. Porsche itself had decided not to bother exporting 959s to the U.S. The engine would have to be altered to meet emission requirements, the bumper reconfigured to meet American standards, and the body structure redesigned to satisfy safety requirements. Then six of the machines would have to be crashed for certification purposes. Gates and Allen stored the cars in a Free Trade Zone warehouse in Oakland, where they remain while their owners pursue legal remedies to get them approved. An Allen employee flies down every few weeks to start the engines and keep them roadworthy.

To feed his Porsche habit, Gates picked up a $60,000 Carrera Cabriolet 964—the model for which the 959 served as something of a prototype. It was, Gates said, "kind of a spare car in case something breaks down." A maroon Lexus replaced the woeful Jaguar as Gates's in-town runabout.

Jon Shirley was intent on the slow lane, about to retire to a house a couple of lots up the lake from Bill's new homesite. If any timing was right to announce his departure, it was the 1989 year-end lull, with the stock market sleepy and the trade papers in their annual two week hiatus. Shirley, fifty-one, joked that the average age at Microsoft would drop by a year upon his departure, and said he would stick around for another six months to smooth the transition.

Although the announcement was unexpected, it had been in the works for more than a year. Shirley had made it clear to Gates when he was hired that he wasn't going to "work there until normal retirement age or something like that, that I had long felt that I would like to reach a stage in my life where I could let them work sixty hours a week or whatever, that I'd been doing it all my life, and there were a lot of other things that I wanted to do." Among them: collecting art, fishing for marlin in the Gulf of Mexico, traveling with his wife Mary, and yachting aboard *Shirley's Temple.*

"We had to work out the timing on the thing," Shirley said. "Obviously, anything was too soon for Bill," who hated losing good people. And Shirley knew he had done a masterful job: "The company is over a billion dollars and thousands and thousands of people. . . . You have a really good staff put together, a lot of very competent people, and you're not facing huge crises. . . . It made sense at that time for me to pull out and let somebody else come in and run this thing." Gates and Marquardt talked him into staying on for a year before making it official, then into hanging around for the six-month extension while a replacement was groomed, and then into remaining on the board of directors.

Finding a replacement wasn't easy. Few executives of Shirley's leadership and organizational caliber willingly eschewed the limelight. "He was effective without having a huge ego and the need to be visible," Stewart Alsop observed of Shirley. The challenge in hiring a replacement, Alsop said, was finding someone who understood Bill Gates as well as Shirley had.

"We looked through everyone that was in the company and kind of thought, 'Oh, is there anybody who's ready at this point?' " Marquardt recalled. "There was only one real candidate that was discussed seriously, and that was Jeremy [Butler, head of international and OEM sales]. And he said he wasn't interested." In February 1991, after having boosted Microsoft's international sales from $50 million to over $500 million—more than half the company's revenues—he too would announce his retirement, saying he wanted to "stop and smell the roses."

It was time for another executive search à la Jim Towne, only this round would be conducted more carefully. "We did a lot of brainstorming," Marquardt recalled. "Bill knows pretty much everybody in the industry, and there wasn't anybody who kind of surfaced that was available or that we had a lot of respect for or that we thought we could get, and we sort of went through that list early on."

So the search, Shirley said, "totally fell on my back." He believed that the retail aspects of the business had become almost routine, and felt it was important to hire someone who knew about the large corporate installations and big accounts that Microsoft was having a tough time cracking.

A corporate guy it was: former IBMer Mike Hallman, chief of Boeing Computer Services. Hallman joined Microsoft in April 1990. At six-foot-five and 240 pounds, the gentle, Bunyanesque executive was as different in physique from the small-boned Gates as he was in style from Bill's aggressive confrontations. Thoughtful, low key, and ten years Gates's senior, Hallman was skilled in the more traditional management style of leadership by example and consensus rather than the shrill disputatious Microsoft Way. It had worked over a twenty-year career at IBM where he had risen through sales ranks to head up Big Blue's southwest U.S. marketing division, accounting for nearly half the company's domestic revenues. It had worked over a three-year tenure at Boeing Computer Services, where Hallman drove revenues up by 50 percent to $1.5 billion by selling systems integration solutions to other corporations. Gates and Shirley believed it would work at Microsoft, which needed a bigger presence in corporate America.

Hallman's charge was to win over the Fortune 500 while keeping the trains running on time in-house. Although nominally president, he considered the job chief operating officer. Gates was the visionary, the products guy, the industry speechifier. "Building new buildings was not a great deal of interest to him," Hallman noted. Neither was hiring 5,000 employees. Nor was talking to die-hard mainframers. Gates didn't believe in big systems and didn't talk the language. He had once managed to insult a gathering of big-corporation software engineers by badgering them about why they still used mainframes when PCs were so advanced.

Hallman knew the lingo and the answer. The computer-aided design "database for an airplane is probably somewhere in the neighborhood of two or three terabytes of code," he pointed out—meaning 2 or 3 trillion characters. "Well,

I'm not going to spread that over 4,000 engineers' desktops and sit there and say, 'How's everybody doing? Everybody back their systems up?' That just isn't going to happen.''

What corporations needed was the kind of support Microsoft had traditionally ignored: ''With many large corporations it's not feature number 86 of Excel that's interesting, or Windows, for that matter. It's how do I install it on 500 machines over a weekend? How do I get my users to be able to be productive when it goes in?'' At Boeing Hallman had done a study showing that it cost ''about twice as much'' to provide training, help, and other support as it did to buy the software itself.

None of this struck a personal chord with a chairman who just a few years before had complained that ''we don't talk to end users'' and had once asked some of his developers, ''What the hell is wrong with the DOS prompt?'' as if the characters **A >** constituted a perfectly adequate user interface. Gates, as Vern Raburn put it, ''still views the world through the eyes of BASIC. He has a programmer's view of the world.'' Gates the technologist seemed to understand only dimly that in the real world there was more involved than just putting good code in the box, that successful competitors such as WordPerfect and Novell were beating Microsoft as much with service as with technology. And even if he understood it and believed it, ponying up the money for it was another matter entirely.

There had been a few efforts, such as Microsoft University, a training program begun when OEM customers and independent software developers began clamoring for technical training, particularly on the devilishly difficult Windows and Presentation Manager. There was *Microsoft Systems Journal,* the company's magazine for hardcore programmers. And there was the perennial game of catch-up in technical support. But actually courting customers on the basis of service was an alien concept to Gates.

Hallman worked to make Microsoft's Management Information Systems (MIS) operations a model for visiting customers—a ''data temple,'' as one small-computer diehard called it with a sneer. In an attempt to teach the MIS world of big corporate computing what Microsoft might bring to their party, Hallman assigned high-level executives to monitor the largest corporate accounts. But Bill just didn't care much about all that, telling Hallman that the MIS journal *Information Week* was ''the biggest bunch of junk ever. There's no technical news in it.'' Hallman would patiently explain why people read the magazine and what Microsoft could learn from it. But somehow Hallman's quiet style didn't put him in the Smart Guy league as far as Bill was concerned, and he could never quite manage to crack the inner circle of a CEO whose company seemed to run perfectly well without an IBM mainframe computer on the premises.

In Redmond, doing perfectly well without IBM was beginning to seem like an excellent idea in general. To Bill, IBM's executives just weren't Smart Guys, particularly the one at the top of the sinking OS/2 effort. As Gates later described it:

> The biggest change in our relationship with IBM is the arrival of Jim Cannavino. So then you get into the Cannavino era where anything can be done. Jim is just gonna fix everything. Everything can be done, there's no problem. He'll be running IBM in a couple of years, and we won't even have any red tape to deal with anymore. It's all gonna be okay. This is a man who never let a few hundred thousand lines of code stand in his way.

Cannavino began making noises that Microsoft was not pulling its weight: When it came to OS/2, IBM had thousands of lines more code and hundreds more programmers. Cannavino thought this was a plus. Gates thought it was a minus. There was talk of renegotiating the royalty. Gates was incensed: The problem isn't the royalty, he told Cannavino, it's the IBM cost structure. The goal was fewer programmers, fewer lines of code, more efficiency.

"Bill got worried about being in partnership, if you will, with the high-cost producer of software," Ballmer recalled. He summed up Gates's attitude as "We may just never make money. These guys will want to have us fund their inefficiency."

By the end of 1989 Ballmer had begun meeting regularly with Cannavino and Hanrahan: "We start this process of famous meetings where I go through and I show them what their P & L should look like, and that means you can only have so many people working on Extended Edition and so many people on Standard Edition. I actually write it all out for them." You got to cut the count, cut the count, Ballmer told them. Cut developers, consolidate projects. Keep it simple: Don't have programmers flying around the world just to look at bugs. Cannavino seemed to be warming.

Then Windows 3.0 got in the way.

▼ In May 1990, two weeks before the Win 3 extravaganza at City Center in New York, Gates was in Boston for the Second Annual Computer Bowl, a "College Bowl" clone featuring industry wizards, East versus West. Gates took the event seriously—a fellow passenger reported that he had boarded the plane in Seattle with an impressive stack of books—and wound up leading the West to victory in a squeaker, 300 to 290. Although he blew at least one question, Gates correctly named two failed computers that led to successes, the PDP-5 and Apple Lisa, and—duck soup!—fingered the industry's highest paid CEO, Apple's John Sculley. For having the highest individual point total, Gates was named Most Valuable Player. Mom, watching by satellite link back in Seattle, was disappointed that he hadn't been more dominant. "He probably wished he'd done better than he did," she said, "being a person who enjoys games as much as he does."

Feeling his oats, Gates invited a group of Lotusians out for drinks. For more than four hours Gates held court while his rapt audience sucked it all in. One week later Lotus's George Gilbert wrote up six pages of notes on the evening and sent them to his immediate superiors under the heading "Another Conversation with Bill Gates." Dubbing the memo "Notes from a Gates Date!" one of those superiors forwarded it to Jim Manzi and the executive suite—and someone leaked it to the press.

If Lotus had retained any doubts about Windows, they would disappear. According to the memo, Gates had no intention of limiting Windows to entry-level systems. On the contrary, Gates said, " 'Six months after Windows 3 ships it will have a greater market share than PM will EVER have—OS/2 applications won't have a chance.' " And just to make sure, he had greased the skids under Presentation Manager, admitting "that Microsoft is dragging its feet on OS/2—OS/2 has been slowed down because of bugs. . . . 'What incentive does Microsoft have to get it out the door before Windows 3?' " Gates asked pointedly.

Bill "strongly implied that now the forces were shifting so that IBM needed him more than he needed them." Besides, IBM would " 'fold' " within seven years—though it could prolong its existence to perhaps twelve years if it did some things right. On the other hand, in two decades, machines would write better software than people, and the computer wave would be over.

His "dates" were dazzled by Bill's industry savvy. "We got the distinct impression that NOTHING happens within IBM without his knowledge. . . . We also got the impression he knows everything going on at Apple." Yet Gates was " 'always running scared,' " avoiding complacency. Products like Lotus's 1-2-3/G, he said, made his developers soft, forcing him to make them run scared by insisting that they imagine tighter, faster, bug-free competition. He admitted that his ability to attack new parts of the market had been financed by such "anchor" products as DOS, PC Works, Word, and the Mac applications. He claimed that Lotus's failure to establish a windowing system of its own enabled him "to overcome the weakness of Windows 2 and bring the Mac conventions over to the PC."

When it came to hiring, Gates looked for four essential qualities: "Ambition, I.Q., Technical Expertise, and Business Judgment." But "according to Gates, there is no substitute for I.Q." So what made *him* tick? "Gates admits his own ambition and drive comes from internal conflicts though his level of self-awareness on those topics was not very convincing."

There were more pressing matters to convince people about. As the crescendo built toward Win 3's release on May 22, 1990, negotiations with IBM had intensified, though Microsoft's public position seemed to be attack, attack,

attack. In late January Gates told a technical briefing "We're very patient people," and suggested that OS/2 would not surpass DOS sales for another three or four years. The following week it was Ballmer's turn: OS/2 was meant to compete with UNIX, not DOS. "There will be a DOS 5, 6 and 7, and a Windows 3, 4 and 5," Ballmer said.

Three weeks before the Win 3 rollout, Microsoft announced that OS/2 2.0, hovering somewhere on the horizon—actually, it would not be released until March 1992, and barely then—would run Windows applications. Microsoft's Peter Neupert characterized OS/2 as a "kind of . . . Windows Plus." Cannavino's collar was getting tighter by the minute. Amazingly, Gates still hoped to get Cannavino onstage at the New York rollout for a thundering endorsement of Windows.

"We were so close to reaching a deal. . . . We almost had a deal," Gates recalled. Royalties became the sticking point. Gates and Cannavino could not agree on who would get what for Windows and OS/2 sales. The problem, as Ballmer put it: "How can two companies which are independent sell the same bits in different boxes and make any money? . . . How will the customer make the decision to buy the Microsoft or the IBM box? Presumably they will pick whichever one is cheaper." Time ran out before a solution was found.

Not showing up at the Windows 3 announcement was Cannavino's loss. Everybody else was there—even Lotus's Frank King, posing as a window washer in the slick video. Lotus's Jim Manzi had in fact unwittingly inspired the global scope of the Win 3 rollout. At the previous Fall Comdex, after the Gates-Cannavino summit, Manzi's declaration that Windows was "neutered" galled Microsoft's PR chief Marty Taucher into thinking big. "We sat around for a while and said, well, how do we make this a big deal? And we came up with the idea of doing not a product announcement but an industry announcement. . . . How can we involve as many people as possible?"

By loosening the purse strings, for openers. Taucher wrote out a $1.2 million budget proposal, including the New York show, a hundred independent software vendors announcing Windows 3 products, fifty OEMs announcing plans to ship Windows, 3,500 people involved in eight cities, from press members to sales reps to interested bystanders. Taucher soon was into budget overrun bigtime, $800,000 or so. He e-mailed Shirley offering to cut the number of cities; Shirley fired back "a note to the effect this is the most important thing the company will ever do. Don't change anything." Taucher tapped City Center Theater, papered the industry with invitations, and wound up with a near-capacity turnout. There were PR kits, demo stations, *Witness the transformation!* buttons, free copies of Win 3.

It may well have been, as Mary Gates told a reporter, "the happiest day of Bill's life." Microsoft had taken on IBM and seemed to be winning. Gates announced that Microsoft would spend $10 million over the next six months to promote Win 3, and the company claimed sales of 380,000 copies in five weeks, an average of nearly 11,000 a day. The raucous momentum spilled out from the City Center into the American consciousness.

No municipality was too small for the Win 3 message. To promote his pet product, Gates appeared in a series of city-by-city satellite television interviews, prompting him to wonder off-camera where Spartanburg was and whether it actually had any computer stores. To assuage his fears, Pam Edstrom had the Chamber of Commerce of Spartanburg, South Carolina, send Gates a postcard inscribed, "We in Spartanburg Love Windows!"

It wasn't all gravy, however. In June, just when he was riding high atop the grand marshal's float of the Windows parade, Gates got word that the Federal Trade Commission was opening an investigation into possible antitrust violations. Although cooperating with the investigation, which also involved IBM, Gates and Microsoft kept the issue quiet. Not until nine months later would the investigation become public.

Still, nothing—certainly not a government investigation that could take years—seemed capable of damping Win 3's success. Within a couple of weeks Microsoft had established a Win 3 800-number hotline: Have credit card ready for ordering Win updates! Need a job? "The Microsoft Corp. has immediate openings for Windows/SDK Systems Support Engineers." In August, in the latest volley in a longstanding rivalry, Bill hired Brad Silverberg, Borland's vice president of engineering, away from Philippe Kahn to become Microsoft's vice president of systems, overseeing DOS and Windows.

After the initial tsunami of attention, users began reporting bugs in Win 3. Once again, Microsoft's testers had not weeded out all the problems. There were problems installing the program on certain machines, troubles with networks, difficulties with mice, data destruction with certain third-party disk management software—along with the usual collection of glitches and documentation errors.

Still, for Windows, three was the charm, assuming you discounted all the interim editions. After all these years, Windows was still not perfect, still not as technically sophisticated as OS/2, but it was good enough. It had a great game of solitaire. You could customize your desktop and display colors and icons for hours on end. And once and for all, the Weise/Wood protected mode solution meant programmers were rid of the 640K barrier.

Vern Raburn would later say that "Microsoft, with a couple of exceptions, has always introduced really crappy products. . . . And ultimately they turn into good products." The running gag in the industry was that Microsoft products were in beta test until version 3. Ann Winblad saw that as a secret weapon. "Hey, talk about willingness to take risks! The company gets a rev one out there, lets all this stuff come back, thinks about how crummy this stuff is, and then goes after the right stuff.''

Most recent evidence: Word for Windows version 1.0, which after its long odyssey as Cashmere and Opus had finally shipped in December 1989, so riddled with bugs it was followed soon after by an only somewhat better version 1.1. Both would later be cauterized in the *New York Times Magazine* by, appropriately enough, chaos specialist James Gleick. But by 1992, the third iteration, version 2.0, though hardly bug-free, would be good enough to begin eroding WordPerfect's hegemony for the first time. At Microsoft, three was definitely a charm.

What helped Windows and the apps most was that the hardware was beginning to catch up with the software. Moore's Law was back in effect, and memory was cheap again, less than $100 per megabyte and falling. The 386 chip was getting cheaper too, and Windows took advantage of it. Most notably, with the 386, Windows could run multiple DOS programs—instead of just one as in OS/2—and run them well. DESQview had been able to do that for years, of course, but DESQview just wasn't sexy. All in all, Windows was good enough to get the PC young and restless to spring $80 or so just to try it out, good enough to be the Anacin for Mac Envy, good enough to push Microsoft to a record $337 million quarter.

Good enough to get IBM's goat. Relations with the Boca brethren continued to deteriorate through the summer, with IBM lobbing occasional volleys in Microsoft's direction. First IBM had snubbed TrueType in favor of Adobe's Type Manager. Next IBM snubbed Microsoft's PenWindows pen-based technology in favor of an allegiance with Go Corp.'s PenPoint. Finally there was the announcement of Patriot Partners, a joint venture with Metaphor Computer Systems to develop a next-generation operating system. It seemed Big Blue was intent on dancing with everyone except the one it brought to the ball.

Not that Microsoft was standing still and taking it. The Gates-Cannavino announcement at Comdex '89 was all but shredded. Promise: After mid-1990 Microsoft will come out with PM versions of graphical applications before Windows versions. Reality: Microsoft's Windows applications ship to much hoopla before and after July, and PM versions are all but invisible. Promise: Windows is meant for systems with less than 2 megabytes of memory. Reality: Win 3 is intolerable without *at least* 2 megabytes. Promise: Windows will never include certain advanced features of OS/2. Reality: David Cutler's NT team is nearly ready to give Windows all those features and more.

In early September, in an agreement that quickly rocked the industry, IBM took over sole development responsibility for OS/2 1.X and 2.0. Microsoft agreed to make available its version of OS/2 1.3, the still-alive 2 meg edition, and remained responsible for OS/2 3.0, temporarily dubbed Portable OS/2, which was actually Cutler's NT project, now in the process of being adapted to Intel chips.

In one of the mad shuffles Microsofties had become accustomed to, the OS/2 operation at Redmond underwent a rapid shakeup. Those whose whole lives had revolved around making OS/2 great were told it was IBM's baby from here on out. A Microsoft OS/2 developer recalled the September massacre:

> In the period of two weeks it was turned around. [They] said we're not doing this anymore, we're handing it off to IBM and going to go do something else. They rationalized it as best they could, but basically they just changed their minds and the fate of . . . hundreds of these employees in this case was affected. . . . They did a very poor job of making people feel that they were worthwhile, that the work they had done was worthwhile.

On September 17 *InfoWorld* reported the story on page 1 as a "rift" between IBM and Microsoft that had led the latter to scrap OS/2 development. "Whatever you say, don't use the word 'divorce,' " Ballmer warned editor Rachel Parker. Naturally, every journal in the country picked up that very word to describe the arrangement. Ballmer insisted they were wrong: "Whatever relationship we've had with IBM in the past, whether it's a 'marriage' or something else, it's strengthened by this agreement." Cannavino echoed him, stating that even if responsibilities were divided, "I wouldn't view that as significant from a relationship point of view."

Was it a divorce? Not quite, not yet—more like a separation with the two parties maintaining separate households. All versions of DOS, Windows, and OS/2 were cross-licensed with royalties, meaning that for the first time IBM had licensed Windows. In effect, Cannavino had gotten what he had wanted earlier: a renegotiation of the JDA. He may even have thought he'd won: One leading software developer heard from an IBMer that "this JDA is considerably better than the last one they got." But speculation was that Gates was glad to be rid of the OS/2 albatross.

"We gave up a lot of our leverage in terms of code ownership and things like that in order to get the relationship unjammed, moving forward in a positive way," Gates said. "We actually thought we're onto a very positive relationship." Echoed Ballmer: "I'll tell you in my heart I didn't think we were separated in any way."

And that was IBM's official position. "I think Microsoft and IBM see Windows as a long-term opportunity, not short-term," claimed Lee Reiswig, IBM's Entry Systems Division vice president of programming. Still, Gates made certain he kept his fingers in the till. Microsoft would "make a lot if they sell it [OS/2] onto a non-IBM machine," Gates insisted, and "a reasonable royalty" if IBM sold it onto an IBM machine. How reasonable? "We make good money every time that thing is sold. We make as much money as we make when an OEM sells Windows," Gates said. If IBM was planning to push OS/2 at the expense of Windows—say, by giving the damn thing away with every machine—Microsoft was still going to come away with a profit.

Gates danced uneasily with the bear, but he stubbed his straightened little toe on a tiny mousemaker. On November 7 little Z-Nix filed an antitrust complaint against Microsoft in Los Angeles Federal District Court, alleging that Microsoft was in violation of Section 1 of the Sherman Act prohibiting tie-ins —using its control of the Windows market to control the mouse market. Z-Nix also claimed that Microsoft was in breach of contract for not following through on a deal allowing Z-Nix to bundle Windows with its mice. Requested: damages of at least $4.5 million.

Microsoft's third mouse design, the sleek "white mouse" vaguely resembling a bar of soap and first released in September 1987, had become a cash rodent for the company, selling millions of units and contributing more than 10 percent of Microsoft's gross revenues. Microsoft's patents on the look of the mouse and on drawing power from the serial port were still in effect. The company was understandably loath to encourage competition to its one successful hardware product since the SoftCard.

"It's time for us to stand up to Microsoft's unfair trade practices and stop the slow death of innovation in this industry," stated Z-Nix attorney Thomas T. Chan. A chronology laid out Z-Nix's allegations. December 1989: Microsoft contacts Z-Nix claiming its Super Mouse II infringes on the Microsoft patents. February 1990: Microsoft sends proposed agreement; Z-Nix agrees with minor changes. March: Microsoft responds with more restrictive proposal. June: Z-Nix files for patent on redesign of Super Mouse II. August: Microsoft quotes $27.50 royalty for each copy of Windows sold with a Z-Nix mouse. Z-Nix says okay and proceeds with ambitious marketing plans. October: Microsoft informs Z-Nix the Windows contract will be signed only when the patent infringement issue is resolved according to the terms of the second, more restrictive proposal. Z-Nix agrees. Microsoft sends a new contract doubling Windows royalties to $55, terminating the deal when the Win 3.1 upgrade ships, and forcing Z-Nix to agree not to sue Microsoft for patent infringement should Microsoft use any of the Super Mouse II features.

Publicized just before Fall Comdex, the complaint was characterized by a Microsoft higher-up as "the nuclear hand-grenade trick. Microsoft is a very attractive target. We viewed this as a terrorist attack." Officially, Microsoft officials expressed complete bafflement. Unofficially, one acknowledged the company "may have been too aggressive" on the Windows pricing for Z-Nix.

As Comdex opened, a settlement was announced, including the withdrawal by Z-Nix of "allegations about Microsoft's conduct." A mousemaker worth

about as much as Microsoft made in a single day had stared the Software
Monolith in the eye and won. Chan had a few choice observations: "At the
beginning, Gates wanted people to write for DOS. But that's not true of
Windows. . . . Microsoft doesn't need Ashton-Tate or WordPerfect to help
them push Windows." Then the prescient bombshell: "If they don't open up
Windows they will definitely get major lawsuits. . . . The FTC and Justice
Department will come in." But Microsoft omitted any public mention of the
still-secret FTC investigation.

Z-Nix could squeak all it wanted: Nothing was going to stop the Bill Gates
juggernaut at Comdex '90. For his opening-day keynote address there would be
no repeat of Comdex '83, where Dad ran the slide projector while Bill craned
his neck backward to see what was being flashed on the screen. This time
everything was fully orchestrated, with Gates departing from his usual routine
of ad hoc speechifying—"my speeches are never written, they're never never
written," he would adamantly insist—to actually prepare, practice, and re-
hearse. This time there would be sound and video, interaction between actors
playing real-life people up on the screen and Bill Gates playing Bill Gates in the
flesh, all based on a campy spoof of "Twin Peaks," the TV series filmed in the
Cascade Range a stone's throw from Microsoft country. Microsoft's aging
Golden Boy Jonathan Lazarus, producer of the extravaganza, had even rustled
up twelve hours of "Twin Peaks" tapes for review by Gates, the no-TV guy
who had never seen the show, so that he would at least know "why I was
cracking those jokes" in his keynoter.

The Las Vegas Hilton auditorium was jammed. Outside, the overflow
crowded around monitors to watch the speech, but latecomers were out of
luck even there. "Bill has packed this place just the way Elvis used to," gushed
Comdex honcho Sheldon Adelson.

The Gates buzzword of the day, the Microsoft catchphrase for the '90s, was
"Information at Your Fingertips," a phrase that was bruited as "World at Your
Fingertips" as early as the 1985 company meeting and that Gates probably
resuscitated from "Information at the Fingertips," the headline of an article in
a January 1988 issue of the *Economist,* his favorite magazine. Under IAYF all
your daily chores would funnel through a computer on every desktop running
Microsoft software: E-mail with not just text but audio and video of the sender
would replace a desktop mess of little yellow slips. A computer in every bread
truck: Handheld pen-based units would recognize handwriting and send orders
through the ether to the system back at the office. No more pencils, no more
books: Everything from Napoleon's birthday to the salaries of high-tech CEOs
would be available on vast computerized databases networked together and
available in a flash. Cool!

It wasn't that IAYF was anything really new. Gates already had a form of it on his desktop in his ability to e-mail anyone in the company for an instant answer to whatever he needed to know. As for the technology, Alan Kay's Dynabook had plowed much of the same ground. So had a grandiose scheme called Xanadu from industry gadfly and pioneer Ted Nelson. So had Knowledge Navigator, a classic demo from Apple's John Sculley. Every half-baked computer visionary had come up with some sort of globally networked, easy-as-a-toaster computer solution to bring microprocessing to the masses. But they'd all faded into the woodwork, except for Sculley. Bill Gates was a guy who shipped product.

"No single company is going to be able to do this," Gates concluded. "It's going to require hardware manufacturers, software developers, and distribution channels all cooperating." An olive branch to those who were rumbling about Microsoft's growing hegemony in the industry? If intended that way, the notion got few takers. Gates—and many others—would consider IAYF his best speech ever, a forty-five-minute-long exposition of The Vision According To Bill. But instead of the industry rallying around him in a groundswell of unity, talk was of how to contain the Gates juggernaut. The day of his keynoter, *PC Week*'s lead headline read "Mighty Microsoft Breeds Fear, Envy." The Bill Bashers were back.

The latest round had started even before the Win 3 extravaganza. Bob Metcalfe, retiring from 3Com after being passed over for the presidency, had predicted that "Microsoft will continue to expand its death grip on the personal computer industry." Jim Manzi, asked by *Business Week* to debate the future of networking with Bill, had sniffed, "If I'm going to break my long silence with Bill Gates, it's going to be in a room where no one can hear us. I don't think we have a lot to talk about." The biggest bash came in a cover story in the November 1990 *Business Month* superimposing Gates's head on a body-builder's torso as "The Silicon Bully." Mitch Kapor called the industry "the Kingdom of the Dead." An anonymous IBMer expressed a desire to put an ice pick in Bill's head. But the Gates luck held again. With that issue *Business Month* breathed its last.

Gates always had an answer at the ready. Asked by *M, Inc.* who was the number-one "miracle maker" of the PC industry, Gates responded that it was "for others less biased than me" to determine but could not resist pointing out, "I will say that I started the first microcomputer software company. I put BASIC in micros before 1980. I was influential in making the IBM PC a 16-bit machine. My DOS is in 50 million computers. I wrote software for the Mac." Those were no small claims and, allowing for a certain amount of Gatesian self-aggrandizement, were largely true.

What was definitely not true was the unchallenged answer to a question posed by the *Washington Post*:

POST: Listening to you today, you seem like such a nice guy, but some people say you are not at all nice to your competitors. Is there a Jekyll and Hyde quality there?

GATES: Well, you can interview me after midnight. We have never sued anyone. Ever.

Microsoft was not particularly litigious, but it had sued at least twenty companies, from Actrix to Wugo, for nonpayment, and a handful of others, including XENIX partner SCO, for a variety of other offenses.

Not all interviewers let Gates off so easy. John Perry Barlow, Grateful Dead lyricist turned Electronic Freedom Foundation crusader, asked Gates if Microsoft was going to be the Standard Oil of computing in the twenty-first century. The chairman snapped back: "That's a pretty nasty question. . . . I don't see any analogy at all. All the businesses we're in are very very competitive. Word processing. Networking. When I name one that's not competitive, tell me. Spreadsheets."

How about operating systems? Barlow asked. Gates praised his old nemesis, Digital Research, for its "very innovative work"—work that Gates was competing against with every bit of his bandwidth. Barlow had no reason to know that in the halls of Microsoft, Gates had in the past told sales executive Mark Ursino that "If somebody would be dumb enough to get DR DOS instead of MS-DOS as their sole bundled operating system," he should "get that deal no matter what it took."

Meaning? According to Ursino, "We'd pull out all the big guns and sit down and say, 'What would it take? How do we buy you out of this deal?' Anything went. . . . That's why the pricing was never published."

Back in 1988, accounts in the press indicated that Atari was considering DR DOS for its clone machines. "We are always after the best price/performance," Atari's Sam Tramiel was quoted as saying. "If there's an alternate . . . we're always willing to talk." According to Mark Mackaman, Microsoft rushed in and matched DR's $6 per-machine quote at a time when others with similar volumes were paying significantly more. But then, every deal was "different," and meeting a competitor's price is within the bounds of the law.

Still, the bashing began to run deeper than headline copy. Out in the industry the term "Microslimed" began to gain common currency. Rich Bader, formerly of Intel, put it this way: "There was a sense of being unethical, a sense of means justifying the ends."

Mark Zachmann of ZSoft had his own "cute story" to tell about his Paintbrush software, which shipped as part of Windows: "We had no name in the 'About' box," where the developer's name was traditionally listed. "We got no credit at all. They said, 'Look at your contract. We're not required to.'

You'll notice the terminal program and other stuff did say who wrote them. To me that's unethical.''

"Resentment against the boys from Redmond grows,'' Piper Jaffray & Hopwood analyst Robert Kleiber reported in December 1990. Seattle comedians had a field day portraying Bill as an awkward, unfashionable ''geek'' and joking that he had given the company his own high school nickname. Not since antitrust complaints about IBM during the '70s had so much vituperation been leveled at a single entity. At computer conventions, conferences, gatherings, the number-one topic was what to do about Microsoft.

Microsoft insiders saw the talk as sour grapes. In their view the company was better: harder-working, smarter, tougher, more competitive. As baseball fanatic Gaudette put it:

> The Yankees were a wonderful team, and people hated the Yankees because they were good. And in fact in '27, '28 they wanted to break up the Yankees. We have some of that here: We're very good and people don't like us for being good. They don't give us enough credit for being a good business, for hiring good people and all the things that we do creating an environment like this.
>
> Like, gee whiz! We're just lucky guys, and Bill just was a lucky guy and luck is everything. So lucky! And some people are breaking their ass working two shifts, working with material resource planning, understanding world-class manufacturing better than anybody, growing 65 percent compounded, and reducing inventory to nothing. All that stuff just whistles by.

"I don't think Bill's deceitful or dishonest or unethical,'' former Apple Macintosh ''evangelist'' Guy Kawasaki would say. ''I think he's extremely tough.'' But pundit Jeffrey Tarter cited ''real concern that Microsoft is a predatory competitor,'' adding ''They really believe the world would be better if there were greater homogeneity.'' Put another way: A computer on every desk and in every home, running *only* Microsoft software.

Circa the changing PC universe of Comdex '90, that meant Windows instead of OS/2, even for ''mission critical'' corporate systems that could not tolerate the flakiness of Windows and its inexplicable crashes. It meant TrueType instead of PostScript, even though designers, typesetters, and print professionals everywhere grumbled that the world needed a new type standard like it needed a new body fungus. It meant PenWindows, a new technology that could turn a stylus and a handheld computer into a digital notepad. It meant Excel, it meant Word for Windows, Project for Windows, PowerPoint for Windows, and everything else for Windows too. Windows was everywhere! Software was everything! Forget the box, forget IBM and Compaq and Apple. Under the banner of Windows, Microsoft software would—just as the slogan said back in Albuquerque—set the standard.

Despite all the industry grumblings, the User Nation seemed to be buying it. By Christmas of 1990, Windows sales were pushing 2 million. The stock was climbing toward a new high on expectations of the company's third consecutive record quarter. The Z-Nix mouse was simply another creature that wouldn't be stirring.

Party time! The annual Microsoft Holiday Party had burgeoned to 8,000-plus employees and guests, many dressed to the teeth in strapless cocktail dresses or Armani sports outfits, others in typical Northwest jeans and Gore-Tex, all jammed into the six floors of the Seattle Convention Center. The theme was "Holiday in Manhattan"—smart-mouthed 42nd Street panhandlers and cops, a Little Italy deli, the Metropolitan Museum of Art, Broadway Lullabye Showroom, Blue Note Jazz Room, Hard Core Cafe, big bands, little bands, slow dancing, disco dancing. For the kiddies—Gaudette was particularly proud of the touch—a Coney Island rumpus room with a merry-go-round, pony walk, midway games. Rumored cost: More than $1 million. Decadence? A local newspaper grumbled about the ironies of hiring actors to portray beggars while the homeless froze outside, but Microsoft made sure the leftover food was donated to a local charity.

Dressed in a striking white tuxedo with red cummerbund, Bill came with Dad and Mom and his girlfriend Melinda French. He made the rounds with baronial grace, chatting, nodding at acquaintances, beaming the whole time. It was a relaxed, sanguine, sociable Bill, not the corporate kingpin, not the haranguing chairman—a Gates the public and the company seldom saw, but one just as much in command as if in a boardroom or behind a computer. Even with the FTC investigation, even with IBM on the outs and the Apple suit still hanging fire, Bill could lighten up and smile, for that particular evening and those particular couple of hours. Looking around the giant hall at thousands of young, driven Smart Guys and Gals dressed to the nines and exuding the cherubic energy of the young and the committed, Gates beamed with exultation. "Have you ever seen so many people at a Christmas party?" he shouted above the din. This wasn't decadence. These were his people.

And they were depending on him. The following morning, a Sunday, he was back in the office as usual. After all, there was still a war to be won: the war for the desktop.

30

HOMEFRONT

And what about the war for the home?

By late 1987 Microsoft's CD-ROM division was heading down a road Microsoft Press had already traveled. At first the idea had been to learn about the business, to become an industry leader, to produce influential products, damn the cost, and hopefully move into profitability somewhere down the road. It was a model that had sunk Nahum Stiskin, founder of Microsoft Press, and led to his replacement by Min Yee, fresh from Ortho's no-nonsense line of gardening books.

Gates was beginning to notice that the new CD-ROM division, never conceived as a profit center in the first place, was not making any money. Even though Bookshelf quickly became the number-one best-selling CD-ROM, its total sales over a period of four years would amount to fewer than 12,000 copies. A product like Windows would sell that many copies in a single *day*. "This is Bill's fault, no question about it," Raleigh Roark said. "Basically what it boiled down to was we're supposed to be developing technology that will be valuable at some future date, but we're supposed to pay our way as we go along."

Microsoft's CD-ROM chief Tom Lopez began pursuing what Gates would later characterize as "the dilettante strategy." The idea was to find "Beta Partners," big companies with databases that seemed ripe for CD-ROM—a Caterpillar tractor manual, say, or a DuPont chemical catalog. With this strategy, as Bill would articulate, Microsoft could "be breaking even and yet learning and developing a generic set of tools." Unfortunately, many candidates had huge programming staffs that could do—and were doing—precisely that kind of work on their own and had no need of Microsoft's services.

Meanwhile, mass-market multimedia was still struggling. After its splash at the 1987 conference, RCA's DVI compact disc video scheme had disappeared from sight. After acquiring RCA, GE had donated the Sarnoff Labs to SRI International and cared hardly at all about the new technology.

How else might Bill Gates trump Philips and Sony and CD-I? One way might be to bring Japanese consumer-electronics giant Matsushita into the picture. Unfortunately, joint talks among Lotus, Intel, Microsoft, and Sony's archenemy went nowhere. Microsoft and Lotus considered teaming to buy the DVI technology, but finally backed away.

At its CD-ROM conference in 1988, Microsoft kept the pressure on. Representatives from Microsoft, Lotus, and Intel endorsed an improved DVI standard—thereby throwing some cold water on Philips's first public demonstration of CD-I, which couldn't do full-frame full-motion video and was technologically way behind DVI's latest stunts. Microsoft itself introduced two new CD-ROM titles, quick-and-dirty disks full of public-domain information and statistics from the U.S. government. In his keynote address, Bill Gates predicted that by early 1991, a 386-based computer with a built-in CD-ROM drive would cost less than $1,000.

That bright-sounding future was not remotely in sync with the grim reality, and Bill's $1,000 CD-ROM computer would not begin to seem a possibility until late 1992. By mid-1988, the CD-ROM division at Microsoft underwent a full-fledged palace revolt. "This idea of you're supposed to do something strategic, long term, but make it pay for itself: It was dumb," said Roark. There were rumblings among the troops, but Lopez had never learned the great Microsoft secret weapon: Stand Up to Bill. So, led by the division's plodding but ambitious young marketing director, Bill Clone Carl Stork, a delegation descended on Gates's office and aired a cornucopia of grievances. Within weeks, Lopez found himself out the door and his division dispersed to the winds.

But though decentralized, CD-ROM efforts at Microsoft refused to die. In October 1988 Intel bought the DVI technology and team, giving them a permanent home at last. And Microsoft was still working both sides of Multimedia Street. Late in 1988, out of the blue, Philips and Sony announced a new standard called CD-ROM XA on which Microsoft and particularly Lopez had been collaborating.

Initiated by Sony's Toshi Doi and implemented with the help of Microsoft's Roark, CD-ROM XA was an audio and graphics standard that would permit the creation of CD-ROM discs that could play on any properly outfitted DOS machine—and also on any CD-I player. It appeared to be a brilliant end run: Anyone producing CD-ROM software would be likely to hedge the development costs by developing a "bridge disc" that worked with both formats. So even though Microsoft wasn't in on CD-I, this intricate backdoor scheme would let its systems play some, if not most, CD-I titles. As Roark recalled, "It was basically annexing half of CD-I and bringing it into the PC world." Amazingly, Microsoft appeared to have snatched at least a partial victory from the jaws of utter defeat on the CD-I platform.

Except, except . . . the yen was still in the stratosphere, and disk drives were still not getting much cheaper, and Sony's proprietary XA chip would add even more cost to each unit. Again and again CD-I kept being postponed until the following Christmas. At Microsoft, Ballmer's systems division, with such things as OS/2 and Windows to worry about, made CD-ROM one of its very lowest priorities, and the software ended up being slow, fat, and hard to find. In 1988 Microsoft Press released a collection of manuals called Programmer's Bookshelf. It might have been interesting to OS/2 programmers, but nobody in the systems division had bothered to make sure its forward-looking new operating system offered any support whatsoever for CD-ROM.

Eventually Microsoft reorganized its CD-ROM efforts yet again—this time under the name "Multimedia," the industry buzzword for everything on your screen all at once, from text to sound to still photos to full motion video. Rob Glaser, another of Gates's Golden Boys, was moved from the sinking network effort to head up Multimedia Systems. XA was abandoned. The new focus was on incorporating multimedia into Windows.

Meanwhile, IBM's Lexington, Kentucky, wing was working with Microsoft on what one participant called "the most incredible machine." At the time, the computers that were destined to become the first PS/1 models were known as "Bluegrass Good" and "Bluegrass Better." But there was also something dubbed "Bluegrass Best" that happened to be a full-fledged CD-ROM-based multimedia monster, originally priced at under $3,000.

The problem—a classic at IBM—was that the Bluegrass Best looked as though it would run rings around most of IBM's underwhelming, expensive PS/2 line—thereby cannibalizing sales. The "Best" was quickly brought under the numbing thumb of the PS/2 wing at Boca. "The PS/2 guys kind of smothered us with kindness," Glaser recalled. The schedule was pushed out more than a year and a half. The projected price doubled.

"So we said, well, let's take a lot of that technology and create an abstract definition that anybody can play with." Microsoft rounded up an oddball consortium including AT&T, CompuAdd, NEC, Olivetti, Tandy, Zenith, and, amazingly, Philips, to develop a standard called "Multimedia PC." The idea was something like the VHS video cassette system or Microsoft's MSX: In theory any MPC machine would be able to play any MPC disc. Microsoft contributed Multimedia Extensions for Windows, plus a Multimedia Development Kit for programmers.

MPC machines began shipping in the fall of 1991 to a chorus of yawns. They suffered from the same problem as prior CD-ROM machines: too high a price, too little software. And IBM weighed in with what it called the "Ultimedia" machine, a direct descendant of "Bluegrass Best." It now cost $6,000.

But Microsoft remained intent on publishing CD-ROM software. It adapted some titles such as Multimedia Beethoven that had long since been available on the Macintosh. It produced Multimedia Works, a CD-ROM-based version of Microsoft Works with jazzy video tutorials and help. And though the attempts of Microsoft Press to crack the world of nontechnical book publishing had not been successful, in March 1991 Microsoft bought 26 percent of Dorling Kindersley, a British publisher best known for its photographically illustrated volumes and *The Way Things Work*—a sort of book-as-multimedia approach that Gates called "a wealth of information that can become multimedia titles."

Late in 1991, the slow-selling Bookshelf got an upgrade from pure dull text to exciting forward-looking Multimedia. The dictionary could pronounce words. The encyclopedia included a few animated sequences—and, if you clicked in the right place, the voice of John F. Kennedy telling Americans to ask not what your country could do for you—just as in the very first demo Microsoft had commissioned. Multimedia sure had come a long way in five years.

▼ If the computer couldn't come to the home, maybe Bill Gates's home could come to the computer. But first the boring manse sitting on his property would have to disappear. At the suggestion of Mary Gates, who could just see the publicity about demolishing a million-dollar house when the homeless were filling up downtown Seattle parks, it was sold in 1990 for less than $100,000, jacked up, and barged up the lake to a new site. Bill Gates had far grander plans.

Under the direction of an architectural consultant providentially named Micheal Doss, Paul Allen had been redoing his place to include a library for his mother and a basketball court for his Portland Trail Blazers and anybody who happened by for a pickup game. After an introduction from Allen, Gates hired Doss to conduct an international architectural competition that eventually included twenty-three entrants from as far away as France and Japan. The three finalists each met with Bill three times during the process of preparing detailed designs.

The two runners-up couldn't have been more different from the winner or from each other: a grandiose, pretentious effort befitting Gates's royal status, and an ultramodern job that assaulted the site, conquered it, and defeated it.

But the winning entry, the one that captured Bill's fancy, was a collaboration between the Pennsylvania firm of Bohlin Power Larkin Cywinski—which had designed the Software Engineering Institute at Pittsburgh's Carnegie Mellon University—and a low-key Seattle-area residential architect named James Cutler who had worked with Peter Bohlin and studied at the University of Pennsylvania under Louis Kahn, the architectural visionary and sage. Under the gray Northwest skies, Cutler's taste had mellowed, and he had designed a variety of wooden houses in a one-with-nature "Northwest contemporary" style.

The winning entry was unassuming, soothing, self-effacing, with 20 percent of the job budgeted for landscaping. "Incredibly understated," sniffed modernist Charles Simonyi, lord of a post-Bauhaus geometric manor about a mile down the lake. "Nobody will guess that is his house, the famous Bill Gates house, because it's not going to look like anything."

From the lake, the passing boater would merely see five large but hardly prepossessing unattached houses terraced into the wooded hillside. Actually, the houses—"pavilions"—would be connected by underground passageways. One pavilion would be the grand entry hall. Another would include the guest bedrooms, the library, and a twenty-seat dining room. A third would be a reception hall with room for 120 people, enough to house the kind of crowd Bill typically bused to his current house for a series of "new hire" parties every summer. A fourth would be a beach house with dock, swimming pool, and hot tub. There was also a twenty-car underground garage whose capacity could increase somewhat in valet-parking situations, room for a dozen or so more vehicles in various turnarounds, and a small, separate, elegant house for the caretaker.

And at the top, overlooking the domain, isolated from the rest, would be Bill Gates's private residence, the master control center, from which like Kane or Hearst or Oz he could make sure his guests were having fun. Visitors, as Cutler put it, "can experience Bill's whole house, and they'll never have really been in his house."

With exquisite environmental sensitivity—and a sense of irony about the absurdity of it—Cutler went out of his way to look for "environmental" angles for this showplace. In a masterstroke of recycling, timber for the house was being pulled out of the structure of an enormous defunct lumber mill a hundred miles to the south in Longview and remilled a hundred miles to the north in Bellingham. A single bigleaf maple tree on the site, where maples grow like weeds, was spared at an estimated expense of $15,000. And a third of the waterfront was slated to be restored to estuary for a salmon run or, failing that, a wetland.

And the exterior, this oasis of natural Rousseauean calm, would be complemented by an interior of more than 30,000 square feet dominated by— *Witness the transformation!*—software! Bill Gates had found a way to turn his house into a business experiment.

Like Citizen Kane plundering the churches of Europe for his Xanadu, like

William Randolph Hearst carting home half of the Old World for his castle at San Simeon, the latter-day software mogul was about to rummage through the art of the ages to furnish his realm. Except he wouldn't bother to buy the art itself: He would simply buy the right to turn it into electronic images, "virtual" art that could at the touch of a button appear and disappear on screens strategically placed just about everywhere. No need for original art, with its messy considerations such as conservation, storage, and eventual overfamiliarity. The Gates house would be a Virtual Xanadu.

The idea had blossomed first at Microsoft. Developing the Bookshelf project had involved the acquisition of electronic rights to such books as the *World Almanac* and the *Columbia Encyclopedia*. Gates thought there might somehow be a business in owning and selling those rights. "What data," he wondered, "do a lot of people want that's not widely available?" Where could Microsoft get "a unique proprietary position?"

Maps wouldn't work; the government owned the data. Music wouldn't work; the industry already had its own schemes for rights payments. Movies wouldn't work: The rights were complicated and they cost a fortune. Business data might work, but it was firmly held by publishers such as McGraw-Hill. Encyclopedias might work, but "Warren Buffett's not selling *World Book, Encyclopaedia Brittanica* can't be bought, and everybody else is losing market share."

The one place where there might be a business, Bill thought, was in creating a massive database of still images. In September 1989 Gates incorporated his own separate company, initially called Home Computer Systems, then changed to Interactive Home Systems—IHS. A skeleton crew of four, including one member of Microsoft's old CD-ROM team, was hired to investigate the photo database idea—meeting with museums, looking into state-of-the-art hardware and software, determining who really owned electronic rights—and, eventually, acquiring some.

By mid-1990 he had the vision down, at least for the house. Behind the scenes there would be a massive computer and the "Wurlitzer," a robotic jukebox that could play CDs and videodiscs and videotapes. And of course, there would be interactive encyclopedias and hypertext and movies at a touch and all the other multimedia wonders.

The scene itself would include big, high-resolution rear-projection screens tastefully placed in all the public rooms and most of the private ones. Fed by a 300,000-image database that could remember what each guest had seen and therefore avoid unseemly repetition, the screens would display new images or call them up with the help of a remote control wand. The underground passageways, lined with screens, would change their images constantly, so that they'd never appear the same way twice. And the "arcade," a room where the walls and ceilings were video, could display such dazzlements as a 360-degree view from Mount Everest in a variety of light and weather. Eventually, robotic

360-degree cameras would roam, say, the Italian countryside, beaming images back to the lakeside palace. Virtual reality! Virtual art! Virtual travel! Virtual life in the twenty-first century!

Yet it would all be tasteful, aesthetically soothing. So as not to dominate the room like the screens in some raucous sports bar, the high-definition television displays would be controlled by sensors that would balance their emissions with the ambient light to blend in unobtrusively with the surroundings. Pointing a magic wand at the screen would make it instantly brighten. And the whole thing would be easy to rip out for the latest technological upgrades. Rear projection would be a mere stopgap, an instant antique. When big flat-panel LCD screens eventually came in—the biggest were still less than a foot across—installing them would be simple, since the house would have easily accessible, interconnected interstices for electrical and mechanical maintenance.

But the business opportunity? Somewhat unclear. When Gates originally drew up a budget for the project and presented it to the Microsoft board of directors, "The board said, nah, it's probably better for you to do it yourself. That's pretty positive," he remarked with sarcasm.

"At the current time it's so clearly not something in which there's a clear large economic potential," board member Jon Shirley said. "At some point in the future it's possible the board could feel that it wasn't proper for this thing to be an independent entity and demand that Bill change the structure and fold it into Microsoft." In the meantime, shareholders potentially dubious over company funds being poured into the boss's house would be soothed.

Gates reviewed the project with the board once a year, and "They can bring it up whenever they feel like it. I mean, there ain't that much going on yet."

That depended on how you looked at it. By 1992 IHS had twenty-five employees, including president Steve Arnold, hired from Lucasfilm to make a go of this. Perhaps you could put together a system that mere millionaires would build into their homes, and eventually, with cheaper technology and a database of big-eyed Keanes, poker-playing dogs, and lush barroom nudes, the whole thing might trickle down to the trailer park. But that seemed unlikely.

The place where the money would come from, at least in theory, was that mammoth image bank, that electronic repository of the World's Great Art, or at least the art that museum directors were willing to cut deals for. Bill's operatives were already flying around the world, dangling contracts for electronic rights on a nonexclusive basis. This alone sounded like the foundation of a business—the digital stock photo business, where anybody putting together a multimedia disc with still images would come to IHS to get them rather than have to contact dozens of museums, artists, photographers around the world. It was yet another variant of the one-stop shopping concept first proposed by the late Blair Newman, who in May 1990 had committed "virtual suicide" at forty-three by erasing hundreds of his on-line messages and then three weeks later did it for real with nitrous oxide.

There were other possibilities: "corporate image management," for companies—say, Walt Disney Productions—that owned a huge assortment of images. But Gates insisted that the home market would one day be the big one. "We are a well-funded company with a smart president who's going to figure out if there's money to be made," he said. "But when it comes right down to it, none of the existing markets—stock photos, museum services—are big enough to justify the size of the investment we're making. So there'd better be some new markets—that is, the equipment for people to browse these hi-res images better come down in price very fast—and people better want to interact with choosing lots of funny little different images, or else we're just wasting a lot of money."

Who knew? Maybe this was the wave of the future. The Gatesian art system might open up whole new realms of scholarship. In a matter of seconds, you could set up a slide show of the art history of the nude, or of Jesus, or of cows. And one IHS wizard was supposedly entering the weight of the various artists into the database. Correlate that with the pictures and you might be able to produce a dissertation exploring cultural and psychological influences on the concept of fatness as beauty.

But there were naysayers too. Photographers worried that selling off their electronic rights would deprive them of their livelihood—reselling images for use in a variety of situations. Museum curators worried about control of their material. If you could call up any picture in the universe in digital form, how hard would it be to draw a political slogan or advertising message across *The Last Supper* and distribute the debased result around the globe?

Bill Gates professed not to worry that his house, his showplace, might never get done. The plans were way past schedule and the budget was ballooning—in part because of what Cutler came to call "the Gates factor." As the architect put it, "I've been doing residences for fifteen years, and all the knowledge you've gained on pricing is out the window. It's like Alice in Wonderland."

Part of that was pride, the realization that this would be the showcase project, the career-maker, the one you could take the time and effort—and the money—to do absolutely right. But part of it was fear mixed with a touch of greed. Engineers kept coming back with incredibly conservative specifications. Contractors factored in extra work to ensure quality. No one wanted even the remotest risk of a lawsuit somewhere down the road if a pavilion sprung a leak or slid down the hill or shook apart in the giant Richter-9 Seattle earthquake that experts agreed was due any century now. "It's driving costs through the roof," Cutler complained.

But work went on anyway. The hillside behind the site was shored up. The pavilion concept underwent substantial modifications that gave the structure more visual unity. In 1992 the underground parking garage, a striking vaulted structure dominated by the huge entry arch, was completed. So was the caretaker's house, all glass and lacquered fir with Oriental-looking hardware joining the posts and beams. Gates would occasionally spend the night there.

And both the garage and the caretaker's house displayed the architects' sly wit. The entire project would adopt elements of the conceit that some of the structures had actually been "found" on the site. Thus the wood-textured concrete vault of the garage ceiling was attacked with jackhammers to reveal through jagged edges a high-tech void above, containing various electrical and mechanical facilities. In the caretaker's living room, a concrete wall crumbled away to reveal stone behind it. The fragments of a broken garden wall were scattered throughout the garden as instant ruins. On one hand: We are all mortal, and all this can come to dust. On the other: We can build on what came before us. It was at once a confirmation and rebuke of Bill Gates's glorious pessimism.

Which the project itself might bear out. Although scheduled for completion by the summer of 1995, the project's final plans had yet to be filed with Medina City Hall as of mid-1992. In monthly meetings, Gates continued to bend the project toward his tastes: "I try and limit the amount of cement, keep the wood content high."

▼ Home not enough? Desktop too limited? How about a computer in every human? This one might require more than BASIC, more than a weekend. In 1990 Gates became interested in a high-powered Seattle biotech startup called ICOS—after "icosahedron," the twenty-sided figure defining the structure of viruses. At the Seattle home of vice president and scientific director Chris Henney, a founder of the Immunex biotech firm, Gates dined with ICOS's principals. George Rathmann, ICOS chairman and a founder of Amgen, one of biotech's big success stories, said his impression was that Gates "was looking for several things—whether we were real, whether we were committed and sincere, whether we were smart, whether we were really honest and straight-forward, whether we really intended to build a first-rate company." Although Gates held his own in discussions about ICOS's scientific plans, "I don't think he was trying to decide whether our science was first class, second class, or third class. I think he was really assessing whether we were first-class, second-class or third-class people."

Rathmann, "anxious to have some people on our board that [had] lived through the formation of a company and carried it all the way into a large company and still kept it dynamic and powerful," had decided to offer Gates a seat whether he invested or not. Gates decided to drop $5 million into ICOS's

$33 million kitty, helping make the company the best-funded biotech startup ever. To Gates, ICOS had the Smart Guys of biotech: Together its three founders had helped account for marketing therapeutic products for anemia and cancer and diagnostic aids for chlamydia, herpes, AIDS, childhood pneumonia, and Legionnaires' disease. On the ICOS board with Bill was Frank Cary, the former IBM chief responsible for getting the original IBM PC rolling a decade earlier.

Licensing technology from the University of Washington and Cold Spring Harbor Laboratory, ICOS promised anti-inflammatory therapies for diseases such as rheumatoid arthritis, multiple sclerosis, and asthma. The elements for success were all in place: all-star board, cutting-edge technology, big-money backing. Rathmann predicted an average 40 percent return on investment. That didn't sound bad to Chairman Bill, even if $5 million was small change, representing only about a 14-cent blip in his Microsoft holdings.

"What's really intriguing to him is that dimension of the conversion of technology into real products that are valuable and can build a company," Rathmann said. "That's the challenge he likes." Gates later confided to an associate that the real reason he invested in ICOS was to have the opportunity "once a month to get together with two or three really smart biologists and learn about biotechnology."

On a breathless schedule, ICOS by spring 1991 was talking of going public, by far the quickest turnaround of a biotech startup. A querulous piece in *Fortune* suggested that a 40 percent return would require a market value of $1 billion by 1997, a valuation achieved by only 2 of 600 biotech companies in the previous twenty years. Further cold water from the article was the disclosure that Paine Webber had fired the initial manager, Stephen Evans-Freke, for opining that the deal was overpriced and refusing to promote it through the PW broker network.

No matter: Gates was golden yet again. In June ICOS sold 4.5 million shares at $8 apiece, though it had hoped for $9. Still, the original investors saw a tidy 166 percent profit on their initial stake. Then the stock rocketed up to $18, riding a whirlwind of speculation in biotech through 1991. By the end of the year it had settled down to $11.

By that time Gates had made a far bigger biotech splash. In October 1991 he announced a gift of $12 million to the University of Washington—the institution's largest donation ever, beating out, in a fit of Gatesian competitiveness, Paul Allen's $10 million grant three years earlier for a new library in honor of his late father Kenneth, a former UW Library associate director. The purpose of the Gates grant: to create a Department of Molecular Biology headed by Caltech's Leroy Hood.

In a reprise of his David Marquardt recruitment a decade before, Gates had attended a U.W. football game with Lee Huntsman, director of the university's

Center for Bioengineering. Huntsman bent Bill's ear about trying to land Hood, one of biotech's bright stars. Like Gates, Hood had big ideas about furthering scientific understanding through computers. He was a key player in the federally sponsored Human Genome Project, a $3 billion effort to map genes and thereby enable scientists to explain and eventually correct human variations in such things as susceptibility to disease. A key factor in the undertaking: accelerating the computerization of gene mapping and other research procedures sufficiently to accomplish in fifteen years a job that by 1991 standards was projected to take hundreds. Talk about the need for fast hardware and software: The metrics were almost unthinkable.

Never one to let a personal investment go unresearched, Gates attended three biotech lectures in a series Hood delivered in Seattle. The two met over dinner, talked for three hours, and hit it off. Although seventeen years his senior, the genial, silver-haired, ruggedly handsome Hood was Gates's kind of guy: smart, energetic, curious, committed, consumed by a singular vision dominating his life. The kind of guy who, upon returning to camp after a brutal day-long hike in the harsh climes of British Columbia, would turn to the rest of the staggering party and ask aloud, "Gee, guys, what are we going to do tomorrow?"—echoing the "where's the next adventure?" Boy Scout Ann Winblad found in Bill.

And Gates was Hood's kind of guy too. "I'd rank Bill as one of the most interesting people I've ever met," he said, citing Gates's "unusual combination of abilities: business on the one hand and computation on the other hand, plus this incredibly bright, inquisitive mind that is interested in all sorts of things." There was the mutually shared vision of computers as well: "I think his view . . . is that there are two things that are going to make a big difference in the twenty-first century, and they both deal with information. One is computers and one is biotechnology, because biotechnology is about developing tools for analyzing biological information."

Auspiciously coinciding with the *Forbes* 400 issue anointing Gates, at a net worth of $4.8 billion, as the second-richest American, the UW grant also softened potential caviling about the charitable conservatism of Gates and his company. The synchronicity was "total happenstance," Mary Gates insisted, pointing out that negotiations with Hood had been under way for more than six months. She wasn't happy about the timing: "My feeling was, isn't it too bad to have it happen on the same day, because then people say, oh well, that's only a small percentage of what he has, just a throwaway gift. So there's two ways to look at it, and I guess I looked at the cup half empty." It was a trait that seemed to have been genetically messengered to Bill's own chemistry.

31

AN INFINITE AMOUNT OF
MONEY

The war for the desktop raged on. Back on January 28, 1991, the eve of a
Microsoft strategy seminar for analysts and press in Redmond, the *Wall Street
Journal* published a story headlined "Microsoft Corp. to Scrap OS/2, Refine
Windows." The article declared what many suspected but few would say and
touched off yet another media firestorm. Microsoft denied the story, with
Chairman Bill himself blandly stating "For customers needing high-end capabilities, deploying OS/2 applications or pursuing IBM's SAA direction, we market
and support OS/2. We will continue to enhance it in the future and enable it
to run Windows applications."

At the next day's seminar Ballmer declared, "Contrary to what you might
suspect, I'm not dropped, scrapped or dead—and neither is OS/2." Yet
moments later Ballmer unveiled Win 32, the Windows API expanded to a 32-
bit arena, with easy conversion from existing Windows programs an apparent
reality instead of an unkept promise. Win 32 offered developers flat address
space, preemptive multitasking and multithreading, integrated networking, interprocess communication, multiprocessor support, and other advanced features—in short, virtually everything that had been reserved for OS/2 in the
Comdex '89 announcement with IBM. There was no mistaking Microsoft's
shift in strategy: Windows was the order of the day. Greg Zachary, author of
the *Journal* piece, said in its defense, "Actions speak louder than words. They
have reasons to deny it, but I do feel the preponderance of their actions
confirms it."

Even Gates, who insisted he continued to hold out hope for OS/2, later
acknowledged "there were signs of weakness in January because of some
statements they [IBM] made and their lack of just visiting us and talking to us."
Gates and Ballmer proposed a joint customer event, proposed a marketing

video, proposed other shows of partnership. No response. Cannavino and Reiswig "just wouldn't answer phone calls, wouldn't talk to us, wouldn't send us letters, and that was strange," Gates recalled. Ballmer was blunter: "I don't think anybody ever at IBM ever thought they could trust us again, even though it was Zachary who decides that we are dropping OS/2 and not us. That was not our strategy."

By March 1, the ongoing FTC investigation of Microsoft became public. "Several industry figures indicated the Federal Trade Commission has recently requested time with them to discuss Microsoft," wrote Goldman, Sachs analyst Rick Sherlund. Microsoft acknowledged what it termed the FTC "inquiry," with Gates stating that it focused on whether Microsoft had made an attempt at "restricting the functionality and features" of Windows, based on the Cannavino-Gates summit at Comdex '89. Never one to shy from a good legal argument, Gates said he had tried to convince the FTC that the issue was moot because of Microsoft's aggressiveness with Windows 3. However, others believed the inquiry would broaden.

While the FTC kept silent, the warlord got busy. Gates brushed off the investigation, claiming "There's no truth to what they are saying" and predicting "This thing will come to an end without any problem." But it did seem to bother him. In the same peevish interview with *USA Today,* Gates charged "Whenever someone asks me about this thing, I say just get somebody who is willing to put their name in print with these lies, because they are just direct lies. You can slander people behind the scenes a lot. But this time somebody might be caught red-handed because this is just out and out baloney."

Analysts and commentators everywhere wondered publicly whether Gates was playing on a level field. Investors didn't seem to mind: After an initial stock hit of $3.50 to $95.75, shares scooted back up toward $100. The number-one investor was typically unruffled: "I have an infinite amount of money," Gates sniffed. Should the stock dive, "I would still order the same hamburger." Within two months, Microsoft declared yet another split, its third since the IPO and fourth overall, this time a three-for-two issue.

A month after the news first broke, the FTC informed Microsoft that it was expanding the investigation: "The purpose of this broadened investigation is to examine allegations that Microsoft Corporation has monopolized or has attempted to monopolize the market for operating systems, operating environments, computer software and computer peripherals for personal computers."

Monopoly! It was Gates's most significant brush with the term since he had uttered it at the Rosen Forum back in 1981. The inclusion of "computer peripherals" in the scope of the inquiry was an intriguing addition, given the Z-Nix case. In the industry there were rumblings that Microsoft might eventually be broken up—perhaps along the model of United Aircraft and Transport, a Northwest institution that under government pressure had been reorganized in 1934 into three separate entities: United Airlines, United Technologies, and the Boeing Company.

Gates knew the FTC investigation promised to take years, but trial by media began almost instantly. Independent developers began airing longstanding grievances, skeletons in the closet, and as-told-tos about Microsoft tactics over the years. The portrait emerged of a company that might or might not have broken the law but that had done things many considered unfair or unethical.

Developers trying to cut deals with Microsoft often divulged their technology and/or their business plans. According to the complainants, Microsoft then used the knowledge for its own gain. The case of Go was the most widely publicized. The Silicon Valley startup, headed by ex-Lotusian Jerry Kaplan and Framework author Robert Carr, had shown Microsoft its technology for a new pen-based operating system with the understanding that Microsoft might want to write applications for it. Instead Microsoft later announced that it would adapt pen-based technology to Windows—a project headed by the chief engineer from the group that got an early look at Go's effort.

"Microsoft stretched the truth a lot," said Dan Bricklin, co-inventor of VisiCalc and vice president of Slate, an independent developer working with both Go and Microsoft. "They'd have you believe they've been working as long as Go. We knew when it became more earnest. They clearly were reacting to Go and OEMs Go was dealing with."

"Stretching the truth," on the other hand, was the way Slate's chairman and CEO Vern Raburn described Go's complaints. "The only thing Go did was they got Microsoft starting to think about it. Did Microsoft plagiarize? Did they lift? Did they take things? No. Absolutely not. Other than, well, what would it be like to use a pen?"

Microsoft agreed: No code was stolen. And upon looking at other systems, the company tended to believe it could do better. As David Weise said of a similar scenario regarding a Micrografx product called Mirrors, "let's just say [they] thought much better of their code than we ever did, and we didn't steal a thing. It was just bad code."

A more common complaint was that Microsoft had used its control of the operating system to gain leverage in the applications market. DOS accounted for 14 million computers sold in 1990, dwarfing OS/2 (300,000), UNIX (400,000), and the Mac (2,000,000), and Windows was coming up fast. What about what had come to be called the "Chinese wall," the old Ballmer separation of church and state? "We bend over backwards to make sure we're not getting a special advantage," Gates told the *New York Times* in March 1991.

Wrong, said independent developers, citing examples of personnel shuffled between systems and applications groups and of technology available to Microsoft apps developers before independents. By the end of April even

Microsoft was backing off: "The divisions are in different buildings and have their own reporting structures, but there's been no attempt to separate the two divisions in terms of information flow," a spokesperson said.

The latest hole in the wall: OLE—Object Linking and Embedding—allowing a chart in a Word document, for example, to be updated instantly and automatically when a related spreadsheet was revised. OLE had been included in Microsoft's PowerPoint in the summer of 1990 and Excel in January 1991, but three months later, Paul Grayson asserted, "we're still waiting for Microsoft to develop the final API and specs to make it all possible" for independent developers. At that time, only big players such as Aldus and Lotus had received sufficient cooperation from Microsoft to be able to include OLE in their software, and then only a provisional version.

Another antitrust concept mentioned in connection with Microsoft was the notion of tie-ins—requiring OEMs to buy Windows with DOS, or making applications sales dependent on systems sales. The tie-in argument had played a major role in the breakup of AT&T on grounds the telecommunications giant could use its control of local service to prevent long-distance competition. Tie-in, in an odd way, had been a foundation of the Z-Nix suit against Microsoft. It was also cited in the case of AlphaWorks, a favorably received integrated program whose biggest OEM customer, Hyundai, switched to Microsoft Works amid rumors of a better deal for DOS.

Then there was the issue of preannouncement of a nonexistent product to forestall competition. Microsoft internal price lists from early 1984 showed the company selling DOS 4.0, the multitasking DOS product that did not appear until late 1986 but competed directly against DESQview and Digital Research's Concurrent DOS. And Windows itself over the course of two years of vapor managed to position itself against every other windowing product on the PC-compatible market at the time, damaging potential competitors from VisiOn to GEM.

The most recent case had involved DR's new DOS-compatible operating system, DR DOS 5.0. In April 1990, a month before DR shipped its product, word filtered out that Microsoft was upgrading MS-DOS "this year" to "dramatically reduce memory usage"—DR's strongest selling point. Yet although Microsoft DOS would not in fact ship until June 1991, a steady stream of updates about its features appeared in trade publications. "Microsoft, in a shift in its policy of not commenting on unreleased products, has been unusually cooperative in confirming details about MS-DOS 5.0," noted *PC Week*'s Paul M. Sherer. According to Microsoft officials, the company was breaking its policy of not discussing unshipped products because "there is no use pretending there is no MS-DOS 5.0 when everyone knows there is." DR president Dick Williams had a different view: "There's no way Microsoft would have spent anything on DOS if we hadn't brought this product to market. Now, instead of competing with a real product, what they're trying to compete with is a lot of FUD''—Fear, Uncertainty, and Doubt, the three horsemen traditionally attributed to the IBM apocalypse.

Also questioned was the concept of selling DOS on a per-machine basis. An OEM paying Microsoft a royalty on every machine it sold would have very little interest in doing a deal for DR DOS. The rumor mill hinted strongly that Microsoft threatened to withhold MS-DOS from any OEM purchasing DR DOS, particularly abroad, where American antitrust concepts don't apply. But those rumors were never substantiated.

Antitrust? Anticompetitive? Or simply pro-Microsoft? For all the complaints and speculation, the only actual antitrust suit filed against Microsoft had been that of Z-Nix—although other firms had contemplated litigation. As one developer put it, "If you just threaten to sue them, it doesn't work. If you play hardball and threaten to go public, they come around." Z-Nix had forced Microsoft into a deal by doing just that.

Up in Redmond, Microsoft house counsel Bill Neukom was playing it cool: "At this point there have been no allegations, no charges brought of any wrongdoing. An awful lot of these investigations don't go very far." The investigation was "essentially as low key an approach as the commission can take." In companywide e-mail billg stood firm: "We want to reinforce our statement . . . that we have NOT [emphasis Gates's] acted in an illegal or unethical manner." Experts who said otherwise were "giving quotes without knowing nearly enough of the pertinent facts and law." Gates blamed a lot of the talk on sheer jealousy: "People don't like a company as successful as ours."

There was no denying that Microsoft was successful. Microsoft's 1990 calendar-year revenues, $1.47 billion, were greater than the combined total of number-two Lotus and number-three Novell, who earlier in the year had proposed to each other a marriage that would never be consummated. And Microsoft's share of the software market was going up.

As suddenly as it had splashed on the front pages of the industry, Bill-bashing quieted down. Since just about every major publication had run an article on the issue, it had become tired copy. The coda was an April *Forbes* cover story, "Can Anyone Stop Him?"

Apparently the answer was no. The FTC continued burrowing away, requesting more boxes of documents. But few held illusions that a Republican administration would actually pursue antitrust action against one of the rare American companies selling more abroad than at home. It became increasingly obvious that relief from the real or imagined sins of Microsoft was not going to come through regulatory channels, or if it did, would be too late to matter.

What happened instead was that the industry itself started ganging up on Bill Gates. The word was out: Don't "open the kimono" to Microsoft. Don't show them new products. Deal the Gator out. IBM wasn't the only major player freezing out Gates and Company. "We don't share product plans with them. Why risk it?" said David Reed, chief scientist at Lotus. Go's Jerry Kaplan warned that developers who showed Microsoft confidential material were "taking a risk." Philippe Kahn observed philosophically that "When you deal with Gates, you feel raped."

Throughout 1991, the message from the field was alliance, consolidation, cooperation—usually without involving Microsoft, often in opposition to Microsoft. In early February, just two weeks after Ballmer's reassurances that OS/2 could still fog a mirror, IBM dealt Microsoft another unpleasant blow, announcing a deal with network rival Novell. Strategically the message was clear: For IBM, the new philosophy seemed to be Anybody But Microsoft. The bear was looking for new dance partners.

So was Gates. A week later Microsoft joined with MIPS, Compaq, DEC, Silicon Graphics, Siemens, and SCO—all entrenched competitors of IBM in the workstation arena—to announce a new lollapalooza workstation strategy based on the hot MIPS R4000 chip and the NT work that had been in the Microsoft lab under David Cutler since 1988.

In a climactic meeting in March 1991, Lee Reiswig and three others from IBM met with Gates, Ballmer, and two other Microsoft executives in Redmond. The game plan: Fold Windows in to run "seamlessly" under OS/2, giving users an all-in-one package handling virtually any PC-compatible app. Ballmer went ballistic as only Ballmer can. "I said, 'It won't work!' " Ballmer recalled. To prove he meant it, he promised to eat a floppy diskette if IBM succeeded by the end of the year. "I think I actually said some other things too about what I'd do, like crawl around on my hands and knees naked or something."

Two weeks later Ballmer talked again with IBM's Lee Reiswig, who laid out Big Blue's OS/2 take-back-the-desktop strategy, designed to win the hearts and minds of corporate users through such stirring sloganeering as "better DOS than DOS, better Windows than Windows," a phrase first bruited by Microsoft. The hapless Extended Edition would be opened to third-party developers for the first time, ending concerns about IBM's proprietary preferences. "I knew we'd hit the end," Ballmer said. For the guy who had insisted there was no divorce, no separation, no death for OS/2, who had served Microsoft as Mr. IBM for long and faithful years, it was a body blow to the corporate corpus.

When the end hit, it hit hard, in the form of an anti-Windows blitz. IBM held a series of seminars where "Blue Ninja" Reiswig reveled in crashing Windows while showing how brilliantly OS/2 2.0 could run DOS and Windows applications. The new OS/2 desktop had a much more Mac-like look and feel. Forget the $340 price tag for 1.3 and $830 for Extended Edition: They were cut to $150 and $690 respectively.

Chairman Bill decided it was time to sever the cord with Big Blue for good. "They did these demos where they personally crashed Windows and they said nasty things about Windows," he recalled. "And then we knew that the name of the product we were working on was Windows NT," not OS/2 3.0 or Portable OS/2 or some other OS/2. The name Advanced Windows had also been rejected, according to Ballmer, because, "that makes the rest of Windows sound like it's not advanced." Which Windows did not need. At the 1991 Computer Bowl, "Examiner" Bill Gates had smirked when the East Coast team blew the question, "What are the three modes of Windows?" From a heckler in the audience came the answer: "Slow, slower, and slowest."

Microsoft wasn't IBM's only problem. In late May John Akers, Big Blue's CEO and chairman of the United Way board that included Bill Gates, issued a companywide memo deriding IBM employees "standing around the water cooler waiting to be told what to do." Flame mail from Mr. Big: "While I know that many IBMers have never worked as hard as they are working today, I am convinced that some of our people do not understand that they have a deeply personal stake in declining market share, revenue and profits." It was time for IBM's 370,000 worker bees to get hardcore! Internally, the memo provoked sniping about Akers's 35 percent raise—to $2.6 million in cash and restricted stock—a figure almost exactly ten times the nominal salary of one William Henry Gates.

Memo wars! Shortly before the Akers flap became public, Bill Gates had gone to the Gateaway complex for one of his "think weeks," a tradition that had begun on the return from Albuquerque, when Bill would take a week off to spend time with Gam at her place on Hood Canal. Alone with his thoughts, he would strategize, read, play with competitors' software, and "write a lot of memos."

In June 1991 one such memo, to a group of Microsoft executives, made its way into headlines after being leaked to the *San Jose Mercury News*—or, some said, planted, which Microsoft denied. The six-page monograph portrayed the chairman as a worried man watching a "nightmare" unfold before his puffy sleep-deprived eyes.

The model for the Gates memo was an impressively literary forty-four-page philippic from Autodesk's John Walker titled "The Final Days," dated April 1, 1991. Concerned that the company he had founded, maker of Auto-CAD computer-aided design (CAD) software, had grown bloated and directionless, Walker painted a "nightmare scenario" in which an "ascetic wunderkind" of software looks out his Seattle window on a gray, drizzly morning and says, "Damn, what I need is MORE MONEY" [emphasis Walker's]. Autodesk's numbers—24 percent after-tax profits, 60 percent market share, and $200 million-plus sales, look pretty good to the chairman, who muses, "And they don't even have a product on Windows." Bill flies into action, assigns teams to do Windows Engineer, promotes the new product the following January with a Super Bowl commercial, and within a year captures 50 percent market share.

Bill's own memo vowed that wouldn't happen. Developing a CAD program "would stretch us too thin," the chairman averred. But he put forth his own grim view of the horrors facing Microsoft: "Our nightmare—IBM 'attacking' us in systems software, Novell 'defeating' us in networking, and more agile, lower cost structure, customer-oriented applications competitors getting their Windows act together is not a scenario but a reality."

At his camp on Hood Canal, Bill was not a happy camper. The Apple case "was a very serious lawsuit" that could be "disastrous." It was "absurd that the lawsuit is taking so long and that we are educating the third federal judge on the case." There was the bane of the FTC investigation: "I am sure it will use up even more executive staff time than the Apple lawsuit has. . . . I know we don't get unfair advantages in any of the markets we are in." Gates hoped we can "quickly educate the FTC on our business."

Then there was IBM. "Other than usability, making sure Windows is the winning OS is our highest priority," Gates wrote. "If we do succeed, then we will be done forever with the poor code, poor design, poor process and other overhead" foisted on the PC universe by Big Blue. "We can emerge as a better and stronger company where people won't just say we are the standard because IBM chose us." BOGU was finished—in part because when you bent over, the world got the impression you might just be prostituting yourself.

Which might account for some of what Bill termed the "dislike of Microsoft." Gates insisted that "Our applications have always succeeded based on their own merit rather than on some benefit of unfair knowledge of system software." The solution? Public openness. "We need to have visible events on a regular basis where we solicit the input of anyone who wants to influence our future direction."

Bill understood that "In large accounts IBM will retain some of its influence—this is where our risk is highest." He even understood that part of the problem was Microsoft's lackluster record of service. "If there is any area we have not paid attention to it is usability/support. It is really embarrassing that people have to wait so long on the phone to talk to us about problems in our products. The number of customers that get a bad impression because of this must number in the millions worldwide." Gates committed to "spend what it takes to have the best support"—but parenthetically added four words that revealed the depth of his commitment to customers: "(without an 800 number.)" WordPerfect, among others, had offered free 800-number support for years. Bill refused to go along, but he did commit funds and manpower to improve Microsoft's support.

The real issue, as Gates saw it, was to improve the usability of the products and cut down on support calls altogether. Here too he was actually backing the idea with cash—in the form of a usability lab intended to learn how real users fared with products while they were still in the design stage. "Usability is incredible stuff," he wrote. "Once it is designed, it is easy to implement, saves money, wins market share, makes customers happier, and lets them buy more expensive software!"

More expensive software! That was the wish, but Philippe was still out there, still Bill's "largest concern about price competition." Gates remembered that "Microsoft priced DOS even lower than we do today to help get it established. I wonder if we would be as aggressive today." He also wondered "why shouldn't some small organization price their product at say $1M for the entire US Government for all time? We would if we were small and hungry." The lowball strategy he had used in the early days to make DOS and BASIC international standards could now be turned against him.

Networking, he admitted, had been a tough nut to crack. "We knew it wasn't going to be easy, but it has been even harder than we expected to build a position in networking. You will see us backing off on some of the spending level, but don't doubt that we are totally committed to the business. Our strategy is to build networking into the operating system." By slaughtering Novell's cash cow with that strategy, Microsoft could then make money by selling add-on products: e-mail systems, "gateways" to other systems, maintenance software. The warlord was not about to take up the concept of "coopetition" popularized by Novell's avuncular Ray Noorda.

Networking would be built into Windows NT, which was one more reason why Windows had to succeed. But there were plenty of others. "Nathan [Myhrvold] (and Kay Nishi before him) has pointed out that the transition of consumer electronics to digital form will create platforms with system software —whether it's a touch-screen organizer or an intelligent TV." By some estimates, Microsoft was only the second largest software company in Redmond, Washington—Nintendo of America being number one. It was time to take the world of Information At Your Fingertips beyond traditional computing environments, and as he had with CD-I, Gates was fighting to control the platform. "Our proposition is that all of the exciting new features can be accommodated as extensions to the existing PC standard. Others propose that start-from-scratch approaches are cleaner and therefore better . . . To win in this we have to get there early before significant development effort builds up behind the incompatible approach."

But as always, the latter-day Napoleon had a fallback plan derived from history: "The key to our Macintosh strategy was recognizing that the graphics and processor of the PC would not allow us to catch up soon enough to prevent Mac from achieving critical mass, so we supported it." Even if Microsoft somehow lost control of the platform, the company could still make money on it. After all, as Gates was fond of pointing out, "We get dramatically more [sales] for every Macintosh that's sold than we get for every PC."

Oddly, there was not so much as a word about the product that had founded the company and carried it for years: languages. The language effort was in shambles. Microsoft, which had been first with a microcomputer language and had remained at the top of the heap for years, was now number three in that market segment, behind KnowledgeWare with its specialized computer-engineering languages and Micro Focus with its industry standard COBOL. Most galling, Borland was number four and gaining ground fast. It was a relatively tiny business—Microsoft's language revenues for 1990 amounted to roughly $79 million—but its slowing growth in the market seemed to be too painful for the chairman even to contemplate.

These were trying times, even for the Smartest Guy. Gates pointed out frustratedly that "it is no longer possible for any person, even our 'architects,' to understand everything that is going on. . . . My role is to understand enough to set direction." He looked at the present from the vantage of the past: "Recently a long-time employee mentioned that we seem to have more challenges facing us now than ever before. Although I agree it feels that way, I can say with confidence that it has felt that way every year for the last 15." Yet Gates praised his executives and said "I love working with people of this caliber —not only do they do a good job but they keep me doing my best. I certainly have no plans to back off from my dedication to the company."

The summary strategy? "Windows—one evolving architecture, a couple of implementations, and an immense number of great applications from Microsoft and others." Or, "for outside consumption . . . more like 'Windows—one evolving architecture with hardware freedom for all users and freedom to choose among the largest set of applications.' "

Hardware freedom: It was device independence all over again. On one hand, it might make the box irrelevant, a Windows machine, a mere commodity, a vector of software. On the other, it might mean hardware makers could innovate, compete on features—better video, faster buses—the way they had tried to in the early days, rather than being locked into some arbitrary standard. Would Windows be a new standard replacing the PC—or would it be Microsoft's version of SAA? The marketplace, buying Windows at the rate of 10,000 to 12,000 copies a day, seemed to be buying into the Microsoft vision. Windows was hot.

Hardware was cold, at least when it came to profitability. Although a depressed U.S. economy was partly to blame, hardware manufacturers were enduring their own private recessions with massive losses and layoffs by fall. Compaq showed its first quarterly loss ever, $70 million for the three months ended September 30. Seventeen hundred of 12,000 employees were laid off, including co-founder Rod Canion, the pioneer whose strategy had led to the first of the clones. Also troubled: IBM, reducing its work force by 29,000, to 344,000 worldwide on the way to an annual loss of $4.23 billion, its first since 1946. Even long-successful direct marketers like Northgate and Zeos were having troubles of their own, although some, like Dell and Gateway, were still doing well.

A dizzying game of musical chairs, partnerships, strategic alliances, and big fish eating little fish dominated the industry for the rest of the year. Philippe Kahn was everywhere, doing deals with Novell and IBM and, in July, buying Ashton-Tate for $440 million, which gave him dBASE and control of 80 per-cent of the PC database market. After the failed merger attempt with Lotus, Novell bought Digital Research, Bill's favorite fall guys, giving every MS-DOS hating, Bill-bashing user another way to run DOS apps on a network.

In April 1991 the MIPS-Compaq-DEC-SCO-Microsoft trial balloon be-came official with the formation of ACE, the Advanced Computing Environ-ment, a twenty-one-member umbrella aimed at putting Windows on a major RISC-based platform. Bill Gates hyped it as "probably the most dramatic thing to happen since the beginning of the PC industry." By mid-1992 it would turn out to be a stunning flop, with defectors running for their lives.

ACE was quickly upstaged by midyear rumblings of the Mother of All Strategic Alliances: IBM and Apple. Proceeding with tanklike deliberation over the desert of common ground, the talks held an on-again, off-again aspect until an official announcement in July and detailed unveiling in October. As it turned out, the two companies, despite radically different corporate cultures, had a lot in common: Both were used to getting top dollar for their hardware on the basis of proprietary advantages, and both disdained the idea of generic, avail-able-to-all third-party operating systems like the ones Bill Gates sold. That was why John Sculley, despite Bill's urgings, had refused to license the Mac. That was why IBM's bureaucrats had refused to cut Bill in on Extended Edition.

Now the two hardware giants intended to create two new companies to focus on delivering new software platforms by the mid-1990s. Taligent would focus on producing an "object-oriented operating system" based on software called "Pink" that Apple already had under development. Kaleida would work on multimedia. Both would aim squarely at elbowing Bill Gates off the desktops and homes of America.

Multimedia! Who had been working on it longer than Bill Gates? Well, IBM, actually, with involvement as far back as its late-1970s investment in Discovision, one of the earliest videodisc projects. And though Apple may have been a relative newcomer, its latest multimedia software for the Mac was getting raves, and Microsoft's was seen as feeble.

As for object orientation, Gates blew hot and cold on it. Object orientation was no simple thing. To programmers, the basic idea was a paradigm involving self-contained bundles of instructions and data called "objects" that could mysteriously interact with one another. To users, the idea might be expressed as "software building blocks" on the Lego model. Jane User might, for example, build her own small-business accounting system, adding or deleting the precise functions she needed, rather than being forced to purchase some overcomplicated do-too-much behemoth.

Alan Kay of Dynabook and graphical user interface fame had been one of the earliest apostles of object orientation as an evangelist for his Smalltalk language. Nearly every forward-thinking visionary in the computer world embraced the concept of object orientation as the next great thing in desktop computers, even though much more attention was being paid to its advantages for programmers than its advantages for users. But within the industry, there was considerable debate about exactly what object orientation meant and even just what an object was.

Maybe "object" meant a data file, as in Microsoft's "Object Linking and Embedding" OLE scheme. Maybe "object" meant the file linked to a little icon on the screen, as in OOUI, the "object-oriented user interface" IBM was now pushing as part of SAA. Bill Gates embraced the term when it seemed to offer a market advantage, spurned it when others touted it as a grail. Pundit Stewart Alsop noticed the contradiction. In his newsletter he had criticized Gates for offering the concept of an "object-oriented file system," an idea that many experts saw as self-contradictory. "Basically in the newsletter I said, 'It's bullshit. He's handwaving because he doesn't know how he's gonna do this.' "

At Esther Dyson's 1991 conference shortly thereafter, Gates spotted Alsop and broke off his conversation midsentence. Bill "comes steaming over towards me," Alsop remembered, saying " 'How the fuck can you get $495 for your newsletter when it's clear you have no fucking idea what you're talking about?!' That was the beginning, and he just went on like that for a full minute, and I know enough about Bill that he does this to everybody, and I'm kind of grinning because I'm thinking, 'Hoo boy, did I hit a soft spot.' "

Still, Taligent was object-oriented, and so far Microsoft wasn't. "It's an opportunity to wrest operating systems control from Microsoft," said Rick Sherlund of Goldman, Sachs. "Software companies are standing up and saluting IBM and Apple, saying we'll support your operating system whatever it is and whenever it is." Philippe Kahn, who had caught Microsoft flatfooted by releasing a compiler for the object-oriented C++ language, banged the drum for object orientation, calling "prehistoric" languages such as BASIC "as bad a habit as smoking."

Bill Gates acknowledged that the concept was important—important enough to be folded into Windows one day. But he dismissed the wild hoopla about object orientation as so much "fairy dust," since nobody was delivering anything close to an object-oriented system at the moment. Just in case anybody might want such a thing, though, Microsoft had super–Smart Guy James

Allchin, the designer of Banyan's Vines network, working on an object-oriented Windows 4.0, code-named Cairo.

Besides, once the fairy emerged from the dust, what would it actually do? Taligent was supposed to run other systems—the Mac, OS/2—as objects. "You can imagine this mulish thing," Gates said, "which has the DOS stuff, the Windows stuff, the OS/2 stuff, the Mac stuff and the Taligent, that's five, count 'em, five user interfaces, five different ways, with different utilities, attributes, device drivers, windows . . . nobody would ever want to use it!"

Of course, people might just develop for Taligent directly and skip the rest. Would Microsoft? "No. I doubt it very much, but not enough is really known to state an answer." No. Probably not. Who knows? The Gator was covering his bets.

A great spec, a perfect sound bite, wonderful column fodder, the Apple-IBM-Taligent-Kaleida deal held promise for the future, maybe. In the meantime, where should users go for advanced technology? IBM was promoting OS/2, but it was clearly a stopgap until Taligent bore fruit. And Apple's message to developers seemed to be that the Mac as such had no future. Macs currently shipped with System 7, and as Alsop hammered repeatedly, there would be no System 8.

Faced with writing a program to run on 7 million installed Macintoshes or 10-plus million machines containing (but not necessarily using) Windows, developers were beginning to pick the latter. To help make it easier, Microsoft released Visual BASIC, the first Windows implementation of the programming language that had founded the empire. By 1992 Apple would announce its intention to bring Macintosh software to Windows, particularly for such advanced technologies as multimedia, imaging, and speech and handwriting recognition. "The Macintosh is not dead," Apple president Michael Spindler would tell a wine-country media seminar, raising the question of who had been asking.

But the livest of operating systems remained good old DOS. Back in 1986, during the "black hole" period of the OS/2 grindout, IBM had taken DOS development into its own hands. The initial result, released with the PS/2 machines, was a version called DOS 3.3 that added a number of useful features, cleaned up a variety of bugs, and was sold to Microsoft for what one IBM insider termed "a fraction of its development costs." But the IBM-developed DOS 4, released in August 1988, was initially incompatible with earlier versions and as buggy as a Boca swamp, in part because IBM didn't bother testing the product on equipment other than its own. Its dubious reputation transferred to Microsoft's OEM version, ensuring that DOS 3.3 would remain the standard for years.

Bill Gates wasn't about to let his former partner tend the cash cow ever again. Microsoft took back the development of DOS. And now it was doing something it had never done before: selling DOS as a retail product. DOS 5 was released June 11, 1991, with a New York gala. The hit of the unveiling was a video of incorrigible ham Ballmer, dressed as Karl Malden complete with oversized nose, starring in "The Streets of Microsoft" and telling users everywhere, "DOS 5! No PC Should Be Without It!" Then it was time to party on the Hudson aboard a cruise ship dubbed *DOS Boat* with entertainment from Dave Brubeck, performing "Take Five."

Here was an operating system that by all rights should have been on the scrap heap but which, as Gates noted, would be installed on an estimated 18 million computers that year alone. With task-switching and memory savings and special utilities, there was just enough in the package—just about as much as in DR DOS's package, oddly enough—to make upgrading worthwhile, especially at the initial lowball street price of $29 to $39. There was also the hint that Windows would run better on top of DOS 5 than on other DOSes, so if you were upgrading to Windows, you might as well get the new DOS as well.

It was another cash cow coup for Chairman Bill. For all its ordinariness, DOS 5 stormed out of the gates. More than 1 million units were shipped within the first six weeks. By the end of 1991 some 8 million copies were in circulation. It was the fastest-selling piece of software Microsoft had ever marketed. To avoid conflict with OEMs, the retail package was offered only as an upgrade, meaning you had to have an earlier version of DOS before it would work. But the retail strategy worked brilliantly, even though it reduced Microsoft margins somewhat. Retail meant that users wouldn't have to hunt up some clone dealer to haggle over their upgrade and what it should cost. Retail allowed Microsoft to put promotional stuff—say, a coupon for other products —in the box. And retail opened up a huge new upgrade market, one that had never before been available to Microsoft: machines that carried three striped initials on the nameplate.

Almost forgotten was the fact that IBM also marketed DOS 5. Before the big rollout, in fact, IBM had formulated plans to undercut Microsoft by offering DOS 5 cheaper, with a toll-free support line and dealer incentives. But IBM had never been successful selling software at retail, and Microsoft's marketers knew the channel like the C> prompt.

Microsoft and IBM both selling DOS—or OS/2—posed the problem of "channel conflict" that Ballmer had raised regarding Windows: The same bits in two different boxes would mean that the two could beat each other up over price to the point where neither made money. According to Gates, "Lowe noticed that it was always better for us that IBM had low market share on DOS, because they had the world's best DOS deal and everybody else paid more. So we were kind of against IBM in a certain sense." On OS/2, the deal had been structured so that Microsoft would pay IBM a rebate of roughly $10 for every copy of OS/2 that either Microsoft or IBM sold. When the compatibles market for OS/2 failed to materialize, it became obvious that this byzantine scheme would give IBM the short end of the stick. Eventually that deal was renegotiated.

In the case of DOS 5, things were simpler. Each company would do its own deal-making, may the better warlord win. "We decided to live with the channel conflict," Gates said. But Gates held back a secret weapon: IBM "never got the RUP code. The RUP was not in the contract." Microsoft's Retail Upgrade Package software automatically preserved previous system settings and worked across networks; IBM's homegrown installation program was untested on non-IBM machines, didn't work on them, and was a pain to use even on IBM hardware. Microsoft won the war in the press and on the shelves. Gates used warlord lingo to describe it: "We cremated—we won on that. There was some channel conflict, but we kept [Microsoft RUP] code out. And we knew our name was more important in software by then."

It was not a humble admission but a true one. More than four years had passed since OS/2 had first been heralded as the heir apparent to good old DOS. Whatever momentum it had built had been in the wrong direction. IBM had also failed dismally in its attempts to develop applications software: The Desktop Software division it had established late in 1988 would be shut down less than three years later, and its 1989 commitment to an SAA-compatible series of applications under the rubric of OfficeVision would be all but abandoned by 1992. And all the while Microsoft was gaining market share in both systems and applications.

Throughout the second half of 1991 IBM and Microsoft traded barbs, dares, and headlines in their battle for the desktop. Punch: IBM discusses selling OS/2 2.0 through third parties if Microsoft won't do it. Counterpunch: Gates memo says OS/2 2.0 is a "poor product with poor Windows functionality." Punch: IBM wins OS/2 endorsements from Lotus and Borland. Counterpunch: Microsoft promises OS/2 features for DOS 6.0. Punch: IBM announces partnership with Apple. Counterpunch: Microsoft discusses partnership with DEC. Punch: IBM negotiates with DR to license DR DOS. Counterpunch: Gates vows to take MS-DOS straight to IBM customers for a big win, since "It's been widely rumored that IBM has a zero-royalty contract with Microsoft on DOS."

In the midst of the enmity, the tenth anniversary of the IBM PC in August passed relatively quietly. Where once IBM and Microsoft might have joined together in celebration, the two were now the Hatfields and McCoys of the desktop. Cannavino appeared on "Today." Gates went on "Good Morning America" and had so much trouble getting a Sony Data Discman to pop open that the nontechnical host had to do it for him. But then, Bill had never pretended to be a hardware guy: Visitors once arrived at his house for a party and found the pool simmering at a temperature of 105 degrees. Sheepishly apologizing, Gates said "somebody screwed up" and admitted he had no idea where the thermostat was.

Mike Maples was turning up the heat on Microsoft's applications. At a seminar on the Redmond campus in early November, Maples told a gathering of press and analysts "If someone thinks we're not after Lotus and after WordPerfect and after Borland, they're confused. My job is to get a fair share of the software applications market, and to me that's 100 percent." Realistically, Maples said, the company hoped to achieve 90 percent within the coming year—at a time when industry figures showed that Microsoft accounted for about a quarter of the total applications market. Despite much press clamor about how this announcement would play with the FTC, there was no comment from the commission. The agency was continuing its questioning nonetheless. A week before the Microsoft seminar, WordPerfect's president Alan Ashton had been interviewed by FTC investigators.

If Maples wasn't kidding, he was being somewhat unrealistic. WordPerfect and Lotus were competing hard, offering new Windows versions of their flagship products, and in the battle for market share, virtually everyone was offering to upgrade users from competitive software for $99 a pop. If you bought 1-2-3 for Windows, Lotus would give you Ami, its word processor, free. Some of the deals were Crazy Eddie specials at their finest: They really were "practically giving it away."

Still, Microsoft's Word for Windows 2.0 made it onto the shelves with one of the rare implementations of "softer software" since the term had fallen into disuse: an automatic envelope addresser refined from a similar feature in Nisus, a competitive Macintosh word processor. Other fall Windows releases from Microsoft—Works, Publisher, and Money (ironically developed by the ascetic Doug Klunder)—aimed squarely at the entry-level market under a new "Solution Series" campaign. Microsoft wasn't just a software factory, it was a software machine, aimed at clear-cutting the competition and planting new trees bearing the Microsoft logo. And perhaps surreptitiously encouraged by spiff-prodded software salesmen, unsophisticated users often believed that a Microsoft application was the only safe choice: After all, someone else's product might not be entirely compatible with Microsoft Windows.

At Fall Comdex 1991, Gates spent the better part of one afternoon observing the scene at IBM's OS/2 booth. Down in Boca land, the year ended with IBM system engineers busily preparing release 6.177H of OS/2 2.0 for limited availability to special customers. But since the final product was still three months away, Steve Ballmer, whose promise to eat a diskette if OS/2 2.0 shipped before the end of the year had hit the press, was spared a mylar diet.

By early 1992 Microsoft president Mike Hallman was out. There had been evidence of unhappiness: From October 23 to October 29 of 1991 Hallman sold nearly all his first vesting of Microsoft stock: 175,000 shares, leaving only 12,500 in the kitty. As far back as the summer of 1991, queries about Hallman drew puzzled comments from aggressive Microsofties. "You look at what [he] does in there . . . it's like the queen," one ex-Softie put it in late spring. "I mean, he wears nice suits and gives keynote addresses . . . we'll see how long he lasts." Asked in January 1992 about Hallman's performance at Microsoft, David Marquardt replied, "The jury's still out." For about two more weeks, it was.

Hallman was unseated because of—take your pick—not enough band-width, too much Mr. Nice Guy, an inability to define and shape his role, and other overtones of Jim Towne Redux. Gates denied there was any historical comparison: "Towne really was a mismatch . . . Hallman did a lot of good things while he was there." But at Microsoft, the immensely likable Hallman had been seen as an ill fit for months. "Not tough enough," said one senior executive. "Didn't have the cutting edge." Veteran developer Steve Wood put it simply: "Mike Hallman was a human being." What you had to be to succeed at the highest levels of Microsoft, he left to the imagination.

Hallman's exit was graceful and classy. He announced he would do con-sulting work for Microsoft, including reestablishing the company in South Africa after an absence of six years. "As this thing began to unfold, my discussion with Bill was 'Look, we're over the bridge and I'm over whatever ego and emotional stuff there is, I'm no longer going to be part of Microsoft. Now what do we do about it? I can help get this thing transitioned well.' "

In Hallman's place was created an Office of the President consisting of the three Smartest corporate Guys—Ballmer, heading worldwide sales; Maples, heading systems and apps; and Gaudette, handling everything else: finance, human resources, manufacturing and distribution. There were other reshuf-flings, but to insiders it was simply a restatement of the obvious: The unofficial inner circle, which Hallman had never been able to crack, was now the official inner circle.

A year and a half after Bill had predicted in his Gates date meeting with Lotusians that IBM would "fold" within seven years, Big Blue was looking more and more like a house of cards. Revenues had declined more than $4 billion; earnings per share were down more than $7. Moody's rating service stripped IBM of its Triple-A rating for the first time since 1979. Within weeks the stock was trading at its fifty-two-week low. The top five executives took major pay cuts, and three left soon afterward. A major restructuring was announced, breaking the company into business units with their own profit-and-loss statements. Meanwhile, *Inc.* magazine crowned upstart Gateway 2000, a cornbelt clone vendor, the fastest-growing company in America, with a growth rate of more than 26,000 percent from 1986 through 1990.

Words like "detente" and "reunification" cropped up now and then regarding the IBM-Microsoft relationship but seldom got much encouragement from Gates. It was true that Jim Cannavino had sat down next to him at Esther Dyson's conference in March, and they did shake hands, but "he didn't buy any copies of Windows from me nor did I buy any copies of OS/2 from him," Gates said. "I didn't detect any particular friendship in the room at that moment."

Ballmer held out more hope. "IBM needs to work with us, and we need to work with IBM. That's a fact. Windows has to work on PS/2s, Windows has to communicate with IBM hosts. That's true from both companies' standpoint. And there's a slight thaw in some of those areas, there's some thawing in that area, and that's good."

But Gates sounded almost wistful when talking about IBM.

> We did our best to make that relationship work. Other people can second-guess us and say we should have given it up sooner, but I think it was worth it to customers and everybody to try and make that relationship work. And we tried super-hard. Our programmers didn't want to keep trying, and it may not have been a good thing from a business point of view to keep trying. But we did, and if they hadn't brought Cannavino into the thing and developed this anti-Windows attitude, we would've succeeded.

One of the industry's best-known figures, with long and intimate knowledge of IBM, insisted that the divorce was for Bill Gates

> the greatest thing that ever happened to him. He needed to get away from that. That, over time, would stifle even Bill Gates. Watch Apple after five years of that: They'll lose market share as a result of that relationship. Bill Gates does not need to be covered up with some giant tarpaulin, some corporate umbrella that stifles the creativity of his people.

And IBM was still a schedule-driven company. In a reprise of the Presentation Manager Death March, this time without Microsoft's participation, OS/2 2.0 slipped out the door electronically at literally the very last second before IBM's self-imposed March 31, 1992, deadline. But it would be six weeks before copies made their way to retailers, and even then only in sorely limited quantities. IBM was finally beginning to understand and adopt Microsoft's low-price, high-market-share strategy, dropping the price of OS/2 to $49 for Windows users, $99 for DOS users, and $139 for everyone else. Members of the press noticed that in public, IBM was even adopting Microsoft-style product-logo tennis shirts. In a move that some saw as savvy and others as desperate, the company deputized its entire work force as evangelists for the product, with prizes and cash bonuses in the offing for each convert made. Although this time OS/2 received better reviews for its technological superiority over Windows, IBM came up short again, delivering promises in place of device drivers for its homegrown video standards known as 8514 and XGA. The *New York Times* called IBM "an unlikely underdog."

For good reason. In January Microsoft's stock had gone on a nine-day roll toward the $125 mark, putting the company's market capitalization at $21.9 billion, ahead of Boeing and General Motors. One analyst estimated the number of Microsoft millionaires at 2,000, although that figure, which assumed no decline in the stock, seemed overstated by at least a factor of two. Some of those millionaires were taking the money and running—or maybe ceasing to run for the first time in their lives. Jim Harris had left in 1987. Ida Cole had left in 1990. Jeremy Butler had left in 1991. Min Yee departed the low-profit Microsoft Press for medical reasons. In 1992, Scott Oki resigned as senior vice president of U.S. sales and marketing to start a baby-blanket business. Fred Gray, head of the floundering languages business unit, left that post. Others were diversifying; a consortium led by Chris Larson and including Rob Glaser, Carl Stork, Jeff Raikes, and former Microsoft chief administrative officer Craig Watjen invested more than $20 million in a minority share of the Nintendo-led buyout of the Seattle Mariners. But even though some Softies were simply marking time until their first set of stock options vested in full, plenty of workaholic millionaires and future millionaires were still on the case.

More would soon arrive. Over the years, the company's database efforts had been an utterly feckless resource sink, but in March 1992, with Cirrus, the successor to the abandoned Omega Windows database, still unfinished, Microsoft bought the best of the dBASE competitors, Fox Software of Perrysburg, Ohio, for roughly $175 million in Microsoft stock—a figure that would have been unthinkably high just a couple of years before, when the two companies began a round of futile discussions. The difference this time around, Fox's David Fulton said only half jokingly, was that "we agreed on a price."

Gates had told associates that he had avoided buying Ashton-Tate because he would have had to lay off huge numbers of people, something he felt he couldn't do. He'd mentioned the deal to Jon Shirley, whose reply was "Sure, Bill. I'm good at firing people; how about you?" It was no idle question: In the Borland buyout, more than half of Ashton-Tate's work force of 1,300 lost their jobs. But a likelier scenario was that the price of Ashton-Tate was simply too high for the parsimonious Bill Gates. In the Fox deal, Bill had no apparent qualms about leaving the impression that more than 250 employees—all but the Smart Guy software developers—would soon be on their own.

In the coming database drama, Philippe would play King of the Hill and Gates would take the unaccustomed role of spoiler. Fox held no more than 10 percent of the market, but Gates insisted that in a couple of years, "I'd be very disappointed if we were anything close to 10 percent. We enter into this with the expectation that we will be the leader, or close to the leader." No one who knew Bill Gates expected anything less.

In early April 1992 Gates unveiled Microsoft's latest scenario—along with Windows 3.1—at the Windows World conference in Chicago. To users, the Windows upgrade was relatively minor, except for the inclusion of TrueType. But it came with a new message: "scalability." Scalability meant Windows everywhere: from small handheld writing tablets capable of translating human scribblings into computer characters via Windows for Pens, to closet-size mini-computers capable of making vast databases available, to networked PCs under the Windows NT banner.

Software emulating hardware! The "scalable" Windows architecture, as Nathan Myhrvold would describe it, was an attempt to do the same thing with software that IBM's System 360 and DEC's VAX architectures had done with hardware: "a single interface with multiple implementations," as intimated in Bill's 1991 memo. There had been another attempt to create a similar software concept: IBM's terminally lame SAA. But this time, Gates was sure, things would be different. From the handtop to the desktop to the mountaintop, Windows was going to carry his vision forward, a vision that, as usual, was blurry and subject to change, Information At Your Fingertips, whatever that might mean.

Sam Furukawa, chief of Microsoft's Japanese division, pointed out that the company "seeks more business opportunity. There are many, many, many different segments." There were chips in facsimile machines, television sets, cable television, vending machines, automobiles, and all of them required software. Windows for VCRs? Windows for fax machines?

And new products were just over the horizon. Before his retirement, Scott Oki floated what he called a "bizarre vision" of "software from someone— hopefully from Microsoft—being sold everywhere you can currently think of batteries or film for a camera being sold. It will be that ubiquitous." It might be diet software to plug into a little palmtop machine. It might be a Nintendo-style game. It might be the swimsuit issue of a popular magazine. With good old Moore's Law plodding inexorably forward, memory chips would soon be cheaper than paper, and by some measures, they already were.

Though the Chicago rollout of Windows 3.1 could not match the New York 3.0 affair for visibility, Microsoft was firmly committed to making it work, with its first television ad campaign ever at a cost of $8 million. Oki recalled it as a very tough three-year sell to the CEO whose home TV set could not receive broadcast television (though the one in his Hood Canal retreat could and, on occasion, did).

Even in the crowded courtroom of San Francisco federal Judge Vaughn Walker, Microsoft was golden. Over four years, Microsoft's lawyers had adopted the strategy of breaking Apple's nebulous "gestalt" and "look-and-feel'' theory into specific identifiable elements and then knocking each one down like uncopyrightable bowling pins. A particularly salient defense was a videotape demonstrating nearly two dozen windowing systems from Xerox, Apollo, and even IBM that used the elements Apple claimed to own. On April 14, 1992, Walker ruled that not one of the ten remaining elements of Windows 2.03 that Apple deemed to infringe upon the Mac was protectable under copyright law. Walker did not yet dismiss the case outright, and Microsoft attorney Bill Neukom cautioned that ''It's not over till it's over,'' but not even Yogi Berra would have taken bets on Apple's chances. Gates claimed the suit had cost Microsoft $9 million in attorneys' fees: ''Thirty man-years of lawyers,'' as he figured it. Wall Street went wild; the day after the judge's announcement, Microsoft stock zoomed nearly $12 a share. Although many in the industry breathed sighs of relief, none were promoting Bill Gates for Fordlike folk-hero status.

The case dribbled on into fall after Walker reaffirmed his April ruling and requested final briefs from attorneys. Although Apple still hoped for a trial or a successful appeal, few were taking the suit's potential impact seriously, especially after Gates and Sculley held a joint press conference in late July reaffirming Microsoft's support for the Macintosh and the PowerPC, a RISC-based computer Apple planned to release in 1993. Of Taligent and Kaleida there was no mention; Gates acknowledged that Apple was not keeping him informed about those systems, but didn't seem especially worried about them. ''The notion that the industry is going to be willing to start from scratch in terms of a user interface and applications is probably not too likely, but we have to pay attention,'' he observed.

In June 1992, Microsoft and IBM announced the final terms of their parting. IBM would relinquish rights to Windows NT, be permitted to use Windows code only until September 1993, and would pay Microsoft a royalty reported at $23—a figure an IBM spokesperson declared too high but not out of the ballpark—for each copy of OS/2 it sold. Microsoft would pay IBM a lump sum of $25 million to $30 million for use of IBM patents. Some saw it more as a declaration of war than a divorce settlement. ''I'd say we're gonna compete,'' Ballmer averred.

Compete they did. Pushed to OEMs with a fervor unseen since the days of DOS, Windows came bundled ''ready to run'' on machines from nine of the top ten vendors. Microsoft's Windows applications were often included, too. Bill Gates was squeezing his rivals with the same low-cost tactics that had choked his original DOS competitors. Despite its tub-thumping for OS/2, even IBM announced it would offer DOS and Windows on its low-end machines. Windows was on its way to becoming as indispensable as DOS.

Plenty of other hardware companies needed allies, and floundering DEC was the biggest. In late April, with ACE in its death throes, Microsoft had joined Digital in Boston to announce Windows NT for a promising new 64-bit RISC chip called the Alpha, aimed at replacing DEC's aging VAX/VMS line of minicomputers. But by July the venerable Ken Olsen had resigned under pressure, just days before DEC announced it had lost as much as Microsoft had sold during fiscal year 1992—$2.8 billion. Around the Redmond campus, wags joked that the chip might be renamed Omega.

And Microsoft's dominance was only increasing. Its fourth-quarter sales, at $815 million, were not far from what Lotus had reported for all of 1991. At $2.8 billion, Microsoft's total revenues were greater than the total of its next five rivals—Lotus, Borland, Novell, WordPerfect, and Autodesk—combined. Microsoft's 1991 after-tax margins beat 25 percent for the second year in a row. The industry, one analyst joked, had turned into Microsoft and the Seven Dwarfs.

In July 1992, Gates told industry analysts that "We will continue to invest in the future." In the long run, that meant Windows, particularly Windows NT. In the short run, that meant Windows multimedia programs such as a Microsoft Golf simulation game and Cinemania, demonstrated by Chairman Bill himself—a CD-ROM movie database containing information on 19,000 films and 3,000 stars. The movie-mad Gates called up *The Maltese Falcon,* clicked on the sound icon, and smiled as Humphrey Bogart's voice emerged from the speakers.

But this was no time to rest on laurels. Frank Gaudette warned the analysts to expect oh, maybe half 1992's 53 percent growth for fiscal 1993. Even as Microsoft appeared destined to win the Apple suit, pesky little Z-Nix waved the antitrust flag once more in a counterclaim after Microsoft hauled it into Los Angeles federal court for allegedly selling Windows 3.1 to customers who hadn't purchased the Z-Nix mouse. OS/2, at a midyear figure of 1 million copies sold, was doing better than expected. Apple was getting a lot of mind-share simply for announcing its Newton "personal digital assistant," a handheld calendar, notetaker, and e-mail communicator not unlike what Oki had in mind but nowhere near ready for release. Hardware prices were dropping so drastically that software prices began to follow, in an attempt to avoid the Altair-era problem of consumer resistance to software that cost nearly as much as hardware. The FTC investigation slogged on. For each new victory there was some looming challenge the chairman could point to as reason for motivation.

Yet to many in the outside world, Microsoft seemed a monolith, a juggernaut, a software factory that would crush everything in its path. In the final six months of 1991 Microsoft had added nearly 2,000 employees at a time when Lotus, Compaq, and other industry leaders were cutting back. By mid-1992 Frank Gaudette presided over a Windows-based war room overseeing international currency trading and the investment of Microsoft's more than $1.3

billion in cash, and the 11,500-employee Microsoft was headed for another record year.

Microsoft's international success was contributing nearly a billion and a half dollars per annum to the American balance of trade. Microsoft was proselytizing the world with even more missionary fervor than it displayed at home, with sales offices in over twenty-five countries and more opening each year. There were development sites in Tokyo and Taiwan, manufacturing plants in Puerto Rico and Ireland. An international e-mail network kept Softies from Norway to Singapore linked closely to Redmond. Despite industry grumblings about Microsoft's increasing power, the company continued to engage in alliances with dozens of firms around the world.

As fiscal 1992 came to a close amid the cranes and cement mixers on the constantly expanding Redmond campus east of Seattle, Bill Gates, at thirty-six, stood alone as the richest person in America. His Microsoft stock was worth roughly $6 billion, and that figure did not include the $450 million worth of shares he had sold over the years for cars, homes, property, market speculation and other purposes only he knew. On June 22, in a Rose Garden ceremony, President Bush presented him with the National Medal of Technology, an award that only Steve Jobs and Steve Wozniak had won at a younger age. Gates had reached the pinnacle of his industry, and now he topped the chart that signified the American Dream: net worth. The ultra-competitive Bill Gates had played hard. He had won.

And yet he hadn't—not as long as there were desktops and homes without Microsoft software. Besides, when you looked at the net worth chart on the global scale that he had mastered since his days of playing Risk, the chairman came out only somewhere around number four. The ever-pessimistic Gates knew well how ephemeral his fortune might be, and was "leery of counting paper assets as wealth." As his good friend Ann Winblad pointed out, "The more successful you get, the higher you climb up the mountain, the farther you have to fall. I think the fear of the fall gets larger and larger. And I don't think Bill is immune to that fear of the fall."

EPILOGUE

THE REST IS SOFTWARE

Fear of the fall, fear of the fall: Despite Bill Gates's stunning successes, the history of the company was a procession of stumbles, blind alleys, bad bets forgotten elsewhere amid the euphoria of the bottom line but remembered all too well in Redmond. Despite the company's public arrogance and braggadocio, that fear of the fall at the top had become internalized at every echelon below. "We've always had an inferiority complex," said the thoughtful Jeff Harbers. "We always believed that we could have done it better. . . . We have low confidence that we're the best guys. We always believed that somebody is over the horizon doing it ten times better, and that philosophy still carries."

Fear of the fall: In spring 1992, from the vantage of his new office-of-the-president position as head of worldwide sales and support, Steve Ballmer would stare in disbelief at the suggestion that Microsoft had won it all. "Won all the victories? We're doing pretty well in operating systems. We're number two in spreadsheets, we're number two in word processing, we're a distant number two in networks, we're number two in mail . . . overall we're probably number three in presentations. Sounds like a company that's good at being number two in general."

It sounded, in fact, a great deal like what Jon Shirley had told a former Microsoft executive years before: "He said the goal at Radio Shack is to be number two in every market. And then what you do is, once you're number two, you hang in there. You hang in there till everybody else goes away, and then you own it."

But Ballmer saw the world through Microsoft's typically jaundiced spectacles: "I see many glasses that are a little less than half full. They're not a little more than half empty: They're a little bit less than half full."

Bernard Vergnes, vice president for Europe, saw the stay-hungry attitude as a global element of the Microsoft culture:

If there is another value worldwide, it is that each dollar we earn is hard to earn, and let's spend it carefully. And the example comes from the top. Bill doesn't go to the best hotel in a city. . . . With an average age of thirty or thirty-one, I would think that 80 percent if not 90 percent, have never, ever known another industry, or known difficult times. . . . It would be so incredibly easy to let them spend lavishly without immediately hurting the company. But in the first instance of rougher times, what do you do?

It was Bill Gates who focused that view: As Harbers put it, "I created a Bill simulator in my head. Before I would go to a meeting with Bill I would actually run Bill in my head and ask all the tough questions and make sure that I thought about the stuff." Software simulating hardware: It was the classic Microsoft development method, expanded to Bill himself.

The question, though, was whether Bill Gates, perhaps not the most self-aware person on the planet, had his own Bill simulator, and, if so, what it was telling him. Although associates claimed he had mellowed, meetings could still be tense. An employee put it this way: "He basically treats everybody as an equal. It's sort of treating them like family, where you don't have to be polite to them because they're family." Gates had not worked for a boss since his days at RODS. Given his dim view of the other companies he saw, he had adopted for his company the model he knew and loved best: the extended family.

In one-on-one interviews, Gates was capable of charming the socks off his questioners—or of high-bandwidth multitasking, skimming the latest trade papers and sipping a family-favorite Fresca while diverting some minor fraction of his attention to the questions at hand. If he yawned or cut you short or blew his top at some offhand question or comment—well, you were no different from his sisters or his parents, so you could always yawn or shout back.

And Gates was fully aware of certain aspects of that style. Challenged when he called one random remark "the most nonsense I ever heard in my life," Gates could mock his own penchant for exaggeration, particularly on the negative side. "The world is full of superlative events. I reach new extremes. It's incredible. There's some kind of attenuation for past events, so I'm constantly running into the most stupid thing I've ever heard. Makes life fun! I know that my climaxes are ahead of me, not just behind me."

But were they? From a standing start, Gates still could jump three feet in the air over an armchair, as he would demonstrate to disbelieving interviewers. His new estate would specify a full-size trampoline. Still, it wasn't quite like the good old days: "I don't jump spontaneously the way I used to, the early years of the company just walking down the hall I just did this all the time"—jumping and touching the ceiling—"or even in a meeting. . . . Now the jumping is not that common."

Gates still drove fast cars, but not as fast, with only one ticket on the record since 1988. Exactly what was off the record remained unclear. Gates could afford the right lawyers, and admitted "there are four or five other cases where the judicial process determined my innocence." Still, every now and then, Gates would take the Porsche out late at night and speed into the Cascade foothills on Interstate 90 east of Seattle. "Nobody expects people to speed going *up* the hill," a close associate pointed out—and most cars don't have the horsepower to do it.

His most fabled recent escapade involved his red Ferrari 348. At Washington's Ocean Shores, where the beach is a public highway, Gates pulled a Thomas Crown spinout maneuver and managed to get the car stuck in the sand. The Ferrari was henceforth known in Gatesian circles as the "Dune Buggy." Speeding "is not a hobby of mine anymore," Gates insisted, though he still drives "fairly fast."

Gates was slowing down, some said, and he was worrying about it. On a good day, he could look like the energetic, boyish wunderkind of the press clips; on a bad one he seemed sallow, tired, jowly. Lefty Gates still played his right-handed game of tennis and at the instigation of his sisters was taking up golf right-handed along with the rest of the Gates clan. His major misgiving, according to his sister Libby: a round of eighteen holes took too much time.

"He is the world's busiest man, bar none," said Charles Simonyi, citing one trip that included "Eleven meetings in five days in Europe—you know, like there were days there would be two countries. And he doesn't fly a private plane, either." Gates still managed a schedule as packed as anyone's, but as he headed toward his forties, he seemed to be modestly tempering his legendary workaholism—and seemed vaguely defensive about it:

Most people have an overblown view of how many hours they work. It's hard: Working eighty hours is very hard. You can't do much else if you're gonna do that. So there's lots of weeks I work eighty hours, but I think my average is lower than that. . . . On average I take every other weekend off. . . . I'm probably more like seventy average now. There are some weeks I work more than eighty. Like those weeks I travel to Europe: That's all I'm doing, is working, sleeping, working, sleeping. So you can get weeks where I'll put in over ninety. I mean, I assume you don't count reading business magazines, the Journal *or the* Economist.

Upon recomputing, he decided that an average of seventy-two hours was the proper figure.

Though in recent years Gates had vacationed in the Dominican Republic, Thailand, and Australia with his girlfriend, he could barely contemplate the idea of a longer period of relaxation: "It's possible I'd take a month off in the next three years. I don't know what that would be like. I've never taken more than a week off with weekends on both ends."

So it was unlikely Bill would join his former mentor Jon Shirley on the arts and leisure circuit. "You must be kidding!" Gates retorted. "We're different people . . . come on, I'm thirty-six years old and this guy was what when he retired, fifty-two, fifty-three? I don't expect to do the same thing myself, but that's sixteen years from now. That's about the length of Microsoft."

"I don't know what he would do if he had some time to spend alone with himself," said one short-term girlfriend who tired of his strange blend of selfishness and selflessness. "He has a significant data storage device. But I don't think he has a lot of wisdom." And she didn't think he was all that happy either. "So many times he complained about how he's got to be here and got to be there. You say 'Why don't you say you're not going to show up?' but he won't do that. He'll stand up for everybody, but he won't stand up for his happiness."

Yet Gates insisted work was his happiness, and others agreed: "I think he actually enjoys his day," said one. "I know that sounds crazy. But in my opinion Bill just honestly loves technology—it's his hobby as well—and it's really kind of a treat to run through the day and chat about it with people."

Ross Perot agreed. "His is an industry where the faster you run the faster you have to run. If he could create software and sit on it for twenty years, he'd probably be bored. But the minute it hits the market shrinkwrapped he'd better be on the next one, right? There is no halftime in his business. You don't even get to go to the locker room and rest. So I think that helps keep a person like Bill motivated."

Gates saw things the same way, minus the football analogies. "It's the most interesting thing, working with smart people. It's a real challenge. It's very interesting how it's gonna develop. There's nothing as interesting as this industry." Not even biotech? "No. Biotech's second."

"I sure do more press stuff than other CEOs," Gates admitted. "But, you know, we have a message. We try to sell millions of copies of stuff that you don't drink or smoke. I guess you've got to do a lot of press interviews." What irritated him most was that

People oversimplify things. I mean, in any month in the history of the company, things are more complicated in terms of keeping people happy, deciding what products to do, keeping partnerships going because you don't know which way the industry's gonna go. I mean, UNIX: Everybody thought UNIX was gonna take off, just to take one issue. So at any point we have a strategy of how we're gonna deal with that, how we're gonna play a role with that. . . . Things are so much more complicated, and dealing with people and their special require-

*ments and partnerships, that to emerge with a lot of successful products and a
lot of profitability is so much harder than it appears.*

Yet Gates seemed to thrive on it. "I choose every day to do exactly what
I'm doing. There's nothing that's going to be as stimulating and have as much
positive impact as this. I don't know anybody else who gets to work with smart
people in a business that's really affecting things." But he was vague about how
the business really changed the world: "Devices that help people who have
ideas communicate those ideas, help people learn, help people try things out.
Tools for the mind—I mean, obviously they'll be a lot better five years out than
they are today, but they've already had an impact."

Was that enough? Aging brought another challenge—what one female
friend called the "fear of not having any more brilliant ideas. The idea that
after thirty, you're kind of over the hill, that you're not being clever anymore." Steve Jobs, she believed, had a similar fear, one he and others confronted by starting second companies just to prove that their initial successes
had not been mere flukes—which in some ways, of course, they had been.

Unlike Jobs, unlike virtually every Silicon Valley upstart who had founded
his own company, Gates was still "tied to the wheel" of Microsoft. Yet despite
its incredible success, it was as if he still had something to prove. But what?

That the company was innovative? The frequent charge that Microsoft was
not an innovator was one of the things that seemed to rankle him most. Yet
Microsoft's innovation always seemed to be of a lesser order, some minor
technological improvement such as Excel's minimal recalc or the data-passing
ability of Windows, rather than brand-new concepts served up fresh. "Word
was innovative," Gates would say, but it was a mere patch on Bravo. "Excel
was innovative," Gates would say, yet that program's first product manager
would admit that at Microsoft "We don't do innovative stuff like completely
new revolutionary stuff. . . . One of the things we are really, really good at
doing is seeing what stuff is out there and taking the right mix of good features
from different products." Bill's house, his multimedia efforts, his still-image
project with IHS all seemed to be attempts to show the world that there was
more to him and his company than a strategy that resembled the Japanese
knockoff efforts immediately after World War II.

Former executive Alan Boyd put it this way:

> *Does Bill have a vision? No. Has he done it the right way? Yes. He's done
> it by being conservative. I mean, Bill used to say to me that his job is to say no:
> That's his job.*
>
> *Which is why I can understand he's real sensitive about that. Is Bill
> innovative? Yes. Does he appear innovative? No. Bill personally is a lot more
> innovative than Microsoft ever could be, simply because his way of doing*

business is to do it very steadfastly and very conservatively. So that's where there's an internal clash in Bill: between his ability to innovate and his need to innovate. The need to innovate isn't there, because Microsoft is doing well. And innovation—you get a lot of arrows in your back. He lets things get out in the market and be tried first before he moves into them. And that's valid. It's like IBM.

Microsoft was in many ways like IBM, particularly the IBM of the Tom Watson Sr. era—not only in its conservatism, but also in its paternalism, and in the fact that it was so closely identified with and ruled by a strong leader. In neither company did unions manage even a toehold. Both corporations exported their cultures around the globe: Even in venues whose labor forces enjoyed siestas and long vacations, Microsoft hired people imbued with what Scott Oki would call "the maniacal work ethic," meaning "six-thirty in the morning until midnight and just pounding away."

And to some, particularly the callow young software developers, Microsoft was what one consultant called "their own little special world," just as IBM was to many of its employees. The early IBM had a corporate golf course; Microsoft had softball and soccer fields and running paths. At Microsoft there was no equivalent of the IBM anthem "Ever Onward," but the self-referential cult of personality was so strong that the on-line tutorial included with Word for Windows repeatedly cited a fictional company called "Trey Research." Softies loved to talk about how their leader danced until the wee hours at company parties or about how, at company meetings, people would keep count of how many times he pushed his glasses back on his nose. The social lives of Microsoft's young programmers revolved around Microsoft, which meant their entire lives centered around what the consultant saw as "this domain that they have under control."

Aside from the stock, one reason the recent collegians accepted low salaries and stayed on was that if they left, they would "have to go out into the real world," where they tended to come up empty when they tried to impress women with their coding styles. That world was the same trying place where their leader inevitably delayed renewing his driver's license until the eleventh hour. Every time he popped in at the local Department of Licensing, he told his long-suffering administrative assistant, the lines were too long. "Welcome to the real world, Bill," she shot back.

Microsoft as IBM? Both Gates and Watson extolled the glories of hard, hard work, and Watson's THINK was a precursor of the "Think smart!" motto Bill Gates had inherited from his grandmother. Longtime IBMer Maples observed that at a 2,000-employee Microsoft picnic, "I got to thinking 'I bet this is exactly like Endicott [N.Y., IBM's original manufacturing headquarters] was fifty years ago.' " Yet Gates was no mere update of Watson—particularly because Tom Watson was a mere businessman, a genius at creating a selling machine. Bill Gates saw himself as a "technologist."

"Hero is a strong word," Gates said. But if Gates had an idol, it was Richard Feynman, the quirky, eccentric physicist who had worked on the Manhattan Project, traced the *Challenger* disaster to defective O-rings, and won the Nobel Prize for his revision of quantum mechanics. Feynman, as Gates put it, "had his own way of thinking about things. He was his own guy who decided what counted and what did not, built his values around what he understood and not some artificial way of looking at things." At one point, Gates and Winblad had planned to meet with Feynman to discuss distributing a videotaped series of his lectures. "It's the coolest way to learn physics ever," Gates said wistfully. "It's funny. It's interesting. I'd love to give a lecture like that someday." But Feynman died before Gates had a chance to meet him, and Bill took the death to heart.

"I admired FDR," said Gates. "I've read even more books about him than about Napoleon, and if there were more Feynman books to read I would have." Still, heroes were hard to find. "I admire lots of people. But it's hard to have this totally pristine way of looking at things unless you're a scientist." And that was it! Despite his astounding financial and business success, despite the fact that Bill Gates was an incredibly smart guy, at bottom he was a business-man—a mere businessman, a Thomas Crown, a Thomas Watson—an entrepre-neur, not a scientist. He was more a Henry Ford than a Thomas Edison. He was less the endlessly inventive Gyro Gearloose, more the wily, opportunistic plutocrat that Andy Hertzfeld had made the subject of the first picture ever drawn on a prototype Macintosh: Scrooge McDuck, the richest duck in the world.

For Gates that was not enough. Thomas Edison himself had admitted to being a "sponge" whose "ideas first belonged to people who didn't bother to develop them." But Edison's admissions would never pass the lips of Bill Gates, who, as one former romantic interest put it, "can never say 'I don't know.' " From his days on the playground, he had told her, it had been a matter of "I'll show them." He had shown them, all right, but the perverse world—and Gates himself—held scientists in far higher regard than mere entrepreneurs. When you came right down to it, Bill knew, scientists were the Smartest Guys.

"Do you ever wish you were back programming on your own again?" Gates had been asked for a Microsoft Press book. "Oh, sure, absolutely," he had replied. "Then you control everything. There's no compromise. Every line is yours and you feel good about every line. It's kind of selfish, but it's like being allowed to do pure mathematics, and yet you have the feedback of making something really work. I sometimes envy my colleagues who get to focus just on the program they're writing."

Business? Business was interesting, but it certainly wasn't pure, and as

Gates told one interviewer, "The business side is easy—*easy!*" Businessmen were interesting, but Gates had no illusions about their general level of brilliance. For him, it was no contest, the reason he could sell them on almost anything. As former IBMer Ed Iacobucci said, "Put a middle manager on one side of the table and Bill on the other, who can deal with technical issues: Who wins that deal?"

A friend from Harvard put it in starker terms: "From my experience, I think Bill is one of the very few CEOs in a corporation that size in America who actually does anything. The average CEO tends not to have hands-on involvement in anything other than negotiating executive compensation." Perot agreed: "Most corporate executives in the United States don't understand their product at all. Guys running huge companies don't understand their product: They're financial men, they're lawyers, you name it. Bill Gates is a guy who knows his product. He can get right down there on the floor with his best programmers and mix it up."

A CEO who had hands-on involvement in pushing Bill's hot buttons was Philippe Kahn. When Gates picked up the *New York Times Magazine* article profiling him as "Mr. Software," a quote from his self-styled "Barbarian" nemesis turned him livid:

> *Oh, here's Philippe. God, fuck this guy! I mean, I really hate this guy. This guy—you know, if it's not rape, if it's not waking up with AIDS—the guy is such an asshole. [quoting from article:] "He's really not a technical guy. It's an image he's trying to put out." I'm so much more technical than that guy is, Jesus Christ! He's the only guy I really don't like.*

Not a technical guy! It was the sharpest rebuke in the lexicon. It was the one that stung Gates hardest. Gates prided himself on his technical talents, used them to separate himself from the rabble. When meeting mere mortals, and particularly journalists, Gates would inevitably preface some explanation with the veiled putdown "I don't know how technical you are." Even Ann Winblad had picked up the trait.

Yet despite his ability to do a quick read, to grasp things faster than his colleagues thought possible, the possibility that he might not be the Smartest Guy after all was his Achilles' heel. Gates had an excellent memory, but it certainly wasn't the "photographic" version countless articles had claimed. As smart as he was, he had a longstanding problem with completion: The near-miss Eagle Scout badge, the Lakeside war game program, the Harvard baseball game, APL—and, you could argue, Cashmere, Omega, multimedia, and even the first version of Windows—all smacked of a certain technical dilettantism.

Not smart enough! Not the Smartest Guy! It was the problem that had rankled him since Harvard. He had told Neil Konzen about it years ago: "He

wanted to make his mark in something but he thought it was going to be math.
. . . So he got there and there was this guy who was so good at it that he
thought, 'Nah, I think I'll find something else.' "

Even in the vastly expanding world of software, as Bill half admitted in his
1991 memo, he sensed he was losing touch. Neil Konzen had witnessed the
transformation:

> He is so spread out. He doesn't have the technical depth in each topic like he
> used to. He really used to know, he could tell you about optimizations in the
> compiler, he could tell you what was going on in DOS, he could talk to you
> about circle algorithms in BASIC. You know, in the old days he knew every-
> thing, really had the breadth and the depth. It was really incredible. And he
> still does, except the business has exceeded his bandwidth.

Bill's personal loyalty to BASIC, his first love, was seen by some as an
indicator of his technical failings. "It's the one thing I understand, I guess," he
said with self-directed sarcasm. And he still insisted on calling products BASIC
when they bore only a glancing resemblance to the original language. "Internally, people will say to me, 'Look, this time let's not call it BASIC.' And they
never succeed in convincing me of that. They show in these focus groups where
BASIC is viewed as lowly, and I say, 'Well, I gotta change those guys' minds.'
BASIC will overcome. Interpreted languages will inherit the world." Still, he
had abandoned BASIC in at least one instance: Peeved over delays in the
Microsoft Mail program, he told one group of developers "I could write this in
Excel macros over the weekend."

The book-loving, movie-loving Gates was also beginning to make investments in "content"—such "software" as the images he was licensing for IHS.
Yet as his emissaries roved the art world to create his image bank, signing deals
with the Seattle Art Museum and the National Gallery of London, Gates was
portrayed as something of a yokel, a rube who might use Michelangelo for
some Microsoft angle, an aesthetic illiterate who didn't understand the rules of
art circles, where, as one museum official told the *Wall Street Journal,* "You can
be walking around dead without knowing it."

In a further omen of the melding of electronics and entertainment, Gates
took a meeting in 1992 with Hollywood power broker Michael Ovitz, the
Creative Artists Agency chairman who had helped put together the Matsushita
purchase of MCA, parent company of Universal Studios. Ovitz had already
spent time talking to Apple's John Sculley, who, like Gates, had deals cooking
with Sony, now owner of Columbia Pictures. With multimedia looking like the
Next Big Thing, the New New Hollywood of software for computer screens
was beginning to close ranks with the Old New Hollywood of software for
television and theater screens.

Yet Gates knew that scientists were the Smart Guys, no doubt about it. He and Winblad had actually talked from time to time about the idea of creating some sort of scientific institute. But "would it be giving monies to an existing institute or creating something new? It's something you'd need a lot of time to think through and figure out. And I just haven't," he said.

By 1991 Gates was hiring Super-Smart Guys—and Gals—to staff a new research facility—a Bill Labs examining voice control, speech recognition, grammar-checking, data-bank access. From IBM's computer linguistics research group Gates lured George Heidron, Steve Richardson, and Karen Jensen. From Carnegie Mellon came Rick Rashid, director of the Mach operating system project. Hail to Redmond PARC!

And if that wasn't enough, Gates commissioned an all-star five-man Technical Advisory Board. The team: Gordon Bell, the great architect of early DEC computers and the VAX machines; John Hennessy, the apostle of RISC architectures and founder of MIPS Computer Systems; Doug Lenat, principal scientist of Microelectronics and Computer Technology Corporation (CMC) and a major figure in the field of artificial intelligence; Dr. Raj Reddy, director of Carnegie Mellon University's Robotics Institute and an expert in speech recognition; and Edward Lazowska, a University of Washington professor specializing in computer systems that run on multiple processors.

Yet Gates would briefly be upstaged by a three-point shot from his old partner and Portland Trail Blazers owner Paul Allen. In March 1992, with former PARC and Metaphor guru David Liddle, Allen established Interval Research Corporation in Palo Alto to look into the implications of high-bandwidth—literally high-bandwidth—communications via satellite and fiber-optic transmission. The expectation: These new media would be the delivery systems for education, information, and entertainment. It was a venture requiring "a more exploratory approach than can be taken when developing competitive products for an existing market," Allen noted.

Gates wasn't about to go quite that far. As Microsoft's newly appointed vice president of advanced research Nathan Myhrvold put it, "we want to have good research, but we also want to be effective at [putting] basic research in products." As Microsoft Press and the CD-ROM group had learned, Gates liked experimentation, but he liked profit even better.

His practicality extended to the spiritual: If there were a Great Programmer in the Sky, Gates was not losing sleep about it. He had come a long way from the Sermon on the Mount. "When I'm in a hotel and have nothing to read around, it's interesting to read the Bible. Or study other religions: Like that time I was in Thailand, I got to know something about Buddhism. Anyway, I'm not a regular churchgoer." Is he a believer? "Oh, I guess agnostic, atheist: I must be one of those things," though he would later hedge that down to "Protestant who hasn't gone for a while." A close friend would put it another way: "He doesn't like the theological. He's not into ghosts, superstition, and the unknown. He has no interest in that. He's a scientist. If you can't touch it and logically and rationally figure it out, he's not interested."

But if he was loyal to no church other than a binary one, he would remain fiercely loyal to his longtime friends. Despite the disapproval of some Microsoft insiders, he remained personally and fiscally close to convicted stockbrokers Andy Evans and Ann Llewellyn. Evans still handled many of Gates's diversified outside investments, and Gates was a godfather to all three Evans children.

Loyalty? When a public outcry arose over the free-spending ways of outgoing United Way president William Aramony, Gates chose to look at the positives: "The guy totally believes in this whole thing, and they're casting a lot of the things he did in a way that's just irresponsible, trying to make things look bad. . . . The guy is a very honest guy. He did a great job with United Way. He made the United Way what it is. He deserves more credit than anyone."

Gates remained loyal to the country that had provided much of his early success. With the help of Kay Nishi, Microsoft had arrived early in Japan and had become at least the number three personal computer software vendor there. Exquisite Japanese prints now graced Microsoft's executive boardroom and conference room. Gates saw comparisons of Microsoft to Japanese companies farfetched, since "They exist in different cultures." But he did admit they had two things in common: "We look at technology as a source of innovation and we think long term."

Gates, whose name was well-known in Japan and whose fictionalized youthful exploits had recently been the subject of a popular comic book called *Young Jump*, believed the Japanese were getting undue negative attention from American media: "You can always find instances where the U.S. and Japan have trade barriers they shouldn't have. The U.S. has plenty, and the Japanese certainly have plenty. But by and large, Japan competes very fairly."

He added, "I happen to be a big believer in free trade and I happen to believe that allowing companies worldwide to contribute products raising the standard of living everywhere is a good thing. I happen to think economics and trade are poorly understood by people and that's played on by politicians in a fairly bad way."

Did Gates have his own political aspirations? "I just don't see it. Well, I can only see ten years, but I don't see it." Looking eleven years ahead? "I think it's pretty unlikely. I mean, it's possible, but pretty unlikely."

But although Bill's father had been active in numerous Republican campaigns, the independent Gates had given money to candidates of both parties. He maintained his personal loyalty to U.S. Senator Brock Adams, his original House patron, contributing to his campaign despite sexual harassment charges against the politician. Although "the differentiation between the two parties is rather small indeed," Gates said, "I'd probably be a Democrat."

And then he hedged even that. "But you're not talking about a huge differentiation. I mean, take an issue: What's the difference? Everybody's into deficit spending like madmen, and not balancing the budget." At a time when his might-have-been boss Perot was about to run for President, Gates sounded like a member of the Capitalist party. "The government can do some good things. It can structure incentives in the market in very good ways. The government mostly does too many things and it does mostly spend too much money, so it's hard to pick between these two parties, and I don't focus a lot of time on it."

But the government didn't have the luxury of gross margins like Microsoft's. "They should," Gates insisted in the tone of a man who had clearly focused some portion of his bandwidth on politics. "They're sitting on some good assets. They can afford to take a long-term approach. They're the leaders. They're number one. Their biggest competitor just folded. It's unbelievable!"

And politics was not out of the question. Gates was one of the most visible CEOs in America, still the embodiment of Microsoft in publications, public appearances, advertisements. He had been featured (without his cooperation) on "Lifestyles of the Rich and Famous," and ABC Television's "20/20" had profiled him as "Billionaire Bill." He still received copious quantities of fan mail, "requests for me to buy something or give money to something or do something. . . . Boats, land, people who've gone bankrupt, people who need saving, there's some girls who want to meet me"—and, rumor had it, occasionally did. "To this day we still get *Time* magazine covers. We still get people ripping off that cover saying 'Please sign my *Time* magazine cover' "— from an issue more than eight years old.

Charitable requests were a constant thorn. Microsoft was relatively generous with its matching funds—matching employees' contributions to the United Way without limit, to other charities up to $1,000. In addition to his pledge of $1 million to the United Way, his million-dollar contribution to Lakeside, and his $12 million donation to the University of Washington, Gates personally had donated $1 million to Seattle's Fred Hutchinson Cancer Research Center and smaller amounts to other charities. "There are a few things in the works right now that are bigger," Gates said in early 1992, "but it's not the focus of my time right now. I'm in my thirties, and even in my forties I'm going to try to contribute by doing a good job at Microsoft. That's my main way of contributing, and there will be plenty of time to decide what charities are worthy of whatever money there is at that time." Yet on the Seattle scene, whatever Gates did was perceived as Not Enough, and locals insisted he could be doing more. It rankled Gates. "Yeah. And when I die I'll have time to do more," he said with a tinge of bitterness.

"Decadence" still bothered Gates. Enumerating his cars produced a hint of embarrassment. The 959 on the docks "effectively I don't have. I've got . . . the red Ferrari, Lexus, Mustang, and then the Porsche [964]. Which is ridiculous, to own that many cars." Same thing with his house: "There was an initial concept of a room that virtually every square inch was screen, and that hasn't survived the design process. . . . I had this idea of a spiral staircase going down to a room that was just all image and—whew! But that," he said without a trace of irony, "was just too expensive."

Too expensive? Marriage was another thing he might well look at that way. Gates was dogged continually by rumors—and family hopes—of impending engagement. "Someday I'll be married. Someday I'll have kids," he insisted. Yet the man with the close family relationship seemed to be ambivalent. Amateur psychoanalysts claimed he would not get married as long as his mother was on the scene, but that analysis seemed the very shallowest of pop journalism. Like Winblad before him, Gates was beginning to worry about the biological clock—not in the sense of fertility, but in the sense of empathy. As Gates neared thirty-seven—the "magic age" Estelle Mathers had twitted him about —friends and colleagues believed he was beginning to wonder about the differences in years between himself and prospective spouses, about the prospect of hanging around with younger women with whom he might have very little in common except a healthy interest in sex. Gordon Letwin viewed Bill as holding a pleasantly romantic notion of marriage—as opposed to the "classic" model, where "you get a young wife from a good family and start turning out kids, but your real interest is in your lovers."

On the other side were the notorious bachelor parties that Bill threw at increasingly shorter intervals as his inner circle began to succumb to the lure of family life—something that one former girlfriend saw Bill as "freaking out" about, along with the idea of getting older. Gates admitted enjoying the talent search for these parties. "It's a very straightforward process. You go to Deja Vu, you sit down and then the girl comes wanting you to buy a table dance. Then you say 'No, I'd like to buy you a drink' . . . And you say, 'Do you do bachelor parties?' And she says no, and you say, 'Oh, come on, you can bring a bodyguard along and come with your friends.'" In the end, two or four strippers occasionally ended up swimming nude in Bill's pool with whichever of the guests chose to join them.

To one married attendee, "It was the ideal bachelor party, because it was decadent enough to make you feel you're really in like the decline of Roman civilization and you're really a decadent kind of guy. But it's not really so decadent that you're worried about getting a disease or feeling ashamed of yourself." Another viewed it less charitably as an example of the strong undercurrent of frat-house sexism that ran rampant in the halls of the company.

Women who got wind of it were even less tolerant. "When I heard it described to me, it was really disgusting. You know, I think that's kind of gross,'' one female ex-Softie recalled. ''My impression is that Bill is still kind of the ugly guy buying beautiful women at some level, and that's obviously my interpretation of it. So I just wouldn't want to be a woman trying to have a real live relationship with him. I think that'd be real hard.''

That was an understatement. Bill's relationship with Microsoft product manager Melinda French since the Winblad breakup had run intermittently hot and cold. It had started out with a lot of visible billing and cooing, a former friend recalled: ''She was really sort of out there and kissing him a lot, and people would be sort of disgusted, and guys would make really crude jokes and I remember going like, 'Oh God, this sounds just sort of like junior high.' But then they've been together sort of off and on for a really long time.'' The ''off'' periods tended to involve Gates's nonexclusive approach to romance, but by mid-1992 the couple was a definite ''on.''

Bill was characteristically private and protective of the relationship, and so was his female friend and employee. The in-house aspect was a particular sore point. ''It affects her position,'' Gates said. ''She'd have to quit her job if this came out in a big way. She'd just have to quit, and you know, what would that mean for our relationship? She'd probably leave. Who knows?''

Yet Gates was seen with French at company functions and in public, and though she certainly didn't qualify as a public figure, her name was an open secret throughout the industry and throughout Seattle. ''Bullshit! Bullshit!'' Gates said when confronted with these facts. ''Maybe in twenty years there'll come a time when it's not such a big deal, but for her career it's a big deal, and it's one of the few things the press has done for me is not use her name.'' Although Gates was almost certainly exaggerating the potential effect of disclosure on his paramour's career, she too felt that being identified would ''make it impossible for me'' within the industry.

Despite Ballmer's segue into family life, despite the marriages of lieutenants like Lazarus and Glaser, Bill Gates, the lone free agent at the top, gave no official signs of settling down, and as late as July 1992 Melinda French, asked about short-term plans for marriage or engagement, flatly stated ''absolutely not.'' But in April 1993, after a trial separation that apparently made their hearts grow fonder, Gates and French made their relationship public by announcing their wedding engagement.

The hints had been there for a while. Gates no longer pointed to infants saying ''That scares me,'' as he had a decade earlier. Instead, like some latter-day W. C. Fields, he said of his younger sister's six-week-old, ''I swear, you could line up twenty-five of these kids and I couldn't pick her out of them. They all look the same till about a year old.'' Christmas 1991 was the first time Uncle Trey managed to establish rapport with his older sister's three-year-old. But when Ballmer's son was born in early 1992, Gates was the first nonrelative to see the newborn child. The second was Melinda French.

For all that, Gates's biological imperative may have been tempered by the sheer rationalism of the Smart Guy. Perhaps the home was not enough, the desktop too limited. Maybe that computer in every human was the ultimate solution?

Why not? Century 21 had not yet arrived, yet the world had already— *Witness the transformation!*—changed far beyond even the imaginings of GE's World of the Future at the Seattle fair of thirty years before. Computers and fax machines and e-mail and networks were essential elements of the American workplace. Projection TV and camcorders and CD-ROM were within the means of middle-class families. Telephone companies and cable TV outfits and broadcasters were locking horns over the idea of piping huge volumes of information and entertainment into households throughout the world to television sets that would become suspiciously like computers.

It was a far cry from twenty years before, when time-shared mainframes were as personal as computers got, or fifteen years before, when Albuquerque was the heart of the PC universe, or ten years before, when the fledgling IBM PC was still a big maybe, or even five years before, when OS/2 had been introduced to thundering disdain. And as hardware became faster, cheaper, smaller, more sophisticated, more complex—almost too easy—software remained the challenge.

After more than a decade of the personal computer, business experts were wondering aloud why office productivity had made marginal gains at best. Bill Gates believed, "One thing economists are not good at is measuring productivity. . . . The output is not defined, it's changing over time, and so the comparison is bogus." Was a business letter with five fancy fonts and a pie chart a more productive output than a dull typewritten sheet of text? Not even software could give a clear answer.

Years after digital watches had become throwaway premiums, befuddled owners could barely figure out how to change them to daylight saving time—a software problem. Years after VCRs had become fixtures in American homes, comedians still made jokes about their flashing "12:00" and the difficulty of programming them—a software problem. Years after computers had conquered the American desktop, puzzled users continued to struggle with their complexity—a software problem. Years after programmers had developed a vast assortment of "personal information management" programs, Bill Gates's administrative assistant would maintain his personal appointment calendar on paper—a software problem. Clearly, solving software problems would be an industry with plenty of room for growth for the foreseeable future.

And the biggest software problem of all was an idea humanist computer scientist Joseph Weizenbaum had treated skeptically back in 1974: "One would have to be astonished," he wrote, "if Lord Acton's observation that power corrupts were not to apply in an environment in which omnipotence is so easily achievable. It does apply. And the corruption evoked by the computer programmer's omnipotence manifests itself in a form that is instructive in a domain far larger than the immediate environment of the computer." Meaning? "The compulsive programmer is convinced that life is nothing but a program running on an enormous computer, and that therefore every aspect of life can ultimately be explained in programming terms."

It was an idea that had captured the imagination of Bill Gates, Technologist:

> The most interesting thing to me is not sequencing the data. It's understanding the program. How does it work? How does evolution and the instructions for the creation of the body, how does all that stuff work? It's there, it's not just a matter of getting the numbers, it's a matter of—like a program. You gotta understand the logic in it: Not just the constants, not just the protein instructions, but the branching, the enforcement, copying. It's the most interesting program there is. It created itself. It solves problems we don't understand.

It was like the old C-Cubed days. The hacker in Gates wanted to disassemble the program, take it apart, find out how it ticked. And then?

> Go, "Wow!" Say, "What a nice piece of work!" Then we can go back and improve the program.

After an *InfoWorld* conference in Seattle in the spring of 1989, Bill Gates joined a group of staffers at the bar of the Four Seasons Olympic Hotel. Toward midnight he began talking about his pet topic, biotechnology: how genetic code was similar to binary code, how in the future humans would be able to be downloaded onto chips, the human spirit would be burned into silicon, and silicon-based life forms would replace those based on mere carbon.

It might just be the ultimate rationale for software, the ultimate recipient of Bill Gates's energy and curiosity and will to power. It was an idea that Gates would return to in social conversations again and again. As reporter Stuart Johnston recalled, it had clearly captured some significant portion of Bill's bandwidth:

> Bill said, "Well, someday they're gonna unravel this and we'll actually be able to put people onto chips." They'd been through plenty of wine at this point without a significant amount of food, and by this point Bill's eyes kind of sparkled. And he smiled in a way that made you know he was feeling the wine, even if he wasn't maybe drunk. But he said something that struck me as the absolute epitome.
>
> He said, "And the rest is a software problem."

. . . *The compulsive programmer's pride and elation are very brief. His success consists of his having shown the computer who its master is. And having demonstrated that he can make it do this much, he immediately sets out to make it do even more. Thus the entire cycle begins again.*
—JOSEPH WEIZENBAUM,
Computer Power and Human Reason

UPDATE

ENVOI: A COMPUTER IN EVERY WALLET?

By mid-1993 the cycle was beginning again, in part because this time the "even more" that programmers were dedicated to making computers do had become "*much* more"—in fact, "everything." Witness yet another transformation! Corporate America busily began carving up the future of computing, communications, entertainment, and education in what was quickly termed "The Digital Convergence" between dowdy computers and sexy consumer electronics. Bill Gates's strategy, as one employee put it, was utterly simple, a tactic that seemed to have been taken directly from the discarded playbook of The Old IBM: Microsoft Everywhere.

It was not a strategy conducive to winning friends. Moments after the release of the film *Jurassic Park,* industry wags noted that the only difference between Gates and a velociraptor was that you didn't have to sign a nondisclosure agreement before the dinosaur devoured you. Gates's reputation for take-no-prisoners aggressiveness left potential friends as wary as foes, throwing up roadblocks to new alliances. Within the industry he was no longer the boyish nerd with a knack for turning a deal, but an insatiable robber baron out to gobble up the competition. After resettling in Gates's Puget Sound stomping grounds, "Outland" cartoonist Berkeley Breathed diabolically transplanted the genetic code of Bill the Nerd into his character Bill the Cat, transmogrifying him into Bill the Gates. Reversing the process accidentally zapped Gatesian genetic material into TV's lovable Barney the dinosaur, who began gobbling small children uncontrollably.

Gates's engagement to Melinda French gave him a broader, mellower celebrityhood. Publications from *People* to the *National Enquirer* and the *Star* ("How 28-Year-Old Beauty Hooked $7 Billion Nerd") trumpeted the match. The Seattle-based TV comedy show "Almost Live" claimed that after his wedding, Gates would eventually "upgrade to Wife 2.0." *Parade* reported that in a survey of high-school males, Gates had finished third as most-admired: Way below Michael Jordan and just behind Mario Cuomo, but well above Luke Perry. Suddenly, Gates was everywhere.

Not unlike Microsoft. Microsoft Everywhere meant the company would move up to mission-critical platforms for corporations; move down to wireless personal communicators; move sideways to televisions, telephones, copiers, and fax machines; and all the while maintain its core business in desktop machines. Result: the digital convergence, if Bill Gates had anything to say about it, would be centered at One Microsoft Way, Redmond, Washington.

On the desktop, Microsoft's lead products—DOS, Windows, Excel, Word, Access, and FoxPro—were all doing fine, at least by such measures as unit volume. But the suicidal price competition that Bill had long feared had finally erupted, sending software prices into a worldwide tailspin. Moreover, as Microsoft vice president of law and corporate affairs Bill Neukom put it, "Piracy is our biggest competitor."

Price warfare, piracy, and bundling deals held down application software revenues. Sales per new PC were so low that vendors tried to maintain their total revenues by selling "suites" of their programs—multiproduct collections such as Microsoft Office—for little more than what just one of the individual components had cost only a short while before. But even that strategy came with drawbacks. As fiscal 1993 closed, Microsoft executives began uttering the grim word "saturation." Translation: Once there was a computer on every desk, and all those computers were loaded up with more software than they really needed, what could you do for an encore, or at least for something that would keep your growth rate on the upside of phenomenal?

Upgrades were one answer. One industry columnist claimed that Microsoft wasn't selling software, it was selling subscriptions. But customers were beginning to rebel against the cost, effort, and often minimal reward of upgrading software. The much-ballyhooed upgrade version of DOS 6, for example, proved to be little more than DOS 5 bundled with a collection of utilities that should have been included in the earlier edition, not to mention a variety of glitches that attracted the notice of the press. Once word got around, the initial rush of upgrade business slowed to a crawl.

But if there still wasn't a computer on every desk in America, some electronic products—such as the telephone—had long since conquered the desktop. Although IBM had spun off its low-end office-machine business, its typewriters and printers and copiers, Bill Gates saw those humble units as just so many potential platforms for Microsoft products. Microsoft was able to convince dozens of office-machine manufacturers—with such illustrious names as Hewlett-Packard, Sharp, Ricoh, and Xerox—to line up behind a new standard called Microsoft At Work (or MAW, though rarely by Microsoft). At a

New York hotel fête reminiscent of the original Windows rollout nearly a decade earlier, Gates trotted out more than 60 vendors supporting the new standard. Taking advantage of microprocessors and connectors in every futuristic telephone, copier, and fax machine, MAW would hook them up to each other with a Windows-based PC acting as the traffic cop and parking lot for the data boulevard.

And if copiers and telephones weren't enough, there were also rumors of a Microsoft appliance-control interface that seemed a throwback to the Blair Newman Home Bus days. Ever since then, Gates had been doing his damnedest to get Microsoft into the home, but with surprisingly little success. The potential was definitely there: According to Paine Webber analyst Michael Kwatinetz, each Nintendo machine generated twice as much software revenue as each desktop computer. But although Microsoft's CD-ROM Bookshelf, Cinemania, and Encarta reference titles were among the bestsellers in the field, a CD-ROM bestseller still sold far fewer units than, say, the equivalent book. Though computers increasingly came bundled with CD-ROM players, the Multimedia PC initiative seemed moribund, and the full-blown audiovisual extravaganzas it promised were beyond the capabilities of most machines on the market or already installed.

Still, Gates publicly stated that he expected Microsoft's consumer products division to be the company's largest within five years. Microsoft was developing more and more content-based titles, aiming at the overlapping home and education markets. Gates's other content company, IHS (Interactive Home Systems), had been renamed Continuum. In August 1993 it split in two, sending nearly half its employees, including CEO Steve Arnold, to Microsoft's multimedia or advanced research divisions. The remainder, divested of most of its technology development efforts, continued to build a digital archive of images. At a press luncheon, Gates admitted ruefully that he would personally lose money on the semimerger.

But Gates had a way of turning short-term losses into long-term gains. The national data highway was coming—even Vice President Al Gore said so—and Gates intended to ride it into the homes of America via potential strategic alliances with such partners as General Instrument, Time Warner, and Tele-Communications, Inc. A salient question, however, was exactly what Gates and Company brought to the communications party. Microsoft's public demonstrations revealed little more than a user interface for a computer-in-a-cable-box, and giant corporations wary of Microsoft's David playing them like an IBM Goliath might well be loath to pay Bill an ongoing royalty for software they could easily develop on their own or purchase outright elsewhere.

A more likely candidate for profit was the "server" technology that Microsoft was said to be demonstrating privately—technology that would store, deliver, and bill for digital movies, games, lessons, or any other bytes someone might be willing to pay for. Competitors pointed out that Microsoft had very little experience at the cutting edge of server technology, which was true enough. However, the company had just hired Craig Mundie, the founder and former chairman of Alliant Supercomputer, to head up a team that would investigate the huge, fast new hardware and software combinations such servers would almost certainly require.

Questioned in August 1993 about rumored deals with Hollywood studios, regional telephone companies, and national cable giants, Gates did acknowledge that "there's no joint venture thing that's been worked out." Nonetheless, he was doubling the size of Nathan Myhrvold's advanced research division to 400 employees and admitted to "spending a lot of time in Hollywood" attempting to explain the forthcoming digital revolution to CAA's Michael Ovitz and his illustrious clients. "There's no doubt we could bomb," said Gates. "I could take fifty million dollars a year and say it'd all be wasted."

The eternal pessimist had reason for his doubts. Microsoft continued to manifest an almost enchanted inability to meet its ship dates. The most recent broken promise involved Windows NT. Microsoft repeatedly announced it as a late 1992 release that would run in 8 megabytes of memory. It finally crept out the door at the end of July 1993, with a minimum of 12 megabytes recommended and at least 16 megabytes sorely needed. The timing was unfortunate: As at the release of OS/2, a freakish confluence of events conspired to send memory prices skyrocketing. NT's prospects looked good, but somewhat less certain than the initial Microsoft hoopla proclaimed. Network competitor Novell strategically delayed support for the new operating system, and NT-compatible versions of Microsoft's own Excel and Word would be even later than NT itself. IBM had actually managed to deliver a respectable version of OS/2, which was beginning to attract a vocal cadre of adherents. Competing operating systems were coming along from the likes of Sun, NeXT, and others. At Microsoft's July 1993 meeting for industry analysts, Gates spoke hardly at all about NT, choosing instead to extol the virtues of Chicago, a combined DOS/Windows upgrade whose ship date had slipped to fiscal year 1995. Cairo, the next version of NT, complete with object-oriented goodies, promised to be a year or two later.

Microsoft Everywhere might have looked like simplicity itself from the inside, but to outsiders the concept appeared confused and unfocused, almost as though Bill Gates were placing a bet on every number on the digital roulette wheel. To stockplayers who preferred to view Microsoft as a monolith able to enforce its will in the marketplace, a surprising number of those bets seemed to return small change. The low-end products, Microsoft Money, Profit, and Publisher, were selling adequately at best. LAN Manager and Windows for Workgroups, Microsoft's major networking efforts apart from NT, were utter duds. And Microsoft didn't even seem to try to come up with new product categories, as Lotus had with Notes, which was gaining a corporate foothold as a relatively painless way of sharing information. Meanwhile, supposedly vanquished competitors were coming back to life. WordPerfect was regaining market share with new updates. Lotus was on the rebound with version 4 of its 1–2–3 spreadsheet; analysts were speaking fondly of the Cambridge company as 1993's Comeback Kid, sending its stock toward one-year highs.

Microsoft stock, meanwhile, lost nearly a quarter of its value in two months and descended toward 12-month lows—putting nearly a year's worth of employee stock options underwater, dropping Chairman Bill's net worth by more than a billion and a half dollars, and threatening his status as the wealthiest American. Although the last three months of fiscal 1993 gave the company its first billion-dollar sales quarter ever and put it within a mere $50 million of its first billion-dollar annual profit, Wall Street was reacting to the company's slowing growth rate. Again and again in the past, CFO Frank Gaudette (who died of cancer in April) had jovially warned that the days of 50 percent year-to-year growth couldn't last, but the market had merely nodded and winked. Now the latest quarter's profits showed only 26 percent growth over the same quarter of the previous year, and Gaudette's successor Mike Brown was warning that the first quarter of fiscal 1994 might show a rare quarter-to-quarter decline. The market was finally taking notice. Still, Microsoft's economies amounted to little more than a broadly rumored hiring slowdown and a widely noticed cancellation of the annual Christmas party.

Despite the Street's gloomy reaction, Microsoft was still golden compared to computing's hardware leaders. Apple's stock nosedived by nearly a quarter of its value when the company reported a third-quarter loss of $188 million following CEO John Sculley's departure. When morale at the Cupertino firm tumbled after it announced that it would lay off 2,500 employees, Gates immediately dangled tantalizing offers to hire the smartest disgruntled Valley smart guys. As for Big Blue, Bill's 1990 prediction to Lotusians that IBM would "fold" within seven years was looking more plausible. Microsoft's agreement to pay some $20 million for IBM patents as part of the two companies' official "divorce" settlement in June 1992 did little to avert IBM's disastrous $5 billion loss for the year, which led CEO John Akers to resign in January 1993. After consulting with (but not, as initially reported, recruiting) Gates concerning the job, IBM hired former RJR Nabisco chief Louis Gerstner. Gates's somewhat self-serving advice to Armonk: cherish the mainframe business and keep key elements of the rest of the operations while dumping deadweight and slimming the workforce. Gerstner met with Gates after the big NT rollout at spring Comdex, but how much attention he paid remains unclear. IBM's downsizing continued with a mind-boggling $8 billion writedown for the second quarter of 1993.

The most visible clouds on Microsoft's legal horizon seemed to have lifted, but the possibility of precipitation lingered. On June 1, 1993, Judge Vaughn Walker granted summary judgment to Microsoft in the Apple look-and-feel lawsuit. Apple threatened to appeal the decision, but its chances of success seemed slim. As a plaintiff, Microsoft was faring even better, winning case after case and big dollar awards of dubious collectability against large-scale pirates of DOS and Windows.

After failing in February 1993 to come to a decision about bringing action against Microsoft for its trade practices, the Federal Trade Commission on July 21 deadlocked twice 2–2, first on whether to issue a formal complaint against Microsoft, then on whether to abandon the investigation. As in a similar February vote on whether to seek a federal court injunction, the fifth commissioner, Roscoe Starek, recused himself because stock he had reportedly inherited, though tied up in a trust, represented a potential conflict of interest. Microsoft was quietly jubilant, but shortly thereafter the FTC's files were trucked over to the Justice Department, whose antitrust division under Clinton appointee Anne Bingaman was expected to be far tougher on anticompetitive practices than the Bush administration had been. Would the government, Gates had to be wondering despite his bravado, become the same long-time thorn in Microsoft's side that it had been in IBM's? On August 20, the FTC voted 4–0 to abandon its investigation, but the Justice Department remained on the case.

At the July 1993 annual meeting for industry analysts, Gates had blamed the competition for the fracas, pointing a finger at Novell's domination of the network server market and its hopes of promoting DR DOS into more than a niche operating system. "The only issues that seem to be active," he said, "have been promoted very heavily by Novell in order to enable them to do a better job of selling their attempted clone product." Gates went on to add, "The goal here is to get us to raise our prices . . . so that they can compete more effectively." In response, Novell general counsel David Bradford pointed out to the press that "When DR DOS came into the market in 1988, the [OEM] price for an operating system was forty dollars. Today it's in the single digits. DR DOS entered the market and provided superior technology and caused Microsoft to innovate."

But Microsoft's major innovation with DOS seemed to be in pricing strategy. The company's real innovativeness continued to be relatively minor: Again and again Microsoft seemed to be developing its own versions of successful products from other companies or translating items from other media into the computer arena. Apple's pen-based Newton portable communicator begat WinPad, a pen-based collaboration with Compaq; the Funk and Wagnalls encyclopedia served as the basis for the digital enhancements of Encarta. Perhaps the one product with the greatest claim to innovation was Visual BASIC—a programming language and environment directly (though by now almost unrecognizably) descended from the first Gates/Allen version for the MITS Altair. The company's technical Smart Guys, however, seemed to be far more enamored of an alphabet soup of proposed protocols and standards (OLE—Object Linking and Embedding, ODBC—Open Database Connectivity, WOSA—Windows Open Services Architecture, etc.) whose names reminded some observers of the tepid IBM acronymic potages of yesteryear.

Yet Gates continued to flog the Microsoft "vision" in venue after venue, repeating the "back in 1975, Microsoft was formed with the vision of a computer on every desk and in every home" tale from podiums throughout the world. At a February 1993 lecture at the University of Washington, Gates took the "Information at Your Fingertips" concept a step farther by describing a wallet PC that would include everything from a global positioning system to a wireless data transceiver and would serve as key, passport, credit card, electronic mailbox, information retriever, and snapshot holder. It was not entirely unlike a "Ubiquitous Computing" project under development at—yes!—Xerox PARC, but that hadn't slowed Bill down before. Although Gates admitted that the whole scenario was many years from fruition and downplayed the many privacy implications, it seemed a particularly incongruous concept coming from a man whose own billfold, as the *Washington Post* reported, was often carried by one of his aides. And even a wallet computer might fail to help Gates with the mundane tasks of daily life. At the Microsoft at Work rollout in New York, a squinty Gates appeared for photo opportunities without his trademark glasses. Somehow he'd broken the only pair he'd brought.

Meanwhile, Gates's lakeside mansion-in-progress continued to be little more than concrete walls, so in the spring he spent a reported $8.5 million for a house just down the lake to serve as an interim love nest for himself and his future bride. Work continued on the grander abode: In keeping with the "found art" and mortality themes, Gates's art consultants were said to be assembling a world-class collection of authenticated prehistoric specimens to complement the virtual museum of the high-tech wall screens. And sources claimed that Melinda French had become involved in architectural decisions, speeding things up considerably when Gates's schedule was tight.

Which it usually was. Although Gates for the first time ever took a vacation marginally longer than his habitual maximum of nine days, his obsessive work habits continued to give lie to the claim (and hope) of some in the industry that marriage would somehow slow Bill Gates down. "It takes a lot of time being single," Gates told a group in London, his tongue only partially in cheek. "I think being married will be very efficient."

FULL DISCLOSURE

We came to call it The Question.

"Is this an authorized biography?" some asked.

"Is this an unauthorized biography?" others demanded.

Finally computer pioneer Jim Warren put it our favorite way: "Is this an authorized biography or an honest one?"

This book is and has always been an independent enterprise. But because Bill Gates and Microsoft have cooperated with many of our requests, some carpers will undoubtedly say we have been unduly influenced or co-opted. We are therefore making full disclosure here.

We developed this project on our own long before we ever discussed a word of it with Microsoft or Bill Gates. Early the morning of February 5, 1991, when Doubleday announced the project under the provisional title *Billion-Dollar Bill,* we immediately called Marty Taucher and Pam Edstrom, Microsoft's inside and outside public relations chiefs. Their private response was that Bill had a book of his own in the works, that writers were still being interviewed for it, and that we weren't in the running. The official Microsoft line, as reported by the Bellevue *Journal American* the following day: "We will not be cooperating in any way with them."

We were prepared for that response and half expected it. From the outset we intended to write the book whether we received cooperation or not. As we began interviewing and researching, we urged Taucher not to shut the door on us completely and reminded him that, in the interest of fairness and accuracy, we continued to hope that Microsoft and Gates would reconsider.

On Monday, May 6, Taucher sent us MCI Mail suggesting we discuss the project. It was the same day that a local newspaper began running a five-part series on Bill Gates that two local reporters had cobbled together. Gates and Microsoft had cooperated with that project at least to the extent of granting a single interview, but the accuracy and tone of the series were exemplified by the horoscope that managed to get Bill's birthdate wrong.

Still fiercely independent, we did something almost unheard of in the journalistic profession when we met Taucher the following Thursday: We paid for the PR man's lunch and our own. We also reiterated that we intended to do a fair, accurate book and hoped that Microsoft would reconsider its attitude toward us. Taucher expressed some concerns involving Gates's personal security, told us that the chairman detested our title, and set up an interview for us with Gates on June 5.

What we told Gates that day was, in longer form, what we had already told Taucher. We agreed to consider changing the title, an idea that was already in our minds, since Bill Clinton was already beginning to wear it out and our wives disliked it. We agreed to respect certain matters of personal security that we wouldn't have reported anyway. But those were our sole concessions. As we told Gates, we intended to tell the whole story and tell it fairly. There would be many things in the book that he wouldn't agree with or like. But we would give neither him nor Microsoft the right to read the manuscript prior to publication; regardless of Microsoft's cooperation, the book would have to remain as independent as when we began it.

Gates soon agreed to be interviewed. Beginning July 22, we began a series of eleven meetings over nine months, amounting to more than twenty hours with Gates. For subjecting himself to the barrage of minutiae we dredged up, and for his gutsy willingness to participate in a project over which he had no control, he deserves our greatest thanks.

From Microsoft we did accept a few items, however, and we hereby acknowledge them. First, cooperation: Although we had interviewed many past and current Softies even before cooperation was afforded us, Gates and Taucher made it possible for us to talk with many who might otherwise have been reticent and who gave us the benefit of their insiders' perspective. Second, research assistance: Bill opened many personal files to us, affording an unprecedented opportunity to clarify many points that had heretofore been misreported. And Microsoft's excellent library, including corporate videotapes and other rare items, was placed at our disposal.

We can't omit food and drink: Three of our interviews with Gates took place in an executive conference room over brought-in Thai, Chinese, and pizza meals for which we never saw a bill. Taucher also bought us two lunches on campus and one off. During our interviews at the campus, we availed ourselves of copious draughts of free soft drinks, consuming perhaps three cases of seltzer between us. However, any potential for influence or taint may have been mitigated by the two meals we bought Taucher, one we bought Pam Edstrom, and the dozens of meals we bought various Softies and non-Softies while we picked their brains.

Finally, just as we began to correct the typeset pages of the book, Gates somehow managed to get his hands on an uncorrected manuscript. Neither he nor Taucher would tell us the source, but evidence suggests a renegade who was solicited to give us a blurb and passed the manuscript to Microsoft instead. Although we had agreed that he would not have the right to read the book before publication, Gates asked to meet with us. We could have said no; since he had already read the manuscript, it seemed unreasonable to turn down the free services of the best-paid fact-checker in the known universe.

In a two-hour in-person session and a seven-hour telephone marathon, Gates forcefully aired his complaints and criticisms. As many of his colleagues told us, and we came to learn intimately, Bill's memory is good but hardly photographic, and though he does have a sense of humor, it peters out when it comes to criticism of Microsoft. The upshot: We scrambled to recheck dozens of facts and opinions, corrected a few horrible errors (at the summer party that was a precursor to Microgames it was indeed Chris, not Gary, Larson, who did the barbecuing), emended some minor gaffes (apparently young Bill did not usually wear a pocket protector), and let stand the vast majority of other items.

Reader, those are the facts: Influence or compromise are for you to decide.

Although returns are still out on the overall effect of computers on productivity—at least one of us played far too many games of Windows Solitaire, Minesweeper, and Tetris during the creation of this book—we cannot imagine how we would have done it without our PCs. Steve Manes used WordPerfect, SideKick, Lotus 1-2-3, PC-File, and Hot Line on his Zenith Z-386 system. Paul Andrews used Nota Bene, WordPerfect for Windows, and InfoSelect on his Gateway 2000 386 system and Nisus and Microsoft Word on his Macintosh IIci. Both of us used various editions of DOS, Windows, and Procomm. But aside from our word processors, no single program was more essential to our work than Magellan, an effortless and wonderful indexing-and-more program that Lotus has irrationally seen fit to essentially abandon. We continue to hope that a Windows version of the program or something very like it will soon appear on the market.

Our gratitude to Karen Novak of U.S. Robotics, whose loan of two 9600-bps modems made short work of transmitting files across town and across the globe. Digital Directory Assistance kindly supplied us with copies of PhoneDisc USA, a national telephone directory on CD-ROM, which was of inestimable value in tracking down important characters who had apparently disappeared from sight. Our thanks, too, to Alyce Perkins and Marilyn Watson of Dow Jones News Retrieval and Kathie Mulvey of Dialog, whose services whittled certain research efforts down to manageability. Ziff-Davis's on-line Computer Database Plus was another particularly valuable resource.

As useful as computers could be, humans proved even more helpful. Pride of place goes to Rita W. Wong, our tireless researcher, for her doggedness and resourcefulness in ferreting out needles of fact from courtroom and library haystacks. The staffs at King County Public Library, Seattle Public Library, and

University of Washington Libraries aided our efforts enormously. Jim Warren gave us unstinting access to his personal collection of journals and ephemera dating back to, and before, the dawn of the microcomputer. His library is a national treasure.

Microsoft's Marty Taucher deserves oak leaf clusters for all his efforts on our behalf. So do Cheri Johnson of the Microsoft public relations staff, Roxanna Frost of the Microsoft library, and Julie Girone of Bill Gates's office.

We received tremendous support from the *Seattle Times,* which made available its vast electronic and more traditional libraries. Alex MacLeod deserves special mention for his encouragement and assistance; thanks also to Alan Berner, Rich Buck, Frank Blethen, Dave Boardman, Casey Corr, Steve Dunphy, Mike Fancher, Carolyn Kelly, Bill Kossen, Carol Pucci, and Mason Sizemore.

Our transcribers turned hundreds of hours of taped interviews into text when computerized speech recognition would have failed dismally. A special mention for services above and beyond to Linda Curtis, Proof Positive. Thanks also to Cheri Fjermedal, Karen Rahl, Professional Dictation, and Eunice Verstegen.

Our appreciation to all those who supplied us with photos, with particular thanks to Paul Gilbert for his untiring efforts on our behalf, to Bob Wallace for his unique documentation of the early era, and to Ann Yow for her help with the later years. Bill Garcia of Seattle's Ivey Seright photo lab helped immensely in transferring the images from fragile snapshots to more permanent forms.

Particular thanks go to Steve Ditlea, Cary Lu, and Matt Mirapaul for their wisdom and counsel throughout the process. Dick Conklin deserves special mention for helping us navigate the vast reaches of IBM. Our gratitude also to Bruce Brown, Chris DeVoney, Grant Fjermedal, John Hedtke, James Lalonde, Fred Moody, and Peggy Watt for their aid and encouragement. Kudos to Frank Zoretich for his yeoman legwork in Albuquerque.

The highest of hosannas to John Brockman, Katinka Matson, and the rest of the staff at John Brockman Associates, particularly Marianne Martens and Elise Pritchard. They are truly the Smart Guys and Gals of agentry.

Thanks to David Gernert of Doubleday for acquiring the project and to Joel Fishman and Renée Zuckerbrot for shepherding it through the editorial process. Special thanks to Marysarah Quinn for her production work and to Sara Goodman for her expert vetting.

For a variety of services rendered, we must also thank June Almquist, Tony Barcellos, Gwen Bell, Sally Brown, Jim Bryant, Sarah Charf, Kelly Corr, John Dickinson, Joel Dreyfuss, Ray Duncan, Bill Gates Jr., Mary Gates, Preston Gralla, Larry Gussin, Darlene Hildebrandt, Jim Impoco, Stuart Johnston, Gordon Lee, Peter Lewis, Eric Maffei, Jill McKinstry, Joe McKinstry, Claudette Moore, Walter Mossberg, Sally Narodick, David Needle, Richard

Oberg, Rory O'Connor, Sam Perry, Charles Petzold, Jerry Schneider, Arnold Shotwell, Pat Simmons, Gina Smith, Paul Somerson, and Fred Wright.

A few individuals inside and outside of Microsoft agreed to be interviewed but insisted on total anonymity. Their contribution must go otherwise unacknowledged, but it has not gone unappreciated. Accolades, too, to those courageous independent-minded Softies who agreed to talk with us, both off the record and on, in the months while their employer was withholding its cooperation. Their assistance got us through the most difficult phase of the project.

Our thanks to all those who gave us hours of their time—a full work day in more than one case—for in-person interviews: Paul Allen, Stewart Alsop, Jeff Angus, Steve Arnold, Steve Ballmer, Jill Bennett, David Berliner, Karen Berliner, Bruce Biermann, Daniel Blom, Jabe Blumenthal, Alan Boyd, Dick Brass, Paul Brainerd, Rod Brock, Richard Brodie, Doug Buck, Lucy Cady, Blanche Caffiere, Hazel Carlson, Robert Carr, Ida Cole, Mike Collier, Christine Comaford, Brian Conte, Casey Corr, Kelly Corr, Mike Courtney, Eddie Currie, Monte Davidoff, G. Gervaise Davis, Doug Dayton, Arthur Dorros, Micheal Doss, Peter Dyer, Pam Edstrom, Mark Eppley, Buck Ferguson, Roger Fisher, Grant Fjermedal, Mary Kathleen Flynn, Sam Furukawa, Margo Gaia, Bill Gates, Bill Gates Jr., Kristi Gates, Libby Gates, Mary Gates, Frank Gaudette, Paul Gilbert, Julie Girone, Rob Glaser, George Grayson, Paul Grayson, Bob Greenberg, Matt Griffin, Mike Hallman, Steve Hallstrom, Rowland Hanson, Jeff Harbers, Portia Isaacson, Ed Johns, Craig Johnson, Stuart Johnston, Jim Karr, Guy Kawasaki, Jessica Kersey, Gary Kildall, Adrian King, Doug Klunder, Neil Konzen, James Lalonde, Jim Lane, Jonathan Lazarus, Richard Leeds, Gordon Letwin, Bobbie Lindsay, Tom Lopez, Cary Lu, Miriam Lubow, Mark Mackaman, Eric Maffei, Basil Maloney, Mike Maples, David Marquardt, Doug Michels, Pam Miller, Barbara Morgan, Mike Murray, Nathan Myhrvold, Bill Neukom, Leo Nikora, Scott Oki, Douglas Oles, Karl Oles, Bob O'Rear, Tim Paterson, Chuck Peddle, Alex Peder, Chris Peters, Charles Petzold, Karl Quackenbush, John Quain, Vern Raburn, Jeff Raikes, Peter Rinearson, Raleigh Roark, Angel Rodriguez, Heidi Roizen, Mark Rolsing, Steve Shaiman, Jon Shirley, Charles Simonyi, Pradeep Singh, Mike Slade, Gina Smith, Steve Smith, Jason Strober, Marty Taucher, Doug Thiel, Tandy Trower, Bernard Vergnes, Melissa Waggener, Bob Wallace, Jim Warren, Bob Wazeka, Ric Weiland, David Weise, Russ Werner, Pauline Westlund, Warren Westlund, Bill Whitlow, Marc Wilson, Ann Winblad, Marla Wood, Steve Wood (the earlier), Steve Wood (the later), Fred Wright, and Mark Zbikowski.

Our thanks, too, to those who took time—entire evenings in more than one instance—to speak with us by phone (or, in a couple of cases, correspond via MCI Mail or CompuServe): Bill Aloof, Marty Alpert, Robert Arnstein, Holden Aust, Rich Bader, Dean Ballard, Bob Barnett, Chris Bayley, Ann Becherer-Petrucci, Bob Belleville, Mike Boich, Dave Bradley, Andrew

Braiterman, Mike Brazier, Daniel Bricklin, David Bunnell, Bill Burgua, Thomas Chan, Thomas Cheatham, Scott Cline, Christine Comaford, Dick Conklin, James Cutler, Glenn Dardick, David Dekker, Donn Denman, Doug Devin, Ewen Dingwall, Jeff Docter, Steve Dompier, William Dougall, Scott Drill, Jim Edlin, Karl Edmark, Lewis Eggebrecht, Gordon Eubanks, Marvin Evans, Will Fastie, Laurie Flynn, Barry James Folsom, Bob Frankston, Rick Galer, Rob Gettinger, Bob Gillespie, Doug Gordon, Ross Greenberg, Bill Gross, Lollie Groth, Dick Gruen, Steve Guild, Martin Haeberli, Diane Haelsig, Mel Hallerman, Dick Hamlet, Steve Hazlerig, Paul Heckel, John Hedtke, David Hennings, Gloria Hennings, Don Herrick, Andy Hertzfeld, Doug Honig, Leroy Hood, David House, Ed Iacobucci, John Jacobson, Jim Jensen, Sergei Kalfov, Mitchell Kapor, John Katsaros, Gary Kildall, Edwin Kiser, Annelise Kolde, Betsy Kosheff, John Kropf, Frank Kulash, Bob Kutnick, Brad Leithauser, Terry Lipscomb, Bill Litchfield, William Lohse, Bill Lowe, Paul Mace, Gary Maestretti, Jeanette Maher, Bob Markell, Estelle Mathers, Bob McCaw, Marc McDonald, Scott McGregor, Sandy Meade, Bob Metcalfe, Mort Meyerson, Darrell Miller, Forrest Mims, Barry Mitzman, Daniel Luzon Morris, George Morrow, Harvey Motulsky, Therese Myers, Phil Nelson, Ries Niemi, John Oellrich, Pat Opalka, Mike Orr, Adam Osborne, Frank Peep, Gerard Pence, H. Ross Perot, Burt Perry, Pete Peterson, Jim Porzak, Jonathan Prusky, Jef Raskin, George Rathmann, Dick Ribas, Melanie Graves Rios, John Roach, Larry Rojas, Tom Rolander, Tom Rona, Philip Rose, Seymour Rubinstein, Stephen Russell, George Ryals, Jonathan Sacks, David Sadka, Jack Sams, Jerry Schneider, Virginia Schultz, Hal Setzer, Hunter Simpson, Richard Sisisky, Michael Slater, Dan Sokol, Michael Stanford, David Stern, Gary Stimac, Paul Stocklin, Sam Stroum, Kathryn Strutynski, Jane Schulte Taylor, John Tibbetts, John Umlauf, Mark Ursino, Bernard Vergnes, Barry Watzman, John Weeks, Tom Weeks, Vicki Weeks, Bill Weiher, John Wharton, Bill Whitlow, Randy Wigginton, Richard L. Wilkinson, Nelson Winkless, Joyce Wrenn, Carl Young, Stanley Youngs, and Sam Znaimer.

To all those we forgot to thank: It was a software problem—software of the brain.

During more than a year of what we came to call "Microsoft hours," our wives, Susan Kocik and Cecile Andrews, tolerated our peevishness and mole-like disappearance from polite society. It is to them that this book is dedicated. We have done our best to make it an honest one.

NOTES

PAGE

PROLOGUE: WITNESS THE TRANSFORMATION!

1–8 On the otherwise . . . : Sources regarding the Windows 3.0 introduction include Microsoft video of the event; Marty Taucher int., Aug. 29, 1991; *PC/Computing*, Oct. 1990, pp. 150–157.

5 "I have . . . of money." *USA Today*, Mar. 25, 1991, p. 4B.

5 "Who is this man?" Lakeside *Numidian*, 1973, unpaged.

5 discuss Microsoft . . . the check: Jonathan Prusky int., Feb. 25, 1992.

5 million-dollar trust fund: This "fact," repeated by a variety of sources, apparently gained currency during Bill's Harvard years, possibly from his own lips. Both he and his parents deny the story today, and no evidence suggests such a fund ever existed.

9 "The Silicon . . . Computer Industry": *Business Month*, Nov. 1990, cover.

9 "unimaginative . . . and slow.": *Business Month*, Nov. 1990, p. 36.

10 "Tell him . . . last night!": Mary Gates int., Aug. 5, 1991.

10 "This is . . . Bill's life.": Gina Smith int., May 29, 1991.

PAGE

1. THINK SMART!

11 "Happy Boy": Bill Gates Jr. int., Apr. 16, 1992.

11–12 Bill's great-grandfather . . . : Sources regarding William H. Gates Sr., William H. Gates Jr., and youth of William H. Gates III (later Jr.) include Merridy Gates Williams, "Gates Clan: From Nome to Microsoft via Bremerton," in *Kitsap: A Centennial History*, pp. 24–26.

12 "On my . . . Gates Jr.": Bill Gates Jr. int., Aug. 5, 1991.

12 "The Indians . . . went back.": *Seattle Times*, Sept. 7, 1950, p. 2.

12 Nicknamed . . . detested: J. W. Maxwell manuscript, "Plan for Biography," p. 2. The name he preferred was Bill.

12 Maxwell spent . . . taking three: Bagley, *History of King County*, pp. 516–517.

13 barrel bolts and oysters: Maxwell, "Plan for Biography," p. 4.

13 Every Thanksgiving . . . people: *Seattle Times*, Oct. 29, 1953, p. 40.

13 Although Maxwell . . . the time.: *Seattle Times*, Apr. 4, 1929, p. 21.

14 "Banker's Hours! . . .

Maxwell'': *Seattle Star,* Aug. 29, 1929, p. 7.

14 ''seven-hour turnaround'': Bennett, letter to author, Aug. 9, 1991.

14 An avid . . . never did.'': *Seattle Times,* Sept. 7, 1950, p. 2.

14 Maxwell kept . . . his garage.: Ibid.

14 Willard, vice . . . Orient.: *Seattle Times,* Aug. 30, 1957, p. 17.

15 ''I think . . . for him'': Mary Gates int., Oct. 10, 1991.

15 ''a huge . . . every pavilion.'': Bill Gates int., July 22, 1991.

15 ''to stimulate . . . science'': *Official Guide Book,* Seattle World's Fair, p. 8.

15 ''quotations . . . material.'': Ibid., p. 35.

15–16 ''a complete . . . creative pursuits.'': Ibid., pp. 30–32.

16 ''colored . . . writing.'': Ibid., p. 53.

16 ''He was . . . invented'': Confidential int., Mar. 1991.

16 ''He'd never . . . thinking.'': Mary Gates int., Aug. 5, 1991.

16 ''It was . . . ever did.'': Bill Gates Jr. int., Aug. 5, 1991.

16 '' 'seven plus . . . record!'': Gates int., July 22, 1991.

16–17 ''get . . . his mind.'': Hazel Carlson int., Sept. 11, 1991.

17 ''He knew . . . organize things,'': Hazel Carlson int., Mar. 12, 1991.

17 On the scent . . . breasts.: Blanche Caffiere int., Mar. 16, 1991.

17 ''I want . . . records.'': Bill Gates, class assignment, Sept. 22, 1964.

17 ''Most . . . or two.'': Hazel Carlson int., Mar. 25, 1992.

17 ''shaped . . . smart dog.'' Bill Gates, class assignment, Feb. 1, 1965.

18 intrusive mother-in-law: Libby Gates int., Feb. 11, 1992.

18 ''Very early . . . think smart!' '': Mary Gates int., Aug. 5, 1991.

18 Hangman: Libby Gates int., Feb. 11, 1992; Kristi Gates int., Feb. 22, 1992.

18 ''A little visitor is coming soon.'' Libby Gates int., Feb. 11, 1992.

18 I remember . . . and everything!'': Gates int., July 22, 1991.

18 ''You were . . . super well.'': Ibid.

19 ''precocious . . . troublemaker.'': Gates int., Aug. 26, 1991.

19 ''viselike . . . his years.'': Dale Turner int., May 21, 1991.

19 ''supermature . . . our minds'': Stanley ''Boomer'' Youngs int., Nov. 12, 1991.

19 ''My most . . . the world.'': Ibid.

20 ''young inventor . . . successful.'': Bill Gates, ''Invest with Gatesway Incorporated,'' May 19, 1967, pp. 1–3.

20 ''He was . . . funny'': Lollie Groth int., Sept. 26, 1991.

20 ''trying . . . this kid.'': George Ryals int., Nov. 12, 1991.

20 ''He was . . . do better.'': Lucy Cady int., Oct. 9, 1991.

21 ''dogmeat'': Gates int., July 22, 1991.

21 According . . . lawnmower.: Ibid.

21 ''things like . . . straight toe.'': Kristi Gates int., Feb. 22, 1992.

21 ''When Trey . . . sign here.'': Contract, Kristi and Bill Gates, May 14, 1966.

21 ''Dirty Boy'': Karl Oles int., May 24, 1991.

22 This return . . . into camp.: Troop 186 *Informer,* fall 1970, p. 2.

22 Gates fell . . . making Eagle.: Gates int., July 22, 1991.

22 He loved . . . happens next?'': Ann Winblad int., July 23, 1991.

PAGE

2. LOGGING IN

23 "Holy smokes . . . I would do." Gates int., July 22, 1991.

23–24 "was . . . in control.": Mary Gates int., Aug. 5, 1991.

24 "He didn't . . . was trouble.": Bill Gates Jr. int., Aug. 5, 1991.

24 "My desk . . . laughing.": Gates int., July 22, 1991.

24 "anxious . . . to attend.": Mary Gates int., Aug. 5, 1991.

24 "thought . . . supportive.": Bill Gates Jr. int., Aug. 5, 1991.

24 "There were . . . them": Confidential int., Sept. 1991.

26 Designed . . . 4:00 A.M.: Kemeny and Kurtz, *Back to BASIC,* p. 16.

27 The Teletype . . . a month.: Fred Wright int., August 14, 1991.

27 "Conceivably . . . sons.": Edgar Horwood, letter to Lakeside School, Sept. 29, 1967.

27 "and explaining . . . those guys.": Paul Stocklin int., Oct. 13, 1991.

27 "I go . . . pass me.": Bill Dougall int., Sept. 17, 1991.

28 "two feet . . . about it.": *GE Time-Sharing Service Reference Manual,* BASIC Language, June 1965, p. 38.

28 Bill Gates's . . . any other. Gates int., July 22, 1991.

28 Tic-Tac-Toe . . . grid.: Ibid.

28 "It was . . . the floor.": Matt Griffin int., Apr. 4, 1991.

29 She wrote . . . on it.: Gates int., July 22, 1991.

29 "It was . . . heaven.": Ibid.

29 We'd just . . . typed BILL.: Dick Wilkinson int., June 11, 1991.

30 "Once you . . . you to.": Steve Russell int., May 29, 1991.

30 "I just . . . playing it.": Harvey Motulsky int., Aug. 14, 1991.

30 "You'd have . . . it worked.": Paul Allen int., Oct. 31, 1991.

30 "It was . . . of learning.": Ibid.

PAGE

31 "Confusion between . . . of bugs." *DDT-10 Programmer's Reference* (Maynard, MA: Digital Equipment Corp., 1968), p. 1–1.

31 At home . . . a problem.: Kristi Gates int., Feb. 22, 1992.

31 "absolute disaster.": Libby Gates int., Feb. 11, 1991.

31 "He never . . . he wore.": Ibid.

31 "We always . . . morning": Mary Gates int., Aug. 5, 1991.

32 "We enjoyed . . . What if?' ": Carl Young int., May 13, 1991.

32 Some years . . . game ever.: Levy, *Hackers,* pp. 59–62.

32 "The novel . . . real people.": Dick Gruen int., June 10, 1991.

32 "I remember . . . go home.' ": Gates int., July 22, 1991.

33 "It was . . . to know.": Allen int., Oct. 31, 1991.

33 "The kids . . . shouldn't have.": Don Herrick int., June 17, 1991.

34 "The school . . . could do.' ": Ibid.

34 "guy from the FBI": Gates int., July 22, 1991

34 "They were . . . hung down.": Wilkinson int., June 11, 1991.

34 The kids . . . year long.: Gates int., July 7, 1991; Allen int., Oct. 31, 1991. As Gates initially recalled it, "We weren't supposed to use computers in any way, shape, or form for a year." Gates later corrected himself: "No, it couldn't have been a year; may have been an entire summer." The version of Gates's hacking exploits in Freiberger and Swaine, *Fire in the Valley,* pp. 21–22, is a myth most likely proffered by Gates himself. "In high school, for about a year and a half, I quit using computers because I didn't want to be a computer nut," Gates said in the *Seattle Times,* Feb. 14, 1982, p. D3. *Fortune,* Jan. 23, 1984, p. 82, reported the absence as two years.

PAGE

34   "When I . . . pretty upset.":
Allen int., Oct. 31, 1991.

34   "get all . . . damn thing.":
Confidential int., Nov. 1991.

34   "That's . . . it's stupid."
Dougall int., Sept. 17, 1991.

34–35   "an extremely . . . been
killed." Confidential int., Nov.
1991.

35   "Will the . . . the lights?":
Gruen int., June 10, 1991.

36   We're sitting . . . in business.":
Gates int., July 22, 1991.

36   Outside . . . magnetic tapes.:
Allen int., Oct. 31, 1991.

3. OPEN FOR BUSINESS

37   "disdain for . . . typing in":
Gates int., July 22, 1991.

37–38   I just . . . were typing: Allen
int., Oct. 31, 1991.

38   "after that . . . grata.": Ibid.

38   "I want . . . computers can't.":
Ibid.

38   "You could . . . collator
thing.": Gates int., July 22, 1991.

38   It was from . . . interpreter.:
Gates int., July 23, 1991.

40   "It was . . . patently obvious.":
Frank Peep int., July 14, 1991.

40   "From the . . . computer
time.": Marvin Evans int., May 1,
1992.

40   "acted like . . . of things.":
Fred Wright int., Aug. 14, 1991.

40   Most kids . . . the time.: Bill
Gates Jr. int., Aug. 5, 1991.

40   "I don't . . . a lot.": Ibid.

41   "the experience . . . gained
thereby.": Letter, Thomas W.
MacLean Jr. to Kent Evans and
Bill Gates, Sept. 28, 1971.

41   "You have . . . very
complicated.": Gates int., July
22, 1991.

41   "It was . . . a program": Allen
int., Oct. 31, 1991.

41   "adding bells . . . payroll
program.": Ric Weiland int.,
Sept. 13, 1991.

PAGE

41   "were much . . . that thing.":
Allen int., Oct. 31, 1991.

41   "really upset . . . of thing.":
Ibid.

42   "What tapes . . . get those?":
Ibid.

42   "made a very good markup.":
Gates int., July 22, 1991.

42   The group . . . effort.: Gates
int., July 23, 1991. Neither Allen
nor Weiland recalled this division,
though Gates has repeated it in
other interviews.

42   more than $25,000 in billings:
MacLean letter to Evans and
Gates, Sept. 28, 1971.

43   "kept wanting . . . difficult.":
Bill Gates Jr. int., Aug. 5, 1991.

43   "In the . . . terminated
immediately." Maclean letter to
Evans and Gates, Sept. 28, 1971.

43   (an amount . . . $10,000):
Seattle Weekly, Jan. 14, 1981,
reprint unpaged.

44   "one of . . . ever lived": Gates
int., July 23, 1991.

44   I want . . . you think.: Ibid.

45   On January . . . were killed.:
Seattle Times, Jan. 31, 1972, p. 1.

45   On May . . . helicopter.: Seattle
Times, May 30, 1972, p. A4.

45   Bill received . . . tears.: Gates
int., July 23, 1991.

46   "classmate, friend, . . . Evans":
Plaque inside entrance, Allen-
Gates Hall, Lakeside School.

46   "he was . . . athletic guy":
Gates int., July 23, 1991.

46   "He didn't . . . the slopes":
Confidential int., Nov. 1991.

46   "I will . . . finishing things.":
Marvin Evans int., May 1, 1992.

46   "I remember . . . stuff done,"
Doug Gordon int., Sept. 16,
1991.

46   "I'm going . . . I'm twenty.":
Melanie Graves Rios int., Feb. 6,
1992.

47   Despite such . . . into view.:
Gates int., July 23, 1991.

47   To avoid . . . requested.: Allen
int., Oct. 31, 1991.

PAGE

47 "a real . . . the school.": Gates int., July 23, 1991. The story has taken a variety of forms over the years.

47 "first call on every sin": Ibid.

47 Gates served . . . taxpayers' dollars.: 93rd Congress, 1st Session, *Report of the Clerk of the House* from July 1, 1972, to December 31, 1972, House of Representatives Document No. 93-51, p. 149.

47 "the most . . . been there": Gates int., July 23, 1991.

48 "that's when . . . some money." Ibid. The reconstruction in the text regarding this incident is taken primarily from Gates's recollections in this interview. One of the earliest reported versions appeared in *People,* Dec. 26–Jan. 2, 1984, p. 37, which had Gates making "a killing buying 5,000 . . . buttons for three cents each and then selling them as collectors' items for $20.25 apiece . . ."

48 Pages on . . . the floor.: Richard Sisisky int., May 22, 1991; William Litchfield int., May 14, 1991; David Sadka int., May 12, 1991; Kevin Pipes int., May 14, 1991.

48 A Ferndale . . . accommodate demand.: *New York Times,* Aug. 2, 1972, p. 20.

48 A Liberty . . . Eagleton himself.: *New York Times,* Aug. 10, 1972, p. 32.

49 McGovern's "1000 . . . Dakota.: *New York Times,* July 27, 1972, p. 1.

49 "billions": *Seattle Times,* Feb. 14, 1982, p. D3.

49 "inflated.": Kristi Gates int., Feb. 22, 1992.

49 "just going . . . engineering guys": Gates int., Feb. 29, 1992.

PAGE

4. PROGRAMMING UNLIMITED

50 "Intel's second . . . expert.": *Electronics,* Apr. 10, 1972, p. 2.

51 "Three hundred . . . chip!": Allen int., Jan. 9, 1992.

51 Intel . . . mainframes.: David House int., Mar. 3, 1992

51 "I wanted . . . at large.": Gates int., July 23, 1991.

51–52 "the guy . . . Boy Scout.": Ibid.

53 "had a . . . on things.": Paul Gilbert int., June 19, 1991.

53–54 "This is . . . come true!": Gates int., July 23, 1991.

54 "way beyond . . . backup system.": Ibid.

54 "He was . . . high-IQ act.": Gates int., July 22, 1991.

54 "I remember . . . No way!' ": Allen int., Oct. 31, 1991.

54 "At first . . . error messages.": Gates int., July 23, 1991.

55 "He hated . . . of it.": Daniel Luzon Morris int., Nov. 25, 1991.

55 "something like $30,000 a year.": Freiberger and Swaine, *Fire in the Valley,* p. 23.

55 "got involved . . . System Integration.": Gates int., July 23, 1991.

55–56 "We had . . . writing code.": Ibid.

56 "Just kidding.": Allen int., Jan. 9, 1991.

56 "totally random": Allen int., Oct. 31, 1991.

56–57 "Let's go . . . injured limb.: Bob Barnett int., Aug. 30, 1991.

57 It was . . . Flathead Lake.: Libby Gates int., Feb. 11, 1992.

57 "It took . . . hours' work.": Barnett int., Aug. 30, 1991.

58 "never met . . . mathematics, ever.": Gates int., Aug. 26, 1991.

58 "We were . . . at Lakeside.": Doug Gordon int., Sept. 16, 1991.

58 "Gates was . . . about

PAGE

everything.'': Andrew Braiterman int., Sept. 5, 1991.

58 "He was . . . the place.'': Thomas Cheatham int., July 17, 1991.

59 When the . . . arouse controversy.: Ibid.

59 "He took . . . monstrous endeavor.'': Sam Znaimer int., August 22, 1991.

59 "One, comma, one, comma, one'': Ibid.

59 "I don't . . . or minus'': Gates int., Aug. 29, 1991.

59 "I used . . . read books.'': Ibid.

59 a mugger . . . voice.: Ibid.; also Frank Kulash int., May 13, 1991.

60 "on a couple . . . the universe.'': Znaimer int., Aug. 22, 1991.

60 "In the . . . outstanding programmers.'': "Description of Lakeside Computer Needs,'' proposal to Lakeside administration, Apr. 17, 1974.

60 ulcerative colitis: Weiland int., Sept. 13, 1991; Allen int., Oct. 31, 1991; Gates int., Feb. 29, 1992.

60 "I was . . . of pressure'': Gates int., Feb. 29, 1992.

60 "because I was nervous.'': Gates int., Aug. 26, 1991.

60 "antsy. . . . job together.'': Ibid.

61 "Tell him . . . last night!'': Mary Gates int., Aug. 5, 1991.

61 a measly $252.67: Traf-O-Data Washington State Combined Excise Tax Returns, fourth quarter 1974. No income was shown on the return for the third quarter of that year.

61 The project . . . $500 job. University of Washington Daily, Sept. 30, 1974, p. 18; Oct. 3, 1974, p. 11.

61 "sciency people'' . . . each day.: Gates int., Aug. 26, 1991.

62 "Gatesing . . . the Gator'': Frank Kulash int., May 13, 1991.

PAGE

62 "Gates gravy train'': Brad Leithauser int., May 14, 1991.

62 "you kind . . . different courses.'': Gates int., Aug. 29, 1991.

62 "the complex . . . Z-plane'': Znaimer int., Aug. 22, 1991.

62 Steve Jobs . . . the rest.: Rose, West of Eden, p. 160; Dan Sokol int., Aug. 2, 1991.

62 Harvard boasted . . . the honors.: American Mathematical Monthly, Nov. 1975, pp. 906–907.

63 "between 1970 . . . go down.'': Bill Gates presentation, Apple Computer, "The Future of Software,'' circa 1984. Gates retailed a variant of the bogus "elevator control'' story on Nov. 18, 1987, at the Sacramento Personal Computer Users Group: Sacra Blue, Dec. 1987, p. 23.

63 "never happened.'': Gates int., Feb. 29, 1992.

63 Gates would . . . Microsoft software.'': Gates int., Aug. 26, 1991. Another variant in Sacra Blue, Nov. 1987, p. 21: "We moved down to Albuquerque, New Mexico, where the very first personal computer company was, and wrote the mission statement of our company, which was exactly as follows, over 12 years ago: 'Our vision: A personal computer on every desktop and in every home running Microsoft software.' '' Paul Allen (int. Jan. 9, 1992) recalled conversations about "a worldwide information network'' as early as 1973, but said "the statement about having Microsoft's software on all those computers was like an early '80s thing.''

63 In early . . . discovered it.: Allen int., Oct. 31, 1991. Gates's version has differed: "We were just walking by Harvard Square and there's that big magazine stand there and he . . . pulled it out and we looked at it and—

PAGE

whoa! This thing's happening without us." (Gates int., Aug. 26, 1991.) "I was in Harvard Square in Cambridge, wandering around on a very cold day, when I saw the cover of *Popular Electronics.*" (Gates at Boston Computer Society, Feb. 2, 1988.)

63 "PROJECT BREAKTHROUGH!" . . . minicomputer.: *Popular Electronics,* Jan. 1975, cover.

63 "EXCLUSIVE. ALTAIR . . . arrived!"*: Popular Electronics,* Jan. 1975, p. 33.

64 It was . . . inoperable.: Mims, *Siliconnections,* p. 43.

5. HARDCORE!

65 Kenbak: Byte, July 1978, p. 66; *Computerworld,* May 19, 1986, p. 33; *Computer Museum Report,* fall 1986, p. 24.

65 Micral: *Computerworld,* May 19, 1986, p.33; *Edge: Work-Group Computing Report,* Aug. 19, 1991; *Computer Museum Report,* fall 1986, p. 25.

65 Scelbi: *Byte,* July 1978, pp. 66–67; *Creative Computing,* Nov. 1984, pp. 12–14.

65 Mark-8: *Radio-Electronics,* July 1974, p. 29–33; *Byte,* July 1978, p. 68; Larry Steckler in Ditlea, *Digital Deli,* p. 37.

66 TV Typewriter: *Radio-Electronics,* Sept. 1973, pp. 43–52; *Byte,* July 1978, p. 68.

66–67 MITS: Freiberger and Swaine, *Fire in the Valley,* pp. 28–53; Mims, *Siliconnections,* pp. 24–46; Les Solomon in Ditlea, *Digital Deli,* pp. 36–41; Levy, *Hackers,* pp. 187–195.

67 "Applications . . . robot.": *Popular Electronics,* January 1975, p. 38.

68 "People lusted . . . reaction.": *Computer Systems News,* Reflections Supplement, undated (Nov. 1988?), p. 115.

PAGE

69 "any of . . . under this.": Agreement, "Ownership of Traf-O-Data," signed William Gates, Jan. 1, 1975.

69 With that . . . royalty agreement.: Letter from Paul Allen to "Sirs," Jan. 2, 1975.

69 According to . . . cross-compilers.: Gates int., Aug. 26, 1991; Allen int., Oct. 30, 1991.

69 "toy language.": Steve Wood [earlier employee] int., Apr. 29, 1991.

70 We have . . . contact us.: *PC Magazine,* October 1982, p. 293. The decimal point after the first dollar sign is almost certainly a typographical error. Otherwise, despite Gates's disclaimers, the text seems authentic: The first and last three words are identical to those in the Allen letter of Jan. 2.

70 Roberts called . . . went dead.: Ibid. The article states that Roberts reached a "Seattle boarding house"; if so, Roberts dialed the wrong number.

71 "We've got . . . on this!' ": Allen int., Oct. 31, 1991. Gates remembered the initial call as being made to Bill Yates: Gates int., Aug. 26, 1991.

72 "many features . . . BASIC.": *BASIC-PLUS Language Manual,* 4th rev. (Maynard, MA: Digital Equipment Corp., 1975), p. iii.

72 "I've written . . . routines.": Confidential int., May 1991.

73 "Wow . . . machine.": Gates int., Aug. 26, 1991.

73 "We're not . . . touches on it.": Allen int., Oct., 31, 1991.

73 The code . . . need 6K: The 6K figure appears in the only available contemporary document dealing with the subject, a proposal from Microsoft re BASIC for the Texas Instruments SP-70, circa May 1977. In an Aug. 26, 1991, interview, Gates said, "I think it was at 5K. It could have been 7."

PAGE

73–74 "Jesus, Paul . . . gonna work.":
Gates int., Aug. 26, 1991.

74 "Oh, my . . . this thing!":
Allen int., Oct. 31, 1991.

74 "there's this . . . was there.":
Ibid.

74 "Yep . . . the truck.": Ibid.

74 "This is . . . I expected.": Ibid.

74 "This is . . . fly-by-night
company": Ibid.

75 "antsy": Ibid.

75 "a little . . . right now": Ibid.

75 "some kind . . . the night?' ":
Ibid.

75 "Have you . . . program yet?":
Ibid.

75–76 "Oh, my . . . I am.": Ibid.

6. UP AND RUNNING

77 ALTAIR BASIC—UP AND
RUNNING: Computer Notes, Apr.
7, 1975, p. 1.

77 Mainframe languages . . . a
month.: Brooks, The Mythical Man-
Month, p. 98.

78 An assistant . . . Gates's.:
Znaimer int., Aug. 22, 1991.

78 "When they . . . the
majority.": Gates int., Aug. 26,
1991.

78 Nor were . . . University.:
Gates int., Nov. 5, 1991.

78 It was . . . Harvard record.:
Znaimer int., Aug. 22, 1991.

78 "Bill was . . . very seriously.":
Ibid.

78–79 He worked . . . Harvard
machines.: Gates int., Aug. 26,
1991

79–80 a young Californian . . . :
sources regarding Steve Dompier,
Homebrew Club, and Altair
BASIC include Steve Dompier
int., Aug. 29, 1991; Levy,
Hackers, pp. 192–195, 203–206;
Freiberger and Swaine, Fire in the
Valley, pp. 38–39.

80 "His article . . . anyone
know?": Computer Notes, July
1975, p. 1.

PAGE

80 "unique marketing . . . BASIC
language": Computer Notes, July
1975, p. 1.

81 "People would . . . or
something.": Eddie Currie int.,
July 23, 1991.

81 Homebrew's pirating of BASIC
tape: Sources include Steve
Dompier int., Aug. 29, 1991;
Dan Sokol int., Aug. 2, 1991;
Levy, Hackers, p. 228.

82 in Computer . . . June 23.:
Computer Notes, July 1975, p. 6.

82 At some . . . was signed: Gates
int., Aug. 26, 1991

82–83 Microsoft was . . . secrecy
agreement.: Agreement between
MITS Inc., and Paul G. Allen and
William Gates, dated July 22,
1975.

83 "we will . . . license
agreement": Computer Notes, Aug.
1975, p. 2.

84 "A BASIC . . . each copy.":
Computer Notes, Oct. 1975, p. 14,
reprinted from People's Computer
Company, Sept. 1975.

84 "for tricky programmers":
Computer Notes, July 1975, p. 8.

84 "the LXI trick": Computer Notes,
Aug. 1975, p. 11.

84 "Some tricks . . . seem
meaningless.": Computer Notes,
Sept. 1975, p. 8.

84 The partnership . . . $606
respectively.: MicroSoft financial
statement circa Sept. 1976.

84 "Even from . . . screwed up":
Gates int., Aug. 26, 1991.

85 "My Way.": Allen int., Jan. 9,
1991.

85 What would . . . the damage.:
Paul Allen, Oct. 31, 1991;
amplified by confidential int., Aug.
1991.

85 "parasite companies": Computer
Notes, Oct. 1975, p. 4.

85 "You have . . . it up.": Micro-8
Computer Group Newsletter, Feb. 10,
1976, p. 7.

86 "we may . . . track record.":
Computer Notes, Aug. 1975, p. 2.

PAGE

86 . . . one thing . . . more than reasonable.: *Computer Notes,* Sept. 1975, p. 2.

86 "MITS should . . . a thief.: *Computer Notes,* Oct. 1975, pp. 3–4.

87 "an excessive . . . are trying!!!": *Computer Notes,* Oct. 1975, p. 3.

7. THIEVES IN OUR MIDST!

88 "pretty hardcore": Weiland int., Sept. 13, 1991.

89 "Those . . . Sphere": *Computer Notes,* Nov.-Dec. 1975, p. 1.

89 "doing too . . . you are": Gates int., Aug. 26, 1991.

89 As Ed . . . $10 an hour: *Computer Systems News,* Reflections Supplement, undated (Nov. 1988?), p. 116.

89 Bunnell . . . minimum wage.: David Bunnell int., Feb. 11, 1992.

89 "I don't . . . for me.": Allen int., Oct. 31, 1991.

89–90 Trey took . . . are murky.): Gates family Christmas card, 1975.

90 The total . . . final quarter.: MicroSoft financial statement, undated, circa Sept. 1976

90 "For a . . . them serious.": *Computer Notes,* Nov.-Dec. 1975, p. 19.

90 "If anyone . . . bugs!": Ibid.

91 "Licenses for . . . detailed information.": *Computer Notes,* Jan. 1976, p. 6.

91–92 To me . . . good software.: *Computer Notes,* Feb. 1976, p. 3.

92 "the software flap.": *Micro-8 Computer User Group Newsletter,* Mar. 28, 1976, p. 1.

92 "misleading . . . time.": Ibid.

92 "I certainly . . . he's really good.": Ibid., circa Mar. 1, 1976, p. 2.

92 "rumors have . . . the results.": Ibid., Mar. 28, 1976, p. 1.

92 "black box": Ibid., circa Mar. 1, 1976, p. 2.

93 "defamatory and insulting": Ibid., circa Apr. 1976, p. 2.

93 "one of . . . eat, too!": *Homebrew Computer Club Newsletter,* Mar. 31, 1976, p. 3.

93 employ twenty people.: Allen int., Oct. 31, 1991.

93 "crazed . . . individuals": Nelson, *Computer Lib,* p. 18.

93 And upstairs . . . the Altair.: Steve Dompier int., Aug. 29, 1991.

94 Moore's Law: *Scientific American,* Sept. 1977, p. 65.

94 "sort of in awe.": Bob Wallace int., Apr. 2, 1991.

94 "why I . . . a closet": Gates, *Computer Notes,* Apr. 1976, p. 5.

94 "the majority . . . be copied.": Ibid.

95 "software should . . . or not.": Ibid.

95 They simply . . . two years.: MicroSoft financial statement, undated, circa Sept. 1976.

95 In April . . . corporate customers. Letter from Bill Gates to American National Standards Institute, Apr. 1, 1976.

96 In drumming . . . alternative transportation.: Gates int., Aug. 29, 1991.

97 "The Legend . . . a manager.' ": Microsoft advertisement, *Digital Design,* July 1976, p. 28.

97 "Microsoft: . . . microsoftware needs?": Ibid.

97 "awe-stricken": *Personal Computing* Sept.-Oct. 1977, p. 123.

97 "I'm *styled* president": Nelson Winkless int., Aug. 12, 1991.

97 "Upcoming Bout . . . 8080.": Microsoft advertisement, *Digital Design,* July 1976, p. 28.

98 A year or so . . . : sources regarding Gates, Allen, and APL include Mike Courtney ints., Aug. 30 and Sept. 11, 1991.

98 In Seattle . . . the fall.:

PAGE

Northwest Computer Club Newsletter,
Sept. 1976, pp. 5–6.

98 "Whatever happened . . . 8080
APL?": *Northwest Computer Club
Newsletter,* Jan. 1977, unpaged.

99 Weiland contacted . . . college
instead.: Robert Arnstein int.,
Oct. 15, 1991.

99 "as a . . . our literature.": Bill
Gates memo to staff, Nov. 14,
1978.

99 Weiland . . . the weekend.
Weiland int., Sept. 13, 1991.

99 But Peddle . . . would win.:
Weiland int., Sept. 13, 1991

100 "dog processor": Chuck Peddle
int., July 30, 1991.

100 "We were . . . PET":
Confidential int., Aug. 1991.

100 "the last . . . BASIC-trained.":
Peddle int., Oct. 21, 1991.

101 What saved . . . the year.:
Weiland int., Sept. 13, 1991.

101 first thirteen . . . bankrupt.:
Fortune, Mar. 26, 1990, p. 72.

101 "I made that up": Gates int.,
Feb. 29, 1992.

101 One estimate . . . MOS
Technology.: *Northwest Computer
Club Newsletter,* Dec. 1977,
unpaged, quoting *Electronics News,*
Aug. 22, 1977.

101 On December . . . annual
budget.: *Impact* magazine,
Albuquerque Journal, Aug. 14, 1984,
p. 7.

101–2 BASIC wasn't . . . Christmas
Eve.: Weiland int., Sept. 13,
1991.

102 "We could . . . did it.": Steve
Wood int., Apr. 29, 1991.

102 "prove . . . that tuxedo": Gates
int., Aug. 29, 1991.

102 "majored in extracurriculars":
Ballmer int., July 29, 1991.

102 "We're just . . . this course":
Gates int., Aug. 29, 1991.

102 "We're golden! . . . we're
not!": Ballmer int., July 29,
1991.

102 "it was kind of rude": Gates int.,
Aug. 29, 1991.

PAGE

8. NEW MEXICAN STANDOFF

103 On this . . . for himself.: Steve
Wood int., April 29, 1991

103 the existing . . . student.:
Partnership agreement between
Bill Gates and Paul Allen, Feb. 3,
1977.

104 The bit . . . workaholic.:
Confidential int., April 1991.

104 "We would . . . theater.":
Allen int., Jan. 9, 1992.

104 "No . . . We're
programmers.": Confidential int.,
July 1991.

104 Employees got . . . a fit.:
Confidential int., Feb. 1991.

104 "Microsoft . . . the job.":
Microsoft internal memo from Bill
Gates to Ric Weiland, Steve
Wood, Marc McDonald, undated,
circa 1977.

105 "normal hourly rate.": Ibid.

105 "louder . . . I say.' ":
Confidential int., June 1991.

105 Insiders . . . party.: Steve Wood
int., April 29, 1991

105 By mid-January . . . to MITS.:
William Gates affidavit, May 9,
1977, p. 3. In MITS v. Allen and
Gates files, Bernalillo County
District Court.

105 MITS told . . . the agreement.:
Letter from H. Edward Roberts to
Microsoft, Apr. 26, 1977.

106 The "hardware . . . to pay.:
Gates affidavit, May 9, 1977,
pp. 8–9.

106–8 Computer Faire: Freiberger and
Swaine, *Fire in the Valley,* pp. 181–
183; Jim Warren int., Oct. 15,
1991.

106–7 "a personal . . . information-
related needs.": Alan Kay and
Adele Goldberg, "Personal
Dynamic Media" (Abridgement of
Xerox PARC Technical Report
SSL-76-1, March 1976), *Computer,*
Mar. 1977, p. 31.

107 I expect . . . software
questions.: *Personal Computing,*
Jan.-Feb. 1977, p. 67.

PAGE

107 "The idea . . . technical background.": *Personal Computing,* Sept.-Oct. 1977, p. 90.

108 "The best . . . multiple versions.": *Personal Computing,* May-June 1977, p. 38.

108 "We would . . . his submarine?' ": Steve Wood int., Apr. 29, 1991.

109 "license, promote . . . the program.": Letter, Bill Gates and Paul Allen to Ed Roberts, Apr. 20, 1977.

109 "Mits, Inc., . . . its competitors.": Letter, Peter J. Broullire to Bill Gates and Paul Allen, Apr. 21, 1977.

109 One week . . . still valid.: Letter, Peter J. Broullire to Bill Gates and Paul Allen, Apr. 29, 1977.

110 someone from . . . currently occupied.: Confidential interview, Aug. 6, 1991

111 "hot, miserable, crowded hall": Nelson Winkless int., Aug. 12, 1991.

111 "until stronger . . . be developed.": Bill Gates, position paper for Personal Computing and Software panel, June 1977.

111 "We were . . . should be.": Mary Gates int., Aug. 5, 1991.

111 In July . . . Bob Greenberg.: Note from Microsoft to Bob Greenberg, July 5, 1977.

111–12 Apple licensed . . . as Applesoft BASIC.: Young, *Steve Jobs,* p. 144.

112 During one . . . to 121.: Gates int., Jan. 15, 1992.

112 "What happened? . . . No. What?": Confidential int., Aug. 1991.

112 "noticed that . . . I could": Gates int., Feb. 29, 1992.

112 The Cement . . . his Porsche.: Ibid.

113 What Bill . . . break-in period.: Letter, Bill Gates to Monte Davidoff, Sept. 20, 1977.

113 "Mr. Gates . . . this fast?": Allen int., Oct. 31, 1991.

113 "one of . . . ever seen.": Allen int., Jan. 9, 1992.

113 "It was . . . in here.": Steve Wood int., Apr. 29, 1991.

114 "How much . . . eventuality": Gates int., Aug. 29, 1991.

114 *Parade* magazine . . . the phenomenon.: *Parade,* Feb. 6, 1977, p. 15; *Kilobaud Newsletter,* Feb. 22, 1977, p. 1.

115 "totally wretched.": *Electronic Engineering Times,* undated clipping, circa December 1977.

115 "a bug . . . been shipped.": Ibid.

115 Another deal . . . for short.: Marc McDonald int., Oct. 12, 1991.

115 "Even on . . . a deal.": Steve Smith int., Apr. 29, 1991.

116 "for comfort . . . fuzzy feeling": Marc McDonald int., Oct. 12, 1991.

116 "still finding . . . it done.": *Creative Computing,* Nov. 1984, p. 295.

116 "We write software.": Miriam Lubow int., July 18, 1991.

11' "Oh," . . . Twenty-one.": Ibid.

11' "standing . . . writing.": Ibid.

117 "I would . . . to that.": Ibid.

117 "they wouldn't . . . weren't interested.": Ibid.

118 "a user . . . over 5000.": Microsoft press release, Nov. 18, 1977.

118 By the . . . roughly equally.: Microsoft income statement for year ended Dec. 31, 1977.

9. FAREWELL TO THE DESERT

119 "People would . . . at night?' ": Allen int., Jan. 9, 1992.

119 "was really . . . miles.": Allen int., Jan. 9, 1992.

120 "just hated the language.": Gary Kildall int., Aug. 13, 1991.

121 "I don't . . . Mary Gates.": Bob O'Rear int., July 13, 1991.

121 The official . . . venerable PDP-

PAGE

10.: Memo from Bill Gates to "everyone," Mar. 13, 1978.

121 "I'd worry . . . behind bars!' '': Lubow int., July 18, 1991.

121 "Got arrested . . . so mad!'': Allen int., Jan. 9, 1991.

121 "People that . . . something wrong.": Gates int., Feb. 29, 1992.

121 "who thought . . . a Porsche.": Gates int. with Steve Ditlea, Aug. 27, 1987.

121–22 Hot dry . . . check it out.: Confidential int., Aug. 20, 1991.

122 "He'd say . . . stopped playing.": Allen int., Jan. 9, 1991.

122 "It wasn't . . . so much.": Wallace int., Apr. 2, 1991.

122 "I put . . . that way.": Ibid.

122 "You want . . . wrote it?" Courtney int., Aug. 30, 1991.

123 "We actually . . . Bill would.": Marla Wood int., May 21, 1991.

123 "I could . . . the weekend": Tandy Trower int., Aug. 12, 1991.

123 "He always . . . brain-damaged.": Wallace int., Apr. 2, 1991.

123 "He could . . . to him.": Confidential int., Oct. 1991.

123 "I had . . . free drinks": Lubow int., July 18, 1991.

124 "It was . . . company office": Confidential int., Apr. 1991.

124 "drug-based companies.": Wallace int., Apr. 2, 1991.

124 A spokeswoman . . . the project.: Computerworld, Aug. 14, 1978, p. 52.

124–25 By April . . . of cash.: Microsoft budget, Apr. 1, 1978–Apr. 1, 1979.

125 "being a retailer sucks.": Vern Raburn int., Mar. 15, 1991.

125 "And in . . . kill you.' '': Raburn int., Mar. 15, 1991.

126 In spring . . . New Mexico," Nishi replied.: Gates int., Aug. 29, 1991; InfoWorld, Aug. 29, 1983, p. 33.

PAGE

126 "For a . . . futuristic, energetic.": Gates int., Aug. 29, 1991.

126–27 As Bill . . . fifteen people.: Gates int., Aug. 29, 1991; Letwin, Inside OS/2, p. ix.

128 "He said . . . in Seattle.' '': Lubow int., July 18, 1991.

128 $1,355,665: "Microsoft Timeline," internal document circa May 1990, p. 8.

128 "I was . . . a hundred.": Wallace int., Apr. 2, 1991.

128 "I handed . . . normal speeding.": Gates int., Aug. 29, 1991.

10. WE SELL PROMISES

129 "gut bombs . . . dripping.": Marla Wood int., May 21, 1991.

130 "When I . . . fired me.": Steve Smith int., Apr. 29, 1991.

130 "We could . . . sold promises.": Ibid.

130 "bought everything": Gates int., Nov. 5, 1991.

130 "In a . . . than anybody.": Steve Smith int., Apr. 29, 1991.

130 "talking to . . . fire hose.": Ibid.

131 "Now, now . . . tickets.": Allen int., Jan. 9, 1991.

131 "An officer . . . I couldn't.": Gates int., Nov. 5, 1991.

131 "I always . . . young people.": Wall Street Journal, Aug. 27, 1986, p. 12.

131 "Kay was . . . the machine.": Confidential int., Aug. 1991.

131 "was the . . . into one.": Ibid.

131 "just kind . . . the marketplace.": Ibid.

131 The Japanese . . . the machine.: Ibid.

132 "We do . . . End Users.": Microsoft internal memo from Bill Gates to "Everyone," Feb. 27, 1979.

133 Microsoft programming . . . of

Adventure?: Gordon Letwin int., Feb. 13, 1992.

134 "I argued . . . small amount.": Ibid.

134 "I was . . . real toy.": Raburn int., Mar. 15, 1991.

134 "Paul . . . this machine.' ": Ibid.

134 "He said . . . to me.' ": Ibid.

134 Gates would . . . been patented.: Gates int., Nov. 5, 1991.

135 Microsoft's Standalone . . . the table.: Tim Paterson int., Apr. 23, 1991.

136 Eventually Kay . . . the closet.: Gates int., Nov. 5, 1991.

136 Gates and . . . had expired.: Letwin int., Feb. 13, 1992.

136 It was . . . (FAT) scheme.: Paterson int., Apr. 23, 1991.

136 The initial . . . "background": Raburn int., Mar. 15, 1991.

136 "We went . . . would crash.": Ibid.

137 "Back then . . . and guises.": Neil Konzen int., Aug. 8, 1991.

137 "I can hit . . . my company!": Konzen, Microsoft videotape of Bill Gates's thirtieth birthday party, circa Oct. 28, 1985.

137 "We would . . . screwed me.": Konzen int., Aug. 8, 1991.

137–38 "The total . . . something working.": Raburn int., Mar. 15, 1991.

138 "He'd come . . . this card.": Ibid.

138 "was Bill's . . . we're showing.": Ibid.

138 "they used . . . that contract.": Ibid.

138 "sporadic business . . . suspend business.": Letter, Paul Gilbert to City of Tukwila, May 20, 1980.

138 Gates would . . . per year.: Gates int. with Ditlea, Aug. 27, 1987.

139 The year . . . to Apple.: Portia Isaacson int., Oct. 20, 1991.

139 "He flew . . . amazing thing": Mary Gates int., Aug. 5, 1991.

139 "We thought . . . about it.": Gates int., Nov. 5, 1991.

139 "I think . . . would go.": Mort Meyerson int., June 11, 1991.

139 "It's this . . . this building": Gates int., Aug. 29, 1991.

139 "He had . . . famous pictures.": Gates int., Jan. 18, 1992.

139 "this guy . . . special elevator.": Gates int., Aug. 29, 1991.

139 "If I . . . you sell?": Gates int., Jan. 18, 1992.

139 "There was . . . was doing.": Ross Perot int., Sept. 17, 1991.

139 "I should . . . needle him.": Ibid.

139 "I don't . . . your life.' ": Mary Gates int., Aug. 5, 1991.

139 "I sent . . . letter": Gates int., Nov. 5, 1991.

140 The highlights . . . in Osaka.: Allen int., Jan. 9, 1992.

140 "one of . . . a gnat.": Paul Heckel int., July 10, 1991.

140 "combative and competitive.": Trip Hawkins, quoted in PC/ Computing, May 1991, p. 136.

140 He and . . . the problem.: Jim Edlin int., May 30, 1991.

141 The state . . . business expense.: Bob Metcalfe, quoted in PC/ Computing, May 1991, p. 138. Steve Ballmer, the board member in question, does not recall the incident.

141 "by the . . . than $20.": Home Bus Standard document, undated, circa 1980.

141 "a modular . . . of the future.": Ibid.

141 "Energy Conservation . . . Convenience.": Ibid.

141 An outfit . . . ultimately killed.: Bob Metcalfe int., July 9, 1991.

142 "It all . . . no mistakes.": Metcalfe int., July 9, 1991.

142 Under the . . . proposal stage: Microsell draft proposal, June 24, 1980.

143 When you . . . to him.:

Microsoft organization chart dated
Aug. 16, 1979.

143 "You're coming . . . right?":
Ballmer int., July 29, 1991.

143 "Ballmer comes . . . working
on him.": Gates int., Nov. 5,
1991.

143 "*Doo-Wah* . . . wants, Bill!":
Ibid.

144 Bill comes . . . tomorrow
anyway.": Marla Wood int., Feb.
3, 1992.

144 "It was . . . principle.": Ibid.

145 "I was . . . about it": Wallace
int., Apr. 24, 1991.

145 "It was . . . based on.":
Confidential int., Apr. 1991.

145 "to waltz . . . in triplicate"
Confidential int., Oct. 1991.

145 "because everybody . . . was
just something.": Alan Boyd int.,
Apr. 5, 1991.

145 "My God . . . the company?":
Doug Klunder int., May 3, 1991.

146 "How can . . . smart guy.":
Gates int., Jan. 18, 1992.

146 "crazy company": Gates int.,
Nov. 5, 1991.

146 "a little flaky": Ibid.

146 "Dare to . . . Never quit.":
Seattle Times, Sept. 29, 1985,
p. D1, quoting earlier *Seattle
Business Journal* interview.

146 "He and . . . our money.":
Gates int., Nov. 5, 1991.

146 "When I . . . were high tech.":
Gates int. with Ditlea, July 8,
1987.

146 "Anybody should . . . were
flaky.": Gates int., Nov. 5, 1991.

147 "Software houses . . . multiple
versions.": *Personal Computing,*
May-June 1977, p. 38.

147 "The system . . . eighties.":
Microsoft Quarterly, fourth quarter
1980, p. 2.

147 "Microsoft is . . . software
crisis.": *Electronics,* Oct. 23, 1980,
p. 320.

148 "abundance of . . . XENIX
OS": *Microsoft Quarterly,* fourth
quarter 1980, p. 2.

11. PLAYING CHESS

149 Radio Shack . . . in Europe.:
Time, Mar. 2, 1981, p. 68.

149 (originally . . . "TOI"): *Byte,*
Apr. 1980, p. 115.

150 Their own . . . publicity shots.:
Larry Rojas int., Aug. 14, 1991.

150 Around the . . . its own.: Bill
Lowe int., Aug. 28, 1991.

150 "I said . . . a year.' ": Lowe
int., Aug. 15, 1991.

150 "wild ducks": Malik, *And
Tomorrow the World?* pp. 209–210.
Watson referred to a Kierkegaard
parable about the inability to make
tame ducks wild again. "At
IBM," he said, "we try not to
tame them." The term "wild
duck" instantly became part of
IBM's corporate culture.

151 "When he . . . ever known.":
Jack Sams int., Sept. 17, 1991.

151 "I was . . . suit-type guy.":
Ballmer int., Aug. 29, 1991.

151 "IBM also . . . initial
meeting.": Letter from Patrick M.
Harrington, IBM to William
Gates, Microsoft, Aug. 21, 1980.

151 "We're big . . . tell them.":
Ballmer int., Aug. 6, 1991.

152 "gave him . . . was needed":
Sams int., Sept. 17, 1991.

152 Sams was . . . these guys.:
Confidential int., Aug. 1991.

152 "We loved . . . our friend.":
Gates int., Nov. 26, 1991.

152–53 Lowe went . . . to do.: Lowe
int., Aug. 28, 1991.

153 "I'm sure . . . was
redundant.": Sams int., March
18, 1992.

153 "our fault . . . machine.":
Microtimes, Nov. 26, 1990, p. 62.

153 The 8088 . . . to work: Lew
Eggebrecht int., Aug. 15, 1991.

153 Charts dated . . . the 8088.:
David Bradley int., July 31, 1991.

153–54 "IBM Confidential information":
Letter from J. M. Snyder, IBM, to
William H. Gates, Microsoft, July
12, 1980.

PAGE

154 "IBM does . . . deemed
confidential.": Ibid.

154 This time . . . BASIC compiler.:
Mark Ursino int., Mar. 26, 1992;
Ballmer int., July 29, 1991.

154 "We were . . . software.":
Ursino int., Mar. 26, 1992.

154 follow-up letter . . . the
languages: Letter from Steve
Ballmer, Microsoft to Pat
Harrington, IBM, Aug. 26, 1980.

154–55 Gates first . . . Gary Kildall.:
Phil Nelson int., Sept. 17, 1991.

155 Gates told . . . arrange it.:
Gates int., Sept. 26, 1991; Ursino
int., Mar. 26, 1992; Ballmer int.,
July 29, 1991; Kildall int., Aug.
13, 1991.

155 "Gary went flying.": Freiberger
and Swaine, *Fire in the Valley,*
p. 272. "Instead of buying
airplanes and playing around like
some of our competitors, we've
rolled almost everything back into
the company," Gates told a
reporter for *Seattle Business Journal,*
Oct. 19, 1981, p. 6. As late as
1987, according to a confidential
document, Gates was still using
the phrase "Gary went flying" to
describe DR's lost opportunity.

155 At the Victorian . . . : Sources
regarding the meeting between
IBM and Digital Research include
Phil Nelson int., Sept. 17, 1991;
Jack Sams int., Sept. 17, 1991; G.
Gervaise Davis int., Dec. 6, 1991;
two confidential ints., Aug. 1991
and Sept. 1991. The version Gary
Kildall offered in an interview
Aug. 13, 1991, conformed to the
version reported in Levering,
Katz, and Moskowitz, *The
Computer Entrepreneurs,* p. 210, but
not to the recollections of any of
the other sources.

155 "not serve . . . the other.":
Letter from Patrick Harrington to
William Gates, July 21, 1980.

156 "My God . . . do now?": Sams
int., Sept. 17, 1991.

156 Seymour Rubinstein . . .

WordStar.: Confidential int., Aug.
1991.

157 They said . . . simultaneous
meetings.: *PC Magazine,* vol. 1,
no. 1, undated, circa Jan. 1982,
p. 18.

157 "developing . . . system.":
Letter from Ballmer to
Harrington, Aug. 26, 1980.

157 Quick and Dirty Operating
System.: Tim Paterson int., Apr.
23, 1991.

157–58 QDOS wasn't . . . CP/M
clone: Paterson int., Apr. 23,
1991; Pat Opalka int., March 21,
1992.

158 SPECIAL NOTE: . . . 86-DOS.:
86-DOS User's Manual, p. 3.

158 Paterson wrote . . . operating
system.: Letter from Bob O'Rear
to Tim Paterson, Aug. 5, 1980.

158 Seattle Computer's . . .
Microsoft's languages.: Letter
from Rod Brock to Paul Allen,
Aug. 13, 1980.

158 Over the . . . capabilities.: Lew
Eggebrecht int., Aug. 15, 1991.

159 "Every time . . . free advice.":
Sandy Meade int., Dec. 13, 1991.

159 "I'm putting . . . of software.":
Eggebrecht int., Aug. 15, 1991.

159 Their secret . . . software
designs.: Eggebrecht int., Aug.
15, 1991; Gates int., Nov. 5,
1991.

160 Frustrated by . . . talking
about.: Sams int., Sept. 17, 1991.

160 "Gotta do . . . do it!": Gates
int., Nov. 26, 1991; Ballmer int.,
Aug. 6, 1991; Allen int., Jan. 9,
1991.

160 "work in . . . several weeks.":
Letter from Rod Brock to Paul
Allen, Sept. 24, 1980.

161 Late the . . . the sun.: Bob
O'Rear int., July 13, 1991.

161 Upon arriving . . . the
president.: Bob O'Rear int., July
13, 1991; Ballmer int., Aug. 6,
1991.

161 "kid that . . . is this?' ": Edwin
Kiser int., Nov. 29, 1991.

PAGE

161   "If you . . . dead body.": Ibid.
162   "Oh, that's . . . Gates's son":
      Mary Gates int., Aug. 5, 1991.
162   "You take . . . I guess.": Ibid.
162   But negotiations . . . at Boca.:
      Ballmer int., Aug. 6, 1991;
      Ballmer deposition, Seattle
      Computer Products Inc. v.
      Microsoft Corp., Aug. 14, 1986.
162   In Boca . . . pay royalties.: Sams
      int., Sept. 17, 1991.
162   "I never . . . big business.":
      Meade int., Aug. 1, 1991.
162   Sources close . . . that BASIC.:
      Ibid.; Ursino int., Mar. 26, 1992.
162   "publish . . . Agreement.":
      Agreement between IBM and
      Microsoft, Nov. 6, 1980, p. 13.
163   Finally there . . . IBM's
      responsibility.: Ibid.
163   "Gates went . . . don't
      know.' ": Meade int., Aug. 1,
      1991.
163   In the . . . a shave.: Kiser int.,
      Nov. 29, 1991.
163   In his . . . inflated "President.":
      Agreement between IBM and
      Microsoft, Nov. 6, 1980, p. 30.
163   "Well, Steve . . . work.": Kiser
      int., Nov. 29, 1991.
163   "I felt . . . the door.": Ibid.

12. DOS CAPITAL

164   "We didn't . . . football
      program.": David Marquardt int.,
      Jan. 22, 1992.
165   "Pretend you . . . add value.":
      Gates int., Nov. 5, 1991.
165   As a . . . computer repairman.:
      Lammers, Programmers at Work,
      p. 7; Charles Simonyi int., Aug.
      15, 1991.
165   "perhaps the . . . the 1970s":
      Seybold Report, Apr. 27, 1981,
      p. 14.
165   "what you . . . night,
      Geraldine.: Charles Simonyi int.,
      Aug. 15, 1991.
165   The Alto's . . . Ethernet.:

PAGE

      Seybold Report, Apr. 27, 1981,
      p. 15.
166   The dream . . . be-all
      metamedium.: Kay,
      "Microelectronics and the
      Personal Computer," Scientific
      American, Sept. 1977, pp. 210–
      244; Kay and Goldberg, "Personal
      Dynamic Media," Computer, Mar.
      1977, pp. 31–41; Kay, The
      Reactive Engine, describes an earlier
      conceptual machine called FLEX.
166   the Cub . . . capabilities:
      Simonyi int., Aug. 15, 1991.
166   "Let's go . . . for it.": Ibid.
166   "The honest . . . a company":
      Bob Belleville int., Mar. 13,
      1992.
166   "It was . . . to nothing.":
      Simonyi int., Aug. 20, 1991.
166   "this crazy guy in Seattle":
      Simonyi int., Aug. 15, 1991.
166   "Bill has to see this!": Ibid.
167   We were . . . like anything!:
      Ibid.
167   "The impression . . .
      exponential thing.": Ibid.
167   In mid-November . . . Apple
      IV.: Ibid.
167   "the messenger . . . PARC
      virus.": Rosen Electronics Letter,
      Oct. 7, 1982, p. 8.
167   "He knew . . . was
      impressed.": Simonyi int., Aug.
      15, 1991.
168   "Bill, give . . . IBM PC.: Ibid.
168   "Paul believed . . . IBM
      project,": Bob O'Rear int., July
      13, 1991.
168   "IBM is schedule-driven.": Mark
      Mackaman int., June 12, 1991.
168   IBM's Dave . . . the hardware.:
      Bradley int., July 31, 1991.
168   "Clean it up, guys!": Confidential
      source.
168–69 Brock submitted . . . deliver 86-
      DOS.: Letter from Rod Brock to
      Paul Allen, Nov. 7, 1980.
169   But there . . . agreed to.: Letter
      from Rod Brock to Steve Ballmer,
      Dec. 12, 1980.
169   With the . . . as president.:

Agreement between Seattle Computer Products and Microsoft, Jan. 6, 1981.

169 The only . . . hung up.: Rod Brock int., May 22, 1991.

169 "it sometimes . . . our time.": Letter from Bob O'Rear to Pat Harrington, Jan. 19, 1981.

169 By February . . . as possible.: Letter from Bob O'Rear to Pat Harrington, Feb. 2, 1981.

169 On March . . . software delivery.: Letter from Steve Ballmer to Pat Harrington, Mar. 12, 1981.

170 As far . . . we were.: Courtney int., Sept. 11, 1991.

171 "random little grit": Konzen int., Aug. 8, 1991.

171 "Sunday afternoon . . . a donkey.' ": Ibid.

171 Parts of . . . appallingly flimsy.: Letter from Ballmer to Pat Harrington, Apr. 17, 1981.

171 kids like . . . see it: Konzen int., Aug. 8, 1991.

171 the delay . . . home.: Eggebrecht int., Aug. 15, 1991.

171 Yet on . . . more software.: Letter from Ballmer to Jerry Schultz, Apr. 17, 1981.

172 Old Retail . . . little closet.: Wallace int., Apr. 24, 1991.

172 "Freedom": Rojas int., Aug. 14, 1991.

172 HAL: Bob O'Rear int., July 13, 1991; Bob O'Rear deposition, Seattle Computer Products v. Microsoft, Oct. 17, 1986, p. 37.

172 In May . . . that too.: Letter from Bill Gates to Don Estridge, May 22, 1981.

172 By early . . . reasonably accurately.: InfoWorld, June 8, 1981, p. 1.

172 "its disk . . . DOS.": Electronics, June 16, 1981, p. 33.

173 Currie was . . . of it.: Eddie Currie int., July 23, 1991.

173 The hint . . . IBM.: G. Gervaise Davis int., Dec. 6, 1991.

173 What did they really want?: Dick Conklin int., Mar. 6, 1991.

173 "blackmailed into it.": InfoWorld, Oct. 5, 1981, p. 38.

174 "You would . . . the mat.": Letter from Paul Allen to Rod Brock, June 25, 1981.

174 "a substantial . . . price tag.": Letter from Rod Brock to Paul Allen, July 10, 1981.

174 "the $150,000 . . . the company": Steve Ballmer deposition, Seattle Computer Products v. Microsoft, Oct. 14, 1986, p. 61.

174 reportedly made . . . very year.: Money, July 1986, p. 56.

174 "At this . . . with it.": Ibid., p. 70.

174–75 "I went . . . was introduced.": Ibid., p. 76.

175 "purchasers of . . . enhancements": Agreement between Microsoft and Seattle Computer, July 27, 1981.

175 "Cash was . . . the license": Brock int., May 22, 1991.

175 "thought it was a fair deal.": Tim Paterson int., Apr. 23, 1991.

175 "Gates doesn't . . . bit different.' ": Fortune, June 29, 1981, p. 87.

175 "As slow . . . an impact.": Microsoft internal memo, Steve Ballmer to "Everyone," June 26, 1981.

176 Gates and . . . percent each.: Marquardt int., Mar. 25, 1992.

176 "My stock . . . for years": Ed Johns int., May 21, 1991.

176 "a lot . . . the overtime.": Confidential int., Feb. 1992.

176 "straighten the . . . people.": Gates int., Jan. 2, 1992.

176 "I said . . . hire people.": Ibid.

177 "Even Paul . . . do this?' ": Ballmer int., Aug. 6, 1991.

177 "I hire . . . every candidate.": Ibid.

177 "He wasn't . . . or not.": Mike Slade int., June 24, 1991.

PAGE

177   "It just . . . the pressure.":
Klunder int., May 3, 1991.

177   "about the . . . would accept":
Ibid.

177   "From the . . . you did.": Ibid.

177   "We hire little Bills.":
Confidential int., June 1991.

177–78   "We were . . . to motivate.":
Simonyi int., Aug. 20, 1991.

178   doctoral dissertation: Simonyi,
Meta-Programming.

178   One visitor . . . slide projector.:
Adrian King int., Feb. 7, 1992.

178   "That was . . . brilliant
products.": Raburn int., Mar. 15,
1991.

178   "I guess . . . and
development.": *Seattle Post-
Intelligencer*, July 19, 1981, p. D9.

178   "Paul always . . . way around.":
Confidential int., Oct. 1991.

178   "You'd see . . . wrung out.":
Raburn int., Mar. 15, 1991.

179   "all the . . . an hour.":
Courtney int., Sept. 11, 1991.

179   Bill was . . . got made.:
Marquardt int., Jan. 22, 1992.

179   "got tired . . . Bill
occasionally.": Ibid.

179   My theory . . . for him.: Ida
Cole int., June 11, 1991.

180   Traffic . . . unspecified.: King
County police precinct records.

180   But some . . . traffic school.:
Gates int., Feb. 29, 1992.

180   "There's this . . . highly
reduced.": Gates int., Nov. 5,
1991.

180   "They had . . . about it.":
Ballmer int., July 29, 1991.

180   "offended": John Katsaros int.,
Sept. 12, 1991.

13. THE REALITY DISTORTION FIELD

181   "a technological . . . technology
guy.": Cole int., June 11, 1991.

182   "Welcome, IBM. . . . to the
world": *Wall Street Journal*, Aug.
24, 1981, p. 7.

182   "We were . . . death warrant.":

Randy Wigginton int., Sept. 4,
1991.

182   Back in . . . desktops.: Rose,
West of Eden, pp. 48–52.

183   "28 percent of . . . the
father.": *Time*, Jan. 3, 1983,
p. 27.

183   "He said . . . heard of ": Jef
Raskin int., Aug. 21, 1991.

183   Gates, Jobs . . . June 5.:
"Microsoft Timeline," internal
document, circa May 1990, p. 13.

184   "I should . . . business sooner":
Gates int., Feb. 29, 1992.

184   "With two . . . in BASIC.":
Raburn int., Mar. 25, 1992.

184   "Basic Strategy: . . . on it.":
Memo from Paul Heckel to Bill
Gates re "Planner," May 8, 1980.

184   "was all junk": Simonyi int.,
Aug. 20, 1991.

184   "very reluctant . . . cleaning
house.": Ibid.

184   "the revenue bomb.": Simonyi
int., Aug. 15, 1991.

185   "We invest . . . the money.":
Klunder int., May 3, 1991.

186   "At one . . . War II.": Simonyi
int., Aug. 15, 1991.

186   "information appliance" . . .
from Raskin.: Jef Raskin int.,
Aug. 21, 1991.

186   "We were . . . dying for.": Jeff
Harbers int., July 17, 1991.

186   "We thought . . . distortion
field.": Harbers int., July 17,
1991.

187   Bill Gates . . . to explain.: Andy
Hertzfeld int., Aug. 12, 1991.

187   The circuitry . . . entire
Macintosh.: Martin Haeberli int.,
Aug. 27, 1991.

187   There was . . . Bill Gates.:
Andy Hertzfeld int., Aug. 12,
1991.

187–88   Aboard a . . . identical cases.:
Harbers int., July 17, 1991.

188   "It was . . . the stuff.": Ibid.

188   "People would . . . just
smile.": Harbers int., Mar. 20,
1992.

188   "undertake in . . . by Apple.":

Agreement between Apple and
Microsoft, Jan. 22, 1982.

189 "Software today . . . a
computer." Bill Gates, "Next-
Generation Software," *Rosen
Research Personal Computer Forum
Proceedings,* May 1981, pp. 43–53.

189 "The hourglass . . . time.": Bill
Gates, "The New Shape of
Software," *Rosen Research Personal
Computer Forum Proceedings,* Jan.
1983, p. 166.

14. A COMPETITIVE PERSON

190 "On the . . . IBM
announcement.": *InfoWorld,* Sept.
14, 1981, p. 14.

190 "Next, a . . . serious
business.": *New York Times,* Aug.
23, 1981, p. C1.

191 I think . . . integrated software.:
PC Magazine, vol. 1, no. 1,
undated, circa Jan. 1982, p. 19.

191 Hardware in . . . other
machines.: Ibid., p. 20.

191 "We're still . . . real tool.":
Ibid., p. 23.

192 He had . . . memory
management.: John Wharton int.,
Mar. 18, 1992.

192 "I'm not a competitive person":
InfoWorld, April 19, 1982, p. 23.

192 In a New York . . . (SB-86).:
InfoWorld, Nov. 2, 1981, p. 9;
Electronics, Oct. 6, 1981, p. 37.

193 "the CP/M record player": Portia
Isaacson and Egil Juliussen, *IBM's
Billion Dollar Baby* (Richardson,
TX: Future Computing, 1981);
Portia Isaacson int., Oct. 20,
1991.

193 "CP/M-86 will . . . personal
computer.": *Computer Systems
News,* Oct. 26–Nov. 2, 1981,
p. 56.

193 "16-bit . . . market.": *Microsoft
Quarterly,* first quarter 1981, p. 3.

193 "what CP/M lacks": Interoffice
memo from Bill Gates to
"Everybody," Mar. 2, 1982.

193 The sales . . . your bet?:
Katsaros int., Sept. 12, 1991.

194 jumping ability.: Jeff Raikes,
Microsoft videotape of Gates's
thirtieth birthday party, circa Oct.
28, 1985.

194 "I actually . . . brief
intermission.": Gates int., Nov.
26, 1991.

194 Gates would . . . the porcelain.:
Confidential int., May 1991.

194 "a healthy . . . IBM Personal
Computer": *InfoWorld,* Dec. 14,
1981, p. 10.

194 "for those . . . Monday
morning.": "Move to New
Building," Interoffice memo,
Craig Watjen to All Employees,
Nov. 12, 1981.

195 By April . . . phone system.:
Microsoft newsletter, Apr. 23,
1982, p. 2.

195 "Once someone . . . go
anywhere": Confidential int., June
1991.

195–96 The Bozo . . . off again.: Slade
int., July 24, 1991.

196 "There were . . . middle
ground": Ibid.

196 "We hire smart guys.": Gates
testimony, Alalamiah Electronics
Co. v. Microsoft, Dec. 26, 1991.

196 And Bill . . . five years.: *Seattle
Business Journal,* Oct. 19, 1981,
p. 6.

15. NATURAL MONOPOLY

197 "was giving . . . things were.":
Ballmer int., Aug. 6, 1991.

198 "a populist president.":
Confidential int., Apr. 1991.

198 "He had . . . about it": Pam
Edstrom int., Sept. 30, 1991.

198 "Bill doesn't . . . than twice.":
Simonyi int., Aug. 20, 1991.

199 "He'd throw . . . other
people.": Confidential int., May
1991.

199 "[He] couldn't . . . good
match": Gates int., Dec. 2, 1991.

PAGE

199   "Go for it!": Estelle Mathers int., Aug. 21, 1991.

199   In her . . . British "super.": Ibid.

199–200   To Mathers . . . become routine.: Ibid.

200   "Bill is . . . for you.": Ibid.

200   "Can you . . . long now.": Ibid.

200   "In some . . . we've remained.": Gates int., *Seattle Times* files, undated, circa 1982.

200   "We spend . . . to Paul.": Ibid.

200   "That scares me": Alan Boyd int., May 20, 1991.

201   "public broadside": *InfoWorld,* Apr. 12, 1982, p. 1.

201   "It is . . . against ourselves": *InfoWorld,* Apr. 12, 1982, p. 1.

201   "Gates claimed . . . the code": *InfoWorld,* Apr. 12, 1982, p. 7.

201   "litigate a . . . the market.": Confidential int., Aug. 21, 1991.

201   "My personal . . . really carefully.": *InfoWorld,* Apr. 26, 1982, p. 9.

201   "Microsoft currently . . . from Japan.": *Microsoft Quarterly,* first quarter 1982, p. 4.

201   In fact . . . American deals.: Seattle Computer v. Microsoft, defendant's responses to interrogatories, pp. 26–28.

201   "Easy Conversion . . . to 8086": Microsoft MS-DOS sales brochure, circa 1982.

201   "the value . . . vastly overrated.": *Microsoft Quarterly,* first quarter 1982, p. 3.

201–2   Yet another . . . delete them.: *Microsoft Quarterly,* second quarter 1982, p. 4.

202   "Why do . . . sell into.": Bill Gates, "Next-Generation Software," *Rosen Research Personal Computer Forum Proceedings,* May 1981, pp. 48–53.

202   "I really . . . that product.": Ibid., p. 54.

203   "We wanted . . . compatible machine.": Gates int., Nov. 26, 1991.

203   On a . . . DOS deal.: Peter Dyer int., Aug. 8, 1991.

203   "Here's some . . . is great.": Gates int., Nov. 26, 1991.

203   In order . . . compatibility loop.: Gary Stimac int., Mar. 16, 1992.

203   "Bill has . . . it back.": Ibid.

204   When Dyer . . . their case.: Peter Dyer, Aug. 8, 1991.

204   "You're going to torpedo us.": Barry James Folsom int., Sept. 13, 1991.

204   "I told . . . went nonlinear.": Ibid.

205   "I think . . . to Rainbow.: Ibid.; Rifkin and Harrar, *The Ultimate Entrepreneur,* pp. 211–212.

205   The credibility . . . by 10.: *New York Times,* Apr. 5, 1982, p. 1.

206   "You're going . . . 2.0 *when?*": Bradley int., July 31, 1991.

206   "Bill and . . . and screaming.": Mark Zbikowski int., Feb. 26, 1992.

206   "There was . . . of BASIC": Gates int., Jan. 2, 1992.

206   "Did you . . . Come back!' ": Courtney int., Sept. 11, 1991.

207   "It didn't . . . doing stuff.": Ibid.

207   "I understand . . . seen before.": Ibid.

207–8   "Hand Top . . . Control": Memo, Kay Nishi to Bill Gates, July 18, 1979.

208   "was not enthused about": Gates int., Nov. 26, 1991.

208   Settling in . . . together somehow.: Sam Furukawa int., Dec. 11, 1991; *Wall Street Journal,* Aug. 27, 1986, p. 1.

208   Gates took . . . the idea.: Jon Shirley int., Oct. 31, 1991.

209   The programmers . . . rudimentary one.: Sam Furukawa int., Dec. 11, 1991.

209   "the incredible madman": Raleigh Roark int., Aug. 26, 1991.

210   "just did . . . business plan": Scott Oki int., Feb. 19, 1991.

PAGE

210 "Steve and . . . myself into?":
Ibid.

210 "How effective . . . eventually
be.": Microsoft internal memo
from Jim Towne, Sept. 27, 1982.

210 "Go conquer the world.": Shirley
int., Oct. 31, 1991.

210 The first . . . Microsoft itself.:
Bernard Vergnes int., Sept. 24,
1991.

211 "There was . . . them stuff.":
Gates int., Nov. 5, 1991.

211 "Literally, we . . . up
products.": Oki int., Feb. 19,
1992.

211 "We danced. . . . some more.":
Ibid.

211 "It was . . . so exhausted.":
Confidential int., May 1991.

211–12 "started feeling . . . hours
straight.": Allen int., Jan. 9,
1992.

212 "I worked . . . keep going.":
Ibid.

212 "think about . . . do before.":
Ibid.

212 I think . . . was miserable.: Jill
Bennett int., Sept. 30, 1991.

212 "I hope . . . paid up": Heidi
Roizen int., June 27, 1991.

212 "there's nothing . . . to Bill.":
Wallace int., Apr. 2, 1991.

213 They come . . . of time.:
Confidential int., Apr. 1991.

213 "Gates is . . . momentum":
Seattle Business Journal, undated
clipping circa 1984.

213 Time . . . personal computer.:
Time, Jan. 3, 1983, pp. 12–39.

16. THE SMART GUYS

214 "It's better . . . the navy":
Rose, West of Eden, p. 56.

215 "It was . . . everything.":
Simonyi int., Aug. 18, 1991.

215 "We helped . . . technical
stuff.": Konzen int., Aug. 8,
1991.

215 Microsoft programmers . . . the

PAGE

screen.: Harbers int., July 17,
1991; Konzen int., Aug. 8, 1991.

215 According to . . . the Mac.:
Hertzfeld int., Aug. 12, 1991.

215 "were the . . . as possible.":
Mike Boich int., Aug. 21, 1991.

216 On Valentine's . . . Window
manager.: Seattle Times, Feb. 14,
1982, p. 1.

216 "device-independent . . .
support": Personal Computing, May-
June 1977, p. 38.

216 Ironically . . . not to bother.:
Boich int., Aug. 21, 1991.

216 "He came . . . see this!' ":
Confidential int., May 1991.

216 he called . . . flight down.:
Simonyi int., Mar. 23, 1992.

217 "metaphor of . . . the user.":
InfoWorld, Dec. 6, 1982, p. 7.

217 Kapor had . . . fatal bug.: Gates
int., Nov. 5, 1991; Mitchell
Kapor int., Feb. 20, 1992.

218 Industry consultant . . . by
Sears.: Isaacson int., Oct. 20,
1991.

218 "sort of . . . his chair.":
Folsom int., Sept. 13, 1991.

220 "Bill called . . . for comfort.":
Confidential int., May 1991.

221 "Mac knockoffs.": Konzen int.,
Aug. 8, 1991.

221 "smoke-and-mirrors": Oki int.,
Feb. 19, 1992; Leo Nikora int.,
May 17, 1991; Mackaman int.,
June 12, 1991.

221 "what the . . . all computers.":
Bill Gates, "The Future of
Software Design: Key Issues Facing
Today's Software Developers,"
Microsoft press release, May 2,
1983, p. 8.

221 "The revolution . . . is soft.":
Ibid., p. 12.

222 "Our engineers . . . little
bigger.": Roark int., Aug. 26,
1991.

222 "Our engineers . . . this
problem.": Microsoft Mouse
Programmer's Reference, p. 6.

222 "It's really . . . much power.":
Roark int., Aug. 26, 1991.

PAGE

222 MicroPro had . . . $5 million.:
Infoworld, Apr. 2, 1984, p. 80.

223 "The bandwidth . . . just
tremendous.": Simonyi int., Mar.
23, 1992.

224 "Steve would . . . at
Microsoft.' ": Mike Murray int.,
Sept. 17, 1991.

224 "I could . . . he was.": Ibid.

224 "and said . . . with me?":
Belleville int., Mar. 13, 1992.

224 "They wouldn't . . . really
doing.' ": Murray int., Sept. 17,
1991.

224 "I wouldn't . . . was
growing.": Belleville int., Mar.
13, 1992.

224 "bet the . . . the Macintosh.":
Murray int., Sept. 17, 1991.

224 "Steve had . . . competitive
advantage?": Ibid.

225 "It just . . . to do.": Ibid.

225 "You guys . . . we do?": Ibid.

225 "It's not . . . the Jobses.":
Boich int., Aug. 21, 1991.

225 "No, Steve . . . TV set!' ":
Ibid. Gates remembered it as:
"You break in first to steal the
TV and I go back and get the rest
of the stuff." Gates int., Dec. 2,
1991.

225 "was very . . . you up":
Folsom int., Sept. 13, 1991.

226 "Magic." Doug Dayton int., Apr.
29, 1991.

226 "There was . . . on this": Paul
Grayson int., Oct. 23, 1991.

227 I kept . . . do it.: Confidential
int., May 1991.

227 "wanted us . . . weren't
right.": Folsom int., Sept. 13,
1991.

227 "When VisiOn . . . the
agreement.: Nelson int., Sept. 17,
1991.

227 "a Chinese warlord.": *Fortune*,
Jan. 23, 1984, p. 84.

227 "I wouldn't . . . to win.":
Confidential int., May 1991.

227 We had . . . the list.: Ibid.

228 "Bill had . . . of view.":
Hertzfeld int., Aug. 12, 1991.

PAGE

228 "Bill didn't . . . ever detected."
Belleville int., Mar. 13, 1992.

228 "I'll tell . . . be there.": Perot
int., Sept. 17, 1991.

228 "Whenever . . . ever sell?' ":
Gates int., Dec. 2, 1991.

229 Companies could . . . on
volume.: Microsoft confidential
internal OEM price list, Mar. 30,
1984.

229 "Microsoft to . . . office
market": *Microsoft Quarterly*, third
quarter 1983, p. 8.

230 "as a . . . savior.": Gates int.,
Dec. 2, 1991.

230 "right down to the wastebaskets":
Seattle *Weekly*, Oct. 26, 1983,
p. 23.

230 "must set . . . publishing
business": *Microsoft Quarterly*,
fourth quarter 1983, p. 5.

230 "pitched me . . . the book.":
Cary Lu int., Apr. 17, 1991.

230–31 "The CMERGE . . . long-term
view.": Internal memo, "The
Microsoft CMERGE Project: A
summary," undated, circa 1980,
p. 4.

231 "the Company . . . desperate
situation.": Internal memo, Bill
Gates to all, May 9, 1983.

231 "We have . . . their
cooperation.": Ibid.

232 "He laughed . . . '32-bit' ":
Bennett, letter to author, Aug. 9,
1991.

232 "We even . . . little alike":
Ibid.

232 "I think . . . 'the' group.":
Ibid.

232 "a huge . . . gets stuck?":
Bennett int., Sept. 30, 1991.

232 "He feels . . . lose him.":
Bennett int., Sept. 10, 1991.

232 "He doesn't . . . eat right.":
Ibid.

232 "He would . . . $2,000 cash.":
Ibid.

232 "He's just . . . dispute that.":
Ibid.

232 "the absent-minded professor.":

PAGE

Bennett, letter to author, Aug. 9, 1991.

232–33 The money . . . Andy Evans.: Gates int., Nov. 5, 1991.

233 There had . . . from Microsoft headquarters.: Bennett int., Sept. 30, 1991.

233 "Estelle, which . . . go to?": Mathers int., Aug. 21, 1991.

233 The resourceful . . . their contents.: Bennett int., Sept. 30, 1991.

233 "always after him": Bennett int., Jan. 2, 1992.

17. THE SOFTWARE FACTORY

234 "real": Shirley int., Oct. 31, 1991.

235 "It was . . . the fire.": Shirley int., Oct. 31, 1991.

235 "I can't . . . the counter.": Marquardt int., Jan. 22, 1992.

236 Steve Ballmer . . . loose cannon: Shirley int., Jan. 22, 1992.

236 When Shirley . . . two employees.: Ibid.

236 The warehouse . . . expensive vendors.: Mark Rolsing int., June 13, 1991.

237 The day . . . the warehouse.: Ibid.

237 Microsoft's clear . . . of salmon.: Ibid.

237 Inventory maintenance? . . . capacious quarters.: Ibid.

237 "resulted in . . . major way.": Shirley int., Oct. 31, 1991.

237 "has told . . . for that.": Ibid.

237 "If you . . . ice cube": Cole int., June 11, 1991.

238 "piles on . . . of 1982.": Marquardt int., Jan. 22, 1992.

238 "You know . . . moisturizers.": Rowland Hanson int., May 30, 1991.

238 "Well . . . doing that.": Ibid.

238 "NFW. . . . to something.": Ibid.

238 "more work . . . was worth.": Sculley, Odyssey, p. 65.

PAGE

238 "You're going . . . Steve Jobs?": Ibid., p. 61.

239 "Do you . . . the world?": Ibid., p. 90.

239 "designed the . . . to think.": Wall Street Journal, Dec. 23, 1983, p. 11.

240 "ultimate environment . . . heard of ": Scott McGregor int., Sept. 3, 1991.

240 "that this . . . all this.": Ibid.

240 "He had . . . windowing environment.": Ibid.

241 "paper machines and phantom computers.": Sobel, IBM: Colossus in Transition, p. 246.

241 "basically announced . . . it yet.": McGregor int., Sept. 3, 1991.

241 "Microsoft Windows . . . this time.": Microsoft press release, "Microsoft Windows: Questions and Answers," Nov. 10, 1983, p. 9.

241 Microsoft was . . . deals impractical.: Microsoft confidential internal OEM price list, Mar. 30, 1984.

241 Lotus, VisiCorp . . . had not.: PC Week, Nov. 29, 1983, p. 73.

242 An early-deadline . . . lower case.: Popular Computing, Dec. 1983, p. 142.

242 Gates told . . . of PCs.: PC Week, Nov. 29, 1983, p. 73.

242 "Microsoft is . . . for president.": Ibid., p. 73.

242 "You could sort of hear".: Edstrom int., Sept. 30, 1991.

242 "You couldn't . . . executive recalled.: Confidential int., May 1991.

242 "sitting there . . . to do.": Ibid.

242 "It was . . . any more.' ": Ibid.

242–43 "The chicks love it!": Confidential int., Apr. 1991.

243 "I want to get laid!": Betsy Kosheff int., Sept. 24, 1991; confirmed by confidential int., Mar. 1992.

18. GROWING PANES

244   "commercializing": Ann Winblad
      int., Mar. 19, 1992.

245   "VisiOn is . . . release it.":
      Byte, Apr. 1986, p. 9.

245   "Microsoft has . . . the
      world.": Raburn int., July 31,
      1991.

245   "Barring a . . . intended
      users.": Byte, Dec. 1983, p. 54.

245   "They pimped . . . and
      BASIC": Gates int., Nov. 26,
      1991.

245   "pretty nice . . . ambitious
      ideas": Gates int. with Ditlea,
      Aug. 27, 1987.

246   "an incredibly fast amount of
      time": Harbers int., July 17,
      1991.

246   "He never . . . always
      pushing.": Rolling Stone, Mar. 4,
      1984, p. 41.

246   "mutual convenience.":
      Agreement between Microsoft and
      Apple, Jan. 15, 1984.

246   "bright little . . . to the
      family": Rose, West of Eden,
      p. 155.

247   Bill Gates . . . long-suffering
      mom.: Macworld, Mar./Apr. 1984,
      p. 43.

247   Bill says . . . that moment.:
      Harbers int., July 17, 1991.

247   Emcee Steve . . . went crazy.:
      Ibid.

247   "wanted to . . . a Mac.":
      Kapor int., Feb. 20, 1992.

248   "sell, lease . . . competitive":
      Agreement between Microsoft and
      Apple, Jan. 22, 1982, p. 5.

248   "Steve Ballmer . . . start
      testing.": Harbers int., July 17,
      1991.

249   "didn't believe . . . three
      months.": Ibid.

249   "All you . . . would crash.":
      Ibid.

249   "He just . . . was it.": Ibid.

249   "The great . . . did
      understand.": Ibid.

250   "Jobs was . . . in India.": Slade
      int., June 24, 1991.

250   "Dropping out . . . from
      software": People, Dec. 26–Jan. 2,
      1984, p. 37.

250   "Microsoft's Drive to Dominate
      Software": Fortune, Jan. 23, 1984,
      p. 82.

250   "You are . . . on it.":
      "Today," Mar. 26, 1984.

250–51 Huddled around . . . sardonic
      laughter.: Jeff Angus int., June
      26, 1991.

251   Time cover story: Time, Apr. 16,
      1984, pp. 62–63.

251   "Best of the New Generation.":
      Esquire, Dec. 1984, p. 284.

251   "They are . . . come along!":
      PC Magazine, May 14, 1985,
      p. 51.

251   "Microsoft Aims . . . of
      Software.": Micro Market World,
      Feb. 20, 1984, p. 49.

251   "We want . . . like IBM.":
      Computer News Weekly, Apr. 9,
      1984, unpaged clipping.

251   Softer software: For a brief period
      it was a consistent theme with
      Gates. "It's Bill Gates' favorite
      expression—'softer software,' "
      wrote Information Age (Oct. 1984,
      p. 44). In Metropolitan Home (July
      1985, pp. 24–25), Gates said, "I
      think that in a couple years you'll
      be able to buy a software package
      that will 'watch' the different
      types of actions you do, learn
      them and anticipate your
      needs. . . . This is what I call
      softer software. It's soft in the
      sense that it's flexible, like a
      human." In Computerworld (July
      22, 1985, p. ID/12), he added
      "In softer software, the fact that
      you've done something before
      allows you to refer back and
      explain how you want to do things
      differently in terms of high-level
      concepts."

251   In 1984 . . . programmers.:
      Microsoft video of Bill Gates,
      "Future of Software," talk at

Apple Computer, undated, circa 1984.

251 "to create . . . every home.": Microsoft Annual Report, 1986, p. 14.

252 "If you've . . . your message.": Gates int., Jan. 18, 1992.

252 "Who would . . . Ramada Inn?": Lubow int., July 18, 1991.

252 Gates trudged . . . a room?: Mathers int., Aug. 21, 1991.

252 "This tragedy . . . with ambition.": Seattle Times, Nov. 16, 1985, p. A14.

252 "seven-hour turnarounds": Bennett, letter to author, Aug. 9, 1991.

253 "I would . . . that's true.": Winblad Int., July 23, 1991.

253 "I said . . . ever met.' ": Ibid.

253 "heavyweight in the gray matter": Frank Gaudette int., Aug. 28, 1991.

253 "lackluster . . . nonusable COBOL.": Winblad int., July 23, 1991.

253 They would . . . the theater.: Kristi Gates int., Feb. 22, 1992.

254 he'd rather . . . in technology.: Nikora int., May 17, 1992.

254 "great white saviors": Ibid.

254 He told . . . of Microsoft.: Letwin int., Mar. 25, 1992.

254 Heuristic reasoning . . . the final.: Byte, Dec. 1983, p. 51.

254 "We did . . . at PARC.": Chris Peters int., Mar. 17, 1992.

255 "He did . . . did it.": Konzen int., Aug. 8, 1991.

255 "Bill didn't . . . couple weekends.": McGregor int., Sept. 3, 1991.

255 "a little shitbox 8088": Konzen int., Aug. 8, 1991.

255 "Bill really . . . thing.": Ibid.

255–56 My personal . . . the PC.": Nikora int., May 17, 1991.

256 postponed . . . to May.: Computer Systems News, June 4, 1984, p. 87.

256 Shirley baldly . . . Windows: InfoWorld, June 29, 1984, p. 9.

256 In June . . . for September.: Micro Software Today, July 1984, p. 8.

256 "You told . . . this change.": McGregor int., Sept. 3, 1991.

256–57 Microsoft believes . . . as possible.: Internal memo from Steve Ballmer and Bill Gates to distribution list, June 28, 1984.

257 "the standard . . . the Mac.": Ibid.

257 "it goes . . . of 1984.": Ibid.

257 having repeated . . . play music.: Slade int., June 23, 1991.

257 "We will . . . and BASIC.": Internal memo from Ballmer and Gates, June 28, 1984.

258 "He would . . . this stuff?' ": Prusky int., Feb. 5, 1992.

258 With Doug . . . or white.: Confidential int., Mar. 1991.

258 "just the . . . wanderlust hitting.": Klunder int., May 3, 1991.

258 "sweeteners": Ibid.

258 "skepticism . . . seven-year voyage.": Jabe Blumenthal int., Feb. 13, 1992.

258 "my baby . . . intelligent recalc.": Klunder int., May 3, 1991.

259 Klunder demanded . . . his baby.: Ibid.

259 "You argue . . . random claims.": Ibid.

259 "Got a . . . back to work.": Ibid.

259 "I've been . . . the documentation?": Ibid.

259 "basically screamed . . . this crap?' ": Ibid.

259 "scared to take on Lotus": Ibid.

260 "was really . . . sweeteners": Ibid.

260 "I don't . . . that day.": Ibid.

260 "Well, Bill . . . "Oh, yeah": Ibid.

260 "We weren't . . . on promises.": Ibid.

260 "They had . . . sticking around.": Ibid.

261 "because Borland . . . Kahn

PAGE

International.": *Inc.*, Mar. 1,
1989, on-line, unpaged.

261 Once you . . . up again.:
Confidential int., Oct. 1991.

262 Gates was beside himself: Trower
int., Aug. 12, 1991.

262 Aside from . . . a loss.:
Microsoft internal product line
sales analysis, June 1984.

263 "PK"—Philippe Killer.:
Confidential int., July 1991.

263 "stick it to Philippe": Rob
Dickerson, memo for presentation
to Dec. 1986 meeting of
Microsoft's languages
group. Borland and Dickerson v.
Microsoft, Exhibit B, declaration
of Steven Snyder, Dec. 8, 1987.

263 "Kick Borland's butt!": Microsoft
Performance Review of Rob
Dickerson, 1987, May 4, 1987.
Exhibit A, Ibid.

263 "Delete Philippe": *PC Week*, Oct.
20, 1987, p. 42.

263 "I think . . . decent product.":
InfoWorld, Oct. 7, 1985, p. 3.

264 "The only . . . could do.":
Confidential int., May 1981.

264 "The next . . . absolutely
right!": Ibid.

264 Televideo guaranteed . . . was
reached.: License agreement for
MS-DOS dated Jan. 7, 1982
[actually 1983]; exhibit in
Microsoft v. Televideo Systems.

264 Pronto Computer . . . for $45.:
License agreement for MS-DOS
dated Apr. 1, 1983; license
agreement for MS-BASIC dated
Apr. 1, 1983; exhibits in
Microsoft v. Pronto Computer.

264 "That was . . . value was.":
Gates int., Dec. 2, 1991.

264 In order . . . per machine.:
License agreement for MS-DOS
dated Apr. 27, 1983; license
agreement for MS-BASIC
Interpreter/GW-BASIC dated May
15, 1983; exhibits in Microsoft v.
Seequa Computer.

264 Amqute's two-year . . . per
unit.: License agreement for MS-

PAGE

DOS dated Mar. 31, 1984; license
agreement for GW-BASIC
interpreter 2.01 dated July 30,
1984; exhibits in Microsoft v.
Amqute Computer.

264–65 "Each of . . . the market.":
Davidow, *Marketing High
Technology*, p. 159.

265 In fiscal . . . $19 million.:
Microsoft internal product line
sales analysis, June 1984.

265 Unlike Compaq . . . to repent.:
Corona Data Systems and
Handwell Corp. were two early
targets who settled with IBM out
of court. *InfoWorld*, Feb. 27, 1984,
p. 15.

265 "a TI-9900 programmer": *PC
Magazine*, July 10, 1984, p. 56.

266 "IBM at . . ." . . . "the
Aquarium.": Zbikowski int., Feb.
26, 1992.

266 "logical address . . . gone
away": *PC Magazine*, vol. 1, no. 1,
undated, circa Jan. 1982, p. 19.

266 Where the . . . same time.:
Gates int., Dec. 2, 1991; Letwin
int., Feb. 13, 1992; Ed Iacobucci
int., Feb. 20, 1992; Sams int.,
Mar. 18, 1992; Mike Maples int.,
Sept. 18, 1992.

266 "TopView . . . of existence.":
Gates int., Jan. 2, 1992.

266 "to come . . . think.
Seriously!' ": Gates int., Dec. 2,
1992.

267 Waiting in . . . as CP-DOS.:
Iacobucci int., Feb. 20, 1992;
Gates int., Dec. 2, 1991.

267 First would . . . of them.:
Iacobucci int., Feb. 20, 1992.

267 "just broke . . . them
anything.": Zbikowski int., Feb.
26, 1992.

267 "For a good . . . the
speakerphone.": Ibid.

267–68 "believed we . . . operating-
system standpoint.": *MS-DOS
Encyclopedia*, p. 39.

268 "the product . . . take it.' ":
Zbikowski int., Feb. 26, 1992.

268 "I left . . . home, left": Ibid.

PAGE

268   "Whatever it . . . do it.": Ibid.

268   "were just . . . the problem.' ": Ibid.

268   "We should . . . about networking": Gates int., Feb. 29, 1992.

269   "the most . . . years ago": Microsoft internal memo, Bill Gates to All Employees, Aug. 14, 1984.

269   "some people . . . user interface.": Ibid.

269   "TopView was . . . bankrupt.": Therese Myers int., Sept. 6, 1991.

270   "We thought . . . than not.": Maples int., Sept. 18, 1991.

270   "In the . . . the reaction.": Shirley int., Oct. 31, 1991.

19. ACTUALLY IN HELL

271   By 1984 . . . Weathervane Window.: *Seattle Post-Intelligencer,* Dec. 4, 1984, p. B5.

271   On August . . . about it.: Internal memo, Jon Shirley to All Employees, Aug. 14, 1984.

271   "stop to . . . mail-reading overhead.": Microsoft *MicroNews,* Apr. 6, 1984, p. 1.

272   "techie nerd . . . in finance": Frank Gaudette int., Aug. 28, 1991.

272   "As soon . . . design issues.": Internal memo, Jon Shirley to All Employees, Aug. 7, 1984.

272   "technical . . . cheerleader.": McGregor int., Sept. 3, 1991.

273   "You don't . . . McGregor's shorts.": Ballmer int., Aug. 6, 1991.

273   "a piece . . . in hell.": Konzen int., Aug. 8, 1992.

273   "felt kind . . . should change.": Ibid.

273   "Bill was . . . do that.": Ibid.

273   "Bill, this . . . good job.' ": Ibid.

274   "And it . . . like twenty.": Ibid.

274   "Windows at . . . fix it.": Ibid.

274   "The internal . . . carried across.": Belleville int., Mar. 13, 1992.

274   "extremely Mac-like . . . in documentation.": *Micro Software Today,* July 1984, p. 7.

274   "We set . . . 8088 processor.": *PC Week,* Oct. 23, 1984, p. 1.

274   "[Windows is] . . . over haste.": *Bellevue Journal American,* Nov. 16, 1984, p. D1.

274   "We announced . . . lead time.": *InfoWorld,* Nov. 19, 1984, p. 18.

274   "There You . . . some more.": Ibid., p. 5.

274   a cartoon . . . as Ballmer.: McGregor int., Sept. 3, 1991.

274   "We were . . . we thought.": Taucher int., Aug. 29, 1991.

275   "this confrontational thing": Nikora int., May 17, 1991.

275   "Well, God . . . the company": Trower int., Aug. 2, 1991.

275   "This is . . . death project.": Trower int., Aug. 2, 1991.

275   Things had . . . and Word.: Harbers int., July 17, 1991; Slade int., June 24, 1991.

275   Program code . . . building nuts.: Simonyi int., Aug. 20, 1991.

276   "go 'Oh . . . really good.' ": Gates int., Dec. 2, 1991.

276   "We were . . . terrified!": Slade int., June 24, 1991.

276   "God, this . . . is bad": Gates int., Dec. 2, 1991.

276   Jeff Harbers . . . called Switcher.: Hertzfeld int., Aug. 12, 1991; Harbers int., Mar. 20, 1982.

276   "I felt . . . the program.": Hertzfeld int., Aug. 12, 1992.

277   A settlement . . . by Microsoft.: Slade int., June 24, 1991.

277   "a long . . . meeting": Ibid.

277   "just draggin'." . . . to know": Ibid.

277   no one . . . was doing.: Ibid.

277   "I'm totally . . . to

PAGE

Microsoft.' ' ": Klunder int., May
3, 1991.

278 "I originally . . . ship Excel.":
Ibid.

278 "lettuce pickers.": Winblad int.,
July 23, 1991.

278 "Bill was . . . really pissed.":
Blumenthal int., Feb. 13, 1992.

278 "the fastest . . . haven't
noticed": InfoWorld, May 20,
1985.

278 "Gates got tremendously upset":
Murray int., Sept. 17, 1991.

278 "really got . . . that one.":
Belleville int., Mar. 13, 1992.

278 Steve got . . . the end.: Ibid.

278 "horsetrading": Donn Denman
int., Aug. 21, 1991.

279 "a chickenshit guy": Gates int.,
Nov. 26, 1991.

279 Denman got . . . Denman's
pride.: Denman int., Aug. 21,
1991.

279 "If you . . . got snookered":
Guy Kawasaki int., Sept. 9, 1991.

279 "one of . . . ever done.": Gates
int., Nov. 26, 1991.

279 "Later to . . . I threatened!":
Ibid.

279–80 "He insisted . . . our head.":
Wall Street Journal, Sept. 25, 1987,
p. 1.

20. SLOW BURN

281 "had reset . . . on us": Gates
int., Nov. 5, 1991.

281 Taming all . . . the year.:
Zbikowski int., Feb. 26, 1992.

282 "the hell with Microsoft":
Iacobucci int., Feb. 20, 1992.

282 Letwin and . . . on four.: Ibid.

283 "he said . . . in color!' ' ": Gates
int., Jan. 2, 1992.

283 "mice weren't . . . very well.":
Ibid.

283 "this thing . . . totally right.":
Konzen int., Aug. 8, 1991.

283 Things like . . . be made.: Gates
int., Jan. 2, 1992.

284 "Her eyes . . . exactly.":

PAGE

Darrell Miller int., Sept. 10,
1991.

284 "You did . . . floppy!": Ibid.

284 "It was . . . to work.": Konzen
int., Aug. 8, 1991.

284 "in excruciating . . . as the
similarities.": InfoWorld, Oct. 7,
1985, p. 1.

285 By August . . . in Dallas.: Wall
Street Journal, Aug. 5, 1985, p. 1.

285 In May . . . Bill Gates.:
InfoWorld, May 6, 1985, p. 15.

285 "That was . . . feel right.":
Ballmer int., Aug. 6, 1991.

285 "We had . . . source code.":
Lowe int., Aug. 15, 1991.

285 "In a . . . to think?": Gates
int., Jan. 2, 1992.

286 There would . . . all out.:
Mackaman int., June 12, 1991.

286 "a framework": Gates int., Dec.
2, 1991.

286 "a set of namby-pamby
documents.": Ballmer int., Aug.
6, 1991.

286 "by far . . . ever signed.": PC
Week, Aug. 27, 1985, p. 8.

286 "Bill is . . . Windows": Bob
Markell int., Sept. 13, 1991.

286 "I already . . . out another?":
Ibid.

286–87 "Competing with . . . the
door.": Kapor int., Feb. 20,
1992.

287 Microsoft actually . . . receive
support.: Management Information
Systems Week, Dec. 5, 1984, p. 38.

287 "We have . . . the business.":
Business Week, Nov. 21, 1983,
p. 115.

287 "Microsoft kept . . . start
over.' ' ": Paul Grayson int., Oct.
23, 1991.

287 "sort of . . . do one.": Ibid.

288 "It's garbage! . . . do it.": PC
Magazine, May 14, 1985, p. 44.

288 "become accustomed to.": PC
Week, Sept. 10, 1985, unpaged
clipping.

288 After its . . . year ever.:
Sculley, Odyssey, pp. 270, 299.

288 Bill Gates . . . Microsoft

customers.: Memo, Bill Gates and Jeff Raikes to John Sculley and Jean Louis Gassée, "Apple Licensing of Mac Technology," June 25, 1985, pp. 2-3.

288 "They aren't . . . discussion." Letter, Bill Gates to John Sculley, July 29, 1985.

288 "We recently . . . on the importance.": Ibid.

288–89 "Ironically, IBM . . . the standard.": Memo, Gates and Raikes, to Sculley and Gassée, June 25, 1985, p. 3.

289 In the . . . competed unfairly.: Supplemented and Amended Complaint, Apple Computer v. Microsoft, May 21, 1991, pp. 9-11.

289 "that we . . . to use"?: Declaration of William H. Gates, Apple v. Microsoft, Apr. 20, 1988, p. 3.

289 "reason to . . . Apple copyright.": Ibid., p. 3.

289 "That was news to them.": Gates int., Jan. 2, 1992.

289 " 'I've tried . . . lost many' ": Ibid.

289 Jon Shirley . . . remarkably like the Mac. *Micro Software Today,* July 1984, p. 7.

289 The message . . . in court.: Declaration of William H. Gates, Apple v. Microsoft, Apr. 20, 1988, p. 5.

290 "problems": Sculley, *Odyssey,* p. 344.

290 "I hope . . . this thing": Ibid., p. 344.

290 Sculley promised . . . the company.": Ibid., p. 344.

290 "They ordered . . . conference room.": Gates int., Jan. 2, 1992.

290 "What I'm . . . good relationship.": Ibid.

290 "I'm glad . . . this stuff": Ibid.

291 "I have . . . Steve Jobs": Microsoft videotape of Gates's thirtieth birthday party, circa Oct. 28, 1985.

291 "at no . . . set forth.": Draft of

proposed license agreement between Apple and Microsoft, Nov. 8, 1985, p. 3.

291 "It didn't . . . just baloney.": Gates deposition, Apple v. Microsoft, undated [probably part of Dec. 22, 1988, deposition], pp. 82–83.

291 "because that . . . livable concept.": Gates int., Jan. 2, 1992.

291 "derivative . . . Macintosh.": Draft agreement, Microsoft and Apple, Nov. 22, 1985, p. 1.

292 "broader than . . . of Windows.": Edwin Taylor deposition, Apple v. Microsoft, Aug. 25, 1988.

292 "It was . . . agreeing to.": William H. Neukom deposition, Apple v. Microsoft, Dec. 7, 1988, p. 82.

292 "non-exclusive . . . software programs.": Agreement, Microsoft and Apple, Nov. 22, 1985, p. 1.

292 "received a . . . including Windows.": Microsoft electronic mail, billg to bobm, buckf, daveme, idac, jeffr, jimh, peteh, steveb, tandyt, cc: jeanri, jons, Nov. 24, 1985.

292 "so we . . . is fine.": Ibid.

292 "Although we . . . behind us.": Ibid.

292–93 "is not . . . make that.": Ibid.

293 "protected the . . . our minds.": Sculley, *Odyssey,* p. 344.

293 "I think that may work": Ibid., p. 346.

293 An industry . . . crunch.: Konzen int., Aug. 8, 1991.

293 "slow burn": McGregor int., Sept. 3, 1991; *Computerworld,* Mar. 2, 1987, p. 15.

293 "we just . . . time ago.": Microsoft Windows roast 1985, video.

293 "so they . . . new job!": Ibid.

293–94 "He starts . . . the afternoon.": Ibid.

PAGE

294   "Ship this . . . doing Windows!": Ibid.

294   Gates and . . . Impossible Dream.": Ibid.

294   Jim Harris . . . product shipped: Ursino int., Mar. 26, 1992.

294   "Windows Arrives . . . Over.": *InfoWorld*, Dec. 23, 1985, p. 34.

294   "impressive" . . . "remarkable.": *PC Magazine*, Aug. 20, 1985, p. 38.

294   "poor" . . . its shortcomings.": *InfoWorld*, Feb. 3, 1986, p. 34.

294–95 "We said . . . favorable terms.": Paul Grayson int., Oct. 23, 1991.

295   Konzen . . . with IBM.: Konzen int., Aug. 8, 1991.

295   "They met . . . the product.": Myers int., Sept. 6, 1991.

295   An offer . . . was had.: Ibid.

295   Next morning . . . no deal.: Ibid.

21. SHARK FRENZY

296   "Bill Gates . . . of it.": Confidential int., Mar. 1992.

296   Gordon Letwin's . . . each disk.: Mel Hallerman int., July 18, 1991.

297   "to raise . . . it's stealing": *InfoWorld*, May 28, 1984, p. 12.

297   "Manufacturers, as . . . our cost?' ": Ibid., p. 12.

297   "Internal security . . . program disk.": *InfoWorld*, Oct. 28, 1985, p. 3.

297   Microsoft's Jeff . . . been excised.: Ibid., p. 3.

297   "How can . . . this idiocy?": *InfoWorld*, Nov. 11, 1985, p. 58.

297   Years later . . . Caltech.: Harbers int., July 17, 1991.

297   In November . . . and Chart.: *InfoWorld*, Nov. 18, 1985, p. 8.

298   "It's a . . . the work.": Cole int., June 17, 1991.

298   cares so . . . the bag.: Ibid.

298–99 "There was . . . the work.": Ibid.

PAGE

299   "What's the . . . you around?": Confidential int., Feb. 1989.

299   "Ida said . . . very unpleasant.: Memo from Charles Simonyi to Handheld PS group, Apr. 3, 1985.

299   "It was . . . beat up": Cole int., June 17, 1991.

299   "sink or . . . or Jill.": Confidential int., May 1991.

299   Protocol was . . . terminated immediately.: Ibid.

299   "There was . . . plenty mad.": Trower int., Aug. 12, 1991.

300   Ballmer's reaction . . . the hall.: Angus int., June 12, 1991.

300   One developer . . . of Windows.: Brian Conte int., June 13, 1991.

300   But to . . . special authorization.: Confidential int., May 1991.

300   "We work . . . that way.": Microsoft Exempt Employee Handbook, circa 1985, p. 23.

300   "No one . . . complete fuckup!": Slade int., June 24, 1991.

301   "Although we . . . first measure.": Microsoft Manager's Handbook, May 1985, unpaged.

301   "the employee . . . further review.": Ibid.

301   "If Paul . . . get rich.": *Seattle Post-Intelligencer*, July 19, 1981, p. D9.

301   "at some . . . some value": *Seattle Times*, May 6, 1984, p. C4.

301   "The ball . . . the grease.": *Fortune*, July 21, 1986, p. 24.

301   "The company . . . pay off.": Roark int., Aug. 26, 1991.

301   "We decided . . . had to.": *Fortune*, July 21, 1986, p. 25.

302   "most visible . . . or ever.": Ibid., p. 26.

302   "We actually . . . public offering": Gaudette int., Aug. 28, 1991.

302   His story . . . public limelight.: *Fortune*, July 21, 1986, pp. 23–33.

PAGE

302 "Instead of . . . the start.":
Ibid., p. 23.

302 "were going . . . beauty
contest": Gaudette int., Aug. 28,
1991.

302 "Better the . . . you don't.":
Fortune, July 21, 1986, p. 26.

302 Windows flops. . . . belly up.:
PC Week, Oct. 21, 1986, p. 57.

302 "The willingness . . .
correspondingly bigger.": Winblad
int., July 23, 1991.

303 The first . . . nest egg.:
Microsoft Prospectus, Mar. 13,
1986, p. 5.

303 "A decision . . . its
customers.": Ibid., p. 5.

303 "It seems . . . consideration.":
Ibid., p. 5.

303 "change in . . . Japan.": Ibid.,
p. 5.

303 "Telephones enhanced . . .
home computers.": Wall Street
Journal, Mar. 17, 1986, p. 24.

303 "even Hello . . . MSX
machine.": Roark int., Aug. 26,
1991.

303 There had . . . Newman's
Microtype.: Gates int., Nov. 5,
1991.

303 With $275,000 . . .
Spectravideo: Ibid.

303 "Sell!" Bill . . . the bottom.:
Roark int., Aug. 26, 1991.

303–4 At 12 percent . . . it off.:
Microsoft Prospectus, p. 27.

304 Finally Nishi . . . MSX
machine.: Roark int., Aug. 26,
1991.

304 "It would . . . the
relationship?' ": Scott Oki int.,
Feb. 19, 1992.

304 "I knew . . . accepted that.":
Ibid.

304 "We can . . . for themselves.":
UNIQUE: The UNIX System
Information Source, June 1986,
p. 3.

304 "was just a disaster.": Marquardt
int., Jan. 22, 1992.

304 As the . . . fiscal 1984.:
Microsoft Prospectus, p. 11.

PAGE

304–5 "reliance . . . the company.:
Ibid., p. 5.

305 For such . . . Shirley's
$228,000.: Ibid., p. 26.

305 For the . . . billion dollars.:
Fortune, July 21, 1986, p. 27.

305 "Ann, I . . . in sales.":
Winblad int., July 23, 1991.

305 "it's possible . . . six years.":
Seattle Times/Post-Intelligencer, Jan.
29, 1984, p. A26.

305 The company . . . to you.:
Marquardt int., Jan. 22, 1992.

305 "Bill figures . . . up here?' ":
Gaudette int., Aug. 28, 1991.

306 "the king . . . big chair": Ibid.

306 "These guys . . . favorite
clients?": Fortune, July 21, 1986,
p. 32.

306 In the . . . a ceiling.: Ibid.,
p. 32.

306 Everything went . . . $4
million.: Ibid., p. 33; Gaudette
int., Aug. 28, 1991.

306 "two-sewer guys . . . to go.":
Gaudette int., Aug. 28, 1991.

306 "a shark . . . Microsoft stock.":
Ibid.

307 "nothing at all decadent": Gates
int., Dec. 2, 1991.

307 "down payment on a house":
Ballmer int., Aug. 6, 1991.

307 FYIFV: . . . Fully Vested.:
Seattle Times, Apr. 23, 1989,
p. 11.

307 the "Brodie": Zbikowski int.,
Feb. 26, 1992.

307 "Is this a distraction?": Fortune,
July 21, 1986, p. 33.

307 "One guy . . . calendar
reform?": Confidential int., Feb.
1982.

308 "To me . . . e-mail name.":
Shirley int., Mar. 7, 1989.

308 "To understand . . . all
adolescents.": Chris Peters int.,
Mar. 17, 1992.

309 A night owl . . . handicapped
space: Video of Microsoft
company meeting, Sept. 13, 1985.

309 "I don't . . . your office.":
Confidential int., May 1991.

PAGE

309 coin flip: Gates int., Apr. 24, 1992.

310 "a computer . . . run on.": Brock int., May 22, 1991.

310 "updates and enhancements": Agreement between Seattle Computer Products, Inc., and Microsoft, July 27, 1981, p. 2.

310 Brock offered . . . came forward.: Letter from James Whelan to Rod Brock, Mar. 26, 1984; Letter from Rod Brock to Kavin Goharderakhshan, Feb. 27, 1985.

310 "see how . . . would stretch": Brock int., May 22, 1991.

310 "Microsoft didn't like that.": Ibid.

310 So maybe . . . $20 million: Letter from Rod Brock to Jon Shirley, Aug. 14, 1985.

310 reporter from . . . in selling.: Information Week, Aug. 19, 1955, p. 10.

310 "We were . . . trademark 'MS-DOS' ": Letter from Jon Shirley to Rod Brock, Aug. 29, 1985.

311 Damages were . . . conceivably be trebled.: Microsoft prospectus, p. 47.

311 "The company" . . . this action.": Ibid., p. 48.

311 By early . . . over $700,000.: Tim Paterson int., Mar. 18, 1992.

311 "any purchaser . . . products business.": Agreement between Microsoft Corporation and Falcon Technology, Dec. 15, 1983, in Microsoft v. Very Competitive Computer Products.

311 Paterson sent . . . disk controllers.: Letter from Tim Paterson to William Gates, Mar. 17, 1986.

311 "reach an understanding": Letter from William H. Neukom to Tim Paterson, Apr. 15, 1986.

312 "Bill Gates . . . in there!' ": Tim Paterson int., Apr. 23, 1991.

312 "merges all . . . contemporaneous communications.": Agreement

PAGE

between Microsoft Corporation and Falcon Technology, Dec. 15, 1983.

312 "He's huffing and puffing": Paterson int., Apr. 23, 1991.

312 "So I'm . . . are $17.": Ibid.

312 "Trey was one of my best students." Kelly Corr int., Aug. 16, 1991.

312 who would . . . the local press.: Seattle Post-Intelligencer, Aug. 19, 1988, p. 1; Seattle Times, Aug. 19, 1988, p. 1.

312 "You mean . . . hardware was": Bill Gates deposition, Oct. 8, 1986, Seattle Computer v. Microsoft.

313 "wasn't what . . . said something.": Tim Paterson int., Apr. 23, 1991.

313 Corr had . . . of the jury.: Corr -int., Aug. 16, 1992.

313 one million dollars.: Brock int., May 22, 1991.

313 When Corr . . . said pointedly.: Seattle Times, Dec. 9, 1986.

314 When the . . . Microsoft stock.: Corr int., Aug. 16, 1991.

22. "WE DAMN WELL CAN!"

315 "This is . . . what's right.": Letwin int., Feb. 13, 1992.

315 "Something that . . . artistic control.": Ibid.

315–16 This was . . . like that.": Ibid.

316 "you make . . . it up.": Ibid.

316 If the . . . code out.: Ibid.

316 "there were . . . programming.' ": Iacobucci int., Feb. 20, 1991.

316 "At IBM . . . the docks.": Ibid.

316 The developers . . . works there.: Ibid.

316 "Microsoft programmers . . . as artists": Ibid.

316 "big development tools": Ibid.

317 "Why does . . . the machine?": Ibid.

317 "IBM was really fragmented groups": Ibid.

PAGE

317 "The image . . . really matter:
Letwin int., Feb. 13, 1992.

317 If we . . . take it.: Ibid.

317 "the second-system effect.":
Brooks, *The Mythical Man-Month,*
p. 53.

317 "Add little . . . big pile": Ibid.

317 "The general . . . first one.":
Ibid.

317 "this is way too complicated":
Iacobucci int., Feb. 20, 1991.

317 "When it . . . a bit": Letwin
int., Feb. 13, 1992.

318 "brain-damaged.": *Micro Market
World,* Jan. 2, 1987, unpaged
clipping.

318 But Intel . . . Gordon Letwin.:
Ibid.; Nathan Myhrvold int., Feb.
12, 1992.

318 And IBM . . . of the 286.:
Confidential int., Mar. 1992.

318 "I thought . . . absolute
disaster.": Markell int., Sept. 13,
1991.

318 What about . . . someone
inquired.: Ballmer int., Aug. 6,
1991.

318 Ballmer and Gates . . . TopView
API: Markell int., Sept. 13, 1991.

318–19 Somebody on . . . buy it.:
Ballmer int., Aug. 6, 1991.

319 "lock, barrel, and stock options":
David Weise int., Aug. 22, 1991.

319 "our kind of guys": Shirley int.,
Oct. 31, 1991.

319 "We said . . . dorky.": Weise
int., Aug. 22, 1991.

319 It's fairly . . . of DOS.: Steve
Ballmer, Windows Development
Seminar, June 5, 1986.

320 "a bunch . . . of them.":
Nathan Myhrvold int., Feb. 12,
1992.

320 "Everybody was . . . silver
bullet": Markell int., Sept. 13,
1991.

320 "a set . . . cross-system
consistency.": Killen, *IBM: The
Making of the Common View,* p. 261.

320 And Earl . . . System/3X
minicomputers.: Ibid., pp. 126–
132, 220–230.

PAGE

320 If IBM . . . seem identical.:
Ibid., p. 131.

321 The SAA . . . same thing.:
Jeannette Maher int., Aug. 19,
1991; John Tibbetts int., Aug. 22,
1991.

321 SAA went . . . one another.:
Killen, pp. 251–263.

321 TopView hadn't . . . it further.:
Ballmer int., Aug. 6, 1991.

321 No problem . . . Hawthorne.:
Gates int., Jan. 18, 1992; Ballmer
int., Aug. 6, 1991.

322 "Test our . . . be happy.: Gates
int., Jan. 18, 1992; Ballmer int.,
Aug. 6, 1991.

322 Lowe was . . . Microsoft's part.:
Lowe int., Aug. 15, 1991.

322 By the . . . graphical system.:
Gates int., Jan. 18, 1992.

322 On the . . . saved it!: Slade int.,
June 24, 1991.

322 "And Bill . . . At anything!":
Ibid.

322 "Get the . . . it takes.":
Ballmer int., Aug. 6, 1991.

322 Back home . . . Grease Up.:
Konzen int., Aug. 8, 1991.

322 "managed to raise enough
doubts": Myhrvold int., Feb. 12,
1992.

322 "We knew . . . them
outnumbered.": Ibid.

322 We thought . . . GDDM layer.:
Ibid.

323 At one . . . the disk.: Ibid.

323 "In general . . . applicable
detail.": Weise int., Aug. 22,
1991.

323 "committed . . . under
286DOS": Charles Petzold int.,
Aug. 13, 1992.

323 "And Bill . . . believed that.":
Mackaman int., June 12, 1991.

323 "They're always . . . to be
over": Ballmer int., Aug. 6,
1992.

323 There were . . . didn't include.:
Ibid.

323 "They don't . . . that period.":
Ibid.

323 "IBM is . . . a maze": Prusky int., Feb. 5, 1992.

324 "Basically this . . . nothing about.": Confidential int., Feb. 1992.

324 "Now," Ballmer . . . CP-DOS 1.1": Ballmer int., Aug. 6, 1992.

324 "Pissed!": Mackaman int., June 12, 1992.

324 "Compaq Introduces . . . 80386-Based Windows.": *InfoWorld*, Sept. 16, 1986, p. 1.

324 "unsell": Ursino int., Mar. 26, 1992.

325 In essence . . . as redundant.: Steve Wood [later employee] int., Apr. 1, 1992.

325 "The biggest . . . people work.": *InfoWorld*, Jan. 5, 1987, p. 8.

23. STORMING THE GATES

326 "I can . . . stupid languages": Gates int., Jan. 2, 1992.

326 "Too confrontational": Ibid.

326 "nervous": Gates int. with Ditlea, July 8, 1987.

326 He spent . . . boning up.: Charles Petzold int., Aug. 13, 1991.

326–27 Solicited for . . . the runner-up.: Ibid.

327 Afterward, emcee . . . that idea.: Ibid.

327 They told . . . winning product.: Presentation of Rob Dickerson to Dec. 1986 meeting of Microsoft languages group. In Borland v. Microsoft, Affidavit of Steven J. Snyder, Dec. 8, 1987.

327 "in order . . . significant": Rob Dickerson, Microsoft Performance Review Form for Exempt Employees, May 4, 1987.

327 "a cheap imitation.": Dickerson, Dec. 1986 presentation to languages group.

328 In a . . . C compiler.: Dickerson, Microsoft Performance Review, May 4, 1987.

328 "we had . . . product plans.": Dickerson, Microsoft Performance Review, Nov. 2, 1987.

328 Boyd flew . . . the Mac.: Boyd int., May 20, 1991.

328 initially opposed: Ibid.

328 pay royalties . . . product.: Cole int., June 17, 1991.

329 "It was . . . beta test": Slade int., June 24, 1991.

329 "That's where . . . bad decision.": Simonyi int., Aug. 20, 1991.

329 In early . . . desktop publishing.: *Computerworld*, Mar. 9, 1987, p. 10.

329 his crew . . . of Vaseline.: Konzen int., Aug. 8, 1991.

329 BOGU had . . . Up, Steve.: Harbers int., Mar. 20, 1992.

329 There was . . . very logo.: Steve Wood int., Apr. 1, 1992.

330 "Bill used . . . him crazy.": King int., Feb. 27, 1992.

330 At one . . . handle more.: Konzen int., Aug. 8, 1991; Steve Wood int., Apr. 1, 1992.

330 "there would . . . other half.' ": Myhrvold int., Feb. 12, 1992.

330 "every part . . . Windows anymore.' ": Ibid.

331 "This thing . . . just gross.": Mackaman int., June 12, 1991.

331 "visual fidelity": Steve Ballmer, Microsoft News Release, Apr. 2, 1987, p. 2.

331 "mechanical recompilation step": Charles Petzold int., Aug. 13, 1991.

331–32 We'd decided . . . still IBM.: Gates int., Jan. 18, 1992.

332 "viewed Microsoft . . . at IBM.": Mackaman int., June 12, 1991.

332 "There was . . . it manhood.": Lowe int., Aug. 28, 1991.

332 The *Wall* . . . in history.: *Wall Street Journal*, Mar. 20, 1987, p. 39.

332 "Why am . . . guy successful?": Lowe int., Aug. 28, 1991.

PAGE

332 "OEMs don't . . . IBM has.' ":
Mackaman int., June 12, 1991.

332 Televideo had . . . the game.:
Agreement between Microsoft
Corporation and Televideo
Systems, Inc., Dec. 1, 1987, in
Microsoft v. Televideo.

332 "Own it or clone it": Gates int.,
Jan. 18, 1992.

24. IN EVERY HOME

335 In 1983 . . . compact discs:
Buddine and Young, *The Brady
Guide to CD-ROM,* p. 15.

335 Among the . . . otherwise
produce.: Ibid., p. 16.

335 Raleigh Roark . . . MSX
standard.: Roark int., Aug. 26,
1991.

335 In their . . . general public.:
Ibid.

335 "There were . . . our lives.":
Gates int., Jan. 2, 1992.

336 Kildall was dumbfounded:
Confidential int., Aug. 1991.

336 Cytation was . . . single disc.:
Tom Lopez int., Apr. 25, 1991.

336 "We have . . . to Japan": Gates
int., Jan. 2, 1992.

337 Microsoft insiders . . . of MSX-
III.: Roark int., Aug. 26, 1991.

337 Though one . . . home-
computer business: *InfoWorld,* Mar.
17, 1986, p. 21.

337 "Kildall started . . . sell yet.":
PC Magazine, June 10, 1986,
p. 103.

337 Initial ploy: . . . was spurned.:
PC Magazine, Dec. 23, 1986,
p. 69; confirmed in part by Gates
int., Jan. 2, 1992.

337 "It's a . . . understanding it":
Confidential int., Aug. 1991.

338 "Are you sitting down?": *PC/
Computing,* Mar. 1989, p. 108.

339 Bill's longtime . . . couldn't
walk.: Mathers int., Aug. 21,
1991.

340 "It's a . . . boat.": Cole int.,
June 11, 1991.

PAGE

340 "And then . . . second
insult?' ": Simonyi int., Aug. 20,
1991.

340 "People were . . . little
pyramids.": Ibid.

340 "There's such . . . great
hams.": Ibid.

340 Roizen had . . . were dating.:
Roizen int., June 27, 1991.

340 "probably a . . . my part.":
Ibid.

340–41 "That's like . . . right there":
Ibid.

341 It's a . . . this pizza.": Ibid.

341 "probably gave . . . good tip.":
Ibid.

341 In countless . . . paid it.:
Playboy, Sept. 1991, p. 168.

341 "out of . . . same price.":
Roizen int., June 27, 1991.

341 "little more . . . of Word":
Macworld, Oct. 1989, p. 135.

341 "And he . . . the water.' ":
Roizen int., June 27, 1991.

341 "one software . . . overcharged
me!": Ibid.

341–42 "I haven't . . . for him.": Mary
Gates int., Aug. 5, 1991.

342 "had a . . . impact on": Bill
Gates Jr. int., Aug. 5, 1991.

342 "The idea . . . different
directions.": Mary Gates int.,
Aug. 5, 1991.

342 "I go . . . detail here.": Slade
int., June 24, 1991.

342 "You're going . . . shitty
sandcastle": Ibid.

342 "They spend . . . you
change?' ": Ibid.

343 "Like, who are these guys?":
Simonyi int., Aug. 20, 1991.

25. "WE WERE PACKAGES"

344 "clearly been controversial ever
since.": Raburn int., Mar. 13,
1991.

344 "lore in . . . that again": Ibid.

344 "I've done . . . we say.":
Myhrvold int., Feb. 12, 1992.

PAGE

344–45 "Every single . . . never happened.": Kapor int., Feb. 20, 1992.

345 "Everybody talked . . . have discussions.": Ibid.

345 "We wanted . . . systems division.": Gates int., Jan. 2, 1992.

345 "Not very. . . . might be.": Kapor int., Feb. 20, 1992.

345 "and I . . . same firm.": Ibid.

345 "Bill doesn't . . . any acquisition.": Raburn int., Mar. 13, 1991.

345 "We called . . . a month.": Gates int., Jan. 2, 1992.

345 "We were . . . I like.": Konzen int., Aug. 8, 1991.

346 Microsoft claimed . . . March 1987: Microsoft press release, Mar. 11, 1987, p. 2.

346 only about . . . hard drives.: Computerworld, Mar. 2, 1987, p. 1.

346 "Frankly, we . . . want it.": Konzen int., Aug. 8, 1991.

346 "begging on . . . not really interested.' ": Trower int., Aug. 12, 1991.

346 At a . . . for PM.: Harbers int., July 17, 1991.

346 "Ballmer just . . . the world.": Ibid.

346 "They just . . . together": Konzen int., Aug. 8, 1991.

347 "We wanted . . . to wait": Peters int., Mar. 17, 1992.

347 When the . . . software company.: Microsoft annual report, 1987, pp. 13–15.

347–48 "So Bill . . . I'm not.": Slade int., June 24, 1991.

348 "as conservative . . . THEM" [emphasis Gates's].: Memo from Bill Gates to top managers, Aug. 16, 1987. Ichbiah and Knepper, The Making of Microsoft, p. 203.

348 Everybody predicted . . . they did that.: Paul Grayson int., Oct. 23, 1991.

349 "confluence of . . . hitting the accelerator.: George Grayson int., Oct. 23, 1991.

349 "Microsoft had . . . Windows application.": Computerworld, Apr. 11, 1988, p. 6.

349 "People are . . . operating system": Computerworld, Mar. 2, 1987, p. 14.

349 "The first . . . Manager": Computerworld, Nov. 2, 1987, p. SR7.

349 "Chernobyl Box.": InfoWorld, June 15, 1987.

349–50 "several developers . . . writing applications?": InfoWorld, May 11, 1987.

350 "If we . . . in applications.": InfoWorld, Oct. 19, 1987, p. 10.

350 "There are . . . the company.: Ibid., p. 10.

350 "There is . . . in Boston.": Conte int., June 13, 1991.

350 Windows developer . . . was implemented.: Steve Wood int., Apr. 1, 1992.

350 "Software Hardball": Wall Street Journal, Sept. 25, 1987, p. 1.

350 "He has . . . biggest winner.": Ibid.

350 "the fox . . . eats you.": Ibid.

351 "virtually . . . Macintosh ideas.": Ibid.

351 "a letter . . . the box.": Bob Kutnick int., Mar. 17, 1992.

351 "We work . . . certain vendors.": Ibid.

351 "We never . . . a proposal.": Ursino int., Mar. 26, 1992.

351 the standard . . . of products.: Ibid.

351 "We were . . . the deal.": Ibid.

351–52 "We felt . . . timely fashion.": Ibid.

352 Gates's Microsoft . . . $971 million: Bellevue Journal-American, Oct. 23, 1987, p. A3.

352 "No one . . . C 5.0.": PC Magazine, Sept. 29, 1987, p. 41.

352 Philippe knew . . . QuickRock.: Deposition of Robert H. Dickerson, Jr., Dec. 2, 1987, p. 72, Borland v. Microsoft.

352 "selling Borland. . . . very exciting.": Ibid., pp. 72–73.

352 $90,000 . . . leaving Seattle.:
Letter, Teresa Zembower,
Borland, to Rob Dickerson, Nov.
10, 1987.

353 On Wednesday . . . to sue.:
Dickerson deposition, p. 87.

353 "solicit, divert . . .
microcomputer software":
Microsoft Employee Non-
Disclosure Agreement signed by
Rob Dickerson, July 9, 1984.

353 "I talked . . . leave it.":
Confidential int., May 1991.

353 "Would you . . . office now?":
Dickerson deposition, p. 118.

353 "No, no . . . honorable man.":
Ibid., p. 118.

353 "There was . . . the office.":
Ibid., p. 119.

353 " 'Microsoft has . . . job
offer.": Ibid., pp. 119–120.

353 Ballmer made . . . a year.:
Ibid., p. 119.

353 Borland's agreement . . . by
Microsoft.: Letter, Robert H.
Kohn, Borland, to Rob Dickerson,
Nov. 14, 1987.

354 "Philippe Kahn . . . job soon.":
PC Week, Dec. 22, 1987, p. 111.

354 "Dickerson's . . . to go.": Bill
Gates int., Apr. 24, 1992.

354 "reading themes. . . . Fitzgerald
vacation.": Winblad int., July 23,
1991.

354 "We were . . . of books": Ibid.

354 She dragged . . . in California.:
Ibid.

354 She gave . . . by Napoleon.:
Gates int., Aug. 29, 1991.

354 "just for the heck of it": Gates
int., Feb. 29, 1992. However,
Gates told his personal assistant
and others that he had adopted
vegetarianism as "a random test
of discipline"; Julie Girone int.,
Apr. 24, 1992.

354 "ran out . . . or something":
Gates int., Feb. 29, 1992.

354–55 "When he . . . of break.":
Winblad int., July 23, 1991.

355 "They tell . . . facedown.":
Ibid.

355 "Ann was . . . a family": Kapor
int., Feb. 20, 1992.

355 "an inspiring domestic example":
Ibid.

355 "It had . . . was hardcore.":
Ibid.

355 "I think . . . Lost Boys.":
Winblad int., July 23, 1991.

355 "wasn't ready . . . other
options.' ": Roizen int., June 27,
1991.

355–56 "I don't . . . very sad.": Kristi
Gates int., Feb. 22, 1992.

356 "No one . . . the business.":
InfoWorld, Dec. 14, 1987, p. 105.

356 "Frankly," he . . . those jobs.":
Ibid., p. 105.

26. LOOK AND FEEL

357 Microsoft's attorneys . . .
notified.: Karl Quackenbush int.,
Dec. 6, 1991.

357 Nor had . . . legal action.: Gates
int., Jan. 18, 1992.

357 "the most . . . ever
experienced.": Ibid.

357 "totally behind us.": Gates e-
mail, Nov. 24, 1985.

357 "I don't . . . New
Wave. . . .": Gates int., Jan. 18,
1992.

358 "Every microcomputer . . .
they're gone.": Computer Language,
June 1986, p. 20.

358 "for some . . . to us.": Letter,
Irving Rappaport to Bill Neukom,
July 23, 1986.

358 "Apparently we . . .
interpretation.": Letter, Bill
Neukom to Irving Rappaport,
Sept. 2, 1986, p. 2.

358 Independent developers . . .
Microsoft's interface.: InfoWorld,
Jan. 19, 1987, p. 8.

358 "The agreement . . . its
developers.": Microsoft News
Release, Dec. 22, 1986, p. 1.

358 "there are . . . our
Agreement": Letter, Albert

PAGE

Eisenstat to Bill Neukom, Jan. 23, 1987.

358 "Specifically, does . . . know this immediately.": Letter, Robert Booth to Jim Harris, Jan. 15, 1987.

359 "However, let . . . infringing.": Letter, Jim Harris to Robert Booth, Feb. 20, 1987.

359 "Apple doesn't . . . "Good"": *Proceedings,* 1987 Personal Computer Forum, p. 239.

359 According to . . . the program.: Declaration, Irving Rappaport, May 6, 1988, p. 3.

359 HP later . . . Rappaport's account.: HP's answer and counterclaims, July 13, 1988, pp. 1–23.

360 "audiovisual works." . . . and Windows 2.03.": Apple v. Microsoft and Hewlett-Packard, Complaint for Copyright Infringement and Unfair Competition, Mar. 17, 1988.

360 "There's nothing . . . for years.": *Computerworld,* Mar. 28, 1988, p. 6.

360 "the intent . . . inhibiting": *Computerworld,* Apr. 11, 1988, p. 105.

360 "may have . . . the art.": *New York Times,* Sept. 25, 1983, p. F2.

361 "BS/2": *PC Week,* Oct. 20, 1987, p. 42.

361 "waking up . . . have AIDS.": *Time,* Apr. 4, 1988, p. 60.

361 "When we . . . artists steal.' ": *Computer Reseller News,* Apr. 4, 1988, p. 134. This "quotation" is likely a variation on T. S. Eliot, in "Philip Massinger," published 1920: "Immature poets imitate; mature poets steal." In a 1960 *Esquire* article, Lionel Trilling adapted the quote to "Immature artists imitate. Mature artists steal."

361 "What do . . . gravity? No!": *Western MicroMarket,* May 1988, p. 10.

361 "We're not . . . some

PAGE

influence.": *InfoWorld,* Mar. 28, 1988, p. 101.

361 "If Gates . . . the lake.": Ibid., p. 101.

361–62 "bring to . . . Windows 1.0.": Declaration of Bill Gates, Apr. 20, 1988, pp. 1–8.

362 "This assertion . . . itself published": Declaration of Paul Norris, May 6, 1988, p. 3.

362 "second-generation . . . advantages": Ibid., p. 3.

362 To illustrate . . . suit would see.: Ibid., Exhibits 1, 2, 3.

362 "more similar . . . Windows 1.0": Al Eisenstat deposition, Sept. 16, 1988, p. 56.

362 "Don't want . . . Mac look!": Bill Neukom deposition, Dec. 7, 1988, pp. 52-54.

362 Neukom countered . . . admonition.: Ibid., p. 82.

362 "It was . . . the Macintosh.": John Sculley deposition, Nov. 2, 1988, p. 145.

362 "when you . . . know it." Jean-Louis Gassée deposition, p. 93 [undated excerpt].

362 "gestalt": Microsoft news release, Mar. 7, 1991.

362 "would accept . . . visual displays.": Microsoft motion and memorandum in support of motion, Jan. 27, 1989, p. 23.

363 "substantially similar": Apple-DR agreement, September 1985, cited in Defendant Microsoft's Motion and Memorandum in Support of Motion, Jan. 27, 1989, p. 24.

363 The chairman . . . from Apple.: Ibid., p. 24.

363 "There will . . . a device.": Lacey, *Ford: The Men and the Machine,* p. 108.

363 "a new . . . stand revealed.": Ibid., p. 109.

363 As we . . . any accusation.: *InfoWorld,* Mar. 28, 1988, p. 6.

363 "IBM was . . . later date.: Lowe int., July 9, 1992.

364 In a . . . box marked YES.: Civil

Cover Sheet, Apple v. Microsoft, Mar. 17, 1988, p. 2.

27. YOU CAN MAKE IT HAPPEN!

365 "feature nymphomania.": Angus int., July 29, 1991.

365 "If you . . . get features.": Richard Brodie int., Feb. 21, 1992.

365–66 "We have . . . mad dog!": Ballmer int., Aug. 6, 1991.

366 "We had . . . enjoying it!": Gates int., Jan. 2, 1992.

366 Konzen . . . OS/2 gang.: Konzen int., Aug. 8, 1991.

366 "a prize . . . first remark.": Kiser int., Nov. 29, 1991.

367 "Mexican school bus.": Iacobucci int., Feb. 20, 1992.

367 "There was . . . identity.": Ibid.

367 It would . . . numbers.: Computer Language, June 1986, p. 20.

367 There was . . . had dropped!: Gates int., Jan. 2, 1992.

367 "Building the world's heaviest airplane.": Myhrvold int., Feb. 12, 1992.

367 "The project . . . was doing.": King int., Feb. 7, 1992.

368 "Who got . . . this room?": Mackaman int., June 12, 1991.

368 "Windows," . . . buy Windows?": Ibid.

368 "There's nothing . . . minute?": Annelise Kolde int., July 30, 1991.

368 "We would . . . perfect.": Myhrvold int., Feb. 12, 1992.

368 "There was . . . or less.": Ibid.

368 "were actually . . . dying out.": Gates int., Apr. 24, 1992.

368 "outrageous": Scott McNealy int., Aug. 10, 1992.

369 "Boy, that . . . got upset!: Lowe int., Aug. 15, 1991.

369 "It did . . . a weekend": Myhrvold int., Feb. 12, 1992.

369 At Spring . . . being

completed.: InfoWorld, May 16, 1988, p. 85.

370 "They're focusing . . . to OS/2": InfoWorld, July 4, 1988, p. 8.

370 "I think . . . to OS/2": Ibid.

370 "didn't get . . . was older.": Cole int., June 11, 1991.

370 "I had . . . to work.' ": Ibid.

371 "Infinite Defects.": Gill, Microsoft Corporation: Office Business Unit, p. 8.

371 "they've been . . . on time.": Harbers int., July 17, 1991.

371 "Products ship . . . them ship": Ibid.

371 "I told . . . so bad.": Mike Maples int., Sept. 18, 1991.

371 "say anything . . . about IBM.": Ibid.

372 "It was . . . a divorce.": Mike Maples int., Sept. 19, 1991.

372 "and you . . . friends good-bye.: Ibid.

372 "We sort . . . hired him": Gates int., Feb. 29, 1992.

372 "Everybody thought . . . everything up' ": Slade int., June 24, 1991.

372 "We're not . . . long time": InfoWorld, Apr. 13, 1987, p. 5.

372 "No wonder it takes longer!": Slade int., June 24, 1991.

372 "We always . . . long time.": InfoWorld, Apr. 13, 1987, p. 5.

372 "How do you know that?": Maples int., Sept. 18, 1991.

373 When one . . . new car.: Jeff Raikes int., Feb. 24, 1992.

374 "the month in hell.": Steve Wood int., Apr. 1, 1992.

374 "What is . . . long day.": Iacobucci int., Feb. 20, 1992.

374 When the . . . a funeral.: Eric Maffei int., Aug. 13, 1991.

374 "Hursley . . . it's complicated.": Gates int., Jan. 2, 1992.

376 "Which one . . . with anything.": Fortune, Oct. 9, 1989, p. 51.

376 "I give . . . paint.":

PAGE

Computerworld, Dec. 11, 1989, p. 107.

376 "He'll come . . . or later.": Steve Jobs int., Mar. 19, 1989.

377 "3Com was . . . spiders mating.": *DBMS Magazine,* Mar. 1991, p. 22.

377 "Everything that . . . do wasn't.": Metcalfe int., July 9, 1991.

377 "Here's Microsoft . . . just unbearable.": Ibid.

377 "Microsoft double-crossed . . . same channels": Ibid.

377 One industry-tracking . . . purchasing OS/2.: *InfoWorld,* Nov. 14, 1988, p. 149.

377 Meanwhile, Windows . . . mid-November.: *InfoWorld,* Nov. 14, 1988, p. 149.

377 A Dataquest . . . of 900,000.: *InfoWorld,* Dec. 5, 1988, p. 5.

377 With an . . . million machines: Jeff Silverstein int., July 24, 1992.

377 "Excel . . . to Windows": Ballmer int., Aug. 6, 1991.

28. HOW THE SUNSHINE WORKS

378 "mining operation": Simonyi int., Aug. 20, 1991.

378 "Part of . . . project?": Confidential int., May 1991.

378 "Where the . . . you from?": Ibid.

378–79 "It may . . . goes 'Okay.' ": Slade int., June 24, 1991.

379 "The last . . . the air.": Jonathan Prusky deposition, Prusky v. Microsoft, Aug. 2, 1990, p. 141.

379 "There's like . . . of résumés.": Confidential int., May 1991.

379 "I made . . . a finalist!": Winblad int., July 23, 1991.

380 "a software factory": Gaudette int., Aug. 28, 1991.

380 "a world-renowned . . . computers.": Weise int., Aug. 22, 1991.

380 "memory, memory, memory.": Ibid.

380 "We're not . . . it down.": Ibid.

380 "It turned . . . wanna be": Ibid.

380–81 There are . . . done it.: Ibid.

381 "This is interesting": Ibid.

381 "Just make it great.": Russ Werner int., Sept. 5, 1992.

381 "Using protected . . . that help?" Ibid.

381 "Did you . . . for it": Weise int., Aug. 22, 1991.

381 "It's like . . . sunshine works.' ": Ibid.

381 "Half the . . . was excited.": Ibid.

381–82 "Okay, let's . . . problem, Steve.": Ibid.

382 "We finally . . . blah, blah.": Ballmer int., Aug. 6, 1991.

382–83 "We were . . . younger horses.": Myhrvold int., Feb. 12, 1992.

383 "The project . . . *que c'est?*": Ibid.

383 "miffed" . . . "Frigate": Confidential source, Sept. 1991.

383 But to Cutler's . . . security facilities.: Ibid.

383 "to develop . . . 1985.": Apple v. Microsoft, Judge William Schwarzer, Memorandum of Decision and Order, Mar. 20, 1989, p. 10.

383–84 "the displays . . . fundamentally different.": Ibid., p. 12.

384 During the . . . $48.91 per share: *Wall Street Journal,* Apr. 19, 1989, p. C21.

384 "a gutsy thing": Gaudette int., Aug. 28, 1991.

384 "similarities in particular features": Judge William Schwarzer, Memorandum of Decision and Order, July 25, 1989, p. 11.

384 "changes . . . 1985 license": Ibid., p. 15.

384 "we'd never . . . of them": Gates int., Jan. 2, 1992.

PAGE

384 "Believe me . . . go tiled.":
Ibid.

384 "minor change . . . overlap
code.": McGregor int., Sept. 3,
1991.

385 "We don't . . . not royalties.":
Gates int., Jan. 18, 1992.

385 "They believed . . . with
them.": Myhrvold int., Feb. 12,
1992.

386 "What I . . . Bill Gates.":
Computerworld, Sept. 25, 1989,
p. 6.

386 "We made John Warnock cry":
Gates int., Jan. 18, 1992.

387 "We did . . . letters.": Ibid.

387 "turned out . . . printer
business.": Ibid.

387 We were . . . confusing
deal. . . . : Ibid.

387 "Every word was negotiated
over": Taucher int., Aug. 29,
1991.

387 "the platform for the '90s": Joint
Microsoft/IBM press release, Nov.
13, 1989, p. 1.

388 "Beginning . . . on OS/2":
Ibid., p. 1.

388 "making . . . effort": Ibid.,
p. 2.

388 "Microsoft stated . . . file
names.": Ibid., p. 4.

388 Mark Zachmann . . . going
anywhere.: Mark Zachmann int.,
Feb. 25, 1992.

388 I say . . . run Windows.": Ibid.

389 "really stuck . . . this
bullshit?": Gordon Eubanks int.,
Sept. 17, 1991.

389 "neutered": Soft•letter, Nov. 27,
1989, p. 3.

389 "That's a . . . will follow.": PC
Week, Dec. 4, 1989, p. 125.

389 "Some guy . . . smart!' ":
Slade int., June 24, 1991.

29. A DATE WITH BILL

390 "Computer wizard . . . of it!":
Star, Oct. 3, 1989, unpaged
clipping.

PAGE

390 "We still . . . friends":
Winblad int., July 23, 1991.

390 "Incredible book! . . . hundred
years.": A Conversation with Bill
Gates, (Framingham, MA:
International Data Corp., Dec.
1987), p. 16.

390 "tunes, ideas . . . arches":
Dawkins, The Selfish Gene, p. 192.

390 "the idea . . . programs": A
Conversation with Bill Gates, p. 16.

391 "When he . . . were off.":
Confidential int., May 1992.

391 "calls me . . . for $380,000.:
Gates int., Feb. 29, 1992.

391 Built in . . . $159,138 each:
Bruce Anderson int., Apr. 3,
1992.

391 For much . . . each way.: Gates
int., Jan. 2, 1992.

391–92 Porsche itself . . . safety
requirements.: European Car, Nov.
1991, p. 97.

392 Then six . . . certification
purposes.: Anderson int., Apr. 3,
1992.

392 "kind of . . . breaks down.":
Gates int., Feb. 29, 1992.

392 "work there . . . to do.":
Shirley int., Oct. 31, 1991.

392 "We had . . . for Bill": Ibid.

392 "The company . . . this thing.":
Ibid.

392 "He was . . . be visible":
Stewart Alsop int., Dec. 28,
1989.

392–93 "We looked . . . interested.":
Marquardt int., Jan. 22, 1992.

393 "stop and smell the roses."
Jeremy Butler int., Feb. 14, 1991.

393 "We did . . . list early on.":
Marquardt int., Jan. 22, 1992.

393 "totally . . . my back.": Shirley
int., Oct. 31, 1991.

393 "Building new . . . to him":
Mike Hallman int., Feb. 28, 1992.

393 He had . . . so advanced.: Jim
Karr int., June 25, 1992.

393–94 "database . . . to happen.":
Hallman int., Feb. 28, 1992.

394 "With many . . . goes in?":
Ibid.

PAGE

394   "about twice as much": Ibid.

394   "What the . . . DOS prompt?":
Confidential int., Sept. 1991.

394   "still views . . . the world.":
Raburn int., Mar. 25, 1992.

394   "data temple": Ray Duncan int.,
Sept. 19, 1991.

394   "the biggest . . . in it.":
Hallman int., Feb. 28, 1992.

395   The biggest . . . his way.: Gates
int., Jan. 18, 1992.

395   "Bill got . . . their
inefficiency.": Ballmer int., Aug.
6, 1991.

395   "We start . . . for them.":
Ibid.

395–96   "He probably . . . he does.":
Mary Gates conversation, Apr. 15,
1991.

396   "Notes from a Gates Date!":
"Another Conversation with Bill
Gates," memo, George Gilbert
and Jenise Ellis to BJohnston,
DWeinberg, SWalsh, KLowe, May
3, 1990.

396   " 'Six months . . . a chance.' ":
Ibid., p. 1.

396   "that Microsoft . . . Windows
3?' ": Ibid., p. 1.

396   "strongly implied . . . fold' ":
Ibid., p. 1.

396   "We got . . . at Apple.": Ibid.,
p. 1.

396   " 'always running scared' ": Ibid.,
p. 2.

396   "to overcome . . . the PC.":
Ibid., p. 4.

396   "Ambition . . . Business
Judgment.": Ibid., p. 4.

396   "according to . . .
convincing.": Ibid., p. 5.

397   "We're very patient people": PC
Week, Feb. 5, 1990, p. 8.

397   "There will . . . 4 and 5":
InfoWorld, Feb. 12, 1990, p. 8.

397   "kind of . . . Windows Plus.":
Computer Reseller News, May 7,
1990, p. 1.

397   "We were . . . a deal": Gates
int., Jan. 8, 1991.

397   "How can . . . cheaper.":
Ballmer int., Aug. 6, 1991.

PAGE

397   "We sat . . . as possible?":
Taucher int., Aug. 29, 1991.

397   "a note . . . change anything.":
Ibid.

397   "the happiest . . . life.": Gina
Smith int., May 29, 1991.

398   "We . . . Love Windows!":
Edstrom int., Sept. 28, 1991.

398   "The Microsoft . . .
Engineers.": CompuServe MSOFT
Windows Forum, May 25, 1990.

398   There were . . . documentation
errors.: Ibid., May 25–June 22,
1990.

398   "Microsoft, with . . . good
products.": Raburn int., Mar. 13,
1991.

398–99   "Hey, talk . . . right stuff.":
Winblad int., July 23, 1991.

399   Both would . . . James Gleick.:
New York Times Magazine, June 14,
1992, pp. 38–42.

400   In the . . . was worthwhile.:
Confidential int., June 1991.

400   "Whatever you . . . word
'divorce' ": Rachel Parker int.,
Sept. 17, 1990.

400   "Whatever relationship . . . this
agreement.": Ballmer int., Sept.
17, 1990.

400   "I wouldn't . . . of view.":
Wall Street Journal, Sept. 17, 1990.

400   "this JDA . . . they got.":
Confidential e-mail, Sept. 1990.

400   "We gave . . . positive
relationship.": Gates int., Feb.
29, 1992.

400   "I'll tell . . . any way.":
Ballmer int., Apr. 1, 1992.

400   "I think . . . short-term": PC
Week, Sept. 24, 1990, p. 8.

400–1   "make a . . . sells Windows":
Gates int., Feb. 29, 1992.

401   On November . . . mouse
market.: Z-Nix Co., Inc., v.
Microsoft Corp., Nov. 7, 1990,
pp. 6, 7.

401   damages of . . . $4.5 million.:
Ibid., p. 8.

401   "It's time . . . this industry":
Miller Communications press
release, Nov. 7, 1990, p. 2.

PAGE

401 "the nuclear . . . terrorist attack.": Confidential int., March 1991.

401 "may have been too aggressive": Confidential int., March 1991.

401 "allegations about Microsoft's conduct.": Microsoft press release, Nov. 12, 1990.

402 "At the . . . come in.": Thomas Chan int., Nov. 21, 1990.

402 "my speeches . . . never written": Gates int., Feb. 29, 1992.

402 "why I . . . those jokes": Ibid.

402 "Bill has . . . used to": Adelson introduction to Gates keynote address, Fall Comdex, Nov. 12, 1990.

402 "World at Your Fingertips": Microsoft company meeting video, Sept. 13, 1985.

402 "Information at the Fingertips": Economist, Jan. 30, 1988, p. 14.

403 "No single . . . all cooperating.": Gates keynote address, "Information at Your Fingertips," Fall Comdex, Nov. 12, 1990.

403 "Mighty Microsoft Breeds Fear, Envy.": PC Week, Nov. 12, 1990, p. 1.

403 "Microsoft will . . . computer industry.": PC Week, June 18, 1990, p. 49.

403 "If I'm . . . talk about.": Business Week, June 4, 1990, p. 110.

403 "the Kingdom of the Dead.": Business Month, Nov. 1990, p. 31.

403 ice pick: Ibid., p. 31.

403 "miracle maker" . . . for the Mac.": M, Inc., Dec. 1990, p. 82.

404 POST: Listening . . . anyone. Ever.: Washington Post, Dec. 30, 1990, p. H3.

404 "That's a . . . Spreadsheets.": MicroTimes, Nov. 26, 1990, p. 66.

404 "very innovative work": Ibid., p. 66.

404 "If somebody . . . it took.": Ursino int., Mar. 26, 1992.

PAGE

404 "We'd pull . . . never published.": Ibid.

404 "We are . . . to talk.": PC Week, June 14, 1988, p. 3.

404 According to . . . paying significantly more.: Mackaman int., Feb. 13, 1992.

404 "Microslimed": Rich Bader int., Feb. 10, 1992.

404 "There was . . . the ends.": Ibid.

404–5 "cute story" . . . unethical.": Zachmann int., Feb. 25, 1992.

405 "Resentment . . . Redmond grows": PJH Research, Pacific Northwest Outlook, Dec. 1990, p. 19.

405 The Yankees . . . whistles by.: Gaudette int., Aug. 28, 1991.

405 "I don't . . . extremely tough." Kawasaki int., June 1, 1992.

405 "real concern . . . homogeneity." Jeff Tarter int., Dec. 4, 1990.

406 Microsoft made . . . local charity.: Buck Ferguson int., Dec. 19, 1990.

406 "Have you . . . Christmas party?": Bill Gates conversation, Dec. 15, 1990.

30. HOMEFRONT

407 "This is . . . go along.": Roark int., Aug. 26, 1991.

407 "the dilettante strategy.": Gates int., Jan. 2, 1992.

407 "be breaking . . . of tools.": Ibid.

408 In his . . . than $1,000.: Transcript of Gates's remarks, Microsoft CD-ROM conference 1988.

408 "This idea . . . was dumb": Roark int., Aug. 26, 1991.

408–9 "It was . . . PC world.": Ibid.

409 "the most incredible machine.": Confidential int., Aug. 1991.

409 At the . . . under $3,000.: Rob Glaser int., Sept. 12, 1991.

409 "The PS/2 . . . kindness": Ibid.

PAGE

409 "So we . . . play with.": Ibid.

410 "a wealth . . . multimedia
titles.": Microsoft Press release,
Mar. 18, 1991.

410 it was . . . new site.: *Seattle
Times,* Apr. 26, 1991, p. 1.

411 "Incredibly understated . . . like
anything.": Charles Simonyi int.,
Aug. 20, 1991.

411 From the . . . the caretaker.:
Micheal Doss int., Mar. 20, 1992.

411 "can experience . . . his
house.": James Cutler int. with
Fred Moody, circa Apr. 1991.

411 A single . . . of $15,000.: Ibid.

411 And a . . . wetland.: Doss int.,
Mar. 20, 1992.

412 "What data . . . proprietary
position?": Gates int., Jan. 2,
1992.

412 "Warren Buffett's . . . market
share.": Ibid.

413 "The board . . . pretty
positive": Ibid.

413 "At the . . . into Microsoft.":
Shirley int., Oct. 31, 1991.

413 "They can . . . on yet.": Gates
int., Jan. 2, 1992.

414 "virtual suicide" . . . nitrous
oxide.: *PC/Computing,* May 1991,
p. 132.

414 "corporate image . . . of
money.": Gates int., Jan. 2,
1992.

414 "the Gates . . . in
Wonderland.": James Cutler int.,
Aug. 13, 1991.

414 "It's driving . . . the roof":
Cutler int. with Fred Moody,
circa Apr. 1991.

415 "I try . . . content high.":
Gates int., Apr. 24, 1992.

415 "was looking . . . people.":
George Rathmann int., Mar. 13,
1992.

415 "anxious to . . . powerful":
Ibid.

416 "What's really . . . he likes.":
Ibid.

416 "once a . . . biotechnology.":
Leroy Hood int., Mar. 10, 1992.

416 A querulous . . . network.:

Fortune, Apr. 22, 1991, pp. 197-
206.

416 In June . . . for $9.: *Seattle
Times,* Dec. 5, 1991, p. B2.

416 Paul Allen's . . . associate
director.: UPI, Oct. 7, 1991, on-
line.

416–17 In a . . . Bioengineering.: *Pacific*
magazine, *Seattle Times,* Feb. 9,
1992, p. 6.

417 Huntsman bent . . . to take
hundreds.: Ibid., p. 7.

417 "Gee, guys . . . tomorrow?":
Ibid., p. 15.

417 "I'd rank . . . biological
information.": Hood int., Mar.
10, 1992.

417 *Forbes* 400 issue: *Forbes,* Oct. 21,
1991, p. 150.

417 "total happenstance . . . cup
half empty.": Mary Gates int.,
Oct. 10, 1991.

31. AN INFINITE AMOUNT OF MONEY

418 "Microsoft Corp. . . .
Windows.": *Wall Street Journal,*
Jan. 28, 1991, p. B1.

418 "For customers . . .
applications.": Microsoft press
release, Jan. 28, 1991.

418 "Contrary to . . . is OS/2.":
Seattle Times, Jan. 29, 1991,
p. C1.

418 "Actions speak . . . confirms
it.": Greg Zachary int., Jan. 30,
1991.

418 "there were . . . to us.": Gates
int., Feb. 29, 1992.

419 "just wouldn't . . . strange":
Ibid.

419 "I don't . . . our strategy.":
Ballmer int., Aug. 6, 1991.

419 "Several industry . . . discuss
Microsoft": Knight-Ridder
Tribune News Service, Mar. 13,
1991, on-line.

419 "inquiry" . . . and features":
Microsoft press release, Mar. 12,
1991.

419 Gates said . . . Windows 3.:

PAGE

Wall Street Journal, Mar. 13, 1991, p. A4.

419 "There's no . . . any problem.": *USA Today,* Mar. 25, 1991, p. 4B.

419 "Whenever someone . . . and out baloney.": Ibid.

419 "I have . . . same hamburger.": Ibid.

419 "The purpose . . . personal computers.": *New York Times,* Apr. 13, 1991, p. 36.

420 "Microsoft stretched . . . dealing with.": Dan Bricklin int., Sept. 23, 1991.

420 "Stretching the . . . a pen?": Raburn int., Mar. 15, 1991.

420 "let's just . . . bad code.": Weise int., Aug. 22, 1991.

420 DOS accounted . . . up fast.: *New York Times,* Mar. 15, 1991, p. C1.

420 "We bend . . . special advantage": Ibid., p. C4.

421 "The divisions . . . information flow": *Computer Reseller News,* Apr. 29, 1991, p. 144.

421 "we're still . . . all possible": Paul Grayson int., Mar. 13, 1991.

421 "this year" . . . memory usage": *InfoWorld,* Apr. 30, 1990, p. 3.

421 "Microsoft, in . . . about MS-DOS 5.0": *PC Week,* Oct. 22, 1990, p. 4.

421 "there is . . . there is.": Ibid., p. 4.

421–22 "There's no . . . of FUD": Ibid., p. 4.

422 "If you . . . come around.": Confidential int., Mar. 1991.

422 "At this . . . can take.": Bill Neukom int., Mar. 8, 1991.

422 "We want . . . and law.": Microsoft e-mail, billg & Mike Hallman to ms–corp, ms–intl, ms–usrg, Apr. 15, 1991.

422 "People don't . . . as ours.": *USA Today,* Mar. 25, 1991, p. 4B.

422 Microsoft's 1990 . . . Novell: *Bernstein Research Weekly Notes,* Apr. 24, 1992, p. 22.

PAGE

422 "Can Anyone Stop Him?": *Forbes,* Apr. 1, 1991, pp. 108–114.

423 "We don't . . . risk it?": Ibid., p. 110.

423 "taking a risk.": *New York Times,* Mar. 15, 1991, p. C1.

423 "When you . . . feel raped.": *Fortune:* Aug. 26, 1991, p. 43.

423 In early . . . rival Novell.: *InfoWorld,* Feb. 11, 1991, p. 1.

423 A week . . . since 1988.: *Wall Street Journal,* Feb. 11, 1991, p. B5.

423 "I said . . . or something.": Ballmer int., Apr. 1, 1992.

423 "better DOS . . . than Windows": *PC Week,* Mar. 25, 1991, p. 1.

423 "I knew . . . the end": Ballmer int., Apr. 1, 1992.

424 "They did . . . Windows NT": Gates int., Feb. 29, 1992.

424 "that makes . . . not advanced.": Ballmer int., Aug. 6, 1991.

424 "Slow, slower, and slowest.": Roizen int., June 27, 1991.

424 "standing around . . . profits.": *Wall Street Journal,* May 29, 1991, p. B1; *PC Week,* June 3, 1991, p. 129.

424 "write a lot of memos.": Gates int., July 22, 1991.

424–25 "nightmare" . . . market share.: John Walker, "The Final Days," Autodesk Information Letter No. 14, Apr. 1, 1991, pp. 24-26.

424–27 All quotes on these pages except the two immediately following are from Bill Gates memo, "Challenges and Strategies," May 16, 1991, unpaged on-line version.

426 "coopetition": *PC Week,* Feb. 10, 1992, p. 1.

427 "We get . . . every PC.": *Soft·letter,* Dec. 26, 1989, p. 6 (quoting *Macintosh News,* Oct. 30, 1989).

427 Compaq showed . . . clones.: *PC Week,* Oct. 28, 1991, p. 1.

PAGE

428   IBM, reducing . . . since 1946.:
      Reuters, Jan. 17, 1992, on-line.

428   Philippe Kahn . . . database
      market.: *PC Week,* July 15, 1991,
      p. 1.

428   "probably the . . . PC
      industry.": *PC Week,* Dec. 23–30,
      1991, p. 19.

429   "Basically in . . . do this.' ":
      Alsop int., Apr. 18, 1991.

429   "comes steaming . . . soft
      spot.' ": Ibid.

429   "It's an . . . it is.": Reuters,
      Oct. 7, 1991, on-line.

429   "prehistoric" languages . . .
      smoking.": Philippe Kahn, on-line
      response to June 3, 1991
      Soft · letter, circa June 3, 1991.

429   "fairy dust": Gates int., Feb. 29,
      1992; *PC Week,* Sept. 30, 1991,
      p. 122.

430   "You can . . . use it!": Gates
      int., Feb. 29, 1992.

430   "No. I . . . an answer.": Ibid.

430   "The Macintosh is not dead":
      InfoWorld, Mar. 9, 1992, p. 127.

430   "a fraction . . . development
      costs.": Confidential int., Sept.
      1992.

431   "The Streets of Microsoft": Video
      from DOS 5 introduction, shown
      by satellite at Bellevue Hyatt
      Regency, June 11, 1991.

431   IBM had . . . incentives.:
      Computer Reseller News, May 27,
      1991, p. 3.

431   "Lowe noticed . . . certain
      sense.": Gates int., Jan. 18,
      1992.

432   "We decided . . . the
      contract.": Ibid.

432   "We cremated . . . by then.":
      Ibid.

432   IBM discusses . . . do it.: *PC
      Week,* June 17, 1991, p. 1.

432   "poor product . . .
      functionality.": Gates memo, May
      16, 1991.

432   IBM wins . . . and Borland.: *PC
      Week,* July 1, 1991, p. 1.

432   Microsoft promises . . . DOS

6.0.: *PC Week,* July 22, 1991,
      p. 1.

432   IBM negotiates . . . DR DOS.:
      PC Week, Sept. 30, 1991, p. 1.

432   "It's been . . . on DOS.":
      Ibid., p. 8.

433   "somebody screwed up": Letwin
      int., Feb. 13, 1992.

433   "If someone . . . 100
      percent.": *PC Week,* Nov. 18,
      1991, p. 1.

433   Steve Ballmer . . . the press: *PC
      Week,* July 1, 1991, p. 102.

434   "You look . . . he lasts.":
      Confidential int., May 1991.

434   "The jury's still out.": Marquardt
      int., Jan. 22, 1992.

434   "Towne really . . . was there.":
      Gates int., Feb. 29, 1992.

434   "Not tough . . . cutting edge.":
      Confidential int., Feb. 1992.

434   "Mike Hallman was a human
      being.": Steve Wood int., Apr. 1,
      1992.

434   "As this . . . transitioned
      well.' ": Mike Hallman int., Feb.
      28, 1992.

434   Revenues had . . . than $7.:
      Reuters, Jan. 17, 1992, on-line.

434   Moody's rating . . . since 1979.:
      Associated Press, Mar. 5, 1992,
      on-line.

434   Meanwhile, *Inc.* . . . through
      1990.: *Inc.,* Dec. 1991, p. 36.

435   "he didn't . . . that moment.":
      Gates int., Feb. 29, 1992.

435   "IBM needs . . . that's good.":
      Ballmer int., Apr. 1, 1992.

435   We did . . . would've
      succeeded.: Gates int., Feb. 29,
      1992.

435   the greatest . . . his people.:
      Confidential int., Sept. 1991.

435   deputized . . . convert made.:
      Computer Reseller News, Apr. 6,
      1992, p. 285.

436   "an unlikely underdog.": *New York
      Times,* Mar. 31, 1992, p. C1.

436   In January . . . and General
      Motors.: *Seattle Times,* Jan. 9,
      1992, p. 1.

436   One analyst . . . at 2,000:

Michael Kwatinetz, *Bernstein Research Weekly Notes,* Feb. 14, 1992, p. 7.

436 "we agreed on a price.": David Fulton, Microsoft press conference, Mar. 24, 1992.

436 "Sure, Bill. . . . about you?": Gates int., Apr. 24, 1992.

436–37 "I'd be . . . the leader.": *Computer Reseller News,* Mar. 30, 1992.

437 "a single . . . multiple implementations": Myhrvold int., Feb. 12, 1992.

437 "seeks more . . . different segments.": Furukawa int., Dec. 11, 1991.

437 "bizarre vision" . . . ubiquitous.": Scott Oki int., Feb. 19, 1992.

437 Oki recalled . . . three-year sell: Ibid.

438 "It's not . . . it's over": Bill Neukom int., Apr. 16, 1992.

438 "Thirty man-years of lawyers": Gates int., Apr. 24, 1992.

438 "The notion . . . pay attention.": Gates int., June 18, 1992.

438 would pay . . . reported at $23: *InfoWorld,* July 6, 1992, p. 111.

438 a figure . . . the ballpark: Scott Brooks int., June 28, 1992.

438 "I'd say we're gonna compete": Steve Ballmer int., June 28, 1992.

439 "We will . . . the future.": Microsoft news release, July 22, 1992.

440 somewhere around number four.: *Forbes,* July 20, 1992, pp. 161, 222.

440 "leery of . . . as wealth.": *Forbes,* Oct. 21, 1991, p. 150.

440 "The more . . . the fall.": Winblad int., July 23, 1991.

EPILOGUE: THE REST IS SOFTWARE

441 "We've always . . . still carries.": Harbers int., July 17, 1991.

441 "Won all . . . in general.": Ballmer int., Apr. 1, 1992.

441 "He said . . . own it.": Boyd int., May 20, 1991.

441 "I see . . . half full.": Ballmer int., Apr. 1, 1992.

442 If there . . . you do?: Vergnes int., Sept. 24, 1991.

442 "I created . . . the stuff.": Harbers int., July 17, 1991.

442 "He basically . . . they're family.": Roark int., Aug. 26, 1991.

442 "the most . . . behind me.": Gates int., Feb. 29, 1992.

442 "I don't . . . that common.": Ibid.

443 "there are . . . my innocence.": Ibid.

443 "Nobody expects . . . the hill": Shirley int., Oct. 31, 1991.

443 "Dune Buggy.": Harbers int., July 17, 1991.

443 "is not . . . fairly fast.": Gates int., Feb. 29, 1992.

443 a round . . . much time.: Libby Gates int., Feb. 11, 1992.

443 "He is . . . plane, either.": Simonyi int., Aug. 20, 1991.

443 Most people . . . the *Economist.*: Gates int., Feb. 29, 1992.

443–44 "It's possible . . . both ends.": Ibid.

444 "You must . . . of Microsoft.": Ibid.

444 "I don't . . . his happiness.": Confidential int., Mar. 1992.

444 "I think . . . with people.": Dayton int., Apr. 29, 1991.

444 "His is . . . motivated.": Perot int., Sept. 17, 1991.

444 "It's the . . . Biotech's second.": Gates int., Feb. 29, 1992.

444 "I sure . . . press interviews.": Gates int., Apr. 24, 1992.

444–45 People oversimplify . . . it appears.: Gates int., Jan. 18, 1992.

445 "I choose . . . affecting things.": Gates int., Feb. 29, 1992.

445 "Devices that . . . an impact.": Ibid.

445 "fear of . . . clever anymore.": Confidential int., Mar. 1992.

445 "tied to the wheel": *Wall Street Journal,* Aug. 27, 1986, p. 12.

445 "Word was . . . Excel was innovative": Gates int., Feb. 29, 1992.

445 "We don't . . . different products.": Blumenthal int., Feb. 13, 1992.

445–46 Does Bill . . . like IBM.: Boyd int., May 20, 1991.

446 "the maniacal . . . pounding away.": Oki int., Feb. 19, 1992.

446 "their own little special world": Confidential int., Mar. 1992.

446 "this domain . . . under control.": Ibid.

446 "have to . . . real world": Ibid.

446 "Welcome . . . Bill": Julie Girone int., Apr. 24, 1992.

446 "I got . . . years ago.' ": Maples int., Apr. 12, 1991.

447 "technologist.": *Upside,* Apr. 1992, p. 74.

447 "Hero is a strong word": Gates int., Feb. 29, 1992.

447 "had his . . . at things.": Ibid.

447 "It's the . . . that someday.": Ibid.

447 "I admired FDR": Ibid.

447 "I've read . . . would have.": Gates int., Nov. 8, 1991.

447 "I admire . . . a scientist.": Gates int., Feb. 29, 1992.

447 Andy Hertzfeld . . . the world.: Lammers, *Programmers at Work,* p. 257.

447 "sponge" whose . . . develop them.": Sculley, *Odyssey,* p. 161.

447 "can never . . . don't know.' ": Confidential int., Apr. 1992.

447 "I'll show them.": Confidential int., Mar. 1992.

447 "Do you . . . own again?": Lammers, *Programmers at Work,* p. 90.

447 "Oh, sure . . . they're writing.": Ibid., p. 90.

448 "The business . . . easy— *easy!*": *Upside,* Apr. 1992, p. 75.

448 "Put a . . . that deal?": Iacobucci int., Feb. 22, 1992.

448 "From my . . . compensation.": Confidential int., Sept. 1991.

448 "Most corporate . . . it up.": Perot int., Sept. 17, 1991.

448 Oh, here's . . . don't like.: Gates int., Aug. 26, 1991.

448 "I don't . . . you are.": Gates int., June 5, 1991; Winblad int., July 23, 1991.

448–49 "He wanted . . . something else.' ": Konzen int., Aug. 8, 1991.

449 He is . . . his bandwidth.: Ibid.

449 "It's the . . . I guess": Gates int., Feb. 29, 1992.

449 "Internally, people . . . the world.": Ibid.

449 "I could . . . the weekend.": Confidential int., Mar. 1992.

449 "You can . . . knowing it.": *Wall Street Journal,* Feb. 11, 1992, p. B1.

450 "would it . . . just haven't": Gates int., Feb. 29, 1992.

450 "a more . . . existing market" Interval Research press release, Mar. 30, 1992.

450 "we want . . . in products.": *New York Times,* May 21, 1991, p. C17.

450 "When I'm . . . for a while.": Gates int., Feb. 29, 1992.

451 "He doesn't . . . not interested.": Confidential int., Feb. 1992.

451 "The guy . . . than anyone.": Gates int., Feb. 29, 1992.

451 "They exist . . . long term.": Ibid.

451 "You can . . . very fairly.": Ibid.

451 "I happen . . . bad way.": Ibid.

451 "I just . . . unlikely.": Gates int., Jan. 18, 1992.

451 "the differentiation . . . a Democrat.": Ibid.

452 "But you're . . . the budget.": Ibid.

PAGE

452 "The government . . . on it.":
Gates int., Feb. 29, 1992.

452 "They should" . . . It's
unbelievable!'': Gates int., Jan.
18, 1992.

452 "requests for . . . magazine
cover' '': Gates int., Feb. 29,
1992.

452 "There are . . . do more":
Ibid.

453 "effectively I . . . many cars.":
Ibid.

453 "There was . . . too
expensive." Ibid.

453 "Someday I'll . . . have kids":
Ibid.

453 "you get . . . your lovers.":
Letwin int., Feb. 13, 1992.

453 "freaking out" . . . getting
older.: Confidential int., Mar.
1992.

453 "It's a . . . your friends.' '':
Gates int., Feb. 29, 1992.

453 "It was . . . of yourself.":
Letwin int., Feb. 13, 1992.

453–54 "When I . . . real hard.":
Confidential int., June 1991.

454 "She was . . . long time.":
Ibid.

PAGE

454 "It affects . . . Who knows?":
Gates int., Jan. 18, 1992.

454 "Bullshit! Bullshit!" . . . her
name.": Ibid.

454 "make it impossible for me":
Confidential int., July 1992.

454 "absolutely not.": Ibid.

454 "I swear . . . year old.": Libby
Gates int., Feb. 11, 1992.

454 Gates was . . . his girlfriend.:
Ballmer int., Apr. 1, 1992.

455 "One thing . . . is bogus.":
Gates int., Feb. 29, 1992.

455–56 "One would . . . the
computer.": Weizenbaum,
Computer Power and Human Reason,
p. 115.

456 "The compulsive . . .
programming terms.": Ibid.,
p. 126.

456 The most . . . don't
understand.: Gates int., Feb. 29,
1992.

456 Go, "Wow!" . . . the
program.: Ibid.

456 Bill said . . . software
problem.": Stuart Johnston int.,
Apr. 19, 1991.

SELECTED BIBLIOGRAPHY

Bagley, Clarence B. *History of King County, Washington.* Chicago: S. J. Clarke Publishing Co., 1929.

Bell, C. Gordon, J. Craig Mudge, and John E. McNamara. *Computer Engineering: A DEC View of Hardware Systems Design.* Bedford, MA: Digital Press, 1978.

Brooks, Frederic P., Jr. *The Mythical Man-Month: Essays on Software Engineering.* Reading, MA: Addison-Wesley, 1975.

Buddine, Laura, and Elizabeth Young. *The Brady Guide to CD-ROM.* New York: Prentice-Hall, 1987.

Butcher, Lee. *Accidental Millionaire: The Rise and Fall of Steve Jobs at Apple Computer.* New York: Paragon House, 1989.

Chposky, James, and Ted Leonsis. *Blue Magic.* New York: Facts On File, 1988.

Crease, Robert P., and Charles C. Mann. *The Second Creation: Makers of the Revolution in Twentieth-Century Physics.* New York: Macmillan, 1986.

Cross, Keith, and Thomas J. Kosnik. *Microsoft LAN Manager.* Palo Alto, CA: Stanford University, Graduate School of Business, 1990.

Davidow, William H. *Marketing High Technology: An Insider's View.* New York: The Free Press, 1986.

Dawkins, Richard. *The Selfish Gene.* Oxford: Oxford University Press, 1989.

Ditlea, Steve, ed. *Digital Deli.* New York: Workman, 1984.

Drexler, Eric K. *Engines of Creation.* Garden City, NY: Anchor Press/Doubleday, 1986.

Eames, Charles and Ray, Office of. *A Computer Perspective: Background to the Computer Age,* new ed. Cambridge, MA: Harvard University Press, 1990.

Espinosa, Chris. *Macintosh User Interface Guidelines,* 2d ed. Cupertino, CA: Apple Computer, 1982.

Feynman, Richard P. *"Surely You're Joking, Mr. Feynman!": Adventures of a Curious Character.* New York: Bantam, 1986.

———. *"What do YOU Care What Other People Think?": Further Adventures of a Curious Character.* New York: W. W. Norton, 1988.

Fjermedal, Grant. *The Tomorrow Makers: A Brave New World of Living Brain Machines.* New York: Macmillan, 1986.

Follett, Ken. *On Wings of Eagles.* New York: Signet Books, 1984.

Freiberger, Paul, and Michael Swaine. *Fire in the Valley: The Making of the Personal Computer.* Berkeley, CA: Osborne/McGraw-Hill, 1984.

Gill, Geoffrey K. *Microsoft Corporation: Office Business Unit.* Cambridge, MA: Harvard Business School, 1990, revised 1991.

Hall, Mark, and John Barry. *Sunburst: The Ascent of Sun Microsystems.* Chicago: Contemporary Books, 1990.

Hanson, Dirk. *The New Alchemists: Silicon Valley and the Microelectronics Revolution.* Boston: Little, Brown, 1982.

Hogan, Thom. *Osborne CP/M User Guide,* 2d ed. Berkeley, CA: Osborne/McGraw-Hill, 1982.

Iacobucci, Ed. *OS/2 Programmer's Guide.* Berkeley, CA: Osborne/McGraw-Hill, 1988.

Ichbiah, Daniel, *Microsoft les Nouveaux Magiciens.* Paris: Editions Micro Application, 1990.

Ichbiah, Daniel, and Susan Knepper. *The Making of Microsoft: How Bill Gates and His Team Created the World's Most Successful Software Company.* Rocklin, CA: Prima Publishing, 1991.

Inside Macintosh. Promotional ed. Cupertino, CA: Apple Computer, 1985.

Johnson-Laird, Andy. *The Programmer's CP/M Handbook.* Berkeley, CA: Osborne/McGraw-Hill, 1983.

Juliussen, Egil and Karen. *The Computer Industry Almanac 1991.* New York: Brady, 1990.

Kawasaki, Guy. *The Macintosh Way.* New York: HarperPerennial, 1990.

————. *Selling the Dream.* New York: HarperCollins, 1991.

Kay, Alan. "The Reactive Engine." Ph.D. dissertation, University of Utah, Salt Lake City, 1969.

Kemeny, John G., and Thomas E. Kurtz. *Back to BASIC: The History, Corruption, and Future of the Language.* Reading, MA: Addison-Wesley, 1985.

Killen, Michael. *IBM: The Making of the Common View.* San Diego: Harcourt Brace Jovanovich, 1988.

Kitsap: A Centennial History. Bremerton, WA: Perry Publishing, 1989.

Kosnik, Thomas J. *Microsoft Corporation: The Introduction of Microsoft Works.* Cambridge, MA: Harvard Business School, 1987.

Lacey, Robert. *Ford: The Men and the Machine.* Boston: Little, Brown, 1986.

Lammers, Susan, ed. *Programmers at Work.* Redmond, WA: Microsoft Press, 1986.

Letwin, Gordon. *Inside OS/2.* Redmond, WA: Microsoft Press, 1988.

Levering, Robert, Michael Katz, and Milton Moskowitz. *The Computer Entrepreneurs: Who's Making It Big and How in America's Upstart Industry.* New York: NAL Books, 1984.

Levy, Steven. *Hackers: Heroes of the Computer Revolution.* New York: Doubleday, 1984. Page citations in notes are from Dell paperback edition, 1985.

Lu, Cary. *The Apple Macintosh Book.* Redmond, WA: Microsoft Press, 1984.

Mahon, Thomas. *Charged Bodies: People, Power and Paradox in Silicon Valley.* New York: New American Library, 1985.

Malik, Rex. *And Tomorrow . . . The World? Inside IBM.* London: Millington Ltd., 1975.

Malone, Michael S. *The Big Score: The Billion Dollar Story of Silicon Valley.* Garden City, NY: Doubleday, 1985.

Microsoft Mouse Programmer's Reference, 2d ed. Redmond, WA: Microsoft Press, 1991.

Mims, Forrest M., III. *Siliconnections: Coming of Age in the Electronic Era.* New York: McGraw-Hill, 1986.

Moritz, Michael. *The Little Kingdom: The Private Story of Apple Computer.* New York: William Morrow, 1984.

The MS-DOS Encyclopedia. General editor, Ray Duncan. Redmond, WA: Microsoft Press, 1988.

Nelson, Ted. *Computer Lib/Dream Machines,* rev. ed. Redmond, WA: Tempus Books, 1987.

Rifkin, Glenn, and George Harrar. *The Ultimate Entrepreneur: The Story of Ken Olsen and Digital Equipment Corporation.* Chicago: Contemporary Books, 1988.

Rogers, Everett M., and Judith K. Larsen. *Silicon Valley Fever: Growth of High-Technology Culture.* New York: Basic Books, 1984.

Rose, Frank. *West of Eden: The End of Innocence at Apple Computer.* New York: Penguin Books, 1989.

Schulman, Andrew, David Maxey, and Matt Pietrek. *Undocumented Windows.* Reading, MA: Addison-Wesley, 1992.

Sculley, John, with John A. Byrne. *Odyssey: Pepsi to Apple . . . A Journey of Adventure, Ideas, and the Future.* New York: Harper & Row, 1987.

Shaffer, Peter. *Black Comedy.* New York: Stein and Day, 1967.

Silverstein, Jeff, et al. *Software Industry Factbook,* 1992 ed. Stamford, CT: Digital Information Group, 1991.

Simonyi, Charles. *Meta-Programming: A Software Production Method.* Palo Alto: Xerox Palo Alto Research Center, 1977.

Slater, Robert. *Portraits in Silicon.* Cambridge, MA: MIT Press, 1987.

Smith, Douglas K., and Robert C. Alexander. *Fumbling the Future: How Xerox Invented, Then Ignored, the First Personal Computer*. New York: William Morrow, 1988.

Sobel, Robert. *IBM: Colossus in Transition*. New York: Times Books, 1981. Page citations in notes are from Bantam paperback edition, 1983.

Thurber, James. *The Thurber Carnival*. New York: Harper & Row, 1945.

Watson, Thomas J., Jr. *A Business and Its Beliefs: The Ideas That Helped Build IBM*. New York: McGraw-Hill, 1963.

Watson, Thomas J., Jr., and Peter Petre. *Father, Son & Co.: My Life at IBM and Beyond*. New York: Bantam Books, 1990.

Weizenbaum, Joseph. *Computer Power and Human Reason: From Judgment to Calculation*. San Francisco: W. H. Freeman, 1976.

Young, Jeffrey S. *Steve Jobs: The Journey Is the Reward*. Glenview, IL: Scott, Foresman, 1988.

INDEX